MW01286318

REDEMPTION

Redemption is a sweeping new history of the largest and costliest campaign waged by US armed forces during the Pacific War. Peter Mansoor surveys the full course of the Philippines campaign from the Japanese invasion and the Filipino guerrilla operations which contested occupation to the US Army's return to Leyte and the subsequent battles of liberation. Central to the book is a reevaluation of the leadership of General Douglas MacArthur, one of the most controversial military commanders in US history. At times brilliant, courageous, and politically astute, MacArthur was also egotistical, publicity hungry, often ignorant of conditions at the front, and self-certain to a fault. In their return to the Philippines, MacArthur and his forces liberated millions of Filipinos and severed a critical Japanese resource lifeline. But he also achieved something much rarer – redemption on the same ground and against the same enemy that defeated him earlier in the war.

Peter R. Mansoor is a retired US Army colonel and the General Raymond E. Mason Jr. Chair of Military History at The Ohio State University. His previous books include *The GI Offensive in Europe: The Triumph of American Infantry Divisions, 1941–1945*, which received the Society for Military History and Army Historical Society distinguished book awards.

"Peter Mansoor applies his talents as a historian and professional soldier (two tours in Iraq) to bear on Douglas MacArthur's World War II generalship. Unsparing in criticism, Mansoor's account acknowledges MacArthur's genuine talent and demanding leadership in fighting and winning the 'I Shall Return' campaign under the war's most trying conditions."

Allan R. Millett, author of *The War for Korea, 1950–1951*

PETER R. MANSOOR

REDEMPTION

MacArthur and the Campaign for the Philippines

CAMBRIDGE
UNIVERSITY PRESS

Shaftesbury Road, Cambridge CB2 8EA, United Kingdom

One Liberty Plaza, 20th Floor, New York, NY 10006, USA

477 Williamstown Road, Port Melbourne, VIC 3207, Australia

314–321, 3rd Floor, Plot 3, Splendor Forum, Jasola District Centre,
New Delhi – 110025, India

103 Penang Road, #05–06/07, Visioncrest Commercial, Singapore 238467

Cambridge University Press is part of Cambridge University Press & Assessment,
a department of the University of Cambridge.

We share the University's mission to contribute to society through the pursuit of
education, learning and research at the highest international levels of excellence.

www.cambridge.org
Information on this title: www.cambridge.org/9781009541190

DOI: 10.1017/9781009541176

First published 2025

Printed in the United Kingdom by CPI Group Ltd, Croydon CR0 4YY

A catalogue record for this publication is available from the British Library

A Cataloging-in-Publication data record for this book is available from the Library of Congress

ISBN 978-1-009-54119-0 Hardback

Cambridge University Press & Assessment has no responsibility for the persistence
or accuracy of URLs for external or third-party internet websites referred to in this
publication and does not guarantee that any content on such websites is, or will remain,
accurate or appropriate.

To the soldiers, sailors, airmen, Marines, and Coast Guardsmen of the US armed forces, their allies, and the members of the resistance who fought in the defense and liberation of the Philippines, 1941–1945

Contents

Preface

Books on Douglas MacArthur are legion; histories of campaigns in the Southwest Pacific, far less so. This book covers the war for the Philippines, from the initial Japanese invasion in December 1941, through more than two years of Filipino guerrilla operations to contest the occupation, to MacArthur's return to Leyte and the subsequent battles to liberate the Philippine archipelago from Japanese control. It examines the Philippines campaign holistically, focusing on the decisions made by American and Japanese leaders at the strategic, operational, and, where warranted, tactical levels of war; organization of military forces; airpower; naval actions; intelligence; logistics; guerrilla operations; and civil affairs. One of its strengths is a thorough discussion of the Filipino guerrilla movement, which receives only passing treatment in most other works. It is both a campaign history and a study in the strategic leadership of General of the Army Douglas MacArthur, for both aspects are required to understand the complexity of the US Army's largest campaign in the Pacific during World War II.

Of course, it is impossible to write a history of the Philippines campaign without focusing on the central role played by MacArthur, one of the most controversial military leaders in US history. Brilliant, courageous, politically minded, and strategically adept, MacArthur was also egotistical, overly ambitious, publicity hungry, and at times tactically suspect. He was sure of himself and craved a place in the history of great men. His subordinates either admired him or they found employment elsewhere.

Rarely in history do commanders who fail on the battlefield receive a shot at redemption on the same ground and against the same enemy. In the Asia–Pacific theaters of World War II, two cases come to mind: Field Marshal William Slim's Burma campaign, and MacArthur's campaign to liberate the Philippines. MacArthur was certain that liberating the Philippines was morally, politically, and strategically the right thing to do. Of course, liberating the Philippines would also redeem his greatest failure – the fall of the Philippines to the Japanese in 1942. Both Slim and MacArthur wrote post-war accounts of their experiences. Slim's memoir, *Defeat into*

Victory (London: Cassell, 1956), is one of the great memoirs of military history. MacArthur's memoir, *Reminiscences* (New York: McGraw-Hill, 1964), most decidedly is not.

In 1941, Roosevelt needed a commander in the Philippines who could unify the American and Filipino forces and provide the needed energy and strategic acumen to defend the islands against a Japanese invasion. Fortunately, he already had an available candidate in Manila. On the same day he signed the embargo against Japan in July 1941, Roosevelt reinstated MacArthur as a major general in the US Army (elevated to temporary lieutenant general two days later and four-star general in December) and gave him command of a new organization, the US Army Forces in the Far East, which would control all US and Philippine army forces in the region. MacArthur formed a staff that would support him over the long war to come. These officers formed the core of the "Bataan Gang" who would serve under MacArthur from Manila to Tokyo. This study also examines their expertise and competence.

Fortunately for MacArthur, Bataan and Corregidor were not the end of the story. Ordered by President Franklin D. Roosevelt to withdraw to Australia, MacArthur set about forming a new command, the Southwest Pacific Area, or SWPA, to blaze an island path back to the Philippines. He then convinced Roosevelt and the Joint Chiefs of Staff of the strategic and political value in liberating not just Mindanao and Leyte, but also the main island of Luzon and the capital city of Manila. Some historians have criticized this campaign as costly and unnecessary, a sop to relieve MacArthur's bruised ego. Yet the Joint Chiefs agreed to the invasions of Leyte, Mindoro, and Luzon for sound strategic reasons. As for MacArthur, he may have desired to liberate the Philippines in part to reverse his earlier failures, but mainly because he deeply cared for the Filipino people. The campaign, rather than being a costly mistake, liberated millions of Filipinos who would have continued to suffer under Japanese occupation had the war progressed into 1946 – a very real possibility as MacArthur waded ashore on Leyte on October 20, 1944. The mere fact that MacArthur was vainglorious does not mean that he was wrong. In his campaign to return to the Philippines, MacArthur achieved his greatest triumph while earning his much-desired redemption.

Note on the Text

Since nearly every Japanese and Australian unit was an infantry unit, I have omitted "infantry" from their titles, but added modifiers where needed (e.g., the Japanese *2nd Tank Division*). To eliminate any confusion, I have denoted Japanese units in italic type.

To reduce wordiness, I have often elided American infantry regiments by eliminating the word "regiment." Thus, the 34th Infantry Regiment can also be rendered as the 34th Infantry. American regiments normally fought as regimental combat teams, with appropriate augmentation such as artillery, tanks, tank destroyers, engineers, and signal and medical units. American regiments noted in the text should be understood to be regimental combat teams.

All other units are designated by their size (e.g., company, battalion, division, corps, etc.). A cavalry troop or artillery battery is roughly equivalent to an infantry company in size, and a cavalry squadron roughly equivalent to an infantry battalion. As for unit strength, at full strength divisions were roughly 10,000–15,000 men; brigades and regiments were 2,000–4,000 men; battalions were 400–800 men; and companies were 100–200 men. Of course, losses meant that many of these units fought with substantially fewer personnel.

Commanders of US and Australian divisions are noted in parenthesis when the division first appears in the narrative, or after a change of command. American division mottos are also noted in the text and are listed at the end of the book for reference.

I have rendered time using a twenty-four-hour military clock, so times from 1 pm to midnight are written as 13:00 to 24:00.

I have not changed the words people used at the time, even if they may be offensive to modern ears.

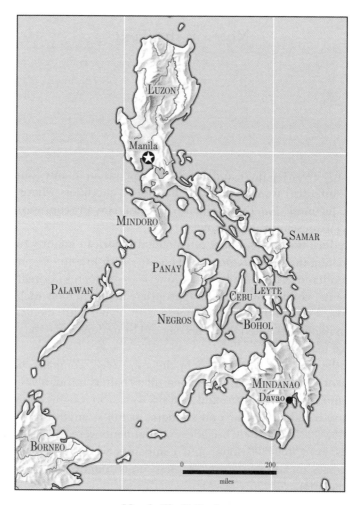

Map 1: The Philippines.

1

CATASTROPHE

We're the battling bastards of Bataan;
No mama, no papa, no Uncle Sam;
No aunts, no uncles, no cousins, no nieces;
No pills, no planes, no artillery pieces.
And nobody gives a damn.[1]

The campaign for the Philippines was the largest and costliest waged by the US armed forces in the Pacific during World War II.[2] For the US Army in the Pacific, it was by the fall of 1944 the main focus. Even so, the Philippines campaign, in particular the liberation of the islands in 1944 and 1945, has received far less attention than has been afforded to the naval battles and island invasions of the South and Central Pacific.[3] Marine invasions of Guadalcanal, Tarawa, Saipan, and Iwo Jima, as well as naval battles in the Coral Sea, at Midway, and in the Philippine Sea, captured the imagination of the American people in a way that fighting in New Guinea, Leyte, and Luzon did not. By the end of the war, however, the US Army had deployed twenty-one divisions to the Pacific, while the Marines deployed just six – the entire strength of the Fleet Marine Force.[4] Of the US Army divisions deployed to the Pacific, all but two served in the campaign for the Philippines. The Philippines campaign was massive, but why it came to pass and how it was waged is shrouded in the mists of time for most Americans today.

Since the end of the Spanish–American War in 1898, the Philippines were US territory. The acquisition of an empire had seemed like a good idea at the turn of the twentieth century, but by the 1930s the US Congress was ready to set the islands on the path to independence. The Tydings–McDuffie Act, signed into law by President Franklin D. Roosevelt on March 24, 1934, granted Philippine independence on July 4, 1946, after ten years of interim Commonwealth government. On March 23, 1935, Roosevelt approved the Philippine constitution, and in September of that year the Philippine people elected Manuel Quezon as their president.

1

He would serve until his death from tuberculosis in 1944, just prior to MacArthur's return to the Philippines at the head of a military juggernaut made possible by the mobilization of the United States for total war. On November 15, 1935, the Philippine Commonwealth came into existence on the steps of the Legislative building in Manila, which would be devastated during combat operations to liberate the city nearly ten years later.

The Philippines campaign is intimately tied to the life and leadership of General of the Army Douglas MacArthur, without whom the campaign to liberate the island archipelago in 1944 and 1945 might not have been fought at all. MacArthur was intelligent, ambitious, personally courageous, a superb orator, and at times strategically brilliant. He was also egotistical, publicity hungry, self-centered, insubordinate, often ignorant of conditions at the front, and so certain of himself that he frequently ignored intelligence assessments grounded in fact but with which he disagreed for no other reason than that to accept them would have forced him to change his preferred course of action. More than two dozen biographers have examined his life, and their assessments range from respect and admiration to criticism and disparagement.[5] For MacArthur, it seems, after death as during his life, there is no middle ground.

MacArthur descended from a storied military family. His father, Lt. Gen. Arthur MacArthur Jr., rocketed to fame after the Battle of Missionary Ridge during the Civil War, in which he planted the flag of the 24th Wisconsin on the crest and shouted, "On Wisconsin!," which the state university later adopted as its motto. Before he had even reached the age of twenty, the elder MacArthur had been breveted to colonel; he would later be awarded the Medal of Honor for his actions on Missionary Ridge. Clearly, his second son Douglas had much to live up to.

After a long period of peacetime service as a junior officer, Arthur MacArthur once again earned fame and promotion, this time in the Philippines during the Spanish–American War.[6] Quickly breveted to brigadier general, MacArthur commanded a brigade in the Battle of Manila on August 12, 1898. After the defeat of the Spanish forces in the Philippines, MacArthur fought against Filipino insurrectionists, earning permanent promotion to major general in the Regular Army. MacArthur led counterinsurgency operations as Military Governor of the Philippines for more than a year before he relinquished command on July 4, 1901. He returned to the United States, where he commanded several different military departments and was promoted to lieutenant general. Passed over for the position of US Army chief of staff, the elder MacArthur retired on June 2, 1909.

2

Douglas MacArthur had by then come to know the Philippines. After departure from the US Military Academy at West Point in 1903, where he rose to the rank of First Captain and graduated first in his class, MacArthur deployed to the Philippines with the 3rd Engineer Battalion.[7] In October 1905, the younger MacArthur traveled to Tokyo to accompany his father on a tour of Asia, which took the pair from Japan to Shanghai, Hong Kong, Java, Singapore, India, Thailand, Vietnam, Canton, Qingdao, Beijing, Tianjin, Hankou, and Shanghai again before their return to Japan in June 1906. The whirlwind adventure solidified both father and son's thinking that America's destiny lay in the Far East, across the vast Pacific Ocean.

As the son of one of America's most famous generals, MacArthur was already a rising star in the US Army (he had served in the White House as an aide to President Teddy Roosevelt and in 1916 as a major he functioned as the army's first press officer – experience that would stand him in good stead in years to come), but he rocketed to fame during World War I as the chief of staff of the 42nd Infantry Division (the "Rainbow" Division – a composite National Guard organization MacArthur had a role in creating) and as commander of the 84th Infantry Brigade. For his bravery in combat, MacArthur received two Distinguished Service Crosses and seven Silver Stars – he was among the most decorated soldiers in the US Army in that conflict. He was gassed several times owing to his refusal to carry or wear a protective mask (most likely because he tended to get claustrophobic), but not severely enough to require hospitalization. While later serving as chief of staff of the US Army, he would create the Purple Heart, and, in typical MacArthur fashion, would award himself the first such decoration.

From his World War I experiences, MacArthur came to believe in the necessity to act first and request permission later – if at all. He often took the initiative after conducting personal reconnaissance forward of the front line armed with nothing more than a riding crop. "Sometimes it is the order one disobeys that makes one famous," he quipped to a subordinate during fighting in the St. Mihiel salient.[8] His later career would verify that thought, but acting on it would also ultimately end his career. MacArthur also learned the value of creating a unique image. He refused to wear a steel helmet and olive drab uniform top, instead opting for a crumpled barracks cap, his gray West Point sweater, and a scarf. His superiors indulged him, and the press and the public ate it up. MacArthur would exit the Great War as America's most distinguished battlefield leader.[9]

Unlike most other brigadier generals in the American Expeditionary Forces, MacArthur retained his rank after the armistice. After the war, he served as superintendent of the US Military Academy, attempting to reform the institution by expanding the curriculum (which the Academy's Academic Board fought tooth and nail), formalizing the honor code, and requiring all cadets to participate in intramural or intercollegiate sports. MacArthur also married socialite Louise Cromwell Brooks, a relationship that ended in divorce seven years later. He served twice more in the Philippines, mapping the terrain of the Bataan Peninsula and commanding a brigade of the US Army's Philippine Division – experience he would put to good use when war again erupted in the Pacific. During his tenure in the islands, MacArthur deepened his friendship with Manuel Quezon and developed relationships at the highest levels of Philippine society – relationships that would become critical in the years to come.[10]

On January 17, 1925, MacArthur became the youngest major general in the army. He was the most junior member of the court martial board for the trial of airman Billy Mitchell (MacArthur claimed he voted for acquittal) and served as president of the US Olympic Committee in preparation for the 1928 summer Olympics in Amsterdam, where the American team set seventeen Olympic and seven world records and earned fifty-six medals – twenty-two of them gold – nearly twice as many as the next most successful country. MacArthur, it seemed, had the Midas touch.

On November 21, 1930, President Herbert Hoover vaulted MacArthur over numerous other candidates and assigned him as the US Army chief of staff, which also brought a promotion to full general. During MacArthur's tenure in this position, he dealt with the budget woes brought forth by the Great Depression, reorganized the US Army into four ground armies controlling a total of nine corps areas, created a general headquarters for the Army Air Corps, and supported army administration of the Civilian Conservation Corps. His most controversial action came in 1932, when he ordered (and personally led) troops to disband the Bonus Army of roughly 20,000 Great War veterans who had descended on Washington, DC, to press their case for early payment of wartime bonus certificates. MacArthur, who was acting on orders of President Hoover, believed the movement was communist-inspired, which was not the case, although a group of communist sympathizers had embedded themselves among the marchers and attempted to spark a riot. It was one of the few times in his career when MacArthur misread public opinion, which sided with the veterans of the Great War and considered his actions – deliberately misrepresented to the public by Communist Party organs – reprehensible.[11]

Upon his relief in 1935 after five years as US Army chief of staff, MacArthur accepted an offer from Quezon to head the newly established

Philippine Army with the rank of field marshal. MacArthur retained his Regular Army rank of major general and served simultaneously as US military advisor to the Philippine government and as head of the Philippine Army. This meant he could retain his annual army salary of $7,500 along with the compensation offered by Quezon's Philippine government – $18,000 per year plus another $15,000 annually in expenses, as well as just under 0.5 percent of the Philippine defense budget as a performance bonus. MacArthur was not just heading back to a land and a people he genuinely loved, but was going to become rich in the process.[12] On the voyage to Manila, MacArthur met Jean Marie Faircloth, who would in April 1937 become his second wife and ten months later bear his only child, Arthur MacArthur IV.[13] Theirs would be an intimate and successful relationship, Jean providing the companionship that MacArthur craved, especially after the deaths of his beloved (and domineering) mother and his brother Arthur.[14]

Taking residence in the penthouse of the Manila Hotel, MacArthur got to work creating an army, assisted by his able chief of staff, Major Dwight D. Eisenhower, and Major James B. Ord. Ord would die in a plane crash in January 1938 and was replaced by Lt. Col. Richard K. Sutherland. MacArthur retired from the US Army at the end of 1937 to avoid being reassigned to a less prestigious (and less lucrative) and duller assignment stateside. In the summer of 1938, Eisenhower returned to the United States for a period of leave and to visit the War Department to attempt to pry more resources out of it for Philippine defense. In his absence, MacArthur, privy to an untrue conspiracy theory that Eisenhower was maneuvering behind his back to replace him as military advisor to the Philippine president, realigned the staff. Upon his return to the headquarters in Manila, Eisenhower discovered he was no longer the chief of staff. Understandably miffed by his effective demotion in the pecking order in MacArthur's headquarters and by this time discouraged with the attempt to create an army with little support from the War Department, he requested and received orders back to the United States, where he could help the army prepare for the war he believed was coming.[15] MacArthur promoted Sutherland to chief of staff, while a year later Maj. Richard J. Marshall, whose expertise was logistics, was brought into the circle as deputy chief of staff.[16] These two officers would serve in those roles throughout the war to come.

Building the Philippine Army from scratch was no easy feat (some would claim it was an impossible task), and MacArthur's record in this regard is uneven at best. He envisioned a military establishment of ten districts based on the Swiss model, with a small core (930 officers and 7,000 enlisted soldiers) of regular army officers and troops, supported by 6,000 members of the paramilitary Philippine Constabulary, who would provide annual basic training for 40,000 Filipino men broken into two cohorts, who would then become reservists until age 50.[17] After 10 years, the army would number 400,000 men. A single regular Philippine Army division would augment these reserve forces. A military academy in Baguio would graduate 100 officers per year. A larger, decentralized national militia, a small air force, and a flotilla of motor torpedo boats would round out the defense establishment.[18]

The Philippine government could not afford modern weapons and equipment, and so the Philippine Army was reliant on whatever surplus arms the United States could provide. Forget artillery and tanks; MacArthur could not even convince the War Department to furnish an adequate number of antiquated Enfield rifles to arm Filipino forces. He was hamstrung partly by the resistance of Philippine High Commissioner Frank Murphy and US Interior Secretary Harold Ickes, who didn't want the Filipinos armed at all, partly because they viewed the Philippines as indefensible, but also because of the worry that some Filipinos might take up arms against the United States.[19] Defense against a modern military power such as Japan would also require the United States to provide a navy and air forces sufficient to control the seas and skies surrounding the Philippines. Given the low priority the US defense establishment placed on the Philippines, these assets were unlikely to be forthcoming.

MacArthur's training program for the Philippine Army failed for a variety of reasons: the difficulty in training officers and noncommissioned officers, some of whom were illiterate; communicating with soldiers who spoke a dozen languages with more than 100 dialects; inadequate training facilities; lack of weapons on which recruits could train; lack of money; lack of support from a young male Philippine populace lukewarm at best about spending five-and-a-half months in military training; and lack of time. MacArthur had deceived himself into believing that if he ordered an army into existence, his capable subordinates could fill in the details to make it happen. When reality sank in, MacArthur turned on his staff, especially Eisenhower, who knew the plan was unaffordable and said so repeatedly.[20] MacArthur's plan envisioned a viable Philippine military establishment by 1946, when the islands would gain their independence. He did not realize it when he accepted the position, but the Philippines would be at war in less than half that amount of time. But perhaps the biggest obstacle was President Quezon, who, seeing war clouds on the horizon, decided that only the immediate provision of independence coupled with a policy of neutrality could keep his nation safe from a Japanese invasion. Quezon distanced himself from MacArthur, even as war approached on the horizon. MacArthur was doing his best to create a defense establishment that seemingly no one else wanted.[21]

The United States military had been preparing for a potential war with Japan since a war scare in 1906 compelled the staff at the Naval War College to plan for one. As a shorthand device, in 1904 the presidents of the Army War College and the Naval War College had assigned colors to the nations involved in planning for future operations.[22] The United States was blue. Japan was orange. War Plan Orange evolved over the years, but since its earliest incarnation it was focused on defeating Japan, presumably embroiled in war on the Asian mainland, by a naval campaign in the Central and Western Pacific.[23]

Projecting power into the Western Pacific was at the heart of the problem confronted by planners. The 1922 Washington Naval Treaty prohibited the United States from building a new major naval base in the region, as the British had already done in Singapore. Relying on the US Navy to sortie to Manila Bay shortly after the outbreak of war was a risky proposition, and in any case the fleet lacked the strength to challenge the Japanese so far from US bases in Hawai'i. By the mid 1930s the planners had settled on a third option – to seize a series of island bases in the Central Pacific and supply the navy by creating a mobile logistics fleet train that would come to number more than 1,000 vessels by 1945. This strategy would take at least two years to implement, however, effectively abandoning the Philippines to its fate.[24]

War Plan Orange – and its Rainbow successors – left the Philippines in an awkward position. The islands were indefensible given the number of troops the United States was willing to commit to their retention, and planners knew it. But successive presidential administrations and the Army–Navy Joint Board could not admit publicly that they were willing to write off the islands.[25] Instead of stating its intention to abandon the defense of the Philippines in the event of war with Japan and accept the political blowback, the Roosevelt administration instead chose a policy of "calculated hypocrisy" that mouthed the right words about supporting the defense of the Philippines without providing the resources to actually do so.[26] The person left holding the bag would be the newest Philippine field marshal, Douglas MacArthur.

As World War II commenced, Army and Navy leaders realized the need to update their war plans. They accordingly directed their planners to draw up a series of Rainbow war plans, which envisioned the United States operating as part of a broader coalition. The final iteration, Rainbow 5, was submitted to President Roosevelt on June 2, 1941.[27] Rainbow 5 gave priority to defeating Germany first, which meant that any offensive in the Pacific would be delayed until resources were available to execute it. Regarding the Philippines, planners estimated an invasion by 100,000 Japanese troops, supported by substantial naval and air assets. American and Filipino forces in the Philippines, guided by the dictates of War Plan Orange-3 (WPO-3), would fight a delaying action, falling back to the Bataan Peninsula, which they would defend to the "last extremity."[28] They would presumably await relief by the US Pacific Fleet, but the navy had long before written off defense of the Philippines as hopeless.[29] The tiny Asiatic fleet, with the exception of a few PT boats and a couple of dozen submarines, would abandon Manila upon the outbreak of war and head for safer harbors. In the event, the US Pacific Fleet would not sortie in the defense of the Philippines, not least because after December 7, 1941, many of its battleships rested on the bottom of Pearl Harbor.

When France fell in June 1940, the United States finally awoke from its peacetime stupor and began mobilizing for war. Even as American industry converted to armaments and munitions production, the Philippines would see little reinforcement. After the passage of the Lend–Lease Act in March 1941, the weapons and munitions rolling off the assembly lines went to Great Britain and, after the German invasion of the Soviet Union in June 1941, to the USSR. The next priority was to arm and equip the expanding US military forces. The Philippines would have to fend for itself.

To paraphrase Leon Trotsky, the Philippines might not have been interested in war, but war would soon be interested in the Philippines. The collapse of France and the Netherlands made their colonial possessions in Asia vulnerable, and it was not long before the Japanese government took advantage of their weakness. To support its ongoing invasion of China, on June 19, 1940, the Japanese government demanded the closure of road and rail links between Indochina and China; the French complied by the end of the month. The Japanese then demanded the ability to station ground, air, and naval forces in the Gulf of Tonkin region. The Vichy government balked, but it was powerless to prevent the inevitable, and acquiesced in an agreement reached on September 22, 1940. In response, President Roosevelt embargoed the sale of scrap metal, steel, and aviation gasoline to Japan.

After the initiation of Operation Barbarossa, the German invasion of the Soviet Union on June 22, 1941, the Japanese military no longer feared a Red Army invasion into Manchuria and became emboldened to reach further. A month later, Japanese forces occupied southern Indochina, which the US government (which had cracked the Japanese diplomatic cipher) properly read as preparation for an offensive against British and Dutch colonial possessions. Cam Ranh Bay, which the Japanese coveted as a naval and air base, was just 800 miles from the Philippines. Further south, the Netherlands East Indies had the raw materials – especially oil – needed by the Japanese war economy, and Japan was willing to take them by force if necessary. In response, on July 26, 1941, President Roosevelt froze Japanese assets in the United States and embargoed oil and gas exports to Japan. In a stroke of the pen, Japan lost 75 percent of its overseas trade and nearly all of its imported oil. Japan could either back down or fight, and it had maybe nine months at most to act before its oil stocks ran out. The United States and Japan were now on the road to war, and the Philippines were squarely in the middle.

Roosevelt needed a commander in the Philippines who could unify the American and Filipino forces and provide the needed energy and strategic acumen to defend the islands against a Japanese invasion. Fortunately, he already had an available candidate in Manila. On the same day he signed the embargo against Japan, Roosevelt reinstated MacArthur as a major general in the US Army (elevated to temporary lieutenant general two days later and four-star general in December) and gave him command of a new organization, the US Army Forces in the Far East (USAFFE), which would control all US and Philippine army forces in the region.

MacArthur formed a staff that would support him over the long war to come. These officers formed the core of the "Bataan Gang" who would serve under MacArthur from Manila to Tokyo. Promoted to brigadier general (and on December 20, 1941, to major general), Sutherland would continue to serve as chief of staff. A graduate of Yale University, he was an intelligent and perceptive thinker with a harsh personality and limited empathy and would rule over the staff with an iron fist.[30] On the other hand, according to MacArthur's press relations officer Carlos Romulo, "no one else seemed so able to interpret the thoughts and plans of the general."[31] Sutherland's deputy, who received a promotion to full colonel and by the end of the year became a brigadier general, was the calm and approachable Richard Marshall, who, unlike his boss, "could be liked."[32] Col. Hugh J. "Pat" Casey would serve as the chief engineer and Col. Spencer B. Akin became the chief signal officer; both would receive promotion to brigadier general on December 20, 1941. Lt. Col. William F. Marquat would become the antiaircraft artillery officer. Lt. Col. (promoted to Colonel on October 14, 1941) Charles A. Willoughby, who was born in Germany and spoke English with a German accent, also joined the staff. MacArthur made Willoughby his intelligence officer – a position in which Willoughby would perform much like his boss: "When he was good, he was very, very good, and when he was bad, he was horrid."[33] In the Philippines in 1941–1942, both fit the latter description.

USAFFE unified the US and Philippine military establishments under one command, giving MacArthur authority over the 22,000 Americans and 120,000 Filipinos in uniform.[34] In theory, MacArthur commanded eleven divisions, all but one of them reserve formations of the Philippine Army. In reality, none of the reserve divisions was properly manned, equipped, or trained; by the time of the Japanese assault on Pearl Harbor, only two regiments in each division had been mobilized, and they lacked critical assets such as artillery and antitank guns.[35] Many of the troops had never fired a rifle before engaging in combat. The troops didn't even speak a common dialect and many were illiterate, making command and control difficult at best.[36] The two most capable ground units were the 26th Philippine Scout Cavalry Regiment and the 10,000-man Philippine Division (Maj. Gen. Jonathan M. Wainwright), composed of the US 31st Infantry Regiment, the 45th and 57th Regiments of Philippine Scouts (PS), and two field artillery regiments armed with 2.95-inch mountain guns and 75mm field guns.[37] Upon the withdrawal of the 4th Marines from Shanghai on November 28, it redeployed to Luzon, where it would provide a defensive force for the island fortress of Corregidor.[38] The US Asiatic Fleet spread throughout the region consisted of the heavy cruiser *Houston*, light cruisers *Boise* (joined after December 7) and *Marblehead*, thirteen World War I-era destroyers, twenty-nine submarines, and six PT boats, among other ancillary vessels.[39] It would be hard pressed to survive, much less interdict a Japanese fleet headed to Luzon.

In Washington, US Army Chief of Staff Gen. George C. Marshall made determined efforts to reinforce the Philippines, at least until the United States was at war. In the fall of 1941, USAFFE received an antiaircraft artillery regiment, two tank battalions with 108 M3 Stuart light tanks, and 25 M3 GMC 75mm guns, mounted on armored half-tracks.[40] Plans to bolster the Philippine Division with an additional US infantry regiment, reinforce USAFFE with a field artillery brigade and a reconnaissance squadron, provide army and corps troops for the tactical commands, and add two bombardment groups and a pursuit group to the USAFFE air forces came to naught as the Japanese invasion commenced before they arrived.[41]

1.1: Gen. Douglas MacArthur, commander of forces in the Philippine Islands, with Maj. Gen. Jonathan Wainwright, commander of the Philippine Division, October 10, 1941. Wainwright would take command of US and Philippine forces when MacArthur escaped to Australia and would be forced to surrender them to the Japanese in May 1942. (Credit: US Army Signal Corps Photo)

These forces were perhaps sufficient to hold the Bataan Peninsula and the island of Corregidor guarding the entrance to Manila Bay for several months until help could arrive, presumably in the form of the US Pacific Fleet. But MacArthur, contrary to WPO-3, which dictated a pullback to Bataan and Corregidor until the Pacific Fleet could arrive (if indeed it ever would before the Philippines fell), decided instead to defend the entirety of Luzon and fight invading Japanese forces at the beaches of Lingayen Gulf, 100 miles to the north.[42] He would not stay on the defensive and passively await defeat. MacArthur divided the command of forces on Luzon among a North Luzon Force (Maj. Gen. Wainwright), a South Luzon Force (Brig. Gen. George M. Parker, Jr.), and a Reserve Force of two infantry divisions in Manila. Additionally, he created a Visayan–Mindanao

Force (Brig. Gen. William F. Sharp), which was tasked with defending the Central and Southern Philippines. Critically, MacArthur ordered supply dumps to be moved north onto the central plain to support the forces defending Lingayen Gulf.[43] With a well-trained and -equipped army enjoying some measure of air support, he might have been able to pull off a forward defense. But USAFFE had neither required force, or at least it wouldn't until well into the spring of 1942 if current deployment projections held, making the decision one of the worst of his military career. For his part, Gen. Marshall, contrary to the dictates of Rainbow 5, approved MacArthur's forward defense plan on November 21, 1941 – unbeknownst to either of them, just two-and-a-half weeks before the outbreak of war.[44]

The War Department placed great faith in the B-17 bombers and P-40 Warhawk fighters being sent to the Philippines: 4 heavy bombardment groups totaling 272 bombers and 2 fighter groups totaling 260 fighters, to be based at a planned two dozen-plus airfields US Army engineers would construct throughout the Philippines. They would come under the control of Maj. Gen. Lewis H. Brereton, as of November 3, 1941, the commander of the newly established Far East Air Force (FEAF). They would presumably control the skies over Luzon and send any Japanese invasion force to the bottom of the South China Sea. But by December 7, 1941, the FEAF possessed only 35 B-17 bombers and 107 P-40 Warhawk fighters in the Philippines, based at just 6 airfields – not enough to stop a full-throated Japanese invasion.[45] Many of the fighters were so new their motors had not yet been slow timed (i.e., broken in), and spare parts were scarce. But even this meager allotment should have accomplished something before succumbing to superior Japanese numbers. Events would prove otherwise.

When war came, there was only one air-warning service company in the Philippines (at Iba on the west coast of Luzon), with only a single operational radar set. The rudimentary system of ground observers used unreliable land line communications to report their sightings. USAFFE lacked sufficient antiaircraft artillery to defend its airfields.[46] MacArthur, Sutherland, and Brereton, warned in late November by air staff officers that the bomber force on Luzon was vulnerable to a Japanese strike, concurred in relocating the B-17s to the Del Monte airfield on Mindanao until engineers could construct air bases in the Visayas that were better positioned and more defensible.[47] But when the Japanese attacked on December 8 (in the Philippines, which was across the International Date Line), only half the bombers had moved south, as Brereton was planning to station the incoming 7th Bombardment Group at Del Monte and there was not enough ramp space there to accommodate all of the planes.[48] But since airfields on Luzon lacked an adequate air-warning system and a robust air defense capability, the B-17s remaining at Clark were vulnerable to attack by Japanese aircraft. It is unclear whether either Brereton or Sutherland informed MacArthur of this change in plans. In his diary, Brereton indicates the move of sixteen B-17s to Mindanao was coordinated with Sutherland, but after the Japanese air attack on December 8, MacArthur was surprised to discover that all the bombers had not been relocated to Del Monte airfield.[49]

Meanwhile, Brereton requested permission to execute a high-level photo reconnaissance of Japanese bases in southern Formosa (Taiwan) to determine the extent of the Japanese buildup of air forces on the island. MacArthur, abiding by War Department instructions not to take any action that could prompt hostilities with Japan, limited the range of reconnaissance to two-thirds of the distance to Formosa (a few days later extended to the international treaty line between the Philippines and Formosa), which could only detect naval activity.[50] The result of this decision was that complete target packages for a B-17 strike against Formosa could be completed only once war had already begun. As it turns out, that timing would be too late for the survival of FEAF.

Nevertheless, as war approached, MacArthur believed that he could defeat a Japanese attack on the islands. The Chinese military philosopher Sun Tzu once wrote, "If you know the enemy and know yourself, you need not fear the result of a hundred battles. If you know yourself but not the enemy, for every victory gained you will also suffer a defeat. If you know neither the enemy nor yourself, you will succumb in every battle."[51] MacArthur didn't see the weaknesses of the forces he commanded, and, blinded by racial chauvinism, he failed to understand Japanese capabilities as well.[52] It was self-delusion at its worst.

As Japanese carrier-based aircraft crippled the battleships of the US Pacific Fleet in Pearl Harbor, Hawai'i, on the morning of Sunday, December 7, 1941, messages flashed to the Philippines warning of an impending attack. Well before daylight, all of MacArthur's subordinate commands had been alerted, so the forthcoming Japanese attack should not have taken his forces by surprise. Instead, a thick fog prevented the Japanese on Formosa from launching a dawn strike, which US airmen expected. The first Japanese strikes on Luzon – at Tuguegararo and Baguio, the summer capital of the Philippines, well north of Manila, did little damage, but as a precautionary measure, the bombers on Luzon took off and circled overhead until the all-clear sounded. P-40 fighters chased after the Japanese planes, without result.[53]

The bombers and fighters then landed to be refueled and armed for their next missions. Brereton wanted to bomb Japanese shipping and airfields on Formosa, a request he made known to Sutherland before daybreak.[54] But MacArthur denied the request until 10:14, when he called and gave Brereton permission to make the decision on offensive air operations, which would begin with a photo reconnaissance of the Japanese airfields on Formosa.[55] MacArthur's delay in authorizing offensive air operations has never been adequately explained, but his eventual approval came several hours too late to catch the Japanese on the ground before they launched their bombing strikes on the Philippines.

Much ink has been spilled about the delay in ordering a bombing strike. Clearly, MacArthur was hesitant to order a strike as he had not yet transitioned his thinking to a wartime mindset. Timelier approval would have enabled a strike on Formosa, although such a mission would not necessarily have been successful. The target packages lacked photo reconnaissance data, fog shrouded the airfields on Formosa, and even if the fog lifted, the B-17s would have flown without fighter escort as the P-40s lacked the range to reach Formosa (though, to be clear, at this stage of the war the Army Air Forces believed that heavy bomber formations were self-defending), making the bombers vulnerable to Japanese combat air patrols. Numbers of available bombers were also an issue; a strike by seventeen B-17s (the others on Mindanao would not be ready for employment against Formosa until the next day) on Japanese military facilities on Formosa on December 8 would not have changed the course of the fighting in the Philippines. But at least the bombers would have been aloft and striking at the enemy, and with a little luck, perhaps catching the Japanese by surprise and destroying some of their airpower. As it was, nearly every plane at Clark Field was on the ground refueling, rearming, or awaiting orders when the main Japanese strike force of 108 bombers and 84 Zero fighters appeared overhead at 12:35.[56]

The result was carnage. Inaccurate intelligence and poor command decisions sent available fighters south to fly combat air patrol over Manila or west into the South China Sea, leaving Clark and Iba airbases – both likely targets for Japanese strikes – undefended.[57] The 20th Pursuit Squadron had eighteen P-40s ready to take off, but Maj. Orrin L. Grover, commander of the 24th Pursuit Group at Clark Field, kept them on the ground until he could definitively determine the direction of Japanese aircraft formations. Only three planes of the 20th Pursuit Squadron took off before Japanese bombs destroyed the rest.[58] Even had they been airborne, the P-40s lacked oxygen and so could not climb to engage the Japanese bombers, which came in overhead above 18,000 feet. They could, however, have engaged Japanese Zero fighters, which attacked next at low level and did much damage to the planes lined up below. Because of a lack of ramp space, FEAF planes were inadequately dispersed, making them easy targets for strafing runs. Antiaircraft fire was ineffective due to poor training and old ammunition that often failed to explode. The bombing cut communications at both Iba and Clark airfields, leaving them isolated. The Japanese attack on Iba Field destroyed sixteen P-40s and the only operational radar set in the Philippines. In one morning, the Japanese destroyed around 100 of the 181 FEAF planes based on Luzon, including 12 B-17s and 53 P-40s, and damaged many others.[59] The facilities at Clark Field had been badly damaged. The P-40s that made it aloft downed just one Japanese bomber and seven Zero fighters.[60] The Japanese strike had effectively eliminated the FEAF as a combat-effective force, significantly reducing MacArthur's already slim chances of successfully defending the Philippines.[61]

In his memoirs, MacArthur brushes off the results of the Japanese attack as inevitable given the odds the FEAF faced.[62] Although the ultimate result of the Japanese offensive might have been inevitable, the fact is that MacArthur's airmen got caught on the ground with insufficient fighter protection overhead. Had the FEAF survived the first strikes by the Japanese, it could have inflicted damage on Japanese invasion forces and delayed the ultimate Japanese victory on Luzon, materially aiding the war effort. But after December 8, 1941, the modern aircraft that the War Department had sent to the Philippines to provide MacArthur with the capability to fight the Japanese on something approaching equal terms were gone.

There is a lot of blame to go around, but, as the saying goes, while victory has a thousand fathers, defeat is an orphan. In his memoir, Brereton blamed the War Department for failing to approve the construction of a sufficient number of air bases in the Philippines and then deploy an adequate air-warning service and enough fighter groups to protect them.[63] After the publication of Brereton's memoir, MacArthur disingenuously attempted to pin the blame on Brereton in a statement to the *New York Times*.[64] Historian William Bartsch pins much of the blame on Grover, stating that he misdirected pursuit planes already aloft to Manila, even though Japanese bombers were clearly heading to Iba and Clark Fields, and then failed to order aloft the 20th Pursuit Squadron when he received a warning of Japanese bombers headed toward Clark Field.[65] But blaming such a disaster on a mid-grade officer seems somewhat insufficient.

MacArthur and Brereton were in overall command, and they were not even reprimanded, perhaps because doing so would have brought into question the leadership in Washington, which had sent heavy bomber squadrons to the Philippines in advance of the creation of a base structure and the air defenses necessary to accommodate and protect them.

Ultimately, Roosevelt, Congress, and the War Department never held a formal inquiry and held no one accountable for the debacle.[66] As one reporter who was on the ground wrote in retrospect, "the picture that emerges is one of confusion and indecision."[67] Within a few months the American people celebrated MacArthur as a hero, and President Roosevelt awarded him the Medal of Honor instead of castigating him for losing more than half of his airpower on the first day of battle. In retrospect, even had everything gone right for the FEAF on December 8, the outcome of the ensuing campaign in the Philippines would not have changed. There were simply not enough bombers and fighters available with the required infrastructure and air defense assets to overcome a determined Japanese attack on the Philippines. MacArthur's airmen were outnumbered, outgunned, and, to be honest, outgeneraled.

Two days later, the Japanese struck Nichols and Nielson Fields, as well as the Cavite Naval Base south of Manila. The Japanese repeated the strikes on December 12 and 13. The results for the Americans were no better than on the first day of the war. Japanese bombs obliterated their targets and made the stationing of air and naval forces in the area untenable. Much to MacArthur's chagrin, the commander of the US Asiatic Fleet, Admiral Thomas C. Hart, withdrew most of his remaining surface vessels from Manila Bay, leaving just two destroyers, a half dozen PT boats, and twenty-seven submarines in Philippine waters. Commercial vessels also made good their escape. The remaining B-17s decamped to Del Monte airfield on Mindanao, and, on December 17, flew from there to Australia. Only a couple of dozen P-40s remained to contest Japanese air supremacy over Luzon. Hopelessly outnumbered, they fought valiantly in a losing effort. MacArthur's ground forces, increasingly isolated, would bear the burden of the battle from this point forward.[68]

With the Pacific Fleet crippled and the FEAF in tatters, MacArthur should have reconsidered his decision to defend forward on the beaches of Lingayen Gulf. He lacked the air and sea power to defend the approaches to Luzon, and his poorly trained ground forces were not likely to overcome an invasion by Japanese forces backed by superior airpower. There was still time, if barely, to implement WPO-3 and position US and Filipino forces in the Bataan Peninsula, as well as to stockpile supplies there for an extended

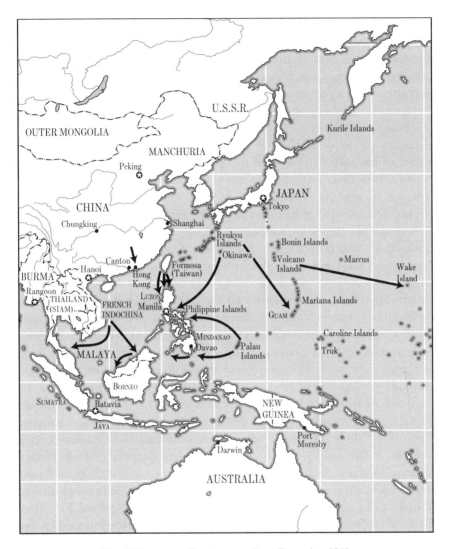

Map 2: Japanese offensive operations, December 1941.

siege. But, confident of his plan and unwilling to reconsider his command's prospects, MacArthur made no changes to his orders.

The Japanese followed up their initial strikes on FEAF airfields and the naval facilities of the Asiatic fleet with small-scale (regimental size or less) landings at Batan Island (December 8), 150 miles off the northern tip of Luzon; Camiguin Island (December 10), 35 miles from Aparri on the northern tip of Luzon; Aparri and Vigan (December 10) in northern Luzon; Legaspi (December 12) on the Bicol Peninsula; Davao (December 20) on Mindanao; and Jolo Island (December 24) on the Sulu Archipelago between Mindanao and Borneo. These locations would provide air bases to cover further operations on Luzon, interdict the San Bernardino Strait, threaten the Netherlands East Indies, and prevent reinforcements from reaching the Philippines.[69] The landings were largely unopposed, although air attacks badly damaged two transports, sank a minesweeper, and hit a light cruiser and a destroyer off the coast near Vigan – the last major effort by the FEAF before it was effectively eliminated as a combat force by Japanese bombing and strafing. From this point forward, remaining FEAF aircraft were used for reconnaissance.[70] The Japanese detachment at Aparri moved around the coast road to Vigan, where it joined forces with the troops there and reunited the *2nd Formosa Regiment*. The combined force then moved south toward the main Japanese landing beaches in Lingayen Gulf.

As Maj. Gen. Wainwright expected, the main Japanese landings occurred in Lingayen Gulf, 100 miles north of Manila. The convoys sailed without interdiction by American air and naval forces, which was the purpose of stationing B-17 bombers and submarines on Luzon. Despite high seas and poor navigation, Japanese troops made it ashore unscathed, although the landing of heavy equipment had to await calmer waters. Lt. Gen. Masaharu Homma's *14th Army* consisted of 43,000 soldiers, with the *48th Division* and part of the *16th Division* as the primary combat elements. MacArthur's forces on Luzon outnumbered the Japanese by at least two to one, but, in this case, quality mattered more than quantity.[71] More combat-effective Japanese forces brushed aside what little resistance the Filipino troops stationed on the beaches offered as succeeding waves swept ashore. By the middle of the afternoon, Japanese infantry, supported by several pieces of artillery and tanks that had made it ashore, controlled the beaches on which they had landed and pushed inland.[72] A timely counterattack by several well-trained divisions might have pushed them back into the sea, but only one such division existed in the Philippines, and it was not stationed in the vicinity. Poorly trained and ill-equipped, the North Luzon Force, according to Wainwright, "were doomed before they started to fight . . .. They never had a chance to win."[73]

The 26th Cavalry (PS) defended Damortis for several hours until ordered to fall back to Rosario. Japanese tanks penetrated the cavalrymen's lines that evening, routing the regiment as it withdrew. The Japanese took Rosario that night. The defense of Baguio proved just as futile, with

Japanese forces seizing the city by dawn on December 24. The 11th, 71st, and 91st Philippine Divisions attempted to stem the Japanese advance to the south, but invariably fell back after first contact with Japanese forces. Only the 26th Cavalry (PS), which fought a heroic delaying action at Binalonan, proved to be combat-effective, and after this fight it was down to just 450 men.[74]

On December 24, the Japanese launched a supporting attack at Mauban, Atimonan, and Siain in Lamon Bay on the eastern shore of Luzon, fifty-five miles southeast of Manila. The 7,000 soldiers of the *16th Division*, minus 2 regiments employed elsewhere, would have to cross the Tayabas Mountains and skirt the shores of Laguna de Bay to reach the Philippine capital. The South Luzon Force, consisting of the 1st Regiment of the 1st Regular Philippine Division, the 51st Philippine Division, the 42nd Infantry of the 41st Philippine Division, six batteries of artillery, and one tank company, was responsible for the area, along with the rest of Luzon south of Manila. A battalion of the 1st Regiment of the 1st Regular Philippine Division, recently inducted on December 19, defended the beach at Mauban, inflicting heavy casualties on Japanese assault forces. After difficult fighting, the Japanese were able to solidify control of the beach and seize the town. Filipino forces likewise fought doggedly for Atimonan, but, by the middle of the afternoon, Japanese forces had secured the town and were advancing into the mountains to the west. Given the small size of the forces employed, Japanese commanders were delighted with their successes.[75]

The results of the first days of fighting had been predictable. Poorly trained and equipped Filipino reserve troops fled quickly after contact with Japanese forces, and US forces and Philippine Scouts lacked the numbers and firepower to stem the Japanese for long. The Japanese had consolidated two major beachheads on Luzon at Lingayen Gulf and Lamon Bay. Heavy equipment and supplies streamed ashore, and Japanese forces were prepared to advance on Manila. American and Filipino forces would have to fight a delaying action back into the Bataan Peninsula after all, in accordance with WPO-3, which MacArthur had derided as defeatist.[76] MacArthur's unwarranted gamble to defend forward had failed.

Despite the failure of his strategy, "General MacArthur's name became a symbol of American resistance to a foe who was meeting with success everywhere."[77] Realizing the galvanizing effect of the defense of the Philippines, and aware of the watchful eyes of the peoples of Asia who would castigate the United States for abandoning the Filipino people in their greatest time of need, President Roosevelt directed the War and Navy Departments to make every effort to reinforce MacArthur's forces. But these efforts ran up against the realities of strategy and logistics.[78] The United States had already committed itself to a grand strategy of defeating Germany first before prioritizing the Pacific War. Moreover, getting arms, ammunition, and supplies to the Philippines was easier said than done. Aircraft, of course, could be flown to their destination, provided that a base structure was in place, but the US Asiatic Fleet was too small to counter Japanese control of the seas surrounding Luzon. Supplies could be flown in, but the number of transport aircraft available was so small that two Pan Am clippers were pressed into service to ferry .50-caliber ammunition to the Philippines.[79] The War Department diverted a convoy containing two regiments of artillery and B-17 aircraft escorted by the heavy cruiser USS *Pensacola* to Brisbane, Australia, where it became the foundation for a new command, US Army Forces in Australia. With Guam and Wake Island now under Japanese control, Australia would become the major logistical hub for US forces in the Southwest Pacific. It would take time to turn it into one, a role that Gen. George C. Marshall gave to none other than newly promoted Brig. Gen. Eisenhower, who became head of the Pacific Section of the War Plans Division.

In his new posting, Eisenhower would do what he could to support MacArthur and his command in the Philippines, even though Ike knew the forces on Bataan and Corregidor were doomed. "In spite of difficulties, risks, and fierce competition for every asset we had, a great nation such as ours, no matter how unprepared for war, could not afford cold-bloodedly to turn its back upon our Filipino wards and the many thousand Americans, troops and civilians, in the archipelago," Eisenhower wrote later. "We had to do whatever was remotely possible for the hapless islands, particularly by air support and by providing vital supplies, although the end result might be no more than postponement of disaster." The peoples of Asia "may excuse failure but they will not excuse abandonment," he argued to Gen. Marshall, who agreed with Eisenhower's assessment.[80]

For his part, MacArthur urged a change not only in the national strategy for the Philippines, but also in the Allied grand strategy for the conduct of the war. He believed that the United States should focus its air and naval power against Japan, which was isolated in the Pacific and vulnerable to a concerted strike. Otherwise, MacArthur warned, "If the Philippines and the Netherlands East Indies go, so will Singapore and the entire Asiatic continent."[81] He was, of course, right about the threat posed by the Japanese, but the Allies, then meeting in Washington, DC, at the first of their wartime summit conferences, were not about to change course. Germany would be defeated first and then Japan – even if it meant having to retake much of the Asian continent and most of the Pacific in the process.

The noose was tightening on MacArthur and his remaining forces. By the end of the year, the last of the submarines of the US Asiatic Fleet had departed, leaving behind just three gunboats, three minesweepers, and six motor torpedo boats.[82] As Japanese forces advanced toward Manila, airfields outside the Bataan Peninsula became untenable. Even had aircraft been available to fly to Luzon, there would have been nowhere for them to land. On December 23, less than two days after the Japanese landing at Lingayen Gulf, MacArthur decided that his forces would withdraw to the Bataan Peninsula and Corregidor after all, in accordance with basic American strategy since the dawn of War Plan Orange. The problem was the lack of supplies to sustain tens of thousands of American and Filipino forces in such a confined area. Because of his insistence on defending forward at the beaches, MacArthur and his staff had neglected to move sufficient food onto Bataan and Corregidor to sustain forces there for more than a couple of months.[83] They had not evacuated Filipino civilians from the area or established the required infrastructure to sustain a lengthy siege. MacArthur's decision not to prepare Bataan for a lengthy defense ranks as his most critical error of the entire campaign in 1941–1942.

MacArthur's decisions required his ill-trained units to conduct a delaying action while in contact with numerically superior Japanese forces, one of the most difficult of tactical maneuvers. That they did so successfully is a testament to the leadership of Maj. Gen. Wainwright and his subordinate commanders. To save the Philippine capital from destruction, MacArthur declared Manila an open city, which allowed the Japanese to occupy it without subjecting it to bombardment or fighting. It took several days before the Japanese in the Philippines got the memo, for Japanese aircraft continued to bomb military installations in the Manila area.[84]

As Wainwright's troops withdrew toward Bataan, MacArthur moved USAFFE headquarters, the Philippine High Commissioner, and the Commonwealth government to the island fortress of Corregidor on Christmas Eve. A week later, Philippine Supreme Court Chief Justice José A. Santos swore in President Quezon and Vice President Osmeña for their second terms in office outside the east portal of the Malinta Tunnel, actually a grid of passages drilled into solid rock beneath Malinta Hill. After a short stay in a house on Topside (the elevated western head of Corregidor), the tunnel would be Jean and Arthur MacArthur's home for the next three months, "both a refuge and a prison," while Gen. MacArthur, no doubt due to his claustrophobia, stayed in a house outside the east entrance. Safe from the ravages of Japanese bombs and shells, the tunnel system was also "a dusty, musty, crowded, dark, damp hole in the ground," which made its denizens yearn "for the sunshine and fresh air outside."[85] Brig. Gen. Marshall stayed behind in Manila and supervised the movement of supplies to Corregidor and Bataan, as well as the destruction of Manila's port facilities and whatever supplies could not be moved in the time available.[86] On Bataan, the newly promoted Maj. Gen. Parker assumed command of the Bataan Defense Force, initially consisting of the 31st and 41st Philippine Army divisions, charged with preparing defenses on the peninsula in advance of the arrival of the North and South Luzon Forces.

The North Luzon Force was to fight a delaying action on five lines, designated D-1 through D-5, anchored on key defensive terrain features from Lingayen Gulf to Bataan. D-1 was aspirational, meant as a position "to reorganize the badly disorganized forces north of the Agno River."[87] The first real delaying position was D-2, situated along the Agno River south of Lingayen Gulf. D-3 and D-4 were each a day's march to the south. The final line, D-5, was anchored on Ft. Stotsenburg, Mt. Arayat, and the Candaba Swamp. Here the North Luzon Force would hold until the South Luzon Force could withdraw into Bataan. Engineers would build obstacles and destroy bridges along likely avenues of approach to further delay Japanese forces.

By Christmas Day, the 21st, 11th, and 91st Philippine Divisions and the 26th Cavalry (PS) were arrayed west to east along line D-2, south of the Agno River. The 26th Cavalry (PS) fought valiantly for Tayug before superior Japanese strength forced a withdrawal from the river. The cavalrymen, reduced to a fraction of their full strength while standing up to Japanese forces in three pitched battles, went into reserve while the Philippine Army divisions continued the fight.[88] A Japanese attack on Carmen destroyed the 1st Battalion, 21st Infantry and forced the withdrawal of the 11th Philippine Division to the south. By December 27, the North Luzon Force was established along line D-3, although fifteen tanks were abandoned when a bridge was prematurely detonated, leaving a tank company stranded north of a stream at Moncada.[89] As Japanese forces had temporarily halted to reorganize, there was no contact along the D-3 line, and the North Luzon Force withdrew to the D-4 line on the night of December 27–28. Wainwright, concerned about retaining the bridges over the Pampanga River at Calumpit over which the South Luzon Force would have to pass to reach Bataan, decided to hold this line "at all costs."[90]

The *48th Division*, supported by tanks and artillery, attacked the Philippine 91st Division at Cabanatuan on December 29, forcing its withdrawal from the line of the Pampanga River. The Japanese quickly advanced south along Highway 5, destroying an attempt to reform the defensive positions near the village of Gapan along the Penaranda River. In the center of the D-4 line stretching from Zaragoza and La Paz, the 11th Infantry Regiment of the 11th Infantry Division, commanded by Maj. Russell W. Volckmann, put up a spirited defense against Japanese attempts to envelop the position from the east.[91] The regiment delayed the Japanese advance for twenty-four hours before receiving orders to withdraw to the D-5 line on the afternoon of December 30. In the west, the 21st Philippine Division likewise put up stiff resistance prior to receiving orders to withdraw south. By dawn the next day, the division was established along the D-5 line. "For the most part," concludes the official US Army historian, "the withdrawal was conducted as well as it could be with the untrained and ill-equipped Philippine Army troops."[92]

The South Luzon Force, now under the command of Maj. Gen. Albert M. Jones, likewise conducted a week-long delaying action from its positions in the mountains west of Lamon Bay to Manila and thence northward to Bataan. The green Philippine troops, unexpectedly reinforced by 300 retired Philippine Scouts who used taxis to move from Fort McKinley to the sound of the guns, did about as well as one could expect of inadequately trained and poorly equipped soldiers. Poorly disciplined soldiers fled when attacked by well-trained Japanese units. Battalions and companies dissolved and had to be reformed in subsequent positions without a coherent chain of command to bring order to the hastily reconstituted units.[93] Nevertheless, the force was able to delay in the face of Japanese assaults and destroy the bridges over which the Japanese would need to pass. On December 28, the South Luzon Force was saved from further combat by Gen. MacArthur, who, concerned about the integrity of the North Luzon Force D-4 defensive line, ordered Jones and his forces to break contact with the Japanese and withdraw through Manila and into Bataan before the Japanese could seize the bridges at Calumpit. The South Luzon Force executed these orders to perfection, establishing defensive positions at Plaridel to block the *48th Division* bearing down from the north and closing on Bataan by New Year's Day.[94]

The defense of Plaridel and, to its north, the town of Baliuag was crucial to ensure USAFFE elements east of the Pampanga River could withdraw into Bataan. As Japanese forces massed for an assault on Baliuag, Jones ordered a preemptive attack by two platoons of tanks from Company C, 192nd Tank

Battalion. At 17:00 the tanks smashed into the northern end of the town, destroying eight Japanese tanks and disrupting the infantry preparing to attack. This action enabled the forces east of the river to cross the Calumpit bridges without disruption, the last ones clearing the river to the west by 05:00 on January 1. They then headed for San Fernando and the road to the Bataan Peninsula. Wainwright ordered the destruction of the Calumpit bridges at 06:15.[95]

As the main strength of the *14th Army* headed for Manila, the 11th and 21st Philippine Divisions delayed Japanese forces along the D-5 line before withdrawing south toward Bataan. The road into the peninsula was jammed with vehicular and pedestrian traffic, for long stretches bumper-to-bumper.[96] But the withdrawal was successful, with Filipino units repelling Japanese attacks and buying time for an orderly move south. By early morning on January 2, the final units of the North and South Luzon Forces had passed through San Fernando, merging into a single command under Wainwright's tactical control.

The 11th and 21st Philippine Divisions defended a line from Guagua in the east to Porac in the west, with their flanks protected by swamps and mountains. The Japanese attacked this line with two reinforced infantry regiments on January 2 and 3, nearly breaking the 21st Philippine Division the next day before being halted by effective artillery fire that reminded one senior officer of Lt. Alonzo Cushing's defense of Cemetery Ridge during the Battle of Gettysburg.[97] The advance of the *Tanaka Detachment* cut off the 11th Infantry Regiment and other portions of the 11th Philippine Division, necessitating a circuitous night march of thirty miles to new positions just north of Santa Cruz. By the morning of January 5, a new line had been formed south of the Gumain River, buying time for the troops in Bataan to prepare defensive positions. Wainwright ordered a withdrawal from the Gumain River at dusk, beginning with the 11th Philippine Division followed by the 21st Philippine Division. The two divisions passed through the town of Layac and across the Culo River into Bataan. The withdrawal was accomplished by 02:00 on January 6, after which engineers demolished the bridge across the Culo River.[98] The US 31st Infantry, 71st and 72nd Philippine Infantry, and 26th Cavalry (PS) defended the Culo River until nightfall under intense Japanese pressure, and then withdrew south under cover of darkness. "It was, in short, a sickening experience to withdraw into the peninsula," Wainwright lamented. "I issued the order with the greatest of sorrow."[99] MacArthur's forces were now in Bataan, but how long they could hold the peninsula was an open question.

Japanese troops entered Manila in the late afternoon of January 2, taking control of the Philippine capital. They interned the roughly 3,000 American and British civilians who remained in the city on the campus of Santo Tomas University, where they would remain until their dramatic liberation 3 years later.

On Corregidor, MacArthur advocated a strategy of securing Mindanao as a base for future operations in conjunction with a relief expedition to keep open the lines of communication to the Philippines. The American and British staffs, then meeting in Washington, recognizing that the basic grand strategy of the Allied Powers was to defeat Germany first, recommended instead the defense of the Malay Barrier from Australia to Burma. The War Plans Division concluded that a Philippines relief expedition was simply not in the cards. Although the planners sympathized with the plight of MacArthur and his troops, the forces, weapons, and equipment – most notably combat vessels and aircraft – required to restore America's position in the Philippine archipelago in the time available before the collapse of the positions on Bataan and Corregidor simply did not exist. It was the same conclusion that successive groups of planners working on War Plan Orange had reached for more than two decades. Secretary of War Henry L. Stimson and Gen. Marshall acknowledged the study, but never wavered in their attempts to send MacArthur whatever aid was available.[100]

Although the strategic situation was far from enviable, the tactical situation on Bataan worked in favor of the Americans and the Filipinos, at least as long as supplies held out. The terrain was well known to the commanders, who had mapped out prospective defensive lines before the war. The peninsula is just twenty miles wide, with only a single highway running north–south down both sides and a single road cutting east–west from Bagac to Pilar across the waist. The rest is mountainous jungle, with ample cover and concealment to protect defending forces from overhead observation. The main defensive line ran from Mauban on the west to Mabatang on the east and was bisected by Mt. Natib, an extinct volcano rising to 4,222 feet. A subsequent defensive line from Bagac to Orion roughly paralleled the east–west road approximately eight miles to the south.

Maj. Gen. Wainwright commanded the 22,500 soldiers of the I Corps on the western half of the peninsula, consisting of the 1st Regular, 31st, and 91st Philippine Divisions, as well as elements of the 71st Philippine Division and the 26th Cavalry Regiment (PS) and supporting artillery.[101] Maj. Gen. Parker commanded the 25,000 soldiers of the II Corps on the eastern half of the peninsula, consisting of the 11th, 21st, 41st, and 51st Philippine Divisions, as well as the 57th Infantry Regiment (PS) and supporting artillery. In the service command area in the southern part of the peninsula were positioned the 2nd Division (Philippine Constabulary), elements of the 71st Philippine Division, provisional infantry units created from air corps personnel no longer needed to service nonexistent aircraft, and a provisional battalion of sailors and marines. The Philippine Division, minus one regiment, plus a tank group, a group of M3 GMC 75mm guns, and corps and USAFFE artillery were in reserve. MacArthur, of course, was in overall command, which he exercised through a Bataan echelon under Brig. Gen. Marshall in USAFFE headquarters on Corregidor.[102]

MacArthur's decision to move supplies northward to support a forward defense of Lingayen Gulf invalidated the plan to move supplies into Bataan to support an extended defense of the peninsula. Movement of supplies did not begin in earnest until December 23, by which time it was too late to provision the peninsula with the amount needed to sustain an extended siege. So, instead of sufficient supplies to support 43,000 soldiers for 6 months, logisticians were able to move only a fraction of the amount necessary to support forces on Bataan that by January 7 had swelled to 80,000 soldiers and 26,000 civilians. Food was the critical shortage, with only a 30-day supply sufficient to support 100,000 soldiers. Because of pre-war stockpiling, Corregidor was better off, with sufficient supplies to sustain 10,000 soldiers for 6 months. Nevertheless, on January 5, MacArthur placed all soldiers and civilians on Bataan and Corregidor, himself included, on half rations, about 2,000 calories a day.[103] Malnutrition and diseases, particularly malaria, would take their toll on the forces in Bataan as the weeks rolled by. "The shortage of supplies of all types," records the official US Army history, "and especially food, had a greater effect on the outcome of the siege of Bataan than any other single factor."[104]

One factor in favor of the US and Filipino troops was Japanese overconfidence. Convinced that little remained of the battle for Luzon other than mopping up, the *Southern Area Army* withdrew the *48th Division* to prepare for the invasion of Java, replacing it with the newly formed and much less capable *65th Brigade*, commanded by Lt. Gen. Akira Nara. Poor Japanese reconnaissance led to an ineffective opening artillery barrage when the battle for Bataan commenced at 15:00 on January 9. The next day, MacArthur made a trip by PT boat to visit the troops on Bataan, the only time he ever left the island of Corregidor before departing to Australia in March. Of course, he needed to remain near his communications center to dialogue with the War Department, and there was a risk in sailing over unfriendly waters to visit Bataan. But his troops needed to see him, and his reluctance to visit them contrasts sharply with his performance in World War I, when he frequently led trench raids. No doubt he was in better shape when younger, and traveling to Bataan was physically draining. Wags among the troops, however, took his absence for cowardice, which was certainly not the case. But the nickname they coined, "Dugout Doug," stuck.[105]

It took two days before Japanese forces uncovered the main line of resistance in the II Corps sector, and their attacks against it met with heavy losses. Japanese units became disoriented in the difficult terrain. They continued to hammer at the II Corps' lines, however, and by January 15 the situation on the western flank of the corps had become unsustainable. Maj. Gen. Parker responded by requesting reinforcements, which USAFFE provided. Upon receiving control of the Philippine Division (minus the 57th Infantry [PS], which had already been committed) and most of the 31st Philippine Division, Parker ordered a counterattack. The 51st Philippine Division scattered in the face of Japanese attacks, but Japanese commanders failed to capitalize on the gap thus created. A counterattack by the US 31st and 45th (PS) Infantry Regiments beginning on the morning of January 17 and continuing for several days failed to restore the main line of resistance along the Balantay River. The Japanese commander realized the weakness of the American and Filipino line and shifted the bulk of his forces to the high ground in the west to envelop their positions. A Japanese attack on January 22 forced the Philippine Division back to its original start line where it had begun its counterattack five days earlier. Maj. Gen. Parker realized the predicament of his corps, threatened by Japanese troops that could drive his forces against Manila Bay. Moreover, the *9th Regiment* had by this time worked its way south along the Abo-Abo River valley to Guitol, where it seized and held the high ground dominating the southwestern flank of II Corps. The situation had become critical.[106]

The *122nd Regiment* contacted Wainwright's I Corps' outpost line on January 16. Reinforced by a battle group of the *16th Division* under the command of Maj. Gen. Naoki Kimura, the regiment attacked the main defensive line on the western side of Bataan beginning on January 18. By January 21, the *3rd Battalion, 20th Regiment* managed to infiltrate through I Corps lines to block its main supply route, creating an emergency so critical that Wainwright personally led a platoon of twenty men in a counterattack in an attempt to destroy the Japanese position. His attack stalled, but other units from the 91st Philippine Division, 26th Cavalry (PS), and Company C, 194th Tank Battalion were marching toward the sound of the guns. Beginning on January 22 and continuing for several days, these forces attempted to reduce the Japanese roadblock and thereby relieve pressure on the 1st Philippine Infantry Regiment to the north, which was defending against heavy attacks. Despite numerical superiority, the counterattacks were unsuccessful. By the evening of January 24, the situation was critical, with the 1st Regular Philippine Division desperately short of rations and ammunition. Col. Kearie L. Berry, in command of two regiments of the 1st Regular Philippine Division, made the decision to withdraw from the main line of resistance. The next morning, the division withdrew along the only route available, the beaches fronting the west coast of Bataan. The route was passable only to foot traffic. Although most of the troops made it south to new positions with their small arms, all the division's artillery was abandoned in the withdrawal.[107]

With both corps under pressure, MacArthur ordered Sutherland to make a personal visit to assess the situation. On January 22, Sutherland arrived in Bataan and spoke to Maj. Gen. Parker near his headquarters in Limay. Concerned by what he heard and with all USAFFE reserves already committed to the fight, Sutherland gave Parker and Wainwright a warning order to withdraw their forces to the subsequent defensive line, an order subsequently approved by MacArthur.[108] Beginning on the night of January 23–24, II Corps began its move to the rear. The first night's movement went smoothly, but poor traffic control on the night of January 24–25 led to a tangle of units and mass confusion, which the Japanese were unable to take advantage of. Japanese aircraft bombed and strafed units that moved during the day, but II Corps moved into its new positions by the morning of January 26. In the west, I Corps withdrew with little difficulty to the subsequent defensive line, reaching it at the same time as II Corps to the east. In its attack against the main defensive line, the *65th Brigade* had sustained nearly 25 percent casualties, but it had forced American and Philippine forces back to their last defensive position on Bataan. Those forces would stand and fight where they now stood. MacArthur wrote to Marshall, "With its [the subsequent defensive line] occupation all maneuvering possibilities will cease. I intend to fight it out to complete destruction."[109]

As I and II Corps began their withdrawal to the subsequent defensive line, a new threat developed to the rear along the southwest coast of Bataan. On the night of January 22–23, a Japanese battalion landed on Quinauan Point and Longoskawayan Point deep in the Service Command Area. The area was thinly defended by a pick-up team of various US and Filipino army, constabulary, naval, and air personnel and a few artillery pieces under the command of the 71st Philippine Division (Brig. Gen. Clyde A. Selleck). Most of the converted infantrymen, who had served up to now as air crews

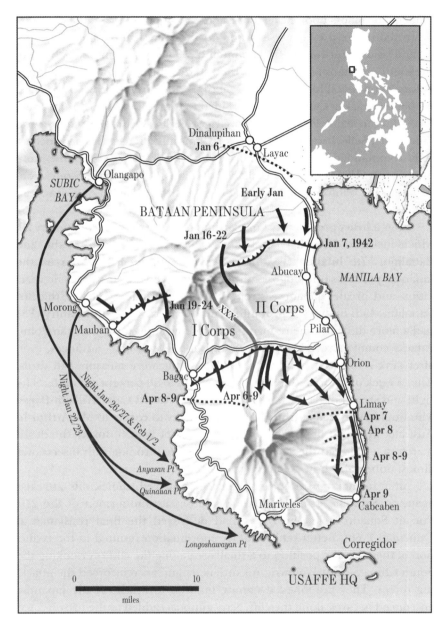

Map 3: Bataan and Corregidor, January–May 1942.

or police, had received only a few days training as such. The Japanese had actually been heading to Caibobo Point further to the north, but inadequate maps, poor navigation, and the opposition of PT 34, which destroyed two of the Japanese landing barges, led to the force being split up and landing further south than intended. The 300 troops that landed in the south at Longoskawayan Point briefly seized the key terrain on Mt. Pucot before a combined force of sailors, marines, and airmen drove them back. A counterattack at Quinauan Point failed to force the 600 dug-in Japanese back into the sea. Believing that more vigorous leadership was required, on January 24, Selleck was relieved by Col. Clinton A. Pierce, who had successfully commanded the 26th Cavalry (PS) during the past month. More importantly, USAFFE dispatched two battalions of Philippine Scouts from its reserve to reinforce the troops at Quinauan Point and Longoskawayan Point.[110]

After a heavy preparatory bombardment on the morning of January 29, which included 12-inch coastal mortars based on Corregidor, the 2nd Battalion, 57th Infantry (PS) attacked and by nightfall had overrun the Japanese positions on Longoskawayan Point. Because of heavy jungle vegetation and greater Japanese strength, the Philippine Scouts of the 3rd Battalion, 45th Infantry (PS) reinforced by Company B, 57th Infantry (PS) had a more difficult time reducing Japanese positions on Quinauan Point. Attacks commenced on January 28 and, for several days, advances, even after tank reinforcements bolstered the assault, were measured in yards. After a week of combat, the Scouts were down to 50 percent strength. "The sight and stench of death were everywhere," recalled Capt. William Dyess, who would later escape from Japanese captivity to report to MacArthur in Australia what had happened to the survivors of Bataan during the death march that followed the surrender. "The jungle, droning with insects, was almost unbearably hot."[111]

After further tank reinforcements had arrived, the Scouts attacked again on February 4. By February 8, the Scouts and airmen of the 21st Pursuit Squadron, led by Dyess, had destroyed the final resistance at Quinauan Point. Better tank–infantry coordination resulted in the reduction of the Japanese position to a small area along the cliff overlooking the South China Sea. At Wainwright's orders, engineers reinforced the attacking forces. They fashioned dynamite bundles to finish off the Japanese ensconced in caves along the cliff. Navy gunboats added to the fire directed at Japanese cave positions.[112] "There were no survivors," Wainwright remarked in his memoirs. "It had at last dawned on me, as it was to dawn on so many commanders who followed me in the Pacific War, that the Jap usually prefers death to surrender."[113]

The Battle of the Points was not yet over, for, at 03:00 on January 27, the Japanese, in an effort to support the *2nd Battalion, 20th Infantry* fighting at Quinauan Point, landed 200 soldiers of the *1st Battalion, 20th Infantry* on the southwest coast of Bataan. Once again, poor navigation led to the force landing astray, this time between the Anyasan and Silaiim Rivers 2,000 yards north of Quinauan Point. The 17th Pursuit Squadron and the 2nd Battalion, 2nd Philippine Constabulary marched to the area, where they found the Japanese dug in approximately 1,000 yards from the beach. The situation remained tenuous until the arrival on January 29 of the 2nd Battalion, 45th Infantry (PS) along with the 1st Battalion, 1st Philippine Constabulary and the 1st Battalion, 12th Philippine Infantry. The combined forces were prepared to attack the next day, when the preparatory artillery barrage landed short, killing or wounding twenty scouts and ending the attack before it began. Pierce, now a brigadier general, ordered the 57th Infantry (PS) into the area, and its commander, Col. Edmund J. Lilly, Jr., assumed control of the operation.[114]

Meanwhile, the commander of the *14th Army*, Lt. Gen. Homma, had finally decided to support the landings, which up to this time had been a local affair. Attempts to supply the troops ashore by air came to naught because of poor navigation. A more significant effort came on the night of February 1–2, when the remainder of the *1st Battalion, 20th Infantry* sailed to reinforce the landing at Quinauan Point. Fortunately for the defenders, a written order detailing the operation had been found on the body of a dead Japanese officer, allowing USAFFE to alert its units and gather reinforcements. A coordinated attack against the Japanese flotilla by artillery, four P-40 fighters (all that remained of the FEAF), and PT 32 destroyed about half of the Japanese force, but the remainder made it ashore at Salaiim Point, where it joined the company already there.[115]

An attack by three battalions of Philippine Scouts at dawn on February 2 hit strong resistance except on the southern flank, where the tortuous terrain slowed the advance to a crawl. It took five days for the 1st Battalion, 57th Infantry (PS) (minus one company) on the southern flank to make contact with the Japanese in its zone and when it did, the Japanese repelled its assault. Lilly reinforced this unit with air corps troops and a battalion of Philippine Constabulary, while a company of tanks reinforced the attack down the trail leading to the beach in the center of the zone between the Anyasan and Silaiim Rivers. The end of the fighting at Quinauan Point on February 8 enabled further reinforcements to flow north. By evening on February 11, the Scouts had reached the mouth of the Anyasan River and the end of the battle was in sight. At dawn the next day the Japanese attempted to break out of their encirclement, exploiting a gap in the lines of the 2nd Battalion, 45th Infantry (PS). The attack succeeded in penetrating the line and overrunning the command posts of the 17th Pursuit Squadron and Company F, 45th Infantry (PS). Lilly ordered the 3rd Battalion, 57th Infantry (PS) into the area to restore the situation. Its attack began at noon and made steady progress that afternoon and the next day. By the middle of the afternoon on February 13, the Scouts had reached the beach, hastily abandoned by Japanese troops who attempted to swim or raft to safety. Few made it – "the beach was befouled with bloated and rotting bodies" – while a group of about eighty Japanese who had infiltrated out of the area to the north were finally located three days later and killed in a two-day battle.[116] The Battle of the Points was over; it had cost the Japanese two battalions of much-needed infantry.

The battle for the new main line of resistance, now positioned on the subsequent defensive line running from Bagac to Orion across the waist of the peninsula, continued to rage. The mountainous, jungle-covered terrain, intense heat, and shortage of provisions tested the resilience of the 90,000 troops packed into the 200 square miles of southern Bataan. The II Corps sector in the east was divided into five subordinate sectors, labeled A through E, while the I Corps sector in the west was divided into a right sector and a left sector, with a south sector controlling the beach defenses of southwest Bataan. As the corps were occupying their new lines, Sutherland (presumably with MacArthur's consent) decided to withdraw the Philippine Division to form a USAFFE reserve. The subsequent confusion of this last-minute decision would profoundly impact the battle to come.[117]

Lt. Gen. Homma, believing the new defensive line was further south than it actually was, ordered an immediate attack. In this case fortune favored the bold, for the attack hit the sectors most affected by the unfortunate shuffling of units caused by the withdrawal of the Philippine Division into USAFFE reserve. In Sector C in the II Corps' sector, Brig. Gen. Clifford Bluemel was caught flat-footed by the repositioning of units out of his defensive line on Maj. Gen. Parker's orders; apparently the corps staff failed to inform Bluemel of the changes to the order of battle.[118] Bluemel did what he could to plug the gaps, but his line was exceedingly thin. Nevertheless, it held. At 15:00 on January 27, Lt. Gen. Nara's *65th Brigade* attacked, but was unable to penetrate the main line of resistance. That night the 41st Philippine Infantry arrived to bolster Sector C, just in time to repulse a renewed Japanese attack the next day. A renewed attack on January 31, preceded by air and artillery support, likewise failed to pierce the defensive line. As the Japanese withdrew their lead units from a bamboo thicket in front of Trail 2, the key terrain in Sector C, a counterattack by the 31st Engineer Battalion on February 2–3 regained the ground lost since the beginning of the Japanese offensive. The danger of a Japanese break-through in this area, for now, was over.[119]

In the western half of Bataan, the *Kimura Detachment* (Maj. Gen. Naoki Kimura, soon to be superseded by Lt. Gen. Susumu Morioka), attacked on January 26 down the road bordering the west coast. Unable to advance in this area, the Japanese found a weakness in Wainwright's lines in the sector occupied by the 1st Regular Philippine Division. The *20th Regiment* assaulted the area on the night of January 28, exploiting a gap created by the attack and advancing south along the Cotar and Tuol Rivers in nearly impenetrable terrain. The Japanese force ended up splitting into two components, each occupying a pocket of terrain behind the main line of resistance. Counterattacks against the pockets quickly discovered that they were occupied by substantial forces, requiring the commitment of reserve forces to reduce. The 1st Regular Philippine Division restored the main line of resistance on January 31, thereby cutting off the Japanese forces in the pockets from resupply. Tank attacks on February 2, 3, and 4 penetrated the larger pocket, but accompanying infantry could not make headway against the dug-in Japanese infantry.[120] On the night of February 6–7, a renewed Japanese attack managed to penetrate 600 yards through the lines of the 11th Philippine Infantry, but remained 800 yards short of the troops surrounded in the larger pocket.[121]

It was now Wainwright's turn to attack. On the morning of February 7, troops from the 1st Regular Philippine Division advanced on the smaller pocket and by the next evening had closed the noose around it, with the exception of an undetected gap on the eastern flank. When the advance resumed on the morning of February 9, the attacking troops found only dead bodies and discarded equipment. The surviving Japanese had escaped the trap to the east during the night, only to be killed later that morning attempting to move north through the main line of resistance. American and Philippine forces now focused their efforts on eliminating the larger pocket of Japanese, which had received orders to withdraw to the north to join with the forces that had created a salient in the main line of resistance. Filipino forces reduced the pocket on the afternoon of February 12, again finding only dead bodies (450 including those already buried in shallow graves) and abandoned equipment and supplies. The rest worked their way slowly north, with 377 Japanese finally regaining the safety of their lines at noon on February 15. The *20th Regiment* had been effectively eliminated as a combat-effective unit.[122]

For the moment, Lt. Gen. Homma had seen enough to know the wiser course of action was to suspend the offensive in Bataan while Japanese forces seized other portions of the Philippines. By the middle of February, the *16th Division's* infantry strength was just over 700 soldiers, while the *65th Brigade* had lost 4,000 of the 5,000 men with which it had entered combat the previous month. The American and Filipino supply situation on Bataan was growing worse by the day, and waiting a couple of months before attacking again would allow malnutrition to take its course on the combat effectiveness of their units. It would also allow time for Tokyo to move reinforcements to the Philippines to bolster the fighting strength of the *14th Army.* On February 8, Homma ordered a general withdrawal northward to defensive positions.[123]

The same day the Japanese began their withdrawal, President Quezon, incensed by the lack of support from the United States for Philippine defense, messaged Washington with a proposal for the United States to grant the Philippines immediate independence, after which Quezon would declare neutrality and request the withdrawal of both Japanese and American forces from the islands.[124] The scheme was wholly impractical and ignored the strategic needs of the Japanese, who would never abide by its terms. As Gen. Marshall and Brig. Gen. Eisenhower worked on a reply to that effect, Secretary of War Henry L. Stimson walked into the office. "There are times when men have to die," he pointedly remarked.[125] After a flurry of messages between Quezon, MacArthur, and President Roosevelt, the issue died.[126]

President Roosevelt made his policy clear by writing MacArthur, "American forces will continue to keep our flag flying in the Philippines so long as there remains any possibility of resistance."[127] Roosevelt also ordered MacArthur to evacuate Quezon and his family from the Philippines, which would end the threat of Filipino capitulation. Quezon and his family left Corregidor via submarine on February 20 to head the Philippine government, first in the Visayas and then in exile. Before he left Malinta Tunnel, MacArthur assured him, "You're going back to Malacañan Palace, Mr. President, if I have to put you there on the points of my bayonets!"[128] Quezon would die of tuberculosis before MacArthur could make good on his promise. As he boarded the boat that would take him to the submarine, Quezon gave MacArthur the signet ring he habitually wore with the words, "When they find your body, I want them to know you fought for my country."[129] He also awarded MacArthur something far more tangible – $500,000 for his service to the Philippines, as well as awarding lesser but still sizable amounts to Sutherland, Richard Marshall, and aide Lt. Col. Sidney L. Huff.[130] Since he was a serving US military officer, MacArthur's acceptance of the money was ethically questionable, but the gift was in keeping with his close relationship with the Philippine president and fell within the norms of Filipino culture. Aware of the transaction, Roosevelt, Stimson, and Gen. Marshall made no objections to it.[131]

Aside from Quezon's gloominess to the rejection of his proposal, after the defeat of the Japanese offensive, morale among the defenders of Bataan soared. MacArthur had earlier, on January 15, issued a message to the troops, promising substantial reinforcements from the United States and urging the troops to "hold until these reinforcements arrive. No further retreat is possible. We have more troops in Bataan than the Japanese have thrown against us; our supplies are ample [not true]; a determined defense will defeat the enemy's attack. It is a question now of courage and of determination. I call upon every soldier in Bataan to fight in his assigned position, resisting every attack. This is the only road to salvation. If we fight we will win; if we retreat we will be destroyed."[132] MacArthur was navigating a fine line between motivating the troops for continued exertions and informing them that they would all be sacrificed to buy time for the United States to marshal its forces for a counteroffensive. To be fair to MacArthur, messages from the War Department seemed to promise aid without making specific commitments, leading him to believe more support was forthcoming than was actually the case.[133] The War Department's deception was deliberate; MacArthur's internal confusion was self-inflicted.

The War Department attempted to run the Japanese blockade to send food, ammunition, and medical supplies to the Philippines, but with scant success. Japanese aircraft and naval vessels were able to interdict cargo vessels, which alone had the requisite capacity to transport sufficient quantities of supplies to Bataan and Corregidor. Submarines and aircraft brought in small amounts of badly needed supplies and took out 220 personnel and part of the Philippines' gold and silver reserves, but they lacked the capacity to transport the one commodity needed more than any other – food.[134]

MacArthur missed an opportunity at this point to prepare the ground-work for an extensive guerrilla campaign against the Japanese. Other than one small party led by his provost-marshal, Major Claude A. Thorp, that infiltrated into the Zambales Mountains region, there were no efforts to establish a guerrilla resistance on Luzon. There were efforts to stockpile supplies and prepare for guerrilla conflict on islands in the Central and Southern Philippines, but a misunderstanding with the War Department would lead to the forced surrender of all US and Filipino forces in the

Philippines after the fall of Corregidor in May. If a guerrilla movement were to begin thereafter, it would have to grow organically.

Although the defenders of Bataan did not know it, this moment was the high-water mark of the campaign. Some among them wanted to launch a counteroffensive, but it was questionable whether it would have succeeded, given the waning strength of the soldiers. Washington – as well as by now MacArthur – had a clearer assessment of the strategic situation, which had not changed. Bataan would eventually fall, and everyone there would either die or be shuffled off to prisoner of war camps. MacArthur was willing to fight it out to the end on Bataan and Corregidor. That was certainly one possible future, for the British fortress of Singapore had fallen on February 15, with 90,000 troops entering captivity along with their commander, Lt. Gen. Arthur E. Percival.

President Roosevelt was unwilling to see MacArthur suffer such a fate, perhaps as much for his party's political prospects in the mid-term elections that year as for genuine concern over losing MacArthur's military expertise. In any case, the collapse of the ABDA (American–British–Dutch–Australian) Command forced a split in command arrangements in the Pacific, with the British commanding forces in Southeast Asia and India and the Americans commanding the broad expanse of the Pacific Ocean, including what would become a new Southwest Pacific Command. MacArthur was the logical choice to command the latter organization, and this role had the added benefit of keeping him away from Washington, where he could interfere with the grand strategy of defeating Germany first. Furthermore, MacArthur was now firmly embedded in the American people's imagination as THE hero of the Pacific War. Much of this was due to MacArthur's masterful and often deceptive manipulation of the media. According to his most recent biographer, MacArthur's communiqués "were masterpieces of verbal pyrotechnics, combining a strong dose of poetic license – or, one might say, heroic license – with artistic ego."[135] Three-quarters of those messages sent in the first four months of the war "mentioned only one individual, MacArthur."[136]

On February 22, President Roosevelt ordered MacArthur to turn over command of the forces on Bataan and Corregidor to Wainwright and decamp to Mindanao, where he would organize a prolonged (presumably guerrilla) defense. From there, MacArthur would fly to Australia to assume command of a new theater of operations in the Southwest Pacific. He was assured a major effort was under way to turn Australia into a robust base for future operations.[137]

MacArthur's initial thought was to refuse to go, and he drafted a message to that effect. But cooler heads among his immediate staff prevailed, and they convinced MacArthur to move to Australia to lead a counteroffensive to relieve the troops still battling on Luzon. MacArthur then accepted the President's order, with the caveat that the general would determine the right departure date, based on the situation in the Philippines. On Corregidor, MacArthur turned over command to Maj. Gen. Wainwright, promising to promote him to lieutenant general if he was still fighting on Bataan when MacArthur returned. Both had been first captains of their respective classes at West Point, and both had to this point thrived in their army careers. "I'll be on Bataan if I'm alive," Wainwright responded. It was a hollow promise; Wainwright survived the war as a Japanese prisoner, but would never see Bataan again.[138]

The right date arrived on March 11, when MacArthur, his wife and son and the son's nanny, and a select group of staff officers – twenty-one people altogether – boarded four PT boats at Corregidor and began a hazardous journey to Mindanao.[139] On the dock, MacArthur looked back at the Rock, but "the desperate scene showed only a black mass of destruction."[140] MacArthur had carefully chosen his fellow travelers. Most of them were

1.2: Gen. Douglas MacArthur and Maj. Gen. Richard Sutherland in Malinta Tunnel, March 1, 1942. Their expressions reflect the dire situation facing the troops in Bataan and Corregidor. (Credit: US Army Signal Corps Photo)

staff officers he would need in Australia; the Bataan Gang would remain largely intact.[141]

After two days of rough sailing in heavy seas, during which at one point the boats became separated and one dumped its spare fuel believing it was under attack by a Japanese warship, thereby necessitating the transfer of its passengers to the other three boats, the small flotilla reached the northern coast of Mindanao. From there the party was trucked to Del Monte airfield, where supposedly B-17s were waiting to ferry them to Australia. Of the four planes initially sent from Australia, only one had arrived, and Maj. Gen. Sharp considered it mechanically unreliable and therefore unsuitable to carry passengers and ordered it to return to Australia. After a sharply worded message from MacArthur to Lt. Gen. George H. Brett, the commander of US Army Forces in Australia, three more B-17s (borrowed from the US Navy) left Australia, with two making it to Del Monte late on March 16. The party was packed aboard the two bombers, which arrived at Batchelor Field fifty miles from Darwin, Australia, at 09:30 the next day in the midst of a Japanese air raid on the city.[142]

MacArthur would undoubtedly be of more use to the United States commanding a theater of war as opposed to being held in a Japanese prisoner of war camp or as a dead martyr, and the President ordered him to withdraw to Australia – the choice had not been MacArthur's, despite what his detractors might claim. "But for those of us who would be left behind on Corregidor and Bataan," recalled Carlos Romulo, "it was like a death sentence."[143]

Back in the Philippines, Wainwright assumed command of forces on Luzon, redesignated as Luzon Force, while Brig. Gen. Sharp would continue to command forces on Mindanao and Brig. Gen. Bradford G. Chynoweth would assume command of forces in the Visayas. Maj. Gen. Jones would assume command of I Corps. MacArthur failed to inform the War Department of these command arrangements, which Gen. Marshall rejected, believing MacArthur's broader responsibilities as theater commander precluded him from directly commanding US and Filipino forces in the Philippines. The War Department confirmed Wainwright, nominated by the President for his third star, as commander of all US and Filipino forces in the Philippines, a command renamed as US Forces in the Philippines (USFIP). This decision would have important ramifications later, when, after the seizure of Corregidor, the Japanese forced Wainwright to surrender all forces in the Philippines, rather than just those on Luzon and in Manila Bay. Upon his ascension to command of

USFIP, Wainwright selected the USAFFE chief of artillery, Maj. Gen. Edward P. King, Jr., to command Luzon Force. It would fall on King's shoulders, when the time came, to surrender the forces on Bataan to the Japanese.[144]

That moment was approaching faster than the new commanders would have wished, if for no other reason than that food was running out. In January, the troops subsisted on 2,000 calories a day, half of the amount required for an active man in combat. By February, the amount had declined to 1,500 calories. On March 22, Wainwright put troops on quarter rations, just 1,000 calories a day, "which according to the surgeon is barely sufficient to sustain life without physical activity."[145] Quartermasters exploited all resources on Bataan to extend the food supply. Rice was harvested and threshed in mills built by engineers. Native carabao were slaughtered for meat, as were the horses and mules of the 26th Cavalry (PS). Local fishermen added tens of thousands of pounds of fish to the food supply. Troops gathered native plants such as camotes (sweet potatoes), mangoes, and bananas, and slaughtered dogs, monkeys, and iguanas for additional meat. Some units had stripped depots bare during the retreat to Bataan and hoarded their food supply; others padded their rolls to receive a greater share of rations. Looting and theft were commonplace. Cigarettes and coffee disappeared, leaving troops desperate for stimulants. The fact that troops on Corregidor ate somewhat better was more a matter of fairness and morale than of substance, for there was simply not enough to go around. When Wainwright assumed command on Corregidor, he shipped some of its food stocks to Bataan to feed the starving troops there. "But it was little more than a crumb for the 70,000 starving men over there," he lamented.[146]

No matter how it was obtained and measured, the supply was limited; by April, the troops had stripped Bataan bare of anything edible. In the wake of malnutrition came maladies of vitamin deficiency such as scurvy, beriberi, and dysentery, adding to the misery of endemic diseases such as hookworm, dengue fever, and, most critically, malaria, as the supply of prophylactics such as quinine ran out. By the end of March, four out of every five soldiers in front-line units on Bataan had been stricken with malaria. The disease hung over the soldiers on Bataan "like a black cloud."[147]

By the end of March, the combat efficiency of the 80,000 defenders of Bataan was fast approaching zero. Starving soldiers could barely defend their positions, much less launch counterattacks or reposition to blunt Japanese advances. "Bataan was a hopeless hell where everything was bad except the will to live, the memories of home . . . and the ever-dimming hope that the great country we represented would somehow find a way to help us,"

Wainwright recalled.[148] He warned the War Department that without provision of additional subsistence to the troops on Bataan, they would be starved into submission by April 15. "In any event," Wainwright concluded, "I assure you that our troops will continue to oppose the enemy as long as they have the physical strength to hold a rifle or wield a bayonet."[149]

The troops nevertheless did what they could to improve their positions. Aided by engineers, the infantrymen arrayed on the main line of resistance had strengthened their fortifications, laid minefields, and strung available barbed wire, of which there was not much. Artillery, tanks, and reserve forces were positioned to counter expected attacks when they came. The Japanese, meanwhile, had reinforced their forces on Luzon in preparation for a final assault on Bataan and Corregidor. The *65th Brigade* and *16th Division* were replenished with individual replacements, while the 11,000 men of the *4th Division* and a 4,000-strong detachment of the *21st Division* arrived on Luzon to bolster Japanese troop strength. Additional aircraft arrived to increase Japanese air strength for the final offensive. Thus, within forty-five days of the defeat of the first Japanese offensive on Bataan, the situation had reversed, with Japanese forces now ready to finish off the American and Filipino garrison.[150]

The final Japanese offensive began on April 3 with a six-hour artillery and air bombardment that devastated parts of the defensive fortifications that the defenders of Bataan had constructed over the past six weeks. Aircraft dropped sixty tons of bombs, while some observers likened the artillery bombardment to the barrages on the Western Front during World War I.[151] At 15:00, Japanese infantry and tanks attacked the western half of the II Corps' line, manned by the 21st and 41st Philippine Infantry Divisions. The reinforced Japanese *4th Division* and *65th Brigade* struck units that were already reeling from the effects of the air and artillery bombardment; by nightfall the Japanese had advanced 1,000 yards against minimal opposition. Maj. Gen. Parker released his reserve, the 33rd Philippine Infantry, to plug the gap left by the disintegration of the 41st Philippine Division, but, by dawn on April 4, the western half of the II Corps line was dangerously thin. Taking advantage of the unexpected success, Lt. Gen. Homma ordered a continuation of the attack.[152]

Japanese air and artillery bombardments once again fell on the luckless remnants of the 42nd and 43rd Philippine Infantry Regiments, causing Filipino infantrymen to flee to the rear. The 41st Philippine Infantry remained intact, but Japanese assaults forced it back east toward the boundary with I Corps, thus opening Trail 29 to penetration southward by the *65th Brigade*. The *4th Division* succeeded in eliminating the last opposition along the main line of resistance in its zone, with lead elements approaching the key terrain of Mt. Samat. The next day, Easter Sunday, began with yet another Japanese bombardment, followed again by assaults by Japanese infantry and tanks. The 21st Philippine Division put up fierce resistance until Japanese infantry overran its artillery, after which it gave way. Japanese infantry seized Mt. Samat, and by evening little remained of the 21st and 41st Philippine Infantry Divisions. The Japanese assault in Bataan was reaching its climax.[153]

If Luzon Force was to survive, its reserve – the Philippine Division, the Provisional Tank Group, and two battalions of combat engineers – would need to counterattack to repulse Japanese forces in the II Corps zone and regain the main line of resistance. It was a tall order for the emaciated soldiers, who lacked sufficient artillery support and air cover. Their attack early on the morning of April 6 would run headlong into the *65th Brigade* and *4th Division*, which were exploiting their gains of the previous days.

The counterattack ran into problems before it properly began, as the US 31st Infantry encountered advance Japanese forces while moving into its jump-off position on the evening of April 5. Faced with the dissolution of the 21st Philippine Division, Lt. Col. Jasper E. Brady, commanding the US 31st Infantry, concluded that he lacked the strength to attack the Japanese or to hold any gains made even if successful. His orders were changed to defend the ground on which his regiment stood. On the II Corps western flank, the 41st Philippine Infantry advanced toward Trail 29 and a hoped-for link-up with the 45th Infantry (PS). The following morning, a reinforced battalion of the *65th Brigade* counterattacked, forcing the Filipino infantry back toward the banks of the Pantingan River. The 45th Infantry (PS) began its attack northward along Trail 29 at 02:00, collapsing Japanese outposts by the middle of the morning and making contact with a strong defensive position at 15:00. The Scouts successfully breached this position before digging in for the night, marking an advance of 2,500 yards for the day, but that was the only success. The counterattack by the 33rd Philippine Infantry and the remnants of the 42nd and 43rd Philippine Infantry Regiments came to naught, as the Japanese scattered the remains of the latter two regiments and surrounded the 33rd Philippine Infantry before it could move. The reserve 57th Infantry (PS) ran into Japanese troops from the *65th Brigade* while moving into position. The counterattack that alone could have saved the Luzon Force had failed.[154]

The commander of the *4th Division*, Lt. Gen. Kenzo Kitano, smelling blood in the water, committed his reserve force, the *37th Infantry*, to the battle. By the middle of the afternoon, Japanese forces were advancing across the II Corps front, compelling Maj. Gen. Parker to order a withdrawal behind the San Vincente River. The 21st and 41st Philippine Divisions had ceased to exist, and the 33rd Philippine Infantry was surrounded. All remaining units were seriously understrength, with the soldiers' energy sapped from lack of food. "The outlook," in the words of the official US Army historian, "was bleak."[155]

The Luzon Force on Bataan collapsed in the following two days as panic and demoralization set in. A Japanese barrage at dawn on April 7 hammered American and Filipino positions along the San Vincente River line, which quickly gave way. Filipino soldiers streamed to the rear, and commanders could do little to stem the swelling tide of refugees from the fighting. Brig. Gen. Clifford Bluemel, commander of Sector C in the II Corps area, attempted to reform a line on the south bank of the Mamala River, but, by this time, any operational plans were merely aspirational as the Japanese attack gained momentum. By evening, Bluemel had already ordered a further withdrawal to the south bank of the Alangan River, to be completed by dawn. I Corps to the west would withdraw to the south bank of the Binuagan River to tie into II Corps to the east.[156]

The Alangan River defenses could not possibly hold back the Japanese assault on April 8. Regiments were now the size of battalions or companies, with the men so exhausted from malnutrition and lack of sleep that they could no longer maneuver effectively. A Japanese air and artillery bombardment once again caused large numbers of troops to flee to the rear, and the Japanese attack in the middle of the afternoon quickly penetrated into the large gaps between the remaining units, which retreated south. Along the East Road bordering Manila Bay, Japanese attacks scattered the Philippine Constabulary troops assigned to the sector and opened the road to rapid penetration. By evening, II Corps was attempting to position troops along the Lamao River, and committed its last available unit, the Provisional Coast Artillery Brigade, to the defense. The commitment of such meager reserves failed to stem the Japanese tide. The food stocks on Bataan were exhausted, the troops incapable of accomplishing the orders issued by Luzon Force. MacArthur was out of touch with the situation, ordering an attack by I Corps to seize Olongapo on the northwest corner of the Bataan peninsula and allow some of Bataan's defenders to escape into the Zambales Mountains to become guerrillas. Maj. Gen. King, aware of the state of I Corps, which was in the process of withdrawing to the Binuagan River, declined to transmit the orders as he knew full well the corps could not follow them. The end of the fighting on Bataan was at hand.[157]

By nightfall on April 8, II Corps had all but disintegrated, sending streams of uniformed refugees south along roads and trails, away from the onrushing Japanese. Command and control of shattered units was not possible, as discipline had vanished. Under the circumstances, Maj. Gen. King took the better course of valor to prevent a bloodbath and sought terms of surrender from the Japanese. MacArthur had prohibited surrender "under any conditions," but MacArthur was no longer in the Philippines and unaware of the reality on the ground. The 78,000 starving, emaciated, disease-ridden soldiers on Bataan had given their last full measure in the defense of the peninsula. They were no longer capable of meaningful resistance. Nothing would be gained from further fighting other than to increase the death toll as Japanese forces rolled through the unprotected rear areas and seized Mariveles on the southern tip of Bataan. King's decision to surrender was both logical and humane. President Roosevelt belatedly came to the same conclusion, rescinding his February order not to surrender the forces on Bataan under any circumstances and giving Wainwright leeway to make "whatever decision you may be forced to make."[158] By the time this order reached MacArthur in Australia, American forces on Bataan had already surrendered.

As King's emissaries approached Japanese lines under a white flag of truce, soldiers began to destroy any equipment and supplies of military value. Around 2,000 soldiers and army nurses made their way on barges and small boats to Corregidor, where another month of bombardment and anguish awaited them.[159] Maj. Gen. King went forward to discuss terms of surrender with Gen. Homma's representative, but the Japanese would only accept unconditional surrender of the entire Philippine archipelago. Now out of options, at 12:30 on April 9, King surrendered his command unconditionally.[160]

Wainwright notified MacArthur of the surrender of troops on Bataan. "Physical exhaustion and sickness due to a long period of insufficient food is the real cause of this terrible disaster."[161] The battle for Bataan was over, but, for the Americans and Filipinos now in Japanese captivity, the suffering was just beginning.

The Japanese viewed surrender as dishonorable and treated their prisoners inhumanely. The 78,000 Americans and Filipinos captured on Bataan were already suffering from severe malnutrition and disease, and needed food and medical care. They received neither; instead, the Japanese forced the exhausted prisoners to march more than sixty miles to a railhead at San Fernando, despite the fact that King had saved enough vehicles and gasoline to transport about half of them by truck. Even had the Japanese attempted to treat their prisoners humanely, three assumptions ensured a degree of chaos in their handling. First, the Japanese estimated they would take 40,000 prisoners, a severe undercount of the number of American and Filipino troops on Bataan. In addition to the soldiers, there were 26,000 Filipino civilians behind the lines in Bataan, and they too needed to be fed. Next, the Japanese had no idea that the prisoners they would take would be seriously malnourished and suffering from disease, primarily malaria. Finally, Homma estimated it would take a month to defeat the defenders of Bataan once the final offensive began, giving his staff plenty of time to work out arrangements for the prisoners they captured. Instead, the Japanese victory came in less than a week, and the Japanese had made none of the necessary preparations for the care of so many prisoners.[162]

The *14th Army* was short on food and medicines, so even had they attempted to treat their prisoners with a degree of compassion, their efforts would have fallen short. But that does not excuse the brutal treatment the Japanese meted out to the prisoners as they made their way north out of Bataan. They could at least have provided water to the prisoners along the route of march. Japanese troops routinely beat the captives and killed any who dropped out of the columns trudging their way north, past the grisly scenes of the recent battlefields and the charred remains of Filipino villages. Some prisoners simply dropped to the ground and died from exhaustion, dehydration, disease, and malnutrition. Japanese wielding swords and bayonets slaughtered wholesale between 350 and 400 officers and noncommissioned officers of the 91st Philippine Division.[163] The prisoners were denied sufficient food and medical care, and there was little attention paid to ensuring that they received enough water, a lifesaving necessity in the tropical heat. The sun was ruthless. Many prisoners drank from stagnant pools, only to suffer later from dysentery. Malaria continued to ravage the ranks. A sickening stench hung over the columns of marching prisoners. The only succor came from Filipino civilians, who lined the route of march and passed what food and drink they could to the trudging masses.[164]

Once at San Fernando, the captives were packed into windowless freight cars and railed the final twenty-five miles past Clark Field to Capas, from which they would march to Camp O'Donnell, their final destination. Heat and lack of air crazed the prisoners as they chugged along, their sweat draining the last ounces of water from their bodies. Dysentery victims relieved themselves at will, and the smell caused others to vomit, adding to the noxious mixture on the floor of the cars. Many men fainted. A few lucky men were able to open the train car doors and jump to freedom. Others died in the enclosed torture chambers during the four-hour trip to Camp O'Donnell, where other horrors awaited the prisoners in the months and years ahead.[165]

By early May, the men of Luzon Force – with the exception of a few thousand still in hospitals on Bataan – were collected at Camp O'Donnell. Several thousand Filipinos and a few Americans had been able to escape during the transit. The number of soldiers who perished can never be known for certain, but, according to Stanley Falk, the foremost historian of the topic, perhaps 600–650 Americans and between 5,000 and 10,000 Filipinos lost their lives in the march. Add to this total prisoner deaths during the first 2 months at Camp O'Donnell, which totaled 1,600 Americans and upwards of 16,000 Filipinos, and the terrible toll of the death march becomes clear. Maj. Gen. Jones later recalled that in Camp O'Donnell, "the hideous presence of death" was all around him.[166] Neither Wainwright nor MacArthur knew the fate of the prisoners taken on Bataan, until three escapees – including Air Corps Captain William Dyess – made their way to MacArthur's headquarters in Australia in July 1943.[167]

Falk blames the death march on poor Japanese leadership, and certainly poor leadership was part of the reason for the failure to take care of the prisoners of Bataan.[168] But, as he points out, the deliberate cruelty of many Japanese officers and enlisted soldiers can best be explained by the culture of the Imperial Japanese Army, which found surrender dishonorable and therefore viewed prisoners with contempt.[169] For his failure of leadership, Homma would find himself convicted by a war crimes tribunal after the war, and was executed by firing squad on April 3, 1946. For their roles in the death march, two of his subordinates, Maj. Gen. Yoshitaka Kawane and Col. Kurataro Hirano, were prosecuted three years later, sentenced to death by hanging, and executed on June 12, 1949.

As the fighting on Bataan ceased, Japanese forces moved to secure Mindanao and the Visayas. Japanese forces had seized the port of Davao on Mindanao in December, but lacked the strength to do anything more until reinforcements reached the Philippines. The three Philippine divisions in the Visayas and on Mindanao, under the command of Brig. Gen. Bradford G. Chynoweth and Maj. Gen. William F. Sharp, respectively, were poorly trained and equipped, even by the standards of the Philippine Army of 1941–1942. Against these units, the Japanese would commit the forces that had landed at Davao in Mindanao on December 20, consisting of elements of a battalion of the *33rd Regiment*; the *Kawaguchi Detachment*, consisting of the *35th Brigade* headquarters and the *124th Regiment*; and the *Kawamura Detachment,* consisting of the *9th Brigade* headquarters and the *41st Regiment.* Filipino forces outnumbered their opponents, but they were no match for the Japanese in terms of combat power. Recognizing this disparity, Chynoweth prepared the Visayas for a guerrilla campaign by stockpiling food, arms, ammunition, and other supplies in the remote interiors of the major islands. These supply caches would prove invaluable in bolstering the Filipino guerrilla movement in the years ahead.[170]

The first Japanese target was the island of Cebu in the Visayas, which the *Kawaguchi Detachment* invaded on April 10. The Japanese made quick work of the defending police regiment in Cebu City and a battalion of Philippine Army troops at Toledo on the west side of the island. Filipino troops defending the approaches to Chynoweth's headquarters at Camp X in the interior fled at the approach of Japanese infantry and tanks. Chynoweth retreated north into the mountains with 200 men to prepare a guerrilla force. His role in the fighting was over; on April 16, Lt. Gen. Wainwright placed all the forces in the Visayas under Maj. Gen. Sharp's command.[171]

Panay was the next target. The 4,000-strong *Kawamura Detachment* invaded without opposition at dawn on April 16. The 61st Philippine Division destroyed anything of military value and moved into the mountains, which had been stockpiled with supplies for an extended guerrilla campaign. Negros, Samar, Leyte, and Bohol were practically undefended, and the Japanese could take them at will. The only island left with significant forces to defend it was Mindanao.[172]

The *Kawaguchi Detachment* invaded the west coast of Mindanao between Cotabato and Parang on the morning of April 29. The 2nd Battalion, 104th Infantry, and the 3rd Battalion, 102nd Infantry of the 101st Philippine Division, along with the 2nd Infantry, 1st Regular Philippine Division, put up a spirited defense for several hours until forced to withdraw east along Route 1. In the Davao area, the *Miura Detachment* assembled at Digos and attacked west along Route 1 toward a junction with the *Kawaguchi Detachment* at Kabacan, the southern terminus of the Sayre Highway. Here the 2nd Battalion, 102nd Philippine Infantry, along with the bulk of the 101st Philippine Field Artillery, led by Lt. Col. Reed Graves, repulsed Japanese attacks for four days before being ordered to withdraw to the west. Graves' troops made their way to Kabacan, which they held against Japanese attacks until the surrender of all forces in the Philippines a week later.[173]

At 03:00 on April 30, the *Kawaguchi Detachment* landed another force south of Malabang, where it engaged the 61st Philippine Infantry, led by Col. Eugene H. Mitchell. After an all-day fight, Mitchell withdrew his forces along Route 1. The Japanese attacked the next morning, and by evening had captured

Michell and shattered his force, which disappeared from the order of battle. The Japanese now had control of Route 1 leading to Lake Lanao, defended by the 73rd Philippine Infantry, commanded by Lt. Col. Robert H. Vesey. His force put up a stiff defense at Bacolod on May 3 before an attempted Japanese envelopment forced a withdrawal into the hills north of the lake.[174]

The *Kawamura Detachment* landed at Macajalar Bay in northern Mindanao beginning at 01:00 on May 3. The 102nd Philippine Division put up a strong defense until Japanese pressure forced a withdrawal toward the northern terminus of the Sayre Highway. Maj. Gen. Sharp committed his last reserves, the Philippine 62nd and 93rd Infantry Regiments, in an attempt to hold the line. By the next morning, Sharp had arrayed his forces parallel to the Mangima Canyon, east of Tankulan and approximately twelve miles from the landing beaches. The Japanese resumed their attack on May 6, but the line held until the night of May 8–9, when the Japanese were able to infiltrate through a gap in the 62nd Philippine Infantry's sector. By the end of the day, the 62nd Infantry had scattered, erased from the order of battle. The Japanese were now in control of all major highways on Mindanao, all but ending the fight for the island.[175]

The island of Corregidor, two miles off the southern coast of Bataan and blocking access to Manila Bay, would hold out for another month after the fall of Bataan. Corregidor had been better stocked with food, was accessible only via an amphibious assault, and possessed formidable fortifications, such as the extensive tunnel system beneath Malinta Hill in the center of the island just east of the low-lying docks area, known as Bottomside. Protected by fifty-six coastal defense guns and mortars, as well as twenty-four 3-inch antiaircraft guns, Corregidor was more than just a nuisance. The Japanese had to take the island to open Manila harbor to shipping.[176]

On December 29, the Japanese launched the first bombing raid on Corregidor. The raids continued until January 6, when Japanese attention shifted elsewhere. Japanese artillery emplaced on the southeast shore of Manila Bay in Cavite Province then took up the battle, pounding Fort Drum, Fort Frank, and Fort Hughes – the three forts located on smaller islands in Manila Bay – and Corregidor until March 22, when the Japanese shifted their artillery to support the final offensive on Bataan.[177]

Japanese army and navy bombers returned to Corregidor on March 24 and bombed round the clock for the next week. Wainwright abandoned his above-ground house – inherited from MacArthur – and withdrew into Malinta Tunnel, taking only MacArthur's old walking stick with him.[178] Because of the construction of additional tunnels and air raid shelters in the wake of the earlier bombing offensive, the bombing achieved little of military value.[179] Nevertheless, with only approximately two months' supply of food remaining, the defenders of Fortress Corregidor were living on borrowed time.

Homma was unwilling to wait until lack of food forced Wainwright's surrender, and instead began planning and preparations for an amphibious assault on the island as soon as the fighting on Bataan had concluded. The *4th Division*, reinforced by the *7th Tank Regiment* and additional artillery, would make the landing. Assembling landing craft under the guns of Fortress Corregidor was no mean feat, but the Japanese accomplished the task by sailing small groups of ships around the southern tip of Bataan under cover of darkness. Japanese commanders also had to overcome an outbreak of malaria in the *4th Division*, which had moved into the malarial flatlands of southern Bataan. The Japanese accomplished the task by the end of the month only thanks to an emergency airlift of 300,000 quinine tablets.[180]

As soon as the fighting on Bataan ended, Japanese artillery positioned there and on the southeastern shore of Manila Bay in Cavite Province opened up on Corregidor, turning its well-prepared defenses into a shambles over the course of the next four weeks. Japanese bombers returned to Corregidor, adding to the damage and destruction. Japanese fire damaged or destroyed most of the coastal defense batteries and antiaircraft guns on the island. After April 18, the Japanese added 240mm howitzers to their arsenal, and the devastation increased by an order of magnitude. The 12-inch mortars of Batteries Geary and Way responded with counterbattery fire until the former was knocked out of commission on May 2 by a direct hit from a Japanese 240mm gun on Geary's powder magazine, which exploded with catastrophic results for both mortars and men alike. By this time, Battery Way was down to two mortars, and the island was all but defenseless against Japanese artillery fire.[181]

By the end of April, the defenders of Corregidor had begun to show the effects of vitamin deficiency. Life in the cramped tunnels under Malinta Hill was increasingly unbearable, with dust, fumes, and unpleasant odors filling the corridors packed with the sick, diseased, wounded, and dying. "We were sharing a democracy of filth," recalled Carlos Romulo, who served with the USAFFE staff on Corregidor before deploying to Bataan.[182] The strain of constant bombardment left nerves raw and tempers short. Damage to the island's power plant often left Malinta Tunnel in darkness, while damage to the island's water supply and distribution pipes resulted in the water ration being cut to one canteen per person per day by the end of the month. Upwards of 100 personnel – key officers, cryptologists, and nurses – were evacuated by Navy flying boats, submarine, and small liaison aircraft, but, for the rest of the 11,000 soldiers, sailors, and marines on Corregidor, captivity in a Japanese prisoner of war camp was nearing.[183]

Beginning on May 1, the Japanese began their pre-assault bombardment. By May 4, the tempo of the bombardment had increased to 16,000 shells per day. The bombardment badly damaged the beach defenses, denuded the island of tree cover and vegetation, and destroyed all but three of the big guns the defenders were counting on to defend the island. The next day witnessed a crescendo of fire, the prelude to the long-awaited amphibious landing.[184]

Under the light of a full moon, Japanese troops of the *61st Regiment*, reinforced by tanks, crossed the channel separating Bataan from Corregidor and landed at 23:10 on North Point on the eastern end of Corregidor, 1,000 yards east of their intended landing point. The American defenders in this area plastered the Japanese landing barges at close range with every available gun, exacting a heavy price for every foot of beach taken. The two battalions that reached shore lost more than 50 percent of their soldiers, while half to two-thirds of the landing boats were destroyed by fire. Despite the casualties, the remaining Japanese troops, after a brief fight with a company of marines stationed in the area, crossed the island to the south shore and then turned west toward Malinta Hill. The commander of the 4th Marines, Col. Samuel L. Howard, who commanded the beach defenses on Corregidor, committed all the reserves he had available, a battalion of sailors along with several batteries of artillerymen turned into infantry after the Japanese had destroyed their guns.[185] The troops moved into position as dawn approached and counterattacked the Japanese on Denver Hill beginning at 06:15. The Americans gained about 300 yards, but the assault faltered due to the lack of artillery, machine guns, and trained troops. When three Japanese tanks (actually, two Japanese tanks and a captured American M3 light tank operated by Japanese crewmen) entered the fray at 10:00, the poorly trained American troops, lacking antitank weapons, panicked and fell back. There were no more reserves to put into the fight, and Japanese artillery fire on James and Cheney Ravines to the west indicated that another Japanese landing was imminent. At 10:30 on May 6, Lt. Gen. Wainwright, certain that the end was near and wishing to avoid a wholesale slaughter of the thousands of soldiers under Malinta Hill, broadcast a surrender message to Lt. Gen. Homma.[186]

To President Roosevelt and Gen. MacArthur, Wainwright broadcast a final farewell. "With broken heart and head bowed in sadness but not in shame I report to Your Excellency that today I must arrange terms for the surrender of the fortified islands of Manila Bay . . .. There is a limit of human endurance and that limit has long since been passed. Without prospect of relief I feel it is my duty to my country and to my gallant troops to end this useless effusion of blood and human sacrifice . . . . With profound regret and with continued pride in my gallant troops I go to meet the Japanese commander."[187] He then sent an officer with a white flag of truce toward Japanese lines to arrange a meeting with Lt. Gen. Homma.

Wainwright traveled to Bataan to meet with Homma and made a vain attempt to surrender only Corregidor and the other three fortified islands in Manila Bay. The War Department's earlier decision to make Wainwright commander of all forces in the Philippines now rebounded badly. Homma would not agree to the terms and demanded the surrender of all US and Filipino forces in the Philippines before accepting the surrender of Wainwright's troops. Wainwright, fearing a bloodbath if the fighting continued, agreed to the terms, and attempted to surrender all forces in the Philippines unconditionally. Homma, incensed that Wainwright initially claimed he lacked authority over the Visayas and Mindanao, refused the offer and sent the Americans back to Corregidor empty-handed. Upon returning to the island, Wainwright surrendered both the fortress and all troops in the Philippines unconditionally to Col. Gempachi Sato, the commander of the *61st Regiment*, which had taken possession of Malinta Hill during the day. The next day, the Japanese ordered Wainwright to travel to Manila to broadcast the surrender over radio station KZRH.[188]

Getting forces elsewhere in the Philippines to surrender was more difficult. Wainwright sent a messenger to Maj. Gen. Sharp on Mindanao, ordering him to have his forces there and in the Visayas lay down their arms. Otherwise, the 11,000 soldiers, sailors, and marines on Corregidor would be treated as hostages and not as prisoners of war, with an implied threat that they would be killed if forces elsewhere in the Philippines did not surrender. Within a matter of days, most US commanders obeyed the instructions to surrender, but a few officers and a large number of Filipino soldiers in northern Luzon and on various other islands disappeared into the hills. Plans for extended resistance in the Visayas and Mindanao, which had begun to be formalized, were scratched. Instead, guerrilla resistance would grow organically, led by US and Filipino junior and mid-career officers and noncommissioned officers who refused to go quietly into the night. But, for now, the fighting ceased. On June 9, the Japanese declared the campaign for the Philippines over.[189] The occupation, which would be contested by one of the great resistance movements in the history of armed conflict, had begun.

2

THE LONG ROAD BACK

The New Guinea Campaign, waged through broiling sun and drenching rain amid tangled jungle and impassable mountain trails, had been a difficult and grueling struggle. In combating the extraordinary problems of climate and terrain, however, many valuable lessons were learned which were to prove of great benefit in pursuing the tasks ahead. This ability to cope with crises and profit from experience was a distinguishing characteristic of the Allied conduct of the war in the Southwest Pacific.[1]

MacArthur had never before felt the sting of a defeat so severe. The fate of the soldiers he left behind on Bataan and Corregidor haunted him. To lessen the blow and counter Axis propaganda that MacArthur had deserted his soldiers, Gen. Marshall convinced President Roosevelt to award MacArthur the Medal of Honor, a decoration MacArthur's father had received nearly eighty years earlier at the Battle of Missionary Ridge. MacArthur's escape from the Philippines and the award of the highest decoration the nation could bestow on a service member resulted in a MacArthur craze back in the United States and even a nascent MacArthur for president movement.[2] But there was no getting around the fact that the Japanese had thoroughly walloped his command in the Philippines. MacArthur would return to the Philippines – he was sure of that, even if his superiors in Washington were not. On a rail platform in Terowie on his way to Melbourne, where he would spend the next four months, MacArthur told the assembled gathering, "The President of the United States ordered me to break through the Japanese lines and proceed from Corregidor to Australia for the purpose, as I understand it, of organizing an American offensive against Japan, the primary purpose of which is the relief of the Philippines. I came through and I shall return."[3] Shouldn't the final three words be "we shall return," asked the Office of War Information? MacArthur demurred. The United States had let the Filipino people down, but he would not. The words were meant for them and the troops he had left behind.[4]

2.1: Gen. Douglas MacArthur and his wife Jean Faircloth MacArthur
at Terowie railway station, March 20, 1942. Upon this platform
MacArthur gave his famous pledge, "I came through and I shall
return." (Credit: John Oxley Library, State Library of Queensland)

Before returning to the Philippines, MacArthur and his subordinates
first had to forge the instrument that would propel the Allies along the road
to Tokyo. These forces next had to learn how to survive in a forbidding and
alien environment. Then they had to learn how to fight and coordinate
their efforts among the various arms and services. Only then could
MacArthur demand that the Joint Chiefs of Staff, to whom the Combined
Chiefs of Staff had delegated Allied strategy in the Pacific, approve an
invasion to consummate a return of US forces to the Philippines.

As he rode the train across Australia, MacArthur had no idea of the
resource challenges that awaited him. Brig. Gen. Richard Marshall, who had

proceeded ahead of MacArthur on a fact-finding mission, flew back to Adelaide and made his way eighty miles northeast to Kooringa to ride with MacArthur the remainder of the journey to Melbourne. Marshall had bad news for the general: American forces in Australia amounted to only 25,000 men, most of them service troops, and no more than 250 combat aircraft. MacArthur's reply was succinct: "God have mercy on us!"[5] There would be no returning to the Philippines, at least not until the Australian base was established and more troops and equipment arrived from the United States.

Unity of command would have been the ideal organizational structure in the Pacific, but interservice rivalry and command personalities precluded such an arrangement. Neither the army nor the navy would allow an officer of the other service to command the bulk of its forces. MacArthur's presence also played an outsized role in the decision to split the Pacific into two areas, one under the command of each service. On March 30, 1942, the Joint Chiefs punted and divided responsibility for the Pacific between MacArthur, whom Australian Prime Minister John Curtin had nominated to command the Southwest Pacific Area (SWPA), and Adm. Chester W. Nimitz, who would command the Pacific Ocean Areas (POA).[6] This division of command would in time have severe repercussions during the Battle of Leyte Gulf, but for now it allowed both the army and the navy to design and control campaigns in their areas of responsibility. SWPA included Australia, New Guinea, the Solomon Islands, the Bismarck Archipelago, most of the Netherlands East Indies, and the Philippines.[7] MacArthur had to supervise the creation of a theater headquarters, oversee preparation of base areas in Australia for arriving US infantry divisions and combat service and support forces, develop joint relationships with US Army Air Forces commanders and US Navy admirals in charge of whatever assets he could convince the US Joint Chiefs of Staff to provide him, and coordinate strategy and operational planning with his Australian allies.[8]

Australian Gen. Sir Thomas A. Blamey commanded Allied land forces. Blamey served with the Australian Army on the Western Front during World War I, rising to become chief of staff of the Australian Corps under Gen. John Monash. He departed active duty in 1925 to become chief commissioner of the Victoria police, but remained in service in the militia and rose in rank to become a major general by the time World War II broke out. Given command of the 6th Division, shortly thereafter he was promoted to lieutenant general and given command of the Australian I Corps, which fought valiantly at Tobruk in North Africa and disastrously in Greece. By September 1941, he was a full general with duties as Deputy Commander in

Chief Middle East Command. On March 23, 1942, just two days after MacArthur pledged to return to the Philippines from the railroad station near Adelaide, Blamey returned to Australia to become commander-in-chief of Australian military forces.[9]

Theoretically, Blamey would command all ground forces in the Southwest Pacific Theater of Operations. After the Buna campaign, MacArthur, contrary to the Joint Chiefs of Staff directive governing his theater, created an independent "Alamo Force" to bypass Blamey and put most US forces directly under General Headquarters (GHQ) SWPA control.[10] Available ground forces in theater included portions of the Australian 6th (Maj. Gen. George A. Vasey) and 7th (Maj. Gen. Arthur S. Allen) Divisions and several territorial divisions in various states of readiness. The 32nd ("Red Arrow," commanded by Maj. Gen. Edwin F. Harding) and 41st (Maj. Gen. Horace H. Fuller) Infantry Divisions, composed of National Guard units from Wisconsin and Michigan and the Pacific Northwest, were the first major American combat formations to arrive in the spring, but the commitment of the Joint Chiefs to the Allied "Germany First" strategy limited further reinforcements for the time being.[11] The two divisions would fall under I Corps, which the War Department had sent to Australia to prevent American troops from falling under Blamey's direct command, a scheme with which MacArthur wholeheartedly agreed.[12]

The I Corps commander was Maj. Gen. Robert L. Eichelberger, an Ohio native who had attended Ohio State University for two years before receiving an appointment to West Point. He graduated with George S. Patton, Jr., and twenty-eight other future general officers in the class of 1909. In 1926, Eichelberger attended the US Army Command and General Staff School at Fort Leavenworth, Kansas, with future General of the Army Dwight D. Eisenhower, and in 1931 he finished his military schooling at the Army War College in Washington, DC. Eichelberger came to MacArthur's attention in 1935 when he served as the Secretary of the War Department General Staff during MacArthur's final year as US Army chief of staff. Eichelberger also served as Superintendent of the US Military Academy at West Point in 1940–1941 as the nation headed into World War II. Among his accomplishments there was the hiring of Col. Red Blaik, who would lead Army to three national championships during his tenure as head coach of the Army football team. After a brief tenure as commander of the 77th Infantry Division, Eichelberger was promoted to command of I Corps and slated to invade North Africa during Operation Torch – that is, until US Army Chief of Staff Gen. George C. Marshall tapped him and his corps staff to deploy to Australia to serve under MacArthur. It was Eichelberger's misfortune to have had the duty to relieve the commanders of both of the divisions in I Corps, both of whom also happened to be his West Point classmates, during operations in New Guinea.[13]

US Army and Allied Air Forces came under the command of Lt. Gen. George H. Brett, while Vice Adm. Herbert F. Leary commanded the Allied Naval Forces. Given the criticality of air and sea control in the Southwest Pacific Theater, allotted air and naval assets were scant indeed and inadequate for the missions MacArthur had in mind. American air units included two heavy and two medium bomber groups and three fighter groups, while Australian elements amounted to seventeen squadrons. The principal naval elements were two Australian heavy cruisers and one light cruiser, a Dutch light cruiser, one US heavy cruiser and two light cruisers, as well as fifteen destroyers, twenty submarines, and assorted escort and auxiliary craft.[14] Maj. Gen. Julian F. Barnes commanded US Army Forces in Australia, a logistical headquarters. Given the vast distances involved in SWPA's forthcoming operations and the lack of base infrastructure, ports, and airfields, shortages of combat service support elements were a constant concern. The distance from MacArthur's headquarters in Brisbane (established there as of July 20, 1942) to the southernmost Philippine island of Mindanao was nearly 3,000 miles, greater than the distance from San Francisco to Boston. As a strategic economy of force effort, SWPA operated on a shoestring. That MacArthur's forces accomplished as much as they did is a credit not just to his strategic conceptions and his subordinate's operational concepts, but also to steadfast Australian support and the minor miracles performed by SWPA logisticians at every step of the way.

The Bataan Gang formed the core of the SWPA staff. MacArthur demanded complete loyalty from those who served under him, and in turn he showed loyalty to them – perhaps to a fault. One of MacArthur's biographers writes (apocryphally) that Chief of Staff Gen. George C. Marshall once told MacArthur that he didn't have a staff, he had a court, a claim taken up by a number of historians since.[15] Certainly MacArthur kept the Bataan Gang around long after some of them should have been replaced with more capable officers.[16] He gave commander's guidance and let his staff fill in the details, which put a great deal of responsibility on the shoulders of his chief of staff. MacArthur was not a micromanager, except for timetables, which often erred on the optimistic side, but nevertheless resulted in successes due to the competence of his subordinate commanders, the power of the joint forces at his disposal, and the courage and abilities of his troops.

Maj. Gen. Richard K. Sutherland rode herd as chief of staff, with Maj. Gen. Richard J. Marshall as his deputy; Brig. Gen. Charles P. Stivers served as G-1; Brig. Gen. Charles A. Willoughby was chief intelligence officer as G-2; Brig. Gen. Stephen J. Chamberlin assumed the role of plans and operations officer as G-3; Brig. Gen. Lester J. Whitlock supervised logistics as G-4; and Brig. Gen. Spencer B. Akin, Brig. Gen. William F. Marquat, and Brig. Gen. Hugh J. Casey became the chief signal officer, antiaircraft officer, and chief engineer, respectively.[17] Sutherland was the "hatchet man" for MacArthur, ruthlessly reigning over the staff without a hint of empathy for the incompetent or inefficient. Historian John McManus contends that Sutherland "was a byzantine operator who seemed to regard Army career advancement as a sort of blood sport."[18] In many ways, he resembled the fictional character Courtney Massingale in Anton Myrer's novel *Once an Eagle.*[19] MacArthur's biographer D. Clayton James describes Sutherland as "fiery, brilliant, and always scheming."[20] Sutherland's intelligence and dedication were balanced by a "nasty temper, brusqueness, and autocratic manner" that limited open communication among the staff and prevented alternative viewpoints from flowing upward to MacArthur.[21]

Nevertheless, Sutherland was essential to MacArthur's command style. MacArthur would issue broad guidance and leave the details of execution to Sutherland and subordinate commanders. He could do this knowing that he and Sutherland thought as one mind on the big issues. "The two men had worked together for so long and had such confidence in each other that there were few situations in which Sutherland could not anticipate with certainty what MacArthur's reaction would be," opines Paul Rogers, who, as Sutherland's stenographer, served closely with both officers throughout the war. "For practical purposes MacArthur and Sutherland were one where official matters were concerned."[22] Sutherland was MacArthur's sounding board, and provided the detailed guidance the staff and subordinate commanders needed. As a result, according to Rogers, "Sutherland, as MacArthur's chief of staff, to a very great extent, ran the war," at least until the end of the Buna campaign, when Sutherland transitioned to a more strategic role and MacArthur became more intimately involved in supervising operations.[23]

MacArthur, Sutherland, and Richard Marshall were a closely knit team. As Rogers notes, "The men could be separated by 10,000 miles and without any communication, but in any single situation all three would come up with the same solution in remarkably similar style and expression."[24] No single incident in the war showed this as clearly as when Sutherland responded in MacArthur's name and without his immediate knowledge when queried by Adm. Chester Nimitz and the Joint Chiefs of Staff regarding the strategic decision to bypass Mindanao and advance the timeline of the invasion of Leyte by two months, from December to October 1944, an episode covered in Chapter 4.

Willoughby, a German-born immigrant who worked his way up the ranks to earn a commission during World War I, would at times challenge Sutherland. But Willoughby "was neither as bright nor as competent as Sutherland. He fluctuated between emotional extremes, shifting from melancholy brooding to temper tantrums . . .. Willoughby's explosive personality, coupled with a physically intimidating 6-foot-3-inch, 220-pound frame, struck terror into field-grade staff officers. He ruled the G-2 shop with an iron hand and seemed paranoid about any outside interference."[25] Known informally among the staff as "Sir Charles" because of his formal Prussian manner, Willoughby was a student of military history who had even recently published a book.[26] Sutherland and Willoughby "sometimes crossed swords, because both men possessed sharp tongues and enlarged egos."[27]

MacArthur tolerated Sutherland and Willoughby's infighting because – for better or worse – he valued both of them as trusted members of his team. The same could not be said for the airmen and logisticians he inherited when he arrived in Melbourne. The general "disliked Brett and derided his staff 'as incompetent, bungling, nincompoop airmen' and was eager to replace them."[28] And for good reason – Brett "was not capable of adapting to the new situation and always seemed to drag his feet, to temporize, and even to maneuver in petty intrigue."[29] As a result, he never developed a functional relationship with MacArthur and the Bataan Gang. Change was inevitable, and it occurred on August 4, 1942, when Maj. Gen. George C. Kenney took command of the Allied Air Forces. Next to go was Barnes, replaced as commander of the newly formed US Army Services of Supply, SWPA, by the quiet but competent Richard Marshall. Both Kenney and Marshall were loyal and committed lieutenants and key facilitators of SWPA operations until the end of the war.

Another key staff officer in the Bataan Gang was Col. LeGrande A. "Pick" Diller, MacArthur's public affairs officer. Given MacArthur's penchant for and emphasis on publicity, it is not hard to figure out why one of the scarce positions in the PT boat flotilla leaving Corregidor was reserved for him. Diller supervised 100 officers and enlisted men in his section, and they in turn ran herd over more than 400 correspondents in the Southwest Pacific Theater. Diller's section took care of the needs of the war correspondents, provided that they took care of MacArthur's image in their stories. He also wrote the first draft of the daily press communiques emerging from GHQ SWPA, which MacArthur personally read and edited with Sutherland's assistance.[30] "Truth was often a casualty of the SWPA publicity machine," writes historian Ian Toll. "Action reports were punched up to make them seem more exciting and dramatic, and in many cases not only was the language improved, but new 'facts' were liberally added. In some instances, statistics concerning enemy losses [such as after the Battle of the Bismarck Sea] were invented wholesale."[31]

The organization of MacArthur's staff was the antithesis of Eisenhower's Armed Force Headquarters in North Africa, Sicily, and Italy, or his follow-on command of Supreme Headquarters Allied Expeditionary Forces in Northwest Europe.[32] Eisenhower demanded an integrated, multi-national headquarters in which American and British officers of multiple services worked together as one staff. Despite the urgings of Gen. George C. Marshall, MacArthur's headquarters was entirely composed of US officers, and the most important of those were the Bataan Gang.[33] GHQ SWPA lacked not only a coalition presence, but an interservice one as well. MacArthur preferred to operate in consultation with his subordinate air and naval headquarters, which were collocated with GHQ SWPA, rather than including joint input in the administration of theater operations, plans, orders, personnel, intelligence, and logistics. While Kenney accommodated MacArthur's preferences, naval commanders chafed at their lack of input, at least until GHQ SWPA hammered out standard operating procedures that improved the planning process.[34]

Blamey was able to escape MacArthur's grasp by arguing that his headquarters was also the headquarters of the Australian Army, and therefore he needed a certain degree of independence.[35] Since MacArthur essentially commanded most US Army ground forces through the fiction of Alamo Force, the location of Blamey's headquarters hardly mattered. As for MacArthur, his "real complaint against Blamey was that he was not entirely under his command."[36]

In Brisbane, MacArthur rarely traveled away from his office in the AMP Insurance Building or his quarters in Lennon's hotel. He was comfortable among his staff and those officers he knew well, but did not enjoy eating or socializing with others and rarely drank. MacArthur confided in Sutherland about professional matters, but he was closest to his aides, Col. Lloyd "Larry" Lehrbas, a former AP reporter who joined MacArthur's circle when the Bataan Gang arrived in Australia, and later Col. Bonner Fellers and MacArthur's personal physician, Col. Roger Egeberg.[37] Most of the generals in the headquarters rarely saw MacArthur; they had to work through Sutherland, an unhealthy isolation that could lead to confirmation bias. When MacArthur did speak to visitors, "out of his blazing ego poured a steady torrent of self-centered oratory: elegant, polished, and sculpted."[38]

According to Egeberg, MacArthur kept a steady routine. He "would occasionally ask one of the general officers, such as Steve Chamberlin, his G3 [Operations and Plans], to drop in on him for discussion of a particular issue. He would receive couriers from the Pentagon, 'eyes only' messages, and orders; he studied his briefings, he read several newspapers, and he talked. While he was thinking or talking he often smoked that corncob pipe, but he consistently paced," an estimated six to seven miles each day.[39] After briefings, MacArthur "never took a vote on the briefing issues, but asked questions, probed, threw in new possibilities, always ended by thanking the group, and then continued his weighing of possibilities, alone or sometimes with General Sutherland."[40]

In the first half of 1942, the primary focus of MacArthur's command was the defense of Australia, which necessitated the retention of Port Moresby on nearby Papua New Guinea.[41] In Japanese hands, Port Moresby was a launching pad to Australia; in Allied hands, it was a gateway to New Guinea. In spring 1942, only a single Australian militia brigade defended the critical port. Two task forces of the US Pacific Fleet formed around the aircraft carriers USS *Lexington* and USS *Yorktown* turned back a Japanese gambit to seize Port Moresby by amphibious assault at the Battle of the Coral Sea (May 4–8, 1942), but Japanese forces seized Buna and Gona on July 22, before US and Australian forces could occupy the area. After Japanese forces began their advance south across the Kokoda Trail, the Australian 7th Division deployed to Port Moresby and Milne Bay, bringing to five the number of Australian brigades in New Guinea. The Australians turned back an assault on Milne Bay between August 25 and September 7, but, by September 14, the Japanese moving south across the Owen Stanley Mountains had reached Iorobaiwa Ridge, just twenty-five miles north of Port Moresby.

Under pressure from MacArthur and the Australian government, Blamey moved to Port Moresby and relieved Lt. Gen. Sydney F. Rowell of command of the New Guinea Force and Australian I Corps.[42] The Japanese advance culminated at that point due to exhaustion, logistical difficulties, and the American landings on Guadalcanal, which forced the Japanese to prioritize support for their forces in the Solomon Islands. Blamey soon had the Australians on the march across the Owen Stanley Mountains. Unsatisfied with the pace of the advance, he relieved the commander of the 7th Division, Maj. Gen. Allen, on October 27 and replaced him with Maj. Gen. Vasey.[43]

Like Blamey, MacArthur believed the only way to effectively defend the Australian continent was to go on the offensive in New Guinea, and he argued for a significant reinforcement of his theater to resource this campaign.[44] His strategy required an offensive across the formidable 13,000-foot-high Owen Stanley Mountains to reach Buna and Gona, although, to be fair, the Kokoda Trail, which was so rugged that even pack horses could not negotiate it, topped out just above 8,000 feet.[45] Once that task was accomplished, the next year and a half would be focused on seizing, and when that proved impracticable, neutralizing, the key Japanese base at Rabaul – Operation Cartwheel – and a leapfrogging offensive up the northern New Guinea coast that would position American troops within striking range of Mindanao.[46] As in the contemporaneous campaigns in North Africa, Sicily, and Italy, the island campaigns of the South Pacific and operations in New Guinea were proving grounds for inexperienced and, in many cases, poorly trained American divisions. Other divisions that would eventually fight in the Philippines endured the crucible of island hopping in the Central Pacific. In time, they too would emerge as effective instruments of American combat power.

By the time the US Army engaged the Japanese in combat, the latter had already been at war in China for more than four years. The Imperial Japanese Army was combat-experienced and had honed its small-unit tactics and night operations in previous battles in Asia. While useful, these experiences were in the end not enough to overcome the overwhelming firepower brought to the battlefield by US forces. The Japanese army attempted to remedy its deficiency in firepower through the inculcation of esprit de corps in its soldiers and by improving small-unit infantry tactics.[47] Neither spirit nor tactical prowess was sufficient on the battlefields of the Pacific War. "Like so much of the Japanese war effort, however, Japanese ground forces were wildly out of balance," writes historian Eric Bergerud, who has written one of the classic accounts of combat in the Southwest Pacific. "Where they were good, such as in the area of small-unit tactics, they were very good. The extraordinary spirit of the troops proved real and astounded the Allies. Yet in every other area of modern land war – planning, interservice coordination, logistics, and intelligence – the [Japanese] Army was second rate."[48]

At first, US Army forces in the Pacific were not much better. The initial American forces at MacArthur's disposal, the 32nd and 41st Infantry divisions, both of which would subsequently participate in the liberation of the Philippines, got off to an inauspicious start in the New Guinea campaign.

The National Guard divisions entering combat in the Southwest Pacific had grave weaknesses. They lacked enough experienced, competent, and steely officers to weed out poor performers, or to overcome the local ties that kept some incompetent leaders in their positions. Many Guard officers were also too old for jungle warfare; the brutal environment of the Pacific War eventually weeded them out, but not before much damage was done to their organizations. The two Australian divisions in New Guinea had been seasoned in combat in North Africa and were more combat-effective than the untried Americans.

The 32nd Infantry Division suffered greatly but learned much at Buna, the first counteroffensive in the Southwest Pacific Theater. Its commander, Maj. Gen. Edwin Harding, was a Marshall protégé (as were most of the other division commanders in World War II), a West Point-educated officer who had worked on infantry doctrine during the interwar period.[49] "It was his fate to be sent to a tropical Verdun without artillery," commanding the only US division in World War II to fight a major battle without this critical supporting arm.[50] Combat readiness was also a problem as, for most of its time in Australia, the division moved from camp to camp without ever settling long enough in one vicinity to train, and what training it did receive did not focus on the jungle warfare awaiting the division in New Guinea. Furthermore, the division was starved of the resources that eventually made the US Army so formidable in the Pacific War: artillery, tanks, M-1 carbines, flamethrowers, jungle fatigues, machetes, and antimalarial drugs were all in short supply or unavailable.[51]

MacArthur deployed the division to New Guinea while awaiting the movement of Australian forces across the tortuous Kokoda Trail; there it sat for a month, its physical condition deteriorating. From October 6 to 28, the 2nd Battalion, 126th Infantry made a harrowing march overland along the Kapa Kapa Trail (which was even more rugged than the Kokoda Trail) to Buna, which served to confirm that better transportation routes were needed. Two regiments of the division finally arrived along the north coast via coastal shuttle and airlift to Pongani (which the troops promptly nicknamed "Fever Ridge"), thirty miles south of Buna, in the midst of the rainy season with ill-conditioned, poorly trained, but overconfident soldiers lacking adequate intelligence, artillery, engineer, or naval gunfire support.[52] Marching north to Buna, they met not the 500 Japanese troops Harding expected (another of Willoughby's intelligence lapses), but more than 2,800 hardened soldiers and naval infantry positioned in excellently prepared and skillfully concealed field fortifications (mostly coconut log bunkers built above ground due to the high water table in the area) in the midst of some of the nastiest malarial swamp on the face of the planet that channeled the attackers along readily identifiable avenues of approach.[53]

The Japanese had fortified themselves in a coconut plantation on patches of dry ground, while the attacking American infantry had to wade through malarial swamp and jungle to reach the front line, harassed by Japanese snipers positioned overhead in coconut trees. Lacking effective close air support or adequate artillery firepower, and without tanks or flamethrowers, the only method to reduce Japanese bunkers was to crawl up to them and throw grenades into the firing slits – a method that failed more often than not.[54] Japanese Zeros sank most of the small coastal craft that carried two Australian 25-pounder guns and the division's supplies (and almost killed Harding in the process), so the soldiers were short of just about everything until engineers could build a road to the local airstrip at Dobodura for tactical resupply.[55] For the soldiers of the 32nd Infantry Division, the situation was bleak.

The first attack on November 19 predictably went nowhere, and those in the following days failed as well. Senior American leaders had earlier complained that Australian troops lacked aggressiveness, but now it was the Australians' turn to complain that American soldiers would not or could not fight.[56] MacArthur stewed at his advance headquarters in Government House at Port Moresby, his irritation increased by the "hot, relatively humid, and uncomfortable" weather.[57] By the end of the month, MacArthur, who had not traveled across the Owen Stanley Mountains to confer with Harding, inspect the troops, or go to the front to figure out why the advance had stalled, was fed up. He ordered the I Corps commander, newly promoted Lt. Gen. Robert Eichelberger, to proceed to Buna to shake the 32nd Infantry Division out of its perceived lethargy. "Bob, I'm putting you in command at Buna," MacArthur intoned as he provided Eichelberger with his commander's intent. "Relieve Harding. I am sending you in, Bob, and I want you to remove all officers who won't fight. Relieve regimental and battalion commanders; if necessary, put sergeants in charge of battalions and corporals in charge of companies – anyone who will fight .... Bob, I want you to take Buna, or not come back alive. And that goes for your chief of staff, too, Clovis."[58] MacArthur then took Eichelberger aside, and in terms that appealed more to MacArthur's vanity than to Eichelberger's professionalism, offered him decorations and publicity should he succeed. "Two thousand dead," he added, "is a small price to pay for Buna."[59]

Proceeding to the front at Buna, what Eichelberger found was disconcerting. Some commanders and many staff officers were out of touch with what was happening at the front. Only a scattered few soldiers actually had contact with the Japanese. Morale among the troops was low, their clothing dilapidated, their weapons dirty and rusting, and they lacked personal hygiene and discipline. Food and ammunition were scarce; the troops were malnourished, and dysentery was rampant.[60] Units lacked critical fire support. The division used two Australian 25-pounder guns and two Australian 3.7-inch pack howitzers, and Kenney's airmen had flown four additional 25-pounders and a 105mm howitzer over the mountains into airstrips cut into the jungle, but resupply was difficult and there was hardly enough ammunition to keep the guns the division had near Buna supplied.[61] Resupply over the Kokoda Trail was tortuous, and there were not enough air transports available for the need. Close air support didn't make up for the shortfall of artillery, as pilots could not locate their targets in the jungle and on at least nine occasions bombed friendly forces.[62]

Blaming Harding and his regimental commanders for the fiasco, Eichelberger relieved them all, as well as five battalion commanders, and put the forward elements of the division under the command of Brig. Gen. Albert W. Waldron, the division's senior artillery officer. Eichelberger appointed I Corps staff officers to replace the rest of the division's senior leadership. He halted combat operations for forty-eight hours, reorganized the division, gave the men their first hot meal in days, and took steps to improve the delivery and distribution of much needed supplies. He circulated among the troops, beginning the process of changing the organizational culture by convincing them that their condition would improve, more support would be forthcoming, and the division would accomplish its mission.[63]

Eichelberger then ordered the offensive to recommence, and he positioned himself at the front, willing the troops forward. Although led by recently landed Australian Bren gun carriers, the attack by Warren Force in the east again failed.[64] Urbana Force in the west also failed to crack the Japanese lines, with the exception of one platoon led by Staff Sgt. Herman J. F. Bottcher, a veteran of the Spanish Civil War, which infiltrated through Japanese positions to reach the coastline and isolate Buna village.[65] The fighting was fierce and, per MacArthur's orders, commanders bled alongside their troops. Waldron lasted three days in command before being hit by a sniper. Eichelberger then gave command to his chief of staff, Brig. Gen. Clovis E. Byers, who supervised the seizure of Buna village on December 14, but in turn was wounded two days later after just eleven days in command. Fresh out of general officers, Eichelberger assumed command of the division himself. Finally realizing what the troops were up against, Eichelberger ordered them to besiege the Japanese positions until logistics improved and reinforcements, artillery, and tanks could be brought forward. The Red Arrow Division would win via a battle of attrition, one bunker at a time. Slowly, combat efficiency, morale, and discipline improved.[66]

American C-47 aircraft brought in much needed supplies by parachute or by landing at a newly constructed airstrip east of Buna Station, which kept the 32nd Infantry Division from disintegrating. The ability of American and Australian engineers to find ground suitable for constructing airfields in the jungle and swampy morass of New Guinea conferred on the Allies a crucial advantage. These airfields made possible the use of tactical airlift to haul troops and supplies to the front when ground routes through the jungle were otherwise nonexistent and shipping was scarce. A trip by foot along the Kokoda Trail over the Owen Stanley Mountains could take anywhere from eighteen to twenty-eight days; soldiers could fly the same distance in the back of a C-47 transport in just thirty-five minutes. The lone 105mm howitzer used in the campaign also arrived via air transport. Airstrips hacked out of the jungle near the front allowed Allied airmen to deliver reinforcements, food, medical supplies, ammunition, uniforms, engineering equipment, and more to units engaged with the Japanese – a chain of supply stretching 1,700 miles back to depots in Australia. By the end of the Buna campaign, twenty C-47s based at Port Moresby delivered 1,000 tons of supplies weekly over the Owen Stanley Mountains.[67]

Blamey committed the Australian 18th Brigade and seven M3 Stuart light tanks to the fight for Buna, which helped to turn the tide of battle. Armor was especially valuable in overcoming Japanese fortifications, as the Japanese lacked antitank weapons. The Australians, led by Brig. George F. Wooten, augmented Warren Force in the east, and they proved instrumental in the next attack that kicked off on December 18 and which, after days of heavy fighting, finally cracked the Japanese strongpoints defending the plantation area east of Buna Station.[68] Progress slowly continued until January 3, 1943, when US and Australian troops destroyed the final pockets of Japanese resistance.[69] Australian forces under Maj. Gen. Vasey, seasoned in combat in the Middle East and more effective at this point than the American troops in Papua, had taken Gona several weeks earlier. MacArthur announced publicly (and erroneously) on January 8 that the battle was all but over, the first of many such pronouncements that annoyed the commanders and soldiers still in harm's way.

Australian and US forces (including a regiment of the 41st Infantry Division flown in from Australia) battled for three more weeks to destroy

Japanese resistance at Sanananda at a cost exceeding that of the battle for
Buna.[70] During this period, the Australian Kanga Force and 17th Brigade
repelled a Japanese assault against the airstrip at Wau southwest of
Salamaua, enabling the Allied Air Forces to use bases in the area in the
next phase of the campaign.[71] The bill was steep: Of the 1,199 men of the
126th Infantry Regiment who entered action on the Sanananda front on
November 22, only 165 survived to see the official relief in place on
January 9, 1943. In the six months of the Papuan campaign, US and
Australian troops suffered nearly 3,100 killed, almost twice the number of
US Army and Marine dead in the contemporaneous battle on
Guadalcanal.[72] The Japanese fared far worse, suffering more than 12,000
dead in all.[73]

MacArthur took credit for the victories won by Eichelberger and the
forces under his command.[74] SWPA communiques inferred that MacArthur
was leading his troops from the front, as he had done as a brigadier general
in World War I.[75] These assertions were wholesale fabrications, and completely unnecessary to burnish the image of a heroic general officer who by
that point had already received the Medal of Honor, two Distinguished
Service Crosses, and seven Silver Stars for gallantry in action. MacArthur
at least visited Bataan once; he never visited the front at Buna, and thus was
ignorant of the challenges facing his soldiers there.

Despite his self-congratulatory and dishonest communiques, which
rankled Eichelberger among others, MacArthur learned his strategic lessons. He would bypass areas of Japanese strength in the future whenever
possible, putting his troops in a position to seize advanced airfields and
base areas with minimal casualties.[76] Having adjusted his strategy for the
better, MacArthur went on to assert that his strategy was somehow different and less costly than the "island hopping" strategy employed by Adm.
Nimitz and his forces in the Central Pacific. It was an unnecessary (and
untruthful) claim and an unwarranted aspersion on Nimitz and his
command.[77]

MacArthur also fully embraced the capabilities of airpower once he
found in Kenney an airman whom he trusted and admired. At the tactical
level, American and Australian units developed the tactics, techniques, and
procedures to overcome Japanese fortifications with fewer casualties, especially as weapons such as flamethrowers and bazookas arrived to bolster the
capabilities of the infantry. Close air support, artillery support, and tank–
infantry cooperation all improved, providing significant advantages to
Allied infantry in future battles.

In New Guinea, as elsewhere in the South and Southwest Pacific, soldiers faced an enemy more prevalent and just as deadly as the Japanese: disease. The tidal swamps and climate in these regions are harsh enough, with "penetrating, energy-sapping heat ... accompanied by intense humidity and frequent torrential rains that defy description."[78] But, in addition to their weather and geography, these regions are also some of the most malaria-infested places on earth. According to the GI publication *Yank,* "Mosquitoes out here [New Guinea] are both monstrous and minute. They are big enough to make you want to dive for a slit trench when they buzz the field yet small enough to penetrate the finest mosquito bar. The females are armed with a hypo needle similar in size to that used by the medics and equally dull."[79] Malaria, dengue fever, scrub typhus, dysentery, ringworm, hookworm, and other tropical diseases weakened and, in many cases, incapacitated soldiers trying to survive in a forbidding and alien environment. The climate and disease in the Southwest Pacific accentuated the psychological issues that led to battle fatigue. Older men did not last long in the Pacific War; their lack of physical endurance led to collapse one way or another. "Disease was an unrelenting foe," recorded the SWPA staff. "New Guinea provided a background in which almost every threat of nature combined with the sudden and unforeseeable dangers of modern war to provide a microcosm of the vast struggle in the Southwest Pacific."[80]

Adequate supplies of food, shelter, and medical care were the best way to negotiate the environment and diseases of the Southwest Pacific Theater of Operations. Well-supplied soldiers had a greater ability to ward off the insects and control the diseases that permeated the jungle, particularly malaria. Without preventative treatments, the rate of infection among soldiers stationed in malarial areas approached 100 percent. Only occasionally a killer, malaria was a disease to be endured, but it significantly lowered the combat effectiveness of infected units. Since the Japanese controlled Java, where 95 percent of the world's quinine supply came from, Allied troops required another prophylaxis to control the disease. Beginning in 1943, Allied soldiers used Atabrine (generic: mepacrine or quinacrine), a drug somewhat ironically synthesized by German scientists in the interwar period, to ward off malaria. By 1944, seven companies in the United States were producing 400 million tablets per month. The drug was so important that officers lined their soldiers up and watched as each soldier swallowed his daily dose; otherwise, rumors that Atabrine caused sterility led many troops to avoid taking it.[81]

Disease was by far the biggest cause of casualties in the war in the Southwest Pacific. By September 1943, the 32nd Infantry Division had to drop 2,334 men from its rolls due to untreatable malaria.[82] The official US history of the campaign concludes, "With the story presumably the same in the case of the Australians, the conclusion is inescapable that the fighting in Papua had been even costlier than had at first been thought, and that the victory there, proportionate to the forces engaged, had been one of the costliest of the Pacific war."[83] Although over time Allied soldiers developed superior combat effectiveness to their Japanese counterparts, they inflicted far more damage by cutting the Japanese off from their sources of supply. Historian Eric Bergerud summed up the dynamic best: "Armies without supplies faced the jungle alone, and, in the South [and Southwest] Pacific, the jungle killed."[84]

The SWPA staff evolved as the New Guinea campaign progressed. Logisticians worked small feats of magic to keep forces supplied over vast distances on a shoestring budget. The quiet but competent Chamberlin oversaw a G-3 section that turned MacArthur's strategic conceptions into viable operations plans and orders. MacArthur considered Chamberlin "a sound, careful staff officer, a master of tactical detail and possessed of bold strategic concepts."[85] As a general rule, the G-3 worked through Sutherland and not MacArthur.[86] But no staff area changed as much over the course of the war as Willoughby's G-2 section. Its structure was in line with pre-war doctrine but adapted for the specific needs of the Pacific War. Willoughby fought a never-ending battle to centralize intelligence activities, especially as newly created agencies such as the Central Bureau and the Allied Intelligence Bureau competed with the G-2 in an attempt to assert their independence.[87]

SWPA theater intelligence comprised sections that provided intelligence summaries, updated situation maps, discerned the Japanese order of battle, created plans and estimates in support of the G-3, and published a variety of information to support combat forces. Beyond this doctrinal application of intelligence, SWPA also developed a number of capabilities, such as interrogating prisoners and translating captured documents, mapping terrain, conducting direct action in Japanese-held territory, and deciphering Japanese communications, to support its unique needs. "Invariably positive knowledge of the enemy's strength and disposition was one of the factors which enabled Gen. MacArthur, with initially weaker resources, to neutralize and by-pass strong Japanese forces, to save American lives, and to carry out his three-dimensional warfare at maximum efficiency," the G-2 concluded after the war.[88]

Willoughby understood MacArthur's priorities, and he created a Philippine section concerned solely with intelligence related to the Philippine Islands. Beginning in December 1942, this group published a monthly Philippines situation report based on all-source intelligence. The section developed over the course of 1943, and, by February 1944, it was turned into a robust, full-time organization of twenty-five staffers that published daily and weekly intelligence summaries along with seventeen special studies on various topics. The section also produced monographs on guerrilla groups operating in the Philippines, making sense of the otherwise confusing organization of the resistance movement in the islands. In essence, the section was "a self contained miniature G-2 for the purpose of handling Philippine matters while the main body of G-2 was devoting its attention to the New Guinea operational picture."[89]

Organized on September 19, 1942, the Allied Translator and Interpreter Section (ATIS) used Nisei (second-generation Japanese American) operators to interrogate prisoners and translate captured documents. Experience on Bataan with Nisei interpreters showed the potential of linguists. The flow of documents and prisoners increased exponentially after the invasion of Guadalcanal and the fighting around Buna and Gona; thereafter, the G-2 pooled available linguists into a centralized organization that could translate thirty-four languages. Initially numbering just thirty-five officers and soldiers, by the end of the war ATIS encompassed more than 1,900 personnel. ATIS field detachments accompanied tactical units on operations and provided responsive translator and interpreter support to field commanders. ATIS publications made available translations of Japanese documents and interrogations; the number of documents distributed rose from 20,000 in January 1943, to 430,000 in January 1944, to 2 million in January 1945.[90]

The Allied Geographical Section mapped areas and provided geographical and terrain information on areas in the Southwest Pacific. The section published terrain studies for use by commanders and planning staffs; prepared special reports on specific areas; developed terrain handbooks for the troops to carry into battle; and distributed special publications for the individual soldier.[91] Despite the best efforts of this staff section, US and Australian troops would sometimes find themselves campaigning in terra incognita, lacking accurate – or any – maps to guide their operations.

One of the most important of the newly created intelligence organizations did not fall under the G-2's control. The Central Bureau, activated on April 15, 1942, was a combined American–Commonwealth codebreaking organization that operated under the overall direction of the competent Brig. Gen. Akin, chief signal officer of SWPA, and under the direct command of US Army Col. Abraham Sinkov, Australian Army Lt. Col. Alastair W. Sandford, and Royal Australian Air Force Wing Cdr. H. Roy Booth. Among those personnel MacArthur ordered to evacuate Corregidor were a cadre of codebreakers who would form the core of the Central Bureau. Other specialists were sent from the United States to join them in Australia. The Central Bureau's strength rose from fewer than 100 personnel upon activation to more than 1,000 in 1943 and more than 4,000 by the end of the war, about half of whom were American and most of the rest Australian.[92]

Special intelligence (code-named Ultra) was one of the keys to SWPA's understanding of Japanese capabilities and intentions. Japanese diplomatic codes (the Purple cipher) were broken before the war, and the Imperial Japanese Navy code (JN-25B8) was broken just prior to the Battle of Midway.[93] Japanese army messages were unbreakable until September 1943, but, thanks to the capture of extensive cryptographic materials in New Guinea in January 1944, by February 1944 the floodgates of special intelligence had opened, with US analysts "deciphering more than twenty thousand Japanese army messages per month."[94] Akin passed raw decryptions through Sutherland to MacArthur. Sutherland in turn authorized Akin to transmit intelligence garnered from decryptions to field commands without going through G-2 channels. Willoughby often had to be content with delayed information copies of Ultra decrypts, even though it was his job to analyze them and produce usable intelligence from raw information by integrating Ultra decrypts with other intelligence sources.[95]

The office of the Special Security Officer (SSO) accompanied MacArthur's forward headquarters as it moved from Brisbane (Australia) to Hollandia (New Guinea), to Tacloban (Leyte), to Manila (Luzon). An SSO always personally accompanied MacArthur to feed him Ultra or Magic information. An SSO was also placed at each army and corps headquarters, although Ultra information was disseminated below army level only on a selected basis.[96]

The G-2 Operations Section initially included Ultra intelligence in its Daily Intelligence Summary, but, as the amount of special intelligence increased, Willoughby created a separate vehicle for its delivery. The Special Intelligence Bulletin allowed Willoughby to evaluate and comment on Ultra decrypts. Its distribution was limited to MacArthur, Sutherland, Willoughby, and Chamberlin, but selected elements were disseminated to subordinate commanders. "Our discreet but distinctly liberal dissemination of this highly classified material must be viewed in the light of the Pearl Harbor debacle when an extreme of secrecy so limited dissemination of similar material [Magic decrypts of the Japanese Purple diplomatic cipher] that responsible commanders were deprived of essential elements of information which, had they been in their possession, might well have averted this disaster," the G-2 wrote after the war.[97]

Army and Navy codebreakers in Melbourne, who operated separately since they dealt with completely different codes, passed Ultra decrypts of interest to one another. Since the Navy controlled the effort to break the Japanese diplomatic cipher, naval liaison officers would show Magic decrypts to MacArthur and Sutherland but not, initially at least, to Willoughby. By early 1944, the chain of Ultra dissemination was streamlined so that Willoughby could receive a Magic summary and Ultra decrypts directly from the Central Bureau and the codebreaking organizations in Washington, DC.[98]

Despite War Department attempts to centralize Ultra codebreaking in Washington, MacArthur jealously guarded the prerogatives of Central Bureau to decode Japanese transmissions locally and provide the information directly to him.[99] MacArthur was the only theater commander who enjoyed his own cryptanalytic capabilities throughout the war. Gen. Marshall attempted to centralize codebreaking efforts at Arlington Hall, but, in the case of MacArthur's Ultra, to no avail. "Only MacArthur's stature stood in Marshall's way, but that enormous shadow allowed Central Bureau to maintain its peculiar relationship with the War Department throughout the war in the Pacific."[100]

Perhaps no newly created agency was as colorful as the Allied Intelligence Bureau (AIB), MacArthur's counterpart to the Office of Strategic Services, which, true to form, he declined to allow into theater because he could not control it. The AIB coordinated clandestine operations throughout SWPA's area of responsibility. The bureau included the coast watchers, who reported ship movements and also provided intelligence on Japanese troop movements in their vicinity. The Inter-Allied Services Department and the Services Reconnaissance Department were subversion–sabotage organizations based on the British Special Operations Executive or American OSS model. The Far Eastern Liaison Office was responsible for propaganda operations, primarily the production and distribution of leaflets dropped by aircraft. During the war, this office dropped more than 50 million leaflets in eight different languages over Japanese-held territory.[101]

In preparing for MacArthur's return to the Philippines, the most important part of the AIB was the Philippine Regional Section (PRS), which established and maintained intelligence networks, including overwatch of the coast watchers in the Philippine Islands; established and operated a radio communication service; developed escape routes from the Philippines to Australia; and supplied guerrilla units with radios, ciphers, weapons, munitions, currency, medicine, propaganda materials, and other supplies. After the first radio messages from the resistance in November 1942 revealed the existence of guerrilla groups in the Philippines, MacArthur ordered his headquarters to organize the resistance and support it with radios, ciphers, equipment, and technical personnel. Col. Courtney A. Whitney, the head of the Philippine Regional Section as of May 1943, oversaw the supply effort, assisted by Lt. Cdr. Charles "Chick" Parsons, who coordinated supply runs by submarine.[102] The PRS established multiple intelligence and communications networks as well as nearly 100 coast-watching and intelligence stations, linked in a vast reporting system. The PRS received and analyzed radio reports, while the Philippines Section of the G-2 collated and distributed the final intelligence products.[103]

Following the seizure of Buna and Gona, the Joint Chiefs approved a campaign directed at seizing Rabaul, which would become Operation Cartwheel. While US Marine and Army forces under Adm. William "Bull" Halsey proceeded from Guadalcanal northward along the Solomon Islands chain to New Georgia and Bougainville, US Army and Australian forces under MacArthur leapfrogged along the northern New Guinea coast and then concluded the isolation of Rabaul by seizing the Admiralty Islands. MacArthur had initially argued for an extension of the campaign to seize Rabaul, but, after the Combined Chiefs of Staff at the Quadrant Conference in Quebec in August 1943 confirmed that US forces would neutralize the Japanese base there and move on to other objectives, MacArthur became a convert to bypassing large Japanese garrisons.[104] Buna had taught MacArthur and his staff valuable lessons, none more important than avoiding enemy strength and ensuring that ground forces were supported in their moves by ground-based air support. SWPA's retooled intelligence apparatus would ensure the former, while Lt. Gen. Kenney's Fifth Air Force provided the latter. Both were essential elements of MacArthur's successful advances up the New Guinea coast in the next eighteen months, which positioned SWPA forces for a return to the Philippines in the fall of 1944.[105]

MacArthur met Halsey during the Solomon Islands campaign. "I liked him from the moment we met," MacArthur later recalled, "and my respect and admiration increased with time. His loyalty was undeviating, and

I placed the greatest confidence in his judgment. No name rates higher in the annals of our country's naval history."[106] Their relationship would be tested during the Battle of Leyte Gulf in October 1944, when Halsey's decision to pursue the Japanese carrier force rather than protect the approaches to Leyte Gulf nearly cost MacArthur's invasion forces dearly.

SWPA required amphibious capabilities if it were to leapfrog up the northern coast of New Guinea, and deficiencies noted in the Buna campaign needed to be rectified. Accordingly, in January 1943 the VII Amphibious Force, commanded by Rear Adm. Daniel E. Barbey, was activated and assigned to the Seventh Fleet, which supported MacArthur's command. Neither force had many ships when formed, but their strength would grow over time. Barbey, or "Dan the Amphibious Man" as he came to be known in the Southwest Pacific, was a 1912 Naval Academy graduate who had honed his expertise in the design and employment of amphibious craft as head of the US Navy Department's Amphibious Warfare Section until ordered to Australia.[107] During his in-brief with MacArthur, the general discussed the strategic situation in the Southwest Pacific and his future plans, then asked Barbey a single question, "Are you a lucky officer?"[108] Barbey found the question "curious," but it was a reference to Napoleon's maxim, perhaps apocryphal, that he would rather have lucky generals than good ones. Barbey noted the friction between the Bataan Gang and other staff officers, as well as the interservice rivalries that permeated GHQ SWPA and its subordinate headquarters. Fortunately for the war effort, however, "the nearer one got to the combat zone the closer became the cooperation and mutual support between the various fighting services."[109]

Like Kenney, Barbey came to admire MacArthur and served him faithfully throughout the war, making possible the campaigns that would make good on MacArthur's promise to return to the Philippines. MacArthur "delegated authority far more than do most commanders," Barbey noted. "He gave his subordinates a job and then left to them the details of how it was to be done. If the job was not being done to his satisfaction, he simply found another man to do it."[110] Barbey's job was to create an amphibious navy. As soon as the Buna campaign ended, training in amphibious and jungle operations commenced. Units designated for amphibious assaults conducted rehearsals. Newly assigned forces and replacement soldiers underwent jungle training. Air–ground coordination was also practiced, ensuring prompt close air support in future operations.[111]

The newly established Sixth US Army would control US ground forces in SWPA as Alamo Force, reporting directly to MacArthur for assigned operations. MacArthur requested that the War Department assign Lt.

Gen. Walter Krueger as the new army commander, which came as a surprise to Krueger, even though the two had known each other for forty years and Krueger had served as head of war plans when MacArthur was the US Army chief of staff.[112] The assignment also came as a surprise to Eichelberger, who had retrieved the situation at Buna and was already in theater. But MacArthur was not entirely happy with Eichelberger's performance (because he had little knowledge of the conditions at Buna and Eichelberger's leadership in that battle), and he certainly was not happy that Eichelberger outshone him in the press after victory was secured, threatening his subordinate with relief if the trend continued.[113] A more plausible reason was seniority; MacArthur wanted a commander who outranked all of the Australian commanders in theater except for Blamey, and Krueger, who was MacArthur's age, fit the requirement.[114] Eichelberger went onto the shelf, relegated to training divisions in Australia as the war seemingly passed him by. MacArthur might also have believed that Krueger was a more aggressive commander than Eichelberger, a trait that MacArthur admired and required in his drive to the Philippines.[115] MacArthur would be proven wrong in the latter assessment of his new army commander.

Krueger was born in 1881 in West Prussia, the son of a former officer in the Prussian Army. In a different universe, he might have fought in World War I as an officer in the Imperial German Army and in World War II as an officer in the Wehrmacht. But his father died when he was young, and his mother brought him and his siblings to the United States to live with her maternal uncle. His mother soon remarried, and the family settled in Indiana, where he received a strict but formative education. Drawn by a sense of patriotism and adventure to enlist in the US Army during the Spanish–American War, Krueger quickly rose to the rank of sergeant and received a commission as a second lieutenant in 1901 while stationed in the Philippines, the first of two tours in the archipelago. Over the next four decades, Krueger proved to be a studious soldier and an outstanding leader. During World War I, he served as the chief of staff of the 84th Division, the G-3 of the 26th Division, and the chief of staff of the Tank Corps. During the interwar period Krueger served nine years on two different assignments in the War Plans Division of the War Department, as well as commanding at the regiment, brigade, division, corps, and army levels before assuming command of the Sixth US Army in the Pacific.

Krueger was no stranger to professional military education institutions. He was a distinguished graduate of the Infantry and Cavalry School (1906) and a graduate of the General Staff College (1907). He served as an instructor at the School of the Line and Staff College from 1909 to 1912.

After World War I, he attended the Army War College in 1921, and the next year served as an instructor at the college. He attended the Naval War College in 1926 and then served in Newport as an instructor from 1928 to 1932. He translated Prussian Generalleutnant William Balck's treatise *Tactics*, which was adopted for use at US Army schools. He commanded at every level, including command of Third Army during the Louisiana Maneuvers just prior to the entry of the United States into World War II. By December 7, 1941, he was a lieutenant general and one of the senior US Army leaders; Col. Dwight D. Eisenhower served as his chief of staff and Col. John W. "Iron Mike" O'Daniel ran his army's junior officers' training camp. His hobbies, strategy and military history, reflected his status as a career military officer.[116]

Krueger, according to Paul Rogers, "was a dour, unimaginative man, whose inner life, if he had one, was hidden by a brusque soldier's manner."[117] With "the appearance of a long-suffering high school principal," Krueger "had none of the majesty that surrounded MacArthur. Where MacArthur inspired awe, Krueger inspired fear and dread."[118] He shunned publicity, which made MacArthur happy and was just as well, for, if his memoir is any indication, he lacked the knack for it. But he was tactically competent and commanded his army skillfully, albeit by the book and with "the bearing of a first sergeant."[119] On the other hand, Krueger was dedicated to his soldiers and their welfare, never forgetting where he had started from at the beginning of his long career.

Krueger, however, was sixty-one years old, which made him an unlikely candidate for an overseas command. His seniority, however, is exactly what appealed to MacArthur, for the reason noted above.[120] The War Department approved Krueger's transfer to the Southwest Pacific to command the newly organized Sixth Army. He could take his key staff officers, but the rest of the Third Army staff remained behind, to eventually serve in Northwest Europe under the iconic Gen. George S. Patton, Jr. Now that he had an army headquarters in his theater, MacArthur allowed Krueger to conduct the operational planning. MacArthur would develop overall strategic goals for the campaign and assign forces, after which Krueger, in consultation with Chamberlin, would complete the detailed plans and execute the operations.

Eichelberger initially was reconciled to Krueger's appointment and thought he might usefully serve as a buffer between his corps and higher headquarters. Later, after Eichelberger was promoted to command of Eighth Army, he thought poorly of his fellow army commander, and the two had a chilly relationship. "If he [Krueger] is a great general or has any of the elements of greatness then I am no judge of my fellow man," Eichelberger would write to his wife during the Luzon campaign. "Beyond a certain meanness, which scares those under him, and a willingness to work, he has little to offer."[121] The unfair assessment reflected more on Eichelberger's jealousy than on Krueger's leadership abilities.

MacArthur, too, did not escape Eichelberger's private wrath. Eichelberger's animus at the time toward MacArthur was revealed in a letter he wrote to his wife the following October, in which he derided MacArthur's absence at the front at Buna despite publicly taking credit for the victory there. "His knowledge of details was so faulty that his directives to me ... indicated that he knew nothing of the jungle and how one fights there – that he had no detailed knowledge of how our forces were divided into many corridors by swamps."[122] According to Paul Rogers, "Eichelberger's psychological world was filled with malevolent demons who were bent on his destruction."[123] According to Barbey, Eichelberger's "outspoken, critical, and sometimes belligerent manner" had "not endeared [him] to the top command in the Southwest Pacific."[124] Perhaps he had thin skin, but there were other, more tangible reasons for Eichelberger's angst. MacArthur, who refused to be upstaged in his own theater, denied the award of the Medal of Honor to Eichelberger, a well-deserved decoration that Marshall was prepared to grant, and likewise prevented Eichelberger's move to the European Theater to assume command of the First or Ninth US Army.[125] Instead, Eichelberger spent the next year on the shelf in Australia training troops for jungle combat. After the war, Eichelberger reflected more thoughtfully that MacArthur's conduct "wasn't a question of what he thought about me but he didn't intend to have any figures rise up between him and his place in history."[126]

In contrast to his relationship with his ground commanders, MacArthur enjoyed a close rapport with his new air commander, Lt. Gen. Kenney, described by Paul Rogers as "an exuberant, uninhibited man, physically small, who gave the appearance of having just climbed out of the cockpit of a World War I SPAD."[127] Kenney was both competent and loyal, the two qualities most highly prized by MacArthur, and MacArthur came to trust him implicitly when it came to the use of land-based airpower in the Southwest Pacific. "One thing that helped, however, was that a very important guy named Douglas MacArthur believed in me," Kenney would write in his memoir. "He would not let me down and I would not let him down."[128] As for MacArthur, he wrote of Kenney, "Of all the brilliant air commanders of the war, none surpassed him in those three great essentials of combat leadership: aggressive vision, mastery of air tactics and strategy, and the ability to exact the maximum in fighting qualities from both men and equipment."[129] MacArthur valued officers who achieved results, and Kenney did just that – in spades.

Kenney grew up in Massachusetts and attended MIT for a time until financial circumstances forced him to seek employment. He was a civil engineer when the United States entered World War I, at which time Kenney enlisted as an aviation cadet. He was an outstanding pilot with the 91st Aero Squadron in France, rising to the rank of captain and earning the Distinguished Service Cross and Silver Star for shooting down two German fighters. He was commissioned in the Regular Army in 1920 and attended the Air Corps Tactical School (ACTS), later becoming an instructor. During the interwar period Kenney graduated from the Air Service Engineering School and became a test pilot. He was a graduate of the Command and General Staff School, and taught attack aviation tactics at the ACTS. In 1940, he served as assistant attaché for air in France and returned with important recommendations, including upgunning aircraft machine guns from .30 caliber to .50 caliber, use of self-sealing fuel tanks, and installation of power turrets in bomber aircraft.[130] He was head of the Air Corps Experimental Depot and Engineering School at Wright Field, Ohio, when the Japanese bombed Pearl Harbor, after which he was promoted to major general and placed in command of the Fourth Air Force on the West Coast. His innovative engineering mentality (he experimented with putting machine guns on the wings of aircraft, which would eventually become standard design) would carry forward to World War II, when, under his command, the Fifth Air Force experimented with modifications to A-20 and B-25 bombers and unique techniques such as skip bombing of enemy ships.[131]

MacArthur had good reason to be displeased with his air forces when he assumed command of SWPA. After Kenney's initial inspection tour of units and facilities in Australia and New Guinea, he discovered poorly maintained aircraft, inadequate facilities, insufficient training, and a broken supply system. Kenney reported back to MacArthur with a determination to fix the issues, gain and maintain air superiority over New Guinea, and then strike at Japanese shipping. MacArthur was pleased; he had found an air commander to his liking. He approved Kenney's program and let him know that "he didn't care how my gang was handled, how they looked, how they dressed, how they behaved, or what they did do, as long as they would fight, shoot down Japs, and put bombs on targets."[132]

Kenney proceeded to do just that. Given the latitude to run the Allied Air Forces as he saw fit as long as he delivered results, he confronted Sutherland and forced the chief of staff to cease his interference with the tactical and technical details of air operations. At one point, Kenney strode into Sutherland's office and drew a tiny black dot in the center of a blank sheet of paper. "That is what you know about air power," he told the chief of staff, pointing at the dot. "The rest of the sheet is what I know about it." He then threatened to take the issue of who ran air operations in SWPA into MacArthur's office, at which point Sutherland backed down.[133]

Kenney quickly cleaned house. He relieved poorly performing commanders and staff officers, rotated tired crews, clarified organizational structure, unclogged an unnecessarily bureaucratic supply system, ordered logisticians to move depots from the Melbourne area 500 miles north to Brisbane, created a functional maintenance system, and instilled a warfighting culture in the Southwest Pacific Allied Air Forces. Within three days of taking command, he launched an eighteen-bomber raid against the main Japanese base at Vunakanau near Rabaul.[134] The strike helped to ensure the success of the landings on Guadalcanal and Tulagi. The bombers then pounded Japanese airfields at Lakunai on New Britain and at Lae and Salamaua on New Guinea to reduce Japanese air strength in the area.[135]

MacArthur had found his airman. Kenney's aggressive attitude pulled MacArthur out of his post-Corregidor funk. According to one war correspondent, "MacArthur's restoration to full health and activity might well be dated from the day that Kenney walked into his headquarters in Brisbane."[136] The extroverted Kenney begged and borrowed resources from his superiors in Washington and improvised new methods of fighting with locally produced matériel. A delighted MacArthur thought his new air chief was "a natural born pirate," and nicknamed him "Buccaneer."[137]

MacArthur received permission from the War Department to activate the Fifth Air Force, which would support his campaigns until the end of the war. Since he would have to collocate his headquarters with MacArthur's in Brisbane, Kenney positioned an advanced headquarters under Brig. Gen. Ennis C. Whitehead in Port Moresby. Whitehead, affectionately known to his men as "Ennis the Menace," would command the air elements in New Guinea while Kenney attended to his wider theater duties as head of the Allied Air Forces.[138] Kenney had a knack for finding fighting airmen to lead his formations and get the most out of the airmen under their command. Brig. Gen. Kenneth N. Walker, commander of the 5th Bomber Command, was killed in action on January 5, 1943, leading a bombing raid on Rabaul, and subsequently awarded the Medal of Honor.

As US industry geared up, the Fifth Air Force gained more planes and parts to fix those already in theater, most of which were badly in need of overhaul. The arrival of the first twenty-five P-38s, which would finally allow fighter escort of bomber formations, was a huge step forward. Among the arriving fighter pilots was Lt. Richard I. "Bing Bang" Bong, who would become the leading ace in US military history, with forty kills to his credit.[139]

The Fifth Air Force proved instrumental in MacArthur's campaign to return to the Philippines. Kenney's transports hauled men and supplies to New Guinea and across the Owen Stanley Mountains. His bombers blasted Japanese airfields near Rabaul on New Britain, and his fighters and bombers gained and maintained air superiority over the battlefields of New Guinea and nearby islands. The airmen attacked Japanese convoys headed to New Guinea with reinforcements and sent a significant number of destroyers and transports to the bottom.

Their biggest success came two months after the conclusion of the Buna campaign. On February 25, 1943, Ultra decrypts informed GHQ SWPA of a Japanese convoy headed from Rabaul to Lae to reinforce Japanese positions on New Guinea. The convoy was spotted by reconnaissance aircraft on March 2 and attacked by seven B-17 bombers, which hit and sank a transport. The next day Kenney sent eighteen heavy bombers, twenty medium bombers, thirteen Australian Beaufighters, and twelve A-20 light bombers, escorted by sixteen P-38 fighters, to attack the convoy. A second strike of sixteen heavy bombers, twenty-two medium bombers, and five light bombers, escorted by eleven P-38 fighters, hit the remaining ships left afloat. Skip-bombing attacks and strafing by specially modified planes carrying eight forward-firing .50-caliber machine guns, techniques and modifications pioneered by Kenney's airmen in the Southwest Pacific with specially modified B-25 and A-20 bombers, were particularly deadly. The attacks, dubbed the Battle of the Bismarck Sea, destroyed all eight troop transports (drowning 3,000 Japanese soldiers) and four destroyers, along with thirty fighters, at the cost of one B-17 bomber, one B-25 bomber, three P-38 fighters, and one Beaufighter.[140] Fewer than 1,000 Japanese soldiers reached their destination. After the Battle of the Bismarck Sea, the Japanese never again attempted to send large convoys from Rabaul to New Guinea; the garrison at Lae would wither on the vine.[141]

During the spring of 1943, Kenney's airmen and Japanese bombers and fighters fought for control of the air over Port Moresby and Dobodura, the airfield near Buna on the north coast of New Guinea, even as American bombers continued to hammer Japanese airfields around Rabaul. The air battles were, according to Kenney, a "slugging match," with US fighters tending to get the better of their counterparts. The fighting took a toll on pilots and machines, and Kenney had to order several of his senior commanders back to Australia for rest. The fighting was a battle of attrition waged in the air, one in which the United States, with its superior production capacity and training pipeline, was better positioned to win over the long term. But, in the summer of 1943, the margin of superiority over the Japanese was thin.[142]

With Kenney's airmen on the path to achieving air superiority over eastern New Guinea and US and Australian forces rested after their strenuous efforts at Buna and Gona, MacArthur could turn his attention to the next step in the campaign. While US Navy, Marine, and Army forces under Adm. Halsey island-hopped up the Solomons chain, US and Australian forces under Gen. Blamey proceeded to assault Japanese forces at Salamaua and Lae. Blamey's idea was to draw the Japanese toward Salamaua, thereby weakening the defense of Lae, which would be taken by amphibious and airborne assault.[143]

As a preliminary operation, on June 30 the 112th Cavalry Regiment and the 158th Infantry Regiment seized the undefended Kiriwina and Woodlark Islands northeast of Milne Bay, adding two additional airfields to the growing base establishment of the Fifth Air Force.[144] Even though the operation met with no Japanese opposition, Operation Chronicle served as a testing ground for amphibious warfare techniques in SWPA that, once perfected, would be used repeatedly until the end of the war.[145]

The seizure of Salamaua would not be nearly as quick or easy. After slowly proceeding overland, the Australian 15th Brigade fought to secure Bobdubi Ridge, key terrain to the south of the town, in action that lasted from June to the middle of August. On June 30, a reinforced battalion of the US 162nd Infantry Regiment landed unopposed at Nassau Bay and moved to link up with the Australian 17th Brigade, which was assaulting the town of Mubo. After seizing Mubo, the two forces advanced toward Salamaua, reinforced by the remainder of the 162nd Infantry, which advanced up the coast to Tambu Bay before encountering strong Japanese positions on Roosevelt Ridge. US and Australian attacks forced the Japanese to withdraw by August 19, and Salamaua now lay vulnerable to bombardment and assault.[146]

As the fighting on Roosevelt Ridge reached its peak, air reconnaissance and Ultra intelligence pinpointed Japanese air units concentrating at Wewak, 300 miles northwest of Lae. The Fifth Air Force had built up a jungle air base at Marilinan, about forty-five miles west northwest of

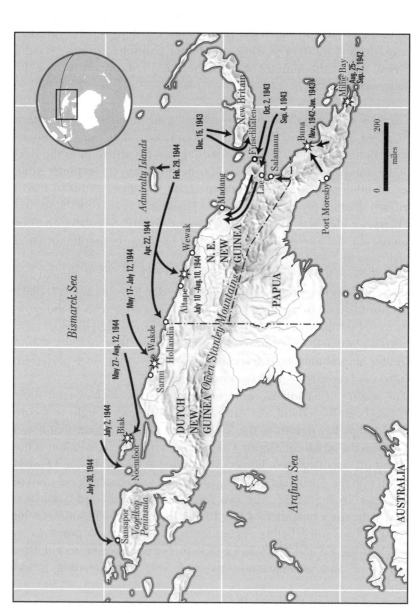

Map 4: New Guinea Campaign, August 1942–July 1944.

Salamaua, housing two squadrons of P-38 fighters for just this moment. Kenney ordered a major attack on August 17–18 on the four Japanese airfields near Wewak. The bombing and strafing caught dozens of Japanese aircraft on the ground, ravaged the antiaircraft defenses, and wrecked numerous ground installations and fuel and supply dumps. Further strikes in the next two weeks increased the toll to upwards of 100 Japanese aircraft destroyed.[147] The attacks on Wewak gave MacArthur air superiority over New Guinea, a crucial advantage in speeding up the campaign before events elsewhere could shut the door on his return to the Philippines.

The fighting around Salamaua continued into September, but it was just a prelude to the main effort, the seizure of the Japanese base at Lae. The Australian 9th Division conducted an amphibious landing on September 4 just to the east of Lae, while the 503rd Parachute Infantry Regiment conducted a parachute assault on an old airstrip at Nadzab, about thirty miles northwest of Lae.[148] MacArthur and Kenney accompanied the airborne armada of ninety-six C-47 transport aircraft in a flight of B-17 bombers, allowing the taking of an iconic photo of MacArthur watching the paratroopers drop to the ground. After the paratroopers had secured the area and restored the airstrip to usable condition, transports ferried the Australian 7th Division into the area. The 7th Division then attacked toward Lae in conjunction with the 9th Division, placing the 10,000 Japanese troops at Lae in a vise. Japanese troops abandoned Salamaua on September 11, and four days later Australian troops seized Lae. The 9th Division followed up this success with an amphibious landing on September 22 that secured Finschhafen ten days later, while the 7th Division worked its way north up the Markham Valley. Aided by an amphibious assault on Saidor on January 2 that severed the Japanese line of retreat, the Allies were now in control of the entire Huon Peninsula. The successful landings at Lae validated the pattern for future operations in the Southwest Pacific.[149]

The Fifth Air Force in the meantime had seriously degraded Japanese airpower at Rabaul. On October 12, a raid by 349 aircraft, "everything that I [Kenney] owned and was in commission," hammered Japanese airfields at Vunakanau, Rapopo, and Tobera, destroying, according to initial (albeit inflated) reports, 100 aircraft on the ground and another 26 in the air, and sinking an estimated 116 naval craft of various sizes.[150] Another raid, on November 2, occasioned "the toughest, hardest-fought engagement of the war" for the Fifth Air Force. Bombers and strafing aircraft sank an oil tanker and three merchant vessels, and damaged twenty-two other vessels in the

2.2: Gen. Douglas MacArthur on the B-17F "Talisman" observing paratroopers of the 503rd Parachute Infantry descend on Nadzab in the Markham Valley, New Guinea, on September 5, 1943. The assault followed by one day the surprise landings of Australian troops on beaches near Lae. (Credit: Associated Press/US Army Signal Corps photo)

harbor. P-38 pilots reportedly destroyed 42 of the nearly 150 Japanese fighters that rose to protect the base, while B-25s shot down 26 others and destroyed 16 planes on the ground. The cost was steep, as the Japanese destroyed eight bombers and nine fighters in the attack.[151] "In the space of twelve minutes we had destroyed or damaged 114,000 tons of Japanese shipping, shot down or destroyed on the ground eighty-five Nip airplanes, and burned out half the town of Rabaul, with a loss of supplies to the enemy estimated at 300,000 tons," Kenney wrote exaggeratedly in his memoir. "Never in the long history of warfare had so much destruction been wrought upon the forces of a belligerent nation so swiftly and at such little cost to the victor."[152] The raids continued as weather allowed until the middle of

November, when Commander, Aircraft, Solomons, a combined, joint command, took responsibility for neutralizing Rabaul. By the end of the war, US airmen had pummeled Rabaul with 20,584 tons of bombs.[153]

In the middle of December, Gen. George C. Marshall, on his way back to the United States from Allied conferences at Tehran and Cairo, visited MacArthur on Goodenough Island, where Krueger had positioned his Alamo Force headquarters, to receive an update on the Southwest Pacific Theater and to discuss future strategy. Not much was decided, but Marshall filled MacArthur in on the infighting among the Joint Chiefs of Staff, and MacArthur made a plea for increased resources for his theater. This was the only meeting of the two senior leaders during the entire war, a function no doubt of the distance between Washington and Brisbane.[154]

Preceded by heavy bombing from the Fifth Air Force, landings on New Britain by the 112th Cavalry Regiment at Arawe on December 15 and by the 1st Marine Division (Maj. Gen. William H. Rupertus) at Cape Gloucester on December 26, as well as an Australian advance on Madang in New Guinea (which concluded four months later on April 24), closed out the operations for the year in the Southwest Pacific. Horrendous jungle and swamps precluded an overland advance by the American forces on Rabaul, but the Vitiaz Strait between New Guinea and New Britain was secured, setting the stage for the next leap westward along the northern coast of New Guinea as MacArthur's forces continued their journey back to the Philippines.[155] They were in a race for time, however, as the Central Pacific campaign had just kicked off with the invasion of Tarawa Atoll in the Gilbert Islands on November 20. For the moment, the Joint Chiefs of Staff gave their support to twin drives across the Pacific, but the time would come when the competing visions of the strategic course of the Pacific War would cause battles inside the Pentagon rhetorically as fierce as the physical ones being waged half a world away.

By this point in the war, Japanese forces in the Southwest Pacific had deteriorated dramatically. Having begun the war with such success, the Japanese could not sustain the combat effectiveness of their forces after the battles of 1943. Furthermore, the organizational culture of the Imperial Japanese Army doomed its soldiers in defeat.[156] In *War without Mercy*, John Dower posits the theory that racism turned the Pacific War into a brutal contest of annihilation.[157] Americans and Japanese killed each other because, influenced psychologically by propaganda and racial stereotypes, they simply hated each other.

Eric Bergerud advances a different and more compelling explanation for the war of annihilation that gripped US and Japanese forces in the Pacific: "A tragedy took place in the South Pacific that stemmed largely from the grotesque manipulation of the Japanese people by the military government. By successfully convincing their soldiers to find meaning in oblivion, and to accept the frightening idea that spiritual purification comes through purposeful death, the Japanese government created the mental framework for total war. If Japanese soldiers would not surrender, American and Australian troops very simply would not take prisoners."[158] Once this cycle of violence was ingrained into the psyche of the troops engaged in combat, it was very hard to break. Even at the end of the war, when Japanese soldiers were somewhat more inclined to surrender, American forces invariably shot first and asked questions later.

To execute operations in the extended distances of the Southwest Pacific, MacArthur needed a navy. There was no chance he would receive command of the big fleet carriers and fast battleships that formed the core of the strength of the US Pacific Fleet, so until his return to the Philippines, MacArthur had to make do with the small number of cruisers and destroyers comprising the Allied Naval Forces in the Southwest Pacific, formed around the US Seventh Fleet, commanded as of November 1943 by Vice Adm. Thomas C. Kinkaid.[159] As was the case with the air commander he inherited, MacArthur was unhappy with his naval commander, Vice Adm. Arthur S. Carpender, who he believed was unwilling to put his ships in harm's way on the northern coast of New Guinea, and had twice asked for his relief. Adm. Ernest J. King responded by tapping Kinkaid, a skilled wartime leader with experience in the Guadalcanal and Aleutian campaigns, for the billet.[160]

Kinkaid had graduated from the United States Naval Academy in 1908 and afterwards served in the surface line on battleships, circumnavigating the globe with the Great White Fleet.[161] He went back to school to receive an education in ordnance engineering and served in a number of gunnery assignments in succeeding years. He commanded the destroyer USS *Isherwood* in 1924, graduated from the Naval War College in the class of 1930, commanded the heavy cruiser USS *Indianapolis* in 1937, and served for more than two years as the US Naval Attache in Rome. Prior to Pearl Harbor, Kinkaid briefly commanded a destroyer squadron. Promoted to rear admiral, Kinkaid commanded the cruisers and destroyers of Task Force 17.2 at the Battle of the Coral Sea and Task Force 16.2 at the Battle of Midway. He then commanded Task Force 16, built around the carrier USS

Enterprise, in the early stages of the Solomons campaign and Task Force 61, built around the USS *Enterprise* and USS *Hornet*, in the Battle of the Santa Cruz Islands. In January 1943, Kinkaid assumed command of the North Pacific Force, supervising the Aleutian Islands campaign that restored Attu and Kiska to US control. For his service to this point in the war, Kinkaid was promoted to vice admiral in June 1943. But his most noteworthy service was yet to come, as the hand-picked commander of what became known as "MacArthur's Navy" in the Southwest Pacific.

Kinkaid had a difficult task to perform, and it had nothing to do with the Imperial Japanese Navy. As commander of Allied Naval Forces, Kinkaid reported to MacArthur, but, as commander of the US Seventh Fleet, Kinkaid was subordinate to Adm. King in Washington. Pleasing both of these headstrong bosses was a nearly impossible chore. GHQ SWPA was Army-centric, and its operational planning often left Kenney's air staff and Kinkaid's naval staff in the dark. According to Kinkaid, MacArthur's staff was paranoid about Navy proposals, suspicious that they were crafted to gain an advantage in interservice rivalries that ran deep. Kinkaid found working with MacArthur's staff difficult, lamenting, "I try to fit in with their methods and organization but they are a bunch of horse traders and horse thieves and don't know the meaning of cooperation."[162] His relations with Kenney, his air counterpart, were similarly colored by interservice rivalry. "General Kenney," Kinkaid remarked, "was a little difficult to deal with because he was an old Billy Mitchell flier, and he thought 'Damn-Navy' was one word."[163]

But the core of the issue of Army–Navy cooperation in the Southwest Pacific ran deeper – all the way back to the basic strategy for the Pacific War. MacArthur desired a strategy that favored his line of advance up the northern coast of New Guinea to the Philippines, and from there onward to Formosa or the Ryukyus, while King favored an advance through the Central Pacific to the Marianas and then to Formosa and the Ryukyus. The reality that MacArthur would command the former line of advance and Nimitz the latter was not lost on anyone. To assuage the services and their senior commanders, the Joint Chiefs of Staff approved both lines of advance, but MacArthur's command was the last priority for the naval vessels now pouring out of America's shipyards. Kinkaid was on the receiving end of MacArthur's angst that was really directed at Kinkaid's other boss in Washington.[164]

Kinkaid was able to improve relations with MacArthur by discussing issues one-on-one on the veranda of the general's quarters at Port Moresby. Command and planning arrangements were at the top of the list of items that demanded attention. Rear Adm. Barbey's amphibious force needed to coordinate planning and remain in command of amphibious operations until the ground forces were established ashore. Only then should Alamo Force – Krueger's Sixth Army – assume command of operations. MacArthur eventually concurred with this sequence of command, albeit with plenty of opportunity for air, ground, and naval commanders to review plans before their final approval.[165] Kinkaid established a fleet intelligence center, and also arranged for air force pilots to serve aboard Seventh Fleet cruisers to provide shipboard fighter direction.[166] But what improved relations more than anything else was Adm. King's intention of starving the Seventh Fleet of significant resources – Kinkaid commanded no aircraft carriers or battleships except those loaned to him for short periods by Nimitz. Kinkaid was supporting cast, and he knew it. More importantly, he acted the part.[167]

In an order dated February 13, 1944, GHQ SWPA ordered the 1st Cavalry Division (Maj. Gen. Innis P. Swift) to invade the Admiralty Islands on April 1.[168] The seizure of the Admiralties, approximately 200 miles off the northern coast of New Guinea at the entrance to the Bismarck Sea, would complete the encirclement of the major Japanese air and naval base at Rabaul.[169] The Admiralty Islands also offered two airfields and a viable naval anchorage at Seeadler Harbor, facilities required for future operations aimed at the liberation of the Philippines. The 1st Cavalry envisioned a two-month training and preparation period before commencing operations. However, low-level air reconnaissance by B-25 bombers on February 23–24 failed to observe enemy activity, and aerial photographs convinced Kenney that the Japanese had deserted the island of Los Negros.[170] Kenney recommended an immediate invasion. On the other hand, based on Ultra decrypts Willoughby estimated (correctly) that the Japanese still had more than 4,000 troops in the Admiralty Islands.[171] Despite the report of an Alamo Scout reconnaissance team that Los Negros was "lousy with Japs," the airmen's reports convinced MacArthur to order a reconnaissance in force on February 29.[172]

The cavalrymen were now in a race against the clock to plan, prepare, and execute a major amphibious landing on a hostile shore with just a few days' notice. They were also under no illusions that the task would be easy. The 1st Cavalry G-2 on February 25 estimated Japanese strength in the Admiralties at 4,600 effective troops, with 2,450 of them on Los Negros – an estimate that proved largely on the mark.[173] "None of the commanders in the forward area liked any part of this 'quickie' assault on the Admiralties," Barbey wrote later. "I did not like the idea of even a small amphibious landing – regardless of what it was called – relying solely on a few destroyers and APDs."[174] Furthermore, because of surf conditions, the force would have to negotiate the fifty-yard entrance to Hyane Harbor to land the cavalrymen on a narrow beach.

The invasion force, dubbed "Task Force Brewer," was a composite group of approximately 1,000 soldiers under the command of Brig. Gen. William C. Chase, the commander of the 1st Cavalry Brigade. Chase served with the 4th Division in World War I, and during the interwar period he had been a professor of military science at Michigan State University, served with the 26th Cavalry in the Philippines, and had graduated from the US Army Command and General Staff School.[175] The bulk of the troops would come from the 2nd Squadron, 5th Cavalry Regiment, under the command of Lt. Col. William E. Lobit.[176] The task force embarked in three destroyer transports and nine destroyers with an additional four destroyers and two cruisers as escorts. Gen. MacArthur and Vice Adm. Kinkaid accompanied the task force aboard the light cruiser USS *Phoenix*; MacArthur wanted to be on the scene in case the landing force met more resistance than expected and he needed to order it to withdraw.[177]

At 08:15 on February 29, the task force invaded Los Negros. As the destroyers entered Hyane Harbor, naval gunfire silenced Japanese shore batteries, a performance so convincing that, according to Kinkaid, MacArthur "became more royalist than the king" when it came to using naval gunfire.[178] The cavalrymen landed under rifle and machine gun fire, but were able to quickly seize their objective, the Momote air strip.[179]

MacArthur and Kinkaid came ashore at 16:00 to inspect the beachhead and talk to the men. MacArthur awarded the Distinguished Service Cross to the first soldier ashore, First Lt. Marvin J. Henshaw of Troop G, and then directed Brig. Gen. Chase to hold the air strip at any cost. "You have all performed marvelously," MacArthur intoned. "Hold what you have taken, no matter against what odds. You have your teeth in him now – don't let go."[180] In fact, there was little chance of letting the Japanese go, since they were at that moment preparing a massive counterattack. Having survived their foray ashore, MacArthur and Kinkaid made their way back to the *Phoenix* and departed for New Guinea in the early evening with all but two destroyers, which remained behind to furnish gunfire support to the troops ashore. Before he departed, MacArthur ordered reinforcements waiting at Finschhafen to set sail for Los Negros.[181]

The task force was not large enough to defend the airstrip, so Chase pulled it back into a tighter perimeter by nightfall. The troops dug in the best they could in the hard coral soil. The Japanese counterattacked in strength at 01:45 and precipitated what would become one of the wildest

2.3: Vice Adm. Thomas C. Kinkaid, Gen. Douglas MacArthur, and aide Col. Lloyd Lehrbas on the flag bridge of the USS *Phoenix* during the invasion of Los Negros, Admiralty Islands, February 29, 1944. MacArthur's calculated risk in launching a "reconnaissance in force" accelerated the New Guinea campaign by several months. (Credit: US Army Signal Corps Photo)

battles of the Pacific War. Cavalrymen fought Japanese attackers hand-to-hand and held their positions. Japanese infantry infiltrated both the squadron and task force command posts and even beheaded one staff officer with a sword. The Japanese assaults lasted until 07:30 the next morning. The beachhead held – barely.[182]

Task Force Brewer badly needed reinforcements. On the morning of March 2, the remainder of the 5th Cavalry, reinforced with engineers, field artillery, and antiaircraft units, arrived in six LSTs and landed to reinforce the beleaguered beachhead, which Chase now expanded to encompass the entire airfield. Bulldozers cleared fields of fire and dug fortifications for the defending troops, while engineers sowed minefields. The last critical point in the battle came on March 3–4, when the Japanese conducted a coordinated night attack in an attempt to drive the Americans into the sea. Japanese infantry penetrated the perimeter and advanced as far as the airstrip, but the cavalrymen held on tenaciously, backed by significant fire from artillery, mortars, and destroyers offshore.[183] The attackers suffered heavily, with several hundred dead Japanese counted within the American lines. In one charge, the Japanese soldiers allegedly belted out a verse of "Deep in the Heart of Texas" to rattle the cavalry troopers. "Let's get 'em," Corporal James Renfro reportedly yelled. "Those guys don't even know the right words."[184] By March 6, the musically challenged Japanese had lost half of their original defending strength and the outcome was no longer in doubt.[185]

The Japanese were on the defensive for the remainder of the battle, driven from one jungle position to another by the relentless attacks of the 1st Cavalry Brigade. Engineers repaired the Momote airstrip, enabling more responsive close air support for the cavalry squadrons. Despite Japanese resistance and forbidding terrain consisting of razorback ridges and deep ravines covered by nearly impenetrable jungle vines and other vegetation, the assault proceeded to destroy the last vestiges of organized Japanese resistance on Los Negros. The cavalrymen cleared the island by April 1; the Japanese defenders on Los Negros died nearly to the last man.[186]

While the 1st Cavalry Brigade secured Los Negros, on March 15 the 2nd Cavalry Brigade assaulted nearby Manus Island to secure its airfield and the western shore of Seeadler Harbor ("Sea Eagle" in German, as the islands were once a German colony), an enormous lagoon large enough to accommodate the majority of the US Pacific Fleet once the Navy turned it into an expeditionary naval base. To support the invasion force, the cavalrymen seized two small islands off the northern coast of Manus and placed three battalions of artillery on them – a tactic learned from previous invasions of the Marshall and Solomon Islands.[187] The artillery augmented the firepower of the destroyers offshore and the close air support provided by Army bombers and Australian P-40 Warhawk fighters operating from Momote airfield. Within four days the cavalrymen had seized Lorengau airfield and defeated the main Japanese resistance on Manus.[188] At a cost of 296 killed and 977 wounded, the 1st Cavalry Division had secured the Admiralty Islands and thereby completed the isolation of the Japanese at Rabaul. In the process, the cavalrymen had killed 4,300 Japanese soldiers, nearly the entire garrison.[189]

The disparity in firepower was the most important factor in the American victory. Naval gunfire supported daily operations. Air superiority over the Admiralties also helped the cavalrymen to fight outnumbered and win. By the time the campaign was over, 616 Allied aircraft had dropped 1,286,000 pounds of ordnance and fired more than 5 million rounds of ammunition on targets in close support of the troops ashore.[190] Besides air and naval support, artillery fired nearly 64,000 rounds during the campaign – an expenditure of munitions that the outgunned and ill-supplied Japanese forces could not come close to matching.[191] Some reconnaissance in force!

The 1st Cavalry Division lost whatever fear it might have had of the jungle, learned a great deal, and validated existing doctrine for small-unit operations. The division after-action report observed, "The lessons which were learned by both the staff and command elements of the Division were not new ones. The Marines [on Guadalcanal and elsewhere] had learned them, the 32d Division [at Buna in New Guinea] had learned them and reams had been written, published and distributed setting forth these lessons for the benefit of the inexperienced. But, like nearly all lessons, they were never fully learned except by experience."[192]

For the next two months, the 2nd Cavalry Brigade cleared the remainder of Manus Island of scattered Japanese forces. The lack of roads, dense jungle terrain, steep mountains, swamps, and ever-present mud made the job of the cavalrymen difficult. But these patrols served to further season the troopers in combat techniques, experience that would prove invaluable during the brigade's next operation on Leyte less than six months later. The Sixth Army G-3, Brig. Gen. Clyde D. Eddleman, later stated the purpose of these patrols: "General Krueger wanted to 'blood his troops' as much as possible so he liked to bring in a new division that was going into one of the later operations and have them go in and clean out the residue of the Japanese forces, put them under fire. Once you've been under fire, it's quite a different feeling. You're always afraid, but you know what it means to have a bullet whizzing past your ear and to be under mortar or artillery fire or bombing."[193]

Manus Island served as the ideal training ground for this purpose. Although the 2nd Cavalry Brigade had cleared Japanese forces from the strategically critical northern shore, many isolated Japanese units remained in the interior – an area the 1st Cavalry Division commander, Maj. Gen. Innis P. Swift, dubbed the "Game Preserve."[194] In June 1944, the division rotated its combat units onto Manus Island to conduct combat patrols to locate and destroy remaining Japanese forces. The island consisted of difficult terrain, a live opposing force, and potentially deadly consequences for careless mistakes. As a result, the soldiers took the training seriously, green junior officers received valuable leadership experience, and new replacements were introduced to their first shock of combat, which was dangerous but not overly so.[195] By the middle of the summer, the newly arrived soldiers had been transformed from untried replacements to semi-experienced jungle fighters, with at least a passing acquaintance with the struggles and fears of the combat soldier on the front line in the Pacific War. By the end of the summer of 1944, the 1st Cavalry Division was a full-strength, battle-experienced, thoroughly trained combat division – qualities that would soon prove their worth on Leyte and Luzon.

MacArthur had taken a calculated risk and won the jackpot. He was a lucky officer, a question he often asked of new arrivals to SWPA. The successful early invasion of the Admiralty Islands, validated with the courage and resourcefulness of Brig. Gen. Chase and his cavalrymen, paid enormous strategic dividends.[196] The US Navy turned Seeadler Harbor into the largest expeditionary naval base in the Pacific to that point, a key to supporting subsequent operations in New Guinea and the Philippines.[197] The seizure of the Admiralties made unnecessary the planned invasions of Hansa Bay and Wewak on New Guinea and Kavieng on New Ireland, and provided inspiration for MacArthur's decision to seize Hollandia, 500 miles to the west. The invasion succeeded due to close joint cooperation in rapidly planning the operation and because of the skill and bravery of the soldiers of the 1st Cavalry Division. The ambitious gambit opened up a number of possibilities for future operations. "Thus endeth the conquest of the Admiralty Islands," the division diarist wrote. "Where do we go from here?"[198] That question would soon be answered.

The rapid seizure of the Admiralties whetted MacArthur's appetite for a more aggressive advance to the west along New Guinea's northern coast. The next planned step, to Hansa Bay, was only 120 miles from Saidor, and the Japanese were expecting an attack there. Kenney, Willoughby, and Chamberlin's Planning Section chief, Brig. Gen. Bonner Fellers, advocated for an aggressive move to Hollandia, where few Japanese forces defended the area. Chamberlin thought the idea was crazy, but Fellers (without Chamberlin's permission) nevertheless briefed the option to MacArthur, who, with access to Ultra intelligence confirming the absence of large numbers of Japanese combat troops at Hollandia, approved it.[199] Hollandia would prove to be one of MacArthur's most brilliant victories of the war; however, incensed that he had been bypassed in the presentation of the plan to MacArthur, Chamberlin fired Fellers. Out of a job, but in MacArthur's good graces, Fellers would serve as the general's military

2.4: Lt. Gen. Walter Krueger, Brig. Gen. William Chase, and Maj. Gen. Innis P. Swift on Los Negros after the destruction of the Japanese garrison on the island, April 10, 1944. The seizure of the Admiralties sealed the fate of the Japanese garrison at Rabaul and provided an anchorage for the US Pacific Fleet in Seeadler Harbor on nearby Manus Island. (Credit: US Army Signal Corps Photo)

secretary and SWPA chief of psychological operations for the duration of the war.[200]

MacArthur now planned on bypassing Japanese garrisons at Hansa Bay and Wewak to seize Hollandia, an advance of nearly 500 miles. Ultra decrypts gave MacArthur confidence that he could pull off this coup, provided that the Joint Chiefs allotted him use of Nimitz's fast carriers to provide air support so deep in the Japanese rear area.[201] Hollandia was essentially undefended, home to rear-area troops with poor combat capabilities. Such a bold stroke would put SWPA back in the game, as it had been relegated to a strategic backwater with the onset of Nimitz's Central Pacific campaign. Given MacArthur's unexpected early success in the Admiralties, the Joint Chiefs of Staff approved the seemingly risky jump to Hollandia. Appropriately, the operation received the code name RECKLESS.[202]

With the invasion date only weeks away, planning at headquarters separated by thousands of miles kicked into high gear. "Krueger and Kenney planned and fought; Barbey planned and transported," Rogers notes. "They all planned, however, and it became the least exciting, most demanding, and possibly the most arduous of their duties."[203] By this point, GHQ SWPA and its subordinate headquarters were a highly functioning machine, making possible relatively rapid changes in operational planning. At GHQ SWPA, Chamberlin had three planning teams, designated red, white, and blue, enabling continuous planning for future operations.[204] Hollandia would be planned in a matter of weeks. A few months later, SWPA would finalize the massive invasion of Leyte in a matter of days.

The Fifth Air Force paved the way for the Hollandia operation by pounding Wewak into dust from March 11 to 16, destroying 100 aircraft on the ground and another 68 in aerial combat. The Japanese had in the meantime moved aircraft into the Hollandia area, ostensibly beyond the range of P-38 fighters operating from the nearest base at Gusap. But, in February, Kenney had received fifty-eight new P-38J fighters with additional wing tanks that gave them the range to reach Hollandia with an hour of loiter time to spare before the return trip. He then had his mechanics fashion wing tanks for seventy-five older P-38s to prepare them for the journey to Hollandia. To lull the Japanese into a false sense of security by making them believe American fighters lacked the range to reach Hollandia, Kenney forbade daylight strikes west of Tadji, a small town just east of Aitape.[205]

Nimitz and his staff traveled to Brisbane on March 25 to coordinate the details of the Hollandia operation. MacArthur extended complete cordiality to the admiral and his party, and, as was usually the case in the later years of the Pacific War, when the two services got together to plan, they cooperated more fully than lingering interservice rivalry would suggest. Vice Adm. Marc Mitscher's Task Force 58 would raid Japanese airpower in the Palaus before heading to New Guinea to support the landings. Task Force 58 would depart the day after the landings, however, to protect the fast carriers from attacks by Japanese land-based airpower. Two task groups containing eight escort carriers would remain behind to provide close support, provided that the Fifth Air Force could base fighters at Aitape within a couple of days after the landings. Krueger's Sixth Army, with its headquarters now at Finschhafen, would command the ground forces in the operation, with the 24th Infantry Division (which would be christened the "Victory Division" after the war) commanded by Maj. Gen. Frederick A. Irving and 41st Infantry Division (which by this point in the New Guinea campaign had been nicknamed the "Jungleers") commanded by Maj. Gen. Fuller under Lt. Gen. Eichelberger's I Corps landing near Hollandia at Humboldt and Tanahmerah Bays, while the 163rd Regimental Combat Team under Brig. Gen. Jens A. Doe would land at Aitape, located between Hollandia and Wewak. Barbey would command the assault force while at sea – 217 ships carrying nearly 80,000 men and 50,000 tons of supplies.[206] MacArthur also ordered a deception operation that included heavy bombing strikes and naval gunfire to make the Japanese believe the assault would occur in Hansa Bay.[207]

Nimitz was concerned about Japanese air strength in the Hollandia area, so the operation hinged on the ability of Kenney's airmen to destroy the Japanese aircraft located in the vicinity.[208] Beginning on March 30, sixty-five B-24s bombed the three Japanese airfields at Hollandia, escorted by eighty P-38s. The Fifth Air Force repeated the strikes the next day and for several days thereafter. By April 3, Japanese air power in the Hollandia area had been eviscerated, with 288 aircraft destroyed on the ground and 50 fighters shot down in the air over the 5-day period.[209] The way was clear for Mitscher's carriers to operate off the coast of New Guinea in support of the Hollandia landings. Adm. Nimitz wired his congratulations, as did MacArthur, who sent his message "uncoded so that even the Japs could read it."[210]

A week later, Capt. Dick Bong downed his twenty-seventh Japanese aircraft, eclipsing the top US ace of World War I, Capt. Eddie Rickenbacker. Kenney promoted him to major and sent him home to Wisconsin on leave.[211] On April 16, disaster struck when the weather closed in on a bombing strike returning from Tadji. Of the 171 planes on the raid, 36 made emergency landings, while 31 aircraft and 32 airmen were lost. "It was the worst blow I took in the whole war," recalled Kenney, but it would not be the worst weather-related disaster to befall US forces in the Pacific.[212]

After a brief bombardment, the troops went ashore on the morning of April 22. The Japanese were completely surprised, offering only slight resistance to the invasions. The 24th Infantry Division, which landed its lead elements at Tanahmerah Bay, could not move inland owing to the unexpected presence behind the beach of an impassable swamp. I Corps diverted the rest of the division to Humboldt Bay, where the 41st Infantry Division had landed and quickly moved inland. The 163rd Infantry likewise seized Aitape against minimal resistance. MacArthur went ashore four hours after the first wave to inspect the beachhead. Upon returning to the *Nashville*, MacArthur, Krueger, Barbey, and Eichelberger celebrated the successful landings with chocolate ice cream sodas. Eichelberger quickly

2.5: Gen. Douglas MacArthur, Commander in Chief SWPA, discusses strategy with Adm. Chester W. Nimitz, Commander in Chief of the Pacific Ocean Areas, at GHQ SWPA in Brisbane, Australia, March 27, 1944. Nimitz and members of his staff had flown to Brisbane to finalize planning for the invasion of Hollandia, which would involve naval assets from the US Pacific Fleet. (Credit: US Navy Photo)

downed his, and then, at MacArthur's invitation, drained the SWPA commander's as well for good measure.[213]

Buoyed by the success of the invasion, MacArthur suggested diverting reserve forces from Hollandia to seize Wakde Island, 125 miles further to the west. Barbey agreed, whereas Krueger was guarded. Eichelberger threw cold water on the suggestion, arguing that the shipping was not combat-loaded and therefore an invasion would succeed only against meager

Japanese opposition, which was not assured. Japanese regiments might still be lurking around Hollandia as well. Apparently, it would take more than two ice cream sodas to buy Eichelberger's acquiescence. MacArthur withdrew his proposal.[214]

The worst calamity to befall the invasion forces was a fire in a Japanese supply dump on the beach at Humboldt Bay that attracted a lone Japanese bomber on the night of April 23. One of its bombs hit an ammunition cache; exploding ammunition then ignited gasoline stockpiled nearby. Fires raged across the beach, destroying 60 percent of the ammunition and rations that had been unloaded during the first two days of the invasion and killing twenty-four soldiers.[215] Troops immediately went on half rations while awaiting resupply. Despite the resulting shortages and difficulties in moving what supplies there were forward to the combat troops, infantry seized the three Japanese airfields four days later, and engineers went to work turning them into usable air bases for Fifth Air Force fighters and medium bombers. US forces killed 3,000 Japanese at Hollandia; another 7,000 Japanese disappeared into the jungle, a green desert that killed relentlessly. Only 1,000 Japanese soldiers emerged to link up with their brethren at Wakde. SWPA declared the operations at Hollandia complete on June 6.[216]

Engineers and Seabees turned Hollandia into an enormous advanced base area housing upwards of 140,000 soldiers that would sustain MacArthur's forces as they continued their advance toward the Philippines. Kenney's fighters and medium bombers moved forward onto three newly built airfields. The seizure of Hollandia had been one of the great coups of the Pacific War. MacArthur, Kenney, Kinkaid, and Krueger all moved their advanced headquarters to a hill overlooking Lake Sentani above Hollandia in September. MacArthur spent only a few days in Hollandia, leaving Sutherland in charge of the advanced headquarters. The collocation of the major headquarters there expedited the planning for the invasion of Leyte, conducted at short notice and on an accelerated timeline.[217]

MacArthur was meanwhile embroiled in domestic politics back home. Interested parties, led by Senator Arthur H. Vandenburg (Republican, Michigan), considered MacArthur's name in connection with the Republican candidacy for the 1944 presidential election. In his memoir, MacArthur denies that he had designs on the nation's highest office, but these protestations are too clever by half.[218] He never uttered a Shermanesque response ("If nominated I will not accept, if elected I will not serve") to tamp down speculation until after the public release of MacArthur's letter to Congressman Arthur L. Miller (Republican,

Nebraska) applauding the representative's disparaging remarks regarding the New Deal and his call for MacArthur to enter the presidential contest. The resulting public furor finally convinced MacArthur, at the time supervising the Hollandia expedition, to definitively withdraw his name from consideration for the Republican nomination. It would not be the last time that MacArthur's communications with elected officials contravening administration policy would get him into trouble, but the next president would be far less forgiving of the transgression than was Roosevelt.[219]

The Japanese attempted to reinforce their positions in western New Guinea with the *32nd Division* and portions of the *35th Division*, but Ultra revealed the route and destination of the nine transports and seven escort vessels in the convoy. The USS *Jack* sank a transport off the coast of Luzon on April 26, but for the Japanese the worst was yet to come. The USS *Gurnard* was positioned along the route in the Celebes Sea, and on May 6 the submarine torpedoed three transports, drowning nearly 1,300 soldiers and sending all of their equipment to the bottom. Altogether the *32nd Division* lost nearly 4,000 soldiers as well as their weapons and supplies, nearly a third of the division.[220]

The 60,000 Japanese soldiers of the *18th Army* were now caught between Australian forces to the east and elements of the Sixth Army in the Hollandia–Aitape area, with no hope of resupply. The Japanese attempted to break out of this strategic vise by attacking US forces along the Driniumor River east of Aitape beginning on the night of July 10–11. Japanese infantry attacked across the shallow river and died by the thousands, but they broke through the thinly manned lines of the covering force and precipitated a month-long battle that claimed the lives of 440 Americans and 9,000 Japanese. An American counterattack finally pushed the Japanese back across the river. By August 9, the Japanese began their retreat east to Wewak and eventually from there into the mountains, where Australian forces left them to wither from malnutrition and sickness until the end of the war brought an end to the suffering of those who had not yet succumbed to starvation, disease, and the elements.[221]

By then, MacArthur's forces had moved on to the west, primarily to seize airfields from which Kenney's heavy bombers and fighters could operate. Forewarned by Ultra intelligence as to the state of Japanese defenses in western New Guinea, the operational pace accelerated to take advantage of Japanese weakness and position SWPA forces to invade the Philippines no later than the end of the year.[222] MacArthur was in a race for time to position his forces to invade the Philippines, as the Joint Chiefs of Staff were considering bypassing Luzon in favor of an invasion of Formosa, an operation that would be under Nimitz's control. "We were definitely on the move," Kenney wrote in his memoirs. "The Philippines didn't look anywhere near as far away as they had just a few months before."[223]

Prodded onward by MacArthur, Krueger's Sixth Army invaded Wakde, Biak, Noemfoor, and Sansapor in rapid succession, with the planning and execution of each operation overlapping one another. Barbey's amphibious force planners and Krueger's army headquarters worked smoothly to synchronize the details of each assault. The Fifth Air Force prepared the way for each landing by demolishing airfields and eliminating the majority of the Japanese fighters and bombers in the invasion area. The 163rd Infantry initiated the sequence on May 17 with an invasion of Arara on the New Guinea coast, followed by a short advance to Toem opposite the island of Wakde to emplace artillery. The regimental combat team then conducted a shore-to-shore invasion of the island the next day, wading ashore against fierce fire from Japanese fortified in caves and coconut log pillboxes and bunkers. After two days of bitter fighting, the regiment had seized the island and its all-important airfield, killing more than 750 Japanese in the process. Engineers restored the airfield to working order, and Kenney positioned two groups of P-38 fighters and two groups of B-24 bombers on it in preparation for the invasion of Biak, now a week away.[224]

Having taken the critical objective with relatively few losses, Krueger erred by ordering an advance on the mainland to seize the heights west of the Tor River. The 158th Regimental Combat Team landed at Arara and began an advance to the west toward Japanese-held airfields in the Sarmi area, which were neither needed nor usable given the pervasive mud that swamped them. The attack began on May 23, and, after three days of slogging through jungle against stiffening resistance, the GIs ran into a nightmare called Lone Tree Hill, which was a 175-foot-high jungle-covered coral wasteland filled with caves and crevices. Two attacks failed to dislodge the Japanese defenders before Krueger pulled out the 158th Regimental Combat Team to send it to invade Noemfoor Island.[225]

The 6th Infantry Division ("Red Star," commanded by Maj. Gen. Franklin C. Sibert), which had not yet experienced combat, now landed at Toem and proceeded to advance toward Lone Tree Hill on June 18. Initial attacks failed, but the 3rd Battalion, 20th Infantry reached the summit on June 22. A Japanese counterattack isolated the battalion on the crest, but the unit held against fierce Japanese assaults. The next day the 2nd Battalion managed to link up with its sister unit on the crest of the high ground, but they remained isolated. On June 24, two companies of the 1st Battalion and the 6th Reconnaissance Troop conducted an amphibious landing behind Lone Tree Hill in an attempt to turn the Japanese out of their positions. The maneuver did not work; nevertheless, the combined efforts of the three forces destroyed the Japanese on the hill mass after another day of brutal fighting in which the GIs killed the Japanese defenders with artillery, flamethrowers, demolition charges, and grenades. The 1st and 63rd Infantry Regimental Combat Teams now took up the gauntlet, finally clearing the rest of the hills overlooking Maffin Bay by July 12.[226]

The next objective in the path of MacArthur's advance was the island of Biak, located 200 miles west of Wakde, and its three coral airstrips populated by what SWPA intelligence thought was a couple of thousand Japanese soldiers.[227] "Coral was good stuff," recalled Kenney in his memoir. "Where there was plenty of coral, the engineers could give us a field in a matter of a few days" as opposed to one to two months for sand or clay soil.[228] Two regiments of the 41st Infantry Division landed on the southern shore of Biak on May 27 and advanced inland. MacArthur issued an optimistic communique which envisioned "the practical end of the New Guinea campaign," but no one told the Japanese. Their robust and well-trained forces, positioned in caves on the heights overlooking the beaches, launched a counterattack that severed the American line of communication to the beachhead. On the evening of June 5, a successful Japanese bombing strike destroyed dozens of aircraft jammed together on the airfield at Wakde, while a torpedo bomber damaged the cruiser *Nashville*, and another aircraft scored a bomb hit on the destroyer *Kalk*.[229]

A Japanese convoy with reinforcements from Mindanao headed to the area, but, alerted to its presence by Ultra, 10 B-25s escorted by 8 P-38s pounced on it about 100 miles west of Biak, sinking a destroyer. As the Japanese approached Biak, two task forces of the Seventh Fleet moved to intercept. The Japanese commander, convinced that discretion was the better part of valor, retreated, leaving Biak isolated.[230] MacArthur courted danger at this moment, for the Japanese were prepared to send a naval task force centered around the super-battleships *Yamato* and *Musashi* against the Seventh Fleet around Biak. The operation was canceled only when the Japanese spotted the Fifth Fleet, which was guarding the amphibious forces that invaded Saipan on June 15. MacArthur's luck – a prerequisite for any successful military leader – held.[231]

The 41st Infantry Division regrouped and received its third infantry regiment as reinforcement before continuing the drive on June 2 against the Japanese positions. The division seized one of the three airfields five days later, but it could not be brought into operation for another week because of the intense Japanese fire directed against it. MacArthur, who had already proclaimed victory and was embarrassed by the failure to take the island, made clear his displeasure to Krueger, who passed it on to Maj. Gen. Fuller, the task force commander at Biak. Neither MacArthur nor Krueger bothered to visit the island to see the situation for themselves. Instead, Krueger sent Eichelberger on June 15 to take command of the task force on Biak and get it moving forward, and once again Eichelberger relieved the division commander, who was, by coincidence, the second West Point classmate he had to relieve during the war.[232] In this he had little choice, as Fuller, enraged at his treatment by Krueger, had already sent a letter announcing his resignation to Sixth Army headquarters. Upon meeting Eichelberger, Fuller lamented that "he does not intend to serve under [Krueger] again if he has to submit his resignation every half hour by wire . . . . He cried when he recalled that it was thirty-nine years ago yesterday since we entered the military academy together."[233]

As he had done at Buna, Eichelberger proceeded to clarify the situation and reorganize the forces on Biak. As with Buna, however, a change of command alone could not turn around a stalemate created by Japanese fortified in horrific terrain and the relative strength of the opposing forces. After further reinforcements landed to bolster the attack, Eichelberger ordered an envelopment of the main Japanese positions, which the GIs overcame by June 27.[234] Engineers immediately turned to the task of putting the island's three airfields into operation. The Jungleers, now under the command of Maj. Gen. Jens Doe, seized control of the remainder of Biak by August 20, although mopping up continued for several months. By the middle of January 1945, Japanese losses on Biak totaled 7,200 soldiers.[235] Once again, Eichelberger had salvaged a difficult situation with exceptional combat leadership, and once again, he received very little praise for his performance from his superiors.

The unexpected resistance on Biak required SWPA to call an audible. Just south of Biak was the small island of Owi, which was "uninhabited, fairly free of tree growth, flat, well drained, and solid coral, except for about a foot of black topsoil."[236] Fifth Air Force engineers quickly created an airfield that filled most of the island, and by June 21 it was in operation. Owi would become "one of [Fifth Air Force's] most important bases."[237]

By this point in the campaign, Halsey had wrapped up major operations in the South Pacific Area. Although fighting was still ongoing on Bougainville, MacArthur recommended that the Joint Chiefs

reapportion substantial elements of the South Pacific Area to his command. The Joint Chiefs concurred with this proposal, and on June 15
reassigned the Thirteenth Air Force, the XIV Corps, the 25th, 37th,
40th, 43rd, 93rd, and Americal Divisions, and the 1st and 2nd
Philippine Regiments to the Southwest Pacific Theater of Operations.
In addition to his duties as Allied Air Forces commander, Kenney
assumed command of the Far East Air Forces, with the Fifth (Maj. Gen.
Ennis Whitehead) and Thirteenth (Maj. Gen. St. Clair Streett) Air
Forces under his command. At MacArthur's request, the War
Department established the Eighth Army on September 7, with Lt.
Gen. Eichelberger in command, to complement Krueger's Sixth Army.
With operations in New Guinea drawing to a close, MacArthur elimin-
ated the fictitious Alamo Force and effectively became his own land
forces commander, leaving Gen. Blamey in charge of two Australian
armies but little else. The Third Fleet, the 15th Marine Amphibious
Corps, and the majority of the naval air forces were transferred to the
Central Pacific for operations in that theater.[238]

Suitably reinforced, MacArthur accelerated his advance along the
northern coast of New Guinea. His next target was Noemfoor, located just
thirty-five miles west of Biak. Kenney's air forces pounded the island in the
days before the invasion, and a heavy naval bombardment prepared the
beaches for the landing forces. The 158th Regimental Combat Team
assaulted the island on July 2, securing Kamiri airfield. Over the next two
days, the 503rd Parachute Infantry parachuted onto the island, bolstering
the offensive.[239] The forces attacked and seized Kornasoren airfield and Hill
201 on July 4–5, destroying the main Japanese resistance on the island. Both
airfields were operational by the end of the month. Combat operations
continued throughout the month to clear the island of remaining
Japanese forces.[240]

The final operation in New Guinea was an assault on the Vogelkop
Peninsula on the western end of the island, 200 miles to the west of
Noemfoor. MacArthur bypassed the Japanese garrison at Manokwari to
land the 6th Infantry Division near Cape Opmarai and nearby on
Middelburg and Amsterdam Islands on July 30. The Japanese were again
caught unawares and offered only scant resistance. Given the beating sustained by the Imperial Japanese Navy in the Battle of the Philippine Sea
(June 19–20) and aircraft losses in New Guinea, the Japanese had few
resources left to defend the area. The next day, troops conducted a shore-
to-shore landing at Sansapor, where airfield construction began
immediately.[241] In addition to the airfield on Owi, the Fifth Air Force

established a heavy bomber base on Biak, and airfields for fighters and medium bombers on Wakde, on Noemfoor, and at Sansapor.[242]

By the end of the New Guinea campaign, MacArthur's forces had honed their capabilities in amphibious operations and island warfare. Their logistics had improved dramatically, as had their transportation capabilities in the air and at sea. More and better equipment, such as flamethrowers and bazookas, enhanced the power and tactical capabilities of the infantry. Large landing craft could now put tanks, trucks, and engineering equipment ashore, creating a powerful combined arms team that overwhelmed Japanese capabilities. Tactical intelligence got better over time, and American commanders learned how to exploit Japanese weaknesses. The medical system learned how to prevent or mitigate tropical diseases such as malaria and to treat wounded and infected patients.

In New Guinea, MacArthur and his subordinate commanders created the powerful joint team that would propel US forces back to the Philippines. With the Bataan Gang at its core, SWPA headquarters had grown from scratch to become a robust theater staff. Also built from humble beginnings, the Central Bureau had cracked Japanese codes, providing MacArthur and his key subordinate leaders with invaluable intelligence. As was the case with German leaders and Ultra in Europe, the Japanese never concluded that the Allies had broken their codes, but instead blamed their seemingly poor luck on Allied air reconnaissance and coastwatchers.[243] SWPA had created a logistics structure that could support operations over oceanic distances. Allied medical personnel had largely eliminated malaria as an impediment to future operations.

In Lt. Gen. Kenney, Vice Adm. Kinkaid, Rear Adm. Barbey, Lt. Gen. Krueger, and Lt. Gen. Eichelberger, MacArthur found commanders of his air, naval, and ground forces who were competent and loyal, the two characteristics he most prized. Under Kenney's leadership, the Allied Air Forces had earned hard-fought air superiority over New Guinea, neutered Japanese air power, and paved the way for multiple amphibious landings through bombardment and strafing of Japanese positions. Together with the PT boats of the Seventh Fleet, the Fifth Air Force destroyed the ability of the Japanese to supply and reinforce their forces by virtually eliminating coastal traffic in the New Guinea area.[244] Denied the use of fast carriers and battleships, Kinkaid and Barbey made use of smaller escort carriers, light cruisers, destroyers, amphibious vessels, and submarines in fashioning "MacArthur's navy." Krueger and Eichelberger created effective combined arms teams that attained their objectives, even when faced with unexpected Japanese strength such as at Buna and Biak.

By October 1944, the time was at hand to test the new capabilities of MacArthur's forces in their return to the Philippines.

3

THE RESISTANCE

When the Spaniards came, they taught us religion; when the Americans came, they taught us education; but when the Japanese came, they taught us prostitution.[1]

Filipino guerrilla saying

Not everyone had to return, because not everyone had left. The Filipino people, tied to a homeland they could not abandon, struggled for three years to free their land from Japanese occupation. Hundreds of thousands resisted, while others collaborated. Most Filipinos did their best to survive, many providing what support they could to the resistance while awaiting the fulfillment of MacArthur's promise to return and liberate their homeland. A few Americans, civilian and military, also remained behind – some who escaped Japanese captivity after Lt. Gen. Jonathan Wainwright surrendered US forces on May 6, 1942, and others who were stationed away from the Manila area and deliberately disobeyed the order to surrender. Theirs was a lonely existence on the run for months on end until the first fragile contact was established with Allied forces in Australia. First, they fought to survive. Next, they fought for recognition from MacArthur's Southwest Pacific Area (SWPA) headquarters, which would bring with it legal protection, promotions, supplies, arms, equipment, money, and prestige. Finally, those active in the resistance often fought one another, sometimes as a matter of ideology, but more often for power. Despite the variegated nature of the resistance, it thrived and grew on the back of Japanese atrocities that turned the Filipino people firmly against the occupation of their homeland. Slowly, steadily, inexorably, American and Filipino leaders formed the framework for a robust guerrilla struggle against Japanese occupation that morphed into one of the great resistance movements of World War II.[2]

MacArthur had directed one small effort to establish a guerrilla movement behind Japanese lines while fighting on the Bataan Peninsula. In January 1942, he authorized his provost-marshal, Major Claude A. Thorp, to lead a party through Japanese lines on the Bataan Peninsula to raid and gather intelligence in the Zambales Mountains region. Thorp gathered local Filipinos to the cause, creating a number of guerrilla bands in the area surrounding Mount Pinatubo.[3] According to Robert Lapham, who served for a period as the group's supply officer, Thorp "was not an imaginative man, but he was tough, fearless, and well liked both by his fellow officers and by enlisted men."[4] As events would show, he was not a natural guerrilla. Nevertheless, Thorp was one of the few leaders of the resistance who had specific orders from the United States Army Forces in the Far East (USAFFE) to operate behind enemy lines. Despite this authority, after the fall of Bataan he allowed members of his group to split off and go their own ways rather than remain under his command.[5] Some of those who did so became major guerrilla leaders in their own right. Thorp's demise came at the hands of a Filipino traitor, who led the Japanese to his position in return for a hefty bribe.[6] The Japanese captured Thorp and a group of his associates on October 30, 1942, sentenced him to death after a perfunctory show trial, and executed him a year later. Thorp's capture left the Filipino guerrilla movement officially leaderless until contact was established between the Philippine Islands and MacArthur's headquarters in Australia.

Thorp had tried to establish relations with the communist guerrilla movement in the Philippines, which was also battling the Japanese occupation. This movement had its origins in the resistance of tenant farmers to rich landowners during the Spanish colonial era. During the American colonial period, better-educated socialist leaders tried to mobilize Filipino peasants against an economic system that repressed them as a permanent underclass. In the wake of the Japanese invasion, Filipino communist and socialist groups met in March 1942 to establish a unified front to resist the Japanese and further their political and economic agendas. The group was christened the Hukbong Bayan Laban sa Hapon (The People's Army against Japan), shortened to Hukbalahap, or simply the Huks.

The Huk guerrillas, led by Luis Taruc, were intent both on fighting the Japanese and on ushering in a post-war socialist government. Centered on the area around Mount Arayat forty miles north of Manila, the Huks vied with other guerrilla groups for power in central Luzon, always with an eye on the post-war future. On July 7, 1942, Thorp dispatched several representatives – among them Air Corps Major Bernard Anderson, Captain Joseph Barker, and Bert Petit – to reach an agreement on cooperation with the Huks. In Thorp's mind, the fact that both his forces and the Huks were willing to fight the Japanese should have been enough to establish the foundation for a working relationship between the groups. The Huks, however, demanded autonomy over their organization and independence in political matters. The result was a weak compromise that promised cooperation but in effect achieved little. Even this agreement was annulled after Thorp's capture and execution by the Japanese.[7]

The Huks were uncompromising. "In my experience with them," writes guerrilla leader Robert Lapham, who led a guerrilla group in central Luzon, "the Huks were shrewd, formidable, and above all, treacherous adversaries . . . . My forces spent at least as much time watching, fending off, resisting, and occasionally fighting Huks as we did Japanese."[8] Guerrilla leader Edwin Ramsey agrees, writing that the Huks "perceived us to be as much a threat to them as the Japanese, and they warred on us equally."[9] Despite their lack of cooperation with other guerrilla groups, the Huks amassed a powerful force during the war, eventually numbering upwards of 15,000 fighters, that harassed Japanese forces.[10] They would become best known, however, for their post-war insurgency against the Filipino government, a rebellion that was eventually suppressed in the early 1950s by Filipino troops under the leadership of Secretary of National Defense and President Ramon Magsaysay (himself a former guerrilla on Luzon) and his American advisor, Edward Lansdale.[11]

Thorp made a number of appointments to bring some order to guerrilla organization on Luzon, none of which panned out. He divided Luzon into four areas, placing each under a US officer: northern Luzon (Capt. Ralph Praeger), western Luzon (Capt. Ralph McGuire), east central Luzon (Capt. Joseph Barker), and southern Luzon (Capt. George "Jack" Spies). None of these officers would survive the war: Praeger was captured in August 1943 and executed sometime in late 1944; McGuire was killed in April 1943 by disloyal Negrito guerrillas; Barker was captured in January 1943 and executed eight months later; and Spies died on his way south before ever assuming command.[12] With Thorp's centralized plan for the guerrilla movement in disarray and Thorp himself out of the picture, American and Filipino leaders would have to mobilize guerrilla formations locally, from the ground up.

Lacking centralized leadership, guerrilla forces grew unevenly and haphazardly. Many unrecognized groups were little more than criminal gangs that preyed on local Filipinos for food, shelter, and women. A complete recounting of the history of all of these resistance groups would require several volumes, but some groups (detailed below) were clearly larger and more effective than others.[13]

Of the hundreds of American civilians and servicemen and thousands of Filipinos who refused to surrender or who escaped Japanese captivity after the fall of Bataan and Corregidor, some died of disease or were killed or captured in the ensuing months, and many simply tried to survive, but only a select few became successful guerrilla leaders. They first had to be willing to disobey the order to surrender, which could lead to a court martial even if they survived the war. Those who became major figures in the guerrilla movement were cunning, resourceful, young and strong enough to endure physical hardships, and mentally tough. They had to be ruthless enough to kill traitors and collaborators among their forces and among the civilian population. They endured physical ailments including repeated bouts of malaria, dysentery, and malnutrition. They also needed a certain amount of guile and political savvy: Leaders vied for control over one another even as they sought to gain Filipino support and fight the Japanese. Individual leaders formed guerrilla groups, made alliances, suppressed local criminal gangs, and competed with one another for territory and popular support. Writing his memoir half a century after the war, Robert Lapham concluded, "[Guerrilla warfare] is a mean, dirty, brutal struggle to the death, devoid of any principle or sentiment save to survive and win."[14] The winnowing process was brutal and Darwinian; many potential leaders met their demise in the first year after the fall of Bataan. Wizened by their experiences and brushes with death, most of the survivors of this formative period survived to the end of the war.[15]

What leaders desired above all else was official recognition from MacArthur's headquarters in Australia, which would make them legal combatants according to the law of armed conflict, and the provision of arms and supplies that would follow in due course. But recognition eluded guerrilla groups in the Philippines for months on end, given the lack of communications with Australia.

Thorp's capture set in place a free-for-all among US officers to assume control of the guerrillas on Luzon. Most US personnel recognized Thorp's authority, given that his orders had come in writing from MacArthur. Few agreed upon his successor. Barker claimed that the succession of command fell to him, but his capture in Manila on January 13, 1943, ended his bid for power. After this misfortune, Lt. Edwin Ramsey, a horse lover who had grown up in Depression-era Kansas and had attended the Oklahoma Military Academy to play polo as much as anything else, assumed command of the guerrillas positioned between Manila and Lingayen Gulf, including the old battlegrounds of the Bataan Peninsula.[16] Ramsey had made history a year earlier on January 16, 1942, as a lieutenant in the 26th Cavalry Regiment (Philippine Scouts) by leading the last mounted horse cavalry charge in US Army history.[17] After the fall of Bataan, Ramsey refused to surrender and, along with Barker, found his way to Thorp, who ordered the two of them to take charge of raising guerrilla forces in east central Luzon.[18]

Barker and Ramsey modeled their organization and tactics after those of the Huk guerrillas, which in turn were based on the writings of the Chinese communist leader Mao Tse Tung, or Mao Zedong.[19] Studying Mao's writings, Barker and Ramsey took a crash course on revolutionary warfare. "For us it was a wholly new approach to warfare," Ramsey noted, "in many cases the reverse of everything we had been taught."[20] Lying awake one night, he ruminated about "what sort of a war this was in which a West Point graduate and a Southern gentleman [Barker], dressed in a uniform of rags and lying in a jungle hut, read from the works of a Chinese Communist revolutionary about tactics, logistics, and the philosophy of the human heart."[21]

Like most guerrilla leaders, Ramsey would adopt the status he felt corresponded to his unconventional duties, assuming the rank of captain by the end of 1942 before being officially promoted by MacArthur to major the following year. Ramsey would write in his memoir:

> In the way of this strange war I supposed I *was* acting on MacArthur's authority. There were so few of us in the guerrilla command, and we were operating under such unorthodox conditions that each of us would have to take extraordinary measures if we were to have any chance not only to succeed but simply to survive. It was no time to stand on ceremony; an army had to be built from scratch, and that army was MacArthur's. I was a twenty-five-year-old lieutenant speaking for the commanding general, but his name was the most potent weapon I had, and for the sake of realizing his promise to return, I would act on his authority.[22]

By early 1943, Ramsey had bounties placed on his head both by the Japanese and by the Huks, but managed to survive and continued to organize the guerrilla groups in what came to be known as the East Central Luzon Guerrilla Area.

Some of the guerrilla leaders under Ramsey's control were intriguing characters who assumed more than military rank. One such man, Charles Putnam, was a hard-drinking mining engineer and reserve artillery captain who controlled the guerrillas in the Lingayen Gulf area and resembled a forerunner of the fictitious Colonel Kurtz of *Apocalypse Now* notoriety.

During one of Ramsey's visits to see him, Putnam, following several long swigs from a bottle of rum, pointed to the hills, inhabited by cannibalistic tribes. "They love Japanese raids, Ramsey," Putnam averred, "they invite them. You know why? Cause that's the only time they have full bellies. That's not military, and it sure as hell's no job. That's guerrilla warfare, and as far as they're concerned I'm no captain, I'm the king." After another long pull from the bottle, Putnam continued, "And if you value your skin, Ramsey, you'll be one too."[23] King or no, Putnam would not live to witness the return; the Japanese captured and beheaded him in September 1944.[24]

After Thorp's capture, Ramsey and Anderson, who led guerrilla forces in Bulacan province north of Manila, competed for command.[25] It was a quixotic endeavor; Luzon was too large, its topography too compartmented, and communications were too fragile for one person to control the entire guerrilla movement on the island. The feud consumed much of 1943 as the two officers sent competing directives to various guerrilla leaders, who in turn were perplexed by the dispute. On October 12, 1943, Ramsey confirmed Anderson as commander of USAFFE Luzon Guerrilla Army Forces and the rivalry dissipated.[26] Ramsey eventually lost interest in controlling other groups, while Anderson moved to Tayabas to make contact with SWPA, leaving Cpt. Alejo S. Santos in charge of the guerrillas in Bulacan.[27] It was no doubt for the best; the egos involved were too big to assuage, centralized control over the guerrilla movement would have done little to improve intelligence collection or operations against the Japanese, and, after the US invasion of Luzon in January 1945, SWPA attached guerrilla groups to various US divisions rather than allowing them to continue to operate independently.[28]

One of the most successful of the early guerrillas was Walter M. Cushing from El Paso, Texas, a civilian mining executive turned guerrilla who terrorized Japanese forces from his first spectacular ambush on January 1, 1942, until his capture and subsequent execution in 1943. More successful in the long run was Col. Russell Volckmann, a 1934 graduate of the United States Military Academy, who began the war as commander of the 11th Infantry Regiment of the Philippine Army's 11th Division. He had been assigned as division intelligence officer just a week before the fall of Bataan, but was in the position long enough to learn of the early guerrilla activities conducted by US officers and others behind the lines.[29] Along with Lt. Donald Blackburn, the division's signal officer, Volckmann would initially serve as a guerrilla under the command of Lt. Col. Martin Moses and Lt. Col. Arthur Noble, regimental commanders in the 11th Division who had also eluded the surrender of US forces in Bataan. Moses and Noble gathered the remnants of several early guerrilla groups under their control and declared their command authority over all other groups in northern Luzon on October 1, 1942.[30] Such control was uncertain at best, but enough guerrilla leaders obeyed their orders for them to begin concerted offensive action against the Japanese. The decision to begin combat operations against the Japanese was a huge mistake, for a devastating counterstrike was inevitable. For nine months, thousands of Japanese troops brutally oppressed the Filipinos in northern Luzon, organized the natives into involuntary "neighborhood associations," armed a Filipino constabulary under Japanese control, and empowered puppet leaders who denounced the guerrillas.[31] These measures severed the vital link between the population and the guerrilla bands. By mid 1943, the Japanese had crushed many of the early guerrilla groups and had captured or killed their leaders, including Moses and Noble.[32] Of the key American leaders in the region, only Volckmann and Blackburn remained.

By the time Moses and Noble were captured, Volckmann and Blackburn had established their own headquarters in northern Luzon at Haliap in Ifugao province, which was linked to other guerrilla organizations through the use of an efficient messenger network. Volckmann issued what he described as a "Lay Low Order," directing guerrillas in northern Luzon to avoid enemy contact and gather intelligence as their primary function. He divided the region into seven districts, appointing a commander for each. He ordered each district commander to raise a regiment of troops, billeting them in company or platoon camps away from the civilian population. Volckmann also organized a general headquarters to assist in control of the districts. Most importantly, he emphasized the need to gain the cooperation of Filipino civilians; by persuasion if possible, by coercion if necessary. Civil affairs officers were among the most important staff personnel in each guerrilla headquarters. Counterintelligence agents worked ruthlessly to eliminate traitors and spies, causing Japanese sources of intelligence to dry up.[33]

Volckmann desired to bring other guerrilla groups in northern Luzon under his control, which put him at odds with several key guerrilla leaders, among them Robert Lapham, whose group, the Luzon Guerrilla Army Forces (LGAF), contested the northern part of the key central plain of Luzon between Lingayen Gulf and Manila. Since this area would be the most likely invasion route for American forces, it was of more than passing interest to intelligence officers and planners at SWPA.

Lapham was caught in the middle, both geographically and figuratively. A 1939 ROTC graduate of the University of Iowa, he joined the 26th Cavalry shortly before the war. In January 1942, Lapham joined Thorp's raiding party and, for the next three-plus years, operated as a guerrilla leader in central Luzon. After the fall of Bataan, Lapham struck out on his own with two noncommissioned officers, moving north through the Zambales Mountains and eventually reaching the town of Umingan. There a group of locals approached Lapham and asked him to lead a guerrilla band they wished to form. Not only did he have military training, but also, in that era, a certain amount of prestige attached to any group led by an American. Together with another nearby group formed by US Army Sergeant Albert Short (who would be killed by the Japanese within a matter of months), Lapham's outfit became the nucleus of the LGAF.[34]

By the end of 1944, the LGAF boasted upwards of 13,000 guerrillas, who contested the northern half of Luzon's central plain in Tarlac, Pangasinan, and Nueva Ecija provinces.[35] Unlike other guerrillas who prized remote locations, Lapham hid more or less in plain sight in barrios on the fertile central plain, protected by the Filipino people and the intelligence and warnings they provided of Japanese raids. Anderson, Ramsey, Volckmann, and others attempted to bring Lapham under their control. Lapham and Volckmann carried on a heated correspondence over the summer of 1944 regarding command authority. Volckmann was adamant that Lapham, as commander of the Second Military District, should report to him, while Lapham believed he was working under Anderson. "For your interest," Volckmann wrote in a strongly worded message, "I would strongly suggest that this is not the proper time to question my authority."[36] Lapham side-stepped the threat and was largely able to retain his group's independence until its link-up with US forces in January 1945.[37]

Unlike in northern Luzon, guerrillas in the southern part of the island were fragmented into "a heterogenous [sic] mass of small units whose command-ers continually bickered with each other and whose operations uselessly overlapped."[38] Most of these groups were led by Filipinos, especially after the capture of Col. Hugh Straughn, commander of the Fil-American Irregular Troops, on August 5, 1943.[39] President Quezon's Own Guerrillas were positioned in Batangas, while two guerrilla groups formed and led by Filipinos, Hunters ROTC and Marking's Guerrillas, dominated the area surrounding Manila.

Upon the Japanese invasion of the Philippines, thousands of ROTC cadets from various colleges and universities reported for duty. On

December 23, 1941, MacArthur ordered these young men demobilized "to preserve the younger generation from the ravages of war." On January 15, 1942, nineteen-year-old Miguel "Mike" Zabala Ver and twenty-three-year-old Eleuterio "Terry" Adevoso decided to form a second front behind Japanese lines, initially to take pressure off US and Filipino forces on Bataan, and, after the peninsula's fall, to maintain a kernel of resistance against Japanese occupation. Together they founded the Hunters ROTC guerrillas, which operated in the mountains just to the east of Manila.[40] They raided armories and other facilities to acquire weapons and military supplies to arm and equip their forces. They took to the jungle to organize and train, emerging occasionally to raid for supplies and ambush Japanese columns. When the young Miguel Ver was killed in action in July 1942, his comrades avenged his death on August 30 by ambushing a large Japanese column along the eastern boundary of Rizal and Laguna and killing 127 Japanese soldiers. Buoyed by this success, the Hunters ROTC began to gain recruits and grow.[41]

Competing with the Hunters were Marking's Guerrillas, formed by Marcos Villa Agustín, a passionate, resourceful, tough man who served with US forces as a convoy escort and scout until he was captured by the Japanese. He made a harrowing escape and took to the mountains in Rizal province. There he teamed up with Valeria "Yay" Panlilio, a Filipina-American who had been born and raised in Denver and had moved to the Philippines when she was eighteen. Yay became the spiritual backbone of Marking's Guerrillas, a superb propagandist (she had been a journalist before the war), as well as Agustín's lover. "War was our marriage, the guerrillas our sons," she would confide to her memoir.[42] Agustín began with just a few dozen fighters, but by the end of 1942 recruitment picked up after the shock of defeat had subsided. The organization, in Panlilio's words, included "full-time fighters in the hills; part-time saboteurs, working for the enemy and undoing all they had done; propagandists writing, printing, passing their down-in-black-and-white defiance; men and women training themselves as intelligence agents, learning to observe and retain and evaluate what they saw and to convey the information accurately and quickly; a countryside, bending its back to a double load: the Jap army that took by force, and their own patriotic army that begged, begged, begged."[43]

Agustín became an accomplished soldier and leader; in Panlilio's words, "None could outshoot him, nor outfight him, nor outthink him."[44] Marking's guerrillas were on average older, rougher, and more seasoned than Hunters ROTC guerrillas, who were young men from middle- and upper-class families filled with nationalist inspiration. The groups coexisted

3.1: Yay Panlilio, a Filipina-American who had been born and raised in Denver and had moved to the Philippines when she was eighteen, became the spiritual backbone of Marking's Guerrillas, led by Marcos Agustín. A pre-war journalist, she was a superb propagandist for the guerrilla movement. (Credit: *Life* Magazine)

in the mountains east of Manila, which made them competitors for local support, women, and territory. Competition soon led to friction and then to violence between the two groups as local communities chose sides in the ongoing struggle. Conflict between the groups erupted into outright war in early 1944.[45]

Other ethnicities on Luzon also formed guerrilla bands, most notably the ethnic Chinese population. The Japanese had ravaged the Chinese homeland on mainland Asia; they were now repeating their atrocious behavior in the Philippines. From a population of around 120,000 Chinese living on the island, several thousand joined the resistance.[46] One of the more unusual guerrilla outfits in the Philippines was composed of Chinese expatriates. Self-titled the Chinese Anti-Japanese Guerrilla Force in the Philippines and numbering at most a few hundred operatives, the unit was loyal to the Nationalist regime of Generalissimo Chiang Kai-shek and made contact with SWPA via Anderson in July 1944.[47]

Sensing the growth of the guerrilla movements, the empire struck back. For much of 1943, Japanese forces conducted a brutal counterinsurgency campaign on Luzon to defeat the guerrillas arising in their midst. "The Japanese tried to camouflage dumps, they instituted prohibited areas, they shuffled their troops, they made suspicion a fatal offense, and they killed and killed," wrote one survivor of the Japanese efforts to defeat the guerrillas. "A vain effort of suppressing this ugly swelling that they felt, but could not see. All in a futile attempt to hold on to a country they knew they could not keep."[48] Most guerrilla groups were hit hard, but Filipino civilians took the brunt of the blows. "Zoning," begun in August 1943 in the provinces closest to Manila, brutally oppressed the population. Japanese soldiers would cordon off an area, separate the population by sex, and have a hooded informant identify men suspected of collaboration with the guerrillas. The hapless suspects would then be tortured in any number of ways:

> Out of the line the victims were yanked to hang in the butterfly-swing[49] or simply be lashed to trees and fence posts; beaten with clubs or rifle butts; burned inch by inch with cigarette ends, matches, or tufts of cotton soaked in gasoline and ignited; slow-roasted head down over an ever replenished fire. Whole bananas sometimes were thrust down their throats at the end of a sharpened pike or trained dogs were sicked on [them] to tear out the calves of their legs and leave them bleeding to death; for others, days of slow starvation and hanging in the ropes intervened before death released the drooping victim.[50]

Wives and children of suspected guerrillas and their collaborators would suffer in turn. Zoning, according to one guerrilla veteran, "almost broke the backbone of the resistance."[51] Yet the resistance persisted.

The Japanese were brutal and unsophisticated counterinsurgents. Their political program of Asia for the Asians in a Japanese-led "Greater East Asia Co-Prosperity Sphere" might have been more appealing had they not acted in such an overweening, rapacious, and sadistic manner. "To be forced to bow to every sentry, as representative of his Imperial Majesty; to be slapped for minor indiscretions or even executed without trial or formal charge; to be tortured by the Kempeitai [Japanese military police] until confession for uncommitted crimes was obtained – these were new experiences for the Filipinos," wrote guerrilla leader Wendell Fertig. "The Americans may have insulted an occasional Filipino through ignorance, but forty years had established their reputation as 'square shooters.' The

Americans had certainly never demanded that the young girls be gathered as prostitutes for the enjoyment of the soldiers."[52]

Captured diaries tell a gruesome story of bloodshed and terror. "Every day we hunt for guerrillas and native inhabitants," wrote a Japanese soldier. "The number of men whom I've killed is well over a hundred and several score. The simple and sentimental days we spent in Japan are gone, and now I'm but a brutal blood-thirsty killer. My sword is always stained with blood. Though it is for my country's sake, it is truly tragic. God, forgive me for these sins!"[53] The Filipinos also recorded their impressions of the Japanese occupation. "Throughout the archipelago these monstrous-like people had displayed their bestialities," wrote one Filipino. "They had beheaded many innocent infants, raped women, confiscated properties, burned houses, and zoned towns. Many civilians met their untimely death because of the wrong suspicion of being guerrillas. During this reign of terror poverty drifted upon the people. Beggars became numerous and death was a frequent visitor of almost every home."[54] Another recalled, "Never was barbarism carried to such unimaginable extremes as was done by the Japanese."[55] Esteban Cruz lamented, "They claim that they are civilized, those men from across the sea. Could they have a right to this claim, they that made life miserable for every Filipino when they ruled the island? They have no right to it for they are all savages."[56] Dionisia Cauam prayed succinctly, "Ah! Heavenly God, put all the souls of the cruel Japanese into purgatory."[57] Japanese tactics were counterproductive; recruiting for guerrilla groups picked up dramatically as news of Japanese atrocities spread.

Even as US forces were reclaiming Luzon, Japanese soldiers were ordered to kill the inhabitants of villages suspected of harboring guerrillas. One Japanese soldier detailed the slaughter in his diary:

> 10 Feb 1945: We began punitive operations against Filipino terrorists and killed 500 of them. This was on direct order from Army.
>
> 12 Feb 1945: Today we left from Calumba [sic – Calamba] by automobile with the mission of punitive operations against the inhabitants of the town. 800 men were disposed of.
>
> 13 Feb 1945: For security reasons, all inhabitants of the town were killed and all their possessions were looted by us. Until yesterday we lived in the hills or in fishing villages and we had salt only to go with our rice. But today we are in Paradise. There is nothing that we cannot obtain. Because there was such a tremendous number of watches, rings, suits, shoes, and dresses, whatever we could not carry with us we had to burn with great regret.

17 Feb 1945: Because 90% of the Filipino people do not have a pro-Japanese spirit but are anti-Japanese, Army Hq issued orders on the 10th to punish all inhabitants. In various sectors we have killed several thousands (including the young and the old, men and women, and Chinese). Their houses were burned and their money and valuables were looted.[58]

He was not alone. Another soldier recorded that his unit "disposed of" 150 guerrillas on February 7, burned to death 1,000 guerrillas on February 9, and burned to death another 1,600 guerrillas on February 13. Since most Japanese concluded that the Filipino population consisted entirely of "guerrillas," the dead most likely included innocent men, women, and children.[59]

Captured messages and instructions also detailed Japanese willingness to commit atrocities:

Message kept by a member of "West of the Lake" Sector Unit: The natives in this sector have become guerrillas, have set up a well-organized communication net, and are greatly hindering our raiding infiltration units .... The Sector Unit will attack these guerrillas and eliminate interference with our infiltration units .... In the infiltration, natives will be killed without fail and their houses will be burned.[60]

Instructions of Group (Heidan) Comdr (presumably Fuji Group), Yamamoto Unit: Kill American troops cruelly. Do not kill them with one stroke. Shoot guerrillas. All who oppose the Emperor, even women and children, will be killed.[61]

These were clearly war crimes and, if the authors are to be believed, were perpetrated on the orders of the Japanese army headquarters. If true, then the Japanese commander in the Philippines, General Tomoyuki Yamashita, had much to answer for.[62]

The Japanese routinely tortured prisoners to extract information from them or tortured captives in public as an example to others. A staff officer with the guerrilla movement on Mindanao compiled a list of "third degree" torture methods used by Japanese forces on captured resistance operatives – or terrorists, in the eyes of their Japanese captors. First on the list was the water cure – a technique that American soldiers had used during an earlier war in the Philippines and the Japanese had recycled:

A person is first tied securely with a rope to a bench, face up and mouth forced wide open by inserting a piece of wood between the teeth. The Japs directed water from a hose at full blast to the open mouth of the prisoners. Before long, the victim is rendered unconscious. When he regains consciousness he is made to confess his guilt. If he answers in the

116

negative, the terrible process is repeated. If he admits his guilt, or owns it even if he is not [guilty], a more heinous fate awaits him. This procedure caused the death of many suspects.[63]

Other techniques included the application of electric shocks, fire, beatings, rape, starvation, pulling out fingernails, hanging by the thumbs, and razor cuts filled with salt.[64] Yay Panlilio of Marking's guerrillas details other forms of torture used by the Japanese in her wartime memoir, including the "sun cure" (forcing a prostrate victim with eyes forced open to stare at the sun for hours on end), pulling out of teeth with pliers, and the suspension of a victim by his heels over an open fire, slowly baking him to death.[65]

The United States and its allies rightly viewed these horrendous techniques as outside the bounds of civilized behavior. The result was a no-holds-barred fight in which quarter was never requested and rarely granted. "Then or later neither side ever took prisoners," wrote guerrilla leader Wendell Fertig. "The Honorable Nipponese desired to die for the honor of their Emperor. We helped them."[66] A number of Japanese personnel who engaged in these acts were tried afterwards as war criminals, some ending their lives on the scaffold. US commanders, aware of public indignation over the use of torture during the Philippine Insurrection at the turn of the century, disavowed the use of such techniques on enemy prisoners of war.

The Japanese were never able to fully suppress the guerrilla movement, even in areas such as central Luzon where they had large numbers of boots on the ground. The reason is simple; successful counterinsurgency requires control over the population, and in most areas of the Philippines the population was decidedly pro-American.[67] Benjamin F. Isidro wrote, "The Filipinos were systematically oppressed and plundered by the enemy under whose rule there was practiced cruelty and robbery. It is not only the buildings and properties that the Japanese looted, they conducted three fierce years of war against the entire Filipino people, in an effort to stamp out by fire and sword the spirit of resistance and of their devotion to democracy, but they never succeeded for, in every Filipino heart the letters in gold 'Pro-American' is engraved."[68] The atrocities they committed quickly eliminated what little goodwill the Japanese had enjoyed after the destruction of American and Filipino forces on Bataan and Corregidor. Fertig admitted that his forces would have faced significant challenges if the Japanese had shown more empathy toward the civilian population, confiding in his diary, "Actually if the Japanese will make friends with and encourage Jap–Fil relations we could not survive."[69]

The Japanese instead attempted to capitalize on racial empathy as fellow Asians, but their actions spoke louder than their DNA. "Too many Filipinos have experienced the brutality and insincerity of the Japanese," reported Edward M. Kuder, the superintendent of schools on Mindanao for seventeen years prior to his involvement with the guerrillas as director of civil affairs and subsequent evacuation to Australia in September 1943 due to ill health. "The people cannot help but contrast their present depressed status with the period of hope and actual progress they formerly had. Nothing the Japanese have been able to do so far has been able to equal it. As often as they gain by their unopposed propaganda they offset it by their stupid compulsion and brutish manners."[70] The American government had already enacted legislation granting Philippine independence in 1946; as a result, many Filipinos felt a debt of gratitude to the United States. They also never wavered in their belief that Douglas MacArthur would one day fulfill his promise to return.

Guerrillas could also keep alive the flame of resistance through the dissemination of propaganda. One example is a poster that was affixed to the wall of the Central Hotel in Manila on April 4, 1944, bearing the inscription "Independence" with a question mark over it. A woman holding a Philippines flag lay prostrate, her neck chained to a block with a Japanese flag on it. The lower right-hand corner was stamped, "Field Headquarters ROTC, The Hunters."[71] Guerrilla organizations also published local newspapers to inform Filipinos of news gathered from broadcasts originating outside the islands, such as "The Philippine Hour," a news program beamed by the US Office of War Information to the Philippines daily from May 1, 1944, to July 31, 1945. These publications had titles such as "Free Philippines," "Echoes of Bataan," "Voice of Corregidor," "United Nations News," and "Allied Nations News of the Day."[72]

Guerrilla warfare in the Philippines was by any measure a deadly business. Many of the most active guerrillas, such as civilian mining executive Walter Cushing, whose meteoric but brief career as a guerrilla ended in a hail of Japanese bullets in September 1942, were captured or killed before the return of US forces to the Philippines.[73] "Nobody knows how many Filipinos died in northern Luzon during the war," writes historian Bernard Norling, "but of the approximately two hundred Americans who were there in the early months of the war, fewer than ten were left when the US Army returned to Luzon in January 1945."[74] Fortunately, there were plenty of Filipinos who were willing to assume leadership roles, and they provided the Philippine people with greater agency in their own liberation.

The guerrillas on Luzon could harass Japanese forces, control large swaths of rural areas, and keep a modicum of order among the people (provided that the guerrillas were not preying on them), but their primary mission according to SWPA was the acquisition of intelligence. MacArthur's orders to the guerrillas in Luzon before contact was lost in the summer of 1943 read, "General policy of USAFIP [US Army Forces in the Philippines] is to limit hostilities and contact with the enemy to the minimum amount necessary for safety. Concentrate on perfecting organization and on developing of intelligence net. Therefore, until ammunition and supplies can be sent, your present mission as intelligence units can be currently of utmost value. Nothing is surer than our ultimate victory."[75] These wise instructions came too late to save many of the early guerrillas in Luzon, who by the summer of 1943 were on the ropes. Direct action invited Japanese reprisals, which fell heaviest on the Philippine people. On the other hand, guerrillas could detail Japanese troop strength on the islands, ascertain the whereabouts and condition of prisoners and civilian detainees, and provide information on naval and merchant ship movements without provoking Japanese military action. All of this would be helpful when the day of the return arrived. But none of it would be useful unless the guerrillas could communicate with MacArthur's headquarters in Australia.

American and Filipino officers further south in the Visayas and on Mindanao also formed guerrilla organizations, in some cases quite formidable ones. They had the advantage of being farther away from the center of Japanese strength on Luzon and also closer to Australia and therefore nearer to aid from and liaison with GHQ SWPA in Brisbane. The beginnings of resistance, however, were not auspicious. MacArthur had expected Major General William F. Sharp's force on Mindanao and in the Visayas to continue to fight on after the fall of Bataan and Corregidor, conventionally if possible but as guerrillas if not. Sharp lacked the necessary physical stamina and mentality required to adapt to this difficult assignment.[76] Despite a radio message from MacArthur urging him to begin guerrilla operations, Sharp surrendered his forces after the fall of Corregidor, believing that the Japanese would slaughter US prisoners and civilian detainees on Luzon if he failed to do so.[77] Many Filipinos, along with a few Americans, refused to lay down arms, believing correctly that Lt. Gen. Jonathan Wainwright had been forced under duress to surrender all troops in the Philippines rather than just those under his immediate command on Luzon.

When Wainwright issued his order to surrender, the chief of staff of the Philippine 61st Division on Panay, US Army Col. Albert F. Christie, informed the Filipino troops that the order did not apply to them. Most of the officers and men took to the mountains with their arms and equipment, and in August 1942 they elected Filipino Lt. Col. Macario Peralta as their leader. Peralta reorganized his guerrillas as a new 61st Division. In control of the shadow Filipino government on the island was the stormy Tomas Confesor, a former governor of Iloilo province, who was "impetuous and determined in his ways at times causing strong differences of opinions and interests."[78] His relations with Peralta were strained and increasingly heated as liberation approached, but they managed to coexist without resorting to violence. Regardless of their differences, the two men successfully organized the political and military wings of the resistance on Panay, which controlled much of the interior of the island by the time of Eighth Army's invasion after three years of Japanese occupation.[79] Peralta had larger designs to control the guerrilla movement in the Philippines, or at least in the Visayas, which also put him at odds with guerrilla leaders on other islands. Some of the first messages to come out of the Philippines, in early October 1942, were from Peralta on Panay, beamed via a weak transmitter and picked up by the Mackay monitoring station in San Francisco.[80] This gave him an advantage in attaining early recognition from MacArthur's headquarters.

Another of those who refused the order to surrender was West Virginia native Wendell Fertig, a forty-one-year-old civilian mining engineer in the US Army Corps of Engineers, who was commissioned as a major before the outbreak of war and soon found himself promoted to lieutenant colonel. He served under Brig. Gen. Hugh Casey, MacArthur's chief engineer, and later as an assistant to Maj. Gen. Sharp, but ignored the order to surrender after the fall of Corregidor since Fertig was adamant that he worked for the US Army Corps of Engineers and only Casey could give him orders.[81] Instead, Fertig took to the mountains of Mindanao with two companions.

On July 4, 1942, the Japanese held a "Victory Parade" of exhausted American prisoners along the highway that ran outside their camp at Dansalan. Fertig watched the sad spectacle from a hiding place near the route:

> First the Americans, many [of whom] were already ragged and barefoot, tied together with wire; then followed the Filipino prisoners. Strutting little Japanese in their sloppy uniforms and with their big bayonets marched on either side of the column. Tired and dejected, our men passed at a forced pace. To myself in silent prayer: "There, but for the Grace of God, go I . . . .." I thanked God that I had been chosen to leave Corregidor in its last agony. Free and in good health, I began to plan my vengeance.[82]

Fertig bided his time, waiting several months before one of the numerous guerrilla groups that sprang up in the summer and fall of 1942, led by the scheming and duplicitous Luis Morgan, asked him to assume leadership of the organization.[83] Following Fertig's orders, the group of 600 or so guerrillas immediately took control of the province of Misamis Occidental in western Mindanao, killing the 125 Japanese soldiers left there on occupation duty.[84]

From this humble beginning, Fertig ultimately would lead one of the most numerous and formidable guerrilla forces in the Philippines, aided greatly by his proximity to MacArthur's headquarters in Australia, initial Japanese neglect of this southernmost major island in the Philippine archipelago, Fertig's diplomatic ability to gain the support of the Moros[85] and the Catholic Church, and the presence of a couple of hundred Americans who would assume leadership roles in the guerrilla movement. He succeeded despite suffering from recurring migraines that occasionally debilitated him.[86] Determining who was loyal, who was competent, and who was a fraud consumed much of his days in this early period.

Mindanao was suitable for guerrillas because of its remoteness, geography, lack of roads, vegetation (both jungle for concealment and arable land for growing food), and the presence of nearly 200 American officers and enlisted men who evaded Japanese capture and threw in their lot with the guerrilla movement. Fertig had to work through the rivalries that divided indigenous groups, unify them into a cohesive organization, find a way to pay them so as to prevent depredations on the civilian population, and develop effective intelligence and counterintelligence organizations to ensure the security of his forces.[87] According to Edward M. Kuder, the former school superintendent in Mindanao whom Fertig appointed as director of civil affairs for the province of Lanao del Sur,

> Colonel Fertig had to exercise great restraint, overlook many breaches of discipline, and ignore some wrongdoing. He won over local leaders by invitation, negotiation, and use of appropriate emissaries, and by calling them in for personal discussion and to see how smoothly things were going in the area under his command. Only in very few instances was the use of force necessary, a great tribute to Colonel Fertig's capacity for leadership.[88]

Fertig engaged in a bit of subterfuge to solidify his position among the numerous guerrilla groups forming on Mindanao. All guerrillas adopted "bamboo" promotions to make themselves seem more important and gain influence among others, but none reached further than Fertig. He pretended to be a brigadier general sent by MacArthur to lead the resistance, which made him the senior ranking officer in the entire Philippines.[89] He even wore silver stars fashioned from coins by a Moro silversmith.[90] With this assumed power, Fertig was able to attract a significant number of Americans and Filipinos to his command, but not all. Some Americans chose to wait out the war in the jungles or mountains without joining the guerrillas, while some Filipinos and especially Moros refused to serve any longer under American leadership.[91] Fertig valued his fellow countrymen for their resourcefulness in making it this far. "To Fertig, any American who had had the courage to refuse to surrender, or the guts to escape, and had proved able to stay alive thus far, was potentially able to help other people. That potential basically qualified him for a commission."[92] Bamboo promotions turned privates into lieutenants; sergeants into captains. But rank did not confer expertise. "Our problem is the same old story of organize, disintegrate under an enemy sustained offensive, then reorganize," Fertig wrote to his old boss, Casey:

> Month after month, the strain begins to tell for I have practically no Filipino officers of field grade .... This is an army of third Lieutenants .... You know that I can move dirt, but to learn soldiering from the top down has been a problem. No TM [technical manual] or other help; no former organization upon which to learn. Just cut and dry, back biting and jealousy, cowardly officers with too much rank and no guts.[93]

Despite the lack of qualified senior leaders, slowly, steadily, inexorably, the guerrilla force on Mindanao grew and gained power. Low-level guerrilla operations progressed from the fall of 1942 until they became more organized by mid 1943.

Fertig did what little he could to help the people of Mindanao. He established organizations and procedures in the key areas of security, justice, and civil affairs. He established a Civilian Relief Administration and a Food Supply Administration, staffed by teachers, to procure and distribute food to the people. These agencies had mixed results, but helped to prevent mass starvation. Meat was scarce, malnutrition common, and malaria took its toll on the population owing to the lack of quinine to control it.[94] Filipinos responded by supporting the guerrillas. The Japanese attempted to appeal to the Filipinos as fellow Asians, but actions spoke louder than words. Leaflets and radio broadcasts had little effect.

Fertig wanted contact with Australia and was not willing to wait for a radio to be delivered to him: MacArthur's headquarters did not even know he was alive. He assembled a team of Filipino radio technicians and put them under the command of newly commissioned 2nd Lt. Bob Ball, a radio operator turned into Signal Corps officer by way of one of Fertig's bamboo promotions. The result, after weeks of effort, was a jerry-rigged contraption that had difficulty maintaining a single frequency. "It gave a strong signal, but week after week of ceaseless calling went unanswered," Fertig later wrote. As 1942 came to a close, "we were still calling, unheard in the darkness."[95] But the transmitter worked, "a monument to the truth that Fertig had learned in a hundred mining camps: 'There is almost nothing a man can't make for himself, once he realizes there is no outside source of supply.'"[96] The signal was strong enough to reach station KFS in San Francisco, where US Navy signalmen interpreted it as a Japanese ruse.

Then fate intervened. Five men – Jordan Hamner, Charles "Charlie" Smith, Athol Y. "Chic" Smith, and two Filipinos – made their way from Mindanao to Australia over the open sea in a small, twenty-six-foot open boat with nothing more than a *National Geographic* map of the Pacific Ocean and a miner's compass to guide them. Debriefed at SWPA headquarters, they revealed the existence of the guerrilla movement on Mindanao, led by Wendell Fertig in the province of Misamis Occidental. Fertig had given Smith a radio call-sign, MSF, to pass on to MacArthur's headquarters so they would know it was Fertig calling if he got the radio to work.[97]

With this new information, on February 2, 1943, Navy signalmen broadcast, "KFS calling MSF." Upon being told of the signal, Fertig rejoiced and had his operator reply. KFS demanded the names and serial numbers of Fertig's group, along with next-of-kin information that did not appear on their dog tags. The War Department contacted Fertig's wife, Mary, in the United States, verifying Fertig's identity by the phrase "pineapples for breakfast," which he had used to indicate he was in Mindanao (where he and his wife vacationed and enjoyed the fruit for breakfast) in his last letter home. After a few more back-and-forth messages, by February 9, Fertig's station had direct contact and codes established.[98] The War Department assigned Fertig a new call sign, WYZB, and passed him off to the control of station KAZ, MacArthur's Southwest Pacific Headquarters in Brisbane. On February 18, the first message from KAZ came through. Another message reported that "C M Smith and companions arrived safely."[99] Fertig now knew he had a friend in court. Contact had finally been established with the one headquarters that mattered most.

Fertig proceeded to inform MacArthur of his activities on Mindanao, including his assumption of rank and attempts to unify the guerrilla movement. His problem was not manpower; he estimated the guerrilla strength at 650 officers and 10,300 men. The problem was weapons and ammunition.

His forces possessed 17 machine guns, 84 Browning automatic rifles, 23 Colt military rifles, 21 Garand M-1 rifles, and 4,000 other assorted rifles, but ammunition was so scarce that his forces could not even "sustain the present harassing guerrilla activities."[100]

MacArthur responded on February 21, informing Fertig that the pre-war military district system would be reinstated. MacArthur made Fertig commander of the Tenth Military District on Mindanao, with additional responsibility to create an intelligence network in the Ninth Military District on Samar and Leyte. The same message made Peralta commander of the Sixth Military District on Panay, with responsibility for the establishment of an intelligence network in the Seventh (Negros) and Eighth Military Districts (Cebu and Bohol).[101] Pointedly, the message cautioned, "No officer of rank of General will be designated at present." Fertig was to remain a lieutenant colonel (albeit now transferred from the Corps of Engineers to the Infantry) for the time being, much to his chagrin.[102] He continued nevertheless to wear his fabricated stars; six months later MacArthur promoted him to full colonel and awarded him a Distinguished Service Cross.[103]

Contact with Fertig's guerrillas on Mindanao forced SWPA to establish a policy toward the resistance in the Philippines. MacArthur's guidance was to "lay low; avoid overt acts that will bring punitive expeditions and retaliatory acts. Receive what modest support we can give them, especially funds and items transportable in subs. Develop internal, discreet organization of guerrillas. Develop intelligence and agent nets, for observation and report."[104] Time would prove the wisdom of this guidance, at least in the early period of guerrilla development.

Communication with SWPA paid immediate dividends. SWPA established regular deliveries of arms, ammunition, radio sets, and currency via submarine. The Allied Intelligence Bureau (AIB) also sent magazines, soap, chocolate, and matches, all emblazed with the words "I Shall Return – MacArthur."[105] To the Filipinos on the receiving end, the phrase was magic. As important as the arms and supplies was a message on April 10, 1943, from President Manuel Quezon authorizing the formation of a Currency Board with the authority to print money, the lack of which had severely hampered guerrilla resistance in the formative months of Fertig's organization. Fertig and the Tenth Military District were in business.[106] With the arrival of more operatives and radios by the end of 1943, Fertig was able to establish an extensive coast-watcher system of thirty-one stations on Mindanao linked together by a comprehensive radio network.

The Japanese attempted to destroy Fertig's organization, but never came close to doing so. In one operation on June 26, 1943, the Japanese landed hundreds of troops from a cruiser, two destroyers, and several transports supported by fifteen aircraft. Fertig displaced his headquarters, but it remained in operation throughout the enemy sweep. Likewise, Japanese ground sweeps and air strikes aiming to destroy the radios they knew were in operation across Mindanao bore little fruit other than continual frustration. In one typical encounter, on May 5, 1944, "six Jap Betty bombers swept over Talacogon, bombing and strafing at a low altitude. After the enemy action, only one cow was found killed. All installations were intact." An immediate evacuation brought all guerrilla personnel and equipment out safely. When the Japanese bombers returned the next day to level the town, Fertig's headquarters was no longer present.[107]

The War Department had offered MacArthur the services of the Office of Strategic Services to fight a clandestine war against the Japanese, but, in typical MacArthur fashion, he declined supervision by an organization based out of Washington. Instead, he set up his own organization to gather intelligence and fight the war in the shadows. SWPA established AIB under the leadership of Australian Col. Caleb G. Roberts on July 6, 1942, with US Lt. Col. Allison Ind assigned as deputy controller. AIB's mission was to gather intelligence on the Japanese in the Southwest Pacific, conduct sabotage, and aid local efforts to weaken the enemy.[108]

The first task was to ascertain what was happening on Japanese-held islands. SWPA had little idea of the guerrilla resistance that was forming in the Philippines until a shortwave station in San Francisco received several weak radio transmissions from the islands and passed them on to Brisbane. After the fall of Corregidor, only two radios capable of reaching SWPA headquarters in Australia remained in operation on Luzon. One transmitted from a station in Nueva Ecija Province southeast of Lingayen Gulf, manned by Filipinos and Americans under Filipino army officer Lt. Col. Guillermo Nakar, at least until the Japanese captured Nakar and destroyed the radio in August 1942.[109] The other radio belonged to the Cagayan–Apayao Forces (CAF) commanded by Captain Ralph Praeger, who began the war as commander of Troop C, 26th Cavalry. The radio was a jerry-rigged operation, but it worked intermittently – at least until the Japanese destroyed the CAF in August 1943.[110] At that point, Luzon went dark.

It would take SWPA nearly a year to reestablish reliable radio contact with guerrilla forces on the island. In the meantime, at least two parties managed to navigate the treacherous seas between the Philippines and

Australia, and "they told AIB of defiant men formed into big elusive guerrilla packs in the main island of Luzon, in the middle Philippines, and most of all, in the big southernmost island of Mindanao."[111] One person who made his way to Australia in December 1942 was Lt. Frank Young, a courier working for Lt. Col. Thorp in Luzon.[112] He delivered a letter written by Thorp for MacArthur, which detailed his efforts in organizing guerrilla resistance in Luzon. The letter requested clarification of Thorp's authority to do so and provided a rosy picture of the guerrilla capabilities. "It is my belief that it will be possible to retake Luzon, by force and without aid, in the months to come, and I am certain we can do it, if we can get aid of bombers for a reasonably short period," Thorp averred.[113] He was off by more than two years and hundreds of thousands of troops. By the time Luzon was finally liberated, Thorp would be dead, executed by his Japanese captors.

Makeshift radios and occasional escapees were not enough to allow SWPA to maintain even a semblance of control over the guerrilla movement. MacArthur and his G-2, Major General Charles Willoughby, wanted their own man on the ground. The objective of Operation Planet was to emplace AIB personnel in the Philippines with adequate radio equipment and ciphers to establish reliable communications with the myriad guerrilla organizations cropping up in the archipelago, in particular Fertig's guerrillas on Mindanao and Peralta's organization on Panay, and to develop an independent intelligence network to provide SWPA with unfiltered reports of what was happening in the Philippines.[114] The head of the mission was Major Jesus Villamor, son of a well-known Filipino jurist and a hero of the fighting on Bataan. Villamor had battled the Japanese over Luzon in an antiquated P-36 fighter (an action for which he was personally decorated by MacArthur) before flying to Australia to continue resistance there.[115] Hearing about Villamor's mission back to the Philippines, Philippine President Manuel Quezon wrote to MacArthur, perhaps prophetically, "I hope his wisdom is as great as his courage."[116]

Villamor selected his team from among the handful of Filipinos who had made their way to Australia. On December 27, 1942, the USS *Gudgeon* departed Australia bound for Mindanao carrying the "Planet" Party – Maj. Jesus A. Villamor, 1st Lt. Delfin C. YuHuico, 1st Lt. Rodolfo O. Ignacio, 2nd Lt. Emilio F. Quinto, Sgt. Patricio Jorge, and Sergeant Dominador Malic – along with two complete radio sets and various other supplies.[117] The *Gudgeon* bypassed the primary landing site on Mindanao because of warnings of hostile activity and landed on Negros instead, much to the disgust of Fertig, who vented in his personal diary after the first supplies from SWPA finally reached

3.2: Capt. Jesus Villamor gets out of his fighter, from which he shot down two Japanese aircraft. As the leader of the Planet Party, Villamor created an extensive intelligence network in the Visayas and on Luzon until his recall to Australia in October 1943. (Credit: Library of Congress, www.loc.gov/item/2017697148)

him via submarine two months later. "Chas had sold Casey on getting help here although Villamor had reported that he could not land here because of hostile Moros. (He did not try). In Villamor's report he said that both Peralta and Fertig were taken. A fact which he shall eat some day."[118]

Despite this misunderstanding, on the night of January 26–27, 1943, Villamor's radio operator on Negros made contact with SWPA Headquarters in Australia. Upon hearing the news, MacArthur's chief of staff, Lt. Gen. Richard K. Sutherland exclaimed, "The first to go in, but not the last. We're on our way!"[119] The return message to Villamor reiterated his primary tasks – to figure out which guerrilla leaders could be trusted, to provide advice on how SWPA should organize their command relationships, and to recommend where SWPA should send supplies, given the limited transportation capability of the few available submarines.[120] These tasks would require political dexterity and a keen sense of observation, as guerrilla leaders "were behaving like kids in dispute for the leadership of a neighborhood gang."[121] Villamor felt the Filipinos could be doing more for themselves; he was proof. "If Fertig was having those dreams of power and glory much of the blame lay on the Filipinos themselves," he later wrote. "Many of them felt more confident if Americans were in charge. Americans were somehow smarter, wiser than Filipinos. And so they were taken advantage of by some opportunistic Americans, and this is what irritated me most of all."[122] MacArthur was not entirely happy with the mission; two months after Villamor arrived the Supreme Commander told Willoughby that "Villamor is delving too deeply into political, financial and personnel questions; operates as an Ambassador rather than an observation-agent; he is to report what he sees and knows, not to reflect the quasi-political views of Fil politicians."[123]

On Negros, Lt. Col. Salvador Abcede, the former head of the ROTC department at Silliman University who had taken command of an infantry battalion after the outbreak of war and refused to surrender after the fall of Corregidor, had established an effective guerrilla organization. Even so, two guerrilla groups on the island refused to accede to his command authority, making recognition by SWPA imperative. Villamor took temporary command of all groups on Negros until MacArthur appointed a permanent commander for the district. Villamor then appointed Alfredo Montelibano Sr., a former mayor, to establish a shadow civil government on the island to control all areas not occupied by Japanese forces. "Under his management the civil government of resistance had grown into a stability that was amazing in time of war," wrote Villamor. "Free Negros not only had treasurers and auditors, it had officials in the municipal level, including policemen and clerks, fiscals and judges."[124] In the summer of 1943, MacArthur appointed Abcede commander of the Seventh Military District, allowing Villamor to focus on his intelligence mission. Unlike the relationship between Peralta and Confesor on Panay, Abcede worked cordially with the civilian shadow governor.

While Villamor gathered information, he trained agents to expand his intelligence network. By the summer of 1943, he had agents in Samar, Leyte, Cebu, Mindoro, and Luzon.[125] He sent YuHuico to carry special ciphers to Peralta on Panay and dispatched Sgt. Jorge to make contact with Ismael P. Ingeniero on Bohol and former Philippine Army Lt. Col. Ruperto Kangleon on Leyte. Villamor recruited Dr. Harold R. Bell, a physics teacher at Silliman University on Negros, and sent him to Cebu to contact James Cushing and Harry Fenton, who had established a strong guerrilla organization on the island.[126] He recruited other trusted agents, many of them old friends or comrades from the Philippine Army Air Corps, to establish communications nodes throughout the Philippines. In a feat of daring, he sent a radio set, disassembled and hidden in vegetable baskets for the journey, to Manila. In the heart of the old walled city of Intramuros, a Filipino-American by the name of Frank Jones reassembled the radio and established a key communications node for the Luzon guerrillas.[127]

Within a short time, Villamor had an excellent intelligence net in Manila, the heart of the Japanese occupation regime.[128] Aside from reporting on Japanese installations and troop dispositions and the rapacious excesses of the occupation, these agents were able to untangle the politics of the collaborationist regime the Japanese had established in Manila. The head of this regime was José Laurel, a former senator and associate justice of the Philippine Supreme Court. He and other key political figures, such as Jorge Vargas, the mayor of Manila, had been persuaded by President Manual Quezon to remain in the Philippines when Quezon fled from Corregidor to establish his government-in-exile in Washington. They would protect to the best of their ability the Filipino people, even while serving in a Japanese-sponsored puppet government. "Keep your faith in America, no matter what happens," Quezon had told them upon his departure.[129] One of the more important of these officials was Manuel Roxas, a key advisor who had served with Quezon on Corregidor and had been captured by the Japanese on Mindanao in April 1942. Roxas served as chief advisor to Laurel, but according to MacArthur was secretly sympathetic to the resistance and passed information to SWPA via Ramsey's guerrilla organization on Luzon.[130]

Agents from the Fil-Americans guerrilla organization also penetrated the Laurel regime, often with the assistance of loyal Filipinos who served the puppet government only to sabotage it from within. The Minister of Home Affairs, Arsenio Bonifacio, and Lt. Col. Antonio Martinez, the executive officer of the Philippine Constabulary, would pass information on to agents, who would then forward it to Major Charles W. Folsom, the American head of the Fil-Americans, and from there on to Anderson's guerrilla headquarters for transmittal to SWPA HQ. Thus, MacArthur was kept well informed of the plans of the Japanese authorities in Manila.[131]

The resistance took an unconventional approach to the collaborationist regime established by the Japanese. Of course, Filipinos had a number of reasons to collaborate with the occupation, with many of the ruling class readily cooperating with the Japanese to maintain their wealth and status at the top of Filipino society.[132] Other elites were more circumspect. The

Japanese-sponsored Philippine Republic nominally gained independence on October 14, 1943, but, instead of boycotting its proceedings, the resistance encouraged loyal Filipinos to run for office in order to control it. This strategy had its greatest success in preventing the institution of a draft.[133] Instead, the thoroughly compromised government did little to support the Japanese administration of the islands and likewise proved of little propaganda value to the Greater East Asia Co-Prosperity Sphere.

AIB was full of colorful characters, none more so than US Navy Cdr. Charles "Chick" Parsons. Parsons made his way to Manila in 1921 at the age of nineteen as a crewman on a freighter. His talent with shorthand and Spanish (then the language of many Filipinos) landed him a job for three years as secretary to US Governor-General Leonard Wood. He stayed in the Philippines afterwards in a variety of business occupations, learning the local dialects and geography and coming to respect the Filipino people. He also joined the US Naval Reserve. Sworn into active service after the Japanese attack on Pearl Harbor, Lt. Cdr. Parsons remained with his family in Manila by convincing the Japanese that he was the Panamanian consul-general to the Philippines and his home was the territory of a neutral nation.[134] Enraged by the Doolittle raid, the Japanese imprisoned Parsons for a few weeks along with other Westerners, but never caught onto his ruse.[135] On June 4, 1942, the Japanese allowed Parsons and his family to leave the country. They sailed from Manila to Formosa, flew to Shanghai, sailed to Portuguese South Africa, and ended up in Rio de Janeiro. From there they repatriated to the United States, arriving in New York on August 29. Several weeks later, the US Army G-2 requested that Parsons come in for an interview. Because of his extensive local knowledge of the Philippines, the War Department requested that he join the "AIB for assignments that were destined to make the Japanese regret that they had ever let him out of their hands."[136]

Parsons became the inaugural member of "Spyron," short for "spy squadron."[137] On March 5, 1943, Parsons led a party of five men, including the redoubtable and newly commissioned Charlie Smith, who had sailed to Australia against all odds, with four tons of supplies, five radio sets, and money destined for the guerrillas on Mindanao – the first installment of the long-awaited "Aid" promised to the Philippines.[138] The submarine USS *Tambor* landed the party in Pagadian Bay on the south coast of Mindanao and then linked up with Fertig's guerrillas and delivered the supplies. As a way of saying thanks, Fertig would load delivery submarines down with bananas, limes, avocados, and pineapples – fruit difficult if not impossible to get in Australia.[139] Parsons then established a coast-watcher station on the small island of Panaon (later moved to the island of Dinagat) along the Surigao Strait, where in October 1944 the US and Japanese fleets would clash in an epic naval battle. Charlie Smith established a coast-watcher station in the Davao area.[140]

After completing these tasks, Parsons crossed the straits to Leyte, where guerrilla groups were engaged in a free-for-all for control, and in the process doing more damage to themselves than to the Japanese. In Parsons's words, there were "at least six first-class wars going on not counting the official one."[141] Parsons convinced Lt. Col. Kangleon, the former district commander for Samar and Leyte who had escaped Japanese captivity, to join the resistance movement on Leyte, with the promise that he would be made commander of the Ninth Military District (Leyte and Samar). Until SWPA made the assignment official, however, it authorized Fertig on Mindanao and Peralta on Panay to establish intelligence networks on neighboring islands. Both thought they had responsibility for Leyte, and they picked different Filipino leaders to lead the effort. This would have worked had the two Filipinos cooperated with one another, but the fact that Kangleon (backed by Fertig) and Blas Miranda (a former member of the Philippine Constabulary, backed by Peralta) were bitter rivals resulted in severe mistrust, as each accused the other of falsely claiming MacArthur's backing.[142] In August 1943, the two groups came to blows.

Because of his closer connections with American officers (Fertig and Parsons) and proximity to the communications hub on Mindanao, Kangleon won the contest for legitimacy, and MacArthur officially recognized him as leader of all guerrillas on Leyte on October 21, 1943.[143] Then, on December 6, Japanese forces used the cover afforded by a typhoon to attack Miranda's base and rout his group, ending whatever chance he had of controlling the guerrilla movement on Leyte. Parsons delivered supplies via submarine to Kangleon, providing him with legitimacy in the eyes of the Filipinos. The guerrillas then united under Kangleon, who reigned supreme from that point on in the shadowy world of guerrilla forces on Leyte.[144] By the time of the US invasion of the island in October 1944, the Filipino guerrillas on Leyte, despite being targeted in brutal counterguerrilla operations by Japanese forces, numbered roughly 3,200 men. The Japanese were never able to shut off the flow of information from the guerrillas on Leyte to SWPA, the provision of which was their greatest accomplishment prior to liberation.[145]

Parsons returned to Mindanao to help unify the guerrillas under Fertig's leadership, a task made easier by promises of aid from MacArthur.

At one point, Parsons narrowly escaped a Japanese raid on the town of Jimenez, where he had taken refuge.[146] His final task on this trip was to accompany Air Corps Captain William "Ed" Dyess, Major Stephen Mellnik, and Lt. Cdr. Melvin H. McCoy, the former officer a survivor of the Bataan Death March, from northern Mindanao, where they had ended up after escaping from a Japanese prison camp, to MacArthur's headquarters in Australia.[147] These officers were the first to relay the reality of Japanese atrocities after the fall of Bataan and Corregidor to US authorities in Brisbane and Washington. Their stories would arouse in the American people a burning desire for revenge that would be satiated only by the unconditional surrender eventually signed in Tokyo Bay in September 1945.[148]

McCoy was a 1927 Annapolis graduate who served as a signals officer on Corregidor until the island's surrender on May 6, 1942. After stints in Bilibid Prison and Camp Cabanatuan, he volunteered to transfer to Davao prison camp in Mindanao, where the Japanese put him to work farming and performing other hard labor. After several months of preparation and gathering supplies, a group of ten Americans, including McCoy, and two Filipino guides escaped the Davao camp on April 4, 1943. After a harrowing journey through a malarial swamp and jungle, the group stumbled upon a group of Filipino guerrillas, who welcomed them as fellow resistance fighters. Escorted by guerrillas and Filipino porters, the group made its way to Mindanao's north coast, where they linked up with American guerrillas and a rendezvous with Parsons. McCoy, Dyess, and Mellnik then had a testy run-in with Fertig (still wearing his fabricated brigadier general stars), who eventually sent word to Brisbane about the first group of Americans who had been able to escape Japanese captivity.[149]

SWPA authorized the three officers to make their way to Australia, which they did after a harrowing jungle trek to board the submarine USS *Thresher* on July 14. Upon arrival in Australia, the three were debriefed by intelligence officers and then met with Gen. MacArthur, who awarded each of them a Distinguished Service Cross. The group recounted the fighting on Bataan, the Death March, conditions in various prison camps, and Japanese treatment of the Filipino people – the first eyewitness testimony to the utter brutality of the Japanese occupation. Dyess would return to the United States to recuperate, where he told his story to Charles Leavelle of the *Chicago Tribune*. The War Department was hesitant to approve its release for fear of Japanese reprisals against prisoners in the Philippines and that subsequent outrage might jeopardize the Allies' "Germany First" grand strategy. The War Department finally allowed the *Tribune* to publish the serialized story four-and-a-half months later, bringing home to Americans the realities of the Death March and conditions in Japanese prison camps. As predicted, the story enraged the American people, who would, in the words of their president, Franklin D. Roosevelt, "in their righteous might . . . win through to absolute victory."[150]

In late summer 1943, the guerrilla situation on Cebu became critical. On that island, Fenton handled guerrilla administration while James Cushing, a US Army mining engineer turned guerrilla leader (not to be confused with Walter Cushing on Luzon), acted as military commander. Fenton, a former radio announcer, was a loose cannon with an inordinate hatred of the Japanese and an unhealthy (and deadly) mean streak. In September, Cushing, despite suffering from malaria, decided to visit Villamor on Negros to discuss Fenton, who had put the guerrilla enterprise on Cebu in danger by his inflammatory broadcasts that were bound to bring Japanese reprisals in turn. During Cushing's absence, one of his Filipino subordinates, Lt. Col. Ricardo Estrella, arrested Fenton and arranged a summary court-martial to try him for the murder of a Catholic priest. The officers found Fenton guilty of murder, sentenced him to death, and executed him.[151]

Villamor provided Cushing with a radio and sent him back to Cebu with the understanding that further supplies and a more powerful radio would be sent his way with a future submarine shipment.[152] But what Cushing wanted above all else was recognition by MacArthur's headquarters and the resources that would flow with it. Currency was in short supply on Cebu and, without financial relief, the economy in guerrilla-held areas would grind to a halt.[153] The long-awaited recognition finally came on January 22, 1944, when MacArthur appointed Cushing commander of the Eighth Military District. Cushing also received a radio, enabling him to communicate directly with SWPA headquarters in Australia.[154]

The recognition and radio came just in time. On March 31, 1944, two flying boats ferrying Admiral Mineichi Koga, commander in chief of the Japanese Combined Fleet, and his staff from Palau in the Caroline Islands to Davao in Mindanao crashed in a storm off the coast of Cebu.[155] Koga died, but his chief-of-staff, Rear Adm. Shigeru Fukudome, survived. Filipino fishermen rescued a group of survivors including Fukudome, along with his briefcase, and turned them over to Cushing's guerrillas. Cushing eventually released Fukudome and his comrades to bring a halt to Japanese depredations on the population of Cebu. The briefcase was hustled to Australia by submarine; inside was a copy of "Plan Z," the Japanese scheme for the defense of the Marianas Islands. Its translation by the Allied Translation and Interpreter Section in Brisbane, relayed in late May to Admiral Chester Nimitz's headquarters in Hawai'i and from there to Admiral Raymond Spruance's Fifth Fleet at Eniwetok, helped to seal the fate of the Imperial Japanese Fleet at the Battle of the Philippine Sea three weeks later.[156]

In late October 1943, Villamor departed the Philippines bound for Australia to report to his superiors at SWPA and then onward to the United States to brief President Quezon in Washington.[157] Despite his desire to journey back to the Philippines to continue to direct the Planet network, he remained on the sidelines for the remainder of the war. Only years later did Villamor discover that infighting among MacArthur's staff, particularly disagreements between his supporters in the G-2 and his detractors in AIB, had tarnished his manifest contributions to the war effort and prevented his return to the land of his birth. In his absence the Planet party withered, and then died altogether – killed off by bureaucratic politics 3,000 miles away from the Philippines.[158]

The initial success of Planet encouraged AIB to send more agents and radios to the Philippines to establish an archipelago-wide communications network that could radio intelligence back to MacArthur's HQ. As more information on guerrilla groups became available, SWPA proffered recognition and sent supplies to them. Parsons made a total of eight trips to the Philippines to deliver supplies, liaise with guerrilla leaders, and develop a coast-watcher system. "Enthusiasm, patriotism, guts, ingenuity, they are all fine things, but they only get you six feet under unless there is knowledge to go with them," Iliff Richardson recalls. "Parsons had it. He knew Navy."[159] In accordance with MacArthur's instructions, most of the supplies went to Fertig's guerrillas on Mindanao, since this large southern island was presumed to be the first objective in the eventual return of US forces to the Philippines.[160] By the end of the war, AIB had established nearly 100 coast-watcher and intelligence radio stations in the Philippines, 70 of them on Mindanao, linked together in a vast reporting system.[161]

In April 1943, the USS *Gudgeon* returned to the Philippines with the "Peleven" party and three-and-a-half tons of supplies for Peralta's guerrilla group on Panay.[162] In late May, the USS *Trout* delivered the "Tenwest" party and supplies to the Sulu Archipelago and Mindanao. In June, the USS *Thresher* delivered personnel and seven tons of supplies to Villamor on Negros, including Dr. Emigdio C. Cruz, the personal physician to the Philippine president-in-exile, Manuel Quezon. Cruz worked his way into

Panay, the Bicols, and then to Manila to gather information, including several meetings with Roxas and officials of the Philippine puppet government, and miraculously returned to report his findings to MacArthur in Brisbane and Quezon in the United States.[163] In late July, the USS *Grayling* departed for Panay with supplies and money, the latter being a critical guerrilla resource as currency was in short supply and the Filipino economy could not function without it.

The most important logistical breakthrough occurred on October 23 when the USS *Narwhal*, specially retrofitted as a cargo carrier, departed for Mindanao and Mindoro. It carried 2 intelligence parties and 46 tons of supplies for Mindoro and another 46 tons of supplies for Fertig's guerrillas on Mindanao, backhauling a group of American civilians (including 8 women, 2 children, and a baby) to Australia on the return trip. The *Narwhal* immediately turned around on November 25 with another 85 tons of supplies for Mindanao and a personnel party designated for the island of Samar.[164]

As the guerrilla forces grew, so did their requirements for arms, ammunition, and supplies. MacArthur made a personal plea to President Roosevelt for increased support for the guerrilla movement, especially cargo submarines to ferry arms, ammunition, and supplies to the Philippines. "Since the fall of Corregidor and the surrender of our Army, there has arisen throughout the Philippines a spontaneous movement of resistance among liberty-loving patriots, both Filipino and American, which would challenge the imagination of the people of the United States if they were informed of its progress," MacArthur informed the president.[165] The Philippine resistance was now on the map at the War Department.

In October 1943, the Seventh Fleet organized a special supply unit composed of the *Narwhal*, *Nautilus*, *Seawolf*, and *Stingray* with the primary duty of carrying out supply and evacuation missions in the Philippines. Designed in the interwar period as scout/cruiser submarines with a cruising range of 18,000 miles and large cargo capacity, the *Narwhal* and its sister ship, the *Nautilus*, were modernized in the early years of the war and later retrofitted specifically for the purpose of transporting large parties of personnel and supplies.[166] A submarine of the *Tambor* or *Gato* class could carry only around 4 tons of supplies, depending on how many torpedoes it carried in addition to other stores; the 2 retrofitted *Narwhal*-class submarines, on the other hand, could carry upwards of 100 tons of supplies in 3,800 cubic feet of cargo space. These large cruiser submarines displaced 2,770 tons, almost twice the weight of the small and swifter fleet submarines.[167]

The large amount of supplies carried by these submarines created different problems; absent docking facilities, unloading this much cargo with the small craft available in the islands would take many hours, putting the boat in jeopardy. Fortunately, in some places docking facilities were available and used, despite the proximity of Japanese forces.[168] Once ashore, all of this hardware had to be moved, usually by pack, and often over rugged jungle and mountain trails. The logistics strained the limited capabilities of the guerrillas.[169] Nevertheless, most missions were successful, and only one submarine engaged in transport of supplies to the Philippines was lost.[170] By the end of the war, 19 different submarines had undertaken a total of 41 missions to the Philippines, delivering 331 persons, evacuating 472 persons, and delivering 1,325 tons of supplies to guerrilla forces. *Narwhal* and *Nautilus* together accounted for fifteen of these missions and the vast majority of the supplies delivered.[171] Guerrillas were delighted by the delivery of arms and ammunition, but by far the more valuable cargo was radio transmitters, by which the guerrillas could maintain contact with each other and with GHQ SWPA.[172]

Money was another crucial resource in short supply in guerrilla-held areas. Without a ready source of cash, the economies in guerrilla-held areas would grind to a halt, and inflation and scarcity would create the conditions for a black market. Guerrilla leaders handled this problem in a number of ways: some printed guerrilla currency (with the hope that the United States would honor the currency when the war was over); some received money via submarine; while others received plates, ink, and paper from Australia with which to print Filipino currency or Japanese occupation script.[173] SWPA put together a scrapbook that contained fifteen pages worth of samples of different notes in circulation in 1943 alone.[174] Control of currency resulted in bitter arguments and sometimes violence. Guerrillas, after all, lived by the Golden Rule: He who has the gold makes the rules.

In April 1943, MacArthur placed Col. Courtney Whitney in charge of the Philippine subsection of AIB, which a month later became the Philippine Regional Section (PRS), a semi-autonomous staff section that reported directly to Lt. Gen. Sutherland, MacArthur's chief of staff.[175] Whitney was an old Philippines hand, a lawyer who had lived in Manila for more than twenty years prior to the outbreak of war. Ind remained as his advisor for technical matters and policy in addition to his duties as AIB deputy controller and finance officer.[176] Maj. Gen. Willoughby in G-2 was in charge of intelligence, but Whitney in PRS was in charge of Philippine guerrilla affairs. This brought them into direct conflict with one another.

Willoughby viewed the guerrilla movement as an adjunct to his intelligence apparatus. Whitney viewed it as an adjunct to AIB operations to pave the way for MacArthur's return to the Philippines, including control of direct action against the Japanese as the return of US forces to the islands approached. If Whitney had his way, PRS would share intelligence with the G-2, but not fall under the supervisory authority of Willoughby's staff section.[177] Above all, he desired to deploy and establish an AIB forward presence in the islands, with Americans firmly in control of the guerrilla movement.

The guerrillas had MacArthur's full support. In a conference on May 30, 1943, with Sutherland, G-2 Philippines Section head Col. Van S. Merle-Smith, and Whitney, MacArthur reiterated his support for the growing guerrilla movement in the Philippines. It had erupted spontaneously, but the guerrillas were fighting the Japanese and for that reason alone they deserved whatever support SWPA could provide. MacArthur would provide certain guerrilla groups with recognition, which would give them legal protection under the law of war. His priorities for the guerrillas were the establishment of a secure communications network and the provision of strategic intelligence. The conference report recorded MacArthur as stating, "One could not hope that these guerrilla bands could long survive if the Japanese made an effort to destroy them. Mindanao had some chance due to its terrain features."[178] MacArthur was right on the second count, but not on the first. The guerrillas proved to be far more resilient than he could ever imagine.

Over the spring and summer of 1943, Whitney, Willoughby, and Merle-Smith debated the merits of different plans to establish intelligence and communications networks in the Philippines. Whitney desired to establish GHQ SWPA-controlled intelligence collection centers staffed by AIB-trained American and Filipino operatives, while Willoughby believed that SWPA should leverage the newly discovered capabilities of the growing indigenous guerrilla movement in the islands.[179] On June 24, Whitney forwarded a plan to Sutherland that recommended the establishment of GHQ-controlled intelligence parties in Manila, Cebu City, and Davao, along with the establishment of coast-watcher stations at Cape Bolinao, Northwest Mindoro, Apo West Pass, Romblon, northwest Samar, Zamboanga, at the Balabac Strait, and at Tinaca Point near Davao. He also wanted to bring 450 Filipinos to Australia for training as PRS intelligence operatives.[180] The G-2 nonconcurred with establishing coast-watcher stations independent from guerrilla forces and likewise rejected Whitney's plan to bring Filipinos to Australia for training, given the pushback from guerrilla leaders who resented the intrusion into their areas.[181]

Whitney responded with a proposal to establish two secret forward intelligence bases in Mindoro and Samar, commanded by Chick Parsons and himself, respectively. "A stevedore and a lawyer – equally devoted to the same cause and the same commander – what a combination – what a headache for Tojo," Whitney wrote. In effect, these bases "would constitute the advanced echelon of the Philippine Regional Section, Allied Intelligence Bureau, and as such become advanced elements of GHQ." They would be kept secret even from the guerrillas, an impractical proposal if ever there was one.[182] Whitney wanted to rely on Filipinos under the control of AIB, rather than relying on local Filipinos affiliated with guerrilla organizations. Willoughby for the moment approved Whitney's proposal as the basis for further development of a plan, which PRS forwarded to Lt. Gen. Sutherland on August 25.[183] Rougher seas were ahead for their relationship, despite Willoughby's note on an endorsement, "At any rate, I think we are en-rapport and I am not the S.O.B. probably identified at first, and mean no harm."[184]

Willoughby replied in a note on August 28 that Whitney's plan was "an honest attempt to reconcile two basically differing propositions" on how to establish the intelligence structure in the Philippines: rely on the guerrillas or establish a network independent of them. Whitney's plan would establish GHQ control of intelligence activities north of Panay and Leyte, while relying on guerrillas in the Visayas and Mindanao. PRS would locate a main intelligence base with Fertig's headquarters on Mindanao, with forward bases on Samar and Mindoro. Willoughby reiterated, however, that the main mission of PRS was to coordinate supplies for the guerrillas, and therefore Whitney would remain at his post in Australia.[185]

Willoughby's goal was to have a comprehensive intelligence network in place by the beginning of the monsoon season in spring 1944. Guerrilla networks would cover Mindanao and the Visayas, while GHQ intelligence parties (using American officers and American-trained Filipinos) would cover Mindoro and Luzon – the latter location chosen without doubt because of the lack of visibility of guerrilla operations on the largest island in the Philippines. Whitney believed that the areas selected for advanced PRS bases were void of either Japanese forces or guerrillas and were suitable for clandestine bases because of their wild, remote nature. "I have given considerable thought to the G-2 reaction heretofore expressed that we should tie in our intelligence moves to the existing guerilla setup," Whitney wrote. "Basically, this is sound. My respect for the potentialities of the guerilla movement is increasing steadily with the advance of knowledge and south of the positions herein discussed we will probably find it necessary to at least collaborate in such matters, possibly go further. But in these more northerly areas, the guerilla movement is not highly developed, if developed at all."[186]

He was, of course, wrong. The fact is SWPA had no communications with the guerrillas on Luzon or Mindoro and therefore knew little of the situation there. In the absence of facts, Whitney made an assumption that would prove deadly to one of the PRS intelligence parties. Contrary to Whitney's reasoning, Americans could not survive in the Philippines without the assistance of the guerrillas or the Filipino people. Carlos Romulo, one of MacArthur's aides who worked on press relations, stated the fact clearly when he wrote, "The Americans in the Philippines could not have survived for two hours without the protection thrown over them by the entire country."[187]

In November 1943, the *Narwhal* delivered PRS intelligence parties to establish forward bases in the Philippines. Charlie Smith returned to establish a communications hub in Samar, the final piece of the trans-Philippines belt of AIB-supported agents that provided information on Japanese movements and acted as way stations for the movement of guerrillas between the Visayan Islands and Luzon. He then expanded the "MACA" net across the San Bernardino Strait on the Bondoc Peninsula.[188] The Japanese picked up the increased radio activity in the area, but could neither locate nor destroy the network. Promoted to lieutenant colonel, Smith strong-armed the indigenous guerrilla leaders on Samar and consolidated the guerrilla movement on the island under his control.[189]

After dropping off Smith's party, the *Narwhal* delivered Major Lawrence H. Phillips, a former employee of Del Monte in the Philippines, and Chick Parsons to establish a forward intelligence base on Mindoro. After accompanying Phillips ashore, Parsons returned with the *Narwhal* to Australia. Phillips established his intelligence base without coordination with the local guerrillas led by Filipino Major Ramon Ruffy and was sloppy with his radio discipline.[190] On February 26, 1944, the Japanese discovered the base and eliminated it, mortally wounding Phillips and capturing or killing many of his men. The survivors scattered to link up with various guerrilla groups.[191]

The harmony between the G-2 and PRS did not last long. After his return from the Philippines, Villamor sensed the tension. "In talks with Ind, Roberts, Merle-Smith, and McMicking," he later wrote, "I sensed a gap between P.R.S. on one side and A.I.B. and G-2 on the other. This was easily noticeable; a strained relationship existed between Willoughby and Whitney, and between Willoughby on one side and Whitney and Sutherland on the other."[192] Whitney wanted PRS to have the maximum latitude and independence in shaping intelligence and guerrilla operations in the Philippines; Willoughby thought PRS needed to be disbanded and its functions distributed to various GHQ staff sections.[193]

The pissing contest between G-2 and PRS played out in the spring of 1944. At one point, Whitney accused the G-2 section of delaying a message to Phillips on Mindoro, with the insinuation that the delay had something to do with the demise of his party. Willoughby shot back angrily in a note to Sutherland:

> I am wearied beyond description with this type of assassination that this undisciplined lot engage in and apparently make sport of every staff supervision or contact. This is very obviously devised by Whitney as a protest to avoid any supervision, which he has fought from the outset.
>
> He knows he is vulnerable in the case of Phillips, who was literally "sneaked" from here without any instruction and the usual briefing by G-2, and who has been conspicuously imprudent; the suggestion that this message had the slightest effect on Phillips' already precarious position is ridiculous.[194]

On March 13, Whitney sent a memo to Sutherland outlining proposed policy and procedures for PRS in the time remaining before MacArthur's return to the Philippines. He stated in one part of the memo, "I shall continue to keep you fully advised of developments and all action taken without burdening you or the staff with requests for specific authorization for projects previously approved or clearly within existing policy."[195] Willoughby was incensed, demanding that PRS be brought under closer staff supervision. "An 'approved' would be tantamount to signing a blank check in view of PRS's broad interpretations of policy and procedure," he wrote.[196]

The gloves were off, the sniping made worse by the demise of Phillips and his party on Mindoro. Sutherland finally had enough of the intramural scrimmage within his headquarters and asked the G-2 to draft a directive clarifying PRS functions. On April 10 Willoughby replied, "G-2/PRS differences have resulted from a lack of a specific directive to PRS outlining its duties, and to its unfamiliarity with staff procedure [a shot at Whitney]. These facts have encouraged PRS to attempt to solve all questions by itself. G-2 had repeatedly referred to the C/S, and had approved by him, SOPs for PRS/G-2 action. PRS has invariably ignored them, or made them ineffective thru inaction (or lack of appreciation)."[197] Three days later, he submitted a directive limiting the powers of PRS to administrative matters and folding its responsibilities into the G-2 and other appropriate staff sections.[198]

Whitney shot back angrily "that the recitation of facts finds no support of record and is for the most part false," and stood his ground that PRS required direct access to Sutherland.[199]

Willoughby ultimately prevailed, and on June 5 Sutherland disbanded the AIB PRS section and distributed its personnel and functions among various GHQ staff sections to facilitate planning for the invasion of the Philippines. Whitney bowed to the inevitable, writing, "Thus PRS, viewed as saint by few and sinner by many, yields to progress and becomes but an historical incident to a great military campaign . . .. PRS retires from the campaign but its guiding spirit, infused in the hearts of many, will carry on."[200]

By 1944, the largest gap in SWPA's understanding of the situation in the Philippines was lack of awareness of the situation on Luzon. As late as May 25, Maj. Gen. Willoughby was unaware of Ramsey's guerrilla force on Luzon. In a note to Lt. Col. Mellnik, Willoughby wrote, "Who is this man Ramsey? Where did he come from?"[201] For his part, Ramsey was trying to make contact with Fertig on Mindanao, sending him a letter via courier asking for updated codes for use with his radio.[202] Ramsey also made the dangerous journey to Mindoro in an attempt to contact Phillips, not realizing that the AIB operative was already dead.[203] The G-2 Philippines Section tried desperately to sort out the various groups, but its confusion is evident in this report from August 20:

> Although it is not known for certain how the original Thorpe [sic]–Praeger group dispersed, after pressure by the enemy knocked out their original leaders, by piecing the bits of information that have come in together it is believed that the following happened. Anderson assumed control. Ramsey, second ranking officer to Anderson, disputed this control and gathered a few remnants of the organization establishing his own command believed to be located in Nueva Ecija. Ramsey attempted to establish himself with the [SWPA] HQ contacting [Lt. Col. Macario] Peralta [on Panay]. Anderson tried by contacting Fertig [on Mindanao]. Later, Volckmann came into the picture. Volckmann apparently controlled yet another remnant of the original Thorpe [sic]–Praeger group in Northern Luzon, but little was known of his activities.[204]

In an attempt to determine the personalities involved, the G-2 Philippines Section developed an enormous database of index cards with information pertinent to various key individuals in the islands. These cards catalogued approximately 20,000 US and Filipino personnel in the Philippines, both those in the guerrilla movement and those collaborating with the Japanese.[205] What SWPA needed more than anything was radio contact with the groups on Luzon, and liaison officers on site to sort out the competent from the pretenders.

Charlie Smith's station on Samar would provide the breakthrough required to establish solid contact with the guerrillas on Luzon. A guerrilla courier arrived at the Samar station in April 1944, informing Smith of the existence of the guerrilla group on Luzon headed by Anderson, an old friend of Lt. Col. Ind at AIB. Smith sent Captain Robert Ball, a former enlisted soldier stationed on Mindanao at the time of the fall of Bataan and Corregidor who had joined the guerrilla resistance after the surrender, to Tayabas to establish a radio station to facilitate communications with the guerrillas in Luzon, beginning with Anderson's group.[206] Contact with other groups followed in due course. Anderson made contact with SWPA on June 20, followed by Lapham on July 12. The first radio contact with SWPA by Volckmann's guerrillas occurred in late August 1944, after Lapham sent a radio with two technicians to his headquarters in northern Luzon. The power pack lasted a week, but technicians devised a seventy-five-watt transmitter powered by a nearby waterfall. At that point, Volckmann sent a constant stream of messages to SWPA.[207] AIB immediately arranged submarine runs to ferry supplies to the various Luzon groups.[208]

Now that the SWPA G-2 PRS was no longer unsure of who Ramsey was, in June 1944 an AIB agent made his way to Ramsey's base near Manila with a coveted radio. After two years of intermittent communications with MacArthur's headquarters in Australia via couriers, Ramsey could now send messages via telegraph key to SWPA via the AIB station on Negros administered by Edwin Andrews, a Philippine Air Force officer. The isolation from the outside world was broken. Ramsey's feelings mirrored others who finally had contact with Australia: "We were connected, we had arrived; the Luzon Guerrilla Force had joined the war."[209] Ramsey now submitted routine daily intelligence reports, while receiving information about the progress of the war, about which he had known next to nothing until then. The only thing that impeded the signal was the chorus of millions of cicadas and frogs surrounding Ramsey's headquarters in the jungle, often so loud they would drown out the dots and dashes from the lone speaker next to the radio.[210]

The contact with SWPA came at an opportune time, as the guerrilla groups on Luzon were at each other's throats. MacArthur's staff noted, "Although the majority of the guerrillas shared a common antipathy for the Japanese, they were often divided among themselves, separated into intractable rival factions engaged in a bitter struggle for power. There was no established demarcation of authority and no defined chain of command. All reports of returning AIB agents stressed the necessity of achieving greater co-operation and more unified control among the guerrilla organizations."[211] One guerrilla memoirist described the situation bluntly, "During these lawless years, the supreme law was the gun. In the towns and in the cities, the Japs, the PCs [Philippine Constabulary], and their armed agents, were the law. In the provinces and in the free hills, the guerrillas were the law. Among the guerrillas, the most powerful was the law."[212] Zonification in the second half of 1943 had hit many groups in Luzon hard. Hunters ROTC and Marking's guerrillas were battling one another over turf and resources. "Early in the war, disputes within and between guerrilla groups had been mainly over what our duties were and what our policies should be, much complicated by rivalry for access to food and arms, all exacerbated by personal grudges," wrote Lapham. "By 1944 we were quarreling mostly over jurisdiction; who should rule whom."[213]

Once he had made contact with SWPA, Anderson played intermediary between MacArthur and Marking's guerrillas and attempted to quell the war between that group and the Hunters ROTC guerrillas.[214] Two American liaison officers, Capt. George Miller and 1st Lt. Brooke Stoddard, arrived at Marking's camp on November 17, 1944, to provide a firmer link between the guerrillas and MacArthur's headquarters.[215] Miller attempted to unify the two groups, but their animosities were too great to overcome. Instead, Miller proposed the formation of a joint command, the Rizal–Eastern Laguna Command, to be advised by him, with a combined staff composed of members of both groups. The two groups accepted this proposal and as the war among the guerrillas abated, the war against the Japanese intensified.[216]

The organization of guerrilla forces progressed rapidly in the second half of 1944 as SWPA was able to establish communications with the various groups and put in place a more viable chain of command. On August 27, the USS *Stingray* landed a party of fifteen Filipinos, led by Lt. Jose V. Valera, at Bangui on the northwest coast of Luzon. They arrived with several tons of supplies, including arms, ammunition, medical supplies, and an all-important radio. The party was unaware of the guerrilla situation in northern Luzon, but finally established contact with Capt. John O'Day of the 121st Infantry Regiment of the US Army Forces in the Philippines – Northern Luzon (USAFIP-NL) at the end of October. The party finally arrived at Volckmann's headquarters in early December, whereupon

SWPA attached it to USAFIP-NL. In late November, the USS *Gar* unloaded twenty tons of supplies at San Esteban on the northwest coast of Luzon, as well as four American officers, two American enlisted soldiers, and ten Filipino radio operators and demolition experts. The submarine returned in early December with another twenty-five tons of supplies, which it off-loaded at Darigayos. Radios were subsequently distributed to the five USAFIP-NL regiments, allowing Volckmann to maintain continuous contact with his forces.[217]

The rise of the guerrillas in the latter half of 1944 coincided with a Japanese effort to redouble their counterguerrilla operations and zoning efforts focused on the supporting civilian populace. "The momentum of this horrible carnage increased in intensity up to the bitter end of 1944 and early months of 1945," the historian of Hunters ROTC writes. "Indeed, the second wave of zonifications was nothing more than an organized butchery of civilian populations by the Japanese Imperial Army."[218]

3.3: Col. Russell Volckmann holding a captured Japanese sword. Volckmann began the war as a major and formed a division's worth of guerrillas in northern Luzon. He is one of the forebearers of the modern US Army Special Forces. (Credit: US Army Signal Corps Photo)

As the day of the return approached, guerrilla groups began the transition from intelligence collection to direct action. On July 16, 1944, Ramsey's guerrillas in Manila unleashed a wave of sabotage that destroyed hundreds of thousands of gallons of fuel in Japanese depots, sank two ships in the harbor, and snarled rail traffic across the city.[219] Japanese pressure against the guerrillas increased accordingly. Japanese sweeps in Manila gathered in dozens of Ramsey's agents, who were tortured for information and then beheaded.[220] Japanese troops converged on Ramsey's jungle headquarters, but its forbidding defenses at the top of a steep waterfall protected by .50-caliber machine guns enabled the guerrillas to evacuate the facility without loss. In northern Luzon, Volckmann's guerrillas wisely avoided combat with the Japanese and instead targeted the Philippine Constabulary, an organization used by the Japanese to police the islands during the occupation. Aided by double agents within the constabulary, the guerrillas were able to neutralize the organization by the end of 1944.[221]

On Mindanao, where both the Japanese and the Americans expected MacArthur's return to occur, fierce Japanese attacks against Fertig's guerrillas beginning in mid 1943 put them on the defensive. Japanese aircraft also bombed villages suspected of aiding guerrilla forces.[222] But here, too, the guerrillas were demonstrating their worth, with one coast-watcher station in June 1944 reporting the transit of the Japanese fleet through the San Bernardino Strait en route to the Philippine Sea, where US naval aviators would destroy hundreds of Japanese planes in what became known as the "Great Marianas Turkey Shoot."[223] The guerrillas also reported the flood of Japanese troops coming into Mindanao in anticipation of an invasion. Fertig used the organizational structure of a Philippine Army Reserve Division to organize the guerrilla forces under his command, and by May 1944 he had formed the 105th, 106th, 107th, 108th, 109th, and 110th Divisions (a loosely applied label, as they lacked the strength of standard divisions) on the island. Fertig's headquarters, which had a full general and special staff laid out along American military lines, moved several times to evade detection and destruction by Japanese forces.[224] Japanese pressure eventually forced Fertig to move his headquarters into the rugged interior of the island, the guerrilla leader watching apprehensively as his food and fuel supplies dwindled.[225]

During the first ten days of September 1944, strikes by land- and carrier-based aircraft pounded Japanese positions in Mindanao and the Visayas. On September 9, Halsey's fleet pinned a Japanese troop convoy of forty-nine ships against the Mindanao coast; naval aircraft sank more than a dozen, and another thirty-two ran aground. Japanese soldiers who swam to shore were butchered by bolo-wielding Filipinos waiting for them in the surf. The episode seriously depleted Japanese strength on the eastern side of the island and gave Fertig and his men a much-needed reprieve as the Japanese forces abandoned their pursuit of the guerrillas to man their fortifications and shore defenses.[226] Fertig confided to his diary, "The airblitz is on . . .. After nearly two weary years of battle, the tide has turned. It should run to flood without serious opposition. I wanted to be home when the aspens turn but impossible. Perhaps by Christmas."[227] Alas, this was also impossible.

Nevertheless, by October Fertig's guerrillas controlled more than 85 percent of the island.[228] By the end of 1944, Fertig's forces had established seven airfields on Mindanao; transport aircraft could now bring supplies to the guerrilla forces, augmenting those carried by submarines.[229] But the return of US forces would not occur for several months, as MacArthur and the Joint Chiefs of Staff decided on the basis of the results of Halsey's raid to invade Leyte first. Upon hearing of the invasion, Fertig remarked in his diary, "Our time of trial and triumph is at hand."[230] But Mindanao had been put on the back burner. By the time the Eighth Army invaded the following spring, Fertig commanded upwards of 35,000 guerrillas, two-thirds of them armed.[231]

President Osmeña issued an executive order on October 28, 1944, which amalgamated guerrilla units recognized by MacArthur into the Philippine Army.[232] Just prior to the invasion of Luzon in January 1945, MacArthur directed guerrillas on Luzon to begin sabotage operations against the Japanese. "The guerrillas were now doing what they had trained for these long years: attacking the enemy at every opportunity; disrupting their preparations to meet the invasion; harassing, crippling, and killing them all over Luzon. The body of the guerrilla resistance that for more than three years had lain quietly, sending intelligence through its vast nerve system and occasionally flicking a finger at the Japanese, was now on its feet and fighting."[233] By this point, Ramsey, at 27 years of age and weighing less than 100 pounds, controlled by his estimate upwards of 40,000 guerrillas – most no doubt serving as auxiliaries, but real combat power nevertheless.[234] As noted by Lapham, all guerrilla strength returns "were notoriously elastic, always depending on whether the totals referred to active, full-time resisters, occasional helpers, or mere sympathizers."[235] The strength of Volckmann's guerrillas in northern Luzon, which he reported as 19,660 men grouped into 5 infantry regiments, or the size of an American infantry division, is accurate, if for no other reason than that the subsequent use of his organization in combat against the Japanese in the spring of 1945 validated its combat power.[236] Volckmann, promoted by then to the rank of colonel, was just thirty-three years old.

4

THE DECISION

The President of the United States ordered me to break through the Japanese lines and proceed from Corregidor to Australia for the purpose, as I understand it, of organizing an American offensive against Japan, the primary purpose of which is the relief of the Philippines. I came through and I shall return.[1]

                                                                Douglas MacArthur

From the moment he arrived in Australia and through the subsequent months and years of the Pacific War, the one overriding goal of Douglas MacArthur was to return to liberate the Filipino people and the American soldiers and civilians, now prisoners and internees, caught in the vortex of war.[2] He had obeyed the president's orders to evacuate to Australia, in the process abandoning his fellow countrymen and the Filipino people to their fates. Undeniably he felt a duty to those he unwillingly left behind. But he also had for the first time in his life experienced defeat, a catastrophic failure of arms that undoubtedly wounded his outsized ego. Avenging Bataan and Corregidor was his motivation and rallying cry, driving him and by extension the Southwest Pacific Theater command along the jungle road through New Guinea and back to the Philippines. On the eve of MacArthur's return to the Philippines, MacArthur's personal pilot, Col. Weldon E. "Dusty" Rhoades, remarked in his diary, "General MacArthur's whole life is wrapped up in this idea of returning to the Philippines. It's almost an obsession with him."[3] He could have eliminated the modifier "almost."

Joint Staff planners mapped out a strategic concept to defeat Japan in the spring of 1943. In late April, the Joint War Plans Committee drafted JWPC 15, "Strategic Plan for the Defeat of Japan." It laid out a strategic concept that included the establishment of bases in China to launch air attacks against the Japanese home islands, which necessitated the opening of the Burma Road and the establishment of a base on the eastern coast of the Asian mainland. US forces would advance either across the Central

Pacific or through the Southwest Pacific to the South China Sea, while British forces would reconquer Burma to open a ground avenue of communication into China. The liberation of the Philippines would ensue, followed by the seizure of Hong Kong. The allies would then launch an air bombardment and naval blockade of the Japanese home islands, followed by a ground invasion if the Japanese refused to surrender. The Joint Chiefs of Staff (JCS) adopted the plan as JCS 287 on May 8 in preparation for the Trident Conference in Washington, DC, where the Combined Chiefs of Staff accepted it as a basis for further study.[4] Although it did not lay out a sequence of specific operations for Allied forces to pursue, the broad strategic outline in this document guided the general strategy of Allied forces in the Pacific War for the next year and a half.

JCS strategy focused on isolating Japan from its overseas possessions and resources, conducting an aerial bombardment to reduce its industrial infrastructure and military wherewithal, and then positioning US forces to invade the home islands if necessary to force a Japanese surrender. As deliberations on US objectives commenced, the JCS believed that bases on mainland China would best position bombardment wings for an air campaign against the Japanese homeland. China, however, was isolated; the logistics of supporting a massive air campaign launched from Chinese bases via the Ledo extension of the Burma Road (which was not complete until January 1945) or by transport aircraft over the "Hump" of the Himalayan Mountains were daunting. Accordingly, the JCS believed that an air campaign launched from China would require a port on the Chinese mainland and control of the "strategic triangle" formed by the southern China coast, Formosa, and Luzon, which would give the allies mastery of the South China Sea and at the same time cut Japan off from the resource-rich Dutch East Indies.[5]

The Combined Chiefs of Staff approved a concept, CCS 417, at the Second Cairo Conference in November 1943 that set as the allied objective the seizure of air and naval bases in the Formosa–Luzon–China triangle in spring 1945. US forces would advance across the Central Pacific and via the New Guinea–Netherlands East Indies–Philippines area in mutually supporting operations. The planners favored an advance across the Central Pacific, but the Joint Chiefs were unwilling at this time to establish a priority between the two avenues of approach.[6] As a result, arguments over the advisability of the Central Pacific versus the Southwest Pacific avenues of approach continued into the new year.

MacArthur knew where he was headed, even if the Joint Chiefs did not. GHQ SWPA issued its first strategic plan (Reno I) in February 1943, with operations proceeding up the coast of New Guinea and ultimately aimed at the island of Mindanao. A second version appeared in August, followed by Reno III on October 20. After the seizure of the Admiralty Islands, Reno IV (March 6, 1944) envisioned a campaign that continued past Mindanao to seize islands in the Visayas and ultimately the liberation of Luzon.[7] The plan used American forces almost exclusively; by spring 1944, MacArthur and his staff had essentially written Australian forces out of the equation. The latter would continue to battle Japanese forces in New Guinea and Bougainville and eventually invade Borneo in the Netherlands East Indies, but they would have little to no influence on the campaign to liberate the Philippines, which is what mattered most to MacArthur. He deleted Australian General Thomas Blamey's land forces headquarters from the command scheme altogether.[8] MacArthur's exclusion of Australian forces from operations in the Philippines was clearly deliberate; redemption was to be an all-American affair.

If MacArthur had his way, the invasion of the Philippines would be the primary focus of the US war effort in the Pacific, but he was only one of many actors in the decision-making process. MacArthur's co-equal in the Pacific Ocean Areas was Admiral Chester W. Nimitz, who commanded the forces that would form one of two major drives in the Pacific Theater of Operations. After seizing Tarawa in the Gilbert Islands in November 1943, Nimitz's forces invaded Eniwetok and Kwajalein in the Marshall Islands in February 1944 before seizing Saipan, Tinian, and Guam in the strategically crucial Mariana Islands in June and July 1944. By that time, MacArthur's forces had taken the key points along the northern coast of New Guinea and had conquered the Admiralty Islands, isolating the major Japanese air and naval base at Rabaul. The question for the JCS, tasked by the Allied Combined Chiefs of Staff with determining the strategy for the war in the Pacific, was what to do once these operations concluded.

On March 2, 1944, the JCS reaffirmed that the first major objective in the final offensive against Japan would be "the vital Luzon–Formosa–China coast area," with a tentative date of February 15, 1945, for the invasion of Formosa. However, the JCS allowed for the possibility of a prior invasion of Luzon "should such operations prove necessary prior to the move on Formosa."[9] The JCS directed planning to commence "for all probable operations" in pursuit of this objective.[10] MacArthur's headquarters natur-ally viewed Luzon as the primary objective, while Nimitz's headquarters looked toward Formosa. This disparity set off a storm of messages, planning, and controversy over the next seven months until the issue was finally decided. MacArthur, of course, argued for an invasion of the Philippines, which would presumably begin in Mindanao, the southernmost major island in the archipelago and the closest to US-controlled airbases in New Guinea, and proceed from there to Leyte in the Visayas. But, for MacArthur, the prize was the island of Luzon and the Philippine capital city of Manila. Admiral Ernest J. King, the Commander in Chief of the US Fleet and Chief of Naval Operations, argued instead for an invasion of Formosa, which had the advantage of being closer to Japan and to Allied forces on the Chinese mainland. There were not enough forces to do both; the Joint Chiefs would have to decide between the two competing operations. The resulting dilemma would dominate the strategic discussions of the JCS vis-à-vis the war in the Pacific for most of 1944.[11]

MacArthur opened the discussion on March 8 by proposing to bypass the major Japanese naval base at Truk in the Caroline Islands, seize a foothold on Mindanao in November 1944, and invade Luzon in January 1945. According to his logic, "This line of action will secure a major strategic victory in November and secure Luzon before the commencement of the heavy rains in July [1945], thus enabling us to initiate V.L.R. [very-long-range] bombing of Japan and establish bases for the advance to Formosa and China."[12] The JCS agreed with the notion of bypassing Truk, but were unwilling to commit to an invasion of Luzon at this time. On March 12, they "decided that the most feasible approach to the Formosa–Luzon–China area is by way of Marianas–Carolines–Palau–Mindanao area." Accordingly, the JCS canceled planned amphibious operations against the Japanese base at Kavieng (on the northwest tip of New Ireland), ordered the development of recently seized Manus Island in the Admiralty Islands as an air and fleet base, and authorized the seizure of Hollandia (April 15), the neutralization of Truk by carrier air strikes and the isolation of the Carolines, an invasion of the Marianas (June 15), the seizure of the Palau Islands (September 15), the invasion of Mindanao (November 15), and an invasion of Formosa (February 15, 1945), or the occupation of Luzon "should such operations prove necessary prior to the move on Formosa."[13]

The Joint Planning Staff considered Formosa the key to the prosecution of the endgame in the Pacific War. According to one official US Army historian, "The island possessed so many obvious advantages and was located in such a strategically important position that most planners in Washington believed the Allies would have to seize it no matter what other operations they conducted in the western Pacific."[14] As with most strategic plans, however, a key assumption underlay this conclusion. JCS planners believed that US forces would have to eventually secure a base on the China coast in order to prosecute the final stages of the war against Japan. Doing so would open up a supply route to the Chinese Nationalist Army, sever Japanese lines of communication to the Dutch East Indies, provide sites for air bases from which to prosecute a bombing offensive against Japan, and offer a port from which to stage invasion forces should the JCS decide to invade the Japanese homeland. Nimitz concurred with this assumption as well, relating to King at a conference in San Francisco on May 6, 1944, that seizing a port on the Chinese coast was essential to funnel arms and supplies to the Chinese Nationalist Army, which would be the main instrument by which the Allies would defeat the Imperial Japanese Army in Asia.[15] Before the summer of 1944, it did not occur to the planning staffs that Luzon and the Mariana Islands could be used in tandem to fulfill the same functions, with the exception of opening a supply route into China proper. By the end of summer, however, it had become clear that China would not play the major role in defeating Japan that many senior military leaders earlier in the war had assumed it would.

During the summer of 1944, the question of the direction of future strategy in the Pacific War came to a head in Washington, Honolulu, and Brisbane. Believing that US forces could accelerate the pace of operations in the Pacific, the JCS began the debate with a message on June 12, 1944:

> The JCS are considering the possibilities of expediting the Pacific campaign by any or all of the following courses:
>
> (a) By advancing the target dates for operations now scheduled through operations against Formosa.
> (b) By by-passing presently selected objectives prior to operations against Formosa.
> (c) By by-passing presently selected objectives and choosing new objectives, including Japan proper.
>
> On basis of over-all situation which will obtain as result of FORAGER operation [the invasion of the Marianas] CINCPOA [Nimitz] and CINCSOWESPAC [MacArthur] directed to present their views and recommendations.[16]

If any phrase would set the planning world afire in SWPA headquarters, it was "by-passing presently selected objectives," which in MacArthur's eyes of course meant the Philippines.

Six days later, MacArthur replied in no uncertain terms. Operations against Formosa without first occupying Luzon were "unsound" and unjustifiably risky, and any plan to attack the mainland of Japan directly with the forces then available in the Pacific was "utterly unsound." Success to date "must not mislead us into a suicidal direct assault without [land-based] air support and with inadequate shipping and bases against heavily defended bastions of the enemy's main position."[17] MacArthur's operations had relied to this point on land-based air support, an advantage of his proposed route of advance from New Guinea to Morotai to Mindanao. Filipino guerrillas stood by, ready to assist with the liberation of their homeland. But MacArthur's opposition to bypassing Luzon ran deeper in his soul.

Beyond purely military considerations that necessitated the seizure of Luzon, the United States had "a great national obligation" to free the Filipino people from Japanese occupation as soon as possible. "Moreover if the United States should deliberately bypass the Philippines, leaving our prisoners, nationals and loyal Filipinos in enemy hands without an effort to retrieve them at earliest moment we would incur the gravest psychological reaction. We would admit the truth of Japanese propaganda to the effect that we had abandoned the Filipinos and would not shed American blood to redeem them; we would undoubtedly incur the open hostility of that people; we would probably suffer such loss of prestige among all the peoples of the Far East that it would adversely affect the United States for many years." MacArthur was not content merely having outlined the military and political factors involved in the future direction of Pacific strategy in a message. He concluded, "If serious consideration is being given to the line of action indicated in paragraphs B and C of your radio, I request that I be accorded the opportunity of personally proceeding to Washington to present fully my views."[18]

Gen. George C. Marshall responded personally to MacArthur in an "eyes only" message. He encouraged the SWPA commander to keep an open mind about future operations in the Pacific. The JCS were considering bypassing certain objectives to avoid Japanese strength:

> All the information we have received from MAGIC or ULTRA indicates the steady buildup of Japanese strength in the area Mindanao, Celebes, Halmahera, Vogelkop, Palau. It is also apparent from the information that the Japanese are seriously limited in their capacity to redeploy or rearrange their troops due to limited shipping. The information available appears to indicate their expectation of an early attack on Palau [which would come in September] as well as continued advances to the northwest by your forces. In other words further advances in this particular region will encounter greatly increased Japanese strength in most localities. There will be less opportunity to move against his weakness and to his surprise, as has been the case in your recent series of moves.[19]

Furthermore, the Japanese summer offensive in China was threatening the collapse of Nationalist resistance, which would have severe consequences for the war against Japan. "For this reason the early capture of Formosa was studied though there was also the thought that, if the descent on Formosa could be organized with a reasonable chance of success, we would profit tremendously in the procedure [if] it were done at an early date and come, therefore, more or less as a complete surprise."[20]

Because of Japanese reinforcement of the Palau Islands, the JCS was considering canceling the operation there (Peleliu) and attacking Formosa or Kyushu instead. "Whether or not the Formosa or the Kyushu operation can be mounted remains a matter to be studied but neither operation in my opinion is unsound in the measure you indicate."[21] The major obstacle to the success of such operations in the view of the JCS was the remaining strength of the Imperial Japanese Navy.

Marshall concluded by addressing the issue closest to MacArthur's heart. "With regard to the last (the reconquest of the Philippines) we must be careful not to allow our personal feelings and Philippine political considerations to override our great objective, which is the early conclusion of the war with Japan," Marshall wrote. "In my view, 'by-passing' is in no way synonymous with 'abandonment.' On the contrary, by the defeat of Japan at the earliest practicable moment the liberation of the Philippines will be effected in the most expeditious and complete manner possible." Finally, Marshall addressed MacArthur's desire to present his views directly to the JCS and the president. "As to your expressed desire to be accorded the opportunity of personally proceeding to Washington to fully [explain] your views, I see no difficulty about that and if the issue arises will speak to the President who I am quite certain would be agreeable to your being ordered home fo[r] the purpose."[22]

The SWPA staff continued to plan operations under the assumption that an invasion of Luzon would be essential in order to provide bases in support of operations on Formosa or the Asian mainland. In a long message to Marshall on July 8, MacArthur outlined his latest operations plan, Reno V, to implement JCS directives in prosecution of the war against Japan:

> Concept is predicated upon assumption that adequate support of Formosa–China Coast Operations will require occupation or control of Central and Northern Luzon prior to the 1945 rainy season. It envisages operations to initially establish necessary land, naval and air bases in the Southern Philippines followed by entry into Luzon at earliest practicable date. Basic scheme of maneuver employed along the New Guinea axis is

continued with appropriate modifications to coordinate land-based air and Pacific Fleet air and surface support to maximum advantage. Operations are scheduled to provide a secure base and land-based air support for each subsequent operation, flexibility being retained by elimination of steps found unnecessary at the time.

In general, operations by-pass [Japanese] strength in Halmahera and Davao. Approach is made via the Vogelkop and Morotai to initial lodgment in southern Mindanao. Thereafter, advance along the Eastern Coast of the Archipelago utilizes Pacific Fleet support to the maximum to seize bases for the final campaign in Central Luzon. Main effort, Luzon Campaign via Balintang Channel into Lingayen Gulf. Subsequently, bases are established and operations into the Formosa–China Coast area supported as directed. Flank protection of advance northward is provided by minor operations and support of Filipino Forces in the Visayas and Northern Mindanao.[23]

The accompanying timeline projected the invasion of Morotai on September 8, Sarangani Bay in Mindanao on October 25, Leyte Gulf on November 15, the Bicol provinces in southeast Luzon and Aparri in northern Luzon in the middle of January 1945, Mindoro in February, Lingayen Gulf on April 1, and supporting operations along the south, east, and west coasts of Luzon sometime later in April. The implementation of Reno V would mean the deferral of the proposed invasion of Formosa until the end of the typhoon season in October 1945.[24]

MacArthur would receive his opportunity to raise his concerns directly with the president in late July at a conference in Hawai'i that also included Nimitz and Admiral William D. Leahy, the president's chief of staff and the only member of the JCS to attend.[25] In his memoirs, MacArthur claims that he received a summons from Marshall to travel to Hawai'i for a conference, for which the agenda and attendees were kept secret. He intimates that he was blindsided upon arrival, having proceeded from Australia with just his personal aides and without plans for his proposed Philippines campaign.[26] This statement is disingenuous, for MacArthur had requested to leave his theater to go to Washington to explain his views on strategy to the JCS and the president. Furthermore, the idea of having MacArthur meet the president in Hawai'i was suggested three weeks earlier, at a meeting in the War Department on July 3:

> The suggestion was made that sometime during the president's Pacific trip, possibly while he was in Honolulu, would be an appropriate time for this conference [between President Roosevelt and MacArthur]. General Marshall approved this suggestion, stating that if circumstances call for it,

General MacArthur should be directed to proceed to Honolulu for
conference with the President and that there should be no interference
with this in any way from here, that is, no one sent out from the War
Department to be parent or anything of the kind.[27]

Upon receiving the summons to travel to Hawai'i, MacArthur complained
to Marshall, "I know nothing of the purpose of my orders."[28] Marshall
replied, "Purpose general strategical discussion. I will be in Washington
but you will see Leahy, etcetera."[29] Since Marshall would be absent from
the meeting, this was clearly not a meeting of the JCS. But, since Admiral
Leahy would be present, he would clearly be attending in his role as the
president's chief of staff. That meant President Roosevelt would be in
Hawai'i to discuss strategy with his two theater commanders in the Pacific.

The idea that MacArthur's meeting with the president in Hawai'i and its
purpose came as a total surprise to him is not supported by the historical
record. For the record, MacArthur noisily protested to aides that he was
being called to Hawai'i to bolster the president's political stature in an
election year, an assertion also made by Admiral King, who had by coincidence preceded the president to Hawai'i at the end of a tour of Central
Pacific battlefields, but tactfully departed before the president's arrival.[30] At
least one senior naval officer in Hawai'i, Rear Admiral Robert Carney, Chief
of Staff to Admiral William "Bull" Halsey, argued with King against bypassing the Philippines in favor of an invasion of Formosa. King shot back, "Do
you want to make a London out of Manila?" "No sir," replied Carney. "I want
to make an England out of Luzon!"[31]

Whatever the circumstances of his visit to Hawai'i, MacArthur was well
prepared for his meeting with the president – two years of preparation for
his return to the Philippines had seen to that. In a conversation during the
flight to Hawai'i, MacArthur's pilot, Dusty Rhoades, listened while
MacArthur opined as to the nature of the meeting. MacArthur was ready
to make his strategic case to the president and told Rhoades "he had been
preparing for weeks to make the strongest possible case" for an invasion of
the Philippines.[32] He didn't need staff officers, studies, and charts to bolster
his rhetoric.

After MacArthur's flamboyant and noisy arrival dockside in a stretch
limo guarded by a police motorcycle escort, an evening reception, and a day
of touring and inspections of military facilities, the president and senior
military leaders got down to work. In two sessions on the evening of July 27
and the morning of July 28, the conferees debated the competing strategic

conceptions for the next phase of the war in the Pacific. Nimitz, dutifully channeling Commander-in-Chief of the US Fleet Admiral Ernest J. King, put forward the strategy for seizing Formosa. The idea was attractive for a number of reasons: seizing Formosa would sever Japan's lifeline to the resources of the Dutch East Indies; the island would provide facilities with which to support Chinese Nationalist forces on the Asian mainland; and B-29 bombers based there could sustain strikes against the Japanese homeland.[33] Formosa would also be an excellent embarkation point for an amphibious assault on Okinawa or Kyushu.

Nimitz did not say so, but by this time he was lukewarm about invading Formosa. He recognized the drawbacks. He would need more forces, and unless Luzon were seized first, any invasion would not be supported by land-based airpower. Nimitz's subordinates, including Fifth Fleet commander Adm. Raymond A. Spruance and Rear Adm. Forest Sherman, Nimitz's deputy chief of staff, were dead set against the operation, code-named CAUSEWAY.[34]

The president then picked up the pointer and aimed it at Mindanao. "Well, Douglas," he asked, "where do we go from here?"

"Leyte, Mr. President, and then Luzon," was MacArthur's reply.[35]

MacArthur then laid out his case for liberating the Philippines, and his heart was definitely in his proposed strategy. Japan's line of communication to the Dutch East Indies could be severed from Luzon as easily as from Formosa, while leaving 300,000 Japanese troops (and their supporting airpower) untouched in the Philippines would entail an unacceptable element of risk should the Americans bypass Luzon in favor of invading Formosa. The Imperial Japanese Navy would be able to strike the US fleet near Formosa under the cover of land-based aircraft. The loyalties of the Formosan people, who had been subjects of the Japanese for half a century, were also suspect in his eyes, which made the island a less than ideal jumping off point for an invasion of Japan. The Filipino people, on the other hand, would overwhelmingly support the American liberators of their islands – MacArthur was sure of that. "The Filipino people will remain loyal at heart and the day we set foot on the islands they will rally as a unit to our call," he had written the Secretary of War nearly a year earlier.[36] But MacArthur's most important arguments were moral and political. The United States, in his view, had failed to support American and Filipino troops on Bataan and Corregidor, and if it were to now forsake the Filipino people and American prisoners of war and internees a second time, America would consign untold numbers to their deaths through starvation and suffer a grievous blow to its prestige in Asia.[37]

Leahy reported favorably on the meeting in his memoirs: "After so much loose talk in Washington, where the mention of the name MacArthur seemed to generate more heat than light, it was both pleasant and very informative to have these two men who had been pictured as antagonists calmly present their differing views to the Commander-in-Chief. For Roosevelt it was an excellent lesson in geography, one of his favorite subjects."[38] As Roosevelt and Leahy discovered, relations between the services on the ground in the Pacific were more cordial than believed by service adherents back in Washington, a premise that also held for Army–Marine relations in the Central Pacific.[39] MacArthur's arguments swayed Leahy and Roosevelt and likely Nimitz as well, although no firm decisions were made at the time.[40]

4.1: Gen. Douglas MacArthur, President Franklin D. Roosevelt, Adm. William D. Leahy, and Adm. Chester W. Nimitz discuss Pacific War strategy at a meeting in Oahu, July 27, 1944. Roosevelt seemed to agree with MacArthur's arguments for liberating the Philippines, but the final decision to invade Leyte and Luzon was made by the Joint Chiefs of Staff in the Pentagon. (Credit: US Army Signal Corps Photo)

Although no definitive record of the meetings in Hawaiʻi has surfaced, Colonel William L. Ritchie, chief of the Southwest Pacific Theater Section in the Operations Division of the War Department General Staff, relayed notes from the meeting to Marshall in Washington.[41] MacArthur had presented to the president his concept of finishing the war against Japan. The campaign would begin with the seizure of Luzon in February 1945 and the establishment of bases there from which to interdict Japanese shipping in the South China Sea. The next step would be the establishment of air bases in the Ryukyus (i.e., Okinawa) and/or the Bonins (i.e., Iwo Jima), followed by an assault on Kyushu and then a landing on the Tokyo Plain in Honshu. Formosa, on the other hand, would be "a massive operation, extremely costly in men and shipping, logistically precarious and time consuming."[42] If US forces bypassed Luzon, Japanese forces in the Philippines would have opportunities to interdict US lines of communication to Formosa.[43]

MacArthur pointed to three major tactical and logistical issues that hindered the proposed Formosa operation:

(1) The ability of SWPA air to neutralize Japanese airfields on Luzon preparatory to the Formosa operation, as required by Admiral Nimitz.
(2) The logistical feasibility of the Formosa operation, which was particularly problematic because of the lack of forward bases and the necessary shipping to sustain a supply line from the United States to Formosa.
(3) The availability of the required number of Army service troops to support the operation.[44]

SWPA could interdict Japanese bases on Luzon only after it seized base areas in the Visayas from which to operate bombers and fighters, which would take time. Naval base Guam had not yet been created, so shipping figures were unavailable. Perhaps most importantly, Nimitz's forces were short 200,000 troops, mostly combat service support forces, and, with the war in Europe still raging, the only source for them would be by stripping them from SWPA. MacArthur cut this option off by stating that he would have to relinquish recent conquests and withdraw to shorten his supply lines should SWPA become the bill payer for resourcing an invasion of Formosa. A final unspoken consideration dealt with interservice relations. MacArthur's staff was convinced "that the Navy desired to place Army units under command of Marine officers . . . . Under this arrangement any logistical set-back would be charged to failure of the Army, whereas victories would be to the credit of the Navy."[45]

The Philippines, in MacArthur's estimation, were a more inviting and important target. His intelligence, much of it gleaned from Filipino guerrillas, indicated that the Philippines were weakly held. Upwards of 50,000 armed guerrillas were ready to rise up at his order, along with 200,000 bolo-wielding auxiliaries. The Filipinos constituted an unlimited pool of labor to compensate for shortages of service troops. MacArthur wished "to assure you that he could accomplish the Luzon campaign faster and cheaper than we have ever possibly imagined and that his losses would be inconsequential."[46] The staff officer relayed MacArthur's wildly optimistic and off-the-mark estimate "that the Luzon campaign could be completed in a maximum of six weeks, and that he was confident it would be completed in less than 30 days after the landing at Lingayen." In a more realistic appreciation, MacArthur believed that, if Formosa were invaded, Luzon would still have to be seized, but, if US forces seized Luzon, then Formosa could be bypassed.[47] Finally, and perhaps most importantly, MacArthur had highlighted "the political implications of by-passing Luzon, particularly emphasizing the effect of blockading Luzon from its food supply and starving out the Filipinos in the process."[48] This argument seemed to resonate with the president.

Even as the president was hashing out strategy with his senior commanders in the Pacific, planning continued apace in Washington and Brisbane. In a planning conference on July 20, Maj. Gen. Stephen Chamberlin, the SWPA G-3, stated, "Our great problem in the Southwest Pacific is the problem of logistics. Anyone who has participated in our campaign realizes that, but I want to again emphasize that logistics constitute 80 to 90% of the problem. Our main objective is to get the ground troops ashore and insure their supply and maintenance."[49] SWPA G-4 Brigadier General Lester J. Whitlock concurred, stating, "Through these newly established bases in the Philippines will have to pass quantities of troops and materials that we have not dreamed of before."[50] SWPA would have to compensate for a severe shortage of Army service forces by using combat troops and Filipinos as laborers.

On July 27, the Joint Staff sent a note to SWPA that laid out a planning assumption that after the seizure of air bases in the Visayas, US forces would bypass Luzon in favor of a landing on Formosa.[51] MacArthur fired back an "eyes only" message to Marshall with his "strongest nonconcurrence." He reiterated his belief that the Philippines were the most important strategic objective in the Pacific, and that Luzon was the most important objective in the Philippine archipelago. If Luzon were seized, then Japan would be cut off from the Dutch East Indies and US forces could bypass heavily defended Formosa and concentrate on more important and less well-defended objectives closer to the Japanese home islands. Bases in the Philippines were essential to support logistically an invasion of Formosa. Political consider-ations, however, were even more important:

> From the highest point of view of national policy the liberation of the Philippines is essential. The Philippine Archipelago is American territory which we failed adequately to defend, with the resultant loss and untold suffering of its loyal people and the death of many thousands of its soldiers and civilians. It is a national obligation to recover the Philippines at the earliest possible date. The President of the United States has acknowledged that obligation and has stated that the Philippines would be redeemed as soon as possible.
>
> The failure to liberate all of the Philippines would subject the Filipino people to continued brutality, potentially cause mass starvation that would kill millions of Filipinos, and "destroy the honor and prestige of the United States throughout the Far East and bring us into disrepute throughout the world."
>
> The failure of the United States to liberate its people would be a blot upon its honor but the imposition of a blockade that would result in the death by starvation of those loyal people presents a course of action that should not be considered by any government even if it were proposed by the military. It is a line of action that would exceed in brutality anything that has been perpetrated by our enemies.[52]

Marshall replied in an "eyes only" message that the Joint Staff message was for coordination among planners only and did not represent approved policy. He cautioned that "in order that the planners messages serve the purpose for which they are intended, it is desirable that answers to them be kept on that level."[53] Nevertheless, MacArthur had made his point.

In late July and early August, planners in Washington and Brisbane looked for ways to accelerate the seizure of base areas on Mindanao and Leyte. MacArthur did not believe the timeline could be accelerated, given the need to recover the assault shipping from the operation at Sarangani Bay on Mindanao and reload it for the invasion of Leyte. Joint Staff planners noted there was sufficient amphibious shipping in the Pacific to execute both operations without reusing vessels from one operation to the next. Perhaps more critically, MacArthur wanted to establish bases from which land-based aircraft could support successive invasions, a phasing of oper-ations he had successfully used in the advance northwestward along the coast of New Guinea. Thus, he desired to invade Morotai on September 15 to provide basing support for a subsequent invasion of the Talaud Islands a month later. Aircraft on the latter islands would support a two-division invasion of Sarangani Bay on Mindanao on November 15 and a smaller invasion elsewhere on Mindanao on December 7. Aircraft stationed in those two locations would support the invasion of Leyte by five divisions on December 20. This final operation would establish the air, naval, and logistical bases essential for any future operations to the north, whether directed at Luzon or Formosa.[54]

Gen. Marshall sent the chief of the US Army Air Forces air staff, Lt. Gen. Barney M. Giles, along with chief of the theater group Maj. Gen. John E. Hull and head of the Southwest Pacific Theater section Col. W. L. Ritchie, to Brisbane in early August to discuss future plans with MacArthur and his staff. MacArthur made clear that the invasion of the Palaus (Peleliu and Angaur) would be required in order to protect his forces as they invaded the Southern and Central Philippines, and once again "repeated with customary eloquence his conviction of the necessity for seizing Luzon and the impracticability of the Formosa operation."[55] Giles came away from the meeting "tentatively convinced of the correctness of MacArthur's position," although he would discuss matters with Nimitz before making a definitive determination. "I realize it is very hard to keep from getting 'localitis' after having talked to MacArthur for five hours (I mean listen)," he messaged to the Chief of the Army Air Forces Gen. Henry H. "Hap" Arnold.[56]

On August 18, Nimitz messaged King with his concept for the sequencing of operations now that the Marianas campaign was over. His desired objective was to seize southern Formosa for development as a base area from which to project power forward, either into Japan or into China. He supported MacArthur's move into the Philippines only as far as Leyte, scheduled for December. "If we are to obtain advantages of establishment of our forces in Formosa Strait region prior to end of typhoon season 1945 CAUSEWAY [invasion of Formosa] must follow as closely after Leyte as movement and preparation of forces will permit."[57] Nimitz recommended a target date of February 15, 1945, for the invasion of Formosa.

On the same day, King presented Marshall for coordination a draft directive, mandating the invasion of Leyte on December 1, 1944, and an invasion of Formosa (Operation CAUSEWAY) by February 15, 1945. This left the status of Luzon uncertain, but priority would most certainly be placed on Formosa, with SWPA in a supporting role after the seizure of Leyte. The liberation of Luzon would be deferred until a later date – or the end of the war. Marshall replied, "Before a directive for the Formosa operation can be issued, the availability of forces and resources in the light of the requirements recently indicated by Admiral Nimitz must be checked."[58] As it turned out, Nimitz's command was short by upwards of 170,000 combat service and support forces to support an invasion of Formosa, even for a limited operation in southern Formosa that did not seize the entire island.[59] Additional service and support troops could come only from SWPA (which MacArthur stated in no uncertain terms was impractical, as taking service troops from his area would require him to withdraw forces from recent gains to shorten his supply lines) or from Europe (which would have to await the end of the war against Germany).

Army planners highlighted the risk incurred in seizing only part of Formosa, which would leave Japanese forces in the northern part of the island free to counterattack the US bastion in the southern half.[60] In this regard, the planners undoubtedly were aware of the situation on Bougainville, where Japanese forces tied down an entire US (and later Australian) corps even after the successful seizure and defense of a beachhead from November 1943 to March 1944. The situation on Formosa would if anything be worse, given the close proximity of the island to Japanese reinforcements on the Asian mainland. Any operation to seize a port on the China coast would only exacerbate the problems faced by the invasion forces, and delay follow-on operations against Okinawa or the Japanese home islands.[61] Furthermore, seizing only the southern part of Formosa limited the logistical and airfield capacity of the bases to be established there, making the island an inferior substitute for Luzon as a forward operating base.[62]

As summer waned, Joint planners continued to struggle with the prioritization of the proposed invasions of Luzon and Formosa. There were not enough service forces to support the latter operation without pulling forces from Europe or SWPA, but both theaters were already short of service troops. The September 3 minutes of the 171st meeting of the JCS noted a shortage of 148,000 service troops for the proposed invasion of Formosa. In the meeting, Admiral King nevertheless argued for CAUSEWAY, followed by operations against Japan. General Marshall believed that it was too early to decide, and the JCS needed to study the implications of an early end to the war in Europe. A month earlier, Allied forces had broken out of the Normandy lodgment area, liberated Paris, and were approaching the German border. The Joint Chiefs agreed on having the Joint Staff Planners begin planning for an invasion of Leyte, but deferred other decisions on the Pacific War.[63]

Planners could not count on an early collapse of Germany, which would have made available service troops redeployed from the European Theater to the Pacific. It was becoming increasingly apparent that either the invasion of Luzon or that of Formosa would have to be canceled or deferred by several months, both unpalatable choices in the view of the Joint Chiefs and the commanders in the Pacific. But, with already scheduled operations either ending (the Marianas) or approaching (Morotai and the Palau Islands), time was running short to select follow-on objectives.

MacArthur sent his deputy chief of staff, Maj. Gen. Richard J. Marshall, to Washington to inform the War Department of SWPA plans and answer questions regarding MacArthur's future operations. Marshall attended the meeting of the Joint Planning Staff on September 4, in which navy planners grilled him on the issue of service troops in support of SWPA operations. The navy wanted SWPA to transfer service troops to Nimitz's command for the Formosa operation. Marshall replied that SWPA could not give up any service forces for other operations as it was already operating on a shoestring.[64] Operation Musketeer (which superseded Reno V and provided detailed plans for the liberation of the Philippines) was practicable only because SWPA planned to use Filipino laborers to supplement American service troops, an option not available in Formosa.[65] A War Department study comparing the value of Formosa with that of Luzon as a base for major operations against Japan made the value of Filipino labor clear: "The natives of the Philippines are a friendly people and there will be a considerable amount of willing and experienced labor available. This will reduce the security problem. English is widely spoken making local contacts easy. Formosa is a foreign country and some of the inhabitants will be hostile. Further there will be very considerable language difficulties in dealing with the local inhabitants. Consequently, practically all Service Forces must be brought in."[66]

Army planners detailed the case against the invasion of Formosa in a memo to their boss:

• When an invasion of Formosa was first proposed, Japanese strength on the island was considered relatively weak. But the projected strength in February/March 1945 was much greater, necessitating a change in the operation from the seizure of the entire island to the seizure of an enclave on the southern part of the island for the establishment of air bases. POA planners did not take into account the need to eventually secure the entire island, a far more costly undertaking than they had initially envisioned.

- No SWPA forces could be released [even if] Luzon were to be bypassed until Japan was defeated. Even so, significant numbers of service forces would still be tied up supporting SWPA forces in the central and southern Philippines, leaving few to support operations on Formosa or an invasion of the Japanese homeland.
- Japanese offensive operations in China had pushed the 14th Air Force out of reach of Formosa, meaning that any air support for CAUSEWAY would have to come from the Navy.
- Unlike on Formosa, on Luzon MacArthur could count on substantial contributions from guerrillas, the Philippine constabulary, and a friendly populace.
- Land-based air support would be more effective in an operation to seize Luzon, given the proximity of bases in the Philippines.
- Luzon could be cleared much more quickly than Formosa, releasing significant forces for the invasion of Kyushu in southern Japan. If Formosa were bypassed, all the forces in the POA would also be available to support future operations against the Japanese homeland.[67]

The last point negated King's argument that Formosa was more important strategically than Luzon. The Strategy and Policy Group in the Operations and Plans Division made the case clearly to their boss, "If we tie up all of our POA [Pacific Ocean Area] forces in Formosa and require the bulk of our SWPA air strength to support them, then the only forces remaining available for a strike against Japan proper are the few combat troops without supporting service troops, remaining uncommitted in the SWPA."[68]

On the other hand, an invasion of Luzon would not require ground forces from Nimitz's command, which would then be immediately available for operations against the Bonins, the Ryukyus, or Japan. Gen. Marshall made use of these arguments in a meeting with the Joint Chiefs on September 5, with the result that "the Navy was thrown into the worst confusion since Pearl Harbor."[69] Arnold did not think an invasion of Formosa was practicable with the available resources and supported the Luzon operation by default. Leahy was also supportive of the Luzon operation for both military and political reasons, leaving King isolated.[70] The Joint Chiefs rejected the proposal to immediately approve the invasion of Formosa, and the matter was returned to the JCS planners for further consideration.

At the same time, the War Department Operations Division pressed for a decision on the invasion of Luzon, writing to Gen. Marshall, "It is important we reach some determination on your question [as to how and when Luzon would be taken], otherwise we may find ourselves in October 1945 with Pacific Ocean Area bogged down in a long land campaign in Formosa, while Southwest Pacific forces are still short of Luzon. Our decisions today ought to be pointing clearly towards an attack on the Japanese homeland in October 1945."[71] For the moment, the Joint Chiefs on September 9 ordered SWPA to invade Leyte on December 20 with support from the Third Fleet, and to prepare bases to support a follow-on operation to invade Formosa on March 1, 1945, or Luzon on February 20, 1945.[72]

Events in the Pacific soon intervened to shape matters. In preparation for the invasions of Peleliu and Angaur in the Palau Islands, and of Morotai, midway between the Vogelkop Peninsula on New Guinea and Mindanao, on September 15, US air and naval forces conducted air and surface attacks on Japanese installations in the Western Pacific. From August 31 to September 2, naval aviation attacked Chichi Jima, Haha Jima, and Iwo Jima, while surface units bombarded Chichi Jima. The task force followed up these raids on September 7–8 by striking Yap. Another task force struck the Palau Islands on September 6–8. Beginning on September 9, Admiral William "Bull" Halsey's Third Fleet conducted airstrikes against Japanese installations in the Southern Philippines to destroy Japanese aircraft that might interfere with either the Peleliu assault or the simultaneous invasion of Morotai by MacArthur's forces. Kenney's Far East Air Force joined in the chorus of bombing, striking airfields, shipping, and troop concentrations on Mindanao, Halmahera, and in the Netherlands East Indies.[73] The success of those strikes and the weak Japanese response led Halsey to extend his strikes into the Central Philippines. For three days, Halsey's airmen hammered Japanese air forces in the Visayas, destroying 75 Japanese planes in the air and 123 on the ground; by the end of the month the fast carriers of Task Force 38 had destroyed 893 Japanese planes and sunk 67 ships in the Philippines.[74]

Halsey was convinced by these operations and the report of a downed airman who had been rescued by Filipino guerrillas that Japanese airpower in the Southern and Central Philippines had been eviscerated and Japanese strength on Leyte was negligible. The timeline for the invasion of Leyte could therefore be accelerated. On September 13, he fired off a message to Nimitz:

> Am firmly convinced FULLCRY [invasion of Yap] not now needed to support occupation of Philippines. Arterial not essential to our operations (except Ulithi which easily defended), can not be used by enemy, and does not offer opportunities for destruction of enemy forces commensurate with delay and effort involved in STALEMATE [invasion of Palau Islands]. Believe that Leyte Fleet Base site can be seized immediately

and cheaply without any intermediate operations if initial landings were covered by Task Force 30 until land air base can be installed. Suggest that Task Force 31 could be made available to CINCSOWESPAC if STALEMATE 2 [invasion of Peleliu and Angaur] cancelled.[75]

Nimitz then weighed into the debate with a message to MacArthur, forgoing cancelation of the landings in the Palau Islands (just two days away) but indicating that the cancelation of the invasion of Yap would make available additional forces for the invasion of the Philippines: "If occupation of Yap is eliminated 24th Corps including 7th, 77th, and 96th Divisions plus Corps Troops and Garrison Forces for Yap would be potentially available to exploit favorable developments in the Philippines. Your views on this and Com 3rd Fleet's 130300 requested."[76] The JCS quickly weighed in with its assessment, stating in a message to SWPA, "The Joint Chiefs of Staff are of the opinion that this operation [Leyte] is highly to be desired and would advance the progress of the war in your theater by many months as well as simplifying the arrangements for further operations."[77]

Both messages reached SWPA advanced headquarters in Hollandia, but MacArthur was located with the invasion armada heading for Morotai under radio silence. In his absence, Sutherland, after consulting with Kenney and Chamberlin, responded for his boss [signing the message "MacArthur"] directly to Nimitz, with a copy to the War Department, which forwarded the message to the JCS, then immersed in the Octagon conference in Quebec:

Reports from air and ground sources of carrier air attacks on Philippines have been awaited eagerly with a view to the creation of the opportunity to eliminate one or both operations scheduled prior to King Two [Leyte] and its consequent acceleration. This has been anticipated as stated in Reno [a series of plans directing US forces along the north coast of New Guinea towards the Philippines] and Musketeer [plans for the liberation of the Philippines] and plans have been prepared accordingly. No repeat no information yet available beyond Commander Third Fleet 130230. Report by rescued carrier pilot [who claimed natives on Leyte told him there were no Japanese defenses on the island] incorrect according to mass of current evidence from our local agents. Concur in elimination of Yap attack. Present limited intelligence indicates probability of elimination prior steps and direct movement against Leyte but consider further information of current air action necessary before final decision. First Cavalry and Twenty Fourth Infantry Divisions immediately available with service elements sufficient to support entire operation. Air elements available. Logistic support practicable. If executed will stage personnel only of Twenty Fourth Corps for rest during final preparations.[78]

For two years the assumption had been that operations in the Bismarck Islands and along the coast of New Guinea would lead to an invasion of the Southern Philippines, most likely beginning with the island of Mindanao, where Wendell Fertig had created a large guerrilla force that could aid in its liberation and Kenney's land-based aircraft could support the landings. Now, within the space of a few days, US military leaders were considering bypassing Mindanao and advancing the date of the invasion of Leyte. MacArthur's headquarters was fully aware that the Japanese had a reinforced division and more than 20,000 troops on Leyte, as reported by Ultra intelligence.[79] Ruperto Kangleon's guerrillas had also kept SWPA fully informed of the strength and disposition of Japanese forces on the island.[80]

The JCS, meeting with their British counterparts at the Octagon conference in Quebec, did not take long to come to an agreement. After just ninety minutes of debate, the chiefs agreed to cancel all scheduled operations, with the exception of Morotai (for use as an intermediate base between New Guinea and Mindanao), Peleliu and Angaur (deemed essential for the provision of airfields within bomber range of the Philippines), and Ulithi Atoll (which would be converted into a fleet anchorage), and to advance the date for the invasion of Leyte to October 20.[81] This meant bypassing Mindanao. It also meant that the date for the invasion of Luzon could be advanced, which gave MacArthur leverage over those who still advocated for bypassing Luzon in favor of invading Formosa in February 1945.

The invasion of Peleliu and Angaur by the 1st Marine Division and the 81st Infantry Division ("Wildcats," commanded by Maj. Gen. Paul J. Mueller) proved costly, as the Japanese had fortified themselves into the volcanic interior of the island and made US forces pay a steep price in blood for their elimination.[82] Guided by Ultra intelligence that indicated Morotai was lightly held, MacArthur had chosen his objective more carefully. XI Corps, consisting of the 31st Infantry Division ("Dixie Division," commanded by Maj. Gen. Clarence A. Martin) and the 126th Regimental Combat Team of the 32nd Infantry Division, invaded Morotai on September 15, observed by MacArthur aboard the cruiser *Nashville.* The 31st Infantry Division rapidly cleared the island of its 400 defenders, and engineers opened 2 airfields for fighter, bomber, and reconnaissance aircraft.[83] The battle against the environment also continued: To reduce the presence of mites (which carried scrub typhus) on the island, aircraft sprayed areas to be occupied with dichloro-diphenyl-trichloroethane (DDT) as the invasion forces reached shore.[84] SWPA officially terminated the operation on October 4.[85] MacArthur and his forces now possessed an air base within 200 miles of Mindanao, which, until Halsey's raid, had been the next planned objective. Elements of the 81st Infantry Division occupied Ulithi Atoll without opposition on September 23, and US Navy Seabees[86] converted it into the largest fleet anchorage in the Western Pacific, eclipsing in importance Seeadler Harbor in the Admiralty Islands.

With the decision to advance the invasion of Leyte confirmed, SWPA and its subordinate headquarters went into a planning frenzy. "The clans were gathering in Hollandia," wrote Lt. Gen. Eichelberger, "a sure sign always that a major campaign is ahead."[87] Significantly, the invasion fleet would advance beyond the range of ground-based air cover, as MacArthur's forces had done just once before – at Hollandia the previous April. Besides the obvious operational consequences, the acceleration of the timeline for

4.2: Rear Adm. Daniel E. Barbey, Commander Amphibious Force, Seventh Fleet (left), and Gen. Douglas MacArthur, Commander-in-Chief, Southwest Pacific Area (center), inspect the invasion beaches on Morotai Island, September 15, 1944. Barbey created the amphibious navy that carried MacArthur's forces from Australia to the Philippines.
(Credit: US Navy Photograph)

the invasion of Leyte had significant logistical impacts and affected the availability of engineer units to support base and airfield construction. Ground combat units would have to depend on carrier-based air support until engineers could construct airfields ashore, as Leyte was 800 miles away from the nearest fighter base, 1,000 miles away from established bomber bases, and 1,600 miles distant from the SWPA supply base at Hollandia.[88] Given the lead time for shipment of supplies and equipment from the United States, SWPA would have to make do with matériel on hand or do without. The official engineer historian recorded, "It was impossible in the curtailed preparatory period with the limited shipping available to overcome existing shortages of such vital items as landing mat, bitumen, and heavy timbers, nor could adequate bridging equipment for an extensive overland operation of the type anticipated at Leyte be moved forward in time."[89]

The substitution of XXIV Corps (assigned to the canceled Yap operation) for XIV Corps (still fighting on Bougainville) had second- and third-order effects on the Leyte operation. XXIV Corps lacked engineer and bridging units, since it did not see them as essential to the invasion of Yap. The force allocation had included only a single Seabee battalion in the initial lift; the corps was also deficient in combat engineers, bridging, construction material, and transportation – assets that would prove crucial on Leyte. Furthermore, XXIV Corps' loadings exceeded by twenty-three the number of LSTs originally allocated to XIV Corps; the result was a forced reduction "by approximately 50 percent the number of engineer units planned for the first 4 critical days on Leyte."[90] It would take more than three weeks to turn around the transport shipping and bring additional engineer units to Leyte.

Maps would also prove to be an issue. There was not enough time available to photograph Leyte and produce military maps for use by the invasion forces, as the island was beyond the range of land-based aircraft. Halsey's forces took some photos of the island during their strikes, and another four dozen photographic missions were conducted by the end of the month. The effort was insufficient; topographical engineers had to rely in many cases on pre-war maps, whose accuracy left much to be desired.[91] The impact on combat units, particularly those engaged in fire support operations, would be palpable.

Given the manifest success of naval air strikes in the Philippines and intelligence indicating a reduced Japanese air presence in the islands, MacArthur recommended moving directly on Luzon after the Leyte campaign, with a target date for the invasion of December 20, 1944, with an interim invasion of Mindoro to establish air bases in support of operations on Luzon. The assault troops would number 148,000 personnel and the invasion flotilla would carry 207,000 dead-weight tons of cargo. This operation required naval support from Nimitz's command and would therefore be hotly debated in the days to come. MacArthur concluded:

> It is anticipated that the central Luzon Plain can be cleared and Manila occupied by February. This will permit of the launching of contemplated operations to the northward on the schedule now projected with the great advantage of Luzon bases and land based air support. The Formosa operation will then be unnecessary and, particularly with a prior attack in Bonin Islands Group, a direct move may be made on Kyushu. Southwest Pacific Forces meanwhile will complete liberation of Philippine Islands, block South China Sea and proceed to the reconquest of Borneo and Netherlands East Indies by attack from Philippine Islands and western New Guinea Island.[92]

On the same day as this message arrived, Gen. George C. Marshall finally came around to the view that an invasion of Luzon should precede a campaign against Formosa. The US Army chief of staff initially conveyed to Maj. Gen. Marshall that his preference was to conduct operations in the sequence Aparri–Formosa–Lingayen Gulf. Maj. Gen. Marshall replied that Formosa was impracticable for logistical reasons, but SWPA could execute an invasion of Lingayen Gulf on the accelerated timeline laid out by MacArthur. Maj. Gen. Marshall then conferred with Operations Division Chief Lt. Gen. Thomas T. Handy, who drafted a memorandum supporting the sequence Lingayen Gulf–Formosa, with Aparri left open for discussion. The chief of staff accepted this memo and directed that it be sent to Admiral King under his signature.[93]

The JCS met in closed session on September 26 to discuss the issue, but the meeting ended without resolution. The Navy objected to tying the Third Fleet down for six weeks to cover the landing beaches at Lingayen Gulf against Japanese air attacks launched from Formosa, a task they believed was necessary to ensure the success of the Luzon invasion. Maj. Gen. Marshall reported to MacArthur that "one of the planners has told me that this is the second worse [sic] battle here in the course of the war."[94]

There were logistical issues associated with the Formosa operation that made an invasion of the island problematic, but MacArthur wasn't about to take any chances. He fired off a note to the chief of staff on September 28 stating his case. MacArthur noted that the Navy would be just as, if not more, vulnerable off the coast of Formosa as it would be off the coast of Luzon, that the Luzon operation would have the advantage of support from land-based airpower based on Mindoro, and that the escort carriers of the Seventh Fleet could protect a beachhead at Lingayen Gulf, leaving the fleet carriers of the Third Fleet free to pursue other missions, provided they were available to halt any sortie by the IJN towards the Philippines.

> It is difficult for me to understand the soundness of the Navy's position on this matter. Should Luzon be bypassed and the Pacific Ocean Areas make an attack on Formosa, the fleet would be tied down to that operation for a period considerably longer than the Luzon attack. Fundamentally the Pacific War can be won expeditiously only by focusing of all available forces on certain critical strategic objectives in succession. Whatever forces are necessary to gain this end must wholeheartedly be utilized to their full capability. Under no circumstances should diversity of objectives be permitted to weaken the assault on each successive strategic locality. The capture of Luzon will provide a location from which the Japanese Empire can be separated from its source of raw materials to the south and will permit of the launching of a more effective attack deeper into hostile territory than now is contemplated by the Navy.[95]

Of course, MacArthur and the JCS did not yet know of the menace of Japanese kamikaze attacks, which would have subjected an invasion fleet off the coast of Formosa to an incessant stream of manned suicide bombers.

What the JCS did know by this point in time was the disaster that had unfolded over the course of the summer on the Asian mainland, where a major Japanese offensive had overrun much of southern China. Phase 2 of Japanese Operation *Ichi-Go* began on August 29, when nine divisions and an independent brigade from the *11th* and *23rd Armies* attacked south from Heng-yang and north from Canton in an effort to seize Kwangsi Province, which contained a number of airbases at Kweilin and Liuchow that housed units of the Fourteenth Air Force. Resistance on the ground was weak, with command and supply problems impeding the effectiveness of Chinese Nationalist forces.[96] On September 15, General Joseph Stillwell, the commander of US Army forces in China, Burma, and India, and Allied Chief of Staff to Generalissimo Chiang Kai-shek, reported to General Marshall that the "situation [in Kwangsi was] now hopeless . . .. The jig is up in South China. We are getting out of Kweilin now, and will have to get out of Liuchow as soon as the Japs appear there."[97] Stillwell blamed Generalissimo Chiang for the "disaster south of the Yangtze," but at this point it really did not matter who was to blame. With the problems of the Nationalist Army and the logistical impracticality of an air offensive from China now clear, the Asian mainland receded from the calculations of Allied planners, who now explored more viable options to end the war in the Pacific.[98] Since those options no longer depended on a foothold on the China coast, Formosa waned in significance compared with Luzon and Okinawa, as Formosa lacked the anchorages and airfields necessary to sustain the logistical infrastructure required for the stationing of fleets, air forces, and ground divisions. With the Marianas now in American hands, B-29 bombers could operate from Saipan, Tinian, and Guam against the Japanese home islands, and, unlike on Formosa, could do so without threat from Japanese land-based aircraft.[99]

The developments in the Philippines meant that US forces could liberate Luzon on an advanced timeline and still become available for an invasion of Formosa in the spring of 1945, should an operation there be warranted. But the loss of US airfields in China and the withdrawal of Nationalist Chinese troops north of the Yangtze obviated the need to establish a base on the Asian mainland to support them, significantly reducing the importance of Formosa, given that it was less suitable than Luzon as a forward operating base for operations against Japan. King led a last-ditch effort to cancel the Luzon invasion by claiming it would draw too heavily on the fast carrier task forces of the Pacific Fleet, to no avail. Maj. Gen. Marshall warned MacArthur of King's objection to the extended use of the Navy's fleet carriers off the coast of Luzon, along with several thoughts on how to address the concern.[100] MacArthur countered that, after the initial invasion at Lingayen Gulf, the fast carriers would be released, while a group of escort carriers provided ground support for forces ashore until engineers could construct landing fields near the beachhead. This argument effectively ended the Navy's final attempt to halt the invasion of Luzon in favor of Formosa.[101]

King flew to San Francisco to confer with Nimitz in a three-day conference beginning on September 29. Nimitz, his subordinate commanders, and his planners had come to the conclusion that an invasion of Formosa was impractical without more combat divisions and army service troops, which would not be forthcoming until the war in Europe was decided. Strong Japanese defenses on Formosa would also result in heavy casualties.[102] Instead, they offered a course of action that included invasions of Luzon in December 1944, Iwo Jima in January 1945, and Okinawa in March 1945, operations that could be conducted with forces already in theater. Although the timeline in each case would be delayed by one month, these operations would conclude the war in the Pacific. Army planners recorded that "Admiral King returned from San Francisco this morning with a considerable amount of data. A memorandum is being written to the JCS which will propose the issuance of a directive which will set up operations as follows:

CINCSWPA to occupy Luzon, target date 20 December, with fleet cover and support.

CINCPOA to occupy (a) the Bonins [Iwo Jima], target date 20 January, (b) Ryukyus (probably Okinawa), target date 1 March.

CINCPOA also to make plans and continue preparations for Formosa and Amoy as soon after 1 March as the required resources can be made available, but execution of the operation to depend upon the situation and whether it is necessary to go there at all or not."[103]

The approval of these proposals in a meeting of the JCS on October 3 set the final strategic objectives for the end game in the Pacific War. SWPA would follow the seizure of Leyte with an invasion of Luzon.[104] Gen. George C. Marshall told MacArthur's deputy chief of staff that "this had been the toughest JCS battle" during the war.[105] It had been decided not in a meeting with the president and his theater commanders in Hawai'i, but in the staff trenches in the Pentagon. Its outcome meant that MacArthur would get his wish after all – to return to the Philippines, avenge the defeat of 1942, and liberate the Filipino people and American and other captives from Japanese occupation. Redemption was at hand.

5

LEYTE GULF

The failure of the enemy main body and encircling light forces to completely wipe out all vessels of this Task Unit can be attributed to our successful smoke screen, our torpedo counter-attack, continuous harassment of enemy by bomb, torpedo, and strafing air attacks, timely maneuvers, and the definite partiality of Almighty God.[1]

Rear Adm. Clifton Sprague

The morning of A-Day, October 20, 1944, dawned clear with calm seas as the largest armada in the Pacific War to date entered Leyte Gulf and approached the eastern shore of the island to execute Operation King II. MacArthur had departed the Philippines two-and-a-half years earlier on 4 PT boats and 2 B-17 bombers; he would now return supported by more than 700 ships and not 1 but 2 air forces. Aboard the transports were 174,000 troops of the Sixth US Army commanded by Lt. Gen. Walter Krueger, composed of the X and XXIV Corps, under the command of Maj. Gen. Franklin Sibert and Maj. Gen. John Hodge, respectively. Krueger was nearing mandatory retirement age, a fact noted by the War Department in a cable to General MacArthur on October 10 as the massive invasion convoy was marshalling at Hollandia in New Guinea: "Do you desire that he be continued on active duty?" Given Krueger's importance to the command of the forthcoming invasion of the Philippines, General Douglas MacArthur's answer to this bureaucratic query was an emphatic "yes."[2] It had been more than two-and-a-half years since MacArthur had last trod the soil of the Philippines, and he was anxious to return to liberate a land and people he had grown to know and admire. The invasion convoys were the products of the arsenal of democracy that had grown exponentially since the summer of 1940, when the fall of France to the Nazi juggernaut had finally awakened Americans out of their isolationist slumber. MacArthur spent the journey aboard the light cruiser *Nashville*, waiting restlessly for the hour of his return.

174

Among the vessels approaching Leyte that morning were 6 old (World War I-era) battleships, 5 heavy and 6 light cruisers, 18 escort carriers, 86 destroyers, 25 destroyer escorts, 11 frigates, 420 transport and amphibious assault vessels, and 135 patrol, mine-sweeping, hydrographic, and supply ships, originating from 9 different bases throughout the Pacific.[3] Covering the invasion force was Admiral William "Bull" Halsey's Third Fleet, consisting of four task groups that included nine fleet carriers, eight light carriers, six fast battleships, five heavy cruisers, nine light cruisers, and fifty-nine destroyers.[4] The combined armada was a colorful array, with warships originating from the Central Pacific painted blue–gray and their landing craft dazzled coral and black, while LCI and LSM landing craft emanating from the Southwest Pacific were painted black and green.[5] In addition, twenty-five submarines prowled the waters around the Philippines, searching for a Japanese fleet that might interfere with the invasion.[6]

Third Fleet strikes in the previous month had largely neutralized Japanese land-based airpower in the Central and Southern Philippines. On October 10, carrier-based aircraft struck airfields in Okinawa, followed by a strike on a Japanese airfield near Aparri in northern Luzon. During October 12–14, land-based and naval air strikes from the fast carriers of Task Force 38 destroyed more than 500 planes on the ground or in the air over Formosa, including a large part of what remained of Japanese carrier-based aircraft. Japanese naval airpower had already been severely diminished four months earlier at the Battle of the Philippine Sea, or, as US naval aviators called it, the "Great Marianas Turkey Shoot." The Japanese were reconstituting their naval aviation in home waters when Halsey's fleet attacked Formosa. The *Combined Fleet* unwisely threw its young pilots into the fight before they had completed their training.[7] After these raids, the Japanese government erroneously claimed (and actually believed) that its airmen had sunk or heavily damaged fifty-seven warships (the actual damage amounted to torpedo hits on the cruisers USS *Canberra* and USS *Houston*, both of which remained afloat and were towed to Ulithi Atoll for repair), including nineteen of the Pacific fleet's carriers (none of which had been hit), to which Admiral Halsey responded in a wryly humorous message to Nimitz, "The Third Fleet's sunken and damaged ships have been salvaged and are retiring at high speed toward the enemy."[8]

Ultra dutifully informed MacArthur's headquarters of the beating the Japanese had taken. A special intelligence bulletin issued just four days prior to the invasion of Leyte stated, "With a rptd [reported] box score of more than 1500 enemy a/c destroyed within the past 30 days by preparatory carrier action alone, the conclusion is that the enemy may not be able to contest effectively from the air our initial opns [operations] against the P.I. [Philippine Islands]."[9] After retiring from the Formosa area, Halsey's carriers targeted Japanese airfields around Manila and in northern Luzon, while the Fifth Air Force pounded targets on Mindanao.[10] Even after the Japanese flew in reinforcements from Formosa, they had fewer than 400 aircraft in the Philippines as the decisive air and naval battle for Leyte began.[11] The evisceration of Japanese land-based and naval airpower over Formosa and on Mindanao limited its role in the upcoming battle for Leyte. Nevertheless, the Imperial Japanese Fleet, still a potent surface navy despite its lack of carrier airpower, lurked somewhere in the South China Sea.

Like MacArthur, the Japanese also foresaw the Philippines as the site of the next decisive battle in the Pacific War. They understood that the loss of the Philippines would result in the severing of the Empire's logistical lifeline to the resource-rich Dutch East Indies and with it the end of Japan's supply of oil to fuel its industry and military forces.[12] According to the Japanese *Shō-Go* (Victory) plan issued on July 24, 1944, an American landing in the Philippines would trigger a decisive naval battle for sea control, without which Japanese forces would be unable to prevent an American buildup and eventual conquest of the islands.[13] By this point in the Pacific War, Japanese naval and land-based airpower had suffered such severe attrition that it could hardly be relied upon to deliver a decisive blow. Japanese commanders therefore counted on the strong surface units of the Imperial Japanese Navy to destroy the American fleet, mainly because they had no other options.[14]

How to come to grips with US naval forces without suffering crippling losses from air attack was the biggest question mark for the operational planners. Japanese commanders tried to solve this dilemma by increasing the number of antiaircraft guns on their ships, and by careful planning that included three fleet war games focused on the execution of *Shō-1* (the defense of the Philippines) in the six weeks leading up to the American invasion of Leyte.[15] Japanese admirals were under no illusions as to their prospects for success. According to Rear Admiral Tomiji Koyanagi, chief of staff to *Second Fleet* commander Vice Admiral Takeo Kurita, "It also appeared that our next sea battle was likely to be our last."[16]

According to Vice Adm. Tasuku Nakazawa, Chief of the Operations Section, *Imperial General HQ*, after the fall of Saipan, "the Philippines [were] the last line of national defense."[17] As soon as the Mariana Islands were lost, Japanese military leaders began to reinforce their forces in the Philippines, shifting air and ground divisions from Manchuria, Formosa, and Southeast

Asia to the archipelago. Ultra intelligence faithfully recorded and reported these movements to American commanders, which enabled naval commanders to vector submarines to intercept the troop convoys bound for the Philippines.[18] US submarines played havoc with Japanese efforts to reinforce the Philippines, halving the number of Japanese merchant ships successfully arriving in the islands.[19] As a result, much of the material required for a successful defense lay on the bottom of the South China Sea.[20]

Because of the number of islands in the Philippine archipelago, defense of the area would require substantial naval and air power, but US superiority in these realms ensured that the Japanese would be unable to stop an invasion short of the beaches. The *14th Area Army* defending the Philippines was hardly in a condition to successfully defend the islands against an American invasion. The army could count on at most 10 divisions and 5 independent brigades in its order of battle: 80,000 troops on Luzon, 50,000 on Mindanao, and 50,000 in the Visayan Islands.[21] Army leaders had difficulties assembling their scattered forces for defense of key areas, since those forces had been dispersed to secure the Philippines against the Filipino resistance.[22] "Staff planning at the newly activated army headquarters was encumbered by this additional requirement, defense plans for the Philippines were retarded, training programs could not be carried out, and the combat efficiency of our troops suffered," recalled Maj. Gen. Yoshiharu Tomochika, chief of staff of the *35th Army* defending the Southern Philippines. "By the time the Americans assaulted Leyte, very little effective training of troops had been accomplished, and none of the specialized training for jungle warfare had been given to the troops or their commanders."[23] Troops that had been used to suppress guerrillas now also had to be converted to more conventional combat roles, a difficult psychological transition for what had been an army used to policing functions.[24]

In the weeks leading up to the American invasion, the Japanese forces underwent a change of command from Lt. Gen. Shigenori Kuroda to Gen. Tomoyuki Yamashita, the conqueror of Malaya and Singapore and one of the most skillful tacticians in the Imperial Japanese Army. Yamashita possessed a brilliant military mind, which made him a political threat to Prime Minister Hideki Tojo, who relegated the "Tiger of Malaya" to a training command in Manchuria, a post Yamashita held for more than two years.[25] Tojo's ousting after the fall of the Mariana Islands resulted in the resurrection of Yamashita's fortunes.[26] He was a gifted commander, courageous and selfless, and admired by the soldiers who served under him. He took command in the Philippines on October 9, less than two weeks prior to the American invasion. He was plagued with inadequate resources and an inexperienced staff unfamiliar with the Philippines. According to the official US Army historian, "The state of affairs was well exemplified by a remark of his new chief of staff, Lt. Gen. Akira Mutō, who arrived in the Philippines on 20 October from Sumatra, where he had been in command of the *2nd Imperial Guards Division*. Told of the landings on Leyte that morning, Mutō is reputed to have replied, 'Very interesting, but where is Leyte?'"[27]

The *35th Army* (*16th, 30th, 100th,* and *102nd Divisions*), under the command of Lt. Gen. Sosaku Suzuki, defended the Visayan islands and Mindanao. Suzuki ordered his subordinates to put covering screens of troops on likely invasion beaches, but largely adhered to the instructions of *Imperial General HQ* to fight the decisive battle in depth rather than risk major losses to air and naval bombardment on the shoreline.[28] He began reinforcing Leyte in the spring of 1944 as the anticipated invasion neared. The movement of the *16th Division* under the command of Lt. Gen. Shiro Makino to Leyte along with some naval troops increased Japanese strength on the island from 14,000 to 22,000 troops.[29] Makino had his troops prepare three defensive lines in depth across Leyte, running from north to south, with significant troop concentrations in the Leyte Valley on the eastern side of the island, although the fortifications were incomplete by the time of the American invasion in October.[30]

The false reports of success against American carriers near Formosa significantly affected Japanese strategy. Maj. Gen. Tomochika recalled, "On the night of 16 October, we celebrated the 'Glorious Victory of Taiwan.'"[31] Upon assuming command, Gen. Yamashita had issued orders to delay the Americans in the Visayas and Mindanao and fight the decisive battle on Luzon.[32] But now Field Marshal Count Hisaichi Terauchi, commander of the *Southern Expeditionary Army Group* based in Saigon, had second thoughts. Terauchi believed that, if US forces were able to construct air bases on Leyte, the *14th Area Army* would not be able to successfully defend Luzon. So, instead of fighting the decisive battle on Luzon, he decided to fight it on Leyte. Lt. Gen. Seizō Arisue, Chief of the Second Department, Imperial Japanese General Staff, remarked that "General Yamashita was a bit skeptical of it at first," which was an understatement.[33]

The decision by the JCS in the middle of September to advance the date of the Leyte invasion to October 20 had given MacArthur, Kenney, Krueger, Kinkaid, Halsey, and their staffs only a few precious days to finalize plans for the operation. Commanders and their staffs converged on SWPA headquarters at Hollandia for coordination and planning sessions. Plans for the invasion of the Philippines (Operation Musketeer) were codenamed King (Mindanao and Leyte), Love (Aparri and Mindoro), Mike (Lingayen Gulf, Dingalan Bay, Batangas, Zambales, and Nasugbu Bay), and Victor (Visayan Islands); the focus now was on King II, the invasion of Leyte. Combat vessels and transports used in the invasions of Morotai and Peleliu were rapidly recovered to Manus and Hollandia, fueled and provisioned, and readied for the Leyte landings. Proximity of commanders and staffs and well understood standard operating procedures made possible the rapid adjustments necessary to make Operation King II a success.[34]

Leyte, 115 miles long and with an average width of 40 miles, is bisected by a steep mountain range on its north–south axis, flanked by the extensive Leyte Valley in the east and the smaller Ormoc Valley in the west. Leyte Valley consisted largely of rice paddies and coconut groves, with native villages positioned on drained areas. Vehicles were road-bound, and swamps limited construction of airfields and logistical bases, much to the future surprise of American airmen and the dismay of engineers, who had planned to build a network of airbases in the valley. Although Leyte had a population approaching a million people, they were spread across the habitable portions of the island. Tacloban, positioned on the northeastern shore fronting San Pedro Bay, was at 9,000 people the largest city and port, although Ormoc on the west coast was also a serviceable port. The heavily vegetated terrain, with few serviceable roads running east–west and none of them capable of supporting sustained heavy military traffic without significant engineering effort, posed an enormous logistics and communications problem.

Sixth Army G-2 correctly calculated Japanese army strength on Leyte at 21,700 troops. The bulk of the combat forces came from the *16th Division*, one of the formations that had conquered Bataan in 1942. The Japanese, the G-2 reasoned, would commit one division on D-Day and another assembled from tactical reserves within seventy-two hours, supported by a limited amount of artillery. Within ten days the Japanese could send up to eight regiments from neighboring islands to Leyte. The G-2 also expected the Japanese navy to play a minimal role in the upcoming invasion. The G-2 concluded that the Japanese would focus their defensive efforts on the town of Tacloban and its nearby port and airfield. The Japanese would hold mobile reserves in the Leyte Valley, ready to be rushed to the decisive battle on the east coast of the island. The port of Ormoc on the west coast, the avenue through which Japanese reinforcements would pour, would be heavily defended, as would the town of Carigara, which protected the northern end of Leyte Valley.[35] The G-2's estimate seemed reasonable, but, except for the initial strength of Japanese forces, it was wrong in most details.

Ten days before the invasion, the redoubtable Cdr. Chick Parsons and Lt. Col. Frank Rawolle traveled to Leyte via a stealthy PBY Catalina "Black Cat" flying boat, which landed them in darkness in Leyte Gulf near Tacloban, the only town of any size on the east coast of the island. The two officers established a hideout in the jungle and then went about their mission of reconnoitering Tacloban, the landing beaches, and the key terrain overlooking them, and contacting Col. Ruperto Kangleon and his guerrillas. Their report, radioed back to SWPA headquarters, noted the absence of Japanese forces or fortifications in Tacloban, sparing the city from pre-invasion bombardment and saving the lives of untold numbers of Filipinos.[36]

Beginning on October 11, the various US Navy task groups began to weigh anchor. The convoy from Hollandia merged with another from the Admiralty Islands, forming the largest naval attack force to date in the Pacific, and one that was larger than the convoys participating in Operation Torch, the Allied invasion of North Africa in November 1942. A typhoon rolled through the invasion area on October 16–17 and gave commanders some pause, but it did not affect operations.

MacArthur was more concerned about the Japanese fleet, which he rightly deemed the greatest threat to the invasion. Assessing Ultra intelligence compiled by the Central Bureau, on October 15 MacArthur wired Nimitz:

> Suggest consideration be given Second Striking Force referred in CINC Combined Fleet orders at 141808 [October 14, 18:08] may still refer bulk of surface strength estimated general Singapore South China Sea area recently under Commander Second Fleet. Total force latter area estimated to include 6 BB 12 CA 4 CL 20 DD representing bulk of enemy's available surface strength excluding carriers. As enemy believes Blue striking fleet [i.e., Third Fleet] including remaining carriers retreating and intends attempting annihilation sortie suggest reasonable to assume South China Sea force will be involved in some way possibly in form of sortie through San Bernardino or Surigao Straits. Orange [i.e., Japanese] recce aircraft over Humboldt Bay early afternoon October 15 reported greatly diminished shipping since last recce Oct 9 suggesting enemy aware departure Blue [i.e., US] assault force. Most dangerous threat to current operation is enemy fleet on our open left flank. If Third Fleet takes position from which it cannot intercept enemy main fleet the result might be disastrous.[37]

The analysis was more prescient than anyone could have guessed at the time. Yet Nimitz had access to Ultra intelligence as well, and intercepts told him the Japanese were moving oil tankers to support the surface fleet based in Lingga Roads on the east coast of Sumatra.[38] If nothing else, American commanders were fairly certain a naval engagement was coming, but they did not know where.

Given the importance of Ultra intelligence, it is surprising how little thought was put into ensuring its providers had space in the invasion convoy. The deputy special security officer for MacArthur's command group, Major John H. Gunn, was left to fend for himself in arranging transportation to Leyte. He finally found space aboard a ship in a Sixth Army convoy. "The trip to Leyte was uneventful," Gunn reported,

> I carried no classified material other than a black handbag filled with cryptographic material. This material I kept stored in a locked closet in the ship's captain's cabin. This seemed the most secure procedure aboard a vessel whose Commanding Officer kept 18 quarts of bourbon whiskey in his ship's safe, and kept his top secret battle plans for several operations on top of the desk in his sleeping quarters.[39]

The assault forces headed for Leyte were preceded by troops of the 6th Ranger Battalion, which seized positions on Dinagat, Homonhon, and Suluan islands at the mouth of Leyte Gulf and installed navigation lights to guide the invasion convoy into the area. Navy minesweepers destroyed 227 mines to clear a 6-mile-wide channel leading to the invasion beaches, while underwater demolition teams reconnoitered the beaches and found no obstacles present.[40]

A-Day dawned "with that quiet beauty which marks the tropics at their best. The sky was clear and bright; the sea calm and blue."[41] Another division recorded, "The sea remained smooth and a brilliant sun beat down. The expected air attacks and the customary October bad weather failed to materialize. So far the gods were with us."[42] Aboard the transport USS *John Land* in Leyte Gulf, the last Resident Commissioner of the Philippines, Brig. Gen. Carlos P. Romulo, mused, "Mine were not thoughts of Christian compassion, this morning of October 20, 1944, in Leyte Bay." Nearby on the bridge of the USS *Nashville*, MacArthur sent Romulo a message, "MY HEARTIEST EMBRACE TO YOU, CARLOS. YOU MAY HAVE BEEN THE LAST MAN OUT [of Bataan] BUT YOU ARE NOW AMONG THE FIRST MEN IN."[43]

Beginning at 07:00, the ships of the Seventh Fleet pounded the invasion beaches with neutralization fire, while aircraft from the escort carriers hit targets further inland. Battleships pummeled the shore for two hours, followed by forty-five minutes of fire from cruisers and fifteen minutes of fire from destroyers. The final salvoes came from rocket- and mortar-firing landing craft, which, in the words of US Navy Capt. Raymond Tarbuck, senior naval advisor to GHQ SWPA, launched "thousands of rockets [that] hit the beach with the rumble of an earthquake. It is impossible to distinguish one explosion from another; it is just a roar."[44]

The roar of the guns could be heard for several miles as cordite smoke billowed over the still waters of the Pacific. "Landings are explosive once the shooting begins, and now thousands of guns were throwing their shells with a roar that was incessant and deafening," MacArthur recalled. "Rocket vapor trails crisscrossed the sky and black, ugly, ominous pillars of smoke began to rise. High overhead, swarms of airplanes darted into the maelstrom. And across what would ordinarily have been a glinting, untroubled blue sea, the black dots of the landing craft churned toward the beaches."[45] As the assault waves debarked from their transports and assembled in their landing craft, carrier-based aircraft roared overhead, bombing and strafing the beaches. Aboard the *Nashville*, Capt. Tarbuck recorded the scene: "The flagship slows down; the transports pass ahead toward the beaches. Destroyers criss-cross the bow and six battleships blaze away with turret fire toward the land. There are so many ships that it is impossible to see the southern shoreline."[46] Standing on the bridge of the *Nashville*, MacArthur viewed Tacloban in the distance, his first assignment after graduating from West Point in 1903. "It was a full moment for me," he reflected.[47]

At 09:36, the first wave started the run for shore, flanked and supported by LCI rocket craft and gunboats. The bombardment left the Japanese defenders incapable of organized resistance.[48] Landing craft carrying the assault echelons of four divisions stormed ashore at 10:00, quickly dispatching the few remaining Japanese infantry on the beach. The 1st Cavalry Division (Maj. Gen. Verne Mudge) landed on White Beach furthest north near the city of Tacloban, with the 24th Infantry Division landing on Red Beach, the 96th Infantry Division ("Deadeyes," commanded by Maj. Gen. James Bradley) landing on Orange and Blue Beaches, and the 7th Infantry Division ("Hourglass," commanded by Maj. Gen. Archibald Arnold) landing on Violet and Yellow Beaches to its south. The 21st Infantry Regiment from the 24th Infantry Division landed seventy miles further south to secure the Panaon Strait, which it did without contact with Japanese forces. The landings were in most areas only lightly contested; the greatest impediment to movement off the beaches was swampy terrain, which enveloped men in mud up to their arm pits.[49] According to one division history, the landing "was a far cry from the reception American troops had become used to on the tiny atolls to the east, and wouldn't have lasted a minute in Hollywood."[50] Compared with other large amphibious invasions in World War II, the landing on Leyte was a milk run.

As the Japanese were unable to contest the landing in strength, troops from all the divisions were able to quickly establish beachheads ashore, although, in the case of the 24th Infantry Division, only after some sharp fighting. The division was not without combat experience. It had been created from the disbanding of the square Hawaiian Division three years earlier.[51] Its 19th and 21st Infantry Regiments had participated in the invasion of Hollandia from April to June 1944, while the 34th Infantry had participated in the Biak campaign in May–June 1944 attached to the 41st Infantry Division.

Colonel Aubrey "Red" Newman, commander of the 34th Infantry Regiment, landed on Red Beach in the fifth wave, only to find a company commander dead and his men pinned down. The soldiers were unresponsive, but Newman knew they had to move inland. "So I stood up and moved forward," he recalled. "And my men went with me."[52] By the end of the day, key terrain on Hill 522 in the 24th Infantry Division's zone and Hill 120 in the 96th Infantry Division's zone overlooking the beaches below was in American hands, the former hill held against a robust Japanese counterattack during the night that resulted in 600 Japanese dead.[53] The 7th Cavalry Regiment of the 1st Cavalry Division seized the airfield near Tacloban, and the 184th Infantry Regiment of the 7th Infantry Division reached the airfield near Dulag, which it cleared the next day. These were key objectives to enable the establishment of land-based airpower ashore.

Engineers followed in the wake of the combat troops to immediately begin work on improving the airstrips and other logistical facilities. A sand bar located offshore from Red Beach, which had been identified during terrain studies, caused LSTs to ground hundreds of feet offshore, exposed to mortar and artillery fire. Personnel and equipment had to be transloaded onto smaller craft and ferried ashore. Meanwhile, inadequate control of logistics flowing ashore severely delayed the construction of the Tacloban airfield; since the airdrome was one of the few dry, flat places in the area, it was soon congested with thousands of tons of supplies, ammunition, and equipment. The single narrow access road leading inland was jammed with vehicles, constituting a near-impassable roadblock.[54] Despite the friction caused by inefficient loading of supplies aboard ships, Japanese fire, and undermanned and harried shore parties, by the end of A-Day a total of 107,450 tons of supplies and equipment had been brought ashore.[55] Sixth Army was activated and in the fight.

The special security officer for Sixth Army, Major C. M. Easley, Jr., was also in the fight, but barely. He had been unable to obtain space on the ship carrying Krueger and his staff. Instead, he was put on a ship that unloaded on the beach on the morning of A-Day under heavy artillery fire. Incredibly, for four days, until the Sixth Army headquarters was established ashore, Easley wandered "up and down the beach, obtaining food and shelter from whatever unit was at hand."[56] This oversight perhaps showed his place in Sixth Army's intelligence pecking order. Sixth Army relied more on combat patrols, intelligence gleaned by its own signal radio intelligence companies, and guerrilla reports than on the strategic intelligence supplied by Brisbane or Washington, which often put its intelligence estimates at odds with those emanating from MacArthur's headquarters.

MacArthur wasted no time in going ashore. Three hours after the assault troops had hit the beaches, MacArthur, along with Kenney, Sutherland, SWPA Chief Signal Officer Maj. Gen. Spencer B. Akin, SWPA G-1 Brig. Gen. Charles Stivers, Col. Courtney Whitney, Lt. Col. Roger Egeberg, senior aides Col. Lloyd Lehrbas and Col. Herbert Wheeler, and pilot Maj. "Dusty" Rhoades, boarded *Nashville*'s motor whaler and headed for the transport *John Land*. They picked up Philippine President Sergio Osmeña Sr., who had succeeded Manuel Quezon in office upon the latter's death from tuberculosis two-and-a-half months earlier, along with Philippine Army Chief of Staff Maj. Gen. Basilio Valdes, Resident Commissioner Brig. Gen. Carlos Romulo, and several other officers. The group then headed for Red Beach, site of the heaviest fighting. The boat could not reach dry land due to the gradient of the beach and, after a fruitless attempt to convince the harried beachmaster to find a shallow draft landing craft to bring the party ashore, MacArthur decided to wade through fifty yards of surf to the beach. The unexpected disembarkation into knee-high water undoubtedly irked the general, who had not planned to arrive back on the soil of the Philippines in waterlogged trousers. But the photo of the group wading to shore, featuring a piqued MacArthur looking like a man on a mission, represented his message of "I shall return" better than he could ever have imagined. Destiny rode on his shoulders.[57]

Once ashore, MacArthur spent an hour walking along the front line and talking to the troops in the vicinity before broadcasting a short speech via a mobile broadcasting unit. Occasional sniper fire from Hill 522 still zinged

5.1: Gen. Douglas MacArthur and party wade ashore on Leyte, October 20, 1944. L to R: Philippine President Sergio Osmeña, Lt. Gen. George Kenney (mostly hidden in back), Col. Courtney Whitney, Philippine Army Brig. Gen. Carlos Romulo, Gen. MacArthur, Lt. Gen. Richard Sutherland, CBS Radio correspondent Bill Dunn, and Staff Sergeant Francisco Salveron. (Credit: US Army Signal Corps, photograph by Clifford Bottomley, Australian War Memorial 017738)

through the area. Undeterred, MacArthur stepped up to the microphone to announce his return:

> People of the Philippines: I have returned. By the grace of Almighty God our forces stand again on Philippine soil – soil consecrated in the blood of our two peoples. We have come, dedicated and committed to the task of destroying every vestige of enemy control over your daily lives, and of restoring, upon a foundation of indestructible strength, the liberties of your people.
>
> At my side is your President, Sergio Osmeña, worthy successor of that great patriot, Manuel Quezon, with members of his cabinet. The seat of your government is now therefore firmly re-established on Philippine soil.
>
> The hour of your redemption is here. Your patriots have demonstrated an unswerving and resolute devotion to the principles of freedom that

challenges the best that is written on the pages of human history. I now call upon your supreme effort that the enemy may know from the temper of an aroused and outraged people within that he has a force there to contend with no less violent than is the force committed from without.

Rally to me. Let the indomitable spirit of Bataan and Corregidor lead on. As the lines of battle roll forward to bring you within the zone of operations, rise and strike! For future generations of your sons and daughters, strike! In the name of your sacred dead, strike! Let no heart be faint. Let every arm be steeled. The guidance of Divine God points the way. Follow in His name to the Holy Grail of righteous victory![58]

Although severely criticized by some at the time as an expression of MacArthur's egotism, the words struck a chord among the Filipino people, who believed in MacArthur and his promise to return one day to liberate their homeland. "If he [MacArthur] wasn't always a hero to his own countrymen, he was to the Filipinos," writes MacArthur biographer William Manchester.[59] The speech was, according to Lt. Gen. George Kenney, "an emotional appeal to an emotional people."[60]

After MacArthur spoke, Osmeña and Romulo gave their prepared remarks. Romulo recalled, "We spoke our words of triumph in the rain, while around us lay three thousand of the enemy who had been our torturers on Bataan, their stiffening bodies sinking into the deepening mud."[61] If the number of dead Japanese was an overstatement, the emotion was not.

Osmeña wrote that night to MacArthur, "It was with overpowering emotion that we returned to our shores after more than two and a half years of forced absence, and witnessed the initial blow dealt the enemy by the United States Armed Forces under your command. May I avail myself of this opportunity to express to you the gratitude of the Filipino people for the persistence with which you fought to secure the means to achieve their liberation and for your careful planning and superb leadership which will unquestionably lead us to victory ... We landed together and together we addressed the Filipino people. It was my privilege to urge them again, as I have repeatedly done in the past, to give you and your forces determined and unqualified support."[62] The president made a plea for the restoration of Filipino civil control over areas in which military operations had ceased, a consideration with which MacArthur was in complete agreement. Osmeña then awarded MacArthur the Philippine Medal of Honor.[63] It was the high point in their relationship, for by the end of the war MacArthur and Osmeña would be at odds over the treatment of collaborators, especially Osmeña's political rival, Manuel Roxas.

President Roosevelt was also effusive in his praise of MacArthur and his troops. "The whole American nation today exults at the news that the gallant men under your command have landed on Philippine soil," he wrote. "I know well what this means to you. I know what it cost you to obey my order that you leave Corregidor in February 1942, and proceed to Australia. Ever since then you have planned and worked and fought with whole-souled devotion for the day when you would return with powerful forces to the Philippine Islands. That day has come. You have the nation's gratitude and the nation's prayers for success as you and your men fight your way back to Bataan."[64]

Upon returning to the *Nashville*, MacArthur's party witnessed an aerially delivered torpedo hit the light cruiser *Honolulu*, killing sixty of the crew and causing it to list to port. Kenney confided that night to his diary, "Halsey notified us that two of his fast carrier groups had to go back for bombs [sic – only one had departed] and the other two 'strategically located' to the north of us. Direct support will have to be furnished by the 12 escort carriers. General MacArthur says get Fifth Air Force [commanded since June 1944 by Maj. Gen. Ennis Whitehead] up here as fast as possible, that he will never pull another show without land based air, and if he does even suggest such a thing I am to kick him where it will do some good."[65] The Seventh Fleet's small carriers housed 400 planes, about a third of which could be airborne at any given time. They would have to support troops ashore with close air support while protecting the invasion forces and ships in Leyte Gulf from Japanese air attacks. Kenney was uncomfortable relying on them.[66] He also decided a sailor's life was not for him. "I would cheerfully have traded my nice comfortable quarters and excellent mess on the *Nashville* for a tent under a palm tree ashore and an issue of canned rations," he admitted.[67]

More diplomatically, MacArthur wrote to Halsey, "Basic plan for this operation in which for the first time I have moved beyond my own land-based air cover was predicated upon full support by 3RDFLT. As planned every possible measure is being taken to expedite the installation in this area of land based air forces but pending achievement [of] our mission[,] shipping is subject during this critical period to raiding enemy elements both air and surface . . . . I consider that your mission to cover this operation is essential and paramount."[68] MacArthur also sent word to the Filipino guerrillas to begin direct action against Japanese forces.[69] Kangleon's guerrillas proceeded to destroy key bridges, blow up Japanese ammunition and supply dumps, and ambush Japanese patrols.[70] For the guerrillas, the day of battle had arrived.

The day of battle had arrived too for the Japanese and American navies. The Commander-in-Chief of the *Combined Fleet*, Admiral Soemu Toyoda, issued a warning order to the ships assigned to *Shō-1* on the morning of October 17 after receiving reports of the US invasion armada from an outpost on Suluan Island. The next day, as American planes hammered Luzon and Leyte, *Imperial General HQ* in Tokyo authorized the activation of *Shō-1*.[71]

Imperial General HQ, the *Southern Expeditionary Army Group*, and the *14th Area Army* all agreed that the decision to execute *Shō-1* would result in a decisive battle in the Philippines. "This meant that our ground, air and naval forces would be concentrated in the Philippines to conduct a 'do or die' battle to decide the issue of the war," a *14th Area Army* staff officer confided after the war.[72] The decision as to whether that decisive battle would be fought in Leyte or Luzon rested with the *Southern Expeditionary Army Group*, however. Yamashita believed the decisive battle should be fought on Luzon and tried on several occasions to convince Field Marshal Terauchi, but without success. Thus, when the *Imperial General HQ* activated *Shō-1*, the Japanese were locked into a decisive struggle for Leyte, which would decide the fate of the Philippines and, more broadly, the Japanese empire in Asia. The ensuing transfer of troops to Leyte (and the deployment of additional forces from outside the Philippines to Leyte instead of Luzon) denuded Yamashita of some of his best forces, leaving insufficient troops to defend Luzon, which he deemed far more important and therefore the logical place to fight the decisive battle for the Philippines.

Both the Imperial Japanese Army and the Imperial Japanese Navy were operating under the mistaken assumption that the US fleet carriers had been badly crippled in the battle off Formosa and that Japanese land-based aircraft had been successful in causing further attrition to US naval airpower off the coast of Leyte.[73] Given these assumptions, the desire for a surface naval engagement to destroy the US fleets near Leyte made sense, but they were dead wrong. Japanese air reconnaissance reported at least thirteen carriers approaching Leyte on the evening of October 19, an indication that US carrier strength was not as crippled as the Japanese had believed.[74] No matter – the *Combined Fleet* would seek a decisive sea battle anyway, staking its continued existence on a single throw of the iron dice.

The *Combined Fleet* suffered from two major shortages: oil, without which it could not move, and aircraft and pilots, which severely reduced the effectiveness of the remaining carriers in the mobile fleet. These constraints affected the positioning of the major fleet units, with the carriers of the *Third Fleet* confined to the Inland Sea training new pilots, and the battleships, cruisers, and other vessels of the *Second Fleet* positioned near Singapore to take advantage of nearby fuel sources.[75] Fuel shortages, along with severe pilot losses in the Battle of the Philippine Sea and over Formosa, severely degraded the readiness of Japanese naval air groups. In fact, by early 1944, newly trained Japanese pilots had completed just 275 flight hours, compared with 525 for their American counterparts.[76] "Gone was the brilliantly skillful, highly integrated naval aviation of the early days of the war – the pilots were all dead," writes one historian of the Japanese fleet.[77] Given the emasculation of Japanese naval airpower, the strength of the *Combined Fleet* rested in its powerful surface units. The *Second Fleet* consisted of seven battleships, eleven heavy cruisers, two light cruisers, and nineteen destroyers, including the most powerful battleships in the world, *Yamato* and *Musashi*, each equipped with nine 18.1-inch guns.[78]

Given the limitations of the carrier force, the Japanese would have to rely on land-based airpower to even the odds. Halsey's raids on the Philippines in September and October 1944 had destroyed nearly 900 aircraft, and although the Japanese flew in reinforcements, by the time of the US invasion of Leyte the *Fourth Air Army* and *First Air Fleet* in the Philippines could muster only 220 bombers, 225 fighters, and 67 reconnaissance aircraft.[79] The Japanese would reinforce the Philippines with the *Second Air Fleet* from Formosa, but it too had taken a beating from Halsey's naval air strikes prior to the invasion of Leyte. The *First Air Fleet*, however, had just formed a new *Special Attack Force*, consisting of volunteers willing to deliberately crash their planes into US ships to increase the chances of damaging or sinking them.[80] These human cruise missiles, or "kamikazes" as they would come to be known, would be the most important tactical development coming out of the Philippines campaign, and they would bedevil the US Navy to the end of hostilities.[81] The first test of the group would come a few days later; meanwhile, Japanese air attacks on the Seventh Fleet in Leyte Gulf were continuous and intense. US Navy Lieut. Dwight C. Shepler recorded that "Leyte Gulf was in a virtually continuous condition of 'Flash Red,'" denoting enemy aircraft approaching.[82] A particularly deadly strike on October 21 resulted in a Japanese plane crashing into the bridge of the cruiser *Australia*, killing its captain and nineteen sailors and wounding fifty-three others, including the senior Australian in the invasion fleet, Commodore John A. Collins.[83]

For the upcoming battle Toyoda divided the *Combined Fleet* into three task forces.[84] The carriers and accompanying escort vessels of the *Mobile Force*, under the command of Vice Adm. Jisaburō Ozawa, would form the *Main Body*, designated in US reports of the battle as the northern force.

Since the majority of its aircraft had been sacrificed over Formosa, Ozawa's ships would be used as a decoy to lure the US Third Fleet to the north, away from Leyte Gulf. Ozawa did not need all of his surface vessels to fulfill this role, and so released the *Fifth Fleet* under Vice Adm. Kiyohide Shima to form the *Second Diversionary Striking Force*, with orders to force Surigao Strait and attack Leyte Gulf as part of what US reports would call the southern force. The battleships, cruisers, and destroyers of the *Second Fleet* would form the *First Diversionary Striking Force*, divided between *Force A* and *Force B* (what US reports would term the center force, under the command of Vice Adm. Takeo Kurita) and *Force C* (the main body of the southern force, under the command of Vice Adm. Shōji Nishimura). Because of the lack of carrier-based fighters and the devastation of Japanese land-based aircraft in the Philippines, none of the task forces would have overhead cover; their defense against air attack would rely solely on shipborne antiaircraft guns.[85]

Toyoda alerted these forces on the morning of October 17 as US Army Rangers invaded Suluan Island east of Leyte Gulf. Kurita's fleet made steam toward Brunei just after midnight. On the afternoon of October 18, the *Combined Fleet* received the order from Toyoda to activate *Shō-1*. Three days later, Toyoda designated October 25 as "X-day," when all task forces would converge on Leyte Gulf to destroy the American armada.[86] The plan, which committed virtually the entire operational strength of the *Combined Fleet* in a risky bid for victory, would precipitate the largest naval battle in history.

Kurita's powerful fleet (battleships *Haruna*, *Kongō*, *Musashi*, *Nagato*, and *Yamato*; heavy cruisers *Atago*, *Chikuma*, *Chōkai*, *Haguro*, *Kumano*, *Maya*, *Myōkō*, *Suzuya*, *Takao*, and *Tone*; light cruisers *Noshiro* and *Yahagi*; and fifteen destroyers), would sail through the Sibuyan Sea toward San Bernardino Strait. Nishimura's smaller fleet (the older battleships *Yamashiro* and *Fusō*, heavy cruiser *Mogami*, and four destroyers) would make for Surigao Strait. Shima's force (the heavy cruisers *Nachi* and *Ashigara*, the light cruiser *Abukuma*, and four destroyers) would join Nishimura's group in forcing Surigao Strait, although fleet headquarters in Tokyo made no provision for coordination between the two groups, and indeed Nishimura initially had no idea that Shima's force would support him.[87] These forces were to navigate these passages on the evening of October 24–25, converging on Leyte Gulf in the morning. Meanwhile, Ozawa's carriers (the fleet carrier *Zuikaku*, light carriers *Zuihō*, *Chitose*, and *Chiyoda*, and converted hybrid battleship/carriers *Hyūga* and *Ise*) accompanied by three light cruisers (*Ōyodo*, *Tama*, and *Isuzu*) and eight destroyers would lure the American fleet to the north. Ozawa's carriers carried only 116 aircraft; the pilots were so unskilled that their aircraft were hoisted aboard rather than risk challenging (for inexperienced aviators) landings on the flight decks.[88] Commanders and sailors understood the importance of the moment. It was not an understatement when Kurita declared, "We are about to fight a battle which will decide the fate of the Empire."[89]

Fuel was the crucial resource; without it the Japanese fleets could not move. However, because of the magnificent performance of the US submarine fleet, by October 1944 nearly the entire tanker capacity of Japan rested on the bottom of the Pacific Ocean.[90] Fleet oilers were pressed into service to transport oil from the Dutch East Indies to Japan; therefore, when they were diverted back to their original duties, intelligence professionals could deduce a major operation was in progress. Tracking the movement of the tankers was an intelligence priority, and, thanks to the workings of MacArthur's Central Bureau in Brisbane and naval intelligence in Washington, their movements did not go unnoticed. A special intelligence bulletin on October 20 asserted:

> Cumulative intelligence, derived principally from orders to fleet tankers, strongly intimates that major fleet units are preparing to sortie in both the Empire–Formosa and Singapore–Brunei areas. As neither group as presently constituted is a balanced striking force, it is anticipated that these forces would join before attempting any attack. The safest and most obvious place for such a rendezvous is the western South China Sea. From here an attack against Allied amphibious forces might be launched from the south through the Celebes Sea [judged unlikely due to Allied airpower based in the Palau Islands and on Morotai], through the Central Philippines [also judged unlikely due to lack of maneuver space], or around the north through the Luzon Strait [judged most likely] .... Whether the enemy will attempt to oppose our landing with a fleet attack against a force which includes more capital ships in all classes than he possesses, depends upon his evaluation of the importance of our Philippine encroachment and his future plans for the employment of his rapidly diminishing naval strength.[91]

In addition to Ultra decrypts, US submarines patrolled the approaches to the Philippines, while naval and land-based reconnaissance aircraft swept the area for signs of hostile forces. Given ample warning and reaction time, Halsey's Third and Kinkaid's Seventh Fleet prepared for battle.

Halsey, a pugnacious, fiery commander with an aggressive disposition, was itching for a fight. He had supervised the campaign in the South Pacific from an office in Noumea on New Caledonia while Adm. Raymond A. Spruance and Vice Adm. Marc A. "Pete" Mitscher had commanded the

Pacific fleet's fast carrier task forces, most recently in June 1944 in the Battle of the Philippine Sea, which to American naval aviators became known as the "Great Marianas Turkey Shoot." In that battle, Spruance, a meticulous and respected professional, decided to hold his fleet close to the invasion force to guard the amphibious vessels and transports. He had taken some criticism after the fact for his lack of aggressiveness in assuming risk to destroy the Japanese carriers. "The Bull" would fix that issue in the upcoming fight. Clark G. Reynolds labels Halsey "a meleeist in the tradition of Nelson," but one who "was also sloppy in his procedures."[92]

Halsey had been away from fast carrier operations for two years and should have relied more heavily on Mitscher and his staff. Unfortunately, Halsey largely sidelined the more experienced Mitscher in the coming fight, perhaps because Mitscher had suffered a heart attack a few days before the battle.[93] Halsey would take the fight to the enemy. "If there were any occasion for criticism of the fast carriers in the future," writes C. Vann Woodward, "it would be for some other failing than want of aggressiveness."[94] Halsey's orders gave him some leeway; although tasked to "cover and support" MacArthur's invasion force, Nimitz had added a caveat. "In case opportunity for destruction of major portion of the enemy fleet is offered or can be created, such destruction becomes the primary task."[95] The addendum to the operations order, a Mahanian vision of decisive sea battle that the navy had embraced during the interwar years in War Plan Orange, was music to Halsey's ears.

Shortly after midnight on October 23, the submarine *Darter* made radar contact with Kurita's center force as it headed up the Palawan Passage. Along with the submarine *Dace*, the *Darter* shadowed the two Japanese columns throughout the night. At dawn the two submarines launched a coordinated attack, sinking the *Atago* (Kurita's flagship) and the *Maya* and heavily damaging the *Takao*.[96] *Darter* reported, "Believe force is Jap first team. Dimly seen at dawn. At least three BBs. Three other heavy ships. Four Atagos. 0530H sank one Atago heavy cruiser. Four hits on another Atago who is stopped."[97] Shadowing the *Takao* awaiting an opportunity to finish off the stricken cruiser, the *Darter* grounded on Bombay Shoal. The *Dace* picked up her crew and then attempted to destroy the grounded submarine with its deck gun, but the *Darter* seemed impervious to its shells.[98] The submarines *Angler* and *Guitarro* picked up the tracking of the Japanese task force, now headed for Mindoro Strait.[99] *Takao* limped back to Brunei, accompanied by two destroyers. Without firing a shot, Kurita's force had already lost the services of three heavy cruisers and two destroyers.[100]

5.2: Adm. William F. Halsey on board the USS *New Jersey* (BB-62). Halsey's
aggressive nature took the Third Fleet away from Leyte Gulf in an effort to
destroy the remaining carrier strength of the Imperial Japanese Navy,
leading to a near-fatal encounter off the coast of Samar between Vice Adm.
Takeo Kurita's force of battleships and cruisers and Rear Adm. Clifton
A. "Ziggy" Sprague's group of six escort carriers and its small group of
escorts. (Credit: US Navy Photo)

Divided into four task groups, Halsey's fleet readied for battle. The ships,
pilots, and crews had been ridden hard over the previous ten months, and
although in need of shore leave, were well trained and combat-experienced.
Operations against Formosa and in the Philippines leading up to the invasion
of Leyte had depleted the fleet's ammunition reserves, so Halsey had begun
a rotation of his task groups to Ulithi Atoll, located approximately 1,000 miles
east of Leyte, for provisioning, beginning with Vice Admiral John S. McCain's
Task Group 38.1 with its 3 fleet and 2 light carriers.[101] US forces had seized
Ulithi Atoll without resistance on September 23 and had quickly turned it
into a major supply base, nearly 800 miles closer to Leyte than the existing
base at Seeadler Harbor on Manus Island. Thus, only three task groups with
five fleet and six light carriers were immediately available for action: Task
Group 38.2 at the eastern entrance to the San Bernardino Strait, Task Group
38.4 east of Surigao Strait, and Task Group 38.3 near Polillo Island off the east
coast of Luzon.[102]

Search planes set off at dawn on October 24 to scour the inland seas in the Philippine archipelago for signs of the Japanese fleet. A plane from the *Cabot* spotted Kurita's force south of Mindoro, a report confirmed by another search plane from the *Intrepid*. The report reached Halsey at 08:10. Minutes later, he ordered the three task groups to concentrate on Task Group 38.2, the closest to the sightings, and launch strikes against the Japanese fleet. Halsey also ordered McCain's task group to reverse course and return to take part in the battle.[103]

A search plane from the *Enterprise* spotted Nishimura's *Force C* in the Sulu Sea. The carrier's air group then launched an attack, which scored two hits on the battleship *Fusō* and narrowly missed the *Yamashiro* at the cost of one plane, but did not significantly impede the passage of the task force. Planes from the *Franklin* spotted three destroyers heading from Manila to join Shima's force; subsequent strikes sank the flagship, *Wakaba*. After embarking survivors, the other two destroyers headed back to Manila.[104] Later in the morning, Shima's force was also spotted, but was not brought under attack as Halsey focused his available airpower on Kurita's stronger force heading for San Bernardino Strait. At 09:50 a reconnaissance plane from the Fifth Air Force again spotted Nishimura's task force, now clearly headed for Leyte Gulf via Surigao Strait. Kinkaid readied the Seventh Fleet for night action.[105]

The Japanese *First Air Fleet* now launched a series of ferocious air attacks against Task Group 38.3, which was closest to their airbases on Luzon. The fleet carriers *Lexington* and *Essex* along with the light carriers *Princeton* and *Langley* had already had a busy morning, launching twenty fighters to attack airfields near Manila and keeping a large number of planes aloft searching for the enemy. Shortly after 08:00, as the task force prepared to launch a strike against the ships sighted south of Mindoro, radar picked up a strike package of forty Japanese planes headed for the task group. Two other waves were quickly detected behind the initial group. Together they would overwhelm the dozen fighters on combat air patrol, so the four carriers swiftly launched all remaining fighters – forty-two in all – to intercept the Japanese air flotilla headed their way. The task group then headed for the cover of a nearby rain squall while the air battle raged overhead.[106]

The fighters of Task Group 38.3 tore into the attacking Japanese formations. Altogether they downed 120 Japanese planes, adding to the 47 destroyed by fighters in their strikes on Luzon earlier in the day.[107] Cdr. David McCampbell of the *Essex* air wing alone accounted for nine aircraft, and his wingman, Lt. (j.g.) Roy W. Rushing, downed six more. Running low on fuel after an hour and a half of combat, McCampbell diverted to the *Langley* and landed with just six rounds of ammunition left in his machine guns and out of gas.[108] Most of the remaining Japanese planes, unable to coordinate an attack against the American ships, headed back to their bases on Luzon.

Most – but not all. As the *Princeton* "emerged from the edge of a rain squall to recover fighters in need of fuel and ammunition," a lone Yokosuka D4Y "Judy" dive bomber appeared "out of nowhere" and dove on the ship. It was shot down, but not before dropping a bomb that penetrated to the hangar deck where it exploded, igniting fuel and ammunition in six TBM Avengers that had been prepared for a strike and hurriedly moved below to make room for the fighters.[109] Fires soon spread throughout the ship. The light cruisers *Birmingham* and *Reno* and the destroyers *Irwin* and *Morrison* came alongside to assist in fighting the fires and rescuing seamen. Heavy swells caused the *Princeton* to bump into the *Birmingham*, causing some damage to the cruiser, while the *Morrison* became lodged on the carrier, causing severe damage to the destroyer's superstructure. But the worst was yet to come. With many of its sailors topside fighting the fires and assisting the *Princeton*'s crew, the *Birmingham* was vulnerable. Tragedy struck at 15:22, when an enormous explosion in the aft section of the *Princeton* showered the *Birmingham* with shrapnel and debris, "ranging from tiny shrapnel to large sections of plating and including 40-mm gun barrels, steel helmets, gas masks, tool chests, and beams from the flight deck," causing severe damage and wounding or killing half of the cruiser's crew.[110] The explosion blew off the *Princeton*'s stern; the ship was abandoned and deliberately sunk shortly before 18:00 by torpedoes fired from the *Reno*.

The carnage aboard the *Birmingham* was beyond words. The ship's diary records, "The spectacle which greeted the human eye was horrible to behold. On the main deck, for 140 to 150 frames, dead, dying and wounded, many of them badly and horribly, covered the decks . . . . Blood ran freely down the waterways, and continued to run for some time. Words will never describe the magnificent manner in which the dying and wounded reacted."[111] The junior medical officer, the only trained physician present on the ship, reported, "To describe the scene would take volumes. However, the outstanding feature was the severity of the wounds – case after case of compound fracture, legs and arms missing, abdominal contents protruding through the belly wall, blood gushing from huge wounds, skull laid open, and intermingled with the living many dead . . . . The carnage was indeed horrifying and terrible."[112] The officer's wardroom, which served as an aid station, was soon filled with wounded and dying men. Within an hour, the ship's chaplain was identifying the dead and committing their bodies to the

5.3: USS *Birmingham* (CL-62) fights the fires aboard the USS *Princeton* (CVL-23) after a Japanese bomb hit the carrier during the Battle of Leyte Gulf, October 24, 1944. An explosion in the *Princeton*'s ammunition magazine caused hundreds of fatalities on the cruiser and doomed the carrier, which was sunk by torpedoes fired by the USS *Reno*. (Credit: US Navy Photo)

deep. The final casualty count was 237 killed, 4 missing, 203 seriously wounded, and 215 lightly wounded. The crew of the doomed *Princeton* had suffered heavily as well, with 108 killed and missing and 190 wounded.[113] Along with the damaged destroyers *Morrison, Gatling,* and *Irwin,* the *Birmingham* retired to Ulithi Atoll, transferring its severely wounded to the hospital ship *Samaritan* along the way.

While the drama with the *Princeton* was playing out, two other task groups launched strikes against Kurita's force as it traversed Tablas Strait and the Sibuyan Sea. Planes from the *Intrepid* and *Cabot,* part of Task Group 38.2, attacked in several waves between 10:25 and 12:15. Despite intense antiaircraft fire, made heavier by extra antiaircraft guns installed in the Japanese fleet after the Battle of the Philippine Sea, the lack of protective fighter cover made the Japanese fleet vulnerable to air attack.[114] Pilots scored several torpedo hits and half a dozen hits from 1,000 lb. bombs;

the cruiser *Myōkō* was damaged severely enough to force her retirement to Brunei, while the super-battleship *Musashi* took on water and fell out of formation. An attack from the air groups of the *Essex* and *Lexington*, which had finally been able to launch their planes after fending off the Japanese air attacks, struck Kurita's force at 12:17. The naval airmen focused their efforts on the super-battleships, scoring two hits on the *Yamato* and four bomb and three torpedo hits on the stricken *Musashi*.[115]

Three more strikes would torment Kurita's force before darkness brought a welcome relief to his ships and sailors. Aircraft from the *Essex* and *Lexington* returned for their second attack of the day at 14:26, hitting the *Yamato* and *Nagato*. Aircraft from the *Enterprise* and *Franklin*, part of Task Group 38.4, then made their appearance in the Sibuyan Sea, hammering the *Musashi* with hits from four torpedoes and ten bombs. The final strike of the day was from the *Intrepid* and *Cabot*, which scored nearly a dozen hits, mostly on the stricken *Musashi*. Five hours later the battleship, having sustained by now upwards of 15 torpedo and at least 16 bomb hits, capsized to port and sank; half of her crew of 2,200 sailors perished.[116] According to Rear Adm. Tomiji Koyanagi, Kurita's chief of staff, "We had expected air attacks, but this day's were almost enough to discourage us."[117] Returning to their carriers, American fliers reported they had crippled Kurita's fleet, which was not true.[118] Kurita had lost a battleship and a heavy cruiser, along with two destroyers detailed to rescue survivors, but his force was still largely intact. Besides reporting the operational status of the Japanese task forces in the Sibuyan Sea, the final reports of the day deceptively indicated the Japanese retiring to the west, away from San Bernardino Strait.[119] And, indeed, they were when the reports were rendered, but that state of affairs would not last long, for at 17:15 Kurita once again turned his ships around and headed for San Bernardino Strait. The change of course went unseen by American reconnaissance until later in the evening. As far as Halsey was concerned, his airmen had devastated the Japanese task force in what became known as the Battle of the Sibuyan Sea.

Two hours later the *Combined Fleet* headquarters in Tokyo radioed, "Advance counting on Divine Assistance," by which the fleet commander meant that losses were not to be considered in the tactical decisions to come. After the war he stated, "The reason for my determination in sending that order was the fact that should we lose in the Philippines operations, even though the fleet should be left, the shipping lanes to the south would be completely cut off so that the fleet, if it should come back to Japanese waters, could not obtain its fuel supply. If it should remain in southern waters, it could not receive supplies of ammunition and arms. There would be no sense in saving the fleet at the expense of the loss of the Philippines."[120] The intent of the order may have been clear to Adm. Toyoda in Tokyo, but from subsequent events it is evident that Kurita either misunderstood the order or deliberately disobeyed it. For the moment, he ordered his task force to transit San Bernardino Strait and converge on Leyte Gulf in conjunction with the two task forces under Nishimura and Shima moving that same night through Surigao Strait.

Ozawa's carrier force was meanwhile bearing down on Third Fleet from the north, and he had no reservations about sacrificing his force for the Empire. The naval air arm was in the process of rebuilding after suffering crippling losses in the Battle of the Philippine Sea when leaders of the *Combined Fleet* threw it into the air battle over Formosa just a week prior to the invasion of Leyte. The partially trained Japanese carrier pilots were no match for Halsey's aviators, who tore into their Japanese counterparts with abandon and downed them by the hundreds.[121] Ozawa thus lacked the punch needed to deal a significant blow to the American fleet.

Japanese search planes discovered the location of Task Group 38.3 in late morning, and at 11:45 Ozawa launched every available plane – just forty fighters, twenty-eight dive bombers, six torpedo planes, and two reconnaissance aircraft – to strike the American fleet. These were the last remnants of the once-proud "Sea Eagles" that had launched the attack on Pearl Harbor and had fought a nasty battle of attrition with their US counterparts for the next two-and-a-half years. Unsurprisingly, the strike was ineffective; only four dive bombers were able to make their way to the American fleet and release their bombs, with zero hits scored.[122] Of the seventy-six planes launched, thirty survivors diverted to shore bases and only three returned to land on the carriers.[123]

If Ozawa were to fulfill his task of luring the Americans north, he would have to put his ships at risk. He was willing to do just that. After some vacillation, given the unclear intentions of Kurita's force, shortly before midnight Ozawa ordered his ships south to fulfill their duty. His task force, divided into an advance guard and a main body, consisted of one fleet carrier and three light carriers, two hybrid battleship/carriers, three light cruisers, and ten destroyers, with a remaining air component of just nineteen fighters, six bombers, and four torpedo planes.[124] It didn't stand a chance against the Third Fleet, but Ozawa never thought it could. He and his crews were sailing south to serve as a decoy to give Kurita's fleet a chance to succeed, all in sacrifice to the Emperor. "I had not much confidence in being a lure," Ozawa confided after the war, "but there was no other way than to try."[125]

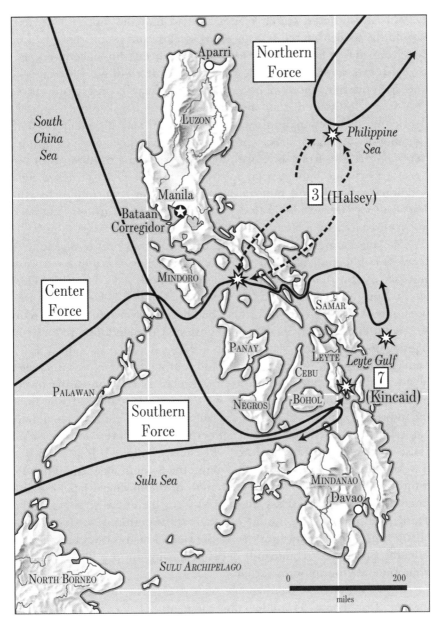

Map 5: Battle of Leyte Gulf, October 23–26, 1944.

Mitscher ordered search planes aloft to find the Japanese carriers. Beginning at 16:40, three transmissions in close succession reported one task group of four battleships or heavy cruisers, five additional cruisers, and six destroyers; another of two destroyers; and a third of two fleet carriers, one light carrier, three light cruisers, one heavy cruiser, and three destroyers.[126] Mitscher's staff aboard the *Lexington* was skeptical, but, after debriefing the reconnaissance pilots, Mitscher and his chief of staff, Commodore Arleigh Burke, concluded that two Japanese task groups were approaching from the north, together consisting of upwards of two fleet carriers, one light carrier, four battleships or heavy cruisers, eight additional cruisers, and nine destroyers.[127] Halsey "concluded that the *Northern Force* [Ozawa's Main Body] was disposed in two groups, estimated to contain a total of at least 17 ships and possibly as many as 24 ships."[128]

The inaccurate reporting of the battleship and cruiser strength of Ozawa's task force, combined with the accurate but misleading report of Kurita's withdrawal to the west, led Halsey to miscalculate. The Third Fleet after-action report stated that "flash reports indicated beyond doubt that the Center Force [Kurita's task force] had been badly mauled with all of its BB [battleships] and most of its CA [cruisers] tremendously reduced in fighting power and life."[129] But this was not the case; other than the *Musashi* (sunk), the *Myōkō* (severely damaged and retiring to Brunei, accompanied by two destroyers), and the victims of the submarine action earlier in the morning (*Atago* and *Maya* sunk, and the *Takao* heavily damaged, now retiring to Brunei), Kurita's task force was still a powerful fighting force of four battleships, six heavy cruisers, two light cruisers, and eleven destroyers. Yet Halsey believed that Kurita's force was damaged enough that, even if it traversed San Bernardino Strait that night, the Seventh Fleet could handle it on its own. Given the reported strength of the northern Japanese task force headed his way, Halsey decided to focus the entire strength of the Third Fleet on it.[130] He would not miss an opportunity to destroy the Japanese carriers, an omission that in the view of many critics had marred Admiral Spruance's command decision-making in the Battle of the Philippine Sea four months earlier.

Halsey activated a contingency plan drafted in the afternoon and formed Task Force 34 under the command of Vice Admiral Willis A. "Ching" Lee, hero of the Naval Battle of Guadalcanal and the premier battleship admiral in the US Navy. Under him on this morning were the Third Fleet's fast battleships – *Washington, Iowa, New Jersey,* and *Alabama* – along with heavy cruisers *Wichita* and *New Orleans,* light cruisers *Vincennes, Miami,* and *Biloxi,* and fourteen destroyers.[131] But Halsey decided to keep this powerful surface force with him to strike at the northern Japanese task force. He contended that leaving Task Force 34 behind to guard San Bernardino Strait would jeopardize his carrier groups if they ended up engaging the reported battleships and cruisers in the northern force, while at the same time subjecting the fast battleships to land-based air attack without benefit of air cover from the carriers. Leaving a carrier task force near San Bernardino Strait to protect the battleships would divide his striking power. Keeping the entire fleet together near San Bernardino Strait, which was perhaps an option the more prudent Spruance would have entertained, would permit Ozawa's force to move south unmolested, but, more importantly in Halsey's thinking, might result in a missed opportunity for the Third Fleet to attack and destroy the remaining carriers of the Imperial Japanese Navy if Ozawa withdrew.[132]

Several hours after the conclusion of the attacks on Kurita's fleet in the Subiyan Sea, night reconnaissance aircraft from the USS *Independence* reported Japanese ships heading east toward San Bernardino Strait and also noted the appearance of navigation lights in the strait, thus indicating their intention to transit during the hours of darkness.[133] Halsey's inexperienced operations staff ignored the information as either unimportant or irrelevant; Halsey himself had retired for the night and was not awakened.[134] Several senior officers in Halsey's fleet, including Task Force 34 commander Vice Admiral Willis A. Lee and Task Group 38.2 commander Rear Adm. Gerald Bogan, had second thoughts about steaming north while leaving San Bernardino Strait unguarded, but Halsey's staff brushed aside their queries to the flagship.[135] Burke and Mitscher's operations officer, Cdr. Jimmy Flatley, urged Mitscher to contact Halsey and recommend leaving Task Force 34 and a carrier task force behind to guard San Bernardino Strait. Mitscher, having been stripped of tactical command by Halsey weeks before, declined, stating, "If he wants my advice he'll ask for it."[136] The comment was a damning indictment of the command climate in the Third Fleet; Halsey and his staff had sucked the initiative out of Halsey's more experienced subordinates.

So, in keeping with his nature, Halsey took the most aggressive course of action and ordered the entire Third Fleet north to deal a death blow to the Japanese carrier task force, leaving not so much as a picket destroyer behind to screen San Bernardino Strait. Doing so kept the fleet together to strike a decisive blow, while mitigating the risk of a surface engagement should the northern task force contain the numbers of battleships and cruisers reported by reconnaissance aircraft the previous day. But the decision rested on an unwarranted assumption. "It was recognized that the Center

Force might sortie and inflict some damage," Halsey later reported, "but its fighting power was considered too seriously impaired to win a decision." In any case, he believed "the Third Fleet forces could return in time to reverse any advantage that the Center Force might gain."[137] Halsey ordered his carrier task groups and Task Force 34 to assemble and proceed north to position themselves for a dawn attack against the Japanese carriers and their accompanying surface forces. Remaining true to his character, Halsey proved in battle to be aggressive, perhaps recklessly so. The stage was set for one of the most dramatic naval engagements in the Pacific War.

Although contact had been lost with the southern task groups of the Japanese fleet during the late afternoon, American commanders knew they had to guard Surigao Strait, the only possible passage these forces could use to reach Leyte Gulf and the American invasion fleet. Kinkaid ordered the commander of Task Group 77.2, Rear Admiral Jesse Oldendorf, to ready his force of six older battleships, three heavy and two light cruisers, and sixteen destroyers for a night engagement. Kinkaid reinforced Oldendorf's command with one heavy and two light cruisers and five destroyers of Task Group 77.3 and the five destroyers of Destroyer Squadron 54.[138] Thirty-nine motor torpedo (PT) boats screened the southern entrance to Surigao Strait as evening descended. Oldendorf's plan was to disrupt the enemy ships with torpedoes fired from PT boats and destroyers, allow any surviving ships to come within 20,000 yards of his battle line, and then destroy them with radar-controlled gunfire from battleships and cruisers steaming in loops on the northern end of the strait. Seventh Fleet's battleships and cruisers had embarked with a large number of high-explosive rounds, many of which they had expended in the shore bombardment of Leyte. The all-important armor-piercing ammunition required to engage Japanese battleships and cruisers was limited, so every shot would have to count.[139]

Nishimura's orders were to transit Surigao Strait in the waning hours of darkness on October 25, emerging into Leyte Gulf shortly before dawn. Kurita's force would move through San Bernardino Strait and then down to Leyte Gulf from the north an hour or two later. At least one historian surmises that Nishimura's force was being used as bait to lure the Seventh Fleet's surface ships south, much as Ozawa's force was being used as a decoy to lure the Third Fleet's carriers and fast battleships north.[140] If so, it was essentially a suicide mission, given the disparity in strength between Nishimura's weak, outdated force and the one he would face. By this point in the war, the superiority of the Imperial Japanese Navy in night fighting was a thing of the past, overcome by US technical superiority in radar tracking and fire control. Or perhaps karma was at work. Nishimura lost his son in a tragic aviation accident only weeks after the outbreak of war, a loss that weighed heavily on the admiral. During the war, Nishimura held a succession of star-crossed commands, yet he continued his upward trajectory despite losses suffered by forces under him. His latest command of pre-World War I (albeit upgraded) dreadnoughts sent on an impossible mission exuded the aura of "a samurai who has found his appropriate place to die."[141] Nishimura nevertheless stoically accepted his fate, signaling in Nelsonian fashion to his ships before the battle, "The fate of the Empire rests on this one battle. Let every man do his utmost."[142]

Kurita's late-afternoon reversal of course had seriously desynchronized the plan to have his and Nishimura's forces debouch into Leyte Gulf within an hour or two of one another. Instead, at 21:45 Kurita radioed that his force would "dash into" Leyte Gulf at 11:00 the next morning, fully five hours behind schedule. Nishimura, perhaps influenced by the superiority of the Japanese navy in night fighting earlier in the war or wary of air attacks against his force in daylight, decided that the best chance for his force to accomplish its mission to penetrate Surigao Strait was to engage in a night battle, and therefore kept on schedule. Inexplicably, he refused to slow down enough to allow Shima's small fleet to join with his ships. Nishimura would attempt to negotiate the strait that night, alone, come what may.[143]

Shortly after 22:30, a section of three PT boats attacked Nishimura's force as it passed between Bohol and Camiguin islands, with all three damaged by Japanese fire before they could get into position to launch their torpedoes.[144] But the battle had been joined, and Nishimura was now committed to moving through Surigao Strait, which his lead elements entered just after 02:00.[145] PT boats, badly outmatched by the Japanese force, launched thirty-four torpedoes without result, at the cost of three dead and twenty wounded.[146] An hour later, all hell broke loose as three groups of American destroyers, operating on the flanks of Surigao Strait, subjected the Japanese force to a torpedo attack of "remarkable precision and effect," just after Nishimura ordered his task force into battle formation.[147] Rear Admiral Joshua W. Cooper, at the time the commander of the USS *Bennion*, recalled, "We were darkened ship, but with the drizzle, rain, proximity of land, and shell fire directly over us from our own ships, and sporadic fire from the Japanese ships, it made a real fireworks."[148] Two torpedoes hit the *Fusō*, fatally crippling the ship, which dropped out of formation and sank sometime around 03:45.[149] Torpedoes also hit and rapidly sank the destroyer *Yamagumo* and fatally crippled the *Michishio* and

Asagumo. At least two and possibly three torpedoes hit the flagship *Yamashiro*, which nevertheless proceeded on course up the strait.[150] Nishimura then broadcast what was to be his last command to his ships, "We have received a torpedo attack. You are to proceed independently and attack all ships."[151]

At 03:51, Oldendorf's cruisers opened fire, followed two minutes later by the older American battleships, all but one of them veterans of the Japanese attack on Pearl Harbor.[152] Restored to fighting trim (and, in the cases of the *California* and *West Virginia*, raised off the harbor bottom), they now had their moment of revenge as for the first and last time in US Navy history they "crossed the T" on an enemy force in combat.[153] The *West Virginia*, *Tennessee*, and *California*, all retrofitted with the latest in fire-control radar, between them fired 225 16-inch and 14-inch rounds.[154] According to Rear Adm. Jesse B. Oldendorf in his flagship *Louisville*, the gunfire "sounded like a train of box cars passing over a high trestle ... cruisers, using flashless powder, were firing so rapidly that the whole sky surrounding them was one incandescent glow."[155]

The Imperial Japanese Navy now paid the price for its technological inferiority, as its ships were unable to respond effectively to the devastatingly accurate American fire, which focused on the battleship *Yamashiro*. A torpedo and gunfire hit the destroyer *Asagumo*, which was still afloat at daybreak when shellfire from several destroyers and the cruisers *Denver* and *Columbia* sent her under. Of Nishimura's task force, only the damaged destroyer *Shigure* and the badly battered *Mogami* escaped. In the confusion of battle, the US destroyer *Albert W. Grant* took twenty hits from both enemy and friendly shellfire, killing thirty-four men and wounding ninety-four others and nearly sinking the ship, which was kept afloat only by heroic measures on the part of the crew. At 04:10, Oldendorf ordered a cease-fire to sort out the friendly fire, which lasted for nine minutes until his ships regained situational awareness and the *Newcomb* arrived to tow the *Grant* to safety.[156] The *Yamashiro*, subjected to terrific punishment from direct fire and hit by several torpedoes, sank around 04:20.[157]

Shima's *Second Diversionary Striking Force* entered Surigao Strait about an hour behind Nishimura's task force. As it did so, a torpedo launched by PT137 hit the light cruiser *Abukuma*, which went down at the bow and fell out of formation. The other ships assumed battle formation and headed into the Strait, unaware of what had befallen Nishimura's task force only a few minutes earlier. At 04:20 Shima's group made radar contact with the American battle line, eight miles distant. Shima ordered his ships to launch torpedoes at the contact, which the two cruisers in the lead did, to no effect.

But, in the chaos of battle, the not quite derelict *Mogami* accidentally sideswiped the heavy cruiser *Nachi*, holing both vessels. Shima had apparently seen enough, or, more precisely, could not locate the American fleet, shielded by a heavy smoke screen, with his inferior radar. His destroyers began a run at the American battle line, but Shima quickly recalled them. He ordered a retirement back down the Strait.[158] Although pestered by PT boats and attacked twice by American aircraft during the course of the morning, all but one of the survivors escaped to fight – and die – another day.[159] The *Mogami* was hit again during the morning airstrikes, finally abandoned, and then deliberately sunk by a torpedo from the Japanese destroyer *Akebono*.[160] The Seventh Fleet had won a decisive victory in the Battle of Surigao Strait.

MacArthur was an unwilling bystander during the fighting. Kinkaid informed MacArthur and Krueger of the coming fight on October 24 and encouraged them to move their staffs ashore. Krueger immediately complied, but MacArthur demurred.[161] He encouraged the captain of the *Nashville* to proceed to the battle area regardless of his presence aboard, which led Kinkaid to order the ship to remain at anchor in Leyte Gulf.[162] Informed on the morning of October 25 by Kinkaid that he required his flagship, the *Nashville*, for battle with a Japanese fleet bearing down on Leyte Gulf, MacArthur replied, "Great, when do we start?" Kinkaid broke the news that MacArthur could not accompany the ship into combat. "I know you are my boss in the overall campaign," he stated, "but the Seventh Fleet is my fleet, and this is its flagship. I have to go and I cannot take the risk of your being aboard, so I shall have to ask you to transfer to another vessel if you will, right now." MacArthur relented, transferring his staff to the *Wasatch* before moving his headquarters ashore to Tacloban the following morning.[163]

As morning on October 25 approached, Ozawa turned his fleet northwards in an attempt to pull the Third Fleet away from Kurita's ships. Halsey took the bait; his task groups had sailed northeast at sixteen knots to put themselves in a position from which to launch a dawn strike against the Japanese carriers. After airstrikes crippled the Japanese ships, the battleships and cruisers of Task Force 34 would move in for the kill.[164] A couple of hours before dawn, the night reconnaissance aircraft that had been tracking Ozawa's fleet developed engine and radar trouble and lost contact. Mitscher nevertheless readied a major strike to take off at dawn, trusting daylight search planes to find the Japanese fleet, and Halsey so informed King and Nimitz.

At 07:35, a fighter vectored into a search pattern northeast of Task Force 38 located Ozawa's force off Cape Engaño on the northern tip of Luzon. A strike group of sixty fighters, sixty-five dive bombers, and fifty-five torpedo planes headed in for the kill. The American airmen were stunned by the sparse fighter cover over the Japanese task force (just nineteen fighters were available, and not all were in the air when the strike hit), mirrored by the lack of planes on the carrier decks. Some believed that the strike had achieved surprise, but others – Halsey included – were simply perplexed by the lack of aircraft. No one suspected the truth, that the Japanese had simply run out of aircraft and the pilots to man them.[165]

American fighters quickly broke up the combat air patrol over the Japanese carriers, and the dive and torpedo bombers went to work. Japanese ships threw up clouds of antiaircraft fire, accounting for ten downed planes by the end of the day, but it was not enough. Bombs and torpedoes tore into the Japanese fleet, sinking the light carrier *Chitose* and damaging several other ships. A second wave struck at 10:00, crippling the light carrier *Chiyoda* and forcing the light cruiser *Tama* to retire. A third strike came in at 13:00 and continued for an hour, sending to the bottom the fleet carrier *Zuikaku*, the last surviving veteran of the raid on Pearl Harbor, as well as the light carrier *Zuihō*. Two additional strikes focused on the converted hybrid battleship/carriers *Hyūga* and *Ise*, but they escaped serious damage. American submarines targeted Ozawa's force as it withdrew to the north, accounting for two more ships. Ozawa had succeeded in luring the Third Fleet north at the cost of all of his carriers, one light cruiser, and two destroyers.[166] But he had accomplished his mission; it remained to be seen whether Kurita could accomplish his.

Kurita's task force – four battleships, six heavy and two light cruisers, and eleven destroyers – passed through San Bernardino Strait just after midnight. It sailed east and then south down the coast of Samar. At 05:32, Kurita received a report that Nishimura's battleships had been sunk and the *Mogami* was seriously damaged, but nothing more. He pressed on. At 06:44, lookouts spotted masts on the horizon; at almost the same time dawn patrol aircraft appeared overhead. Within five minutes Kurita reported seeing on the horizon "a gigantic enemy task force including six or seven carriers accompanied by many cruisers and destroyers." This was a surface admiral's dream. Kurita's force seriously outgunned the American task group ahead, and three hours steaming beyond those ships lay the vulnerable supply ships of the Leyte invasion force.[167] At 06:59, the *Yamato* opened fire at a range of 35,000 yards, and soon dye markers bracketed the

American ships in "vivid splotches of red, yellow, green, and blue."[168] Kurita's plan was "first to cripple the carriers' ability to have planes take off and land, and then to mow down the entire task force."[169] He had enough ships and firepower to do it.

In Leyte Gulf, Kinkaid had been monitoring the action in the Sibuyan Sea and Halsey's maneuvering against the Japanese task force bearing down from the north. During the afternoon of October 24, Kinkaid had intercepted a message from Halsey to the Third Fleet (with information copy to Nimitz) indicating his intention to form Task Force 34, a force of four fast battleships, five cruisers, and fourteen destroyers under the command of Vice Admiral Willis A. "Ching" Lee, but he lacked the critical context that this was a contingency plan, and furthermore Halsey intended for the battleship force to sail with him to the north, leaving San Bernardino Strait unguarded.[170] At 18:24, Halsey notified Nimitz and King, with Kinkaid on the information line, that he was "proceeding north with three groups to attack the enemy carrier forces [northern force] at dawn." Since Kinkaid believed that Task Force 34 constituted a fourth group apart from the three carrier task groups, he assumed the message meant that it would stay behind to guard San Bernardino Strait. It was a deadly and incorrect assumption.[171] In fact, Halsey was sailing north with three task groups – his entire fleet – as Task Force 34 did not come into existence until 02:40 the next morning.[172]

Kinkaid, who had committed his old battleships to battle in Surigao Strait under Oldendorf's command, spent the evening with his staff aboard the *Wasatch*. As dawn crept closer, Kinkaid asked his staff the key question: What might have been overlooked? Capt. Richard H. Cruzen, the operations officer, suggested they confirm that Task Force 34 was in fact guarding San Bernardino Strait.[173] Kinkaid agreed and sent an urgent query to Halsey at 04:12 as to the status of Task Force 34. But MacArthur had prevented the establishment of a direct communications link between Kinkaid (who reported to him) and Halsey (who reported to Nimitz). The result was delay and confusion as messages had to go through a naval communications station on Manus Island in the Admiralties rather than directly between fleets; the resulting flood of message traffic overwhelmed the communications personnel stationed there.[174] A communications backlog delayed the message for two-and-a-half hours. To compound the fog and friction of war, night reconnaissance aircraft launched by the Seventh Fleet were provided with inaccurate coordinates and so missed the passage of Kurita's force through San Bernardino Strait and down the east coast of Samar.[175] Halsey's eventual answer to Kinkaid's query that Task Force 34 was sailing with his carrier task groups caught all the addressees off guard, no one more so than Kinkaid. The message arrived at 07:05, just five minutes after the Japanese armada had opened fire on Kinkaid's escort carrier battle group.[176]

Task Unit 77.4.3 (call sign Taffy 3), commanded by Rear Adm. Clifton A. "Ziggy" Sprague, consisted of six escort carriers (*Fanshaw Bay*, *St. Lo*, *White Plains*, *Kalinin Bay*, *Kitkun Bay*, and *Gambier Bay*), three destroyers (*Hoel*, *Heermann*, and *Johnston*), and four destroyer escorts (*Dennis*, *John C. Butler*, *Raymond*, and *Samuel B. Roberts*). The carriers had just finished launching their morning anti-submarine patrols when Kurita's task force appeared roughly seventeen miles to the north, spotted by a TBM Avenger launched from the escort carrier *St. Lo*. Sprague's first reaction was to chew out the pilot for breaking radio silence. Lookouts soon spotted the pagoda-like masts of Japanese warships on the horizon. As the chilling realization dawned that these were in fact Japanese warships bearing down on his severely undergunned task unit, Sprague immediately ordered all available aircraft launched to attack the Japanese fleet with whatever ordnance was available, while the escorts laid a smoke screen to conceal the carriers from enemy fire. After launching their planes, the carriers retired due east at flank speed into the cover of a nearby rain squall.[177]

Taffy 3's situation was desperate. Kinkaid belatedly recalled some of his surface units (*Tennessee*, *California*, and *Pennsylvania*, along with five cruisers and two destroyer squadrons) from Surigao Strait, but Task Unit 77.4.3 would likely perish before they arrived. He also directed all aircraft not involved in strikes against the Japanese fleet retiring from Surigao Strait to attack the Japanese force descending on Leyte Gulf from the north. Finally, Kinkaid sent an urgent dispatch to Halsey, steaming north on the battleship *New Jersey*, for fast battleships to come to his assistance.[178]

Halsey hedged, for he believed Seventh Fleet had the wherewithal to defend itself. Furthermore, in his mind Third Fleet's mission was offensive, and it was on the verge of a crushing victory over the Japanese northern task force. If he redirected Task Force 34 to the south, at least some of the Japanese ships in the northern group would likely escape to fight another day. Instead, for the moment Halsey kept Task Force 34 steaming north, while directing McCain's Task Group 38.1, now refueled and heading west, to assist Kinkaid's forces in Leyte Gulf.[179] This was another missed opportunity, for, had Halsey turned Task Force 34 around when first informed of the plight of Kinkaid's escort carriers, he could have caught Kurita's fleet as it withdrew back north toward San Bernardino Strait and likely annihilated it.[180]

Completely outgunned by the heavy Japanese ships, Taffy 3 was fighting for its life. Japanese salvoes soon straddled the formation and, in Ziggy Sprague's estimation, "it did not appear that any of our ships could survive another five minutes."[181] If so, no one told Cdr. Ernest E. Evans, commanding the destroyer *Johnston*, whose nickname was "GQ Johnny" because the ship seemed to be continually at general quarters. Nor did he require an order to know what he needed to do. Evans ordered his crew to charge the Japanese formation, putting his ship in harm's way.[182] At 07:10, the *Johnston* opened fire on the Japanese cruiser *Kumano*, hitting it forty times, albeit with 5-inch shells that could not penetrate the ship's armor.[183] Taken under fire in return, the *Johnston* closed the range to 10,000 yards and launched a spread of 10 torpedoes, scoring a hit on the *Kumano* and ripping off its bow.[184] Evans was injured by a Japanese salvo from the *Yamato* that hit the radar mast, damaged the bridge, and turned parts of the ship into twisted wreckage. Lt. Robert C. Hagen, the ship's gunnery officer, recalled, "It was like a puppy being smacked by a truck."[185] But the *Johnston* kept fighting. According to Hagen, Evans had "two fingers blown off, an unknown number of shrapnel holes in his back and superficial wounds about his face and neck, all of which were drawing considerable blood. Despite these things the captain fought that ship as no other man has ever fought a ship."[186]

At 07:16, Sprague ordered his destroyers and destroyer escorts to launch a torpedo attack against the closing Japanese fleet. The *Hoel* and *Heermann*, along with the *Samuel B. Roberts*, their severely outgunned 5-inch guns blazing, charged Kurita's ships. Amazingly, Evans brought the damaged *Johnston* around to provide gunfire support to their torpedo attack. The remaining destroyer escorts followed ten minutes behind. "It was as if a bantamweight were put in the ring with a ham-fisted heavy," wrote several officers who worked on battle reports for the US Navy after the war. "For destroyers with their five-inch guns to take on the Japanese heavies was plucky enough, but for DE's with only two 5-inchers – well, it was unbelievable."[187]

Edward J. Huxtable, the commander of a composite air squadron, had taken off in an unloaded TBM Avenger and made several dummy bombing runs over the line of Japanese cruisers to deflect their attention from the vulnerable carriers. He watched the outgunned escorts charge the Japanese fleet. "The destroyers were taking a terrible beating, and some were afire. They were magnificent in their actions from the first attack all through the battle .... I really felt for them when I saw them turn to go into their first attack. Here were six destroyers and destroyer-escorts making a run on the mightiest main battleline of the Jap fleet."[188] Guns and torpedoes scored numerous hits on the enemy and disrupted the Japanese formation, but the escorts paid a stiff price for their bravery: over the course of the morning Japanese gunfire sank the *Hoel, Johnston,* and *Samuel B. Roberts* and badly damaged the *Heermann* and *Dennis*. The escorts of Taffy 3 went down fighting in what Adm. Kinkaid called "one of the most gallant and heroic acts of the war."[189]

Aircraft from the escort carriers dove on the Japanese ships, scoring a number of hits and adding their influence on the battle. But the hastily launched planes were for the most part not armed with the type of ordnance that could inflict lethal damage on the Japanese warships. One exception was a flight from the *Kitkun Bay* of sixteen F4F Wildcat fighters and eight TBF Avengers armed with torpedoes and 500 lb. bombs. Led by Lt. Cdr. Richard L. Fowler, four Avengers descended on the already damaged *Chokai* and hit it with nine bombs, causing significant damage.[190] Another group struck the *Chikuma* with a torpedo, taking off a portion of her stern and knocking out her power.[191] The *Suzuya* was also hit by bombs and sank around 13:00.[192] A number of the pilots made emergency landings on the incomplete airstrips at Tacloban and Dulag, where ground crews did their best to service and refuel those who survived the risky landings and get them back into the air.[193] Twenty-five aircraft crashed on the immature airstrip at Tacloban and, while the pilots were saved, the wreckage was bulldozed into the sea. As planes ran out of torpedoes and bombs, pilots resorted to making strafing runs against Japanese ships.[194] By the end of the day, the jeep carriers had launched 453 sorties, which dropped 191 tons of bombs and launched 83 torpedoes at the Japanese ships.[195]

Taffy 3's carriers attempted to make good their escape, but at only seventeen knots they were seriously outclassed by the Japanese warships. Japanese fire was hampered throughout the battle by obscuration from smoke and rain, the use of armor-piercing shells which failed to detonate when they passed clean through the unarmored escort carriers, and poor gunnery, a result of constant manuevering to avoid bombs and torpedoes, and perhaps damage done to fire control systems in the Sibuyan Sea. The *Kalinin Bay* took her first hit at 07:50 and suffered fourteen more before the battle was over. The *Gambier Bay* was hit at the waterline at 08:20, lost speed, and sank at 09:11 after Japanese cruisers shelled her at point-blank range.[196] The *Fanshaw Bay* suffered the first of four hits at 08:50, but survived with minor damage. Japanese shells straddled the other three escort carriers, but scored no hits. The 5-inch guns of the carriers joined in the melée as Japanese cruisers and destroyers came within range, but after two hours

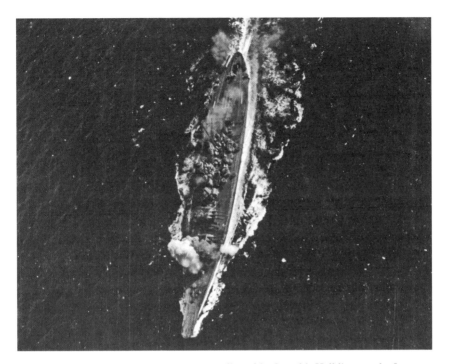

5.4: Lt. Cdr. Arthur L. Downing scoring two direct hits from his Helldiver on the Japanese battleship *Yamato* off the coast of Samar, October 25, 1944. Although damage to the battleship did not take it out of action, repeated aerial attacks disrupted the Japanese attack on Rear Adm. Ziggy Sprague's Task Unit 77.4.3, call sign Taffy 3. (Credit: US Navy Photo)

of battle were running low on ammunition. The escorts waged a valiant effort to keep the Japanese fleet at bay, but it seemed only a matter of time before it would close to finish off Taffy 3 and descend on the shipping in Leyte Gulf, which might not have been as fatal as it seemed. The amphibious task forces had so efficiently unloaded their cargoes that by this date the only shipping remaining in Leyte Gulf amounted to three amphibious command ships (AGC), one amphibious cargo ship (AKA), twenty-eight Liberty ships, twenty-three LSTs, and two medium landing ships (LSM).[197] The Japanese ships could have bombarded supply dumps ashore, damaging Sixth Army's logistical structure, but that would have taken some amount of time that the Japanese didn't have.

Around 09:30, Japanese cruisers and destroyers had closed to within 10,000 yards of Taffy 3 and the situation was, in the words of Adm. Kinkaid, "black, black, black."[198] Aboard the *Blue Ridge* in Leyte Gulf, Capt. Tarbuck sensed imminent disaster. At 07:20, he had written in his observer's log, "The successful completion of the remaining phase of our trans-ocean amphibious operation is very seriously threatened. Armor piercing ammunition shortage in our slow battleships and cruisers has been partially sacrificed for shore bombardment [HE] shells, our ammunition is practically exhausted, torpedoes have been expended, fuel is low and the situation is desperate." Feeling his own mortality, he wrote, "As soon as the Jap finishes off our defenseless CVE's we're next, and I mean today." He also had empathy for Taffy 3, remarking, "Radio dispatches from our beleaguered force are pathetic and unbelievable."[199]

Two hours into the battle, Kinkaid messaged Halsey, "Enemy force attacked our CVEs composed of 4 BBs 8 cruisers and other ships. Request Lee [commander, Task Force 34] proceed top speed to cover Leyte. Request immediate strike by fast carriers."[200] Halsey shrugged; he had decided not to send Task Force 34 to Leyte Gulf and had already ordered McCain's Task Group 38.1 to launch air strikes when within range. "There was nothing else I could do except become angrier," he confided in his memoirs. Twenty-two minutes later, Halsey received Kinkaid's message, sent two hours earlier, that his old battleships were low on ammunition.[201] Communications friction was clearly playing a role in American command and control on this day.

Kinkaid, who was partly to blame for his own misfortune, was growing desperate. He sent a final plea to Halsey in the clear, the lack of encoding indicating its urgency: "My situation is critical. Fast battleships and support by air strike may be able to keep enemy from destroying CVEs and entering Leyte [Gulf]."[202] Three thousand miles away in Pearl Harbor, Adm. Nimitz had been monitoring the battle. He now for the first time interjected, sending a message to Halsey: "Turkey trots to water gg From CINCPAC action Com Third Fleet [Adm. Halsey] info COMINCH [Adm. Ernest J. King] CTF Seventy-Seven [Rear Adm. Thomas L. Sprague] x Where is rpt Where is Task Force Thirty Four rr The World Wonders."[203]

The first and last sentences separated by double consonants were random "padding" used to confuse potential Japanese eavesdropping and decoding by burying the first and last words of the actual message, which tended to be scripted and therefore vulnerable to cryptologic attack. But the last part of the message seemed plausible to the radiomen on Halsey's flagship, so they included it in the version sent to the bridge.[204] Upon reading it, Halsey erupted, believing that Nimitz was criticizing his decisions. "I was as stunned as if I had been struck in the face. The paper rattled in my hands. I snatched off my cap, threw it on the deck, and shouted something that I am ashamed to remember. Mick Carney [Rear Adm. Robert Carney, Halsey's Chief of Staff] rushed over and grabbed my arm: 'Stop it! What the hell's the matter with you? Pull yourself together!'"[205]

Halsey retired to his cabin to do just that, but it took him an hour to emerge and issue new orders. Finally awakened as to Seventh Fleet's plight, he turned Task Force 34 south, too late, as it turned out, to have an impact on the battle. He had also "turned [his] back on the opportunity [he] had dreamed of since [his] days as a cadet [sic – midshipman]" of destroying an enemy fleet through battleship gunfire.[206]

This was the golden opportunity Adm. Toyoda had dreamed of when he devised the battle plan. The decoy had worked; Third Fleet's fast carriers and battleships had been lured to the north, away from Leyte Gulf. Kurita's surface armada had breached San Bernardino Strait at night without opposition and was now bearing down on the Seventh Fleet, which had suddenly become vulnerable to a strong surface attack. The Japanese task force had lost one cruiser and one destroyer, with severe damage sustained by several other cruisers, but it still had formidable combat power. Then the inexplicable happened – at 09:11, Kurita ordered his force to regroup to the north just as its heavy cruisers came to within 10,000 yards – killing distance – of Taffy 3's carriers.[207] Taffy 3's commander, Rear Adm. C. Sprague, commented, "Had this decision not been made, the Jap main body could have, and should have, waded through and completed the destruction of this Task Unit, and continuing to the south, would have found our naval opposition very low on ammunition following their night action. In Leyte Gulf they could have successfully accomplished their mission and retired through Surigao Straits [sic] as was originally intended."[208] A signalman on the bridge of the *Fanshaw Bay* was more expressive, yelling out defiantly, "Goddammit, boys, they're getting away!"[209] Kurita's ships could have continued southwest to regroup, but instead he ordered them to rendezvous to the north, taking them away from Taffy 3.[210]

Despite the losses, the outcome of the fighting could have been much worse. American commanders from the Philippines to Hawai'i to Washington breathed a huge sigh of relief. Rear Adm. Thomas Sprague (no relation to Rear Adm. Clifton Sprague), commander of Task Force 77, messaged: "At 0924 Jap main body and cruisers now at 120 [degrees] suddenly turned away to opposite course. It was unbelievable …. Impossible to understand why heavy cruisers failed to close in promptly or encircle force and polish off this entire outfit."[211] Writing four days later, Rear Adm. Clifton Sprague could hardly believe what his task unit had experienced:

> The success attendant upon the efforts to escape the devastating enemy fire was remarkable almost to the point of being unexplainable. After being under enemy fire for two and one half hours at ranges closing to under 10,500 yards this Task Unit lost one carrier, and two DD's and one DE. These escorts were lost as a result of their heroic torpedo attack into the center of the enemy under very heavy fire. U.S.S. *St. Lo* [CVE 63] was lost sometime later after enemy had begun retirement as a result of a successful suicide dive into the middle of her flight deck and subsequent explosions. From almost the beginning of the action heavy funnel and FS smoke was laid by all vessels; this, together with a providential rain squall, seemed to bother the enemy fire control parties to an unusual degree, resulting at times in lulls in the firing, and perhaps indicating lack of use of fire control [radar] for surface gunnery .... In summation, the failure of the enemy main body and encircling light forces to completely wipe out all vessels of this Task Unit can be attributed to our successful smoke screen, our torpedo counter-attack, continuous harassment of enemy by bomb, torpedo, and strafing air attacks, timely maneuvers, and the definite partiality of Almighty God.[212]

Nimitz concurred that the survival of Taffy 3 had required divine intervention, writing to King on October 28, "That the San Bernardino detachment of the Japanese Fleet, which included the YAMATO and the MUSASHI, did not completely destroy all of the escort carriers and their accompanying screen is nothing short of special dispensation from the Lord Almighty."[213]

Why did Kurita break off the pursuit of Taffy 3 just when his task force was on the verge of success? The admiral was undoubtedly exhausted after swimming for his life after the torpedoing of his flagship and three days of continuous operations, but his failure to press home the attack according to his orders is baffling.[214] Poor intelligence had a great deal to do with his decision. One historian who has studied the Japanese side of the battle in detail concludes,

> Utterly lacking information on anything beyond his field of vision, his two observation planes shot down, ignorant of the fact that over the horizon to the southwest his cruisers were within five miles of the American carriers, Kurita thought that his enemy had escaped. Still intent on penetrating the Gulf, mindful of the need for fuel conservation, especially in his destroyers, engendered by the morning's chase, and anticipating that he would soon be subjected to increasingly heavy air attack, he decided to break off and reform his widely scattered force.[215]

To this could be added the overestimation by Kurita of what he was facing, as his lookouts assessed American escort carriers to be *Independence*-class light carriers, destroyers to be *Baltimore*-class cruisers, and destroyer escorts to be destroyers.[216] In this sense, Taffy 3 had indeed punched above its weight.

In what went down in history as the Battle off Samar, Taffy 3 and its aircraft had surprisingly fought the *First Diversionary Striking Force* to a draw, ending any chance for Japanese victory. Although Kurita, after reforming his scattered ships, made one more turn to the south shortly after noon, he would not follow that course into Leyte Gulf. At 12:36, Kurita turned 180 degrees and headed north to chase an imaginary US carrier task force mistakenly reported off the north coast of Samar, never again to make contact with the enemy.[217] He had traded the certainty of battle in Leyte Gulf for the possibility of engaging a fast carrier task force in the open sea.[218] When no force was located and with his ships running low on fuel, Kurita decided to withdraw back west through San Bernardino Strait. There is little doubt but that he had badly fumbled the tactical aspects of the battle.

Japanese suicide bombers, or kamikazes, had more success. As Taffy 3 was battling the enemy to the north, Task Unit 77.4.1 underwent attack from six kamikazes, which hit and seriously damaged the *Santee* (which also took a torpedo from a Japanese submarine) and *Suwanee* and narrowly missed the *Petrof Bay* and *Sangamon*.[219] Later in the morning, Taffy 3 also came under suicide attack, sinking the *St. Lo* and damaging the *Kitkun Bay, Kalinin Bay,* and *White Plains.* Fighters from Task Unit 77.4.2 fended off an attack in the afternoon by more than twenty-five aircraft, splashing most of them without damage to friendly ships.[220] Noting the effectiveness of the suicide attacks, Tarbuck commented, "If the enemy knows [their] effectiveness we can expect plenty more in future operations …. A countermeasure must be found soon."[221]

Halsey admitted he had initially underestimated the importance of the kamikazes. "I think that most of us took it as a sort of token terror, a tissue-paper dragon …. We could not believe that even the Japanese, for all their hari-kiri traditions, could muster enough recruits to make such a corps really effective."[222] Halsey found room for optimism; the use of kamikazes illustrated to him the deterioration of the skill of the remaining Japanese pilots, who could do little more than take off, fly level, and attempt to crash their planes into ships. "To me," Halsey confided in his memoirs, "the *kamikaze* was a weapon not of inspiration, but of desperation – an unmistakable sign that the Japanese war machine was close to collapse."[223] If the kamikaze was an omen, it was a deadly one. Within a month after their first

5.5: The ammunition magazine of the USS *St. Lo* (CVE-63) explodes sometime after the ship was hit by a Japanese kamikaze on October 25, 1944. The use of these human-guided bombs in the Battle of Leyte Gulf inaugurated a new phase in the US Navy's war with the naval and air forces of Imperial Japan. (Credit: US Navy Photo)

use in the Battle of Leyte Gulf, kamikazes damaged three carriers seriously enough to require repairs in Ulithi Atoll or Pearl Harbor; damaged four other carriers; hit two battleships, two cruisers, two transports, and seven destroyers (one of which sank); destroyed upwards of ninety planes; and killed several hundred sailors.[224] The Japanese indeed took notice. If bombs and torpedoes could not find their marks, human guided weapons could and would. The army and the navy "expanded and institutionalized" the kamikaze corps "with remarkable speed."[225]

Upon receiving word of the Japanese attack on Taffy 3 and Halsey's order to come to its assistance, McCain had ordered his carrier division to sail at flank speed toward Leyte Gulf. At 10:30, his carriers launched a ninety-eight-plane strike at extended range against Kurita's task force, which was now withdrawing northwards toward San Bernardino Strait, with a second follow-up strike launched at 12:55.[226] The strikes hit Kurita's force with upwards of twenty bombs, but did not cause fatal damage to its warships.[227] Halsey sent a subunit of Task Force 34 consisting of his two fastest battleships, the *Iowa* and *New Jersey*, along with three cruisers and eight destroyers, in a vain attempt to intercept Kurita's force before it could negotiate San Bernardino Strait. They were able to catch only one destroyer, the *Nowake*, which they quickly sent to the bottom. The rest of the Japanese center task force escaped through the Strait.[228] Halsey's fast battleships had spent the crucial day of battle sailing up and down the coast of Luzon without making contact with either Ozawa's or Kurita's task force.

While Halsey was making "Bull's Run" with his fast battleships and Task Group 38.2, Task Groups 38.3 and 38.4 continued to attack Ozawa's fleet in what became known as the Battle of Cape Engaño. Submarine packs with colorful names such as "Roache's Raiders" (*Haddock*, *Tuna*, and *Halibut*) and "Clarey's Crushers" (*Jalleo*, *Atule*, and *Pintado*) were also directed to intercept the retreating Japanese ships.[229] Ozawa's force, its mission of decoying Third Fleet a success, suffered heavily. All four carriers went to the bottom, along with the light cruiser *Tama* (torpedoed by the submarine *Jalleo* on the night of October 25–26) and two destroyers; the two battleships and two surviving cruisers all sustained damage of varying degrees.[230]

The next morning scouts from the *Wasp* found Kurita's task force off the northwest coast of Panay.[231] Attacks from naval aircraft sank the light cruiser *Noshiro* and damaged the *Yamato*. Carrier planes also located and sank the stragglers *Hayashimo* and *Fujinami* off Mindoro. US Army B-24s located the cruiser *Abukuma* from Shima's force northwest of Mindanao and sank it, while naval aircraft sent the destroyer *Shiranui* to the bottom. Carrier planes attacked a Japanese convoy that had just offloaded 2,000 troops at the port of Ormoc on the west side of Leyte, sinking the lighter cruiser *Kinu*, the destroyer *Uranami*, and two transports.[232]

With these attacks, the Battle of Leyte Gulf came to an end. Sailors on the ships sunk in combat floundered helplessly in the cruel sea, beset by thirst, exposure, wounds, and sharks. More than 1,000 survivors of Taffy 3 eventually were rescued by a small ad hoc task group arranged by Captain Charles Adair, an amphibious planner serving under Vice Adm. Barbey. Adair noted reconnaissance reports of men in the water but could find no mention of efforts to retrieve them. With Barbey's permission, he put together a task group of two patrol craft and five landing craft (LCIs, or landing craft, infantry) to search for and rescue survivors. Most of the survivors spent two harrowing nights in the water, with hundreds succumbing to wounds, shark attacks, or the hazards of the sea before salvation arrived. In all, Adair's task group rescued 1,153 men.[233]

Despite the mistakes made and the fog and friction of battle, the outcome was a decisive victory by the US Pacific Fleet over the last viable fleet of Imperial Japan in the largest battle in the history of naval warfare. Lack of air parity doomed the Japanese fleet to fighting on unequal terms (Spruance's victory at the Philippine Sea and Halsey's strikes on Okinawa, Formosa, and Luzon prior to the invasion had seen to that), and communications difficulties hampered the coordination of its efforts. Its gunnery was not up to the standards set by the Imperial Japanese Navy earlier in the war. Japanese commanders made several questionable decisions, most notably Kurita's decision to withdraw from battle off the coast of Samar on the morning of October 25. US commanders also made mistakes and suffered their share of communications failures, but, given American superiority in ships and planes, not enough to make a difference in the final outcome. One senior Japanese admiral concluded in retrospect, "However majestic a fleet may look, without a carrier force it is no more than a fleet of tin."[234]

Both sides fought courageously. It had been a very human battle, full of unexpected twists and mistakes and subject to the capricious dictates of chance, but in the end decided by weight of resources. Japanese losses amounted to one fleet carrier and three light carriers, three battleships, six heavy and four light cruisers, and eleven destroyers. In comparison, the US Navy suffered the loss of one light carrier, two escort carriers, two destroyers, one destroyer escort, and one submarine.[235] Japanese naval airpower was broken for good, and no fleet of sufficient numbers or power remained to contest control of the seas. The US Navy had gained command of the sea over the full expanse of the Pacific Ocean. From this point forward, kamikazes would be its primary opponent.

On October 29, MacArthur sent a note to Halsey thanking him and his command for their support of the Leyte invasion:

> I send my deepest thanks and appreciation to your magnificent forces on the splendid support and assistance you and they have rendered in the Leyte operation. We have cooperated with you so long that we are accustomed and expect your brilliant successes and you have more than sustained our fullest anticipations. Everyone here has a feeling of complete confidence and inspiration when you go into action in our support.

During the height of the battle and in private, however, MacArthur's thoughts had taken on a darker tone. The following handwritten note, penned by Sutherland, appears on the file copy of the message:

> This follows verbal castigation of Halsey by Gen. MacArthur who repeatedly charged him with failure to execute his mission of covering the Leyte operation. When Halsey failed to get into the Battle of Leyte Gulf [sic – the Battle off Samar], thus threatening the destruction of our shipping, Gen. MacArthur repeatedly stated that Halsey should be relieved and would welcome his relief, since he no longer had confidence in him; that he would never again support us.[236]

These thoughts, expressed in private at a time of high anxiety, were quickly forgotten. At dinner in Tacloban on October 26, MacArthur chastised some of his staff who disparaged Halsey and his conduct in the recent battle. "That's enough!," MacArthur retorted. "Leave the Bull alone. He's still a fighting admiral in my book."[237] MacArthur continued to support Halsey, and they would remain good friends throughout the rest of their lives.

Naval officers, pundits, armchair admirals, and historians would evaluate Halsey's performance for decades to come. Clark Reynolds contends that Halsey "was in fact the fast carrier task force commander at Leyte, and not a very good one at that. Audacious he was by nature, prone to *ad hoc* rather than detailed planning, guilty of sloppy techniques and often vague dispatches."[238] Trent Hone has provided the latest and perhaps soundest assessment:

> Had Halsey retained focus on his responsibilities as a fleet commander, made more effective use of the initiative of his subordinates, and created an atmosphere of decentralized decision-making, he might have won an unparalleled victory. However, his fatigue, his predisposition for aggressive action, and the importance [in US Navy doctrine] of concentration prevented him from considering alternative courses of action.[239]

Halsey's best course of action, both at the time and in retrospect, was to allow his fast carriers under Vice Adm. Mitscher to destroy the Japanese carriers, while his fast battleship task force under Vice Adm. Lee dealt with Kurita's battleships and cruisers at the mouth of San Bernardino Strait.

Leyte Gulf was still a major victory; these judgments concern whether disaster could have been prevented had Kurita pursued his course into Leyte Gulf, which he did not, or whether the battle could have been even more decisive than it was, had Halsey made different decisions. The strategic outcome, however, would have been the same even had the Third and Seventh Fleets destroyed the entire Japanese fleet. The outcome of the Battle of Leyte Gulf meant that the liberation of the Philippines and subsequent operations could proceed unhindered by Japanese naval power. Cut off from its oil supplies, the Imperial Japanese Navy would never again threaten to derail US amphibious operations; only the kamikazes could do that from this point forward.[240] The focus now turned to the fighting on the ground, which turned out to be much longer and more difficult than anyone had anticipated.

6

THE BATTLE FOR LEYTE

Leyte went on forever. Heavy fighting, daily bombing, sickness and rain, and death near at hand, week on week of it.[1]

Roger Olaf Egeberg

While the Japanese and American fleets were dancing their minuet of death in the seas surrounding the Philippine Islands, MacArthur's forces were expanding the beachhead and seizing the high ground leading to Leyte Valley. The campaign on Leyte would last for two-and-a-half rain-soaked months and clearing operations several months longer. Japanese *Imperial General HQ* decided to put forth a determined effort to defend Leyte, realizing that an American victory there would inevitably lead to the projection of American power onto Luzon and the ultimate fall of the Philippines.[2] American submarines and aircraft based in the Philippines would sever the Japanese lines of communication to the Dutch East Indies – and thus drain the lifeblood of raw materials upon which the Japanese war economy depended. But, by pouring reinforcements into Leyte, the Japanese high command made the successful defense of Luzon impossible. The troops fighting through the swamps and over the tortuous mountains of Leyte did not know it, but they were fighting in the decisive battle of the Philippines campaign.

The landing on Leyte took the Japanese by surprise. They had expected the Americans to invade Mindanao, which was within range of SWPA's airfields on Morotai – and, indeed, until Halsey's September raid, that had been the American plan as well. A tropical storm that passed through the area had kept the invasion fleet hidden from Japanese reconnaissance. The failure of Japanese naval forces in the Battle of Leyte Gulf meant that success or failure now rested on Japanese ground forces on Leyte. The defense of the island centered on the *16th Division*, a veteran of the Bataan campaign. The SWPA G-2, Maj. Gen. Charles Willoughby, assessed that, because of American air strength and the losses inflicted to date on Japanese shipping, the Japanese could either regroup and defend in a last desperate stand or withdraw from the island.[3]

But the ensuing battle for Leyte proved the old adage that, in warfare, the enemy gets a vote. As the American invasion fleet appeared off Leyte, the fog of war clouded Japanese vision. The *Southern Expeditionary Army Group* believed that the American invasion was only the remnants of the force that it believed had attempted to invade Formosa. The *35th Army* on Cebu chose "to believe that the full force of the American invasion force had been lost in an unsuccessful attempt to invade Formosa and that the survivors had been decimated by the great tropical storm, and were now straggling onto the Leyte shore." The *14th Area Army* in Manila concurred with the estimate. The commander of the *16th Division* on Leyte also believed that the fleet entering Leyte Gulf was taking refuge from the tropical storm that had recently blown through the area. Only after the full force of the invasion armada had become clear did Yamashita understand that this was a full-scale invasion.[4]

The commander of the *Southern Expeditionary Army Group*, Field Marshal Count Hisaichi Terauchi, convinced the American fleet had suffered heavily off of Formosa and the Imperial Japanese Navy had won the Battle of Leyte Gulf, opted to fight the decisive battle for the Philippines on Leyte rather than cede the island to the Americans.[5] Yamashita "protested vigorously" against the decision, as a concerted effort to hold Leyte would denude Luzon of troops and thwart its successful defense.[6] Nevertheless, he followed orders and heavily reinforced the forces on Leyte. Over the next several weeks, the crack *1st Division* (from Manchuria), two regiments of the *26th Division*, the *68th Independent Mixed Brigade*, and elements of the *30th* and *102nd Divisions*, for a total of 45,000 reinforcing troops, flowed to Leyte.[7] The operational scheme entailed the *16th Division* defending Burauen and Dagami, with an element forward on Catmon Hill. The *102nd Division* would occupy Jaro and the area to the north to screen deployment of the *1st Division* through Ormoc and the arrival of the *26th Division* and the *68th Brigade* in Carigara. Elements of the *30th Division* would land at Albuera and proceed to Burauen. The *1st* and *26th Divisions* would then assemble and launch a counterattack to seize Tacloban.[8]

Japanese commanders were confident of their chances. On November 2, the headquarters of the *35th Army* deployed from Cebu to Leyte to assume direct control of the battle. After receiving reinforcements along with orders to fight the decisive battle on Leyte, Maj. Gen. Yoshiharu Tomochika, the chief of staff of the Japanese *35th Army*, recalled, "We had hopeful discussions of entering Tacloban by the 16th of November. We were determined to take offensive after offensive and clean up American forces on Leyte Island according to original plans. We seriously discussed demanding the surrender of the entire American Army after seizing General MacArthur."[9]

Japanese aspirations would run headlong into advancing American forces. In the northern portion of the beachhead, X Corps advanced with the 1st Cavalry Division on the right, or northern flank and the 24th Infantry Division on the left, or southern flank. The 1st Cavalry was a Regular Army division that had been de-horsed and converted to infantry. It still maintained its square, two-brigade structure, albeit with each brigade containing only two regiments, each of which had only two squadrons (battalions) of dismounted cavalrymen. The division experienced combat in the Admiralties before the Leyte campaign; its combination of Regular Army cadre and combat experience made it one of the most tactically competent divisions in the Pacific.

On the afternoon of October 21, the 7th Cavalry Regiment liberated Tacloban, the provincial capital of Leyte, to the delight of its citizens, who lined the streets and waved American flags as they welcomed their liberators.[10] Radio reporter William Dunn recalled, "I expected a welcome from the Filipino people. But never in my wildest dreams did I expect to witness scenes such as those that greeted the returning Americans .... The first American troops to enter the city were greeted with mingled tears and laughter, with cheers that were almost inarticulate because of the emotion behind them."[11] Carlos Romulo opined, "[The liberation of Tacloban] was not only military victory. It was victory of the soul we saw on the road to Tacloban."[12]

Of perhaps greater import to the cavalrymen was the seizure of an enormous cache of San Miguel beer, which the division commander, Maj. Gen. Verne Mudge, immediately ordered issued to the front-line troopers. According to the 1st Cavalry Brigade commander, Brig. Gen. William C. Chase, "It was warm but its tactical effect was truly miraculous."[13]

The cavalrymen continued on to clear the high ground north and west of the city, a task barely accomplished in time for MacArthur to restore the Philippine civil government under President Sergio Osmeña in a ceremony in front of the provincial capitol building on the afternoon of October 23. Capt. Raymond Tarbuck, the senior naval observer at MacArthur's headquarters, recorded the scene: "Guerrillas are filtering in, some of whom are equipped with Enfield rifles. All of them salute as we pass. The civilians wave and give the victory sign with emotions of gratitude, as we pass the outskirts of Tacloban which our patrols entered 24 hours ago."[14]

6.1: Gen. Douglas MacArthur (left), Lt. Gen. Richard K. Sutherland, Lt. Gen. Walter Krueger (back to camera), and Lt. Gen. George C. Kenney discuss the invasion of Leyte, October 22, 1944. (Credit: US Army Signal Corps Photo)

An honor guard of two troops of the 1st Cavalry Division, dirty and tired from the fighting, graced the front of the government building in Tacloban. If there was any doubt about the loyalty of the local civilians, they greeted President Osmeña by singing "God Bless America."[15] After speeches and raising of Philippine and US flags, MacArthur decorated guerrilla leader Ruperto Kangleon with a Distinguished Service Cross, after which Osmeña appointed Kangleon governor of Leyte "as a tribute to all who had resisted the Japanese."[16] MacArthur approved the site for his new headquarters at the Price House in Tacloban before returning to the *Nashville* for the evening.[17]

On October 24, the 8th Cavalry Regiment invaded Samar to begin a two-month operation, aided by Filipino guerrillas, to clear the weakly garrisoned island of Japanese forces. That same day the 1st Squadron, 7th Cavalry

launched an amphibious invasion of Babatngon on the northern coast of
Leyte, leapfrogging Japanese resistance along the coastal road. The squadron made another amphibious leap forward on October 29, landing at
Barugo, while the 2nd Squadron, 8th Cavalry seized San Miguel and the
1st Squadron, 5th Cavalry took Cavite further south. The division then
advanced on Carigara.[18]

To the south of the 1st Cavalry Division, the 24th Infantry Division attacked
through the high ground into the northern end of Leyte Valley and then
toward Carigara Bay on Leyte's northern coast. After overcoming stiff opposition, the 19th Infantry reached the town of Palo late on October 21 and was
met by a scene of jubilation. As the troops entered the town, the Filipinos

> poured out in a great welcoming crowd. The Church bell rang, and the
> people brought gifts of food and a type of Japanese soft drink which they
> proffered to their liberators. Ragged and dirty as they were – many only
> recently bereaved through the deaths of family members killed during one
> phase or another of the fighting – the Filipinos were nevertheless almost
> beside themselves with joy at the return of the Americans ... even the
> smallest children held up their fingers in the "V" sign.[19]

During the night of October 21–22, the Japanese launched
a counterattack against the troops in Palo. After three-and-a-half hours of
bitter fighting, the Japanese withdrew. Artillery played a major role in the
fighting, with barrages called down as close as 100 meters in front of friendly
positions.[20] The division then fought to secure the high ground leading to
Leyte Valley – Hill 331 and Hills B and C as marked on its battle maps. These
maps were not always helpful. Small-scale maps of 1/200,000 scale were
available for planning, but such maps were unsuitable for combat requirements such as land navigation and artillery targeting. Larger-scale 1/25,000
and 1/50,000 maps made available just prior to the invasion

> were hastily prepared, incomplete and inaccurate to the point of being
> more misleading than helpful. This fact, combined with the lack of suitable
> early photo coverage beyond the coast, made the pinpointing of enemy
> targets impossible. Artillery fire adjustment was dependent upon air
> observation or forward observer parties until surveys could be made.
> Ground troops were likewise unable to accurately locate on their maps
> their own front lines and patrol activities.

The Japanese suffered from the same deficit, as "captured Japanese maps
were no better than our own."[21]

On October 22, the 2nd Battalion, 34th Infantry, attacked to secure the Hill 331 ridge, which it did by having the infantry closely follow artillery fire to the crest. The 3rd Battalion, 34th Infantry, took Hill C on October 25, overcoming Japanese forces using a reverse-slope defense. Hill B was taken in a most unusual fashion. Companies E and G of the 2nd Battalion, 19th Infantry, attacked the hill on the morning of October 25 after an artillery barrage. Heavy Japanese fire from fortified positions repelled E Company, but G Company succeeded in taking its objective. By twilight, it had moved further west onto the crest of the hill, where it dug in for the night. The battalion commander, Lt. Col. Robert B. Spragins, decided to consolidate the battalion on Company G's position that night, which meant a night move of approximately 900 yards. The column moved out, but lost its way in the dark. Spragins then set a compass course for G Company, which he failed to find. At midnight the troops stumbled upon an undefended Japanese fortified position on the crest of the hill and stopped to dig in for the night. The morning sunrise illuminated Highway 2; the battalion had finally – and quite to its own surprise – taken the last piece of key terrain in its path to Leyte Valley.[22]

For the next week, the 24th Infantry Division attacked up the Leyte Valley to reach Carigara. A rapid pursuit of disorganized Japanese forces paid dividends, as the division met little organized resistance. Destroyed bridges across the numerous streams were the major obstacle to the advance. On October 28, the 34th Infantry reached the Mainit River along the Palo–Jaro highway. The 1st Battalion ran headlong into the teeth of a Japanese infantry company dug in on the far bank. The regimental commander, Col. Aubrey S. Newman, ordered 2nd Battalion to cross a ford 500 meters downstream and flank the enemy position. F Company took the lead and accomplished the task with a bayonet charge. "We are all trotting again," Capt. Paul Austin recalled. "Some men run at times, dashing up to clumps of bushes, leaping over small ditches. Some are yelling. We are moving faster – an explosion rips the air 10 yards in front of me. A Jap mortar shell." Dazed but still mobile, Austin continued to lead the attack. "I did not hear anyone shout 'Remember the Alamo' that afternoon, but had I heard it I would have understood. It would have meant remember Joe Bartnichak, Louis Farber, Ralph Dyer, and other F Company men who had fallen on Hill 331 a few days before."[23] The 1st Battalion seized a steel truss bridge across the river after a battle with Japanese defenders lasting until the middle of the afternoon. The bridge had been wired for demolition, but the defenders failed to detonate the explosives.[24]

The 3rd Battalion, 34th Infantry took Jaro on October 29, after destroying the Japanese positions inside the village. The next day the battalion continued the advance. When Japanese fire pinned down the attacking platoon, Col. Newman, remembering his actions that had motivated his men on Red Beach, declared "I'll get the men moving!" and started to walk toward the Japanese positions. The men followed, but a shell landed near Newman, wounding him severely in the stomach and killing the man next to him. Newman recalled his wounding was "just like in a story book – the regimental commander fell at the head of his regiment. But when I lay helpless on the ground, I was no longer a leader. Just another burden to be taken care of. I had made a great mistake, and became a casualty needlessly."[25] Newman was awarded a Distinguished Service Cross, but had to be evacuated for medical treatment.[26] For two days the 34th Infantry fought against stiff resistance, suffering 108 casualties on October 31 alone.

On November 2, the 24th Infantry Division took part in an attack on Carigara in conjunction with the 1st Cavalry Division. The attack began with a rolling barrage of 3,000 rounds fired by the 4 battalions of the 24th Infantry Division artillery. The 34th Infantry Regiment then attacked, only to find the town abandoned.[27] Leyte Valley was now in American hands. Fred Hampton of the Associated Press wrote,

> Truly NIPPON felt the full fury of American arms and American guts in this smashing battle of the roads, a battle fought through one typhoon storm and many days of crucifying heat. We fought at the crossroads, in the villages and along the banks of sluggish rivers. We rooted the Jap from his dugouts; we stalked him over the hills, and we slaughtered him at the edge of the roads. He lies today from JARO to the coast in grotesque huddles, and in sprawling masses of blood, brains, and guts. It is not a pretty picture, this backwash of war, but it is, to some extent, revenge for BATAAN and PEARL HARBOR.[28]

In the southern portion of the beachhead, XXIV Corps advanced with the 96th Infantry Division on the right, or northern flank and the 7th Infantry Division on the left, or southern flank. The 1,400-foot-high Catmon Hill dominated the 96th Infantry Division's beachhead area. On A+1, the 1st Battalion, 383rd Infantry moved toward the southern side of the hill, while the other two battalions of the regiment attempted to envelop it. The flanking maneuver was easier said than done; there were no roads in the division's zone, and vehicles could not traverse the swampy ground behind the beach. "It was a hard job for a man to get through with just a rifle; it was a prodigious one for him to carry a machine gun or mortar on his back," records the division history. "At times the men had to crawl on hands and knees to keep from sinking into the grasping muck."[29]

After three days of slogging through the swamps, the 2nd and 3rd Battalions of the 383rd Infantry reached the village of San Vincente on the northwestern slope of Catmon Hill. The 1st Battalion assaulted the southern end of the hill mass on October 27, followed the next day by the 1st and 2nd Battalions of the 381st Infantry, supported by forty-five tanks from the 780th Tank Battalion which had found a route off the beach. By October 29, the entire Catmon Hill mass was in American hands.[30]

On the division's left flank, the 382nd Infantry Regiment advanced west to seize Tabontabon, which it did in a two-day battle on October 26–27. By October 30, the division had secured its entire beachhead area. It then assumed control over the entire corps beachhead to enable the 7th Infantry Division to move to the west side of Leyte and advance north on Ormoc. The "Deadeyes" advanced to the foothills of the mountain range separating Leyte on its north–south axis, where it hit a Japanese defensive line manned by the remnants of the *16th Division*, barring further progress. The 96th Reconnaissance Troop conducted a long-range patrol across the mountains to within range of the west coast port of Ormoc, where it witnessed the destruction of a Japanese convoy bringing reinforcements to the island.[31]

In the southern portion of the American beachhead, the 7th Infantry Division advanced off Yellow and Violet Beaches to seize Dulag airfield on A+1. The "Hourglass" was a veteran division, having fought to liberate Attu in the Aleutian Islands in May 1943 and to seize Kwajalein in the Marshall Islands in February 1944. Many of the soldiers were veterans of these campaigns, with attendant battle scars to prove it. Of the fighting in these early battles, Pvt. John Shult of Toledo, Ohio, stated, "We learned the hard way. But it was the quick way. The one-lesson way."[32] Now, on Leyte, the soldiers would again put their experience to the test.

The division advanced to seize the town of Burauen on October 24 and the three airstrips nearby. The 17th Infantry Regiment then advanced north, meeting heavy resistance along the Burauen–Dagami Road. The regiment succeeded in seizing Dagami on October 29 after "vicious hand-to-hand fighting" and liberal use of flamethrowers to clear Japanese infantry from the vaults and graves of the local cemetery.[33] This action completed the initial objectives for XXIV Corps, which had secured the southern end of the Leyte Valley along with its airstrips, without which portions of Lt. Gen. George Kenney's land-based airpower would be left stranded back in New Guinea.

With all beachhead areas secure, the race was now on to reach the west coast before Japanese reinforcements could stymie forward progress. One unit that succeeded in doing so was the 2nd Battalion, 32nd Infantry, preceded by the 7th Reconnaissance Troop, which moved south down the coast to Abuyog. From there, the units advanced west along the road to Baybay through the mountains along the narrow waist of the island, reaching the west coast of Leyte on November 2. The 3rd Battalion, 32nd Infantry joined up with these units on November 8. The Japanese had unwisely left this avenue of approach unguarded because of the reported destruction of the road crossing the island.[34] This movement provided the division with the opportunity to advance north up Highway 2 to Ormoc, provided that it could mass its combat power to do so. This would happen only after reinforcements arrived to assume responsibility for the critical area around Burauen.[35]

MacArthur kept track of Sixth Army's progress from his advanced headquarters in Tacloban and through visits to command posts near the front. He did not micromanage Krueger's conduct of the battle. MacArthur supported Krueger's request for reinforcements, adding considerable combat power to Sixth Army when its advance stalled in the face of Japanese reinforcements, but otherwise left the fighting to Krueger and his men.[36]

For MacArthur's staff, "Leyte was Tacloban and Tacloban was a town of one-story houses in a sea of mud . . .. Tacloban was a place where the sun rarely shone, where the narrow streets and roads were of mud, where the color was gray . . .. The people seemed shadows."[37] The large advanced headquarters at Hollandia was probably better suited to future planning, but, now that MacArthur was ashore in the Philippines, he "couldn't, he really couldn't, go back – and he didn't want to."[38] In his office in the Price House, MacArthur would conduct the majority of his business, pacing endlessly while sucking on his long-stemmed corncob pipe. The exercise, according to his doctor, was "important to his health."[39] When not working or pacing, he would sit in a rocking chair on the porch, relaxing or bouncing ideas off his personal staff and lamenting his resource woes. "You know, Doc," MacArthur confided to his personal physician in one of these moments, "the way I have to bargain for a few extra days of a carrier's time, you might think the Navy was almost out of them."[40]

The Price House was also marked for destruction by the Japanese, who knew that MacArthur's headquarters was located there. Amazingly, they were never able to put a bomb on target, although machine gun bullets were another matter altogether. One night a Japanese fighter strafed the house while MacArthur was asleep. According to MacArthur's doctor, "The tile on the roof shattered and danced, but two bullets came through a wall and landed in the beam about a foot-and-a-half from the General's head."[41] MacArthur slept through the commotion and later had the staff dig out the bullets to send to his son. "Arthur will like that," MacArthur commented, to which staff member Bonner Fellers replied, "His mother won't."[42] On another occasion, after Japanese aircraft strafed the building, MacArthur's aides rushed to his office, yelling, "Did it get you?" "Not yet," MacArthur coolly replied, nodding at a bullet hole a foot away.[43]

Others were not so fortunate; Japanese bombs targeting Tacloban killed and wounded soldiers and civilians alike, many within a stone's throw of the Price House. Repeatedly for the first week after the invasion and periodically thereafter, Japanese aircraft bombed Tacloban. Nearby, at the airfield that was under construction, Lt. Gen. Kenney "spent most of the time getting in and out of slit trenches because of Jap air raids."[44] Carlos Romulo, who had waded ashore with MacArthur, wrote, "Death was in the air, all around us, all the time."[45]

MacArthur's troops had battled the Imperial Japanese Navy, land-based airpower, and Japanese soldiers. They were now about to confront elements every bit as difficult to control: weather, terrain, and refugees. After seizing Carigara, the 24th Infantry Division attacked west along the narrow coastal corridor in an effort to enter the Ormoc Valley and reach Ormoc on Leyte's west coast. The 34th Infantry attempted a company-strength amphibious envelopment on November 3, but the force was not strong enough to dislocate the Japanese defenders. After a difficult fight, in which the beach-head was saved by massed artillery fire, the force was withdrawn by nightfall. Nevertheless, Japanese forces, subjected to massed artillery fire throughout the night, withdrew from their positions, enabling the 34th Infantry to advance the following day.[46] But the *1st Division* had beaten the American forces to the high ground dominating the entrance to the Ormoc Valley. These reinforcements, discovered by air reconnaissance and reports of Filipino guerrillas, made a quick advance into the valley impossible. "A feeling grew among staff officers that the ORMOC CORRIDOR would become another GUADALCANAL," lamented one division history, "and they were right."[47] As the reality of a long slog ahead dawned, the rains set in. "Heavy rains impeded maneuver," recorded the division's historical report. "Inadequate roads became increasingly more inadequate as heavy equipment battered them. The individual soldier, his clothing, and his equipment were constantly wet. At times even more than spirits were dampened. Living in a foxhole is a muddy business."[48]

The 1st Cavalry Division found the going no easier. With the seizure of Tacloban and Carigara complete, there "began a battle with an enemy that all through the Leyte Campaign caused more trouble and difficulty than the Japanese ever did. It was mud, and rain, and mud, and typhoons, and mud, mud, mud."[49] According to Brig. Gen. Chase, "We lived in mud at least knee deep most of the time, and as a result, we lost hundreds of men to sickness and to tropical skin diseases."[50] As the weather deteriorated, the 5th and 12th Cavalry Regiments made a long and exhausting march west, "toward the green cloud topped mountains which divide the eastern sides of the island like a tall fence."[51]

Thus began the long and bitter struggle to secure the high ground and mountain passes between the Leyte and Ormoc Valleys, a struggle that tested the endurance and mental fortitude of the American forces. "This struggle was to continue for nearly two months under the most depressing and difficult conditions known since the famous march over the Kokoda Trail in New Guinea," the division after-action report stated. Torrential rains, steep slopes, razorback ridges, thick jungle foliage, heat and humidity, inaccurate maps, and poor or nonexistent roads proved difficult obstacles to overcome.[52] Just knowing where a unit was located in the trackless terrain was an enormous challenge. Rain, mud, and typhoons made the steep mountain terrain even more difficult. "For the Cavalrymen the routine became endless – climbing, slipping, sliding patrols through the mountain jungle by day; wet shoes, wet clothes, and wet foxholes for sleeping at night .... Large scale fighting was rare but the total success of a thousand odd patrol missions enabled the troops and squadrons to gradually pull their way to the top of the ridge."[53]

Further south, the 96th Infantry Division had also found the mountainous interior of Leyte tough going. The terrain was so severe that the division sometimes had to use small liaison aircraft to locate friendly units, which often could not accurately locate their own positions because of the poor quality of the maps they were issued.[54] Indeed, Col. Henry Muller, G-2 of the 11th Airborne Division, reasoned that the mountains bisecting Leyte presented such an obstacle to movement "that the people on opposite sides spoke different languages."[55] Progress slowed to a crawl as the troops negotiated a succession of ridges separated by deep gorges and covered with dense vegetation, defended by Japanese infantry determined to hold the ground until reinforcements could arrive to enable a counteroffensive.[56] Sixth Army tasked the division to find a trail across the mountains, but trails did not exist. Troops had to cut them as they progressed, hauling supplies and evacuating wounded on the backs of horses, mules, carabao (native water buffaloes), or infantrymen.[57] "The terrain, to use the favorite but inadequate phrase of the doughboy, was 'rugged,'" recorded the 96th Division history. "The trails ran up and down in an endless series of ridges and gorges. The jungle was thick, providing ideal spots for Jap ambushes. The altitude was high – the clouds hung in a low mist, and it was usually raining. Altogether, it was about the least pleasant place one could imagine."[58]

The newly arrived 11th Airborne Division ("Angels," commanded by Maj. Gen. Joseph Swing) was ordered to move into the mountains west of the airfields at Burauen to defend them against the *26th Division*, which was offloading at Ormoc on the west coast of the island. The 11th Airborne Division was the smallest division in the Pacific Theater, with just over 8,300 men in one parachute infantry regiment and two glider regiments, the latter units consisting of just two battalions each. What it lacked in quantity, it made up for in the quality of its soldiers, all of whom were self-selected volunteers. The division's performance on Leyte and Luzon would earn it an enviable and well-justified combat record. According to Muller, the division had additional motivation to battle the Japanese on Leyte:

> We knew the 511th [Parachute Infantry] was likely to make contact with stragglers from the 16th Japanese Division which had been virtually destroyed by our 1st Cavalry and the 7th Infantry Divisions in the initial assault on Leyte. The 16th, incidentally, was the same infamous division that was in charge of the Bataan death march three years earlier. Since the Japanese did not rotate their soldiers home during the war, most of its members who were wiped out on Leyte were the same soldiers who had so cruelly mistreated the American and Filipino soldiers captured on Corregidor and Bataan. The Division Commander, Major [sic – Lieutenant] General [Masaharu] Homma [sic – Homma commanded the *14th Army* during the invasion of the Philippines in 1941–1942], somehow eluded capture on Leyte, but the 511th apprehended him later on in Japan. He was tried as a war criminal and was hanged.[59]

For some, revenge would go hand in hand with redemption.

Swing was an artillery officer commissioned in the West Point class of 1915 – the "Class the Stars Fell On."[60] He had served with the 1st Division in World War I and was aide-de-camp to US Army Chief of Staff Peyton C. March, whose daughter Josephine he married while the war was still raging. Swing was the honor graduate of the Command and General Staff

School in 1927 and also attended the Army War College in 1935, marking him for higher duties once war broke out. He had commanded the division since its activation in February 1943 and now was to oversee its entry into combat. Among the many difficulties faced by the division was the lack of maps for the area. Muller recorded, "All the rest of Leyte had been mapped neatly and completely down to the last schoolhouse and cemetery, but where our mountains were supposed to be was a patch of white rather like Outer Mongolia used to appear on world maps when I was a schoolboy."[61]

The Division Reconnaissance Platoon was sent to locate trails leading across the mountains, and what they discovered was disconcerting – such trails as existed were little more than animal tracks. Any movement across the mountains would include only what could be carried on the backs of soldiers, porters, or animals.[62] Despite the foreboding terrain, Swing ordered the 511th Parachute Infantry Regiment into the mountains to find the Japanese. According to Muller, "the flow of intelligence from the guerrilla units swelled into a virtual flood. They were especially helpful in providing us with the location of Japanese forces."[63] The paratroopers soon contacted the *26th Division* in the mountains to the west. Their hard-nosed commander, Col. Orin D. "Hard Rock" Haugen, reported to Swing, "Hell, General! We are surrounded. We don't have to look for the Nips to kill 'em!"[64] Swing committed his other two regiments into the mountains. The division then fought a knock-down, drag-out fight with the Japanese division for the next several weeks.

Stormy weather added to the misery, for in 1944 Leyte was subjected to near record rainfall – nearly twenty-four inches in the first month after the landing. The outcome of the campaign would depend heavily on the ability of engineers to keep the roads inland from the beaches on Leyte Gulf trafficable to support offensive operations. After almost perfect weather on A-Day, rain descended on Leyte in buckets and did not let up, turning choking dust into glutinous mud. Combat troops could never really get dry, leading to jungle rot – a catchall term used by the troops for all sorts of tropical skin diseases made worse by the inability to stay dry.[65] "Foot travel, even on level terrain, was laborious because of the heavy, sucking, clinging, knee-deep mud," recorded one division's history. "The slopes and tops of mountain ridges were as boggy as the valleys, but the infantrymen slipped and slid and crawled forward. They slept and ate and fought in a sea of mud, while supply troops conquered the same tenacious footing to give them the wherewithal to continue."[66] Clothing quickly fell apart in the wet, tropical climate, necessitating periodic issue of new uniforms and boots to the troops.

Typhoon season, which runs from October through December in the Visayas, descended upon American and Japanese soldiers alike. Sixth Army commander Lt. Gen. Walter Krueger recalled three typhoons with torrential rains hitting Leyte in late October. These storms

> flooded the whole country, made roads and trails practically impassable, created havoc in Army Headquarters and in other installations, carried Treadway and other bridges out to sea, made it extremely difficult to establish dumps, hospitals and the shops of ASCOM, the Army supply agency, and inordinately delayed construction of airdromes, which deprived us of adequate air support for a considerable period and enabled the Japs to bring large reinforcements to Leyte.[67]

Soldiers living out in the open felt the full fury of Mother Nature. Medical Corps officer Captain George E. Morrissey recalled living through one of the storms on October 30:

> We rigged up a long shelter with three ponchos for three men and felt secure for the night, but we had a genuine typhoon lasting from 9 P. M. to 4 A. M. It was the most miserable night I've ever spent. The rain was unbelievably hard and accompanied by a 50 mile [per hour] gale. My foxhole filled up with a foot of water and after midnight the air seemed bitterly cold. The night seemed endless.[68]

On the night of November 8–9, another typhoon blew through the area, collapsing buildings, causing streams and rivers to flood their banks, and washing out roads and bridges. Bonner Fellers, MacArthur's military secretary, wrote to his wife Dorothy, "There is a typhoon blowing. Winds estimated at 100 mph for tonight. There are many thousands of American lads sleeping on the ground – if there is sleep possible."[69] Elizabeth James, an American civilian living in the Bicols region of southern Luzon, wrote in her diary, "The wind sounded like a heavy express train overhead, and when it hit us, it shook the frail little edifice we call 'our house'!"[70] Radio reporter William Dunn informed his listeners, "The rain came down as it seems to come down only in the tropics – by the barrel instead of the drop. Then the wind, sweeping across the water, caught the downpour and swept it ahead of it in great blinding sheets."[71]

Henry Muller had just landed on Leyte with the 11th Airborne Division when the typhoon struck:

> We were no sooner ashore when the worst typhoon in a decade dowsed the island. It was an amazing phenomenon. Torrential rains accompanied by

violent winds produced an actual horizontal rainfall. All we could do was stake down our tent flaps and try to keep ourselves and our equipment dry. The roads on the island, not designed to support heavy military traffic, soon turned into ribbons of deep mud. Everything came to a halt as hundreds of trucks submerged to their axles, blocked the roads and even the infantrymen on both sides became mired in a sea of mud. Worst of all, construction of the vital airfields was suspended, disrupting the critical timetable for the attack on Luzon.

The three airfields near Burauen were now seas of mud, with construction equipment "bogged down in the mud along with several Navy fighter aircraft which had been forced to make emergency landings but ran off the ends of the unfinished, steel planking runways."[72]

Units improvised to keep supplies moving forward. Heavy rain rendered roads untrafficable and necessitated supply via parachute drops, water transportation, carabao, and native carrying parties.[73] Guerrillas assisted US forces as guides, while thousands of "intelligent, friendly and cooperative" Filipinos were used for carrying parties and road maintenance – just as MacArthur had foreseen.[74] The Tacloban–Ormoc highway in northern Leyte "became slippery, then deeply rutted, and finally between Carigara and Pinamapoon [sic – Pinamopoan] it became bottomless," recorded the 32nd Infantry Division history.[75] Engineers worked in twenty-four-hour shifts to keep the roadway open and its bridges intact. The road, built on swamp and rice paddies, was capable of handling light traffic, but it "literally disintegrated under the pounding of heavy trucks, tanks, and artillery …. Long lengths of corduroy [logs placed transversely along a road to improve trafficability] were laid on the apparently bottomless mud. Gangs of Filipino laborers were employed to bolster weak spots by hand-patching. But the road remained an uncertain supply line at best during subsequent actions."[76] In the end, persistent rains prevailed and the stopgap measures failed. Quartermasters used landing craft and amphibious trucks to move supplies along the coast in order to skirt impassable stretches of roadway.[77]

As hard as resupply was along the coast, resupply in the mountains was even more difficult. The 12th Cavalry Regiment's supply chain, for instance, began at warehouses in Tacloban, where laborers would load trucks with supplies. The trucks would then haul the supplies thirty miles to Carigara. There, laborers would trans-load the supplies onto amphibious tracked vehicles for a three-mile journey through flooded rice paddies to Sugud. Laborers would again transfer the supplies, this time to trailers hauled by artillery tractors. These tractors would labor their way into the foothills, across boulder-strewn rivers, up steep inclines, and through the never-ending mud that often required soldiers to winch the vehicles forward. High in the foothills, the supplies would end up at the regimental supply base, where 300 Filipino laborers, or *cargadores*, would carry them forward, two men to a 50-pound load, to a forward supply point staffed by another 300 native bearers that was yet another day's march from the forward line of troops. "To describe the terrain is impossible," the division history relates. "Narrow, slippery trails, waist deep rivers and streams, heavy undergrowth and the never-ending climb to gain altitude, forced consumption of five hours over a track that measured less than three miles on the ground."[78] From warehouse to soldier, the journey took four days. The way back was no easier; during the 1st Cavalry Division's attack across the mountains, it took twenty-four native stretcher bearers twelve hours to carry a litter patient from the front line to the division's supply base. In the worst of the mountainous terrain, a single battalion – the 1st Squadron, 12th Cavalry – was supported by 1,500 Filipino laborers.[79]

Indeed, the 1st Cavalry Division would have been hard-pressed to have accomplished its mission on Leyte and Samar without Filipino assistance. On the island of Samar, one engineer troop built over 50 bridges and repaired 71 miles of road without heavy equipment by employing more than 3,000 Filipinos.[80] In the operations over the mountains that separated the Ormoc and Leyte Valleys, each cavalry regiment used a minimum of 1,000 Filipinos each day to haul supplies and evacuate casualties.[81] The division initially had difficulties in recruiting enough laborers to work in the mountains, and then had even more difficulties transporting them to the mountains every day. The solution was to build labor camps in the mountains, where Filipino bearers would live for a week at a time; as an inducement, the division paid the Filipino laborers overtime, fed them well, and provided them with work clothes.[82] By the end of the campaign, the division employed more than 6,000 Filipino laborers in various work details, thereby substantially adding to its authorized strength.

The Filipino people treated the Americans as liberators and assisted them in maintaining order, in rebuilding key infrastructure, and by working as paid laborers. Filipinos in Tacloban greeted the arrival of American forces on October 21 by lining the streets and porches of the main street and waving American flags. "The universal attitude of all Filipinos contacted in the initial stages of this operation was one of complete confidence in the American Army and great gratitude for the liberation from the Japs," the 1st Cavalry Division reported. "The entire atmosphere was charged with the spirit of appreciation and happiness of these peoples in contacting our

American soldiers."[83] Filipino appreciation for their liberation from the brutal Japanese occupation was not limited to the urban areas. American soldiers observed "a spirit of friendliness and gratitude sincerely manifest" as they moved forward.[84] The 24th Infantry Division reported similar findings:

> On the whole, it was found that the Filipinos were loyal and extremely cooperative. Those who were collaborationists were ever watched by the civilians and guerrillas and were quickly apprehended when the opportunity presented itself. The pro-Japanese were very much in the minority and some of these could be better described as opportunists. If Leyte is a criterion, willing aid will be given the American Army in all parts of the Philippines.[85]

The Filipino civilian population, while overwhelmingly supportive of US forces, also presented challenges to commanders trying to move inland and to come to grips with the Japanese. According to SWPA policy, US forces were to provide food, fuel, clothing, shelter, medical care, sanitation, and other supplies "necessary to preserve lines of communication, to maintain the health and working capacity of the population, and to preserve public order." The War Department informally referred to this as the "disease and unrest" policy.[86] Civilian looting was a problem wherever US forces eliminated the Japanese presence. There were not enough military police to guard warehouses and other facilities, and combat forces could not be diverted for this purpose. One solution was to use guerrillas to secure rear areas, but commanders had difficulty distinguishing the real guerrillas from pretenders who came forward only after the invasion. Only when guerrilla leaders emerged was any value derived from these forces as scouts and security personnel.[87]

Within a day of the assault on Leyte, civil affairs issues arose to plague the assault divisions. In the 1st Cavalry Division area, nearly 50,000 hungry Filipinos demanded food and shelter. The division set rules on fraternization, placed guards on warehouses and supply dumps, and distributed captured Japanese rations and clothing to the neediest Filipinos. Commanders placed a higher priority on unloading rice from ships lying offshore. Guerrillas came forward and were soon in great demand as security forces to keep order in Filipino towns and villages.[88] Refugees also challenged the 24th Infantry Division as Filipinos streamed into the liberated zone. The division established a temporary refugee camp on the beach, but soon moved the people to Palo, where they were organized "to clean the church, bury dead humans and animals, and dig latrines." The division established a local police force, instituted a curfew, and recruited hundreds of laborers to assist with such tasks as road construction and maintenance.[89]

Army or area commanders were responsible for administration of civil affairs in their zones. On Leyte, Sixth Army exercised this responsibility through eight Philippine Civil Affairs Units (PCAUs), self-sufficient units composed of ten officers of various specialties and thirty-nine enlisted soldiers of Filipino descent. PCAUs followed US forces ashore as they liberated Leyte, the vanguard of thirty such units that would deploy to the Philippines in 1944 and 1945. PCAUs were trained to reestablish governance and restore essential services in areas under their control. They administered civil affairs and humanitarian relief, using Filipino leaders and laborers to assist in the process to the maximum extent possible, until the Commonwealth government could assume responsibility for these functions. Their work brought vital relief to the Filipino people, but, just as importantly, it kept the civilian population from interfering in military affairs. PCAUs kept the local population informed of military activities and recruited local labor for military and reconstruction activities. Once areas were deemed secure, the PCAUs worked to restore civil administration and economic life by appointing temporary public officials, reestablishing the court system, administering relief, restoring public safety, reopening schools, restoring public utilities, improving public health and sanitation, managing local currency, stimulating local food production and fishing, and recruiting labor for combat units and reconstruction.[90]

PCAUs were a key link to the restoration of Filipino civil society and self-governance. Lt. Col. Joseph Rauh, Jr., a Harvard graduate who worked as a civil affairs planner on MacArthur's staff, recalled that he used John Hersey's 1944 Pulitzer Prize-winning novel *A Bell for Adano*, about an Italian-American officer who rehabilitates a Sicilian town in the wake of the Allied invasion, but is eventually fired by a micromanaging and hard-hearted general, as the template for the civil affairs effort in the Philippines.[91] Areas liberated were quickly transitioned to Filipino control. The American army in the Philippines was a force of liberation, not an instrument of occupation.

MacArthur, guided by Courtney Whitney and Bonner Fellers, resisted the reinstatement of the US High Commissioner to the Philippines before the war concluded. In this regard, MacArthur wrestled with Secretary Harold Ickes and the Interior Department, whom MacArthur accused of wanting to treat the Philippines "as another of his national parks."[92] Ickes wanted to reinstate the US High Commissioner in the Philippines as soon as the fighting on Leyte ended. MacArthur would have none of it. "My plan for civil administration and relief in the Philippines throughout the period of military operations contemplates two phases," MacArthur wrote. "During actual combat, civil administration and relief will be handled by United States Military Detachments which will utilize, when possible, local Philippine governmental organizations and individuals. Administration by these detachments will be closely coordinated with Commonwealth Government officials. After cessation of combat in a particular area, I shall delegate to the Commonwealth Government, insofar as may be practicable, the administration of civil government and relief under my supreme authority."[93] In MacArthur's opinion, reinstating the High Commissioner before the Philippines had been completely liberated smacked of imperialism and would lead to divided authority and confusion. Roosevelt sided with MacArthur, but the bad blood would boil over into MacArthur's memoirs.[94]

The key point, in MacArthur's view, was the need to reinstate and empower the Filipino civil government as soon as possible, rather than appointing military governors of liberated areas. The army of liberation would never become an army of occupation. The Filipinos had made great strides toward the day when they would become independent; the United States needed to bolster the foundations of constitutional government rather than supplanting it for the sake of expediency. That the Filipino people, the civil affairs section recorded, "have never been deprived of the right to constitutional government by the United States, despite compelling reasons ofttimes for its temporary sacrifice, gives added strength to the democratic basis upon which the Filipino people may now build toward their future political destiny."[95]

In Tacloban, President Osmeña did what he could with his limited staff to see to the interests of liberated Filipinos. He appointed officials, organized the recruitment of civilian labor to assist US forces, distributed food, worked to suppress black marketeering, opened schools and hospitals, and issued currency. He had less interest in apprehending collaborators, an issue that MacArthur turned over to his counterintelligence officer, Brig. Gen. Elliott R. Thorpe, who headed an enormous roundup of suspected collaborationists. Osmeña desired to give each suspect a trial to determine their motives for collaboration, which he believed absolved them of the worst of their crimes in appropriate circumstances. Unfortunately, lack of judicial capacity left this issue in abeyance for the time being, but it would certainly resurface once US forces liberated Manila.[96]

MacArthur's forces were now in a race with the Japanese to build up combat power on Leyte. Logistics in the beachhead area dwarfed the previous efforts of SWPA logisticians and engineers. The challenge was so significant that MacArthur labeled his chief engineer, Maj. Gen. Hugh J. "Pat" Casey, as indispensable to the operation. Casey had wrenched his back just prior to embarkation for Leyte and then herniated a disk aboard ship, which immobilized him. Ordered by MacArthur to get Casey ashore, his doctors "dosed him up with codeine and aspirin and other things that would help him with his pain," strapped him to a stretcher, and took him via boat and jeep to the engineer headquarters in Tacloban.[97]

According to one observer, on Leyte logistics refused to conform to the doctrinal templates. "No instructor ever perpetrated such a requirement on hapless students, nor did any student ever offer such a solution in the history of the Command and General Staff School."[98] The school solution did not work on Leyte. During the planning for the invasion, SWPA planners relied on a rosy timetable for airfield construction, which they believed would be sufficient to station two fighter groups, one bomber group, and seven other squadrons in less than a week. The SWPA engineer, Col. Samuel Sturgis, Jr., and his Sixth Army counterpart, Col. William J. Ely, pointed out the weather and terrain conditions that would inhibit construction, to no avail.[99] Seaborne replenishment of Leyte was retarded by the presence of only one dock at Tacloban, the need to dredge an approach channel (which was not completed until December 4), and the resulting need to move supplies ashore by landing craft.[100]

According to Vice Adm. Daniel E. Barbey, successful amphibious movements in the Pacific were "made possible because of the slow, awkward, wonderful LSTs," without which "it is difficult to imagine how the war could have been successfully fought."[101]

Planned construction included four airfields capable of housing 380 aircraft, with facilities for 2 fighter groups and a squadron of night fighters in place by A plus 5; a naval air base, PT boat base, naval repair base, and Seabee facilities; petroleum storage and distribution facilities in support of 11 petroleum barges anchored offshore for immediate use and even more extensive petroleum storage and distribution facilities for longer-term use; and a base area to support 200,000 troops that included port facilities capable of accommodating 4 Liberty ships, warehouses, hospitals with a total capacity of 12,000 beds, a replacement depot, and headquarters facilities for various commands.[102] The engineer troop list included eighteen engineer aviation battalions, three engineer construction battalions, six engineer construction brigade and group headquarters, an engineer aviation headquarters, two engineer port construction groups, and numerous other engineer units, totaling 21,322 personnel and 6,258 vehicles.[103] Rainy

6.2: A flotilla of Coast Guard-manned and Navy LSTs unload their cargoes on the beach on Leyte. LSTs, with hinged doors that could allow vehicles to drive from the ship to shore without need of a crane, were the workhorses of US and British amphibious operations during World War II. (Credit: US Coast Guard Photo)

weather, extensive swamps, and poor drainage bedeviled the engineers throughout the campaign.

The engineers had a near-impossible job, with too many priorities and too few units. They concentrated on preparing or improving exit roads so that equipment and supplies could be moved inland. But there were few places for them to go; the dump locations selected from aerial photography proved in most cases to be swamps or rice paddies. Units claimed ground as they came across suitable dump and bivouac areas, only to be forced to move as other units arrived. As engineer reconnaissance parties determined the scope of the problem, an area allocation board reallocated the few areas of dry ground to the most critical installations. It was a Sisyphean task, as the heavy rains would often turn what once appeared to be usable ground into quagmires.[104]

The most pressing problem was the construction and maintenance of roads. Roads on Leyte were too narrow for two-way military traffic and quickly collapsed under the strain placed upon them. By early December, the road inland from Dulag was impassable along a four-mile stretch centered on Burauen; the only way to get through was to pull vehicles with tractors across the rutted, muddy stretch. Engineers eventually repaired the road by dumping three feet of gravel on top of it. Keeping open lines of communication to forward combat elements competed with maintenance and improvement of the service areas inland from the beaches for the services of the inadequate number of available engineer battalions. The situation only gradually improved after the middle of December as the rains subsided.[105]

Commanders diverted engineers to road repair and combat duties as both rain and Japanese opposition increased, delaying the development of the critical airstrips on which Kenney's fighters depended. In New Guinea, the engineers chose airfield sites with the subsequent concurrence of the air task force commander. Prior to the invasion of Leyte, this procedure was reversed; the air force commander chose airfield locations on the basis of flawed geographical studies and then tasked engineers to build on these sites. All this proved is that airmen are not engineers; most of the sites chosen were under water during the rainy season. Only the airfield at Tacloban and smaller fields at Dulag, San Pablo, Bayug, and Buri were viable – the latter four problematically so.[106] Kenney was never able to base bombers on Leyte during the campaign because of the restricted runways on the available airfields.

Hampered by enemy air raids and LSTs attempting to unload their cargo directly onto the airstrip, engineers (supported by 1,500 Filipino laborers) raced against time to finish construction on the Tacloban airfield before carrier-based air support departed, leaving US forces ashore highly vulnerable to air attack. Engineers installed steel mat on the crushed coral base to put the airfield into limited operation.

The carriers and battleships of the Imperial Japanese Navy might have retired from the field, but Japanese airpower continued to contest the land, seas, and skies on, surrounding, and over Leyte. During the three months beginning in the middle of October, *Imperial General HQ* augmented the Philippines with more than 2,300 planes from Japan, Formosa, and elsewhere.[107] While the Japanese fleet battled its American counterpart in the battle of Leyte Gulf, upwards of 250 land-based aircraft operating from Luzon attacked the beachhead and the ships anchored offshore.[108] They succeeded in hitting two fuel dumps and an explosives cache, as well as striking at shipping in the gulf.[109] The escort carriers in the

Gulf required all their fighters to protect the fleet, leaving none to spare for close air support of troops fighting ashore. To protect the ships in the gulf from kamikaze attacks, smoke-laying landing craft belched out a continual fog to create "a heavy pall of smoke around and over them."[110] Japanese attacks disrupted logistics and hindered efforts to put Tacloban and Dulag airfields into service. These airfields were crucial, for by the end of the month Halsey and Kinkaid had to withdraw their carriers for replenishment, leaving US forces for the time being dependent solely on land-based fighter cover.[111]

The Japanese aerial assault was the most intense since the dark days on Corregidor two-and-a-half years earlier. MacArthur confided to Kenney, "Stonewall Jackson's last words were 'Tell A. P. Hill to bring up the infantry.' If I should die, today, tomorrow, next year, anytime, my last words will be 'George, bring up the Fifth Air Force.'"[112] Kenney lamented in his diary, "P-38's must clean this place up. There is a continuous red alert, ackack and bombing both getting the troops and I regret to say many officers jittery. Everyone is kept awake, unloading of boats is prevented and so is work of every kind. At the strip the only way I could keep the men out of the slit trenches was to go out on the [steel] mat myself and yell at them."[113] The arrival on October 27 of thirty-four P-38s of the 49th Fighter Group was a moment for celebration. As the first fighter landed, troops and civilians alike erupted in cheers and threw helmets and tools into the air in triumph.[114] By the end of the day, the P-38s had bagged four Japanese bombers.[115] The land-based fighters finally gave the forces ashore consistent air cover, forcing the Japanese to limit daylight bombing runs. P-61 Black Widow night fighters arrived to fend off nighttime attacks.

With the arrival of the first of Kenney's P-38 fighter squadrons, air cover over US forces on Leyte improved. One of the instructor-pilots deployed to Leyte was Major Richard "Bing-Bang" Bong, the top aerial ace in the US Army Air Forces. Given that he was already an American hero who had shot down thirty Japanese planes, Kenney ordered him not to push his luck and to refrain from aerial combat. This admonition was of little use. Five hours after arriving at Tacloban on October 27, Bong shot down his thirty-first aircraft; a day later he downed two more. Kenney wrote tongue-in-cheek to his boss Hap Arnold in Washington that "Bong is trying to be careful but the Nips won't do their part."[116] Arnold replied in kind: "Major Bong's excuses in shooting down three more Nips noted with happy skepticism by this HQ. Subject officer judged incorrigible."[117] By the end of the Leyte campaign, Bong had increased his kill count to forty Japanese planes. Kenney reported with mock sheepishness to Arnold, "He is still trying to get in his flying time without interruption."[118] Kenney also nominated Bong for a Medal of Honor, which was awarded to the aviator by MacArthur in a special ceremony before Bong left the combat zone for good.[119]

Despite Bong's heroics, Fifth Air Force could achieve only so much, for weather and terrain hampered Kenney's engineers and fliers. Rain reduced sources of sand and gravel, hampering construction of the airfield at Dulag. Engineers eventually placed 23,000 cubic yards of sand and gravel on the runway to provide the foundation for steel matting. The airstrip went into limited operation on the morning of November 18, with thirty-five P-38s transferred from Tacloban that day.[120] Given the cramped conditions and immature facilities, these airfields remained insufficient to serve as intermediate staging bases for bombers and had only limited space for P-38 fighters from the 49th and 475th Fighter Groups, P-47 fighters from the 348th Group, Marine Corsair and Hellcat fighters from Marine Aircraft Group 12, and a Marine night fighter squadron, VMF(N)-541 – enough force to achieve local air superiority over Leyte, but not enough to provide

6.3: Gen. Douglas MacArthur awards the Medal of Honor to Maj. Richard I. Bong at Tacloban, Leyte, airstrip. With forty kills to his credit, Bong was the top US ace in World War II. (Credit: US Army Signal Corps Photo)

close air support to the forces fighting inland or to prevent Japanese reinforcements from reaching the island.[121]

The airstrips further inland were in even worse shape. The airstrip at Bayug was so unstable once the heavy rains started that "it became a veritable graveyard for P-38s." Because of the unstable silt surface, Sixth Army engineers recommended its abandonment, but Fifth Air Force remained firm that it needed the capacity. Steel mat arrived in the middle of November, but constant rain, emergency use of the runway by aircraft, and a Japanese paratroop attack delayed completion until December 22, thirty-five days after the first mat was laid.[122] The Buri airstrip was used for dry-weather operations beginning on November 5, but lack of engineers and its low priority meant that it was never upgraded, and it was abandoned at the end of the month. The airstrip at San Pablo suffered a similar fate; by November 23 heavy rains had turned the area into a quagmire, forcing the engineers to abandon it as well.[123] Maj. Gen. Ennis C. Whitehead, commanding the Fifth Air Force, observed, "Mud is still mud no matter how much you push it around with a bulldozer."[124] To replace the capacity lost by the abandonment of these airstrips, engineers convinced Krueger to relocate his army headquarters so that they could convert the relatively well-drained ground underneath into an airfield. Construction at Tanauan, located halfway between Tacloban and Dulag, began on November 28 and was completed eighteen days later with the installation of a steel-mat runway over a sand and coral base.[125]

The issue of air cover over the beachhead area came to a head on November 1, when Kinkaid sent a message of concern to MacArthur:

> At the present time there is in operation at Tacloban 1 air strip from which can be operated possibly 125 planes. My last information was that a second strip at Dulag would not be ready until 10 November. In the meantime the Japs are steadily adding to their air strength in the Manila area. For 10 days or more it is possible that the enemy will dominate in the air. An attack in strength might readily make the strip at Tacloban unserviceable and wipe out the planes. Following attacks without air opposition would destroy the town, sink shipping and harass our troops.

Getting to his point, Kinkaid recommended that MacArthur request Nimitz to order Halsey's fast carriers to strike Japanese airfields on Luzon and in the Visayas. "I believe the above recommended action is essential for the security [of] the whole operation."[126]

If this message wasn't clear enough, Kinkaid fired off another an hour and a half later to nearly every major commander in the Pacific. "Naval forces covering Leyte report 2 heavy air attacks today. 1 destroyer has been sunk by torpedo plane. 3 additional severly [sic] damaged. If adequate fighter cover not maintained over combatant ships their destruction is inevitable. Can you provide the necessary protection?"[127]

At this point, Halsey weighed into the debate. "I will beef up repeat beef up your surface forces at Leyte if needed but the fast carriers must not repeat not be risked in close or defensive CAP [Combat Air Patrol] job. I am presuming from our long association that Kenney repeat Kenney is being called on for heroic measures." MacArthur replied, "CAP will be maintained over your ships from – 1 hour before sunrise until 1 hour after sunset. Continuous strength 4 P 38's. 16 P 38's on Tacloban available on call. No night fighters available. Regret exceedingly your losses today but know your gallant ships played their usual magnificent part."[128]

The inability to bring sufficient ground-based air power to bear forced MacArthur to request the assistance of Halsey's Third Fleet to attack Japanese airfields in the Visayas and on Luzon. After replenishing his ships at Ulithi Atoll, Halsey's fast carriers steamed west to bomb Japanese air bases near Manila, beginning on November 5. For the next three weeks, Halsey's naval aviators hammered the Japanese air forces on Luzon, downing 245 Japanese planes in aerial combat and destroying another 502 on the ground.[129] The pounding continued until kamikaze strikes on November 25 damaged four carriers stationed in Leyte Gulf, compelling Halsey to again withdraw all but one fast carrier task group back to Ulithi Atoll for replenishment and repair.[130] MacArthur and Nimitz realized the threat the kamikazes represented and censored news of them to keep both the Japanese high command and American civilians unaware of the damage and casualties they had inflicted on the fleet.[131]

The insufficient capacity of the airfields on the east coast of Leyte limited available land-based airpower, which was needed to provide fighter cover over Leyte and to prevent Japanese reinforcements from reaching the west coast port of Ormoc, especially after the withdrawal in late October of the bulk of the Seventh Fleet and portions of the Third Fleet to Ulithi Atoll for replenishment. Lack of air superiority over Leyte and the absence of sea control over the western approaches enabled a number of Japanese convoys to reach Ormoc. Code-named the *TA operation*, the Japanese reinforcement of Leyte portended a longer and more costly battle for control of the island. Yamashita was less than enthusiastic about the plan; by the middle of

November he had realized that the battle for Leyte would be a meat grinder, one the outnumbered and outgunned Japanese forces could not win. He argued instead for a curtailment of operations on Leyte to husband resources for what he viewed as the more decisive battle upcoming on Luzon. Yamashita's superior, Field Marshal Terauchi, overruled him.[132]

MacArthur's intelligence analysts failed to pick up on these intentions until November 2, when they reversed their assessment that the Japanese were withdrawing from Leyte.[133] A week later, they concluded that the Japanese now had 3 divisions and 43,500 troops on the island, a fairly accurate estimate.[134] In all, 9 *TA* convoys delivered 45,000 troops and 10,000 tons of weapons, supplies, and ammunition to Leyte between October 25 and December 11, including the *1st* and *26th Divisions* from Luzon and portions of seven other divisions and brigades.[135] So, instead of facing 22,000 Japanese troops, as the Sixth Army G-2 estimated, US forces ended up battling more than 60,000 in the 2-plus-month struggle for the island. The reinforcements came at a steep price, as US land-based and naval airpower and PT boats sent to the bottom the light cruiser *Kinu*, nine destroyers (*Uranami, Shiranui, Shimakaze, Hamanami, Naganami, Wakatsuki, Kuwa, Uzuki*, and *Yuzuki*), two dozen merchantmen and naval transports, and eight smaller combat vessels, drowning tens of thousands of soldiers and sailors in the process.[136] The reinforcements extended the Leyte campaign and exacted a greater toll on American combat forces, but, as Yamashita foresaw, this came at the expense of the *14th Area Army*'s ability to successfully defend Luzon.

The Japanese began to ship reinforcements to Leyte even as the Battle of Leyte Gulf raged. With American forces distracted by the movements of the Imperial Japanese Navy, the first *TA operation* – 3 destroyer-transports and 2 landing ships carrying more than 6,000 soldiers of the *30th* and *102nd Divisions* – proceeded without loss.[137] Two other convoys followed closely thereafter. No reinforcement meant more to Japanese chances of success than the *1st Division*, one of the oldest units in the Imperial Japanese Army, which deployed from Shanghai to the Philippines to counter the American invasion. The division landed unmolested at Ormoc on November 1 and moved up Highway 2 toward Carigara, harassed by a flight of P-38s which attacked the column as it headed north.[138] As American forces arrived at Carigara first and the opportunity to counterattack had been lost, the Japanese instead fortified the high ground at the northern entrance to the Ormoc Valley. There the *1st Division* would fight to the death with the US 24th and 32nd Infantry Divisions over the next several weeks. Lt. Gen. Krueger confided in his memoirs that the reinforcement of the *1st Division*

247

to Leyte "did more than any other enemy unit to prolong the Leyte operation."[139]

From November 11 onward, US naval and air forces began to interdict the *TA* convoys. On that morning, 347 aircraft from 10 carriers of Task Force 38 attacked the 5 transports and 7 escorts of *TA3*, sending all but 1 destroyer and 1 subchaser to the bottom. Since the attack took place while the ships were near Ormoc, most of the soldiers made it to shore, but all of the heavy weapons and equipment being carried by the convoy, which belonged to the *26th Division*, ended up on the bottom of Ormoc Bay.[140] Codebreakers then pinpointed the timing and route of convoy HI 81, carrying two regiments of the Japanese *23rd Division* from Pusan to the Philippines. On November 15, American submarines attacked, sending to a watery grave the division headquarters, four infantry battalions, and an artillery battalion.[141] Airstrikes sank most of the ships in *TA5* on November 24–25; the two surviving vessels returned to Manila without reaching Leyte.

On November 27, passage into the Camotes Sea was swept clear of mines, allowing portions of the Seventh Fleet to patrol the west coast of Leyte for the first time. Destroyers and PT boats took a toll on reinforcing Japanese convoys from that point forward, adding to the carnage.[142] Marine Corsairs stationed at Tacloban joined the battle during the final two reinforcement convoys on December 7 and December 11–12, sinking upwards of a dozen transport and cargo ships and three destroyers and seriously damaging several other vessels.[143] In their attempt to reinforce their forces in the Philippines, the Japanese overall lost forty-six merchantmen and attack transports, twenty-four of them bound for Leyte. Betrayed by broken ciphers and hammered by land-based and naval aircraft as well as destroyers and PT boats, thousands of Japanese soldiers went to the bottom in their doomed transport ships, along with thousands of tons of equipment, supplies, and ammunition.[144]

By November 1, Krueger embraced a new intelligence assessment that the Japanese would fight a decisive battle for Leyte. Dutifully recorded by Ultra intelligence and confirmed by guerrilla reports and aerial reconnaissance, the presence of tens of thousands of Japanese reinforcements headed for Leyte became clear. XXIV Corps also captured a document confirming the presence of the *1st Division* on Leyte. Worried about Japanese intentions, Krueger halted the X Corps advance south into the Ormoc valley and reoriented it north to defend the shores of Carigara Bay against a possible amphibious assault.[145] The loss of momentum would cost X Corps dearly, as

6.4: A medium bomber from the 38th Bomb Group attacks a Japanese destroyer in Ormoc Bay, Leyte. The bombing attack destroyed the ship. In their attempt to reinforce their forces in the Philippines, the Japanese overall lost forty-six merchantmen and attack transports, twenty-four of them bound for Leyte. (Credit: US Army Air Forces Photo)

Japanese reinforcements reached the high ground overlooking the north coast and dug in.

Krueger's fear of an amphibious assault in the rear of X Corps shows the limitations of MacArthur's special intelligence. Ultra was of much greater value in planning campaigns and operations than in executing them. Although Ultra did give lots of information about the enemy order of battle, it did not always give away enemy dispositions and intentions at the tactical level. Intelligence officers gathered information from patrol reports, aerial reconnaissance (of limited value because of jungle foliage and the near-constant inclement weather), civilians, guerrillas, captured documents, and to a lesser extent, prisoners (who normally had been wounded and separated from their units and whose information was therefore out of date). Inevitably, corps, divisions, and regiments had to gain intelligence the old-fashioned way, by fighting for it.

Three weeks into the campaign, MacArthur knew he was up against Japan's best ground commander and some of the best troops in the Imperial Japanese Army. SWPA G-2 struggled with the presence of Japanese soldiers from the *1st Division* for several days. The supposition was that the unit was still in China and that the soldiers found in Leyte were from an ad hoc organization. On November 6, the G-2 Order of Battle section cast these assumptions aside. On the basis of pocket litter found on enemy dead, it confirmed the presence of the *1st Division* from Manchuria.[146] Two days later, the G-2 informed MacArthur of Gen. Yamashita's assumption of command in the Philippines. Guerrilla reports had earlier cited Yamashita's presence in Manila, but a captured document confirmed the sightings. "Gen. Yamashita conducted the Singapore campaign and is probably the foremost hero of the war insofar as the Jap soldier is concerned," wrote the G-2 analyst. A hand-written note on the memo reads, "He is the original Jap blitzkrieg kid – undoubtedly explains the change of Jap tactics in the P.I. [Philippine Islands]."[147]

After two days of defending against a threatened Japanese seaborne assault on Carigara that never materialized, the 24th Infantry Division began a renewed push into the Ormoc Valley on November 5. A rugged, densely overgrown mountain barrier separated Leyte Valley from Ormoc Valley, with only one road and one track leading from one to the other. The key feature was Breakneck Ridge, actually a series of ridges covered with tall grass ideally suited to the defense. The *1st Division* had fortified the area, blocking the road from Pinamopoan as it ascended over the ridges and twisted through the hills. Rain, mud, and inaccurate maps plagued the attack, which tended to splinter into a series of uncoordinated small unit fights.[148]

The 21st Infantry Regiment, so far unbloodied in the battle for Leyte, met a wall of resistance from entrenched Japanese forces. The 19th and 34th Infantry Regiments attempted to envelop Japanese positions by striking through the trackless mountains, but the going was treacherous and slow, and troops had to be supplied by air drop. "This enemy was combat trained, skillful in individual warfare, and apparently quite willing to die fighting," recorded the division's history.[149] The battle continued without letup until the 1st Battalion, 21st Infantry, supported by a platoon of tanks, finally gained the crest of the ridge on November 11. The battalion then called in an artillery barrage of 350 rounds of white phosphorus, which cleared its fields of fire in the tall grass and burned the remaining Japanese soldiers hunkering down in spider holes. An attack by the 3rd Battalion, 21st Infantry seized the rest of Breakneck Ridge the next morning, and further attacks over the next three days secured the remainder of the high ground in the area.[150] Attacking forces used flamethrowers extensively to clear Japanese troops from their positions.[151] It had taken the regiment 12 days to advance just 2,000 yards over this difficult piece of terrain defended by veterans of the *1st Division*. The commander of the 21st Infantry, Colonel William J. Verbeck, noted the professionalism of the defending Japanese troops, especially their fire discipline, counterattacks supported by artillery and mortars, camouflage, entrenchments, and reverse-slope defensive tactics.[152]

During the fighting on Breakneck Ridge, Lt. Col. Spragins' 2nd Battalion, 19th Infantry was tasked with seizing the high ground south of the village of Limon to block the Ormoc Road that ran along its base. Hampered by unreliable maps and guides, the battalion advanced on November 11 and within three days had established a blocking position that obstructed Japanese reinforcements and supplies headed for Breakneck Ridge. The isolated battalion suffered greatly from supply shortages, and wounded soldiers could not be evacuated for lack of a line of communication to the rear. Small supply parties and often inaccurate airdrops kept the unit going. The Japanese resorted to using tanks to run the blockade, but they could carry only a small amount of supplies. The battalion repulsed Japanese attacks on the morning of November 20, but that afternoon began a withdrawal to Hill 1525, which it completed two days later with the assistance of the 3rd Battalion, 34th Infantry. The column then continued over the next two days to Pinamopoan, where the "bearded, mud-caked soldiers came out of the mountains exhausted and hungry. Their feet were heavy, cheeks hollow, bodies emaciated, and eyes glazed." There the survivors were treated to a Thanksgiving dinner of carrots, bully beef, and coffee, which the soldiers agreed was "the finest Thanksgiving dinner they had ever eaten."[153] The battalion had played a crucial role in the battle by denying Japanese forces supplies and reinforcements, earning a well-deserved Distinguished Unit Citation for its interdiction of the Ormoc road.

The division also tried to envelop the other Japanese flank. On November 10, the 1st Battalion, 34th Infantry moved via eighteen tracked amphibious vehicles around Japanese lines and landed unopposed seven miles up the coast. Assisted with orientation and intelligence by Filipino guerrillas, the battalion then marched over a period of three days to a position on Kilay Ridge.[154] Supplied by air drop, the battalion fended off Japanese attacks in combat that was often hand-to-hand "in the pitch blackness of torrential tropical rains." Thousands of bats, gorging on the ubiquitous mosquitos, would fly over the men each night as they lay in their foxholes. By December 1, when the unit received orders to withdraw, soldiers were "either in a dull, stale, apathetic state or jittery as hell," according to battalion surgeon Captain George E. Morrissey,

> The latter because the proximity of Japs and proximity of our own artillery bursts go hand in hand. I gravitate from one state to the other, but usually just sit and stare. Smoke three times as much as usual. Wanting to get off this hill is one of the greatest wants I've ever had. At times it even supersedes wanting to go home.[155]

The battalion commander, Lt. Col. Thomas E. Clifford Jr., was a former all-American football player from West Point. The message ordering the withdrawal of the battalion noted, "You and your men have not been forgotten. You are the talk of the island and perhaps the United States," adding as an aside, "Army beat Notre Dame 59 to 0, the worst defeat on record."[156]

As with units elsewhere on Leyte, the climate and terrain took as great a toll on the troops as the enemy. Rain and mud plagued the infantry, who could not keep dry. Already hungry and tired when the mission began, the troops had to pack all supplies, ammunition, and equipment over the tortuous terrain to reach their positions. Rations and sleep were both scarce. Under these conditions, soldiers suffered from trench foot, dysentery, and fever. Only the truly debilitated were evacuated; "the remainder fought with what strength they had left, and often on sheer nerve alone."[157] The fighting was relentless. "You can see our own artillery concentration hammering away at the Japs in their almost impregnable positions on the reverse sides of slopes," wrote Morrissey, the battalion surgeon, in his diary. "The sound of artillery magnified by valley echoes shatters the air day and night around us."[158]

The fighting along Breakneck Ridge had significantly reduced the combat effectiveness of the 24th Infantry Division. The 21st Infantry Regiment alone had lost 630 men killed, wounded, and missing, along with 135 non-battle casualties evacuated from the front.[159] Twelve thousand men short by the end of the first week of November and now facing three times as many Japanese forces as predicted, Sixth Army needed replacements and reinforcements. SWPA, on the tail end of the priority list for the former, sent 5,000 men – all it had – to Leyte.[160] More importantly, MacArthur authorized the reinforcement of Sixth Army by the 32nd Infantry Division, the 11th Airborne Division, and the 112th Cavalry Regiment. Krueger, unaware of the extent of Japanese reinforcements that were now digging into the high ground on Leyte, relieved the commander of the 24th Infantry Division, Maj. Gen. Frederick Irving, presumably for his inability to break into the Ormoc Valley.[161] The 24th Infantry Division, minus the 34th Infantry Regiment and three artillery battalions that remained behind to augment the strength of the 32nd Infantry Division, assumed a position on the southern flank of X Corps in the Jaro–Cavite area to defend against a possible movement along the Dolores–Daro trail that ran over the mountains between the Ormoc and Leyte Valleys.

Krueger committed the 32nd Infantry Division, which itself was 2,000 men understrength, into the line to relieve the depleted 24th Infantry Division. For the next six weeks, the "Red Arrow" Division would fight the *1st Division* to the death in a cage match, a battle "characterized by close hand to hand combat in densely jungled, mountainous terrain, during torrential tropical rainfall throughout the period."[162] The division history compared the fighting to "a boxing bout for a heavyweight crown, but there was no limit on the number of rounds, no referee, no rules, and no bell . . .. From Pinamopoan on 16 November to Lonoy on 22 December every yard of the 6 1/2 miles was a bitterly contested mountain stronghold. Maneuvers and flank movements were of no value."[163] Of the 13,000 men in the Japanese *1st Division* that arrived in Leyte, fewer than 500 survived the war.[164]

The *1st Division* proved a formidable enemy. During the night of November 19–20, elements of the *49th Regiment* took advantage of a gap in American lines (caused by inaccurate maps) to penetrate north to the coast between Pinamopoan and Culasian Point, where they blocked the highway.[165] The US 126th Infantry Regiment attacked and destroyed the Japanese forces after a three-day battle. The ferocity of the fighting is highlighted by a battle that began on the night of December 5–6, when the 127th Infantry Regiment attacked Japanese entrenched on the high ground 1,000 yards south of the Leyte River and to the west of Limon. There the GIs fought Japanese entrenched in "numerous foxholes and spider holes 10 feet deep ... connected by [well-camouflaged] interlacing communication trenches."[166] A week later, on December 13, another attack by the 3rd Battalion, 126th Infantry south along Highway 2 met defending Japanese in

> foxholes dug into the banks of the road and spider holes dug underneath the roots of trees and under logs on the hillsides. It was bitter, close, hand to hand fighting and because of the steepness of the terrain, the denseness of the tree growth, the inaccuracy of maps and nearness of adjoining units, artillery and mortar fire could not be used to its full advantage in reducing these positions.[167]

Medium tanks proved valuable in supporting the attacking infantry, but for the most part "the enemy troops encountered had to be blown from their foxholes with hand grenades or killed in them with bayonets and flame throwers."[168]

To the south of the 32nd Infantry Division, the 1st Cavalry Division also found the defending Japanese forces formidable and the terrain challenging. By November 20, the 12th Cavalry ran into the enemy's main defenses on the Hill 2348–Mt. Cabungangan line. Heavy rains limited visibility and protected Japanese positions from observed artillery fire. Artillery fire had to be right on the mark; otherwise, the shells would sail over the Japanese fortifications atop the ridge and explode harmlessly several hundred meters below. For more than a week, the 12th Cavalry battered itself against Japanese positions, built into knife-edged ridges and well concealed by thick undergrowth. On November 29, disaster arrived on the cavalrymen's doorstep, as a Japanese infantry battalion maneuvered around the American positions and established a strongpoint astride their supply line. What had been a difficult situation had now become a crisis.[169]

The supply line meant everything to units in contact. With the 12th Cavalry's supply line severed, the fight for survival commenced in earnest. Counterattacks over the next two days failed to dislodge the Japanese. On the morning of December 1, B and C Troops of the 12th Cavalry and A Troop, 5th Cavalry again attacked the Japanese strongpoint. Fighting raged at close quarters until 18:00, when resistance ceased. The attackers counted 218 dead Japanese, not including those who had fallen or jumped to their deaths from a cliff. After some further mopping up the following day, the supplies flowed forward once again.[170]

The 1st Cavalry Division continued to fight for and clear the high ground of Japanese forces for the next three weeks. Nothing could be accomplished quickly, given the terrain and weather conditions in the mountains. The division spent nearly a week resupplying and reequipping the 12th Cavalry, which had been reduced to 60 percent effectiveness after its grueling battles for Hill 2348 and Mt. Cabungangan.[171] The attack continued relentlessly, grinding the Japanese defenders down until their defenses collapsed. The battle's intensity is reflected in the actions of the 2nd Squadron, 7th Cavalry to seize "George Hill." Over five days from December 10–14, the cavalry troopers of the Gary Owen regiment fought a tenacious Japanese enemy over a series of narrow, rugged, razor-back ridges in rain-soaked mountains. The cavalrymen had to attack the Japanese position frontally, as the terrain on the enemy flanks sloped downwards at sixty degrees. American artillery had fired more than 5,000 rounds at the Japanese position with minimal effect. On December 14, Troop G finally seized George Hill the hard way, by killing fifty-five Japanese soldiers in vicious hand-to-hand fighting.[172]

Further south, the 96th Infantry Division, the 11th Airborne Division, and the 7th Infantry Division found the going no easier. In the mountains to the west of Burauen, the 96th Infantry Division wrestled with resupply operations, which consumed one out of every three companies in the advance. The 2nd Battalion, 383rd Infantry reported,

> It took the work of one company a day to keep the forward units supplied with rations and ammunition. The haul was an all-day trip, and the men soon began to fade out from the hard march, some of it up steep vertical slopes on hands and knees. The dampness and filth led to a great many cases of jungle rot, especially on the feet. In addition, there was much dysentery. The battalion suffered approximately fifty per cent casualties from these diseases.[173]

On another occasion, the battalion used eighty-five men in shifts over an eight-hour period to carry three casualties one-and-a-half miles to the aid station.[174] During a ten-day period from December 15 to December 24, the battalion "suffered eighty per cent non-battle casualties from fungus infections, leeches, dysentery and other ailments caused by the miserable living conditions."[175] "The story of these December patrols," recorded the division's historians, "is not one of fighting as much as it is one of hard marches up and down steep trails, of leeches by the thousands, of dysentery, dengue fever and jungle rot, of laboriously packing supplies on tired backs."[176]

The 11th Airborne Division, initially not intended as part of the troop list for the Leyte campaign, relieved the 7th Infantry Division in the vicinity of Burauen between 22 and 28 November, allowing the latter unit to

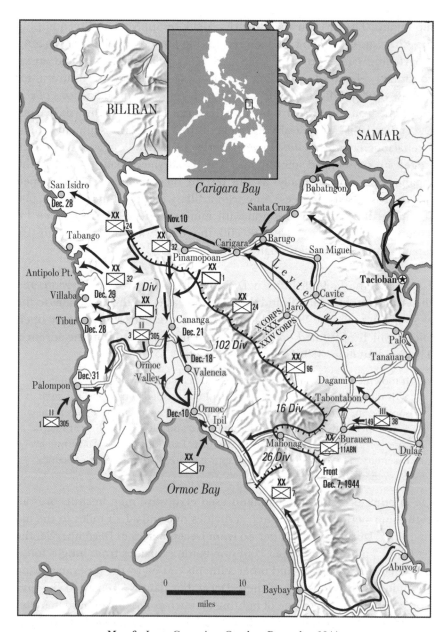

Map 6: Leyte Campaign, October–December 1944.

consolidate along the west coast at Baybay and advance northwards toward
the port of Ormoc.[177] As the 11th Airborne Division advanced across the

mountains, it became clear that it would have to rely on air transport to sustain its attack. There were no roads in the mountainous interior of Leyte, just steep, narrow, muddy foot trails where there were any trails at all. It took ten hours for a soldier to traverse the trail over razor-backed ridges linking Burauen to Lubi, a distance that a plane could negotiate in just ten minutes. The division decided to drop a battalion of 75mm pack howitzers on Manarawat, a small plateau rising 150 feet above a nearby river. Normally such a drop required thirteen C-47 aircraft. Only one was available on San Pablo Airstrip No. 2, so, on December 3–4, it made thirteen sorties to deliver Battery A, 457th Parachute Field Artillery Battalion to the plateau. Division artillery observation aircraft carried the division forward command post to the same destination.[178]

11th Airborne Division logisticians improvised to keep the forward units resupplied. Bad weather and postage-stamp-size drop zones limited the use of larger C-47 cargo planes for aerial resupply. Each division, however, was allocated a small number of liaison planes, Piper L-4 Grasshopper and Stinson L-5 Sentinel aircraft used mainly for artillery spotting. Logisticians pressed them into service to ferry small units, supplies, and ammunition from the airstrip at San Pablo to the front. Pilots dropped material onto crude strips hacked from the jungle. They dropped more sensitive bundles such as medical supplies by parachute. The work was dangerous. "On many days, a thick gray fog hugged the mountain areas, and the pilots had to circle to find an opening near the drop zone. Once under the ceiling, they made the drop and spiraled upward, hoping to break out on top before encountering a mountain peak."[179]

The division established two forward hospitals at Lubi and Mahonag, complete with surgical teams dropped in by parachute, to care for the wounded until they could be evacuated. Additionally, these small planes could land on rough strips to evacuate the wounded to field hospitals in the rear. Because of the tortuous nature of the trails through the mountains, ground evacuation was impractical. Each litter would have required twelve bearers and a security escort, with the journey taking a full two days. Instead, evacuation by air enabled the wounded to be on an operating table within twenty minutes of take-off. These "flying jeeps" altogether delivered 470 tons of supplies, with the peak day's total amounting to 176 flights that delivered 18 tons of cargo.[180] The airborne troopers affectionately nick-named them "biscuit bombers."[181]

The arrival of the 11th Airborne Division enabled the XXIV Corps commander, Maj. Gen. John R. Hodge, to begin shifting the 7th Infantry Division to the west coast. The muddy road from Dulag to Baybay was often flooded out by the incessant rains, so the movement took a full two weeks to accomplish. The 2nd Battalion, 184th Infantry moved to Baybay on November 20 to bolster the 32nd Infantry Regiment, which was defending "Shoestring Ridge" (so named because the troops positioned there were operating at the end of a logistical shoestring) south of the Palanas River. The 17th Infantry Regiment and the remainder of the 184th Infantry Regiment moved to Baybay by stages, beginning on November 22. The entire division had closed on the area by December 4 and began preparations for an attack north toward Ormoc, in conjunction with a planned amphibious turning movement scheduled for December 7. The logistical problem was hellish: The 7th Infantry Division line of communication from Abuyog to Baybay was kept open only through the herculean efforts of division and army engineers. The tenuous, narrow road through the mountains was simply not designed or constructed for the heavy traffic inflicted upon it by upwards of 300 vehicles per day.[182]

The *35th Army* commander, Lt. Gen. Suzuki, was well aware of the vulnerability of Ormoc to an attack from the south. On November 13, he ordered elements of the newly arrived *26th Division* to establish positions in the Albuera area and along the Palanas River. The unit was a division in name only. Tipped off by Ultra intelligence, Task Force 38 aircraft had savaged one of its two convoys, sinking most of the division's heavy weapons, ammunition, and supplies. Five transports went to the bottom, along with four destroyers and several smaller escort vessels. Although several thousand troops managed to swim ashore, another 2,900 drowned.[183] What remained was the division headquarters and five infantry battalions, equipped only with small arms and a few machine guns.[184] Its main purpose was to cut a road across the mountains in preparation for an attack on the US airfields near Burauen, but it also received orders to contain the US drive north from Baybay to Ormoc. To accomplish the latter mission, the Japanese attacked the US forces on Shoestring Ridge on the evening of November 23 with four infantry battalions supported by artillery. The battle raged for the next five nights as Japanese infantry attempted to overrun the American positions. The arrival of the 184th Infantry Regiment into the line turned the tide of battle. By the end of the month, US forces had retaken all the ground lost and were firmly positioned on Shoestring Ridge, this time to stay.[185]

The Japanese could still surprise their American adversaries, even in ways that were self-destructive. In late November 1944, Yamashita and Suzuki embarked on a desperate and ultimately suicidal scheme – Operation *Wa* – to neutralize

American airpower on Leyte by attacking the airfields at Dulag, Tacloban, and around Burauen via airborne and ground assault. Yamashita ordered the *35th Army* to launch a counteroffensive to retake the airfields around Burauen, which he erroneously believed would reduce the amount of ground-based air support available to US forces and even the odds in the battle for Leyte. The operation entailed elements of the *16th* and *26th Divisions* attacking from the mountains to retake the airfields, while an airborne drop of 1,000 soldiers would support the assault. The commitment of the *26th Division* to the battle of Shoestring Ridge hampered its readiness for the attack on Burauen, significantly reducing the odds of success, which were not great to begin with.[186] The attack would begin on the night of December 5, but Suzuki subsequently delayed the airborne attack by twenty-four hours to allow more time for preparation. Unfortunately for the Japanese, the *16th Division* never received the postponement order due to a faulty radio.[187]

In this case, Ultra was up to the task of divining Japanese intentions. During an orientation session with Willoughby in Australia, 11th Airborne Division G-2 Col. Henry Muller received a one-time cipher pad for beyond top-secret messages from MacArthur's G-2. Willoughby, hinting at a unique source of intelligence (without a doubt Ultra), stated,

> Sometime during future operations you may receive a message from me, using our two-way pad, which will begin with the words 'crystal ball states.' After this there will follow a report of a coming enemy activity. You must believe it absolutely. You must not question it or inquire back for further details. Most importantly, you must not reveal the source of the report to anyone.[188]

Two days before the Japanese attack, Muller received a coded message from GHQ SWPA. Using the one-time pad provided to him by Willoughby back in Australia, Muller decrypted the message, which made his pulse quicken: "FOR MULLER G2 11ABN DIV EYES ONLY. CRYSTAL BALL STATES: JAP FIRST PARACHUTE BRIGADE FROM LIPA, LUZON WILL MAKE PARACHUTE ASSAULT BURAUEN AIRSTRIPS SEVEN DECEMBER 1800 HOURS SIGNED WILLOUGHBY G2."[189] It was an invaluable piece of intelligence provided by the Ultra codebreakers. Since he could not inform Swing of the source of the intelligence, Muller decided to present a Japanese airborne assault on the airfields as a distinct possibility in his daily G2 summary. Swing wasn't buying it; he ordered the G2 summary amended to delete the reference to a possible airborne assault.

Despite the ground and parachute assault achieving a degree of surprise, seizing Buri airstrip and overrunning some rear-echelon troops, the

Japanese plan was overly ambitious. A consolidated battalion – all that was available of the Japanese *16th Division* – attacked at dawn on December 6 toward Buri, with a couple of hundred making it as far as a heavily wooded area on the northern end of the airstrip, where they killed a number of service troops. The 1st Battalion, 187th Glider Infantry counterattacked that afternoon and destroyed most of the force.[190]

Four hundred Japanese paratroopers landed at dusk on the San Pablo and Buri airstrips, but not enough to make a difference.[191] The drop resulted in a chaotic night for both sides. Most of the Japanese paratroopers landed at San Pablo, site of the command post of the 11th Airborne Division. The attack was so unexpected that the GIs did not realize the planes were Japanese until paratroopers started to spill out of them. The Japanese landed with a hazy mission to destroy targets of opportunity, which became even murkier after all the senior leaders, who had traveled together in the same plane, were killed when their chutes failed to open. The ensuing battle pitted paratrooper against paratrooper at close range. Expecting to find the airstrip packed with fighters and bombers, the Japanese found just eight Piper Cub planes. Japanese troops destroyed half a dozen light aircraft along with some stores of fuel and other supplies, but did not come close to achieving their goal of destroying US airpower on Leyte, most of which was based at the airfields at Dulag and Tacloban.[192]

The next morning, portions of the 127th Airborne Engineer Battalion, the 674th Field Artillery Battalion fighting as infantry, and a miscellaneous assortment of headquarters and service troops counterattacked and cleared San Pablo airstrip of Japanese forces. The fighting around Buri airstrip was more challenging. At least 200 Japanese paratroopers, reinforced by remnants of the *16th Division*, had to be rooted out of their positions. Krueger requested that SWPA release a regiment of the 38th Infantry Division, in theater reserve, to counterattack the paratroopers, which MacArthur granted.[193] The 1st and 2nd Battalions, 149th Infantry, attacked on December 7 and reached the edge of Buri airstrip, where they linked up with the 1st Battalion, 187th Glider Infantry and the 1st Battalion, 383rd Infantry, 96th Infantry Division, which was also placed under the operational control of the 11th Airborne Division. Over the next three days, these units cleared the Buri airstrip of Japanese paratroopers, while the 11th Airborne Division destroyed what remained of the other Japanese ground forces in the area.[194]

The *26th Division* was to move two regiments through the Mahonag–Anas pass, down the Lubi River Valley, and then advance on Burauen. The order was based on wishful thinking and ignorance of Leyte's geography.

Staff officers in the Japanese *14th Area Army* believed that the trail west of Burauen was a highway.[195] Leyte's imposing geography prevented the Japanese from building even a supply trail to support an advance over the mountains. Instead of concentrating an entire division for an attack on the American airfields in the vicinity, only one regiment reached the Mahonag–Lubi area, and only a single consolidated battalion made contact with the 11th Airborne Division, albeit five days later than planned. On December 10–11, the Japanese executed a weak night attack and then withdrew into the mountains. The American airborne troops protecting the division supply trail contacted this force, scattered it, and annihilated it piecemeal.[196]

Operation *Wa* would never have achieved its objective of destroying American airpower on Leyte in any case, because, by the time the Japanese executed it, the Fifth Air Force had already abandoned the three airstrips that were the main targets of the attack. The Japanese *35th Army* then ordered the remnants of the *16th* and *26th Divisions* to withdraw over the mountains to the Ormoc plain, but shortages of food and limited trails resulted in the loss of most of the soldiers along the way. The 11th Airborne Division commander, Joseph Swing, informed his corps commander that "if he wants to walk from Burauen air fields to Ormoc beach all he has to do is put a clothes pin on his nose and let a man with a strong stomach guide him," due to the stench of the rotting Japanese corpses along the route.[197] Neither unit played a significant role in the fighting from this point on, except for those elements of the *26th Division* defending the western coast of Leyte.[198]

Krueger had planned to conduct an amphibious turning movement along the west coast of Leyte since early November. The operation aimed to seize the port of Ormoc, the last major gateway to Leyte available to Japanese forces. Lack of air support to cover the invasion fleet as well as shortages of shipping and ground forces to execute the landing caused Krueger to shelve the plan, at least for the remainder of the month.[199] The latter shortcoming was rectified by the arrival of the 77th Infantry Division ("Statue of Liberty," commanded by Maj. Gen. Andrew D. Bruce), which was in Sixth Army reserve until October 29, when MacArthur released the division to control of the Pacific Ocean Areas.[200] The division had fought in Guam from July 21 to August 11, 1944, after which it prepared for Operation Stalemate, the invasion of Yap. When the Joint Chiefs canceled that operation, the division, with MacArthur's concurrence, sailed to New Caledonia to rest and refit. Given the difficulties of the fighting on Leyte and at Krueger's urging, on

November 10 MacArthur requested Admiral Halsey to transfer control of the division once again to SWPA. Halsey acquiesced and redirected the division while still at sea to Manus Island in the Admiralties.[201] After a brief forty-eight-hour stop, the division deployed to Tarragona and Dulag on the east coast of Leyte, landing on November 23. The rushed deployment caught the division short of equipment and supplies and worsened the already critical supply situation on Leyte.[202]

On December 1, SWPA ordered a ten-day postponement of the invasion of Mindoro, which had been scheduled for December 5. The purpose of that operation was to seize an area for the construction of airstrips to support landings in central Luzon. But the delay in construction of airfields on Leyte jeopardized air cover for the invasion, so MacArthur agreed to delay the landing. The sudden availability of shipping now made an invasion on Leyte's west coast possible, albeit hazardous, given the threat of Japanese air strikes and kamikaze attacks. The arrival of five Marine fighter squadrons on Leyte mitigated to some extent the threat to the invasion convoy. Admiral Kinkaid agreed to provide the shipping, and along with Krueger assumed the risk to the invasion force. Sixth Army ordered the 77th Infantry Division to prepare for the landing.[203]

The division worked over the next several days to gather its scattered forces and prepare them for the operation. Loading of supplies into landing craft began on the night of December 5–6, even while some units of the division were still moving toward their debarkation points. Given the threat of Japanese air and naval attack, the assault shipping would remain on the far shore for only two hours. As a result, all supplies going ashore had to be assault-loaded onto the limited number of available vehicles. The invasion flotilla of 8 APDs, 25 LCIs, 10 LSMs, and 4 LSTs would carry these vehicles along with 8,500 soldiers – a tight squeeze for both men and equipment. The plan was for the division to land on a narrow beach three-and-a-half miles south of Ormoc and then attack north to the port, shutting down the ability of the Japanese to land additional reinforcements on Leyte. In support of the invasion, the division could call on naval gunfire and air support, along with the fire of the 226th Field Artillery Battalion, positioned near Jaro on the east side of the mountains.[204]

The ships carrying the 77th Infantry Division assembled in Leyte Gulf, where they rendezvoused with twelve destroyers that would provide their naval escort. The convoy then set sail under cover of darkness and moved south around Leyte and then north into the Camotes Sea without incident. As the convoy approached the invasion area on the morning of December 7, air reconnaissance reported a Japanese convoy of thirteen ships – carrying the *68th Independent Brigade* – approaching Ormoc. Fifth Air Force scrambled nearly every available plane to attack the convoy and its accompanying fighters, sinking 4 transports along with their complement of 4,000 Japanese soldiers and supplies and reportedly shooting down 56 planes.[205] The 77th Infantry Division could now land unimpeded.

The landing force of seven infantry battalions and one field artillery battalion, along with divisional combat support and combat service support forces, arrived at its destination and, after a twenty-minute barrage by the 5-inch guns of the destroyers and rockets launched from two LCI(R)s, the first wave went ashore shortly after 07:00. Landing on such a narrow beach in just the two hours available was a calculated risk, but Maj. Gen. Bruce, the division's commanding general, deemed it acceptable after evaluating intelligence from aerial photos and information gathered from guerrillas and civilians familiar with the area. Still, as he and other senior leaders "stood on the bridge we were jubilant over reaching the landing area without opposition as it was a hazardous operation."[206] By 09:30, the division was established ashore and had reached its initial objectives without opposition.[207]

The amphibious turning movement took the Japanese by surprise. Maj. Gen. Tomochika recalled, "The Ormoc landing came as a complete surprise because the strait between Bohol and the southern coast of Leyte had been mined and Japanese Army Headquarters considered that not even LSTs could navigate through these waters. Furthermore, it was thought that the Bohol Strait was controlled by the Japanese navy and that the Americans would not attempt a maneuver so daring as a movement of troop transports into the landlocked waters."[208] The Japanese response was disrupted by the movement of the *35th Army* headquarters from Ormoc to the vicinity of Burauen to direct the counteroffensive there. Lt. Gen. Suzuki returned to his headquarters on the west coast of Leyte only on the evening of December 13, well after the battle for Ormoc had been decided.[209]

The Japanese attacked the withdrawing invasion convoy with more than seventy aircraft, two-thirds of which were shot down.[210] Kamikazes struck five vessels. The destroyer *Mahan* and high-speed transport *Ward*, damaged beyond recovery, were abandoned, leaving "towering columns of smoke mushrooming into the sunny sky as we sailed on."[211] Both ships were later sunk by friendly gunfire and torpedoes. It was an especially ironic moment for the *Ward*, which, before its conversion to transport duty, had struck the first blow against the Imperial Japanese Navy by sinking a midget submarine at the entrance to Pearl Harbor on the morning of December 7, 1941 – exactly three years earlier. Compounding the irony was the fact that the commanding officer of the USS *O'Brien,* which sank the *Ward,* was Cdr. William W. Outerbridge, who had skippered the *Ward* at Pearl Harbor on that fateful day.[212]

The plan was for the division to establish a defensive line and await more supplies and reinforcements. However, Bruce determined that the division had landed in the Japanese support zone, with few combat troops in the area. He therefore determined to attack north toward Ormoc as quickly as possible rather than give the Japanese time to organize a counterattack. By 16:00, the 307th Infantry Regiment had captured Ipil. The next day the division continued the attack, with Japanese resistance increasing as the American troops moved north. The 307th Infantry Regiment seized Camp Downes by 16:00 on December 9 after a difficult battle. The 306th Infantry Regiment and the 305th Field Artillery Battalion moved into the division's beachhead south of Ormoc, bringing more infantry and artillery into the fight. By this point in the battle, Bruce could see Ormoc in the distance, and he issued orders to seize it the next day.[213]

After a ten-minute preparatory barrage, the 306th and 307th Infantry Regiments began their attack at 09:30 on December 10. Rocket-firing LCMs of the 2nd Engineer Special Brigade contributed to the fight by launching their ordnance into the center of Ormoc, which turned the town into "a blazing inferno of bursting white phosphorus shells, burning houses, and exploding ammunition dumps, and over it all hung a pall of heavy smoke from burning fuel dumps mixed with the grey dust of destroyed concrete buildings, blasted by our artillery, mortar, and rocket fire."[214] The 307th Infantry Regiment crunched into Ormoc, killing its defenders in house-to-house combat with mortars, artillery, tanks, tank destroyers, self-propelled guns, grenades, rifles, and bayonets. The 306th Infantry Regiment meanwhile enveloped Ormoc to the east, forcing its remaining defenders to withdraw. By the end of the day, the 77th Infantry Division had cleared the blasted ruins of the town, sealing the fate of Japanese forces on Leyte. Bruce, with an eye on the dramatic, sent a message to the commanders of the 7th Infantry Division and the 11th Airborne Division, which were nearby. "Have rolled 2 sevens in ORMOC. Come 7 and 11. Bruce."[215]

The next day, the 306th and 307th Infantry Regiments launched an attack against Japanese forces north of the Anilao River, which met with stiff resistance even after a massed time-on-target artillery barrage and direct fire from tanks and tank destroyers. But Sixth Army was winning the battle to build combat strength in the area. During the night of December 10, a Japanese barge, unaware that American forces now held the port, attempted to dock at Ormoc, only to be riddled with fire from machine guns, 40mm guns, and tank destroyers. Another Japanese landing craft attempted to land northwest of Ormoc. It managed to offload 150 men and 2 tanks before being taken under fire and sunk.[216] The *Takahashi Detachment* (the *5th Regiment* and an artillery battalion – about 4,000 men – roughly one-third of the *8th Division*), departed Manila on December 9 for Ormoc, but American aircraft engaged the convoy 2 days later west of Palompon and destroyed most of the units except for 1 battalion.[217]

The 305th Infantry Regiment attacked Japanese positions north of the Anilao River on December 13, supported by a barrage from four artillery battalions. The Japanese had decided to defend this position to the last man and managed to hold onto it for another day despite losing upwards of 500 soldiers in its defense.[218] The attack continued the next day, with the 305th Infantry Regiment finally gaining the main Japanese position astride a now thoroughly pulverized three-story stone building. Self-propelled howitzers and tank destroyers moved up to fire directly into Japanese firing slits. An engineer officer used an armored bulldozer to reduce several dozen Japanese emplacements. The bulldozer operator lifted the top cover off each fortification and then killed the occupants with his submachine gun. After his ammunition ran short, the bulldozer operator proceeded to bury the occupants alive.[219] Infantry mopped up the remaining defenders with flamethrowers and by dropping grenades into their positions. The division reported that the fighting in this area was "the bitterest thus far experienced [by the 77th Infantry Division] in the Pacific war."[220]

For the next two days, the 305th Infantry Regiment continued its attack along Highway 2, clearing out remaining Japanese resistance near Cogon. Division artillery and airstrikes pounded Valencia, which fell on December 18 after a determined two-day assault by the 307th Infantry Regiment.[221] After hard fighting, the division reached Libungao on December 21. At 16:45 that day, the division made contact near Cananga with elements of the 1st Cavalry Division attacking south through the Ormoc Valley, completing the destruction of Japanese forces in the corridor. The 32nd Infantry Division finally cracked the last resistance along the so-called Yamashita line on December 22, and, from that point on, the offensive south gained momentum.[222] The 1st Cavalry, 24th Infantry (Maj. Gen. Roscoe B. Woodruff), and 32nd Infantry Divisions descended into the Ormoc Valley. They then attacked to clear the area between the Ormoc Valley and the west coast of Leyte, guided by Filipino guerrillas through the trackless terrain, while meeting only scattered resistance from the few remaining organized Japanese units.[223] The 1st Cavalry Division was unable to get rations over the mountains, so Christmas dinner for its soldiers consisted of sugar cane and camotes (native sweet potatoes).[224]

On Christmas Day, an amphibious turning movement by the 1st Battalion, 305th Infantry seized Palompon. On New Year's Eve, they linked up with the 3rd Battalion, 305th Infantry moving west from Cananga. The latter force and its accompanying engineers fought the "battle of the bridges," as forty bridges along the route had to be strengthened or replaced to carry military traffic. The successful landing at Palompon denied the Japanese forces on Leyte the use of the last viable port in their possession. The relentless attacks had shattered Japanese resistance on the island and sealed the fate of the scattered pockets of enemy troops that remained. The remnants of the *35th Army* withdrew into the northwest portion of Leyte, where they were strategically isolated and suffered greatly from lack of food and supplies. From the time it landed at Ormoc until the link-up of its forces on December 31 along the Palompon Road, the 77th Infantry Division had killed by its estimate 14,384 Japanese soldiers – nearly a quarter of the total Japanese strength on Leyte.[225]

True to form, MacArthur officially ended the Leyte campaign on Christmas Day despite continued fighting on the island. There was some justification for this pronouncement: An Ultra summary accurately reported that the *14th Area Army* had conceded defeat on Leyte a week earlier and noted that the time for the battle of Luzon was "drawing near."[226] MacArthur celebrated the next day by donning his newly authorized five-star insignia as a General of the Army, with rank precedence that placed him behind Leahy, Marshall, and King, but in front of Nimitz, Eisenhower, and Arnold. MacArthur's staff wondered how they would obtain a set of the stars, a problem that was solved when they hired a Filipino silversmith in Tacloban to fashion two sets of the new insignia from US coins and "a collection of Australian shillings, Dutch Guilders and Philippines pesos," which represented the Allied forces in his command.[227]

Christmas 1944 also represented the end of MacArthur's close relationship with his chief of staff. The previous March, during a trip to Washington, Sutherland had convinced US Army Deputy Chief of Staff Joseph McNarney to commission his Australian secretary and mistress, Elaine Bessemer Clark, into the Women's Army Corps (WAC), against the advice of WAC director Col. Oveta C. Hobby.[228] A month later, Sutherland brought Clark from Brisbane to Port Moresby, where she was the only woman in the advanced headquarters. MacArthur ordered her back to Australia, an order that

Sutherland apparently took as more of a suggestion, much to his boss's annoyance. Sutherland then brought Clark forward to Hollandia when the advanced headquarters moved there in September, where her presence, according to Paul Rogers, "was a disruption and a constant source of conflict."[229] Sutherland's insubordination led to a caustic showdown with MacArthur, who in no uncertain terms ordered Sutherland to send Clark permanently back to Australia.[230]

The climax came on Leyte on December 14, when MacArthur's staff learned that Sutherland had once again brought his WAC "friend" forward, this time having a house built for her near SWPA rear headquarters at Tolosa, ten miles south of Tacloban. Not only was this in contravention of MacArthur's wishes, but also it was a violation of an agreement with the Australian government not to bring Australian women or conscripts north of the Equator.[231] MacArthur's aides conferred and nominated Doc Egeberg to deliver the news to the boss that "Captain Z" was on the island. Egeberg went to sit on the porch of the Price House with MacArthur, wondering how to broach the sensitive subject, finally resorting to mental telepathy:

> I sat there and said to myself, "Captain Z, Captain Z, Captain Z," and concentrated on her. I suppose only a minute or two went by before the General said, "Say, Doc, whatever happened to that woman?" I said, "Woman, what woman, General?" "Oh, you know, *that woman.*" I waited a second or two before I said, "Oh, you mean Captain Z?" "Yes, Captain Z – where is she now?" "She's in that cottage I told you about down at Tanauan." The *WHAT* that came out of the General even startled the officers in the street.[232]

Egeberg quickly excused himself as Sutherland arrived, but anyone within earshot could hear MacArthur's "violent, pent-up, end-of-the-rope loss of temper" in the minutes that followed.[233] According to another member of the staff, Captain Z left Leyte "with all the suddenness of the [man] shot from the cannon" in a circus stunt.[234] MacArthur temporarily relieved Sutherland of his duties and put him under house arrest. He had put Sutherland firmly in his place, as subordinate to the commander-in-chief.[235] Sutherland would not long survive the falling out. He would be replaced as MacArthur's consigliere by Courtney Whitney, who, if anything, was even more "despised [than Sutherland] by other members of the GHQ staff."[236]

Although the Leyte campaign was officially over, American forces now under the command of the Eighth Army continued to clear scattered enemy elements for months to come in combat "characterized by battalion level actions against the stubborn pockets of Japanese entrenched in the mountain ridges and along the swampy valleys."[237] Eichelberger despised the term mopping up. "The only difference between a big fight and mopping up," he wrote to his wife, "is that when victory is obtained nobody can call it that. It is just as difficult and the bullets go by just as fast."[238] Despite his chagrin at the lack of mention of his army in MacArthur's press releases, Eichelberger admired the handling of the campaign by his boss. "We have had a very successful movement back to the Philippines," Eichelberger opined to his wife. "It has not been easy and it has been very costly for the Japs. In American lives the cost has been cheap. If [MacArthur] had not had the courage to take chances this campaign for the Philippines would have ended a thousand miles before it started. Certainly not further than Hollandia."[239]

When Sixth Army handed control of the Leyte operation to Eighth Army, Krueger's G-2 estimated that 8,000 Japanese troops remained on Leyte.[240] By the end of May, Eighth Army had cleared most of the island, killing or discovering dead around 27,000 Japanese in the process.[241] Only 1,100 Japanese were able to make their way to Cebu; the remainder faced their fate on Leyte.[242] Altogether, Sixth and Eighth Army forces engaged and killed around 60,000 Japanese troops on Leyte, more than 3 times as many as intelligence estimated to be on the island before the invasion. Victory came at the cost of more than 3,500 killed and nearly 12,000 wounded.[243] Thankfully, malaria was not the challenge it had been further south. After devastating units during campaigns in the Solomon Islands and on New Guinea, malaria was much less of a factor in the outcome of the Philippines campaign. Three factors explain this: the availability of Atabrine, use of DDT to eliminate mosquito breeding areas, and differences in climate and geography.

Leyte never became the major base American commanders intended it to be, but the campaign had more important consequences. The Japanese, unwilling to cede the island, reinforced Leyte as the campaign progressed with some of their best forces, subjecting them to relentless air and sea attack. Tens of thousands perished – victims of poor strategy, inferior intelligence, inadequate logistics, and unrelenting American firepower. Regarding intelligence, Maj. Gen. Tomochika stated, "American intelligence was so far superior that a comparison is useless. It seemed to me as if we were fighting our battles blindfolded, while the enemy seemed to have ten times the intelligence we possessed."[244] Given American access to Ultra information, he was, of course, correct.

The Leyte campaign eviscerated Japanese air and sea power. The Battle of Leyte Gulf had gutted the Japanese surface fleet. According to statistics compiled by Kenney's staff, the Japanese lost 3,864 aircraft in the Philippines–Formosa–Ryukyus area during the period from 1 October to 31 December, a level of attrition Japanese factories and pilot-training facilities could not replace.[245] On Leyte alone, between October 20 and December 31, US combat aviators and antiaircraft gunners shot down somewhere between 606 and 763 Japanese planes at a cost of just 23 American aircraft.[246] By fighting a decisive battle for Leyte, the Japanese high command had also sacrificed Yamashita's ability to successfully defend Luzon – which was now squarely in MacArthur's sights. After Leyte, MacArthur wrote in his memoirs, "The dark shadow of defeat was edging ever faster across the face of the rising sun of Japan."[247]

7

THE INVASION OF LUZON

> It was awe-inspiring to see one of the mightiest armadas of ships ever to be assembled. As we sped by these powerful ships my spine tingled with excitement at this display of the power of the United States – the power that had driven thousands of miles back across the Pacific to the Philippines and that would sweep on to Tokyo itself![1]
>
> Guerrilla leader Russell Volckmann

The Luzon campaign would be the largest US ground campaign of the Pacific War and the second-largest American campaign of World War II, eclipsed only by the campaign in France and Germany following the Normandy invasion. Planning for the invasion of Luzon continued concurrently with ongoing operations on Leyte. According to operations plan Musketeer III, Sixth Army would land in Lingayen Gulf, in roughly the same area used by the Japanese in their invasion three years earlier and for the same reason – the dictates of geography. The beaches in Lingayen Gulf could support a multi-division assault, and, once ashore, the forces would have access to the northern end of the central plain, an optimal avenue of approach leading to Manila, with its vital dock area that could support US forces on Luzon and serve as a base for the invasion of Japan. Leading the Sixth Army ashore would again be Lt. Gen. Walter Krueger. Few Americans were as well acquainted with the terrain. Krueger had fought on Luzon during the Philippine Insurrection; on a previous tour of duty in the archipelago, he led a topographical party that mapped Luzon's central plain.[2]

Admirals King, Nimitz, and Kinkaid determined that the invasion fleet would require support from land-based aircraft to operate safely on the northern tip of Luzon. MacArthur's airman, Lt. Gen. George Kenney, agreed.

> It [the invasion of Leyte] was a glorious headache for a while but we are out of the woods now with about two hundred more Nip scalps added to the collection of our fighters. For the Luzon show we will have our aircraft

based on Leyte and Mindoro so that we can do the job right. Halsey's big carriers will support us by keeping Jap air down in Formosa and the islands to the north. Kinkaid's escort carriers will provide cover for themselves and for the troop and supply vessels. Long jumps like the Leyte show are practicable only if we have indisputable evidence that the enemy is shattered and we can therefore afford to gamble

he wrote to General Hap Arnold in the middle of the Leyte campaign.[3] Maj. Gen. Stephen Chamberlin and his planners at MacArthur's headquarters accordingly planned operations to seize lodgment areas suitable for the construction of airfields: Aparri on the northern tip of Luzon, if the fleet were to sail up the eastern coast of Luzon, or in southern Mindoro, if the fleet were to take the western route through the Visayas. In early November, MacArthur and Nimitz's staffs agreed on the western route, which could assure better air coverage from Japanese air attacks, and planning for the invasion of Mindoro, scheduled for December 5, intensified.[4]

The extended campaign for Leyte put the schedule for the invasion of Mindoro at risk. Airfield construction on Leyte was so delayed by the monsoon rains and swampy terrain that the Mindoro invasion fleet required air support from escort carriers, something Kinkaid was loath to risk in the confined waters of the Mindanao and Sulu Seas. The debate was ugly. According to Kenney, a meeting at MacArthur's headquarters on November 26 turned into a brawl:

> Kinkaid refused to put CVE's into Mindoro show or even use them to cover shipping in Leyte Gulf to release our fighters for the convoy cover. Said if he did they would not be ready for Luzon show. I argued that if we could risk LST's and 26,000 men, he could risk his CVE's; that if he could just escort the convoy until troops were ashore he could beat it full speed to Leyte and be ready in plenty of time for the Luzon show, and I would take over the rest of the cover job besides helping his CVE's out whenever I could. He said that his CVE's had to return to Manus to refuel and rearm, that it was too dangerous to do it in Leyte Gulf on account of Jap suicide bombers. If his argument is good he will lose all of them before he gets to Lingayen Gulf. Told him so. Kinkaid sore. Krueger mad – joined me.[5]

By the end of the meeting, Kinkaid reluctantly agreed to escort the Mindoro invasion force with six escort carriers plus supporting surface units. Kenney breathed a sigh of relief: "While the Mindoro show is still a risky one, this takes the curse off."[6]

Four days later, Kinkaid met MacArthur and Sutherland in Tacloban and argued against launching the Mindoro operation until Japanese airpower in the vicinity had been reduced to an acceptable level to reduce the risk to his fleet. MacArthur refused to budge. Kinkaid then retreated to his cabin on the *Wasatch* and drafted a note to Adm. King in Washington regarding the situation that would have effectively ended Kinkaid's career. Later that afternoon, Kinkaid went ashore for further discussions with MacArthur, Sutherland, and Kenney, during which Kinkaid made a detailed argument for the postponement of the Mindoro operation. According to Kenney, "MacArthur hit the ceiling, questioning Kinkaid's loyalty."[7] The group adjourned for dinner and, as they were finishing, a memo arrived from Nimitz outlining Halsey's need to refit and resupply his fast carriers at Ulithi, which necessitated a delay of the Mindoro invasion. Nimitz urged a ten-day postponement, which MacArthur, after conferring in private with Sutherland, approved. Kinkaid never sent the message he had drafted, much to his relief.[8]

The delay had an upside; it would allow allotted invasion shipping to be used by the 77th Infantry Division in its amphibious turning movement to the west coast of Leyte and gave more time for engineers to complete the construction of airfields on Leyte. This decision, along with other considerations such as moon and tide conditions, replenishment of Kinkaid's fleet, and airfield construction on Leyte and Mindoro, would delay the invasion of Luzon from December 20 to January 9.[9]

The Japanese garrison on Mindoro numbered roughly 1,000 men, few of whom were organized into trained combat units. The Western Visayan Task Force, commanded by Brig. Gen. William C. Dunckel, would invade the island with an overwhelming force centered on the 19th Regimental Combat Team (reinforced) of the 24th Infantry Division and the separate 503rd Parachute Infantry Regiment. The latter unit was initially scheduled to drop on Mindoro, but was reassigned as part of the seaborne invasion force because of the lack of space on Leyte's airfields for an adequate number of transport aircraft. Four US engineer battalions and an Australian engineer squadron would land behind the combat forces to immediately begin construction of airfields capable of basing two fighter groups, a light bomber group, a tactical reconnaissance squadron, and two commando fighter squadrons.[10]

Task Group 78.3 weighed anchor on December 11 and headed through Surigao Strait into the Mindanao Sea. The Japanese launched a small but deadly attack against the flotilla the next afternoon, with kamikazes

272

seriously damaging the cruiser *Nashville* and the destroyer *Haraden*, both of which suffered severe casualties and had to retire for repairs.[11] Halsey's fast carriers meanwhile hammered Japanese airfields on Luzon. Fighters from the accompanying escort carriers downed nearly three dozen Japanese planes attempting to hit the invasion fleet as it neared Mindoro.[12] As the troops headed for shore on the morning of December 15, kamikazes struck again, fatally damaging two LSTs and causing lesser damage to several other ships. Nevertheless, the landing proceeded without resistance, with the troops met by ecstatic Filipinos on the beaches. By nightfall, the two combat teams had seized a beachhead seven miles deep. As Dunckel's troops established a solid beachhead ashore, Halsey's naval aviators racked up 461 kills, while the escorting jeep carriers accounted for another 66 Japanese aircraft.[13]

The Third Fleet suffered the largest losses of the operation when Admiral Halsey, headed to strike Luzon, unwittingly sailed his ships into the center of Typhoon Cobra, resulting in the capsizing of 3 destroyers, damage to 27 other ships, 146 aircraft wrecked or washed overboard, and the loss of 790 sailors.[14] Third Fleet was out of commission for several weeks as it retired to Ulithi Atoll for repairs, which made the establishment of airfields on Mindoro even more significant. Admiral Nimitz personally attended a Court of Inquiry at Ulithi to investigate the tragedy. The court concluded that Halsey had committed an "error of judgement," but stopped short of recommending disciplinary action. A month later, command of the fleet (renamed the Fifth Fleet) passed to Admiral Raymond A. Spruance.[15]

The geography of Mindoro protected the San Jose area from the torrential rains that had impeded the Leyte operation, and airfield and base construction proceeded expeditiously. Within five days engineers had an airfield in operation. No sooner had the first fighters arrived than twenty Japanese kamikazes attacked a resupply convoy headed for Mindoro, damaging two LSTs (which were abandoned), two destroyers, and a Liberty ship. A second airfield was in limited operation three days later and ready for continuous operations on December 28; two additional airfields were added later. The airfields on Mindoro accommodated P-38 Lightning, P-40 Warhawk, and P-47 Thunderbolt fighters, A-20 and B-25 bombers, as well as a squadron of P-61 Black Widow night fighters.[16]

The Japanese reacted by dispatching a naval force consisting of two cruisers and six destroyers to shell the airfields and sink any shipping they found in the nearby area. The force arrived off the south coast of Mindoro an hour before midnight on December 26 and shelled the area for forty minutes, causing minor damage ashore and sinking a Liberty ship and a PT boat. Aircraft sent to interdict the Japanese force helped to sink one destroyer and damage other ships, but twenty-six planes crashed while attempting to make their way back to airfields on Leyte in the darkness.[17]

The Japanese also launched a number of air attacks against Allied shipping; by January 4, when Japanese attention turned to the invasion convoys headed for Lingayen Gulf, they had sunk or forced to run aground six Liberty ships, a tanker, two LSTs, a destroyer, and two LCMs, while damaging another Liberty ship, an oiler, two destroyers, an LCI, a mine sweeper, a PT tender, and two PT boats. Air strikes on Mindoro on the night of January 2 destroyed fifteen P-38s and seven A-20 Havoc bombers.[18] Japanese attacks diminished the effectiveness of the air squadrons on Mindoro, but by January 9 there were still enough aircraft and pilots stationed on the island to provide meaningful support to the invasion of Luzon.[19]

The 19th Regimental Combat Team and the 503rd Parachute Infantry, reinforced by the 21st Infantry Regiment and aided by Mindoro guerrillas, secured the remainder of Mindoro by the end of January. Units sent out patrols to hunt down Japanese stragglers. On January 1, 1945, SWPA transferred control of these forces from Sixth to Eighth Army; the latter headquarters would be responsible from this point on for operations outside of Luzon. The seizure of Mindoro proved to be of great value to the upcoming invasion; by January 9, the airfields on the island housed three fighter groups, two night fighter squadrons, three tactical reconnaissance squadrons, an air photography squadron, and an air–sea rescue squadron.[20] These aircraft would secure the seas on the western side of Luzon and support Sixth Army forces ashore, reducing the need for carrier-based airpower which had proven so problematic in the Leyte campaign. In addition, Marine Aircraft Group 14 deployed to Samar and was available for operations in the Central Philippines and southern Luzon.

Fifth Air Force plastered Japanese aircraft based on Luzon, destroying hundreds of planes on the ground or in the air in preparation for the invasion of Lingayen Gulf.[21] From the beginning of October 1944 through January 1945, US Army Air Forces airmen and naval and Marine aviators destroyed more than 1,500 Japanese aircraft on the ground on Luzon, to which could be added hundreds more finished off in air-to-air combat.[22] "The airstrips there [Mindoro], like stoves in an all-night diner, never got cold," wrote Lt. Gen. Robert Eichelberger in his memoirs.[23]

Maj. Gen. Charles Willoughby, MacArthur's chief of intelligence, estimated in the middle of October that the Japanese would defend Luzon with the

121,000 men (4 infantry divisions and 3 independent brigades, among other units) on the island, reinforced by other units as the invasion neared. Willoughby predicted that the Japanese would defend the beaches at Lingayen Gulf and then create successive defensive lines across the central plain to defend the central bastion at Manila. The battle on Leyte sucked in some of the forces on Luzon, but the Japanese replaced them with other forces brought from the Asian mainland and elsewhere.[24]

By late 1944, US and Commonwealth cryptanalysts were reading traffic sent in the Japanese army's four-digit cipher, several other army and air force codes, the Japanese army's water transport code, the military attaché code, the Imperial Japanese Navy's code, and the foreign ministry's code (broken before the war by Magic).[25] Together with information derived from Filipino guerrilla reports, Japanese prisoners of war, captured documents, and aerial reconnaissance, Ultra gave US commanders an intimate look at Japanese capabilities and intentions. It could also be deceptive. By the end of December, Willoughby incorrectly estimated Japanese strength on Luzon at 152,500 men (5 infantry divisions, a tank division, 6 independent brigades, 2 infantry regiments, and a plethora of naval and air troops who could be pressed into service as combat forces).[26] His assessment was precise, logical, backed by Ultra intelligence, and mostly wrong.

Krueger's intelligence officer, Col. Horton V. White, instead estimated that the Japanese had 234,500 troops on Luzon (107,000 combat troops and 127,500 support troops). White and his intelligence section placed far greater reliance on guerrilla reports than did their counterparts at SWPA.[27] At a meeting at the Price House in Tacloban, Brig. Gen. Clyde D. Eddleman, Krueger's G-3, briefed Sixth Army's plan for the Mindoro landing and Luzon campaign. Present were MacArthur, Eddleman, Willoughby, and Maj. Gen. Dunckel, who commanded the Mindoro Task Force. After MacArthur had approved the Mindoro invasion plan, Eddleman addressed the Luzon operation. As usual, the briefing started with an assessment of the enemy situation. As Eddleman discussed Sixth Army's intelligence assessment, MacArthur became agitated. According to Eddleman, MacArthur

> kept removing his pipe and saying, "Bunk!" I'd go a little further and he'd say, "Bunk!" I broke out laughing and I said, "General, apparently you don't like our intelligence briefing," and he said, "I don't. It's too strong. There aren't that many Japanese there." "Well," I said, "Most of this information came from your headquarters." Willoughby jumped out of his chair. "Didn't come from me! Didn't come from me!"[28]

MacArthur refused to believe there were that many Japanese on Luzon, partly because Willoughby had briefed otherwise and partly because, if Sixth Army's numbers were true, the Luzon campaign was under-resourced and therefore at risk. When confronted with an estimate that did not fit his preconceived notions, MacArthur remained true to form: He ignored it. After the briefing ended, MacArthur grabbed Eddleman by the arm and took him into his bedroom. MacArthur then provided his view of intelligence officers. "There are only three great ones in the history of warfare and mine is not one of them."[29] According to MacArthur, the three great ones belonged to Alexander the Great, Hannibal, and Grant – which shows how little MacArthur understood intelligence, a specialty that came into its own only after the conclusion of the US Civil War.

In fact, the guerrilla reports were spot on. In late November 1944, Russell Volckmann's guerrillas captured documents from a crashed Japanese aircraft that included notes from a conference convened by Gen. Yamashita, the newly installed commander of Japanese forces in the Philippines. The translated document indicated that Yamashita would forgo a defense of Lingayen Gulf or the central plain, and instead shift his forces to the mountainous interior of Luzon. Before then, the Japanese had about two divisions stationed in northern Luzon, but reinforcements soon arrived. By the end of December, the Japanese had, according to Volckmann's estimate, six divisions in northern Luzon, and Gen. Yamashita had moved his headquarters and the puppet government of José Laurel to Baguio, the summer capital of the Philippines.[30] Volckmann was so sure of his intelligence that on January 7, 1945, he sent a short but important message to MacArthur: "There will be no – repeat – no opposition on the beaches."[31] A reduction in pre-invasion bombardment would save Filipino lives and husband ammunition that could be used to better effect elsewhere.

Willoughby's overreliance on Ultra intercepts led his intelligence section to badly miscalculate Japanese strength on Luzon.[32] Instead of 152,500 troops, the Japanese had nearly twice as many (275,000) men on the island.[33] Willoughby's estimate significantly undercounted the myriad combat support, administrative, logistical, and air and naval personnel on Luzon, because these units used telephones as their primary means of communication and therefore their messages were not picked up by radio intercept operators.[34]

Willoughby also misread Japanese intentions. Because the Japanese high command had committed to fighting the decisive battle of the Philippines campaign on Leyte, General Yamashita found the defense of

Luzon to be "an almost impossible matter," just as Gen. MacArthur had discovered back in 1942. Besides the difficulties of terrain and weather, the *14th Area Army* had sent three divisions to Leyte, where they were destroyed. They were replaced by three divisions new to Luzon (the *10th*, *19th*, and *23rd Divisions*), but because of losses to submarines and aircraft en route, they arrived at only two-thirds strength.[35] Shortages of troops, weapons, transportation, and supplies as well as lack of air parity made a mobile defense impossible. Many Japanese units were "badly organized, ill equipped, poorly officered, and miserably trained."[36] Morale was low and unit cohesion uneven at best.

By this point in the war, Japanese military leaders also understood that defending forward along the beaches against an American amphibious force was the equivalent of a death sentence. Yamashita therefore ordered his army to cede the landing beaches to the Americans and defend inland. Furthermore, he would not attempt to defend the central plain – the rice granary of the Philippines – or Manila, the capital. Instead, Yamashita organized his army into three groups, each of them responsible for defending a rugged mountainous area of Luzon, where they could fortify themselves on high ground and force the Americans to pay a heavy price in blood and treasure to root them out.[37] To mitigate the impact of American firepower, the Japanese constructed elaborate cave defenses that included spaces for soldiers to live, work, and fight underground.[38] Belatedly, *Imperial General HQ* and the *Southern Expeditionary Army Group* agreed and gave Yamashita the latitude to conduct the defense of Luzon as he saw fit.[39]

The *Kembu Group*, 30,000 troops commanded by Maj. Gen. Rikichi Tsukada, would defend Clark Field and the Zambales Mountains to its west, including the Bataan Peninsula. The hodgepodge of units in the group consisted of naval engineers, air ground crews, antiaircraft personnel, various service units, and a few infantry, tank, and field artillery units, the latter being the only combat-trained organizations in the assemblage.[40] To the south lay the *Shimbu Group*, commanded by Shizuo Yokoyama, 80,000 troops centered on the *8th* and *105th Divisions* but also including 16,000 naval troops of the *31st Naval Special Base Force* in Manila. Although the *Shimbu Group* covered the southern half of Luzon, its center of gravity focused on the defense of the mountains east of Manila. Yamashita ordered Yokoyama to evacuate supplies from Manila, which was the major Japanese supply hub on Luzon, after which his forces were to destroy critical infrastructure in the city before retiring to the mountains to fight on. The problem was that the naval forces in Manila, under the command of Rear

Adm. Sanji Iwabuchi, were not under Yamashita's direct command, and Iwabuchi had other plans for the city's defense.[41]

The largest concentration of forces was the 152,000 troops of the *Shobu Group* in northern Luzon, commanded directly by Yamashita from his headquarters in Baguio, the summer capital of the Philippines in the mountains northeast of Lingayen Gulf. The *Shobu Group* had elements of four infantry divisions (the *10th, 19th, 23rd,* and *103rd*), most of the *2nd Tank Division,* the *58th Independent Mixed Brigade,* and various other service and support organizations and provisional units. Unfortunately for the Japanese, they had not yet completed moving supplies and troops from the Manila area to northern Luzon when the Sixth Army invaded, and guerrilla action and American airpower inhibited Japanese troop movements from that point onward.[42] Nevertheless, in the remote and rugged terrain of northern Luzon, Yamashita would delay American forces as long as possible, exacting a price in blood and, in theory at least, buying time for the Japanese government to negotiate an honorable end to the war.[43]

The army Yamashita commanded in the Philippines in no way resembled the well-trained juggernaut he commanded in Malaya in 1942. It was haphazardly organized, ill-equipped, poorly trained, and in many cases ill-disciplined. Units were still on the move to their assigned locations when the Americans invaded, and some, particularly the Manila garrison, would never reach them. But, as 1945 dawned, Yamashita readied his forces for battle. "All things considered, the outcome of the Philippines operation will have a bearing on the rise and fall of the nation," he wrote in a message to the troops. "The units will fully materialize every concrete plan at once, and annihilate the enemy when the opportunity presents itself, thus setting His Imperial Majesty's mind at peace. The units are so instructed this New Year's Day. Long live the Emperor!"[44]

The Luzon campaign entailed the commitment of eight infantry divisions, a dismounted cavalry division, an airborne division, an armored group, and five separate regimental combat teams. Lt. Gen. Walter Krueger's Sixth Army would control the majority of these forces, although MacArthur assigned certain missions to Eichelberger's Eighth Army to simplify Krueger's span of control and, to be honest, to play off the rivalry between the two army commanders. Sixth Army planners in Hollandia planned the Luzon campaign, while Krueger and his staff directed ongoing combat operations on Leyte. MacArthur, Chamberlin, and the SWPA planners considered several alternatives, but they chose Lingayen Gulf as the site of the landing for the same reason the Japanese had landed there in 1941 – excellent beaches and access to the central plain and its roads leading to Manila.[45]

The Sixth Army plan, Mike I, envisioned an amphibious assault on the southern shore of Lingayen Gulf with the four divisions of I Corps (6th and 43rd Infantry Divisions) and XIV Corps (37th and 40th Infantry Divisions) landing on S-Day. Planners rejected the more traversable ground to the east, given intelligence reports of Japanese strength in the area. The separate 158th Regimental Combat Team would land on S+2 on the eastern flank of I Corps and attack northeast to secure the army's left flank. The 13th Armored Group would remain under Sixth Army control, with elements attached to supplement the fighting power of the corps and divisions as required. The 25th Infantry Division ("Tropic Lightning," commanded by Maj. Gen. Charles L. Mullins, Jr.) was designated as the army reserve. Filipino guerrilla forces, although not always well armed and lacking substantial artillery and supporting arms, provided at least another two divisions' worth of combat power to the force pool. SWPA planners envisioned a five-phase operation, entailing (1) air, naval, and sabotage operations to disorganize enemy defenses, (2) seizure of beachheads in Lingayen Gulf, (3) attack to secure crossings of the Agno River, (4) operations to destroy enemy forces and occupy Manila, and (5) destruction of remaining Japanese forces and the occupation of the rest of Luzon.[46]

Assembling the convoys for the invasion of Luzon was no easy feat, but, by this point in the Pacific War, the various staffs were well versed in the procedures and details of coordinating shipping, forces, and logistics dispersed throughout the vast distances of the Southwest Pacific. Vice Adm. Daniel E. Barbey's VII Amphibious Force transported I Corps, while Vice Adm. Theodore S. Wilkinson's III Amphibious Force transported XIV Corps. Units came from staging areas in the Solomons, New Guinea, New Caledonia, Leyte, Morotai, and Australia; the 25th Infantry Division had the longest distance to travel – nearly 4,300 miles from its base in New Caledonia to Lingayen Gulf.[47]

XIV Corps worked diligently to fill equipment shortages and prepare loading plans for the 130 ships allocated to it for the invasion. "The magnitude and complexity of the problem involved reached stellar magnitude," recorded the corps after-action report:

> When 53,116 troops, 9,228 vehicles and 34,908 tons of supplies and equipment are to be embarked on 129 miscellaneous type ships, long arduous hours must be spent trimming, piecing and patching the data in order to meet the requirements of a plan for unloading troops and

equipment in such order as to achieve maximum effect. Assault infantry and weapons, beach reconnaissance parties, reserve infantry, armor, artillery, beach working parties, service troops, supplies and vehicles must be woven into the pattern which is designated as an amphibious operation.[48]

The official US Army historian summed up the challenge nicely: "The wonder is not that some problems arose during the loading and staging, but rather that the problems were so few and relatively minor in nature."[49]

The convoys assembled in late December and, after conducting rehearsals, weighed anchor for Leyte Gulf, where they rendezvoused with combat elements of Admiral Thomas Kinkaid's Seventh Fleet. MacArthur and members of his personal staff went aboard the light cruiser *Boise*, the *Nashville* having been hit by a kamikaze on December 13 during the invasion of Mindoro, requiring extensive repairs back in the United States. Krueger and key members of his staff sailed in the *Wasatch*, the amphibious force flagship. Among the destroyer escorts guarding the fleet was the *Ulvert H. Moore*, skippered by President Franklin Roosevelt's son, Lt. Cdr. Franklin D. Roosevelt, Jr. By January 6, the entire fleet, encompassing a convoy more than forty miles long, was en route to Lingayen Gulf.[50] Lieut. Dwight C. Shepler, a graduate of Williams College who the US Navy had commissioned as a combat artist, recalled,

> The voyage as far as Leyte was one of great suspense but no action. We steamed across the endless sea, glassy in the equatorial calms and reflecting the patterns of the towering cumulus clouds gleaming on the long swells …. Looking aft we could see only a part of the three attack forces as they faded hull down out of vision, and the pips of light [washed out] on the periphery of the surface radar scope. Escort carriers joined the procession and the big Grumman fighters and torpedo bombers kept roaring across the sky.[51]

As he puffed on his corncob pipe, MacArthur's "thoughts went back to that black night three years gone, when I churned through these same waters with only the determination to return."[52] Fortunately, the crew's thoughts were on the here and now, as the *Boise* maneuvered to evade a torpedo aimed at the ship by a Japanese submarine, which was soon sent to the bottom courtesy of an accompanying destroyer.[53] The crew later fended off a kamikaze attack, destroying the Japanese plane 100 yards away.[54] Outwardly calm, MacArthur had several days before confided to his aide and confidante Bonner Fellers that, "If the Lord will let me land this one, I'll never ask so much of him again."[55] Now, as the invasion armada neared Luzon, MacArthur stood at the rail of the *Boise*, staring at the familiar sites on the horizon. "At the sight of those never-to-be-forgotten scenes of my family's past," he later wrote, "I felt an indescribable sense of loss, of sorrow, of loneliness, and of solemn consecration."[56]

As the invasion convoys headed for the Philippines, Kenney's bombers and fighters attacked Japanese airfields on Luzon, while Halsey's Third Fleet returned to strike Formosa. With four kills on December 26, Maj. Thomas B. McGuire, Jr., took Bing Bang Bong's place as the leading ace in theater with thirty-eight kills to his credit.[57] Japanese air strength was reduced to perhaps 200 combat aircraft in the Philippines, a shadow of its former strength, but still a dangerous figure given the adoption of kamikaze tactics, which effectively made each aircraft a human-guided bomb. Kamikaze attacks on the invasion convoys began on the morning of January 3 and increased in intensity as the American ships approached Lingayen Gulf. Maj. Gen. Oscar Griswold, XIV Corps commander, wrote in his diary on January 6, "Tomorrow weather promises to be good, and serious air attacks are probable. I hope none of my boys get hit. It's bad enough to die in battle – but worse, I think, to drown."[58]

Japanese pilots, eluding combat air patrols and attacking through a storm of antiaircraft fire, hammered the invasion fleet as it neared its objective. On January 6 alone, kamikazes sank the destroyer minesweeper USS *Long* and damaged fifteen other ships.[59] Kamikazes posed a significant threat to Vice Adm. Jesse Oldendorf's bombardment and fire support group, and he feared the worst if the transports took a similar beating. Adm. Kinkaid sent an urgent message requesting reorientation of the Third Fleet to strike Japanese airfields on Luzon before returning to the waters off Formosa.[60] Beginning on January 7, carrier aircraft joined in the air battle over Luzon. Vice Adm. John S. McCain, who now led the fast carrier task forces, and his operations officer, the innovative Capt. John S. "Jimmy" Thach, had developed a tactic called the "Big Blue Blanket" to position aircraft over all known airfields within striking distance of Lingayen Gulf. If Japanese planes could not take off, they could not crash dive into US ships. The Big Blue Blanket helped to reduce the kamikaze threat, although it could not eliminate it altogether.[61]

The Imperial Japanese Navy, largely destroyed in the Battle of Leyte Gulf in October, made a cameo appearance in the form of sorties by three destroyers; American aircraft heavily damaged two of them while American destroyers sent the third Japanese ship to the bottom of the West Philippine Sea.[62] Japanese commanders formed special suicide boat squadrons known as "Fishing" units to defend the long coastline of Luzon. "Q" boats operated by Japanese naval personnel would attempt to ram American ships and detonate explosives, thereby sinking both vessels. Dozens of suicide boats and divers attacked the invasion flotilla, ramming an LST, the transport *War Hawk*, and two LCIs; depth charges and explosives placed by swimmers damaged three other LSTs and the destroyer *Robinson*.[63] The reckless sacrifice of the Japanese occasioned grudging admiration in the eyes of the Americans. Griswold confided, "You've got to hand it to the Jap – he has guts!"[64]

The attacks finally came to an end on January 13, only because the Japanese, saving their strength for the defense of the home islands, had run out of aircraft to throw at the American armada.[65] Kenney's airmen, with assistance from Kinkaid's and Halsey's naval aviators, had finally achieved air supremacy over the entire Philippines archipelago. In all, the Japanese sank twenty-four ships and damaged sixty-seven others in the month leading up to the invasion of Lingayen Gulf.[66] Among them were the escort carrier *Ommaney Bay*, scuttled after being fatally damaged by a kamikaze attack; the heavy cruiser *Australia*, which suffered its fifth kamikaze strike in less than a month, but survived the battle; and the battleship *New Mexico*, hit in the bridge by a kamikaze that killed British Lt. Gen. Herbert Lumsden, Winston Churchill's special military representative to MacArthur's headquarters, Capt. R. W. Fleming, the ship's commanding officer, and William Henry "Bill" Chickering, a correspondent with *Time* magazine whom MacArthur liked.[67] The carnage was a preview of what awaited the US Navy off the shores of Okinawa in a little less than three months.

Despite the best efforts of the kamikazes to turn back the invasion fleet, the bombardment and fire support group (six old battleships – five of which, the *West Virginia, Maryland, Tennessee, California,* and *Pennsylvania* – had been damaged or sunk in the Japanese raid on Pearl Harbor and subsequently raised from the bottom and repaired, five heavy cruisers and one light cruiser, nineteen destroyers, ten high-speed transports, a seaplane tender, and eleven LCIs modified for gunfire support of amphibious operations) began pounding the invasion beaches on January 6, while minesweepers cleared the approach lanes and underwater demolition teams swam ashore to destroy beach obstacles. To the surprise of all, only four mines and no beach obstacles or defenses were found. At one point, a reconnaissance aircraft noted Filipinos in the town of Lingayen preparing a parade to welcome their American liberators. Aircraft dropped leaflets instructing the crowd to disperse, after which Oldendorf's ships gratuitously pounded the town with gunfire. Aside from the kamikazes and the suicide boats and divers, the Japanese put up virtually no resistance, as Yamashita had ordered his forces inland and away from the firepower he knew they would encounter on the shoreline.[68]

On S-Day, January 9, 1945, "the sun came up over Baguio Hills to witness the greatest flotilla ever assembled in the West, its guns roaring, its airplanes droning and the landing troops poised for the Luzon victory."[69] Griswold confided to his diary, "How those poor devils fighting there [Bataan] three years ago now would have welcomed this magnificent armada!"[70] As the guerrilla Russell Volckmann eyed the invasion flotilla in Lingayen Gulf from his headquarters fifty miles away, he reflected on what it meant. "This was the day we had dreamed about and prayed for during three long years! To us on Luzon, 'I shall return' was now a reality."[71] His report suggesting that

7.1: Battleships USS *Pennsylvania* (BB-38) and USS *Colorado* (BB-45) and cruisers USS *Louisville* (CA-28), *Portland* (CA-33), and *Columbia* (CL-56) move into Lingayen Gulf preceding the landing on Luzon, January 1945. (Credit: US Navy Photo)

a preparatory bombardment was unnecessary, however, had gone unheeded. The final preparatory bombardment of the invasion beaches began at 07:00, shifting to targets inland just prior to the landing of the first wave at 09:30. Rocket-firing LCIs delivered the final barrage, accompanied by naval fighters that strafed the area.

The assault waves met little resistance. Lieut. Shepler reported the scene:

> After what seemed a hundred years the amphibious tractors of the assault waves churned up and we started in with our brood down the navigational center of the assault lane of White Beach Two. Behind the combatant ships were pouring their naval artillery onto the beachhead until the LCI rocket ships flanking us took over with their incredible rain of fire. At 1800 yards from the beach we came to a stop and held our position to control succeeding waves. Mortar fire, which was to continue for several days on this particular beach, reached out to greet the oncoming waves . . . . At 0930 the attack hit the beach with little resistance, for the Japanese infantry had fled to the hills.[72]

The local Filipinos who remained in the area took the brunt of the American firepower. "No scene could better express the plight of captive peoples of this war than the Filipinos waving white flags along the shores of Lingayen Gulf as the fury of the H-Hour bombardment subsided," Lieut. Shepler recalled. "Bedsheets, old shirts, anything white on a bamboo pole served as a signal for the pitiful little groups waving at our shoal-draft LCI gun boats which cruised the shore in support of the troops."[73]

The battalion landing teams of XIV Corps (Maj. Gen. Oscar W. Griswold) on the right, or western, flank and I Corps (Maj. Gen. Innis P. Swift) on the left, or eastern, flank swam ashore in their landing craft without opposition except for the heavy surf. A number of landing craft grounded on sand banks offshore, forcing soldiers to wade to shore through waist- and chest-high water. MacArthur, forgoing the opportunity to land with dry trousers on a makeshift pier and sensing a publicity opportunity, waded ashore in the wake of his troops as he had done on Leyte.[74] Filipinos greeted the invasion forces with open arms, but lamented that they had waited "three long years" for the return of the Americans. "Nine out of ten males claimed to be members of guerrilla bands," a division historian related. "Later, it became apparent that eight and one-half out of every nine had become active guerrillas about five minutes after the landing."[75]

But there were tens of thousands of actual guerrillas on Luzon, and they had been busy. A Japanese staff officer with Yamashita's *14th Area Army* recorded after the war,

> AMERICAN and PHILIPPINE guerrillas were prevalent on the many islands of the PHILIPPINES group, and they were in constant contact with the US forces by means of radio and submarines. These guerrillas were very powerful and active, especially in the districts of MINDANAO, BESSIE [Visayas] and LUZON. Such being the case, each unit had to resort to punitive actions in order to maintain public peace and order.[76]

But after American forces returned, the Japanese consolidated units to prepare for conventional operations and curtailed counterguerrilla operations. Guerrilla units gained freedom of action, with the result that "guerrilla activities against our mobile transportation and the great deduction of military strength greatly influenced the LUZON campaign."[77]

As the invasion neared, MacArthur ordered the guerrillas to shift from intelligence gathering to direct action. The guerrillas were hampered by lack of arms and training, inadequate fire support, and their paucity of experience in direct combat, but they had the advantage of knowing the terrain and were motivated to liberate their country. They quickly went about their work of cutting telephone wires to disrupt communications, blowing up bridges, ambushing Japanese supply columns, and destroying Japanese supply dumps. "When the enemy garrisons were left standing in magnificent isolation from their other scattered units, the real work began," recorded Volckmann's after-action report.[78] This work included interdicting Japanese transportation moving supplies from the Manila area to the three groups defending the mountainous regions of Luzon. A Japanese staff officer reported that "all movements required the fighting off of guerrillas attacks while the convoys were enroute" to their destinations.[79] By the end of January, the flow of supplies from the Manila area had ceased altogether.

In northern Luzon, Volckmann had organized the 20,000 men of his command into the USAFIP-NL (US Army Forces in the Philippines, Northern Luzon), with 5 infantry regiments and a composite field artillery battalion. His men were not as well trained or equipped as the US forces of the Sixth Army invading Luzon, but Volckmann's organization nevertheless became a killing machine, accounting for tens of thousands of Japanese in the weeks and months to come. In January 1945 alone, Volckmann's forces killed 3,333 Japanese, wounded 306, and took 7 prisoners, while suffering just 40 killed and 70 wounded.[80]

By nightfall on S-Day, the 37th ("Buckeye," commanded by Maj. Gen. Robert S. Beightler) and 40th ("Sunburst," commanded by Maj. Gen. Rapp Brush) Infantry Divisions had moved on average four miles inland to establish a secure beachhead, delayed more by swamps, rice paddies, and fish ponds than by the Japanese. According to the XIV Corps, "The extent of the advance far exceeded the wildest dreams of those who had planned the operation."[81] MacArthur was especially pleased by the day's events. According to senior aide Bonner Fellers, upon returning from a tour ashore, MacArthur "sat down plide [i.e., pleased and proud] in his room and ate a quart of ice cream – just like a kid at a circus. He is very happy tonight for he was playing high stakes and again he was right and out thought Yamashita."[82] This was not true, since Yamashita's strategy did not rely on repelling the invasion at the beaches, but, for the moment, MacArthur was delighted by the progress made.

The next day the assault divisions secured the Army Beachhead Line in their zones and in some areas linked up with Filipino guerrillas, who had already liberated some of the towns in the vicinity. Volckmann left his headquarters to meet the Sixth Army commander. As he was whisked by PT boat to Lt. Gen. Walter Krueger's headquarters at Lingayen Gulf, he marveled at the sight of the invasion armada. Upon meeting Krueger and delivering his intelligence report, the general exclaimed, "Damn it, Volckmann, if there are that many Nips, why don't they drive me back into the sea?" "Sir," Volckmann replied, "They're going to sit and force you to dig them out of the mountains."[83]

Japanese forces were now faced with hybrid war, fighting against a combination of conventional and irregular forces that has proven throughout history to be difficult to beat.[84] As Volckmann realized, the Japanese could concentrate their forces to face Sixth Army to their south, or they could disperse them to counter the guerrillas to their north. They did not have enough forces to do both.[85]

On the left flank of the Sixth Army, the 6th ("Red Star," commanded by Maj. Gen. Edwin D. Patrick) and 43rd ("Winged Victory," commanded by Maj. Gen. Leonard F. Wing) Infantry Divisions met scattered Japanese resistance on the high ground behind the beaches, slowing their momentum. On January 10, the 169th and 172nd Infantry Regiments ran into heavy Japanese resistance on the hills to the east and northeast of Lingayen Gulf. The Japanese in this area had dug deep, fortifying themselves into the sides of the treeless hills. The difficulties faced by the 43rd Infantry Division, a National Guard outfit from the New England area that had seen extensive service in New Georgia and at Aitape in New Guinea, in overcoming the resistance in this area presaged the fighting that awaited Sixth Army in the mountains of northern Luzon.[86] Given the difficulties encountered by the 43rd Infantry Division and the gap developing between I Corps and XIV Corps, Krueger decided to position the army reserve, the 25th Infantry Division, in the I Corps zone. It came ashore on January 11, as did the 6th Ranger Battalion and the 13th Armored Group.[87]

For a week after S-Day, Mother Nature played havoc with Sixth Army's logistics. The beaches remained heavily congested until several days into the operation. Heavy surf and poor beach conditions in Lingayen Gulf caused by a winter storm hampered the unloading of heavy equipment and bridging material and forced logisticians to temporarily abandon the beaches in the XIV Corps zone. Bailey bridges were especially needed to span waterways whose bridges the Japanese had destroyed before withdrawing, but they were in short supply.[88] As always, units improvised. On January 19, the 37th Infantry Division discovered that the railroad between San Carlos and Bayambong was serviceable, albeit lacking locomotives. The division ordnance officer fashioned flanged wheels on two jeeps, which could then pull four loaded sixteen-ton cars. Two days later Sixth Army assumed control of the railroad.[89]

By January 16, three of the four assault divisions of Sixth Army had reached the Army Beachhead Line and the XIV Corps was across the Agno River. The 43rd Infantry Division (with the 158th Regimental Combat Team attached) on the army's left flank continued to face stiff Japanese resistance from the *158th Independent Mixed Brigade* and elements of the *23rd Division* on the defensive edge of the *Shobu Group* in the vicinity of Mt. Alava and Rosario. Attacking infantry had to reduce fortified cave defenses with flame-thrower and demolition teams as they otherwise proved immune to artillery fire.[90] Thankfully, because of the predations of American submarines, on Luzon "only a few wire entanglements were utilized for obstacles because of the shortage of material."[91]

To allow I Corps to focus on the battle in this area, Krueger committed all but one regiment of the 25th Infantry Division in its zone. The beachhead now measured thirty miles across and up to thirty miles in depth, granting Sixth Army room to emplace logistical installations, airfields, headquarters, and other necessary infrastructure to support the next stage of the campaign. Engineers, assisted by Filipino laborers, soon made usable an airfield near the town of Lingayen, and several fighter squadrons flew in on January 16, allowing the escort carriers offshore to depart.[92] A second airstrip near Mangaldan was ready by January 22, housing more fighters,

A-20 Havoc bombers, and two squadrons (growing to seven squadrons by the end of the month) of Marine Dauntless dive bombers.[93] A delighted MacArthur decorated his chief engineer, Brig. Gen. Leif J. Sverdrup, with a Distinguished Service Cross and promoted him to major general.[94] But Lingayen Gulf was intended to be only a temporary base, until the Sixth Army could seize and renovate Clark Field and the port facilities of Manila.[95]

MacArthur was already thinking about the next stage of the campaign. He wanted to get to Manila, the sooner the better. On January 12, he held a meeting aboard the *Boise* with Krueger and his G-3, Brig. Gen. Eddleman. MacArthur broached the possibility of landing XI Corps (38th Infantry Division and the 34th Regimental Combat Team from the 24th Infantry Division) on the Zambales coast north of Bataan Peninsula, an idea with which Krueger concurred. MacArthur then got to the heart of the meeting: When could Sixth Army begin its advance on Manila? Sixth Army's losses had been small and Japanese resistance in the southern part of the beach-head negligible. MacArthur stated his belief – backed by Willoughby's seriously flawed estimate of Japanese strength on Luzon – that the Japanese would not defend the capital.[96] Krueger explained his need to keep I Corps focused on defending the Lingayen beachhead, leaving only the two divisions of XIV Corps for the drive to Manila. Given the issues with bridging material, the corps would soon outrun its supplies and its flanks would be vulnerable to a Japanese counterattack. A full-throated attack toward Manila would have to await the arrival of the 32nd Infantry Division and the 1st Cavalry Division. An irritated MacArthur appeared unconvinced, but did not direct Krueger to alter his plans, at least not yet.[97] According to Eddleman, it was "the only time I ever saw the two of them when they had cross words."[98]

The next day MacArthur moved his headquarters ashore to the coastal town of Dagupan. Meeting with Maj. Gen. Griswold a day later, MacArthur asserted "that the battle of the Philippines had already been won on Leyte."[99] "MacA is fine," Bonner Fellers wrote his wife. "Full of drive – in complete personal command."[100] Not all was well in the headquarters, however. By this point, the relationship between MacArthur and his chief of staff had broken down. "Sutherland could no longer stand MacArthur," Paul Rogers recalls. "It was not just petty pique over one matter. It was a complete revulsion based on many events over the three-year period. Sutherland threw his career aside in one act of rebellion after another, which made him appear indecisive, weak, afraid, or smitten by passion."[101]

Claiming a severe toothache that needed to be fixed, Sutherland decamped for two weeks to Leyte and then Brisbane, leaving Maj. Gen. Richard Marshall to fill the gap left by his absence.[102]

Ultra revealed that Yamashita had packed up the *14th Area Army* headquarters and moved it north to Baguio.[103] If MacArthur needed any more convincing that Manila was ripe for the taking, he received it a day later from Capt. Bartolomeo Cabangbang, a Philippine Army Bataan–Corregidor vet who was evacuated to Brisbane in November 1943. Cabangbang returned to Luzon in September 1944 aboard the submarine USS *Nautilus* and established a communications station near Manila. Within three months Cabangbang was transmitting intelligence from Lt. Col. Bernard Anderson in Tayabas, Major Alejo Santos in Bulacan and Manila, and Lt. Col. Gyles Merrill in the Zambales–Pampanga area.[104] One piece of information sent through Cabangbang to SWPA HQ on January 13, 1945, may have reinforced in MacArthur's mind the ability of US forces to seize Manila in a quick strike:

> In a conference between President Laurel [leader of the Japanese puppet state known as the Second Philippine Republic] and General Yamashita on or about December 15th, it was decided that due to the indefensibility of the city and to avoid heavy loss of civilian lives most of the Jap Army forces would be moved out of Manila and the national government under the protective custody of Army would be moved to Baguio .... In conference between Benigno Aquino [Sr., Speaker of the National Assembly] and Yamashita, Yamashita admitted the indefensibility of Manila but when asked why Manila was not declared an open city replied that it would reflect [negatively] on the might and reputation of Jap forces by doing so .... Yamashita did not accept the proposal [to declare Manila an open city] and he explained that the complete demilitarization of the city would lay it open to a possible paratroop invasion from Mindoro .... He will remove his troops from the city and it is up to the Americans to take notice that the Japanese have already left the city. I understand the military police will remain and perhaps enough troops to cope with a surprise attack by paratroops.[105]

Cabangbang added a comment that, as of January 7, there were few Japanese troops left in Manila, but those that remained had constructed fortifications on practically all street corners. The clarification should have given him pause to consider Japanese intentions.

Krueger understood the need to accelerate XIV Corps' attack to the south, a task made clear via a radio message on January 17 from MacArthur

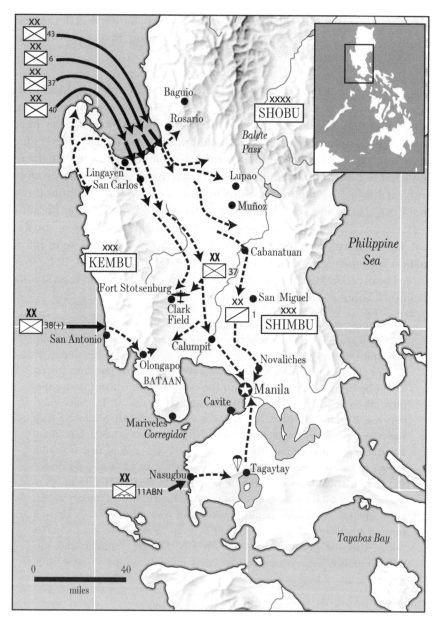

Map 7: Invasion of Luzon, January 1945.

emphasizing the need to seize Clark Field – a massive installation consisting of a half-dozen airstrips, revetments, taxiways, and maintenance facilities – as soon as possible. If Krueger needed a boost, he got one the next day when MacArthur recommended his promotion to four-star rank. A day later MacArthur visited Krueger in the Sixth Army headquarters near Lingayen Gulf, telling Doc Egeberg he wanted "to see if I can persuade [Krueger] to go down the plain a little bit faster." After the conclusion of the meeting, MacArthur opined, "Walter's pretty stubborn. Maybe I'll have to try something else."[106] MacArthur proceeded to move SWPA headquarters to Hacienda Luisita, a sugar plantation at San Miguel, fifty miles in front of Krueger's headquarters on the road to Manila, a not so subtle message to prod the Sixth Army commander into action.[107]

Krueger got the message, but by then Col. Horton White, Krueger's intelligence officer, had correctly deduced that the Japanese were not going to defend the central plain, which meant XIV Corps could advance south without fear of a massive Japanese counterattack. Krueger remained concerned about the concentration of the *2nd Tank* and *10th Divisions* near San Jose, which could jeopardize the Lingayen Beachhead if it were left lightly defended. Krueger need not have worried about a Japanese counterattack. Yamashita did not believe maneuver was possible due to the threat of US air power, and so ordered the tanks of the *2nd Tank Division* dug in as pillboxes.[108] Regardless, Krueger ordered XIV Corps to attack south with the 37th and 40th Infantry Divisions, while positioning troops along its left (eastern) flank to maintain contact with the 6th Infantry Division of I Corps. Sixth Army would assume the risk until the 1st Cavalry and 32nd Infantry Divisions arrived on or about January 27.[109]

The reinforced 43rd Infantry Division remained locked in a bitter contest for the high ground near Mt. Alava and Rosario. Infantrymen struggled to clear Japanese defenses in close combat with bazookas, flame-throwers, dynamite, and grenades.[110] Preceded by massed air strikes and artillery fire, a coordinated division attack commenced on January 25 and three days later managed to seize Rosario and other key terrain on the division's front. Further south, the 25th Infantry Division encountered a regiment of the *2nd Tank Division* in San Manuel on January 23 and destroyed it in a five-day battle. The Japanese defenders of the *Shigemi Detachment*, determined to fight to the death, "resisted fanatically from pillboxes and dug-in positions under buildings, supported by fire from tanks hulled down as pillboxes and anti-tank guns placed at strategic street intersections throughout the town," but were finally rooted out of their positions by the 161st Infantry Regiment on January 28 after a "pulverizing air and artillery bombardment."[111] The desperate stand of the *Shigemi Detachment* had little effect on the outcome of the campaign, but was "illustrative of a sort of tour de force to which the Japanese Army seemed peculiarly addicted during World War II."[112] On January 29–30, the 27th Infantry Regiment destroyed another small armored task force of the *2nd Tank Division* at Pemienta. Sixth Army's base in Lingayen Gulf was secure.

While I Corps battled significant elements of the *Shobu Group* near Rosario and San Manuel, XIV Corps attacked toward Manila. The 37th and 40th Infantry Divisions met with minimal resistance from withdrawing Japanese forces. As the divisions marched south, they were confronted with the task of establishing governance in newly liberated Filipino towns. Philippine Civil Affairs Units and counterintelligence detachments would establish boards of reliable civilians to screen governing officials, removing those who had collaborated with the Japanese and replacing them with pre-war officials. They would then publish regulations on restrictions, curfews, possession of weapons, and other matters. Of course, determining which citizens were "reliable" was more of an art than a science.[113]

XIV Corps ran the risk of a Japanese counterattack into the exposed eastern flank, and the corps supply lines originating at Lingayen Gulf were stretched to breaking point. As the XIV Corps front extended southward, Maj. Gen. Griswold echeloned the 37th Infantry Division along the left flank to protect the corps against potential Japanese counterattacks. The 40th Infantry Division would begin the attack to seize the high ground near Clark Field. On January 23, the Sunburst Division encountered the leading edge of the *Kembu Group* near Bamban and engaged in heavy fighting for control of the town and the high ground to its west and southwest against "fanatical and suicidal" opposition.[114] Japanese defenders had created strongpoints in the numerous caves on the ridgelines, forcing the attackers to destroy them in an agonizingly deliberate process using flamethrowers, white phosphorus and thermite grenades, and demolition charges.[115]

By January 26, the 37th Infantry Division was positioned across the Bamban River, prepared to seize Clark Field and nearby Fort Stotsenburg, a military installation named after a US Army officer killed during the Philippine–American War in 1899. Griswold decided on a coordinated attack to clear the two military installations and the high ground to the west, known locally as "Top of the World," before driving on Manila to the south. The hills had to be cleared if Clark Field were to be opened again to air traffic; otherwise, Japanese gunners on the high ground would have a field day with the targets beneath them. While the 40th Infantry Division continued to chew through the Bamban Hills, two regiments of the 37th Infantry Division attacked on January 28 to seize Clark Field and Fort Stotsenburg, a task they accomplished in two days of fighting.[116]

While the Buckeyes fought to seize Fort Stotsenburg, six officers and men – 2nd Lt. Henry C. Conners, Corp. Robert T. Mailheau, Pvt. Frank Gyovai, Sgt. Bob A. Campbell, Staff Sgt. Willard A. Bresler, and Pvt. First Class Doyle V. Decker – descended from the hills, passed through the lines of the 37th Infantry Division, and reported into the XIV Corps command post at Conception. They were malnourished and suffering from vitamin deficiencies that left them nearly blind. After the fall of Bataan, the group had escaped into the hills near Fort Stotsenburg, eventually forming a guerrilla group in the provinces of Pampanga, Tarlac, and Nueva Ecija. They carried an American flag that once belonged to the 26th Cavalry, saved from Japanese capture by the regiment's last Filipino color bearer, who spirited the flag away to his village and gave it to his wife, who protected it by sewing it inside a pillow. In spring 1943, he presented the colors to Conners, who flew them over his guerrilla hide-out until the time of the American invasion. The group presented the colors to Maj. Gen. Oscar Griswold in an emotional ceremony on January 28.[117] Three days later, Lt. Gen. Krueger raised the flag over the largely demolished ruins of Fort Stotsenburg, a symbolic but no doubt heartfelt act of liberation that also invited fire from "almost every Japanese gun within range."[118] GIs reached the crest of the Top of the World the next day, against Japanese resistance made more deadly by the use of antiaircraft guns moved from Clark Field to bolster the defense of the high ground to its west. Clark Field was now secure, and the Fifth Air Force had the base it needed to support further operations on Luzon.

With the seizure of Clark Field and Fort Stotsenburg nearly complete, Sixth Army issued a field order on January 26 directing XIV Corps to attack south to the Pampanga River.[119] The only forces able to do so immediately were the reconnaissance troop and the 148th Infantry Regiment from the 37th Infantry Division, aided by Filipino guerrillas who assisted in seizing the road and rail bridges over the San Fernando River. By January 30, patrols were closing on the Pampanga River at Calumpit. MacArthur drove south along Route 3 to check on progress and reported back to Krueger his displeasure at the rate of the advance. The issue was lack of troops to make a full-throated attack toward Manila, but the commander-in-chief's irritation rolled downhill to the Buckeyes.[120]

The arrival of the 1st Cavalry Division (Maj. Gen. Verne Mudge), 32nd Infantry Division (Maj. Gen. William H. Gill), and the separate 112th

Regimental Combat Team in Lingayen Gulf on January 27 eased many of Krueger's concerns. The 32nd Infantry Division (minus one regiment in army reserve) would move into the line on the right of the 43rd Infantry Division, allowing the 6th and 25th Infantry Divisions to shift south. With the army flank now secure, XIV Corps – reinforced with the 1st Cavalry Division – would resume its drive on Manila. Sixty-six days of combat in Leyte and an additional ten days of patrolling to mop up the enemy had reduced the 1st Cavalry Division's strength and depleted its matériel, but there was little time between the Leyte and Luzon campaigns to make good the losses. Few of the units in the Luzon campaign operated at full strength. Replacements had brought the division up to about 93 percent strength, but they were of varying quality.[121] Commanders complained that replacements joined their units too late, arrived poorly trained, and were in "miserable" physical condition.[122] The replacement system was also slow to return wounded soldiers to their units once healed. The cavalrymen would have to carry on with what they had. Instead of training onboard the ships en route to Luzon, troopers were encouraged to rest and take advantage of the excellent rations afforded by the Navy – red meat, real butter, eggs, and fresh vegetables.[123] "The spirit of the Division was high," the division history recorded, "but the means – replacements, new equipment, rest – had not been provided."[124] On the other hand, nearly every soldier in the division was now a battle-hardened combat veteran, and units functioned confidently as cohesive teams. They would soon be put to the test on the road to Manila.

MacArthur traveled with minimal staff and delighted in pointing out landmarks from his father's campaign on Luzon at the turn of the century. On one excursion, he pointed out to his personal aide, "Doc" Egeberg, the location where his father's aide had been killed. Not relishing MacArthur's sense of destiny, Egeberg urged the driver to move on.[125] Arthur MacArthur Jr. was never far from his son's thoughts. "The General didn't often speak of his father," Egeberg recalled, "but when he did, it was with the warmest admiration, pride, and a certain wistfulness, as though he wished that that famous general could see what his son was doing now."[126] His father had earned a Medal of Honor before the age of twenty leading a charge up Missionary Ridge at Chattanooga during the Civil War; the son had earned his at age sixty-two in a failed effort to prevent the Japanese conquest of the Philippines, the land that his father had pacified. The distinctions no doubt weighed heavily on Douglas MacArthur's psyche.

Regardless of what triggered his actions, some of MacArthur's habits alarmed his staff and irritated his subordinate commanders. Perhaps believing in his own destiny, MacArthur repeatedly traveled with insufficient escort too close to the front, far closer than a commander-in-chief needed to move to sense the direction of the fighting. He relished his visits to the front and enjoyed sharing the dangers of frontline combat, however briefly, with his soldiers. "We went forward at least every other day," Doc Egeberg recalled. "Sometimes he would stop at division headquarters and ask the division general to join him. Sometimes he would go directly to the front with both Larry [Col. Larry Lehrbas, MacArthur's aide de camp] and me or one of us, in the jeep."[127] And sometimes those personal reconnaissance trips would land the general in serious and unnecessary danger. At one point on the attack south as the 37th Infantry Division neared Clark Field, MacArthur drove in his jeep with Doc Egeberg to locate the front, only to find himself in the middle of a firefight between US and Japanese forces.[128] Egeberg believed that these trips to the front "fulfilled some inner need or compulsion in taking the risks that the fighting men took."[129]

MacArthur also often announced accomplishments before their realization. He had declared an end to the Leyte campaign on December 26, 1944, much to the chagrin of Lt. Gen. Eichelberger, whose Eighth Army had to clear the remaining Japanese on the island. Told there were only 6,000 or so Japanese left on the island, Eichelberger's forces killed upwards of 27,000 Japanese on Leyte by the real end of the campaign in May 1945. "I must admit that, after serving under him for over six years, I never understood the public relations policy that either he or his immediate assistants established," Eichelberger confided in his memoir. "It seemed to me, as it did to many of the commanders and correspondents, ill advised to announce victories when a first phase had been accomplished without too many casualties."[130] The habit carried over to Luzon. On January 26, 1945, as the 37th Infantry Division was still fighting for Clark Field and Fort Stotsenburg, MacArthur's headquarters announced their capture. "Why does he do this?" grumbled Maj. Gen. Griswold in his diary.[131]

MacArthur appeared to the Filipinos larger than life and was mobbed wherever he went. According to radio reporter William Dunn,

Since his arrival here General MacArthur has been cheered and toasted, he's been serenaded and made the recipient of more presents than he can possibly use .... I've met Filipinos in the past two days who insist that the General, after death, must belong to these islands. "We'll bury him in

Manila, right beside President Quezon," one man assured me today . . . . He belongs to the Philippines.[132]

MacArthur recalled that the people would "crowd around me, try to kiss my hand, press native wreaths around my neck, touch my clothes, hail me with tears and sobs."[133] The Japanese had worn out their welcome in the Philippines by treating the Filipinos as inferiors. Dunn reported, "They not only failed to convert the vast majority of Filipinos who were already satisfied with the American method of life, but they also succeeded in alienating a great many Filipinos who were giving serious thought to the Asia for Asiatics theory . . . . There has been no common ground."[134] The vast majority of Filipinos greeted American soldiers as liberators, erecting welcome signs along the roadways and flashing the V for Victory sign at every opportunity.[135]

The same day the reinforcements arrived in Lingayen Gulf, guerrillas informed Sixth Army that several hundred American, British, and Dutch prisoners of war were being held at a small stockade just east of Cabanatuan. The facility was twenty-five miles inside Japanese lines, but was lightly guarded. Krueger immediately decided to send a force to free the prisoners. That evening three officers and ten men from the Alamo Scouts – a special Sixth Army reconnaissance unit – departed to reconnoiter the route to the camp. Lieutenant Colonel Henry A. Mucci, commander of the 6th Ranger Battalion, would lead the raiding party of a reinforced Ranger company consisting of 5 officers and 115 enlisted soldiers, supported by 286 of Lapham's guerrillas. The force departed the next day and rendezvoused with the reconnaissance party early on January 29. Filipino guerrillas reported a large number of Japanese soldiers moving through the area near the camp, which caused Mucci to delay the rescue attempt by twenty-four hours. On the morning of January 30, a joint US–Filipino reconnaissance party determined Japanese strength in the camp at 73 men, with another 150 transients bunking down in the facility. An additional 800 Japanese with tanks and trucks were stationed 2 miles away at the small town of Cabu. The Alamo Scouts returned to the Ranger assembly area with details of the camp and its defenses.[136]

The Rangers infiltrated to an assault position in the late afternoon of January 30 and commenced the attack on the camp at 19:45. The Rangers gained complete surprise, and within thirty minutes they had killed the entire Japanese garrison and rescued the prisoners. With guerrillas covering their flanks and providing rear security, the Rangers and the newly freed prisoners withdrew. The column moved slowly, held up by 100 litter-bound patients who had to be carried in carabao (water buffalo) carts. Just after the column crossed over the Pampanga River, 800 Japanese soldiers reinforced by tanks approached a guerrilla roadblock on the bridge. Taken by surprise, the Japanese lost 300 men in the ensuing firefight. The guerrillas held for an hour before withdrawing, allowing the Ranger column the time it needed to make good its escape. At 08:00 the next morning, the column linked up with ambulances at Sibul, which transported the 512 freed prisoners to hospital facilities at Guimba. Krueger was on hand there to greet the former prisoners, "most of [whom] were in pitiable condition and could not realize that they were now actually safe."[137] The Rangers suffered just two killed and one wounded, while the Filipino guerrillas sustained nine wounded.[138]

While XIV Corps tangled with the Japanese defenders on the high ground west of Fort Stotsenburg, on the morning of January 29, XI Corps (Maj. Gen. Charles P. "Chink" Hall) invaded the Zambales coast under the control of Eichelberger's Eighth Army. The corps had originally been scheduled to invade further north at Vigan, but SWPA was concerned about the threat of kamikaze attacks originating from Formosa against an invasion force that far north. As the strength of Russell Volckmann's guerrillas in northern Luzon became clearer, MacArthur calculated that XI Corps could be better used further south. Its mission was to drive across the neck of the Bataan Peninsula to prevent Japanese forces from withdrawing into the enclave (something they had no intention of doing), as MacArthur's forces had done after the Japanese invasion in 1941. The corps was also tasked to seize Subic Bay and nearby airstrips for use by naval and air forces. The area was defended by the 4,000 troops of the *Nagayoshi Force*, no match for the 40,000 troops of the XI Corps and all of its organic firepower.[139]

As the invasion flotilla appeared off the Zambales coast, Filipino guerrillas sailed out to warn the task group commander, Rear Adm. Arthur D. Struble, that no Japanese forces were in the vicinity. Accordingly, he called off the pre-invasion bombardment. The 38th Infantry Division ("Cyclone," commanded by Maj. Gen. Henry L. C. Jones), reinforced with the 34th Regimental Combat Team from the 24th Infantry Division, landed without opposition.[140] Saved from the terror of a pre-invasion bombardment, local Filipinos happily greeted the arriving American forces and helped to unload cargo. The 149th Infantry Regiment moved to seize the San Marcelino airstrip, only to find the field under the control of guerrillas led by Capt. Ramon Magsaysay. The next morning MacArthur's headquarters transferred XI Corps to Sixth Army control.[141]

The next day the 34th Infantry Regiment seized Olongapo on Subic Bay, completing the initial mission of the XI Corps. But Subic Bay as an anchorage was untenable if the Japanese controlled Bataan, and XI Corps now commenced the task of cutting off the peninsula and then clearing it of Japanese forces. Col. Sanenobu Nagayoshi had fortified an area around Zig Zag Pass astride Route 7 on the northern end of the peninsula. Japanese emplacements were well camouflaged by the dense jungle foliage. Despite warnings from guerrillas, the 152nd Infantry Regiment stumbled into the Japanese emplacements on February 1 and made little headway against tough resistance. Japanese counterattacks and mortar fire took their toll of the attacking troops, who had difficulty even accurately locating themselves on their maps. The corps commander, Maj. Gen. Hall, berated Jones for the poor performance of his division. Jones in turn relieved the commander of the 152nd Infantry Regiment, Col. Robert L. Stillwell. Neither action helped the situation, which was the result of inexperienced troops experiencing combat for the first time coming up against unexpectedly strong enemy positions in difficult terrain. On the morning of February 3, the 34th Infantry Regiment passed through the 152nd Infantry Regiment to resume the attack, which went nowhere. By the next evening, even Hall had to concede that his forces were up against the Japanese main line of resistance.[142]

Jones regrouped the two regiments for a more coordinated attack on February 5. Japanese artillery and mortar fire mauled the 34th Infantry Regiment, leaving it combat-ineffective. The 152nd Infantry Regiment fared little better. The next day Hall, unhappy with the performance of the 38th Infantry Division in the fighting for Zig Zag Pass, relieved Jones of command. Krueger sent newly promoted Maj. Gen. William C. Chase from the 1st Cavalry Division to take command on February 7. Over the next week the division fought to reduce Japanese defenses, the 151st and 152nd Infantry Regiments attacking from the west, while the 149th Infantry Regiment, which had reached Dinalupihan along a more northerly route to link up with XIV Corps on February 5, attacked from the east to surround the Japanese defenders. P-47 Thunderbolt fighters operating from San Marcelino Airstrip began smothering Japanese positions in Zig Zag Pass with napalm, aided by corps and division artillery, which finally registered their guns to make their fire accurate. The 152nd Infantry Regiment linked up with the 149th Infantry Regiment on February 14, bringing the battle for Zig Zag Pass to a close. The Cyclone Division had sustained 250 killed and

1,150 wounded, but had killed nearly 2,400 Japanese in the 2-week battle. Col. Nagayoshi lived to fight another day, retreating into Bataan with 300 survivors from his command.[143]

After underestimating Japanese strength in the Zig Zag Pass area, XI Corps overestimated the remaining Japanese strength on Bataan, which numbered fewer than 1,400 troops. Krueger reinforced Hall's forces with the 1st Infantry Regiment, 6th Infantry Division, to attack down the east coast of the peninsula. Its attack began on February 14, just as the battle for Zig Zag Pass ended. The next day the 151st Infantry Regiment executed an amphibious turning movement, landing on the southern tip of Bataan at Mariveles against slight opposition. It then advanced north along the east side of the peninsula to establish contact with the forces moving south, meeting only scattered resistance. The 1st Infantry Regiment repelled a Japanese counterattack on the night of February 15–16, effectively ending organized Japanese resistance on Bataan. The 1,000 or so remaining Japanese troops on the peninsula holed up on the slopes of Mt. Natib, hunted by American infantry and Filipino guerrillas and plagued by starvation and disease until they met their ultimate fate.[144]

While XI Corps struggled to clear Bataan, the 40th Infantry Division to its north battled the 25,000-strong *Kembu Group* in the Zambales Mountains on the west coast of Luzon. The Japanese were strongly entrenched on high ground, with mutually supporting strongpoints and infantry entrenched in cave positions. Maj. Gen. Tsukada's forces were cut off from resupply and reinforcement, but Krueger determined that they had to be pushed out of artillery range of Clark Field lest they endanger that critical airbase. Beginning on February 6, the Sunburst Division, supported by close air support, artillery, tanks, and tank destroyers, attacked Japanese positions on McSevney Point, Snake Hill, the high ground to the west of Top of the World, Scattered Trees Ridge, and Object Hill. The division history recorded the ferocity of the fighting:

> As our infantry advanced, enemy machine guns deep in the cave recesses opened fire. Lumbering M-7's [self-propelled guns] and M-10's [tank destroyers] were brought into positions on the undulating slopes at the foot of the hills and faced toward the cliffs. With deadly accuracy the caves were blasted until sealed or silenced. Our artillery concentrations, setting fire to the hillsides, disclosed individual rifle and machine gun pits when the camouflage was burnt away. As infantry advanced, small arms fire and hand grenades were used to clean out the positions and flamethrower teams destroyed possible survivors in the larger caves.[145]

After two weeks of hard fighting, the division had killed upwards of 5,000 Japanese soldiers, cracked the *Kembu Group*'s main line of resistance, and ended any threat to Clark Field. On February 21, XI Corps assumed control of the fight against the *Kembu Group*, directing sequential operations by the 40th, 43rd, 38th, and 6th Infantry Divisions from that point until the end of June. Organized resistance had long since ended, as on April 6 Maj. Gen. Tsukada ordered his remaining forces to disperse and fight on as guerrillas. The *Kembu Group* ceased to exist; only 1,500 survivors lived to surrender at the end of the war.[146]

If XIV Corps were to make the drive for Manila, it needed its eastern flank protected against potential Japanese counterattacks. Of particular concern to Krueger were the Japanese *2nd Tank* and *10th Divisions* stationed in the vicinity of San Jose, Muñoz, and Lupao. These divisions were still redeploying to their mountain redoubts when the invasion interrupted their movement. Krueger tasked I Corps with clearing the area and eliminating the threat to the Sixth Army's flank.[147] Yamashita had no intention of launching a counterattack; rather, he wanted to hold on to San Jose long enough to move the ammunition and supplies located there into northern Luzon and to transfer the *105th Division* north before American forces severed the last link between the *Shimbu* and *Shobu Groups*.[148]

The 25th and 6th Infantry Divisions began their attack on February 1, the latter running into heavy contact from a Japanese combined arms task force built around the *6th Tank Regiment* in the heavily fortified town of Muñoz. The 20th Infantry Regiment's assault on Muñoz was particularly intense, with the Red Star soldiers fighting against entrenched Japanese tanks. An attempt by a column of Japanese tanks to withdraw from the city on February 7 led to a wild engagement, as GIs engaged the column with machine gun and antitank fire, as well as howitzers engaging in direct-lay mode over open sights. "While the enemy vehicles and tank-riding infantry turned to attack the battery positions and were held off by perimeter guards and roadblocks, artillery shells knocked the turrets off some tanks, tore through others, or sent armored cars and tractors turning end over end into the irrigation ditches that paralleled the road," the division history records. "Blazing vehicles illuminated the highway and the roar of exploding ammunition in the burning tanks almost drowned out the noise of the 'Sightseers' [another nickname for the 6th Infantry Division] fire . . . . Daylight found the highway from Muñoz to Santo Tomas littered with smoking Jap tanks, trucks, prime movers and enemy dead."[149] The town – or what was left of it, as "only wood and tin debris, smoking tanks and charred bodies of enemy soldiers" remained – was cleared by late morning. While the 20th Infantry Regiment struggled to seize Muñoz, the 1st and 63rd Infantry Regiments bypassed the Japanese strongpoint to the south and drove toward San Jose. In a week of fighting, the 6th Infantry Division had destroyed 52 tanks, 4 armored cars, 41 trucks, 5 105mm howitzers, and 16 47mm AT guns, and killed nearly 2,000 Japanese soldiers.[150]

The 25th Infantry Division meanwhile took two days to clear the town of Umingan and then advanced across rice paddies to Lupao, where it encountered a ferocious defense on the same lines as the Japanese defense of Muñoz. "Attacking across the rice paddies was like crawling across a series of pool tables; each time a soldier attempted to cross the dike separating one paddy from another, Japanese tankers, machine gunners, and riflemen laid down withering fire."[151] As the 27th and 35th Infantry Regiments battled for those towns, the 161st Infantry Regiment enveloped the Japanese positions to the south. After the difficult fighting for Lupao and Muñoz, the seizure of San Jose turned out to be a cake walk. On the morning of February 4, elements of the 1st Infantry Regiment entered the city unopposed. Lupao and Muñoz both fell three days later, when Japanese forces, hammered by air and artillery, attempted to withdraw from the towns only to be destroyed by American forces.[152]

Although Yamashita had sacrificed much of the *2nd Tank Division* in the process, he had bought the time needed to evacuate ammunition and supplies from San Jose and to move the *105th Division* to the mountains of northern Luzon.[153] There the *Shobu Group* would make its final stand, forcing the Americans to fight on ground of its choosing in an effort to exact a heavy price in blood for the complete liberation of the island. For Krueger, this was not an immediate concern. I Corps could now deal with the isolated Japanese strongpoints at its leisure and attack toward the east coast of Luzon, which it did, reaching Baler Bay on February 12 and completing the isolation of the *Shobu Group*. For the moment Krueger's anxieties dissipated; XIV Corps could continue its attack to seize Manila without threat of Japanese counterattack from its flank and rear.[154]

MacArthur wanted to get to Manila quickly, and his patience was wearing thin. Aside from the significance of the city as the seat of government and the importance of its docks and other logistical facilities, the fate of nearly 3,700 internees (mostly American, but also British, Australian, New Zealand, Canadian, French, and other nationalities) at the Santo Tomas Internment Camp in Manila was much on his mind.[155] He had reason to worry. On December 14, 1944, Japanese guards on Palawan, worried that the Mindoro invasion convoy was heading in their direction, targeted 150 American prisoners of war in Puerto Princesa Camp 10-A for execution. Around 14:30, two P-38s circled overhead and the Japanese ordered the prisoners into the three air raid trenches they had dug for themselves. The guards then threw aviation fuel into the openings of the covered trench and ignited the mixture with flaming torches. As the prisoners fled the resulting inferno, the Japanese mowed them down with rifle and machine gun fire, killing 120 of them. Approximately thirty Americans were able to escape the inferno by climbing down a cliff to the rocks on the beach below. Of these, only eleven would survive by negotiating their way through the jungle or by undertaking a long swim to the opposite shore of shark-infested Puerto Princesa Bay.[156]

One badly wounded escapee, Corporal Elmo "Mo" Deal, was discovered in the jungle by Filipino guerrillas, who arranged for his evacuation by a US Navy PBY Catalina flying boat.[157] His report of the atrocity was sent to MacArthur's headquarters on January 1, 1945.[158] Three other escapees, Marine Sgt. Douglas W. Bogue, Marine Pfc. Glenn W. McDole, and Navy Radioman 1st Class Fern J. Barta, eventually made their way to a guerrilla headquarters in southern Palawan, where they were picked up by a Catalina flying boat and flown to Leyte. They arrived aboard the seaplane tender USS *Tangier* on January 21, 1945, where they relayed their harrowing story to the American command.[159] These reports convinced MacArthur that the lives of the men and women he had left behind on Bataan were in jeopardy. Speed was of the essence to rescue them and ensure their survival.

MacArthur was also convinced that the Japanese would give up the capital without a fight.[160] "General MacArthur was naturally anxious to secure Manila at an early date, preferably on January 26, his birthday," Krueger commented after the war. "He considered that feasible, since he did not believe that the Japs would defend the city, whereas I felt certain that they would do so."[161] On January 30, Sixth Army issued a field order directing the 1st Cavalry Division and the 37th Infantry Division to attack south toward Manila.[162] The same day Griswold, perhaps feeling the pressure, relieved his G-3 for "inefficiency."[163] The next day Gen. MacArthur visited the 1st Cavalry Division command post and ordered its commander, Maj. Gen. Mudge, "Get to Manila. Go around the Nips, bounce off the Nips, but get to Manila. Free the internees at Santo Tomas. Take Malacanan Palace and the Legislative Building."[164] Krueger also visited the 1st Cavalry Division to speed it on its way, stopping briefly at Guimba to reminisce about the day forty-four years earlier when, in a different war, he had been commissioned as a second lieutenant, "little dreaming that one day troops of an army under my command would reconquer the town from the Japanese."[165]

Mudge, whom Krueger's G-3, Clyde Eddleman, deemed "the finest division commander I saw during the whole war," was the right person for the job.[166] He formed a motorized "flying column" under the command of Brig. Gen. Chase that would race ahead of the division along Highway 5. The first serial, commanded by Lt. Col. William E. Lobit, consisted of the 2nd Squadron, 5th Cavalry reinforced by a tank company, a field artillery battery, a platoon of engineers, a reconnaissance platoon, an antitank platoon, and a medical platoon. The second serial, commanded by Lt. Col. Haskett L. Conner, Jr., consisted of the 2nd Squadron, 8th Cavalry similarly reinforced. The third serial, commanded by Lt. Col. Tom Ross, consisted of the remainder of the 44th Tank Battalion and the 302nd Reconnaissance Troop. Fifth Air Force would support the advance from recently completed airstrips near Lingayen Gulf with P-40 Warhawk fighters and Marine SBD Dauntless dive bombers on continuous air alert, while a squadron of A-20 Havoc bombers remained on ground alert.[167]

The 37th Infantry Division would parallel the advance of the 1st Cavalry Division, attacking south along Highway 3 until it merged with Highway 5 at the small town of Plaridel. On the same day he met Mudge, MacArthur visited Maj. Gen. Beightler and made it a race to the Philippine capital. MacArthur "stated he would like to see the Division commanded by his old Rainbow comrade reach Manila first, but the cards were stacked against the Buckeyes."[168] MacArthur was referring to the greater mobility afforded the 1st Cavalry Division. Beightler and his soldiers took up the challenge, even though most of the division's infantry would have to march on foot to the capital. Lt. Col. Jim Gall's 1st Battalion, 148th Infantry would lead the advance down Highway 3.

The biggest challenge for Beightler's division was not the Japanese but crossing the many rivers on the road to Manila. Patrols had reconnoitered to the Pampanga River in the vicinity of Calumpit on January 30, but found both the highway bridge and the rail bridge destroyed, the result either of Japanese demolitions or of the pre-invasion preparation of the battlefield by the Fifth Air Force. Sixth Army engineers arrived to build a pontoon bridge, but, "when the bridge was 100 feet from completion it was discovered that the engineers lacked 60 feet of decking to cover the pontons, and [they] stopped work pending the arrival of the materials which, however, did not arrive for some time."[169] The bridge at Calumpit was the longest span that engineers had to replace on the road to Manila, and, until it was repaired, infantry could cross the river only in boats. The 1st Battalion, 148th Infantry did so in the early morning hours of February 1 and then marched to Plaridel, where it engaged a Japanese infantry battalion from the *Shimbu Group*. The soldiers cleared the town by noon, their first taste of urban combat in the war.[170] It was not to be their last; a much greater challenge lay ahead in Manila. Meanwhile, division engineers had improvised decking for the bridge at Calumpit, and, at 13:00 on February 3, the division's vehicles "poured across the bridge."

Two columns of Buckeyes advanced on Manila, followed by the engineers who "were three bridges behind the infantry."[171] "These last few miles were just more distance to be covered on the not-so-glory road," recorded the division historian. "More hiking, more sweating, more blisters, more dust."[172] But the troops moved with a purpose, pulled from the front by the presence of American internees waiting to be liberated in Manila, and pushed from behind by MacArthur and the chain of command beneath him.

The 1st Cavalry Division's flying column departed for Manila at one minute past midnight on 1 February and moved under a moonlit sky along primitive roads past rice paddies and over rivers. By dawn the column approached the Valdefuente bridge over the Pampanga River. Maj. Gen. Mudge led a group of engineers onto the bridge to remove demolition charges and throw them into the river below. Suddenly a Japanese truck approached, heading for the bridge at high speed. A bazooka hit the truck, which was loaded with explosives, causing an enormous explosion that created a twenty-foot-deep crater.[173] Lt. Col. William E. Lobit's 2nd Squadron, 5th Cavalry (nicknamed the "Buck Rogers Squadron" by its men) bypassed the obstacle and forded the river.[174] The column crashed into Cabanatuan and battled all day for the town. Lt. Col. Ross, commander of the 44th Tank Battalion, was killed in the fighting on the road south to Gapan.

The 7th and 12th Cavalry Regiments, moving by foot, arrived to take over the fight and free the column to continue its dash southward to Manila. The 1st Cavalry Division bypassed Japanese forces positioned in the hills to the east, relying instead on two Marine aircraft groups, MAG 24 and MAG 32, colloquially known as the "Diving Devildogs of Luzon," to provide reconnaissance and flank protection for the flying column as it dashed south. The Marine flyers were equipped with the outdated SBD Dauntless dive bomber, which nevertheless worked just fine for its role in the Luzon campaign.[175] Nine SBDs flying overhead covered the flying column at any given time, warning of enemy movement ahead, behind, and on its flanks.

The First Team troopers appreciated the air–ground coordination and precision of the Marine aviators.[176]

The column raced southward on February 2, overcoming minor Japanese resistance and roadblocks with the help of Filipino guerrillas. Jubilant Filipinos lined the road shouting, "Veectory, veectory" and offering flowers and fresh produce as gifts.[177] "In fact," remembered Brig. Gen. Chase, "the whole column seemed to be eating its way toward Manila."[178] In the town of Baliuag, recorded radio journalist William Dunn,

> we met the greatest ovation these islands ever witnessed. Thousands of people thronged the streets, screaming, singing, and dancing about our armored column until it was difficult to move ... an aged woman wept openly as she waved the V for victory sign and two young boys in a church steeple were banging the bells with rocks. From then on, the procession was a triumphant parade.[179]

Briefly held up at the Angat River, the 2nd Squadron, 5th Cavalry improvised. Bulldozers filled the deeper holes, and tanks towed wheeled vehicles across the river.[180] By midnight on February 2, the lead elements of the 1st Cavalry Division were within fifteen miles of the capital and had made contact with elements of the 37th Infantry Division at Plaridel. With the 37th Infantry Division and 1st Cavalry Divisions now together south of the Candaba Swamp, Krueger greenlit the final advance to Manila.[181]

The next morning Lt. Col. Haskett L. Conner, Jr.'s 2nd Squadron, 8th Cavalry approached the bridge spanning the Tuliahan River, which was still intact but covered by Japanese fire and in the process of being demolished. Navy Lt.(jg) James P. Sutton, a bomb disposal expert who was with the column, ran onto the span under fire to cut the burning fuse.[182] After an hour-long fight for the town of Novaliches, the column then continued southward in a "movement [that] resembled a Wild West movie," reaching Grace Park just north of the Manila city limits as dusk descended.[183] The 2nd Squadron, 5th Cavalry approached Manila in the wake of the 2nd Squadron, 8th Cavalry. As the squadron approached the city, the column sped up to forty to fifty mph as it traveled down a paved two-lane road.[184] As the column approached a crossroad just outside the city, four Japanese trucks turned onto the highway. As the two columns passed each other, cavalry troopers poured volleys of fire into the Japanese trucks, setting them afire.

The flying column of the 8th Cavalry would reach Manila first. After a journey of 100 miles in just 66 hours, a tank named "Battling Basic" battered down the gate of the Dominican campus of Santo Tomas

University at 20:50 on February 3, thereby announcing to the nearly 3,700 internees housed there that their liberation was at hand. The Japanese garrison (actually mostly Formosan soldiers led by Japanese officers and noncommissioned officers) took 221 hostages to use as human shields and retreated into the 3-story education building.[185] Troop F, 8th Cavalry moved to secure Malacañan Palace, the official residence of the President of the Philippines. Soon a Cadillac with lights ablaze moved in through the palace gates. In the car were four Japanese officers, all of whom were killed.[186]

The 2nd Squadron, 5th Cavalry entered Manila an hour later. As it moved down Quezon Blvd., four Japanese trucks moved into its line of march. A pitched battle erupted between the two moving forces, and two Americans were killed and several wounded, but the Japanese trucks and their occupants were destroyed. The squadron closed on the rear of G Troop, 8th Cavalry, which had taken a wrong turn and run into fierce opposition at Far Eastern University, where the Japanese halted the advance.[187] Brig. Gen. Chase (who was riding in the column) decided at that point to disengage and reinforce the perimeter around Santo Tomas.[188]

The Buckeyes were not far behind. When the infantry reached the Tuliahan River on the outskirts of Manila, they were rewarded with beer confiscated from the Balintawak brewery. While the infantry slaked their thirst, Capt. Morgan Griffiths, commanding the antitank company of the 148th Infantry Regiment, improvised the construction of a floating bridge over which flowed a steady stream of trucks and jeeps after its completion at 06:30 on February 4. The 145th Infantry Regiment joined the 148th Infantry Regiment in the attack south, fighting a series of short, sharp engagements in the northern suburbs of Manila. By the evening of February 4, the 2nd Battalion, 148th Infantry reached Old Bilibid Prison, used by the Japanese during the occupation as an internment camp, and unexpectedly liberated the occupants without a fight as the guards had already fled. Inside the walls were 1,275 internees: 447 civilians and 828 American service personnel.[189]

Infantrymen reached the Pasig River later that night. "As the liberators came marching down the New Road and the Old Road from the north they saw vast globes of fire whirl skyward, and blaze in the inky blackness punctuated by mighty roars and crashes," records the division history. "If the Japanese could not hold Manila at least the Americans would never fall heir to Manila's beauty and wealth."[190] The Japanese were destroying critical installations in the area, but wind whipped the fires into the vulnerable buildings nearby. As the business district went up in flames, GIs discovered in a lumberyard the first evidence of Japanese atrocities against Filipino civilians that would come to define the fight for Manila – 115 Filipinos, including women and children, indiscriminately bayoneted by Japanese soldiers, their bodies left to rot in the sun.[191]

The liberation of the internees at Santo Tomas elicited a joyous celebration only those who have been freed from years of captivity can comprehend. Internee Emily Van Sickle remembered the weary days of captivity. "Like prisoners everywhere, we left the day behind us and entered a world of twilight – a drab, grey world, only half-real, like nightmares that haunt our souls in sleep."[192] Stunned by their liberation, the internees "came suddenly face to face with our soldiers: twice as big as life to our starvation-ridden eyes, those husky young giants of the 1st Cavalry Division. Our joyful thoughts were too turbulent for articulation."[193] Gene Hungerford, who had endured 1,135 days in captivity, confided to his diary,

> The psychological feeling of being free is one of undescribable [sic] joy and relief. The feeling of heaviness and strain had vanished, as if one had just lifted the entire weight of the universe from your shoulders. The feelings I have are too difficult to express in mere words. One has to live through such an experience; one must squeeze from each new moment of the experience the utmost of exultation and joy and thanksgiving which the moment has to offer.[194]

Radio reporter William Dunn recalled "a loud cheer – dominated by the shrill soprano of women and children, shook the night air ... we encountered scenes of the greatest jubilation you can ever envision. Laughter mingled with tears and shouts of joy and audible prayers of thanksgiving. Small children clung to the hands of the cavalrymen and both men and women hugged and kissed them."[195]

Sherman tanks riddled the education building with machine gun fire, but the camp commandant, Lieutenant Colonel Toshio Hayashi, refused to surrender. Brig. Gen. Chase arrived the next morning and received a note from Hayashi proposing safe conduct of his troops out of Santo Tomas in return for the release of the hostages. Chase played for time, not wanting the Japanese to know just how small the force holding Santo Tomas was. Elements of the 37th Infantry Division arrived during the day, bolstering the cavalrymen holding the campus. Chase sent his executive officer, Lt. Col. Todd Brady, to finalize the release of the captives. Brady agreed to allow the Japanese to retain their personal weapons and leave the compound. Shortly before 07:00 on February 5, cavalry troopers escorted sixty-five Japanese officers and men through the front gate of the camp and four blocks east into the city. The Japanese "hurriedly disappeared into houses down the street to escape a civilian mob that was anxiously waiting for them."[196] A few guards lingered too long and paid the price, killed in revenge by Filipinos. "Three Japs were caught and brained just outside the Prison gate," Gene Hungerford recalled. "They were left, mashed and gory, to attract flies in the hot sun."[197]

Later in the morning an American flag – provided by Sam Wilson, a former Manila businessman who spent the war as a guerrilla on Mindanao as his wife and two sons were interned at Santo Tomas and who had arrived with the forces of liberation – was hoisted above the courtyard. "As it caught the breeze – still tinted with the smoke of a hundred fires – the hungry thousands, without signal, began to sing God Bless America in voices choked with obvious emotion." William Dunn stood next to Col. Fred Hamilton of the 1st Cavalry Division, who shed tears at the sight of the simple but solemn ceremony.[198]

As the Japanese retreated south of the Pasig River, they laid waste to the city behind them, dynamiting buildings and setting them ablaze. At 13:30 on February 4, an observation post atop Santo Tomas University reported three large fires burning in the business district along the Pasig River. By 17:30 there were seventy-eight large fires burning. The Japanese were systematically destroying Manila. Artillery shells started to land on the grounds of Santo Tomas University, but the Americans balked at returning fire, under orders from Krueger to not fire artillery into Manila in order to save it from the destruction that the Japanese were now wreaking on the beautiful city.[199]

The carnage continued the next day, as recorded by the 5th Cavalry:

> With the coming of darkness large explosions followed by streaks of flame lit the western part of the city like a huge candle. At the mercy of the Japs the once most beautiful city in the Orient would soon be nothing more than a blackened skeleton. Each hour saw one section after another burst into flames .... To many a soldier this night would not be forgotten and a feeling of retaliation, if and when the opportunity presented itself, ran high.[200]

Gene Hungerford recalled, "We might have been beholding some unearthly chimeric panorama, or a vision of the consummation of Sodom ... one could easily have believed the world was coming to an end, and the day of Judgement was upon us."[201]

MacArthur attempted to reach Manila on February 4. Tasked with escorting the commander-in-chief, the chief-of-staff of the 37th Infantry Division reconnoitered the route and gathered a security force. MacArthur and his escort drove through Plaridel and into the zone of the 1st Cavalry Division, only to find that its lead elements at Santo Tomas were now cut off by Japanese forces that had moved in behind the spearhead of the flying column and destroyed a bridge across the Tuliahan River at Novaliches along the line of advance.[202] Until it could be repaired, the forces at Santo Tomas were isolated and outnumbered by the Japanese garrison. MacArthur's arrival in Manila would have to wait while the Buckeyes reestablished contact with the cavalrymen and the two divisions cleared the rear area of Japanese forces. MacArthur would later write in his memoirs of this day, "For all strategic purposes, Manila was now in our hands."[203] Nothing could have been further from the truth. The strategic value of Manila lay in its docks and port area, which had not yet been cleared of Japanese forces or refurbished to allow the transit of supplies and equipment. The former task would take weeks; the latter task would take months. But, having prematurely announced Manila's liberation, MacArthur basked in the flood of congratulatory notes that streamed into his headquarters.[204]

Griswold was incensed at the folly of the expedition. "Gen. MacArthur tried to enter Manila accompanied by Gen. Mudge and myself," Griswold wrote in his diary.

> He is insane on this subject! With just a handful of scouts we passed along a road where our dead and enemy dead could often be seen. Enemy in close proximity. Finally prevented from getting in by enemy action. Why we didn't all get killed I don't know! This, in my opinion, was a most foolhardy thing for a C in C to attempt. Our route – Sante Marie–Novaliches. An unforgettable trip.[205]

It would not be the last time on Luzon that MacArthur would, for personal gratification, endanger himself and those accompanying him.

The cavalrymen made one final attempt to seize an intact bridge across the Pasig River on the evening of February 4. Brig. Gen. Chase ordered a small task force under the command of Maj. F. W. Mayfield consisting of E Troop, 5th Cavalry, a heavy machine gun platoon, and three tanks to secure the Quezon bridge. One block from the bridge the small force encountered a tank trap guarded by a roadblock. As the convoy began to turn around it came under fire from antiaircraft guns and machine guns on both sides of the street. As fires lit up the area, the soldiers worked to turn the vehicles around and withdraw back to Santo Tomas. The Japanese blew the bridge, ending whatever hope there had been of a quick seizure of Intramuros and the government quarter.[206] The battle for inner Manila would have to wait for more units and heavier artillery to arrive from the north.

The liberation of Santo Tomas did not immediately end the suffering of the internees. The camp's liberators were but the spearhead of a corps that stretched back dozens of miles to the north of the city. For a time, the internment camp became the front line. The Japanese shelled the camp on February 7, killing twenty-two people (including twelve internees) and wounding twenty-seven others. Another bombardment on February 10 added another six dead to the list. Most of the internees suffered from malnutrition, in some cases severe – thirty internees had died of starvation in the previous month. By the end of their internment, the residents had been living on fewer than 900 calories per day.[207] Civil affairs teams brought food into the Santo Tomas campus, alleviating the malnutrition that had taken hold of the internees and that was claiming nine lives per day by early February 1945.[208] For some it was too late, as deaths ascribable to malnutrition continued even after liberation, despite the best efforts of the Army Medical Corps. Amelia Mary "Millie" Bradley's husband Noble, a purchasing agent for the Army Quartermaster Corps, died one week after liberation from complications arising from malnutrition.[209]

The internees in Bilibid Prison, in danger of becoming engulfed in the inferno now raging in the immediate vicinity, also had to be evacuated. On the evening of February 5, troops of the 2nd Battalion, 148th Infantry escorted several convoys to remove the American internees from the prison – those able to move walked to freedom, whereas litter-bound patients were transported on trucks and ambulances. Japanese machine guns raked the area with fire, wounding and killing some of the infantrymen. The operation took three harrowing hours to complete, but the detainees made it to safety unharmed. The detainees were returned to the prison, judged by the 37th Infantry Division to be the safest place for them, given the conflagration engulfing the city, the next morning.[210]

MacArthur made sure to visit the internees both in Bilibid Prison and at Santo Tomas. The visits were emotional and heart-wrenching for the general, who had left these people behind when ordered by the President to evacuate to Australia. At Bilibid prison – now a hospital for all intents and purposes – he was greeted by an emaciated Major Warren Wilson, a Medical Corps officer from Los Angeles who had been captured on Bataan and whose leadership was instrumental in the survival of many of the former prisoners. One of the newly freed prisoners, Archie L. McMaster, commented, "We were surprised the American soldiers' skin looked yellow from taking atabran [sic] to prevent malaria. Their bodies also looked thin. They were perhaps awed by our looks, especially our skin and boney upper bodies, and swollen legs from edema."[211] MacArthur spent a good bit of time in Bilibid, greeting former comrades, many of whom were so emaciated they could not even stand. Those that could, stood at attention as MacArthur greeted them, tears in his eyes, apologizing for not liberating them sooner.[212] MacArthur "recognized several of them, put his hands on their shoulders and said that he regretted that it had taken him so long to liberate them," recalled Chase, who accompanied the general on his visit.[213]

The liberated internees at Santo Tomas were frantically joyous, reaching out to grasp MacArthur by the hand and to thank him for their liberation.[214] After an hour or so, MacArthur told his staff it was time to leave; the emotional toll was just too much. He wanted to head to the front line, which was fairly fluid at this point in the battle. Escorted by a fireteam of BAR men and accompanied by Andres Soriano, president of the San Miguel Corporation, MacArthur and his aides headed to Malacañan Palace. After touring the palace and paying respects to the late Filipino President Manuel Quezon with a moment of silence in his former office, MacArthur strode down the middle of the street to the San Miguel Brewery, mobbed by joyous, flag-waving Filipinos shouting "Viva!! MacArthur!!," which they pronounced "Mock-a-tour," but which the general nonetheless recognized.[215] The entourage celebrated the brewery's liberation with beer, MacArthur sipping from a bottle and others gulping down entire pitchers. In typical MacArthur fashion, the general then walked down the street toward the front, bullets from a sniper plinking around him, before turning around upon encountering a Japanese machine gun.[216]

MacArthur had another asset at his disposal, one with special training and a unique skill set. The 11th Airborne Division (Maj. Gen. Joseph Swing) had proven its combat abilities on Leyte and was now available for operations on Luzon. In the planning for Musketeer III, planners considered and rejected an airborne operation into the central plain because of the lack of transport aircraft, and likewise rejected separate regimental-size amphibious assaults at Nasugbu Bay and Tayabas Bay as insufficiently robust to upset the Japanese defensive scheme. They eventually settled on a division-size amphibious assault at Nasugbu Bay, forty-five air miles southwest of Manila. Its advantages were its proximity to Manila, fifty-five road miles distant; its defensibility; and its location south of Manila, which would put US forces on both sides of the Philippine capital.

On January 20, Eichelberger, who would oversee the assault, recommended the operation to MacArthur. Two glider infantry regiments would conduct an amphibious landing, while the 511th Parachute Infantry Regiment would drop later onto Tagaytay Ridge, the key terrain along Route 17 linking the landing beaches with Manila.[217] Concerned about reports of Japanese strength in the area, MacArthur limited the initial landing to a single regiment and labeled the operation a reconnaissance in force, which provided an alibi for withdrawal should Japanese strength in the area prove too robust.[218] The assault would commence on January 31, two days after the landing by XI Corps north of Bataan.

The 11th Airborne Division was slightly larger than half the size of a standard infantry division and lacked its robust firepower. In theory, the Japanese forces south of Manila were a match for it, but in practice the Japanese forces were spread out in small detachments throughout the area. Only 100 troops were located near the landing site, while 1,000 were positioned further back along the key approaches to Tagaytay Ridge.[219] "I am very keen about this 11th Airborne," Eichelberger wrote to his wife. "They are small in number but they are willing to fight."[220]

The division embarked on four APDs, six LSTs, and forty LCIs, escorted by four destroyers and the USCGC *Spencer*, a command ship. After an hourlong shore bombardment, the landing craft carrying the 188th Glider Infantry swam ashore in Nasugbu Bay at 08:15; the soldiers met only light and scattered opposition. Two hours later Eichelberger directed the landing of the remainder of the sea-based force, turning the reconnaissance in force into a full-blown assault on Japanese forces south of Manila. Infantrymen rapidly seized the steel-trussed bridge over the Palico River five miles inland, considerably speeding the division's advance. Eichelberger smelled blood and ordered the attack to continue through the night. He also moved the airborne drop of the 511th Parachute Infantry forward a day to February 2, by which time he believed the entire 11th Airborne Division could be consolidated on Tagaytay Ridge.[221]

The next day at 01:00, a group of thirty Q boats attempted to destroy the American invasion shipping off the coast of Nasugbu Point, but American forces destroyed or dispersed the entire force with damage sustained by only a single landing craft.[222] Ashore, the 188th Infantry ran into prepared Japanese defenses anchored on Mt. Cariliao and Mt. Batulao straddling Route 17. The 1st Battalion fought to seize Mt. Aiming southeast of Mt.

Cariliao, which provided a tactical position between the heights and split the Japanese defenses. The attack was successful, but the delay in moving past the defile caused Eichelberger to move the airborne drop on Tagaytay Ridge back to February 3.[223] More than 1,000 Japanese remained in the area, but, given their limited means of resupply, they remained immobile, to be hunted down and destroyed several months later.[224]

The 1st Battalion, 188th Glider Infantry and the 1st Battalion, 187th Glider Infantry, supported by P-38s and P-47s flying out of Mindoro, advanced the next day through the small town of Aga, forcing the Japanese to abandon their area command post. By nightfall the latter unit was just two miles short of the western slopes of Tagaytay Ridge. There it halted, ready to resume the advance the next morning after the paratroopers commenced their airborne drop.[225]

Pathfinders infiltrated through Japanese lines during the night to mark drop zones for the 511th Parachute Infantry on Tagaytay Ridge. The airborne troopers jumped at 08:15 the next morning, while the 188th Infantry attacked to reach Tagaytay Ridge. The commander of the 188th Glider Infantry, Colonel Robert H. "Shorty" Soule, was wounded while directing the attack. After receiving treatment for his injuries, Soule led his men to seize the spur for which they were fighting. In his honor, they named the area "Shorty Ridge."[226] Filipino guerrillas had already seized much of the high ground, easing the entry of the paratroopers onto Luzon. This was just as well, for two-thirds of the paratroopers, confused by the accidental drop of a supply bundle several miles short of the target, dropped upwards of six miles northeast of their intended drop zones.[227] Despite this mishap, the infantry and parachute forces linked up at 13:00, and the 511th Parachute Infantry was consolidated on Tagaytay Ridge by 14:00. The 11th Airborne Division took charge of the 2,000 or so guerrillas in the area and readied itself for a rapid advance on Manila by consolidating enough wheeled vehicles to move a battalion at a time. The division command post was established atop the ridge in the annex of the Manila Hotel. Thirty miles to the north lay Manila, glistening in the setting sun. Within a few days, the Pearl of the Orient would be covered in black smoke, its white buildings reduced to rubble by Japanese demolitions and American artillery.[228]

At first light on February 4, the 2nd Battalion, 511th Parachute Infantry set out in trucks and jeeps along Route 17 toward Manila, the way cleared by Filipino guerrillas for several miles. For Eichelberger, speed was the order of the day to disrupt the Japanese before they could create a defensive line to stop the advance of the airborne troopers.[229] Along the two-lane concrete highway, jubilant Filipino crowds waved, wept, threw fruit into the trucks, and saluted the paratroopers by yelling "veectorie."[230] A brass band greeted the column at Silang, while Filipino guerrillas with a mixture of Japanese and American weapons and displaying a large American flag were drawn up along the road at present arms.[231] The column halted at the town of Imus, where the Japanese had destroyed the highway bridge across the Imus River and fortified themselves in an old stone Spanish church. Paratroopers from Companies E and F crossed the river by walking across an intact dam to establish a bridgehead. Tech. Sgt. Robert C. Steele reduced the Japanese fortification by knocking a hole in the roof, pouring gasoline into the building, and igniting it with a white-phosphorus grenade. Eighty-eight Japanese soldiers were killed defending the town.[232]

The column crossed the Imus River at an alternate intact bridge and reentered the highway to continue its march, delayed somewhat in Bacoor, where

> the Filipinos had thrown together a 17-piece band, which blared the National Anthem and a pot-pourri of Sousa marches, while nearly three thousand other Filipinos crammed the streets, wringing the hands of paratroopers and thrusting such gifts as bananas and cucumbers and even fried chicken on the tired soldiers. Many people, especially women and old men, wept with joy and cried over and over "God bless you, God bless you."[233]

Disentangling themselves from the warm embrace of the populace, the paratroopers continued to the Las Piñas River, where they seized a bridge intact after a short firefight. At this point, the 1st Battalion, 511th Parachute Infantry passed through the lines to continue the drive on Manila. As daylight waned, the battalion reached the town of Parañaque, where a destroyed bridge and Japanese resistance halted the advance, four miles short of the capital. Thus far, casualties had been light.[234]

"The 11th Airborne Division," one GI said, "has established a beach-head 200 yards wide and 65 miles deep."[235] The statement was not quite true, but it was close enough. While the 511th Parachute Infantry and the 188th Glider Infantry battled on the road to Manila, the 187th Glider Infantry protected the division's line of communication stretching back to the beachhead. Units of Hunters ROTC, President Quezon's Own Guerrillas, Fil-Americans, and other guerrilla forces protected the division rear, freeing up combat resources. At Nasugbu, the beaches proved unsuitable for discharging LSTs, resulting in what could charitably be called just-in-time delivery of supplies to the paratroopers at the point of attack.

Supplies airdropped directly onto Tagaytay Ridge alleviated the worst of the shortages.[236] The division also took control of all guerrillas in Batangas and Cavite provinces, and soon a couple of thousand had assembled to support the American operations in the area. They proved useful in containing Japanese forces that had been bypassed in the rapid advance north toward Manila.[237]

MacArthur was thoroughly pleased with Eichelberger's handling of the invasion and advance on Manila, awarding him the Silver Star and, perhaps just as telling, given MacArthur's penchant for publicity, releasing several press communiques on Eighth Army's performance.[238] For his part, Eichelberger was convinced MacArthur was using his operation as leverage to spur Krueger on to Manila, which was undoubtedly true.[239]

By February 5, MacArthur's forces had conducted three amphibious landings on Luzon, created a massive logistical base at Lingayen Gulf, built or rehabilitated numerous airfields, and advanced to Manila in dramatic fashion, liberating thousands of Filipinos and American detainees along the way. The 1st Cavalry (now christened the "First Team" for being the first to reach Manila) and 37th Infantry Divisions had penned in Japanese forces in the heart of Manila south of the Pasig River, while the 11th Airborne Division was closing in from the south. "Indications early in the campaign that the enemy might not defend Manila had proven false," the Sixth Army after-action report recorded with more than a bit of understatement. The stage was now set for what would prove to be one of the most tragic battles in the Pacific War, "a battle distinguished for its ferocity and destruction," as Japanese and American forces grappled for control of the heart of the Pearl of the Orient.[240]

8

THE BATTLE OF MANILA

Monuments to Filipino loyalty and American valor were the masses of
twisted steel and shattered concrete, the staring, vacant windows of
gutted homes and public buildings, the wandering civilians who sought
food and shelter, and the piles of rotting Japanese bodies.[1]

Stanley A. Frankel

The Battle of Manila was the largest – indeed, the only – urban battle of the
Pacific War involving US forces. The divisions of the Sixth Army that fought
for Manila had been sharpened in jungle, atoll, and mountain warfare in the
Solomons, the Admiralty Islands, and Leyte. The regulars among them might
have understood US Army doctrine for urban combat, but virtually none of
the troops had ever experienced fighting in cities. But the same could be said
of the Japanese garrison, most of whom had never even experienced ground
combat. Both sides improvised, with the American forces adapting their
tactics, techniques, and procedures quickly to the urban jungle.

The 100-square-mile city was a mixture of architectural styles, with broad,
tree-lined boulevards, modern concrete structures, the old Spanish walled
city of Intramuros, modern port facilities made possible by land reclamation
along the shores of Manila Bay, and American-style suburbs, transitioning to
native nipa huts as the city limits gave way to more rural areas. The walls
surrounding Intramuros, forty-feet thick at the base and twenty-five feet high,
were constructed of stone, as were most of the buildings inside. More modern
structures in the business and government districts were made from
reinforced concrete, while the old city presented a significant fortified zone
that American troops would have to overcome. Manila is bisected by the Pasig
River, which flows east to west into the bay, and this waterway would present
another obstacle to American forces. The city's population numbered
around 800,000, with another 300,000 in the outlying suburbs. Manila had
been only lightly touched by the war by the beginning of 1945, but it would
suffer tremendously in the fighting to come.[2]

MacArthur had declared Manila an open city on December 26, 1941, during the Japanese invasion of the Philippines. He now expected the Japanese to likewise abandon the city with minimal fighting. This was, in fact, Yamashita's intention. Manila was indefensible, with a large population that required sustenance, and was located outside the mountainous zones upon which Yamashita had decided to anchor his defense of Luzon.[3] Yamashita left a small, three-battalion garrison in Manila to destroy bridges and other critical infrastructure to hamper US operations. Once this mission was completed, they would withdraw to link up with Japanese forces of the *Shimbu Group* in the mountains east of Manila. But Yamashita's plan was poorly coordinated with the naval component in the Philippines, the *Southwestern Area Fleet* commanded by Vice Adm. Denshichi Okochi.

Okochi created the *Manila Naval Defense Force* under the command of Rear Adm. Sanji Iwabuchi, who oversaw the base forces in the area. Iwabuchi had commanded the battleship *Kirishima* during the Naval Battle of Guadalcanal in November 1942, losing his ship to devastating fire from the radar-equipped USS *Washington*.[4] He survived, and capably led Japanese forces in the ultimately unsuccessful defense of New Georgia. In his view, perhaps by fighting for Manila he could restore his honor or die like a samurai. History will never know, for Iwabuchi committed ritual suicide before the battle was over. By the time Yamashita vacated Manila for his new headquarters in the Philippine summer capital of Baguio, Iwabuchi had upwards of 17,000 mostly poorly trained troops and naval personnel under his command, and he had no intention of going anywhere until he had at a minimum accomplished his assigned missions.[5]

Technically, Iwabuchi's forces were under the operational control of Lt. Gen. Yokoyama, commander of the *Shimbu Group*. But interservice cooperation in the armed forces of Imperial Japan was so poor that the army and navy had different definitions of such basic terms. Iwabuchi refused to obey *Shimbu Group* directives until he believed he had accomplished his assigned missions in Manila. It might not have mattered anyway, as the number of naval troops in Manila far exceeded the *Shimbu Group*'s ability to transport them out of the city. American forces also arrived in Manila more than two weeks ahead of Japanese estimates, which complicated any withdrawal from the city.[6] In any case, Iwabuchi and his staff made it clear to Yokoyama that they would remain in Manila whether ordered to withdraw by the *Shimbu Group* or not. Acceding to the inevitable, Yokoyama agreed to allow Iwabuchi's forces to defend the city and attached the available army troops in Manila to the *Manila Naval Defense Force*.[7]

Iwabuchi organized his forces into northern, central, and southern forces, each with roughly 5,000 men. The northern force would defend the business district and suburbs north of the Pasig River as well as Intramuros; the southern force would defend Nichols Field and Fort McKinley, which the Japanese believed would be the most likely avenue of approach into the city; and the central force defended everything in between, including the government district. Buildings were fortified inside and out with available material, but fields of fire were generally not mutually supporting. Japanese troops tunneled to connect buildings via their basements. Roadblocks as well as thousands of mines and improvised explosive devices prevented easy vehicular access along the streets. The heart of the defense consisted of the government buildings and walled city of Intramuros just south of the Pasig River.

The force was armed with a large number of automatic weapons, many of them stripped from naval vessels and aircraft and adapted for ground use. Antiaircraft weapons were also used in a ground role. Fire support included around fifty 120mm guns, smaller numbers of 76.2mm and 75mm pieces, and 200mm and 447mm rockets, as well as a large number of mortars.[8] Most of the troops were untrained for ground operations, so Iwabuchi planned a static defense, or, in the prosaic words of the US Army official history, "a suicidal fight to the death in place."[9] He ordered the destruction of military installations, which "once started by a body of half-trained troops hastily organized into provisional units and whose only future is death in combat . . . are impossible to control."[10]

Yokoyama did his best to exhort his soldiers to supreme effort and sacrifice. On January 16, he issued combat instructions to his command that were heavy on encouragement but light on substance. "The officers and men to participate in this battle will, by deeply impressing upon themselves their grave responsibility and by exerting their supreme efforts, inspired by the glory involved, destroy the invading American devils, and thus avenge the deaths of the great number of our comrades who have fallen since Guadalcanal." Realizing the odds stacked against the *Shimbu Group*, Yokoyama demanded that "the officers and men will each account for at least three enemy casualties." Appealing to a famous Japanese Samurai warrior, Kusunoki Masashige, Yokoyama implored, "Every effort will be made to take the enemy by surprise from its rear while checking the front in which the enemy is prepared. The Kusunoki tactics will be applied to the fullest extent . . . . Every possible means will be used to hold out. Remain undaunted despite failures. Retain faith in the Divine Power to the very end." Yokoyama realized he could do little to assist in the coming battle.

"The existing supply of arms, ammunition and medical supplies cannot be replenished until the decisive phase of the Greater East Asia War," he wrote.[11] One wonders when exactly Yokoyama believed that decisive phase would be fought.

Despite their rhetoric, neither Yamashita nor Yokoyama intended the Manila garrison to defend the city to the last man, but it did not matter. Iwabuchi was determined to stand fast at all costs. The stage was set for a catastrophe of the first order.

By February 5, the 37th Infantry and 1st Cavalry Divisions were closing on the north bank of the Pasig River, while the 11th Airborne Division was approaching Manila from the south. By this time, it was clear to commanders not named MacArthur that the Japanese were going to defend the heart of the city, nullifying MacArthur's premature declaration of victory, which he issued on February 6, and his plan to lead a victory parade through the liberated Philippine capital.[12] AP War Correspondent Yates McDaniel, who had been reporting on the Pacific War ever since the Marco Polo Bridge incident in July 1937, knew a battle when he saw one. He wrote a story describing the fighting, which MacArthur's censors banned from publication. McDaniel headed fifty miles north to MacArthur's headquarters, situated in a sugar plantation, to protest. MacArthur erupted when confronted with the facts, but after a dinner with some of his staff officers, who accurately described the ongoing fighting in Manila, the general relented. "Go back and tell your correspondents to see everything they can in Manila and write what they see as they see it," he told Yates.[13]

In an attempt to save the city from wanton destruction, MacArthur forbade air strikes and unobserved artillery fire within the city limits.[14] Krueger directed XIV Corps to seize the facilities that ensured Manila's water and electricity – the Novaliches Dam, Balara Water Filters, San Juan Reservoir, various pipelines, and a steam generator plant.[15] The idea was to liberate Manila intact to the extent possible, thereby ensuring the wherewithal necessary for the care of the Filipino residents of the city. By the time the battle was over, the water system was saved – but little else remained intact.

The initial XIV Corps plan envisioned the 37th Infantry Division seizing Manila from the north, while the 1st Cavalry Division moved into the mountains east of the city. With Japanese resistance firmly established, Maj. Gen. Oscar Griswold divided Manila. The Buckeyes would clear the northern half of the city and the 1st Cavalry Division would clear the southern half, both units driving from east to west once they had crossed the Pasig River. Eighth Army would control the operations of the 11th Airborne Division to the south until February 10, when the division passed to the control of Sixth Army, which gave operational control to XIV Corps. Griswold would command all American forces in the battle for the city from that point on.

On February 6, the 37th Infantry Division finished clearing its zone north of the Pasig River, except for a strong pocket of resistance in the Tondo district along the waterfront, which would hold out in fierce fighting until the morning of February 9.[16] The 145th Infantry Regiment took a week to clear the area to the west of the division's line of communications to the shores of Manila Bay, battling through flooded fish ponds, sluggish streams, swampy terrain, and Japanese strongpoints.

The 7th Cavalry Regiment seized the Novaliches Dam on February 6, followed the next day by securing the Balara Water Filters. A day later the regiment seized intact the San Juan dam.[17] Manila's proximate water supply was now largely in American hands. The 7th Cavalry would protect the various facilities while the remainder of the division fought a raging battle for the city.

On February 7, the 8th Cavalry Regiment encountered its first significant resistance east of the San Juan River in the New Manila Subdivision, where nearly 1,000 heavily fortified Japanese naval troops covered by heavy weapons and automatic cannon halted the regiment's attack. The battle was a portent of engagements to come. Artillery fired 1,360 rounds of 105mm and 350 rounds of 155mm high explosive at Japanese strongpoints. Tank support from a company of Shermans of the 44th Tank Battalion was hampered by mines, which prevented vehicular movement along the streets. Infantry cleared the area the old-fashioned and time-proven way, by moving building by building through the urban jungle. It took the next three days for the cavalrymen to clear the subdivision, destroying much of the area in the process. The 5th and 8th Cavalry Regiments closed on the north bank of the Pasig River by February 10.[18]

On the morning of February 7, MacArthur toured the northern part of Manila with Griswold. As the group stopped at the 37th Infantry Division's advanced combat post at Malacañan Palace, MacArthur remarked to Maj. Gen. Beightler that "it was so quiet in the area that XIV Corps could cross the river and clear all southern Manila with a platoon."[19] It was the usual MacArthur hyperbole and underestimation of the enemy, the same hubris that had led MacArthur to plan a victory parade through the main avenues of Manila.[20] Griswold noted,

He [MacArthur] seemed to think the enemy had little force here. Was quite impatient that more rapid progress was not being made …. Gen. MacArthur has visions of saving this beautiful city intact. He does not realize, as I do, that the skies burn red every night as they [the Japanese] systematically sack the city. Nor does he know that enemy rifle, machine gun, mortar fire and artillery are steadily increasing in intensity. My private opinion is that the Japs will hold that part of Manila south of the Pasig River until all are killed.[21]

Griswold's private opinion was spot on. MacArthur's headquarters postponed the victory parade indefinitely.

The Buckeyes would be the first to cross the Pasig River. At 15:15, the 3rd Battalion, 148th Infantry using LVTs (tracked landing vehicles, nicknamed alligators by the troops) and thirty engineer assault boats crossed the river under a blanket of smoke just east of the palace, where a gap existed in the concrete sea wall that lined the river. The first wave took the defenders by surprise, but the Japanese plastered succeeding waves with mortar and machine gun fire. The 2nd Battalion followed next into the bridgehead, which the Buckeyes securely established by nightfall. Engineers installed a floating bridge to enable vehicles to cross to the far embankment. Around 18:00, the Japanese unleashed salvos of 200mm and 447mm rockets onto the bridgehead, their concussive effects unnerving the soldiers in the impact zone. The rockets were finally silenced the next morning by counter-battery fire. A Filipino nicknamed "Chico," who had fought on Bataan and was now ready to rejoin the fight, assisted the infantry in their efforts. He donned an old "soup bowl" helmet and his former technical sergeant rank insignia and served as a medic on the grounds of Malacañan Palace, saving a number of lives as the battle raged. The Filipino sergeant became a liaison of sorts between the 148th Infantry Regiment and the civilian population, earning accolades from the regimental commander for his courage and devotion to duty.[22]

At 09:00 on February 8, the 2nd and 3rd Battalions attacked south against heavy opposition from a battalion of Japanese naval infantry fortified in and around the Paco Railroad Station, Paco School, and Concordia College. While the 148th Infantry Regiment vied for possession of the station, the 1st and 2nd Battalions, 129th Infantry, crossed the Pasig in LVTs and assault boats in the late afternoon. Their objective was the Municipal Power and Light Building on Provisor Island, which the 2nd Battalion attempted unsuccessfully to seize the next morning. The Buckeyes had run into the Japanese main line of resistance, featuring heavily fortified buildings, pillboxes, minefields, obstacles, and an opponent who "preferred death to surrender."[23] From this point onward, the battle for Manila turned into a building-by-building slugfest.

The fighting in the vicinity of Paco Railroad Station and Paco School on February 9 was fierce. During the assault, Pfc. John N. Reese and Pfc. Cleto Rodriguez dashed to within sixty yards of the station, armed with Browning Automatic Rifles and all the ammunition they could carry. In two-and-a-half hours, they fired 1,600 rounds, killing 82 Japanese soldiers and destroying a 20mm antiaircraft gun and a heavy machine gun. They withdrew only when their ammunition ran out, Reese being killed in the process.[24] Pfc. Elmas W. Harrell and Pfc. Billie Muenster halted a Japanese counterattack with their .30-caliber machine gun, killing thirty-three Japanese and destroying seven machine guns. At one point, Muenster picked up the gun and led his company in a counterattack, shooting from the hip.[25] Pfc. Joseph Cicchetti led a medical litter team that saved the lives of fifteen soldiers. At one point, he exposed himself to enemy machine gun fire to allow the litter team to rush past to safety. He then killed the two Japanese machine gunners with his rifle. After four hours of effort, Cicchetti's luck ran out when shrapnel hit him in the head. He nevertheless carried a final stricken soldier to safety before collapsing, and was soon dead.[26] Casualties in the 37th Infantry Division on February 9 (19 dead and 216 wounded) were the highest single-day total of the entire Luzon campaign.[27]

Faced with a determined, fortified enemy, the Buckeyes resorted to the use of massive amounts of firepower. Artillery blasted the railroad station and nearby school, causing the bulk of the remaining Japanese to withdraw during the night of February 9. The 148th Infantry attacked again at 10:00 the next morning and took the buildings with fewer casualties than expected. The 3rd Battalion was committed to the fight and, together with the 1st Battalion, gained 700 yards, an impressive achievement by the standards of urban combat.[28] At 15:15, the regiment contacted a patrol from the 8th Cavalry Regiment, which had crossed the Pasig without opposition near the Philippine Racing Club. The 5th Cavalry Regiment crossed further east near Makati and quickly established a bridgehead on the southern bank. Within hours, engineers had erected a pontoon bridge to allow vehicles to cross. The Japanese now faced not one but two divisions in the battle for central Manila, and the noose was tightening.

At 02:30 on February 10, Company E, 129th Infantry crossed over to Provisor Island in assault boats, gaining the dubious safety of a coal pile where a day earlier fifteen men of Company G had been pinned down. Sometime after dawn, the company had cleared the boiler plant, but could advance no further against Japanese fire raining down on the area. Division artillery, tanks, and tank destroyers struck the Japanese-held buildings on the island. By dawn on February 11, Japanese resistance had collapsed, enabling Company E to clear the island by the middle afternoon. Unfortunately, the power plant, which Krueger had hoped to seize intact, had been for all intents and purposes wrecked.

Also wrecked was MacArthur's stipulation on the pinpoint use of fire support to save Manila. The Japanese had fortified every major building in the heart of the city, requiring massive amounts of artillery, tank, and tank destroyer fire to support the infantry, which otherwise would have taken losses out of all proportion to the ground gained. Given the paucity of replacements flowing to SWPA, such massive casualties would have been a show-stopper.[29]

"The fighting in South Manila is very bitter," Griswold noted in his diary. "Japs organize each big reinforced concrete building into a fortress, and fight to the death in the basement, on each floor, and even to the roof. This is rough. I'm getting a lot of unavoidable casualties."[30] The only way to reduce the number of casualties was to increase the use of heavy weapons against Manila's buildings, which would kill military personnel and civilians alike. MacArthur lifted restrictions on the use of artillery and direct-fire weapons within a few days into the battle for Manila, after it became clear that the Japanese were going to fight to the death. Maj. Gen. Beightler deliberately ignored warnings from XIV Corps to conserve artillery ammunition, instead opting for large bombardments to save the lives of his soldiers. The division did its utmost to spare civilian lives, "but as the tactical need for heavy fire power increased permission was sought and obtained to place area artillery fire in front of our advancing lines without regard to pinpointed targets. Literal destruction of a building in advance of the area of friendly troops became essential."[31]

When MacArthur was informed by Brig. Gen. Bonner Fellers of the massive use of firepower by the 37th Infantry Division, MacArthur ordered Griswold to restrict use of weapons heavier than 37mm – which were wholly inadequate to penetrate the reinforced concrete structures in the city. Beightler refused to obey, telling Griswold he would have to relieve him of command instead. Since Beightler was a World War I Rainbow Division comrade of MacArthur's, MacArthur sent his chief of staff, Lt. Gen. Sutherland, to hear him out. When Sutherland reported back and validated the need for the use of heavy guns, MacArthur backed off, allowing the massive use of artillery fire to continue.[32] His aide Bonner Fellers confided in a letter to his wife, "Mac is very depressed over the destruction."[33]

While the 37th Infantry Division and 1st Cavalry Division fought to establish bridgeheads south of the Pasig River, the 11th Airborne Division entered the fight to their south. Since this was the direction from which the Japanese believed the Americans would attack, fortifications were better established and more numerous. On the other hand, the 11th Airborne Division was permitted to use close air support to reduce Japanese fortifications in this more sparsely inhabited area, unlike the divisions to its north fighting in the center of the city.

The Japanese defended southern Manila from the Genko Line, which consisted of a line of concrete pillboxes that extended 6,000 yards from the Manila Polo Club through Nichols Field to the high ground at Fort McKinley. Nichols Field, its runways now useless to the defenders, housed numerous 5-inch naval guns, antiaircraft guns, and heavy mortars that were now trained against a potential ground attack. Fort McKinley was another strongpoint that the airborne troopers would have to reduce.[34]

At 05:00 on February 5, the 2nd Battalion, 511th Parachute Infantry crossed the Paranaque River and entered the southern outskirts of the greater Manila area under fire from Japanese artillery, naval guns, and antiaircraft guns. Improvised explosive devices consisting of 500 lb. bombs with low-pressure detonators barred advance along the roads.[35] The battle for Manila was joined, and advances were now measured in yards rather than miles. Soldiers attacked house to house and reduced Japanese positions with flamethrowers, demolition charges, and mortar-delivered white phosphorus, but the advance was costly to friend and foe alike.[36] Filipino refugees streamed out of the city, bringing with them tales of horror and Japanese atrocities against the city's inhabitants.[37] On February 11, the 511th Parachute Infantry Regiment lost its commander, Col. Orin D. "Hard Rock" Haugen, when he was hit in the chest by shrapnel from a Japanese antiaircraft gun, one of seventy men from the regiment killed up to that time in the fighting on Luzon.[38]

The advance was impeded by the Japanese guns positioned at Nichols Field, which would have to be taken. The attack needed more weight, so Swing ordered the 188th Glider Infantry Regiment (reinforced with a battalion of the 187th Glider Infantry Regiment) to launch an attack in conjunction with a battalion from the 511th Parachute Infantry Regiment. The attack, which began on February 7 and continued for four days, barely succeeded in creating a foothold on the western side of the airfield. Referring to the Japanese 5-inch naval guns hindering his unit's advance, one company commander messaged his headquarters, "Tell Bill Halsey to stop looking for the Jap fleet. It's dug in on Nichols Field."[39]

The infantry needed more fire support, which the 11th Airborne Division, armed with 75mm pack howitzers and short-barreled 105mm howitzers with an insufficient supply of ammunition, lacked. Once the division came into range of XIV Corps artillery, the heavy 155mm howitzers and 8-inch guns of the corps artillery could assist it.[40] The lack of a boundary between Sixth and Eighth Armies was a challenge. XIV Corps and the 11th Airborne Division mutually agreed to a fire support coordination line on February 8 to prevent friendly fire incidents between the converging forces. Finally, on February 10, SWPA transferred the 11th Airborne Division to Sixth Army control.[41]

XIV Corps halted the 11th Airborne Division's attack northward into the city on February 11 to avoid friendly fire, given the imminent arrival of the 1st Cavalry Division along its line of advance. Griswold authorized the Angels to attack Nichols Field again on February 12, but this time supported by Marine Corps SBD Dauntlesses based at Lingayen Gulf and the full weight of XIV Corps artillery. The heavy fire support did the trick; the 187th and 188th Glider Infantry Regiments cleared the field against "heavy opposition … from the Imperial Jap Marines and Naval forces who held each position until killed."[42] From this point to the end of the battle for the city, the 11th Airborne Division would focus on clearing Cavite naval base, destroying remaining Japanese forces in its zone, and seizing Fort McKinley, the latter mission coordinated with the adjacent 1st Cavalry Division.

Advances by the 1st Cavalry Division completed the encirclement of Japanese forces in Manila. The 5th Cavalry Regiment made significant headway on February 12, blitzing across Nielson Field all the way to Manila Bay and contacting the lead elements of the 11th Airborne Division. Japanese resistance in this area was light; the far larger problem for the cavalry troopers on this day was civilian looting and violence. Thugs "ran people from their homes, looted all of their personal belongings, confiscated their cars, and in general presented a difficult problem. One half of the [2nd] Squadron spent the rest of the day rounding up these disorganized 'Guerrilla' bandits, took their arms away from them, and drove them out of the city."[43] The 12th Cavalry Regiment, which had been relieved of its duties guarding the division's line of communications by the 112th Regimental Combat Team, skirted past Nielson Field, made contact with the 5th Cavalry Regiment, and reached the shore of Manila Bay in the middle of the afternoon.[44] Japanese forces in Manila were now isolated, leaving them

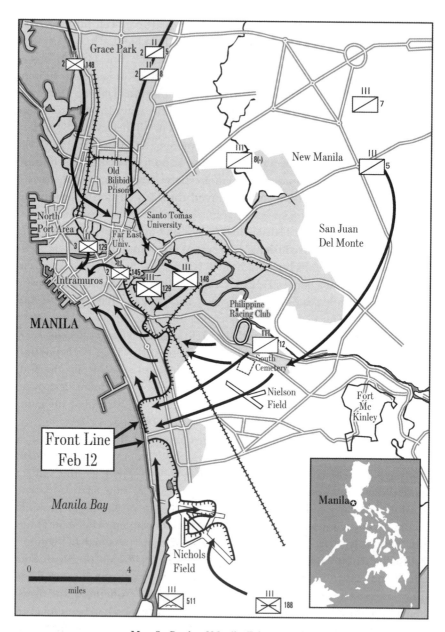

Map 8: Battle of Manila, February 1945.

with the choice of surrender or death. Of course, Rear Adm. Iwabuchi had already made that decision weeks previously.

Or had he? The fast pace of the American operations had confused the Japanese commanders responsible for operations in Manila. After the 37th Infantry Division had crossed the Pasig River, Iwabuchi decided that the situation required a withdrawal after all. He moved his headquarters to Ft. McKinley, planning from there to direct the movement of his forces out of Manila to link up with the *Shimbu Group*. At the same time, Yokoyama, seriously underestimating American strength, planned a counterattack to open a corridor through which the Japanese forces in Manila could withdraw. Before any of these operations could be executed, Iwabuchi decided the situation had deteriorated to such an extent that withdrawal was no longer an option. He moved back into the city on the morning of February 11, just missing the regiments of the 1st Cavalry Division slicing across his path back into the city, to resume his tenuous control of the battle. Four days later, Gen. Yamashita chimed in from his headquarters at Baguio, censuring his two subordinates and demanding the immediate withdrawal of all Japanese forces from Manila.[45]

The order came two weeks too late. By February 12, XIV Corps had isolated Manila, making impossible any withdrawal from the city. The counterattack by seven battalions of the *Shimbu Group* during February 15–18 came to naught, being repelled by the 112th Regimental Combat Team, guarding the 1st Cavalry Division's line of communication north of Manila, and the 7th and 8th Cavalry Regiments, guarding Manila's water supply. Despite Yokoyama's urgings to break the *Manila Naval Defense Force* into small groups and withdraw at night, Iwabuchi by this point once again had decided to fight and die in Manila. On February 23, communications between Iwabuchi and the outside world ceased; the Manila garrison was on its own.[46]

While this drama within the Japanese chain of command played out, the 11th Airborne Division completed its conquest of the southern Greater Manila area. A guerrilla force under the direction of US Army Maj. John D. Vanderpool had isolated a force of Japanese troops, the *Abe Battalion*, on the high ground just west of Laguna de Bay on February 14. The Japanese should have broken the encirclement to join the *Shimbu Group*, but inexplicably remained in position to be destroyed by the 11th Airborne Division. During February 18–23, a task force of three reinforced infantry battalions attacked the *Abe Battalion*, wiping it out with the use of generous amounts of airpower and artillery. Another four battalions attacked east to clear Japanese forces from the approaches to Ft. McKinley. On February 17, following an airstrike employing napalm on Japanese positions, the 188th

Infantry seized the Ft. McKinley annex. A patrol sent the next day reported no contact with Japanese forces in Ft. McKinley. The 1st Cavalry Division entered the fort the next morning to find it vacated. The *4th Naval Battalion* and the remnants of the *3rd Naval Battalion* defending Ft. McKinley had exercised the better part of valor before the 11th Airborne Division launched its final attack and withdrew to rejoin the *Shimbu Group,* leaving 961 dead comrades behind.[47]

Japanese strength in central Manila now numbered around 6,000 men, who were progressively stripped of their heavy weapons and artillery by American counterbattery fire. But they still had small arms and hand grenades, along with a will to fight to the death. Once the 1st Cavalry Division had completed the encirclement of the Japanese garrison, the days of rapid advances were over. The fighting was now confined to individual buildings in a grinding urban war of attrition.[48] "During the drive down the Central Plain, the doughboys fought one day and then hiked uneventfully the next five; now, the infantrymen expended all of their strength to occupy a few yards," records the 37th Infantry Division history. "For those who missed Normandy or Cassino, Manila would do."[49] The Buckeyes had trained platoons in assault techniques for use against fortified positions before embarking for the invasion of Luzon, and this training was now put to the test.[50] The civilian population, caught between a rapacious and cruel occupying force and liberators who were all too willing to use massive amounts of artillery, mortar, tank, and tank destroyer fire to reduce their losses, suffered the most.

After the battle for Provisor Island, the 37th Infantry Division had consolidated its lines along Marques de Comillas Street, and now began the long, slow process of collapsing the Japanese back to the stronghold of Intramuros. On February 11, the 148th Infantry continued its assault after the battle for Paco Railroad Station. The Japanese had fortified Paco Cemetery with underground emplacements, the dead sharing their graves with those desperately trying to stay alive. 1st Battalion attacked with mortars and flamethrowers, but three Japanese 75mm guns kept the infantry at bay. That night American artillery pulverized the area, adding new dead bodies to those already interred. A resumption of the attack the next day met stiff resistance, but a second artillery concentration backed up by infantry attacking with bazookas, flamethrowers, and pole charges carried the position.[51]

To the north of its boundary with the 148th Infantry Regiment along Isaac Peral Street, the 129th Infantry Regiment attacked on February 12 after a thirty-five-minute artillery preparation. 2nd Battalion gained a couple of hundred yards along the Pasig River toward the General Post Office, but 1st Battalion's attack went nowhere, as Japanese troops fortified in the Manila Club, St. Theresa College, San Pablo Church, a shoe factory, and the New Police Station barred the way. Machine guns raked the approaches with fire, while mines blocked vehicular movement. Infantry attacked the buildings with flamethrowers, bazookas, and pole charges, supported by mortars and artillery, and, after engineers reinforced the bridges over the Pasig River to allow heavier traffic, by tanks and tank destroyers as well. "The fires of Manila are burning tonight," reported William Dunn. "The rumble of artillery can be heard as the Japanese continue their fanatical effort to spread as much destruction as possible before their final annihilation."[52]

The Buckeyes hammered away at the heavily defended buildings for three days. On February 14, Company B managed to enter the Manila Club, while Companies A and C managed to breach the east end of the New Police Station, only to withdraw at dusk to allow artillery to plaster the building again. At an abandoned gas station on Isaac Peral Street, infantrymen discovered a grisly mound of bodies, Filipinos who had been bayoneted by the Japanese and left for dead. The GIs found one eight-year-old girl and her mother clinging to life, rendered first aid, and evacuated them for treatment.[53] Columns of haggard refugees streamed out of the city, screened by counterintelligence detachments for foreign nationals, collaborators, and Japanese sympathizers. Those suspected of aiding the Japanese were interned in Bilibid Prison.[54]

"The stories that come out of south Manila, borne on the drooping shoulders of homeless refugees, are both harrowing and unbelievable," reported William Dunn. "The Japanese, in his dying frenzy, seems determined to take as many innocent civilians with him as possible."[55] Viewing the scene, Bonner Fellers wrote to his wife, "It takes all one's strength to see the refugees .... The suffering, the mental torment, and the losses which these people endure are indescribable," adding, "If anything should happen to Tokyo, the Japanese have asked for it."[56]

For two days after reaching Manila Bay, the 5th and 12th Cavalry Regiments cleared Japanese holdouts northwards to Vito Cruz Street. "Clear" is a doctrinal term meaning the removal of enemy forces and elimination of organized resistance in an assigned objective area, but it does not convey the degree of violence involved. "All day the fighting in this area raged with the buildings being subjected to artillery, tank and bazooka fire," the 12th Cavalry regimental history recalled. "One by one they were reduced to rubble and their occupants eliminated by hand-to-hand fighting. In the meantime, on the right flank elements of the 1st Squadron had pushed forward through the wrecked residential district of Taft Avenue, searching out Japanese stragglers as they moved forward."[57] By the evening of February 14, the 1st Cavalry Brigade was poised to attack the Japanese 2nd Naval Battalion, which defended Harrison Park, Rizal Stadium and the nearby baseball park, and La Salle College.

Following a one-hour artillery barrage, the attack commenced at 08:15 on February 15. Progress was slow; while the 1st Squadron, 12th Cavalry seized La Salle College and advanced west toward the old Spanish Fort Abad, it took five hours for the lead troop of 2nd Squadron, 12th Cavalry to cross Taft Avenue and seize some buildings east of the baseball park. The 2nd Squadron, 5th Cavalry, positioned west of the 12th Cavalry Regiment, attacked north along Dewey Boulevard. The pressure worked; by nightfall the Japanese in Harrison Park had retreated to Rizal Stadium, and G Troop, 12th Cavalry had breached an entrance into the facility with the assistance of attached tanks and tank destroyers. The attack continued the next day, following another artillery barrage, and the brigade destroyed organized resistance in the area, with the most difficult fighting in the baseball park. In this facility, the Japanese had built bunkers on the ball diamond, created sand-bagged positions under the grandstands, and positioned snipers in the rafters overhead. E and G Troops, 5th Cavalry, supported by three Sherman tanks, fought for two hours to clear the facility. Japanese holdouts under the grandstands were finished off with flamethrowers and dynamite. At a cost of 40 killed and 315 wounded, the GIs had killed around 750 Japanese troops and captured 25 Formosans, who were more than ready to surrender, effectively eliminating the Japanese *2nd Naval Battalion*.[58]

While this battle raged, Maj. Gen. Griswold decided to consolidate the battle for the shrinking pocket in central Manila under a single division commander. He gave operational control of the 1st Cavalry Brigade (minus one squadron) to the 37th Infantry Division. Maj. Gen. Beightler ordered the cavalrymen to continue their attack to clear a zone adjacent to Manila Bay extending north to Isaac Peral Street. This area included a number of reinforced concrete buildings, including the High Commissioner's residence and General MacArthur's pre-war home, the Manila Hotel.[59] "Bitter fighting and slow progress," Griswold wrote in his diary.[60] Bonner Fellers was more explicit in his comments to his wife, "Manila is slowly crumbling. The Jap is putting up a stubborn, suicide[al] fight and as he retires building by building, he sets them on fire. It's a horrible thing . . . . In view of the atrocities these beasts have committed, it is impossible to sympa-thize with them."[61]

On February 15 and 16, heavy artillery and mortar concentrations, along with direct fire from 105mm self-propelled cannon, tanks, and tank destroy-ers, blasted the Japanese positions in the buildings facing the 1st Battalion, 129th Infantry. Probing attacks resulted in dozens of casualties but little else. The 3rd Battalion, 129th Infantry attempted to breach City Hall, without success. The 148th Infantry Regiment made better headway; it cleared Japanese strongpoints in the Malete traffic circle, but could not overcome Japanese positions in the Philippine General Hospital. To make matters worse, the Japanese had taken several thousand Filipinos in the hospital hostage, using them as human shields to discourage the use of heavy firepower against the buildings. The 3rd Battalion skirted the hospital to the south and reached the shore of Manila Bay by 19:40.[62]

The 129th Infantry Regiment had borne the brunt of the battle to date and needed rest. On February 17, the 145th Infantry Regiment effected its relief, taking up the fight. The next day the 1st and 3rd Battalions, 145th Infantry attacked behind a preparatory bombardment from tanks and self-propelled cannon. The bombardment ripped huge chunks out of the buildings, leaving St. Theresa College looking "hollow, desolate, and forlorn."[63] In the north, the 3rd Battalion seized the three-story, reinforced concrete YMCA Building and a portion of the Manila Trade School. Further south, GIs from 1st Battalion wielding small arms, bazookas, and flame-throwers seized the shoe factory and St. Theresa College and gained entry into the eastern side of the New Police Station.[64] The infantrymen were unable to seize the western half of the structure, so they withdrew to enable supporting fire to reduce the Japanese defenses.

Wash, rinse, repeat. On the morning of February 19, tanks, self-propelled cannon, and a battalion of 105mm howitzers worked over the building. 1st Battalion cleared the San Pablo Church, while Company B again entered the eastern wing of the structure. Once again, the hold proved untenable, and the troops withdrew by dusk. Wash, rinse, repeat. The next morning, for a final time, American guns again blasted the New Police Station again. Company C occupied the ruins, finally ending the battle after eight days of brutal combat.[65]

While the 1st Battalion seized the New Police Station, the 3rd Battalion continued its attack toward Taft Avenue. On February 20, infantrymen seized the remainder of the Manila Trade School and the girls' dormitory of the Normal School. Working its way through ruined small factories, homes, and assorted piles of rubble, the battalion prepared to assault City Hall, a four-story, stone building constructed around a central courtyard, and the Metropolitan Water District Building. Under cover from artillery-delivered smoke and supported by direct fire from self-propelled cannon and a 155mm howitzer that blasted a hole in the east wall, a platoon gained entry into the building, only to be repulsed by heavy fire. The attack recommenced the next morning, and by 09:30 Company L had seized the Water District Building. The battalion continued on through mine-strewn gardens to seize the Metropolitan Theater and the rest of the Normal School. The fight for City Hall was vicious; Company I lost two commanders and had just eighty men left by the end of the day, but managed to secure a foothold in the building. The Japanese then set off explosives under the GIs, setting fire to the building, which became a death trap. The Americans withdrew to lick their wounds.[66]

As the fight for City Hall raged, the 1st Battalion left a company to defend its newly won positions along Taft Avenue, maneuvered to the rear of the 3rd Battalion, and attacked the Cold Storage Plant and the General Post Office. The latter building was particularly imposing – 5 stories and 500 rooms, with thick walls and a deep basement, fortified with sand-bagged bunkers, barbed-wire entanglements, and minefields, and further protected by the Pasig River on the north and a raised roadway to the south. While Company C seized the western half of the Cold Storage Plant, Company B fought to breach the General Post Office. After hours of fire from tanks and self-propelled cannon, two platoons gained entry into the building, but were immediately repulsed by a Japanese counterattack. The next morning the entire battalion, minus elements left to hold the Cold Storage Plant, converged on the General Post Office. By now, troops had learned to rush to the upper floors and work their way down.[67] The fighting went on throughout the day and into the night, not ending until the GIs had seized the building during the middle of the morning on February 23. Japanese holdouts were dispatched by pouring oil and gasoline into the basement and igniting the mixture with flamethrowers.[68]

On the night of February 21–22, tanks, tank destroyers, self-propelled cannon, and two 155mm howitzers moved through mine-infested streets to engage City Hall with direct fire. Led by Company I, the 3rd Battalion, 145th Infantry charged through the resulting breach, the infantry blasting their way from floor to floor and from room to room using rifles, machine guns, grenades, demolition charges, and flamethrowers. The final twenty Japanese soldiers, holed up in a first-floor room, refused to surrender and

8.1: Soldiers of Company F, 145th Infantry, move past the General Post Office Building on the banks of the Pasig River. Artillery and tank fire inflicted heavy damage on the building before it was taken by assault. The fighting in Manila destroyed a third of the city and seriously damaged another third, requiring years of reconstruction. (Credit: US Army Signal Corps Photo)

were incinerated with flamethrowers.[69] By dark, the building was secure, with 382 Japanese dead "sprawled in heaps throughout the smoky ruins."[70]

The city was also fast becoming a casualty. "Hope of saving beautiful downtown Manila had been reluctantly discarded long before," recorded the 37th Infantry Division history.[71] The division's after-action report stated,

> To occupy and secure any one of these virtual fortresses without prohibitive and decimating causalities, required the constant employment of direct fire weapons such as Cannon Company M-7s, tank destroyers, medium tanks, and 155mm howitzers, to blast openings in walls and sufficiently neutralize enemy fire power to permit Infantry assault units to penetrate the buildings and eliminate the enemy forces remaining therein. This slow, deliberate, but ultimately successful process continued throughout the [final] phase of the Battle of Manila.[72]

Firepower would save American lives, but it indiscriminately destroyed both the buildings it targeted and their occupants.

While the 145th Infantry fought its way through the New Police Station, City Hall, and the General Post Office, the 148th Infantry faced Japanese units fortified in the Philippine General Hospital and the University of the Philippines, the former act a war crime under the Geneva and Hague Conventions, which prohibited the militarization of medical facilities.[73] Initial contact was made on February 14, when the 2nd Battalion discovered the extent of Japanese defenses in the area. Movement down streets was impossible; infantrymen had to assault through adjacent buildings to work their way to Taft Avenue, the jumping-off point for an attack on the hospital grounds. On February 15, the 3rd Battalion on the left flank reached Manila Bay and then turned ninety degrees to the north to face the hospital grounds. The regiment began its main assault on the morning of February 17, after which forty-eight hours of combat decided the issue.

At 08:30, the 2nd Battalion, 148th Infantry crossed Taft Avenue to assault the Science Building from the east. The Americans limited use of artillery and heavy-caliber fire on the buildings for fear of injuring the civilians in the area, whom the Japanese had forbidden to evacuate. After fierce close quarters combat, the Japanese repulsed the first attack. A second assault led by T/4 Eugene J. Callaghan, who, though wounded, was able to blanket the entrances to the building with searing liquid from his flamethrower, succeeded in securing the building and killing its twenty-eight occupants. The 1st Battalion, which had relieved the 3rd Battalion on the left flank, attacked north to reach the Medical School by 11:30. Two thousand civilians streamed out of the hospital grounds, seeking the safety of American lines.[74]

During the afternoon, the 2nd Battalion seized the Administration Building, the Nurses Dormitory, and the two eastern wings of the hospital. The GIs worked to evacuate patients and internees being used by the Japanese as human shields as the battle for the hospital continued. Fighting at close quarters in the various wings of the hospital continued for hours. Company E attempted, but failed, to enter the Medical Science Building, which the Japanese set on fire at nightfall. During the night, infantrymen seized the west wing of the hospital, while civilians in the area were successfully evacuated.[75]

On February 18, the 2nd Battalion consolidated its gains, which included the entire hospital complex with the exception of the Medical School and five buildings in the northwest corner of the hospital grounds.[76]

At 10:00 the next morning, the 5th Cavalry Regiment relieved the 148th Infantry Regiment in place. "The area we are moving into is a cauldron of complete wreckage with the ever-present litter of battle and the stench of enemy dead," recorded the 5th Cavalry Regiment.[77] The cavalrymen would finish the battle for the hospital and the University of the Philippines.

After a short bombardment of the Medical School by a platoon of tanks and a platoon of tank destroyers, G Troop began the assault by entering the second floor via an adjacent building. Liberal use of flamethrowers and bazookas forced the Japanese to the first floor and basement. Additional use of flamethrowers and grenades dropped from above ended resistance by 16:00. Other units seized nearby Assumption College and the other buildings on the hospital grounds. By nightfall on February 19, the hospital complex was in American hands.[78]

The next objective was the University of the Philippines, just across Padre Faura Street from the hospital complex. The attack would begin on the morning of February 20 with an assault by B Troop on Rizal Hall, a large, rectangular, reinforced concrete structure with an open patio in the center and a wing jutting off the west end of the rectangle. There were two staircases on either side of the building on the eastern end. On each floor was a hallway that ran the length of the building. The Japanese had heavily fortified the structure. Machine guns firing through openings in the foundation could rake with fire any attack at ground level, while additional machine guns were positioned on rooftop bunkers and in the interior hallways. The defenders had barricaded all doors and windows.

After a two-hour preparation by a platoon of tanks and a platoon of tank destroyers, a platoon from B Troop entered the east side of the building at 11:30. The platoon gained the second floor after two hours of fighting, and the third floor three-and-a-half hours later. At this point the Japanese, fearing the building would be lost, set off explosives that shook the entire structure and collapsed the center of the building. Fearing further explosions, the 1st Battalion commander withdrew the platoon from Rizal Hall.[79]

Meanwhile, G Troop assaulted the Administration Building on the southwest corner of the campus. Gaining entry into the building with the help of a platoon of tank destroyers, the cavalrymen had occupied the first two floors by 17:00. As if on cue, a series of explosions then rocked the building as the Japanese detonated explosives with the intent to collapse it. The cavalrymen then exercised the better part of valor and withdrew, renewing the assault the next day and taking the building for good.[80]

Over the course of the night, small groups of Japanese attempted to infiltrate the 5th Cavalry positions around Rizal Hall. The cavalrymen killed 134 Japanese during the evening and early morning hours. The cavalrymen then continued their assault. Two platoons of Sherman tanks, two 105mm self-propelled howitzers, and a platoon of tank destroyers fired on Rizal Hall for two hours, which opened up numerous holes in the structure. An assault team from Troop C attempted to enter the southwest corner of the building, but Japanese machine gun fire hit five soldiers as they crossed the street. A flamethrower operator, hit during his approach, sent a burst of flame into the building as he pitched forward, dead. From 13:00 to 14:30, the regiment repeated the preparation with direct fire, after which an assault team from C Troop entered the building, reinforced by a platoon from B Troop. By 16:30 cavalrymen occupied the three above-ground floors, where they hunkered down for the night. During the night the Japanese again attempted to infiltrate American lines, with ninety-two of them killed in the process. The mounting strain of sleepless nights took a physical and psychological toll on the cavalrymen.[81]

US forces now occupied the eastern end on all three floors, but a Japanese sniper located inside the patio wall on the second floor at the western end of the building made movement dangerous. Firefights raged in the enclosed space during the afternoon of February 22. At 20:00 the Japanese attacked along the second floor with machine guns, rifles, and grenades. For two hours the cavalrymen battled the Japanese at close quarters, but successfully defended their positions in harrowing and deadly combat.[82]

At 01:30 the troopers holding the eastern end of Rizal Hall heard chanting that soon rose to the level of full-throated singing. After forty-five minutes, a final burst of song was followed by loud shouting and reports of exploding grenades and dynamite charges that continued for more than two hours. The next morning an assault team moved forward to reconnoiter the premises and found on the west end of the building seventy-seven dismembered Japanese who had committed suicide during the night. The cavalrymen secured the building by 13:00. In four days of fighting, the 5th Cavalry Regiment had killed 243 Japanese inside Rizal Hall.[83]

While 1st Squadron cleared Rizal Hall, 2nd Squadron assaulted the adjacent University Hall on February 22. The usual preparation from tanks, tank destroyers, and 105mm guns sent the Japanese down into the deceptive safety of the basement. At 11:30, an assault team from E Troop entered the building and cleared the upper floors. GIs emptied the contents of flamethrowers into the basement, but finally resorted to pouring a mixture of oil and gasoline into various openings and igniting the mixture. The building was secured by late afternoon, only to be relinquished when the occupying platoon misunderstood its orders.[84]

As the fighting for the Philippine General Hospital and the University of the Philippines raged, the 12th Cavalry Regiment added its weight to the fight for central Manila. At 10:00 on February 19, the regiment (minus 2nd Squadron, positioned at Fort McKinley) relieved the 148th Infantry from the shore of Manila Bay to the boundary with the 5th Cavalry along Mabini Street and an hour later attacked north to seize the High Commissioner's Building and the Manila Hotel, the latter building Gen. MacArthur's pre-war home. By 15:00, B Troop had closed on the pre-war office and residence of the US High Commissioner, while A Troop cleared its zone to the east. After an artillery preparation, B Troop attacked the building at 07:15 the next morning and cleared it within an hour. It then continued on to the Army–Navy Club, clearing it by 10:30. The 1st Squadron then consolidated its gains.[85]

On the morning of February 21, 1st Squadron, reinforced with two M7 105mm self-propelled howitzers and a platoon of Sherman tanks, attacked the Manila Hotel behind an artillery preparation and entered the structure by 09:30. The Japanese had heavily fortified the interior of the building and held the basement and underground passageways in strength. Fierce hand-to-hand fighting, including liberal use of flamethrowers and demolition charges, resulted in the cavalrymen seizing the upper two floors by noon and the remainder of the building, minus the basement areas, by dark. Mopping up continued for two days.[86]

On February 23, Gen. MacArthur and his personal staff raised the Stars and Stripes outside the High Commissioner's Building, after which he visited his old residence on the top floor of the Manila Hotel. It was not a happy homecoming. During the war the Japanese had left the suite vacant as a gesture of respect.[87] But the penthouse apartment was destroyed in the fighting, leaving just ashes behind. "I was tasting to the last acid dregs the bitterness of a devastated and beloved home," MacArthur later wrote.[88]

Griswold noted the strain on commanders and soldiers alike. "Very slow progress, with bitter fighting," he confided to his diary.

We are constricting the enemy in a smaller space day by day. The Army–Navy Club, Manila Hotel, Legislative Building and Post Office have all been assaulted and taken. Remaining are the Mint of Finance Building, the Walled City and the port section, including Wallace Field area. The

> Intramuros is a formidable obstacle. I plan a river crossing and assault from the north across the Pasig River, supported by the biggest artillery concentration from 155s, 105s, 8″ howitzers and 240 mm howitzers, with emphasis on much direct fire. Plans are being perfected now.[89]

The Battle of Manila was reaching its climax.

As the Japanese perimeter shrank to the old city of Intramuros and the few modern government buildings still in their possession, "block after bloody block [of Manila] was slowly mashed into an unrecognizable pulp."[90] The medieval stone walls of Intramuros and the modern reinforced concrete buildings of the government district would prove to be no match for modern American firepower. The sixteen-foot-high walls of Intramuros, built in 1571, were forty feet thick at their base. A moat surrounded the area on the east and south, while the Pasig River bordered the north and Manila Bay bordered the west. Inside Intramuros were cathedrals, monasteries, and

8.2: Accompanied by Col. James Corbett (with cane), Gen. Douglas MacArthur visits his old residence in the Manila Hotel, February 23, 1945. MacArthur's pre-war home in the penthouse was destroyed in the fighting. (Credit: US Army Signal Corps Photo)

residences, along with the old Spanish Fort Santiago in the northwest corner. The Japanese defenders had built an extensive tunnel system to move soldiers from one part of the area to another. Rooting them out of these positions would be difficult.

Beightler initially requested to use dive bombers and napalm strikes from P-38s to level Intramuros, significantly reducing (in his view) the potential for friendly casualties. Griswold and Krueger agreed, pending approval by MacArthur. "I hated to ask for it since I know it would cause death of civilians held captive by the Japs," Griswold lamented in his diary. "We know, too, that the Japs are burning large numbers to death, shooting them and bayoneting them. Horrid as it seems, probably death from bombing would be more merciful."[91] But thousands of noncombatant Filipinos were trapped inside the walled city of Intramuros. XIV Corps broadcast a message in Japanese granting safe passage for these innocents, but Japanese commanders ignored it.[92] William Dunn reported, "The consistent refusal of the Japanese to allow civilians to evacuate contested territory, together with their unbelievable orgy of murder and arson, has taken a toll of life and property without parallel in the Pacific."[93] Worse yet, Japanese soldiers were to commit atrocities that would claim the lives of thousands of civilians. The coming battle would prove to be a horrific experience for the Filipino residents of the old city.

MacArthur was adamant; air strikes would inevitably kill large numbers of civilians and, while they might speed the conclusion of operations, their use in Manila was "unthinkable."[94] The decision angered Griswold, who wrote in his diary,

> I fear that the C in C's refusal to let me have bombing will result in more casualties to my men. However, I understand how he feels about bombing people – but it is being done all over the world – Poland, China, England, Germany, Italy – then why not here! War is never pretty. I am frank to say I would sacrifice civilian Philipino [sic] lives under such circumstances to save the lives of my men. I feel quite bitter about this tonight.[95]

Despite Griswold's concerns, MacArthur's veto required Beightler and his planners to go back to the drawing board.

The choice now confronting Beightler was whether to continue the attack from the south and east, to eliminate Japanese resistance in the large government buildings on the periphery of Intramuros, or to conduct a crossing of the Pasig River to the north in conjunction with an assault on the eastern walls. The latter option would require careful planning and a massive artillery preparation, but would avoid the main areas of Japanese strength. Griswold and Beightler chose to conduct the river crossing.[96] The attacking forces would use direct and indirect-lay artillery, tank, and tank destroyer fire to penetrate the walls in two places: just south of the Quezon Gate and between the Parian and Victoria Gates. The amphibious crossing by the 3rd Battalion, 129th Infantry would target the area on the northern side of Intramuros where the thick stone wall gave way to a much more scalable seawall. The 145th Infantry Regiment would penetrate through the two breaches made by the artillery in the eastern wall.[97]

The firepower amassed for the assault on Intramuros was considerable. The division artillery of the 37th Infantry Division, XIV Corps artillery, and tanks, tank destroyers, mortars, and self-propelled cannon assigned to or supporting the division all contributed to the bombardment: all or part of nine battalions of field artillery in all, ranging from 105mm to 240mm howitzers. The preparation would last a full week, from February 17 to 22. Eight-inch howitzers hammered a clean breach between the Parian and Victoria Gates, while a 155mm howitzer formed a breach just south of the Quezon Gate. The resulting piles of rubble were "smoothed over" by indirect-lay artillery fire, producing ramps of debris over which infantrymen could scramble. Meanwhile, 240mm howitzers produced a breach along the north wall near the Government Mint, aided by tank destroyers that blasted small footholds amidst the rubble created by the bigger guns along the riverbank.[98]

The final barrage began at 07:30 on February 23 and continued for an hour, after which the artillery switched to indirect fire to support the assault. The howitzers and other weapons fired a total of 7,896 rounds, or 185 tons, of ammunition during the final preparation for the assault; each minute of the barrage entailed 131 rounds, or more than 3 tons of ammunition, crashing into Intramuros. One observer recalled, "The noise and concussion was so great even on the sending end that one wondered how any of the recipients could possibly survive."[99]

At 08:30 the artillery fire shifted to hammer the interior of Intramuros and to lay a smoke screen to shield the assaulting infantry from Japanese fire.[100] The 2nd Battalion, 145th Infantry attacked the east wall overland, while the 3rd Battalion, 129th Infantry loaded into engineer assault boats and crossed the Pasig River without opposition to scale the northern wall. "It was a breathless moment," reported William Dunn:

> The first boats reached the south shore and the men clambered onto the levee. A lone sniper under Jones bridge opened up with a machine gun and was immediately silenced. It was the only opposition. As dazed, half crazed

civilians moved out of the north wall, toward the boats, our troops moved in and the fighting within the walls began. Beside me, Major General Oscar W. Griswold, 14th [sic – XIV] Corps commander, wiped the perspiration from his hands as the first men disappeared inside. "God bless them," he said.[101]

The battle for Intramuros had commenced in earnest.

Infantry penetrated the breaches created by the artillery within a matter of minutes. The soldiers climbed over the debris and into Intramuros, where they cleared the area building by building, supported by the medium tanks of the 754th Tank Battalion once armored bulldozers had cleared paths into the walled city. At one point the Japanese released 2,000 to 3,000 Filipinos being held in the San Agustín Church and Del Monico Hotel, which halted the battle for a time as the GIs shepherded them to safety.[102] A Filipino, the lone survivor of his family, described the siege of Intramuros:

> At times the incessant explosions from the American bombs and shells were so intense and the resultant rain of brick and concrete was so excruciating as to defy sanity in the lives of those still remaining. Within those walls, life waned further as the very sources of existence dried up and vanished, and [the detainees] were cut off from the outside world. The wave of starvation spread to the Jap troops and with it the scourge of and pestilence of disease, bringing to all its own forms of death. Unable to retaliate upon the Americans, the Japs went berserk, [and] tried to retaliate upon the Filipinos …. Death was omnipresent, attacking from without, from above, and from within.[103]

The result was the slaughter of the Filipino population of Intramuros.

Japanese troops, stunned by the weight of firepower directed against them, put up minimal resistance, except for those in the Del Monico Hotel and the garrison of Fort Santiago. The former building was pummeled by tanks and self-propelled howitzers, while in the latter infantrymen reduced strongpoints with the usual weapons: grenades, demolition charges, bazookas, and flamethrowers. The air was full of dust that "filled men's lungs as roofs and walls toppled over to the ground, loosening the dirt collected over decades and sending great clouds of fine, desert-dry sand billowing over the section like a tidal wave."[104] The tunnels under Fort Santiago were sealed with demolition charges or by pouring gasoline into the entrances and igniting it with white phosphorus grenades.[105] During the fighting, soldiers stumbled upon scene after scene of horror as the full scale of the Japanese crimes against Filipino civilians became clear. In the dungeons of Fort Santiago, soldiers of the 129th Infantry discovered the grisly remains of upwards of 3,000 Filipino men who had been doused with gasoline and incinerated by their Japanese captors.[106] Bodies were layered several deep, and the decay and stench were nearly unbearable. At least 400 men and 1 woman were found in 3 other rooms, where they had died from gunshots, bayonet wounds, and starvation.[107] The XIV Corps operations report concluded, "These and a hundred more stories could be told of unbelievable torture, rape and death . . . .. Never once during the entire Manila Campaign did the enemy show the attributes of civilized man. This program was one of complete destruction and annihilation."[108]

The 145th Infantry cleared most of Intramuros in its zone, with the exception of the Aquarium, which was shielded by Japanese fire from the government buildings still in their possession. Troops discovered an unguarded tunnel leading to the Aquarium, and the next day Company C used this avenue of approach to assault the building. The 3rd Battalion, 129th Infantry continued to mop up scattered remnants of Japanese opposition in Fort Santiago and its environs. By nightfall on February 24, Intramuros – or what was left of it – had been secured. In all, the 37th Infantry Division suffered 25 killed and 265 wounded while inflicting nearly 2,000 Japanese casualties (almost all killed) in the fighting for the walled city – reflecting the massive disparity in the firepower available to the two sides.[109] Delighted with the results, Beightler called the assault on Intramuros "the perfect operation."[110]

While the Buckeyes assaulted Intramuros, the 1st Squadron, 12th Cavalry and the 2nd Squadron, 5th Cavalry cleared the port area north of the Manila Hotel and west of Intramuros. The only serious resistance came from Japanese soldiers holding the Customs Building, but the usual treatment by direct fire from tanks and tank destroyers led to a successful infantry assault at noon on February 24. All Japanese resistance ceased by 16:00.[111]

The final Japanese holdouts were fortified in the Legislative, Finance, and Agricultural Buildings on the southeast corner of Intramuros along with a few other smaller structures in the vicinity. The three governmental buildings were modern, multi-story structures made from reinforced concrete and could be approached only over streets that lacked both cover and concealment. Approximately 300 Japanese defended the Finance Building, while 200 soldiers defended the other two structures.[112] As the Japanese had fortified the exterior entryways and the interior passageways, they would be difficult to assault. Generals Griswold and Beightler considered allowing the Japanese in the buildings to starve, but Filipino hostages who had escaped

Japanese control provided intelligence that the Japanese had stockpiled sufficient supplies to outlast anything but a lengthy siege. SWPA needed the port and headquarters facilities that Manila could offer, and Japanese forces in these three buildings could fire upon logistical sites in downtown Manila. There was no other choice but to take them by force.[113]

Faced with a difficult tactical problem, American commanders resorted to what had worked so well for them to this point in the battle: massive firepower. The 5th Cavalry, tasked with assaulting the Agricultural Building and a nearby apartment complex, directed tank, mortar, and artillery fire on the area during the night of February 23–24. An assault the next morning failed, so additional weapons were brought to bear. Maj. Gen. Beightler, aware of the strength of the Japanese positions, ordered the buildings to be pulverized with preparatory fire during the night and throughout the next day. The howitzers of the 136th Field Artillery Battalion were brought to bear on the Legislative Building, at some cost to the artillerymen, who were thereby exposed to Japanese fire.[114] Mortar concentrations blasted the buildings overnight, while four 105mm self-propelled howitzers, two 155mm howitzers, a company of medium tanks, and two platoons of tank destroyers hammered away at the Agricultural Building throughout the day on February 25. In the words of the 5th Cavalry's regimental history, "With this array of weapons there was one hell of a lot of shooting going on."[115] As the day gave way to night, mortar fire again rocked the buildings. Several hundred Japanese soldiers attempted to withdraw from the area, leading to a wild night of firing that led the regimental commander to believe his troops had become trigger-happy. But, by 09:00 the next morning, 422 dead Japanese had been counted in front of the 5th Cavalry's lines.[116]

After additional direct-fire preparation of the Agricultural and Legislative Buildings, infantry and cavalrymen attacked on the morning of February 26. The 1st Battalion, 148th Infantry assaulted the Legislative Building, gaining entry but meeting stubborn Japanese resistance inside. The troops withdrew in the afternoon under the cover of smoke.[117] Meanwhile, A Troop, 5th Cavalry supported by medium tanks attacked the apartment complex near the Agricultural Building, only to be repulsed by heavy Japanese fire. Braving mined streets, a Sherman tank commander was able to maneuver his vehicle to within forty yards of the apartment complex, taking it under fire. Since there was only room for a single tank to fire at the building at any given time, the assault on the complex was postponed to the morning of February 27 to allow time for the fire to have an effect. During the night, another 141 Japanese were killed attempting to withdraw from the area.[118]

At 07:30 on February 27, tanks, tank destroyers, self-propelled howitzers, and artillery took the Finance Building, the Agricultural Building, and a nearby apartment building under fire. The assault was led by a platoon of Troop A under the leadership of Lt. W. Kinser, who exhorted his men prior to the battle "like a football coach" giving a halftime speech:

> See that building over there? It's full of Japs now, but it is going to be ours by the time the sun goes down. As soon as that last artillery round is fired I want you men following me as hard as you can go. Once we start for that building there will be no stopping. Get that, there will be no stopping!

The cavalrymen gained control of the first floor of the apartment building by 09:40, with the stalwart lieutenant leading his men until wounded by a grenade.[119]

As the cavalrymen concluded their assault, the Buckeyes once more entered the fray by assaulting the Legislative Building at 14:00. Following another intensive preparation that turned "parts of this massive stone structure to sand and dust," the 1st Battalion, 148th Infantry assaulted the badly damaged building, "literally digging their way into the building since most of the entrances had been closed by the bombardment." By nightfall, the battalion had secured the structure, minus the basement. The Buckeyes cleared the building of its remaining Japanese defenders the next morning.[120]

A three-hour preparatory bombardment pummeled the Agricultural Building from 08:00 to 11:00 on the morning of February 28, with the result that "it did not seem possible that any soul could be living in such a mass of rubble and twisted steel."[121] Platoons from Troops F and G entered the building without loss and began to clear it. A flamethrower tank reduced a strongpoint in the southeast corner, while infantry cleared the upper three floors using rifles, grenades, flamethrowers, and bazookas. By nightfall they had cleared the building, minus the Japanese trapped in the basement below. The next day, after an appeal for the Japanese to surrender, the basement was sealed. Troops poured a fuel–oil mixture into the only remaining opening and ignited it, after which they used satchel charges to blow shut the entrance, entombing the Japanese who remained below.[122] Somewhere in the rubble of the Agricultural Building lay the body of the Japanese commander, Rear Adm. Iwabuchi, who met his demise in the fighting.[123]

8.3: After a three-day barrage of artillery fire, members of Company C, 148th Infantry move up in the early morning to take the Legislative Building in Manila, February 27, 1945. The Battle of Manila resulted in the deaths of more than 16,000 Japanese soldiers, along with thousands of Filipino civilians. (Credit: US Army Signal Corps Photo)

The last structure to fall was the Finance Building, which was subjected to intense direct fire for two days. At 14:30 on March 1, an appeal was broadcast for the remaining Japanese inside to surrender; twenty-one soldiers came out with their hands in the air while others attempted to escape from the other side of the building. The escapees were gunned down, while twenty Japanese were taken into captivity; the final soldier committed suicide in lieu of surrender.[124] After yet another preparatory bombardment on March 2, which left the Finance Building "standing only from sheer force of habit," the 1st Battalion, 148th Infantry assaulted the structure and killed most of the remaining Japanese, finally clearing the last resistance in the pre-dawn hours the next day.[125]

Manila, or what was left of it, had been liberated. Amid the ruins lay the dead bodies of 16,665 Japanese soldiers, nearly the entire garrison of the once great city.[126] Astonishingly, given that XIV Corps had just concluded the largest urban battle in US military history, for which it had not extensively trained, its after-action report concluded, "Street fighting in Manila was normal and advanced no principles or tactics not already covered in FM 31-50."[127]

"All organized resistance in Manila has ended," Griswold wrote in his diary on March 3. "Again Gen. MacArthur had announced its capture several days ahead of the actual event. The man is publicity crazy. When soldiers are dying and being wounded, it doesn't make for their morale to know that the thing they are doing has been officially announced as finished days ago. The one weakness of a really great man – publicity!"[128]

While the battle for Manila raged, another battle was playing out on the island of Corregidor in Manila Bay. Its seizure was essential to opening Manila Bay to seaborne traffic once the port area was restored to working condition. The port facilities in Manila were badly needed, for the beaches at Lingayen Gulf and at Nasugbu could not sustain the logistical throughput required for the forces on Luzon or those that would gather for the planned invasion of Japan. Corregidor would be a difficult objective to assault. The island was only three-and-a-half miles in length, a mile and a half wide at its western and larger side, and tapered to a narrow band on its eastern tail. The western head of the island, or "Topside," consisted of elevated high ground under which were numerous tunnels, caves, and fortifications. Malinta Hill and the tunnel underneath dominated the center of the island, while the eastern tail of the island contained an airstrip, Kindley Field. Both SWPA and Sixth Army intelligence officers, the former exhibiting what historian John McManus appropriately labels a "seemingly inexhaustible talent for inaccuracy," believed the island was defended by roughly 850 Japanese troops in solidly fortified positions. Their estimate was off by a factor of six.[129]

While the 38th Infantry Division cleared the southern portion of the Bataan Peninsula, XI Corps would launch a combined airborne and sea-borne invasion of Corregidor. The 503rd Parachute Infantry Regiment, flying from airfields in Mindoro, would jump onto the island, while the 3rd Battalion, 34th Infantry would cross from Mariveles Bay on Bataan to the beach at San Jose near the key terrain of Malinta Hill, which towered 350 feet above the nearby beaches. The obvious drop zone, Kindley Field, was vulnerable to artillery and mortar fire directed from the high ground on the west side of the island. Therefore, planners chose instead to drop the airborne forces on Topside, the area above the fortified heart of the island, despite the tiny drop zones available on the parade ground and a nine-hole golf course that would require precise navigation by the transports carrying the paratroopers. Provided the troop carriers could land them safely, the paratroopers would then have the advantage of fighting from the high ground and could seize key terrain to cover the amphibious landing, which would otherwise be vulnerable to interdicting fire.[130]

The 2,000 soldiers in the initial landing forces would be enough to overcome the predicted Japanese strength on the island. Together the units involved in the assault were labeled "Rock Force," and, once on the ground and ashore, would come under the command of Colonel George M. Jones, commander of the 503rd Parachute Infantry Regiment. To ensure that the Japanese did not interfere with the airborne drop or amphibious landing, naval and air forces subjected the island to intense bombardment for several days prior to the assault.[131] Lt. Gen. Kenney

> sent word to [Maj. Gen. Ennis] Whitehead to 'gloucesterize' [a reference to the heavy bombing of Cape Gloucester on New Britain in December 1943] Corregidor and Mariveles prior to the 12th when troops are to land at both places. It will be a mess if there are any Jap machine gunners still alive to oppose it or if a bad crosswind interferes with the landing on the narrow parade ground …. It should be all right if, as I expect, the Air Force will have taken out practically all the Nips beforehand.[132]

Fifth Air Force bombers went to work on the island as directed, turning large portions of it to rubble.

The fighting for Zig Zag Pass tied up the 38th Infantry Division longer than expected, so Sixth Army attached the 1st Infantry Regiment, 6th Infantry Division, to XI Corps for operations on the east coast of Bataan and delayed the scheduled assault on Corregidor by three days to February 16. The same order added a parachute 75mm pack howitzer battalion and a parachute engineer company to the airborne forces, giving them added strength. More than 4,000 soldiers would be involved in the airborne and seaborne assaults or would land as follow-up reinforcements.

Nevertheless, there was great risk involved in the landing. There were only two possible drop zones on Topside: the parade ground, which measured 150 yards by 250 yards, and the golf course, which measured 150 yards by 325 yards. Both landing areas were cluttered with the ruins of pre-war buildings, debris, bomb craters, and splintered trees, and ended in a sheer drop-off over cliffs into Manila Bay. Planners assumed jump casualties of upwards of 20 percent of the force. To minimize the chances of an errant drop, transport planes would fly in columns over each landing zone, dropping a single stick of six to eight soldiers on each pass. Paratroopers would drop at an altitude of less than 500 feet to prevent drifting outside the landing area. Each lift would require multiple passes, taking upwards of an hour to complete, after which the transport aircraft would return to Mindoro. Two-thirds of the force would land on February 16 in two lifts separated by more than four hours, with the balance arriving the next day.[133]

The attack down the east coast of Bataan commenced on February 13 and met only scattered resistance. By the end of the first day, the column had reached the town of Pilar, half-way down the peninsula. On February 15, the 151st Infantry Regiment conducted an amphibious assault on Mariveles on the southern tip of Bataan and established a beachhead against light opposition. The two forces then maneuvered to link up with one another. On the same day, the 3rd Battalion, 34th Infantry reached Mariveles, where it loaded onto twenty-five LCMs in preparation for its landing on Corregidor.[134]

The following morning MacArthur and his aides, accompanied by Maj. Gen. Hall, Brig. Gen. Eddleman, a number of other officers and war correspondents, and a security team of BAR men, drove in an eight-vehicle column down the east coast of Bataan and past the scene of devastation from the previous night's fighting. Eddleman and Bonner Fellers urged MacArthur to stop at this point as the area ahead had not yet been cleared. Eddleman remarked, "You're liable to get a bullet through your heart," to which MacArthur replied, "That wouldn't hurt as much as it's been hurt ever since we lost our lads here."[135] MacArthur admitted to how the journey was "easing an ache that [his] heart [had] carried for three years." He told the group, "You can't stop me here! We'll go on. This is my personal patrol."[136]

Much to the chagrin of the other senior officers present, the now six-jeep column moved on past the lead scouts, driving through dense jungle until arriving at an unfordable stream, where it could go no further because of a blown bridge. Miffed that he couldn't move forward far enough to watch the scheduled airborne drop on Corregidor, but somewhat satisfied with his return journey to Bataan, MacArthur turned around to return to his headquarters at San Miguel.[137] Unbeknownst to MacArthur, friendly aircraft had spotted the column and were prepared to attack it, but were denied permission by Maj. Gen. Chase, who was located in Manila Bay with Rear Adm. Arthur D. Struble, whose naval forces were supporting the invasion of Corregidor Island.[138] Doc Egeberg, who was (rightly) as concerned about being strafed by friendly aircraft as he was about the Japanese, "was thanking God and the Japanese for destroying that bridge."[139] But the emotional journey back to Bataan "was the real cleansing of the old defeat, of the ignominy and the starvation and death of his earlier troops."[140] Redemption was at hand.

With or without MacArthur as an observer, the assault on Corregidor would proceed. The pre-invasion preparation – "the heaviest bombing to which any comparable area had been exposed in the whole Southwest Pacific fighting" – accomplished the goal of keeping Japanese troops pinned down under cover so the paratroopers could land on Topside with minimal interference.[141] In the three weeks prior to the assault, Fifth Bomber Command dropped 3,128 tons of explosives on the 1-square-mile island. Air bombardment and naval gunfire on the day of the assault added another 185 tons of explosive to the total.[142]

At 08:30 on February 16, the airborne drop on Corregidor commenced. Sporadic antiaircraft fire hit some of the planes and wounded a few paratroopers, but all of the aircraft survived the initial lift. Twenty-five-mile-per-hour winds interfered with the drop, causing a number of paratroopers to miss the tiny drop zones. Paratroopers who landed in the right place quickly organized to subdue the Japanese defenders, who were clearly not expecting an airborne landing. The Japanese commander on Corregidor, Imperial Japanese Navy Captain Akira Itagaki, was killed in the ensuing melée. Two hours later, the 3rd Battalion, 34th Infantry landed on the beach at San Jose on the center of the island. Mines caused some casualties, but the infantry quickly reached the crest of Malinta Hill. The second drop of paratroops at 12:50 proceeded without mishap, as the drop zone was now firmly in American hands.

The Japanese defenders had been taken by surprise and had lost their commander as well as the island's communications center, with the result that the defense was poorly coordinated. By the end of the day, US forces were in control of the key terrain on Topside and Malinta Hill. The paratroopers suffered 12 killed and 267 wounded that day, most of them in the first lift. Still, the casualty rate was less than had initially been feared. To avoid further jump casualties, the parachute infantry battalion scheduled to drop on Corregidor on February 17 was flown instead to an airstrip near Subic Bay, where it was loaded onto landing craft and transported to the beach at San Jose.[143]

For the next ten days, the 503rd Parachute Infantry Regiment (reinforced) would face the difficult task of eliminating Japanese resistance in the numerous caves, tunnels, dugouts, and fortifications on the island, which would "develop into some of the bloodiest fighting of the Luzon campaign."[144] In the process, they would discover a disturbing fact. In keeping with the underestimation of Japanese strength by SWPA and Sixth Army intelligence, the Japanese strength on Corregidor was not 850 troops as initially believed; rather, more than 6,000 Japanese were on the island. Japanese troops defended their positions to the death, on occasion blowing up portions of their own positions in the process. An explosion that collapsed part of the Malinta tunnel on the night of February 21–22 caused a number of casualties in the 3rd Battalion, 34th Infantry, while the detonation of an ammunition dump at Monkey Point on February 26 killed or wounded more than 200 soldiers in the 1st Battalion, 503rd Parachute Infantry and nearby units.[145]

Aided by extensive use of napalm by attacking aircraft and flame-thrower teams, Rock Force cleared the western and central portions of Corregidor in a series of small-unit assaults by February 23. Japanese not killed in the attacks were often sealed in their cave fortresses by demolition teams. Many Japanese committed suicide rather than surrender. On February 24, the 503rd Parachute Infantry Regiment attacked to clear the eastern tail of the island. The 2nd Battalion, 151st Infantry relieved the 3rd Battalion, 34th Infantry, which moved to Subic Bay to prepare for movement to Mindoro and its next mission with the 24th Infantry Division on Mindanao. By nightfall on February 27, GIs had cleared Corregidor of Japanese forces. The fighting was ugly. According to Chase, who observed the battle, the process of convincing the Japanese to surrender "was time consuming so we evolved a new 'boil 'em in oil' tactic which was brutal but successful. We pumped diesel fuel and gasoline down into the old caves, tunnels, and gun emplacements and then set them on fire with phosphorus grenades. This usually brought the Nips out screaming and we could mow them down with Tommy guns."[146]

XI Corps officially ended the Corregidor operation on March 2. On that day MacArthur returned in a flotilla of four PT boats, along with many of the same group that had departed the Rock with him, mirroring in reverse his departure from the island nearly three years earlier.[147] Krueger, who accompanied MacArthur for the ceremony, recalled, "Corregidor itself was a shambles, with its buildings and gun emplacements in ruins, its tunnels blown up and dead Japanese everywhere."[148] After a short tour, MacArthur drove Topside to congratulate Col. Jones and his troops, who presented Fortress Corregidor to the general.[149] The group then witnessed the raising of the American flag over the island in a simple but meaningful ceremony. The fighting had cost Rock Force more than 1,200 casualties, while the Japanese had lost the entire garrison of 6,000

soldiers and sailors. The stench of decomposing flesh was so bad commanders ordered their men to spread quicklime over the rotting corpses.[150]

In an epilogue of sorts to the seizure of Corregidor, US forces cleared
Japanese forces from the south shore of Manila Bay and three small islands
south of Corregidor over the course of the next month and a half. The 11th
Airborne Division and attached Filipino guerrillas cleared the Cavite
Peninsula and Ternate by March 3, leaving in Japanese possession only
Caballo Island, Carabao Island, and El Fraile Island, the latter in reality
a concrete pre-war fortress christened Fort Drum by the US Army. Although
there was no great rush to clear Japanese forces off the islands, they had to
be taken eventually. On March 19, a platoon from the 38th Infantry Division
landed on Caballo Island and discovered approximately 400 troops dug in
on the high ground on the island's center. After a naval and air bombardment, the 2nd Battalion, 151st Infantry landed in force on the island on
March 27 and by the end of the next day was in possession of the island's
high ground. Two hundred or so Japanese troops withdrew into a series of
pre-war mortar pits and tunnels and for more than a week defied attempts to
wrest control of the fortifications from them. A solution emerged when
engineers devised a pipeline and on April 5 injected more than 2,500
gallons of diesel into the Japanese positions via an unguarded ventilator
shaft. Ignited by white phosphorus mortar shells, the resulting fire and
explosions were, according to the division's after-action report, "most grati-
fying." Engineers repeated the procedure on April 6 and 7, adding three
large demolition charges to the mix on the final day. After several days of
probing what was left of the Japanese positions, infantry killed the remaining Japanese holdouts on April 13 and, with that, Caballo Island was
cleared.[151]

Fort Drum, a battleship-shaped fortress built atop a reef, posed similar
challenges to the Japanese troop positions on Caballo Island. Although its
guns had long since been neutralized, taking the fortress would be no easy
feat, given its thirty-six-foot-thick walls and twenty-foot-thick roof that were
pretty much impervious to fire. Taking a cue from the experience on
Caballo Island, on April 13, 1945, a small party of engineers, guarded by
Company F, 151st Infantry, approached the fort in an LSM rigged with
a drawbridge. After the infantry had clambered over the drawbridge and
secured the top of the fort, engineers aboard an LCM pumped 2,200 gallons
of a gasoline–oil mixture into a ventilator opening. The infantry withdrew,
and engineers detonated the mixture via a delay fuse that ignited white
phosphorus grenades wrapped in primacord along with 600 pounds of

TNT. The initial explosion seemed disappointing, but fires soon reached the fort's ammunition magazine. The resulting explosion sent concrete and steel fragments several hundred feet into the air and obliterated the facility. The fort was too hot to approach for several days after the explosion, but, on April 18, a reconnaissance party probed the fort's interior and found sixty dead Japanese inside.[152]

After these two episodes, the seizure of Carabao Island was anticlimactic. Troops from the 1st Battalion, 151st Infantry invaded the island on April 16, only to find that the Japanese garrison had previously withdrawn. GIs found only "one very badly shaken pig" on the island, leading the official US Army historian to surmise that some of them "had fresh pork chops for supper" that evening.[153]

As the battles on Corregidor raged, another drama unfolded to the west. On the night of February 21–22, 1945, a special task force of the 11th Airborne Division assembled for a raid to secure the Los Baños Internment Camp, with the objective of liberating its 2,146 civilian internees. The camp was twenty-five miles behind Japanese lines, with several thousand Japanese troops in the vicinity. To prevent a mass slaughter of the detainees, commanders decided to conduct a lightning-quick hit-and-run raid on the camp, rather than to move against it more deliberately. On February 22, fighters bombed gun positions around Los Baños and strafed targets of opportunity in the area. The 11th Airborne Division Reconnaissance Platoon then rode in Filipino bancas (canoes) across Laguna de Bay to infiltrate into position around the camp by moonlight. They carried with them information concerning Japanese guard positions and machine gun emplacements, provided by Filipino guerrillas and a recently escaped internee.[154]

Shortly after dawn, 123 paratroopers from Company B, 511th Parachute Infantry Regiment dropped from 9 C-47 aircraft at an altitude of 700 feet onto a tiny landing zone, secured by Huk guerrillas, 1,000 yards from the camp. Simultaneously, the remainder of the 1st Battalion, 511th Parachute Infantry, under the command of Lt. Col. Henry Burgess, hit the beach, guarded by Marking's guerrillas, in Amtracs after a twenty-mile, six-hour ride that was timed to perfection. Guerrillas of President Quezon's Own Guerrillas guided the unit to the camp. The raid took the Japanese, who had just lined up the detainees for morning roll call, completely by surprise. The internees were wildly excited, but soon took cover as the shooting started. The reconnaissance platoon, along with more than 100 guerrillas of the Hunters ROTC, entered the camp and killed the few Japanese soldiers who hadn't taken to the hills. Guerrillas of the Philippine Chinese Anti-Japanese Guerrilla Force 48th Squadron guarded the approaches to the camp against potential Japanese counterattacks.[155] By 17:00 the paratroopers had evacuated all of the detainees to friendly lines. The 240 or so too sick to walk were evacuated on stretchers by Amtrac. The last soldier left the Los Baños beach a few minutes before Japanese reinforcements arrived. The internees were taken to an Army hospital established in the New Bilibid Prison south of Manila and given medical care, food, and clothing.[156]

The raid had been executed to perfection. Of note, the participation of Filipino guerrillas was essential to its success. Col. Henry Muller, G-2 of the 11th Airborne Division, remarked, "Everything which could have gone wrong, did not. Everything which should have gone right, did go right. For a 12-hour period, 'Murphy's Law' had been inoperative!"[157] Griswold visited the newly liberated internees and lamented their plight. "The gratitude of [the Los Baños] refugees is pathetic. Some of the little children, mere babies three years ago, didn't even know what to do with candy. It is pathetic to see how they unconsciously still hoard their food. How their eyes glistened at the sight of coffee. Hunger is a terrible thing." Krueger visited XIV Corps to celebrate the successful raid, and "for once he was beaming."[158] The Angels of the 11th Airborne had delivered the sweetest sort of victory.

At least the Los Baños internees were alive, which is more than could be said for the thousands of Filipinos who died in the fighting for Manila or who fell victim to Japanese atrocities.[159] For this slaughter the Japanese commanders in Manila were fully responsible. They refused to allow civilians safe passage outside the battle zone, even when cease-fires for that purpose were offered by American commanders. Furthermore, they lost control of their soldiers, who murdered, mutilated, and raped tens of thousands of Filipino civilians. Documentary evidence confirms the deliberate killing of civilian noncombatants by Japanese forces, who suspected most Filipinos of collaboration with the resistance. They were not wrong on that score, but their actions were war crimes of the first order. One document seized in Intramuros read,

> When Filipinos are to be killed, they must be gathered into one place and disposed of with the consideration that ammunition and manpower must not be used to excess. Because the disposal of dead bodies is a troublesome task, they should be gathered into houses which are scheduled to be burned or demolished. They should also be thrown into the river.[160]

XIV Corps noted in its operations report, "The wanton murder of innocent men, women and children is evidence of the extreme truculence of the enemy. On every hand there was evidence of unprovoked murder. Spanish, Chinese, and Filipinos alike suffered sadistic torture and finally death. Volumes of evidence have been compiled recording atrocities on all races and creeds."[161]

The "volumes of evidence" make for difficult reading.[162] "As the elements of the XIV Corps crossed the Pasig and in conjunction with the 11th Airborne compressed the ring about the enemy in South Manila," noted the operations report, "there was being perpetrated crimes which were to make all the civilized world shudder. These crimes included the destruction of property by burning and the taking of human life by torture, bayoneting, grenading and burning alive."[163] Guerrillas were targeted for killing, and, in the eyes of some Japanese commanders, any Filipino qualified. A *Kobayashi Force* order dated February 13, 1945, read, "Even women and children have become guerrillas. All people on the battlefield with the exception of Japanese Military personnel, Japanese civilians and Special Construction Units will be put to death."[164]

Other reports were more specific:

> On the 17th of February, nineteen Japanese, twelve of whom were officers, forced several hundred Filipinos and Chinese to the second floor of a house in the Singalong District where after a ritual, the victims were beheaded and their bodies thrown into a ravine. Men were told that they were to be forced into labor only to find themselves taken in groups of ten to be bayoneted, shot, burned alive or the victims of grenades. Women were bayoneted trying to shield their babies while young women were carried off for rape.[165]

Indeed, systematized rape was widespread. Dozens of Filipino girls ranging in age from thirteen to twenty-seven were held in the Bay View Hotel, where they were serially raped by Japanese troops.[166] One of these girls, Zenaida Lyons, was held in the hotel from February 9 to February 12. While there, she witnessed Japanese soldiers raping approximately 100 Filipino women. Women were raped multiple times, and the ordeal stopped only after the hotel caught fire. Lyons was raped ten times over the course of three days. She and her two sisters escaped to the Paramount Hotel, where they were again raped multiple times by Japanese soldiers.[167]

Another, much larger group held in the San Agustín Church were preyed upon for several days by labor troops, who "would prowl the Church dragging the young girls to the choir loft, cloisters, dug-outs, and even to the front of the altar where they were forced to submit to the most brutal indignities."[168] The 125 men in the church were gathered together and marched to bomb shelters in the foundations of the Palace of the Governor General in Plaza McKinley, where they were locked in, doused in gasoline, and set afire.[169] Similar incidents happened in dozens of places, some unknown to history because everyone involved died in the subsequent slaughter.

After the battle for Manila had ended, investigators compiled reams of evidence of Japanese atrocities. The US Senate conducted its own investigation that summer. Even in abbreviated form, a sampling of the reading is appalling. The torture and murder of tens of thousands of civilians was purposeful and indiscriminate. In Concordia College, the Japanese "closed the doors with chains, surrounded the building with machine guns to prevent anyone from leaving the premises alive, then set fire to the building." On February 10, a squad of Japanese soldiers entered the Red Cross building, shot and bayoneted more than fifty civilians inside, including doctors and nurses, and then looted the premises. The same day, Japanese marines set fire to the German Club, incinerating more than 500 civilians, but not before raping and killing dozens of women.[170]

On February 12, a platoon of Japanese soldiers entered La Salle College and killed sixty Filipinos. Japanese soldiers bayoneted more than fifty people at the Spanish Consulate. In Intramuros, priests and lay brothers were forced into shelters in front of the Cathedral, after which "Japanese soldiers threw hand grenades among them, then covered the entrances to the shelters with gasoline drums and earth – literally burying them alive." Thousands of other bodies were discovered killed, burned, mutilated, often with hands bound behind their back. "The individual atrocities, as told by the survivors, were countless and barbarous. Women were slashed with sabers, their breasts cut off, their genitals pierced with bayonets; children were cut and stabbed with sabers and bayonets."[171]

Maj. Gen. Griswold ordered an investigation into the atrocities committed in Manila and elsewhere in his corps' area. On April 9, the investigators released a thirty-four-page report detailing the atrocities committed in the XIV Corps area in just a short time in February 1945. The investigation concluded,

> Because of the number and extent of the killings of civilians and the destruction of public and private buildings in Manila and other towns and cities in the Philippine Islands ... it is concluded with unmistakable certainty that the wanton destruction of the greater part of the city of

Manila and the mass murdering of large numbers of defenseless civilian men, women and children, the majority of whom were Filipino, was not the result of caprice or impulsiveness of individuals in the confusion of battle, but was instead the consequence of a preconceived plan executed by the Commander of Japanese Armed Forces in the Philippines, under orders from higher military command in Tokyo.[172]

No such plan ever surfaced, but there was plenty of evidence that the wanton slaughter of Filipino civilians in the pursuit of counterguerrilla operations was an unintended result of *14th Area Army* policy.

The city of Manila – the Pearl of the Orient – was ruined by the fighting. A report compiled by a US Senate committee "listed 613 blocks containing approximately 11,000 buildings destroyed or badly damaged."[173] Utilities were either demolished or severely damaged and would take months to repair. Public sanitation was a nightmare, and the populace escaped a cholera outbreak only by the slimmest of margins. Other damage would take years to repair. Thirty-nine bridges were destroyed. The business district north of the Pasig River was reduced to ashes. Major buildings such as the University of the Philippines, the Philippine General Hospital, and many of the government buildings that bore the brunt of the fighting would have to be rebuilt. Cultural landmarks such as churches and cathedrals, as well as the centuries-old walled city of Intramuros, were heavily damaged or reduced to rubble. Of greatest import for US forces, the port and industrial areas had been demolished by the Japanese and would have to be reconstructed to make them usable.[174]

Gene Hungerford, who had survived more than three years of Japanese captivity, described the center of Manila as being in

complete and utter ruin. Most of the buildings are completely gone, all that remains of them are heaps of broken brick and concrete – cold ashes of their former glory. A wall left standing here or there, iron roofing, twisted girders, contorted wires, pieces of plumbing, parts of furniture all jumbled together in a purposeless hodgepodge. Sticking out here and there were dead bodies and parts thereof. The few buildings seemingly whole were burned and gutted completely from top to bottom, interior walls and ceilings were entirely absent, or if still there, cracked and blistered beyond recognition.[175]

Touring the city, he entered

a sea of crumbled bricks, debris, and dust. The acrid stench, oxidation, and decay burned into my nostrils, which together with the merciless heat of the sun and my profound weakness produced by three years of incarceration produced a stroke of extreme nausea in me. I sat down on the wall, until the dizziness past [sic] and [I] took stock of the situation. What I first imagined to be an interesting sightseeing tour was turning out to be anything but pleasurable. That man should be able to wreak such complete destruction of his own works without regard to the future held me in troubled wonderment beyond my small powers of understanding. I felt lost, alone, afraid and engulfed in this vast grim vastness of death.[176]

Millie Bradley, whose husband had passed away a week after his liberation, despaired at the sight of destruction as she was driven through the streets a month after the battle: "We bumped over the scarred streets, or what was left of them. My heart thumped and thumped. The beautiful city of Manila was completely destroyed. Buildings not entirely demolished looked frightening. They seemed to wave in the air like clothes on a clothes line."[177] Driving past her former home, she realized that "it too had gone." "With a stifled sob," she realized that the war had consumed "both my husband and my home."[178]

One soldier, Pvt. Thomas Woebke from New Ulm, Minnesota, visiting Manila six weeks after the conclusion of fighting there, wrote home to his parents,

> The news of the President's death shocked us considerably, and all indications of the terrific struggle waged here before us – the shattered and burned buildings, pathetic natives with clean but ancient remnants of clothes, torn up roads, abandoned and destroyed equipment – all that filled us with a sense of pity and sadness. The sight of a once beautiful but now destroyed city seems to instill in us a greater respect for the destructive powers of war than does the distant rumble of artillery fire.[179]

The cost in blood and treasure was a far cry from MacArthur's expectations when he landed at Lingayen Gulf. Liberation – and redemption – came at a price.

On February 27, MacArthur restored constitutional authority to Filipino President Sergio Osmeña in a ceremony at Malacañan Palace. MacArthur's journey to the palace was somber:

> As I passed through the streets with their burned-out piles of rubble, the air still filled with the stench of decaying and unburied dead, the tall and stately trees that had been the mark of a gracious city were nothing but ugly

scrubs pointing broken fingers at the sky. Once-famous buildings were now shells. The street signs and familiar landmarks were gone.[180]

According to MacArthur's biographer, "Manila had joined the ranks of Warsaw, Stalingrad, Dresden, Nanking, and other great cities of Europe and Asia that became victims of the horrors of World War II."[181]

As MacArthur and his staff entered the reception hall where the ceremony would be held, the general endured "a soul-wrenching moment" as he thought of the great Filipino and American statesmen he had known but who were not present: his father Arthur MacArthur, President Manuel Quezon, Governor-General William Howard Taft, commander of the Philippine Division Leonard Wood, Governor-General Henry Stimson, Governor-General Dwight Davis, President Theodore Roosevelt, and Governor-General Frank Murphy. "In this city, my mother had died, my wife had been courted, my son had been born; here, before just such a gathering as this, not so long ago, I had received the baton of a Field Marshal of the Philippine Army."[182] For an Army officer whose career began in 1903 with his graduation from West Point and who had served multiple tours in the Philippines, Manila was the closest place he had to call home.

In a short speech, MacArthur recounted the years of "bitterness, struggle, and sacrifice" since he had declared Manila an open city to spare it "the violence of military ravage." The Japanese chose a different path that resulted in the city's devastation, "but by these ashes he has wantonly fixed the future pattern of his own doom." The power of the United States and its allies has "turned the tide of battle in the Pacific and resulted in an unbroken series of crushing defeats of the enemy, culminating in the redemption of your soil and the liberation of your people. My country has kept the faith." MacArthur then announced the restoration of constitutional authority to the Filipino government. "Your capital city, cruelly punished though it be, has regained its rightful place – citadel of democracy in the East. Your indomitable ..." – at this point MacArthur faltered – "the culmination of a panorama of physical and spiritual disaster. It had killed something inside me to see my men die." And it had pained him to see the city that he had once called home shattered. After a long pause, MacArthur led the assembled group in a recitation of the Lord's prayer.[183]

The Battle of Manila was over. The battle for the rest of the Philippines continued to rage.

9

CLEARING LUZON

> Positions will not be yielded to the enemy even though you die. Our only
> path is victory or death; therefore, defend to the last man. Those who
> retreat without orders will be decapitated.[1]
>
> Japanese 10th Division order

With the seizure of Manila and its nearby ports and airfields, Sixth Army had
gained control over a vital logistical hub required for SWPA forces to
participate in the anticipated invasion of Japan. But MacArthur was not
satisfied with this achievement; having now returned to the islands, he
would settle for nothing less than the complete liberation of the
Philippines from Japanese control. Although there was no military necessity
for clearing the rest of Luzon and the few towns still occupied by Japanese
forces, it was American territory, and thus leaving it under Japanese control
would have been an afront to American (and MacArthur's) honor.[2] Even as
the battle for Manila raged, MacArthur directed the reassignment of the
41st Infantry Division, geared up for deployment to Luzon, to Lt. Gen.
Robert Eichelberger's Eighth Army, now readying itself for the liberation
of the Central and Southern Philippines. Gen. Krueger would also lose the
24th and 40th Infantry Divisions, as well as the 503rd Parachute Infantry
Regiment once it had finished fighting on Corregidor Island.[3] Sixth Army
would have to make do with the nine divisions and two separate regimental
combat teams left at its disposal. Prolonged combat would steadily erode the
combat effectiveness of those forces, even as they strove to clear Luzon, the
largest and most important of the islands in the Philippine Archipelago, of
Japanese forces.

MacArthur believed that these forces would be adequate to clear Luzon
on the basis of faulty intelligence. He overly relied on Ultra intelligence,
which failed to reveal an accurate count of Japanese forces in Luzon and
likewise failed to divine Yamashita's intention of fighting an extended
campaign of attrition in the mountains of northern and central Luzon.
Radio communications tapered off as the campaign progressed and

Japanese forces reverted to wire and messenger for much of their tactical communications.[4] With the inability of codebreaking efforts to give an accurate reading of Japanese capabilities and intentions, Sixth Army and its commanders had to rely on less advanced methods of intelligence gathering: patrols, guerrilla reports, prisoners, captured documents, and aerial reconnaissance. They all told a similar story: the Japanese would have to be dug out of their fortifications, one hill and mountain at a time.

In a series of division fights, Krueger's forces would, over the next several months, destroy Japanese forces in their mountain redoubts. US divisions were aided by local guerrilla forces, which proved to be welcome additions to the forces of liberation and gave agency to the Filipinos in their own deliverance. Osmeña's government integrated guerrilla units as components of the new Philippine Army, which gave them recognition and, more importantly, pay. This policy also opened the flood gates to a host of specious claims, which inundated the Sixth Army Special Intelligence section.[5]

Sixth Army had as many as 51,000 guerrillas under its control, a huge boost to its combat power.[6] It used teams of Alamo Scouts to evaluate guerrilla groups and coordinate their activities.[7] Although arming and equipping the guerrillas put severe strain on Sixth Army's stockpiles, the results were worth the effort. Indeed, their addition to the US force pool was essential, for the divisions on Luzon were seriously understrength.

As the Philippines campaign ground on, unit losses mounted, with insufficient replacements arriving to replenish the ranks. By late February, the 43rd Infantry Division was at 71 percent strength, the 32nd Infantry Division was at 81 percent strength, the 1st Cavalry Division was at 85 percent strength, and the 40th Infantry Division was at 88 percent strength. Only the 37th Infantry Division was in comparatively good shape at 95 percent strength. "Even these figures, impressive as they are, do not give a realistic picture of the reduced fighting strength of units," MacArthur wrote to the War Department:

> Some Rifle Companies are down to total strengths of 30, 40, 60, and 80 [men]. These losses are not from Luzon alone but are cumulative from Leyte and further back. The shortage of service troops to support current operations and to tackle the huge problem of developing Manila and the Philippines as a base to support future operations is critical.[8]

The situation became so serious that MacArthur and his staff considered breaking up a division and using it to fill the others to full strength. The replacement shortage would not abate until the end of the war in Europe aimed the personnel spigot at the Pacific, but by then the fighting in the Philippines was nearing an end.

For the Japanese, the fall of Manila signaled the start of the decisive part of the campaign, when Japanese forces would attempt to force the Americans to pay a high price in blood and treasure to dig them out of the mountains of Luzon and thereby, they hoped, convince the US government to forgo an invasion of the home islands in favor of a negotiated settlement of the Pacific War. By this time, Japanese soldiers had little hope of surviving the war. Prisoners recounted the generally high morale of the Japanese army on Luzon as the battles commenced in January and February, at least until US artillery and airpower began to take their toll and the disparity in firepower became obvious. But, as the winter and spring of 1945 wore on, most Japanese troops in the Philippines suffered from severe malnutrition, bordering in some cases on starvation, and logistical shortages relegated them to the status of scavengers. Voluminous prisoner interrogation reports from Sixth Army repeatedly mention the lack of food as the key to deteriorating Japanese morale.[9] But hungry soldiers could still fire their weapons.

The destruction of the *Shimbu Group* in the mountains east of Manila was a difficult and bloody operation. Even before the Battle of Manila was over, XIV Corps began to shift forces to secure the mountains east of the city, key terrain that dominated Manila's water sources – particularly Ipo Dam, which provided half of the city's water. The *Shimbu Group* – composed of numerous ad hoc units interspersed among units of the *8th* and *105th Divisions* – was dug in on this high ground, prepared to fight to retain the area at all costs. The Sixth Army G-2 estimated that there were 20,000 Japanese troops in the area – an estimate that was short by 250 percent. The units were a heterogeneous mass of mostly second-rate, ill-trained troops, but they were dug into fortified positions and still had to be attacked and destroyed in close combat. To provide XIV Corps with the striking power needed to begin offensive operations against the *Shimbu Group*, Krueger redirected the 6th Infantry Division south from I Corps. Along with the 2nd Cavalry Brigade of the 1st Cavalry Division, the 6th Infantry Division would begin offensive operations to destroy the *Shimbu Group* and complete the liberation of central Luzon.[10]

On February 17, the 6th Infantry Division entered the line east of Manila between the 112th Regimental Combat Team to the north and the 2nd Brigade, 1st Cavalry Division to the south. The division's attack made slow progress, the infantry crossing the Marikina River near San Mateo. The

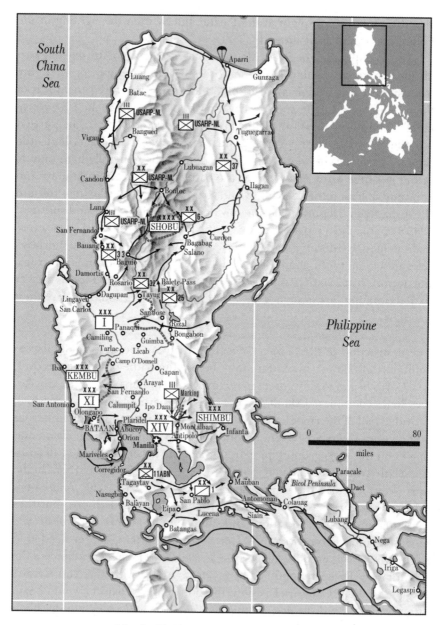

Map 9: Clearing Luzon, March–August 1945.

2nd Brigade of the 1st Cavalry Division kept pace, crossing the river in the vicinity of Rosario. By February 22, XIV Corps had identified the Japanese main line of resistance running from Antipolo to Montalban and Mt. Oro, with additional concentrations around Ipo Dam to the north. The Japanese had strongly entrenched their positions amid the numerous limestone caves in the area. Ammunition shortages reduced the impact of Japanese artillery fire, which nevertheless included some monstrous 447mm rockets. Counterbattery fire was hampered by the positioning of Japanese guns, which would expose themselves to fire a few rounds before retiring into the relative safety of caves. The attack now slowed considerably as infantry and dismounted cavalrymen reduced the Japanese positions in a slow, grinding, time-consuming advance.

The existence of infantrymen amounted to a daily monotony of combing draws, sealing caves, destroying machine gun emplacements, and taking cover from mortar and artillery fire, while nighttime brought mortar fire, infiltration by small parties, and fierce Japanese counterattacks. P-47s and Marine SBD dive-bombers attacked Japanese positions, but only 1,000 lb. bombs with delay fuses could destroy the caves, and then only if they scored a direct hit. Supporting aircraft dropped napalm to clear away camouflage and vegetation and make Japanese fortifications visible to forward observers. Among the casualties in the fighting was the 1st Cavalry Division commander, Maj. Gen. Mudge, who was wounded in action. Brig. Gen. Hugh F. T. Hoffmann, commander of the 2nd Cavalry Brigade, assumed command of the division.[11]

Maj. Gen. Griswold decided a more concentrated attack was needed to crack the Japanese line. Preceded by two days of intensive air bombardment, XIV Corps launched a coordinated assault on the southern portion of the *Shimbu Group* on March 8. The 1st Cavalry Division, now with both brigades on the line with the conclusion of the battle for Manila, attacked Japanese positions in the vicinity of Antipolo, while the 6th Infantry Division attacked to its north on a narrower front. But, at this point in the Luzon campaign, neither unit packed the punch they once did, as the infantry strength of both divisions had declined by roughly a third. Nevertheless, after four days of heavy fighting, the 1st Cavalry Division secured the high ground over-looking Antipolo.[12] The 6th Infantry Division met fierce resistance in the hills east of Montalban, but its 1st Infantry Regiment was able to penetrate a mile and a half into Japanese lines and secure the northern portion of the corps' objective. On March 12, the 103rd Infantry Regiment was attached to the 1st Cavalry Division and seized Antipolo. The next day the 43rd Infantry Division relieved the 1st Cavalry Division, which moved to the western shore of Laguna de Bay to prepare for its next mission in southern Luzon.[13]

The commander of the *Shimbu Group*, Lt. Gen. Yokoyama, decided at this point to pull back the *Noguchi Force* in the vicinity of Antipolo to

9.1: Members of the 1st Cavalry Division push toward the town of Antipolo on Luzon Island, March 14, 1945. Filipino guerrillas, working with American combat troops, carry a litter case, hit in the neck by enemy machine gun fire, from the front lines. Guerrillas were instrumental in assisting US forces in the liberation of their country. (Credit: US Army Signal Corps Photo)

a supplementary defensive line several miles east of the town, while ordering a counterattack to push back the American forces of the 6th Infantry Division that had penetrated his line further north. His inexperienced units, which lacked sufficient fire support, could not execute his detailed scheme of maneuver, and the counterattack went nowhere. American air bombardment and artillery fire forced Japanese guns under cover, interdicted units moving along the few trails in the area, and disrupted command, control, and communications. Four Japanese battalions ran headlong into the 20th Infantry Regiment, which was attacking north from the salient created by the Red Star Division's attack toward Wawa Dam. The Japanese attack was so ineffectual that the division did not even record a Japanese counterattack in its operations reports, and XIV Corps learned of the counterattack only from a captured Japanese order. Rather than pushing the Americans back, the only accomplishment of the counter-attack was the destruction of several Japanese battalions and the dispersal of several others into the hills.[14]

On March 14, the 43rd Infantry Division attacked, unaware that the Japanese forces to its front were withdrawing to a new defensive line. In just one day, it advanced a mile and a half against scattered resistance, but for the next three days the 172nd Infantry only

> made slow, bitterly contested advances of 600 to 1000 yards along critical ridge lines defending in succession positions in depth. In this zone a sheer volcanic hill, heavily wooded, appeared to be the focus of the enemy's defenses. Parallel ridges emanating to the west from this feature were the only means of advance for our forces. Densely forested ravines between the ridges were held by the Japs, and were a constant threat to our lines of supply and evacuation.[15]

Skillful Japanese infantry whittled the attacking infantry companies down to an average of fifty men.

The 20th Infantry Regiment attacked north toward Wawa Dam, gaining a mile of ground in the tortuous terrain. The Sixth Infantry Division sustained a heartbreaking loss that day when a burst of Japanese machine gun fire killed its commander, Maj. Gen. Edwin D. Patrick, and the commander of the 1st Infantry Regiment, Col. James E. Rees, as they were conferring over a map on the ground at an observation post near the front line. The next day, XI Corps took over control of forces on the Antipolo front.[16]

Little changed in the scheme of maneuver under Maj. Gen. Charles P. Hall's leadership, other than that the attack north toward Wawa Dam was deferred to a later date. The 6th (now under the command of Brig. Gen. Charles E. Hurdis) and 43rd Infantry Divisions continued to attack to collapse the southern flank of the *Shimbu Group.* Japanese infantry made effective use of the many limestone caves in the area, making "every hill a small fortress in itself."[17] The only real success came on March 21, when the 103rd Infantry Regiment seized Mt. Qutago and Mt. Tanauan. The 6th Infantry Division, on the other hand, was on the verge of becoming combat-ineffective, having suffered excessive casualties. Just when the situation looked bleakest, Yokoyama ordered his units to withdraw behind the Bosoboso River. When XI Corps resumed its attack on March 23, the regiments of the 6th and 43rd Infantry Divisions tore through the retiring Japanese opposition. The 6th Infantry Division seized Mt. Baytangan, while the 43rd Infantry Division seized Mt. Yabang. Within five days they had turned the left flank of the *Shimbu Group,* destroying much of the *Noguchi Force* in the process. XIV and XI Corps had achieved this result despite "operating on shoestrings holding out scant reserves and expecting normal results from generally understrength units."[18]

XI Corps now shifted its attention northward toward Wawa Dam, defended by the *Kobayashi Force.* The 6th Infantry Division began the attack on March 28, with the 1st and 20th Infantry Regiments attacking abreast. The attack went almost nowhere against stiff Japanese opposition on Woodpecker Ridge, so named because of the constant chatter of Japanese machine guns defending it, but the real problem was the lack of replacements to bolster the infantry regiments, which were now operating at less than 50 percent strength. Brig. Gen. Hurdis inserted the 63rd Infantry into the line, and, in an eleven-day battle from April 6 to 17, the regiment was finally able to seize the key terrain atop Mt. Mataba. The 1st Infantry Regiment's attack, however, failed to seize Woodpecker Ridge.[19]

The 6th Infantry Division was largely spent and needed reinforcements. Salvation came in the form of the 145th Infantry Regiment, part of the 37th Infantry Division that had spent the last month on garrison duty in Manila. The regiment went into the line on April 21, supported by the equivalent of six artillery battalions and other fire support. It took ten days for the 145th Infantry Regiment to seize Mt. Pacawagan, at a cost of 55 killed and 220 wounded in action.[20] Engineers made a heroic effort to keep the regiment supplied. They constructed a supply road up the southwest face of Mt. Pacawagan, blasting the upper part of the road through solid rock. Bulldozers had to be secured by cable from above to keep them from overturning. The upper two-thirds of the road was so steep that only tractors and bulldozers could carry supplies up it.[21] On April 30, the 38th Infantry Division relieved the tired 6th Infantry Division and took over the mission of seizing Wawa Dam.

The attack continued on May 4, with the 145th Infantry Regiment attacking east toward Mt. Binicayan overlooking Wawa Dam and the 152nd Infantry Regiment attacking north along Woodpecker Ridge. The 145th Infantry Regiment seized its objective on May 9, while the 152nd Infantry Regiment on Woodpecker Ridge ran into reserves of the *Shimbu Group* that were being repositioned for a counterattack. The Japanese counterattack, which amounted to little more than a series of nighttime raids, delayed the seizure of Woodpecker Ridge, which Maj. Gen. William C. Chase, the commander of the 38th Infantry Division, deemed a necessary precondition for securing Wawa Dam. Engineers bulldozed a road to the front, and, suitably reinforced by flamethrower tanks and other mobile fire support, the 152nd Infantry Regiment attacked again on May 21, broke through Japanese lines, and seized Woodpecker Ridge and the junction of the Marikina and Bosoboso Rivers four days later. Meanwhile, the 151st Infantry Regiment attacked north of the Marikina River, and by May 26 had seized the western slopes of Mt. Pamitinan and Mt. Hapunang-Banoi, clearing the way for the seizure of Wawa Dam, which the 149th Infantry Regiment secured on May 28. The *Kobayashi Force*, no longer capable of organized resistance, dissolved into the mountains to the east of the Marikina River.[22]

GHQ SWPA, since March 5 located in Manila, was becoming increasingly worried about the water situation in the capital, and directed Sixth Army to expedite the seizure of the Wawa and Ipo Dams lest waterborne diseases overwhelm the city's inhabitants.[23] The former objective, for which the 6th Infantry Division and the 145th Infantry Regiment had bled out to the point of combat-ineffectiveness, turned out to be a fool's errand; unbeknownst to GHQ SWPA, Wawa Dam had not provided water to the city of Manila since 1938. It was a major error in intelligence that cost the lives of hundreds of American soldiers for little gain.

Krueger directed Maj. Gen. Hall to plan an operation to seize Ipo Dam, which would begin with a night attack at 22:00 on May 6. Hall repositioned the 43rd Infantry Division to the north as the main effort, with 3,000 soldiers of Marking's guerrillas – the equivalent of an infantry regiment – attached. For three days prior to the attack, 238 fighters pounded Japanese positions in the Ipo Dam area, dropping bombs along with a quarter-million gallons of napalm, the largest quantity used in support of a single operation in the Southwest Pacific to that point. Later estimates attributed 2,000 Japanese dead to these airstrikes alone.[24]

The 103rd Infantry Regiment attacked as the main effort through difficult terrain against the southern flank of the *Kawashima Force*, supported by the 172nd Infantry Regiment, which aimed to seize Osboy Ridge in the center of the division's zone, and Marking's guerrillas, which would attempt to envelop the Japanese flank on the north side of the Angat River. The attack took the Japanese defenders, who had expected an attack along Route 52 rather than through the foreboding terrain further south, by surprise, with the 103rd Infantry Regiment advancing six miles toward Ipo Dam on the first day. Japanese defenses, aided by torrential rains and tortuous terrain, stiffened as American and Filipino forces neared the dam. After ten days of fighting, the 103rd Infantry Regiment and Marking's guerrillas had closed to within 500 yards of their objective.

On May 17, the 43rd Infantry Division launched a final effort, supported by 673 fighters dropping more than 70,000 gallons of napalm on Japanese positions, turning "the area into a sea of flames."[25] The 103rd Infantry Regiment and Marking's guerrillas captured Ipo Dam intact against negligible opposition. The division then reduced the positions of the *Kawashima Force* on Osboy Ridge and the bend in the Angat River to open its supply corridor along Route 52. By May 21, the Japanese forces remaining in the area were no longer combat-effective, and they were hunted down during the remaining weeks of the campaign.[26]

The last unit of the *Shimbu Group*, the *Kogure Detachment* positioned east of Laguna de Bay, also met its fate in May as attacks by the 7th and 8th Cavalry Regiments of the 1st Cavalry Division destroyed it. The main Japanese position was at Kapatalin Sawmill along Route 455 leading to Lamon Bay on the east coast of Luzon. The 7th Cavalry Regiment gathered adequate intelligence and extensively prepared the battlefield. Artillery and napalm denuded the area of concealment, while air bombardment and artillery fire demolished the Japanese fortifications. The cavalrymen overran the Japanese positions on May 9, destroying much of the remaining strength of the *Kogure Detachment* in the process.[27] The 7th Cavalry Regiment reached Lamon Bay on May 13, moving north along the shore to link up with a battalion of Lt. Col. Bernard Anderson's guerrillas and liberate the town of Infanta twelve days later. There the cavalrymen discovered still more evidence of Japanese atrocities in the village of Alitas, where they were welcomed by "excited and thankful" Filipinos who reported that the Japanese had killed between 200 and 300 civilians in the area before the arrival of American forces.[28] The regimental intelligence officer noted, "In most cases these reprisals were ordered by higher headquarters."[29]

An attack by the 38th Infantry Division seized Santa Iñez, the last place of organized resistance by the *Shimbu Group*, on June 9. The 38th Infantry Division was able to use new medical evacuation helicopters for the first time in this attack, and they proved their worth in transporting casualties in the rough terrain of the Sierra Madre. Air evacuation of casualties became more widespread during the Luzon campaign, with more than 31,000 casualties evacuated via transport plane and helicopter by the official end of the campaign on June 30.[30]

Whatever Japanese forces were left melted into the Sierra Madre, where they foraged for food while being hunted down by 10,000 Filipino guerrillas commanded by Anderson and Maj. Edwin Ramsey. At the end of the war, only 6,300 ragged Japanese survivors remained to surrender out of the 50,000 in the *Shimbu Group* at the start of the campaign.[31]

9.2: An ambulance at Grace Park airstrip waits to pick up wounded retrieved by helicopter from the battlefield, June 23, 1945. Experimental use of helicopters in the Philippines proved successful, leading to their widespread use for medical evacuation in the Korean War. (Credit: US Army Signal Corps Photo)

Clearing the southern part of Luzon was an easier task than destroying the Japanese forces ensconced in the mountains of the central and northern parts of the island, but just as important. Operations to clear Batangas and Balayan Bays would enable the establishment of logistical installations in those areas in preparation for the invasion of Japan, while the clearance of the Bicol Peninsula would open shipping lanes through the Visayan Passages, shortening the distance for transports from Leyte Gulf to Manila by 500 nautical miles. Defending southern Luzon were the 13,000 troops of the *Fuji Force*, of which only 3,000 troops of the *8th Division* were trained infantry. The primary mission of this force, however, was not to hold southern Luzon, but to protect the southern flank of the *Shimbu Group* fortified in the mountains east of Manila.[32]

The 11th Airborne Division, with the 158th Infantry Regiment attached, began the offensive into southern Luzon on March 7. The division was at

75 percent strength and, even with this reinforcement, the division had only two-thirds the strength of a standard infantry division.[33] It is unsurprising that its attack made only slight gains against the Japanese defenses around Tanauan. The 158th Infantry made greater headway against weaker opposition, driving from Balayan to Batangas and destroying Japanese forces on the Calumpan Peninsula. By March 23, when the 1st Cavalry Division entered the line near Tanauan on the northern end of the Lipa Corridor, the 11th Airborne had cleared the shores of Balayan and Batangas Bays and had closed on the Japanese main line of resistance. Maj. Gen. Griswold then ordered the 11th Airborne to consolidate between Batangas and Mt. Macolod in preparation for a two-division attack in coordination with the 1st Cavalry Division to its north. To strengthen its attack, the 11th Airborne was augmented by Filipino guerrillas, tanks, tank destroyers, and additional artillery.[34]

To make up for shortfalls in its strength, the 11th Airborne Division made considerable use of guerrilla forces. On March 1, 1945, the division centralized control of guerrilla forces and assigned sectors of responsibility to them. Some units were attached directly to regiments and battalions, participating in combat operations until the end of the fighting. In a letter to his father-in-law, retired US Army General (and former US Army Chief of Staff) Peyton C. March, Maj. Gen. Swing wrote,

> The only thing that keeps my lines open and allows me to be spread so thin is the fact that we have organized 5,000 guerrillas and have them attached to all the infantry, artillery and engineer units. We let them wear the 11th A/B shoulder patch over their left breasts, they are proud as punch and really fight. Put artillery forward observers with them [and] give them all the captured Jap machine guns and mortars and they keep on pushing.[35]

According to division records, "these units made an enviable record by killing 2,349 Japs and capturing 35 prisoners."[36]

The XIV Corps attack began on March 24. The 188th Glider Infantry Regiment made quick work of the Japanese forces to the east of Batangas, closing on the badly battered town of Lipa three days later. Near Tanauan, the 2nd Cavalry Brigade destroyed the Japanese resistance to its front and advanced south, seizing Lipa and linking up with the airborne forces on March 29. The 1st Cavalry Brigade advanced steadily eastward along the southern shore of Laguna de Bay. Only at Mt. Macolod did the Japanese, heavily fortified on the high ground, put up stiff resistance. The 187th Glider Infantry managed to surround the Japanese position, but an attack on April 1 failed to dislodge the defenders. There matters stood until April 18, when the regiment, further reinforced by 500 guerrillas and a company each of tanks, tank destroyers, and 4.2-inch mortars, overran the remaining Japanese resistance.[37]

While the 187th Glider Infantry seized Mt. Macolod, the 1st Cavalry Division attacked on March 30 to clear its zone and link up with elements of XI Corps on the eastern shores of Laguna de Bay. The 12th Cavalry advanced on San Pablo from the north, while the 5th and 7th Cavalry Regiments attacked from the west and seized the town on April 2. The two forces linked up three days later, after the 12th Cavalry destroyed Japanese resistance on the heights between Calauan and San Pablo. On April 6, the 5th Cavalry made contact with elements of the 103rd Infantry Regiment on the southeast shore of Laguna de Bay.[38]

Meanwhile, the 11th Airborne Division, tasked with conducting a reconnaissance in force toward Tayabas Bay, punched far above its weight, given the limited assets at hand. The 188th Glider Infantry Regiment advanced from its positions south of Lipa to the north and east, linking up on April 3 with patrols from the 5th Cavalry eight miles south of San Pablo. The regiment then advanced to the east to enter Lucena three days later, finding most of the area under the control of Filipino guerrillas. Little remained other than mopping up scattered Japanese elements in southern Luzon, a task largely accomplished within the next week.[39]

The final act was the destruction of the last organized elements of *Fuji Force* on Mt. Mataas na Bundoc, a hill mass located half-way between Lipa and San Pablo. Reconnaissance from April 6 to 12 located these Japanese positions, which were then compressed into a compact perimeter by probing attacks from April 17 to 21. To finish the destruction of *Fuji Force*, XIV Corps amassed a force that included the 188th Infantry, the 8th Cavalry, and a squadron of the 7th Cavalry, along with 1,000 guerrillas and 7 battalions of artillery under the control of the 11th Airborne Division. After two days of bombardment, the 11th Airborne Division attacked and caught *Fuji Force* attempting to withdraw to the east. The attack cleared the hill mass by the end of the month, effectively ending operations in southern Luzon. The Japanese commander, Colonel Masatoshi Fujishige, managed to elude capture and spent the remainder of the war with about 2,000 soldiers hiding out on the slopes of Mt. Banahaw.[40] After the war, Fujishige, known locally as the "Butcher of Southern Luzon," was tried, convicted, and hung by the International Military Tribunal for the Far East for the killing of 25,000 unarmed Filipinos during his tenure in command.[41]

Finishing the campaign in southern Luzon, the Bicol Peninsula, and northern Samar would open a sea passage through San Bernardino Strait into the Sibuyan Sea, saving 500 nautical miles and obviating the need for vessels to pass through Surigao Strait into the Sulu and South China Seas. While XIV Corps cleared the northern side of San Bernardino Strait, Eighth Army eliminated Japanese forces on Samar and several nearby islands. In the middle of February, the Americal Division (Maj. Gen. William H. Arnold) cleared Japanese forces on Capul and Biri islands off the north coast of Samar and then established a base on the northwestern tip of the island. The 1st Battalion, 182nd Infantry destroyed the weak Japanese forces in the area and then turned over responsibility for patrolling northern Samar to the 1st Filipino Infantry Regiment, a unit formed from Filipino residents of the United States. Other elements of the Americal Division cleared Ticao and Burias, eliminating 100 Japanese soldiers on the latter island. On March 11, Filipino guerrillas took over responsibility for both islands.[42]

Elements of the 24th Infantry Division, based in Mindoro, cleared a Japanese company and three artillery pieces on Verde Island, located between Mindoro and Luzon, between February 23 and March 3. The 1st Battalion, 21st Infantry landed on Lubang, located on the western end of the Verde Island Passage, on February 28 and forced the small Japanese garrison into the interior of the island. By the end of March, responsibility for securing the island passed to local Filipino guerrillas. East of Mindoro, the 1st Battalion, 19th Infantry landed on the islands of Romblon and Simara on the stormy night of March 11–12. The GIs dispatched most of the Japanese garrison of 120 men on the latter island in 10 days, and then left the remainder to be rounded up by Filipino guerrillas. Resistance on Simara took longer to quell, but by April 3 the 19th Infantry had killed most of the Japanese garrison of 140 men. Guerrillas had already secured the islands of Tablas and Sibuyan, which allowed Lt. Gen. Eichelberger to report to MacArthur on April 5 that Eighth Army had secured the Visayan Passages in its area. A final operation to clear 400 Japanese troops on Masbate, west of Samar, was facilitated by Filipino guerrillas, who had already taken control of much of the island. The 2nd Battalion, 108th Infantry, 40th Infantry Division landed on Masbate between April 3 and 7 and worked with the guerrillas to clear the island, killing some 120 Japanese in the operation. On May 4 the Americans departed, leaving Masbate in control of the Filipinos.[43]

The Bicol Peninsula, the area of southern Luzon jutting southeast toward Samar, was the final area south of Manila to be cleared of Japanese forces.

Given the lack of roads on the peninsula, the most expeditious manner of clearing the area would be to use the amphibious capabilities of the Seventh Fleet. Lack of resources delayed the proposed landing of the 158th Regimental Combat Team on the shores of Albay Gulf to April 1, but by that date the Fifth Air Force would presumably have destroyed beach defenses in the landing area and forced the 1,500 Japanese defenders inland. Indeed, that was the case, as the two companies of infantry in the first wave met no resistance.

Infantry secured the beachhead and advanced south, running into the Japanese main line of resistance at Daraga astride the only road leading to the regiment's objectives further south along the northern shore of San Bernardino Strait. After directing his forces in battle with the Japanese at Daraga for several days, Brig. Gen. Hanford MacNider decided to conduct an amphibious turning movement on the Sorsogon Peninsula. On April 6, Antitank Company, 158th Infantry boarded five landing craft, landed on the northern shore of the peninsula, and advanced five miles to the town of Sorsogon. The company reconnoitered Japanese positions in the area, finding the largest concentration in the hills overlooking Bulan on the western shore of the peninsula. After overcoming the Japanese opposition at Daraga, the 2nd Battalion, 158th Infantry, arrived on April 12 and attacked, destroying the Japanese positions four days later. As in so many other places in the Philippines, local guerrillas then took over security of the area.[44]

The remainder of the 158th Infantry attacked northwest to clear the remainder of the Bicol Peninsula. The terrain and lack of roads delayed progress as much as Japanese resistance, but, by the end of the month, the regiment had killed 700 Japanese soldiers in their positions in the Quituinan Hills near Camalig. After this action, the remaining Japanese melted away, allowing a rapid link-up between the 158th Infantry and the 5th Cavalry moving down the peninsula from the north on May 2. The 5th Cavalry had begun its attack on April 13, its progress determined more by the ability of engineers to restore bridges and lines of communication than by the ferocity of Japanese resistance. Filipino guerrillas hunted down Japanese stragglers until the final surrender brought the remainder in from hiding.[45]

Other than Gen. Yamashita's main body, the *Shobu Group*, there were no critical objectives in northern Luzon. Nevertheless, given MacArthur's desire to liberate all of Luzon, Krueger ordered I Corps (Lt. Gen. Innis P. Swift), to this point in the campaign a holding force while other elements of Sixth Army liberated Manila and its environs, to prepare to attack toward Baguio, where Gen. Yamashita had established his headquarters. The largest concentration of Japanese forces was located in the area between Baguio, Bambang, and Bontoc, although control of the agriculturally rich Cagayan Valley would prove crucial once the *Shobu Group* lost its ability to move supplies north from other parts of Luzon. The mountain ranges bordering the Cagayan Valley – the Sierra Madre to the east, Cordillera Central to the west, and Caraballo to the south – were steep and rugged, with few passable roads capable of handling military vehicular traffic. Supplying combat forces in northern Luzon required heroic efforts by the engineers, who operated short of bridging matériel; the use of Filipino cargadores; and hundreds of airdrops, which were often hampered or canceled due to inclement weather. Sixth Army would require the better part of four months to gain control of northern Luzon, and, even then, never succeeded in destroying all of Yamashita's forces.[46]

By the end of February 1945, the Japanese had consolidated their defensive line in front of Baguio and southeast from there along the southern slopes of the Caraballo Mountains. To say the ground was rough would be an understatement. In the area southwest of Santa Fe, "patrols discovered that most of the trails through the [Caraballo] spur seemed to have been used before February 1945 by wild pigs rather than human beings."[47] Battalion-size reconnaissance efforts up the Villa Verde Trail and Route 5 toward Santa Fe revealed Japanese forces fortified in strength. *Shobu Group* would not go quietly into the night.[48]

The Villa Verde Trail was named after a Spanish missionary, Juan Villa Verde. It snakes over a rugged razorback ridge winding through mountains separated by deep ravines. Some of the slopes were sparsely covered, while others were matted with rain forest vegetation. Some slopes were so steep that infantrymen could ascend them only on all fours. Frontal assaults were futile against Japanese infantry bunkered in caves. Infantrymen discovered that caves were most successfully assaulted in pairs, with artillery and mortars suppressing Japanese positions on the flanks. Once the infantry had painstakingly reached a cave entrance, a white phosphorus grenade thrown into the opening would reveal other entrances. Soldiers would use demolition charges to seal cave entrances, which was usually followed by "the dull, faint thud of an exploding grenade coming from inside of the sealed cave," indicating that the Japanese inside had killed themselves.[49]

Krueger lacked the forces required to be strong everywhere, and, by the end of February, he had decided that I Corps with the 25th and 32nd Infantry Divisions would constitute the main effort in northern Luzon in an attack toward Santa Fe, while the 33rd Infantry Division ("Prairie," commanded by Maj. Gen. Percy W. Clarkson)[50] would await reinforcement by the 37th Infantry Division before attacking on the Baguio front. Lacking sufficient strength because of MacArthur's decision to strip divisions from Sixth Army for operations in the Visayas and on Mindanao, Krueger found an unexpected resource in Col. Russell W. Volckmann's guerrillas, the USAFIP-NL. Volckmann's forces would go a long way toward making up the shortfall in troops in I Corps during its operations in northern Luzon.

By the end of 1944, Volckmann had organized five Filipino infantry regiments, selected their leaders, and armed and equipped them to the limits of his abilities. In early January 1945, Volckmann moved his regiments into key terrain to hinder Japanese movement prior to Sixth Army's invasion of Lingayen Gulf. Once Sixth Army was ashore on Luzon, the spigot of arms, ammunition, and supplies was opened, and Volckmann's regiments were turned into lethal killing machines, albeit not trained to the standards of other American forces.[51]

By the end of February, USAFIP-NL had 18,000 armed effectives, adding roughly a division of infantry (albeit without the robust artillery component of a US Army division) to Sixth Army's rolls. Volckmann's forces performed yeoman service in clearing the western and northern coasts of Luzon, as well as menacing Japanese lines of communication north of Baguio. Yamashita was compelled to reposition the *19th Division* to the north near Bontoc to deal with this threat. These were no mean accomplishments, and the success of Volckmann's forces convinced Krueger to bolster efforts to provide the guerrillas with the wherewithal to take their place alongside Sixth Army's conventional infantry units. The guerrillas of USAFIP-NL fought for 218 days of continuous combat operations after the invasion at Lingayen Gulf. At any given time, only three US combat divisions were engaged with Gen. Yamashita's main body in the mountains and valleys of northern Luzon; the guerrillas made up the difference in combat power that Krueger's forces lacked.[52]

The 32nd Infantry Division, under the command of Maj. Gen. William H. Gill, had been overseas since May 1942 and had already fought in New Guinea and on Leyte before its arrival on Luzon. The lengthy combat service of many of the leaders and soldiers would lead to numerous cases of combat exhaustion in the attack along the Villa Verde Trail. Voicing the ultimate compliment, however, Yamashita after his surrender told his interrogators that "he considered the 32nd Division the best his troops had encountered both on Leyte and Luzon."[53]

The division began its attack toward Sante Fe on February 22, with the 127th Infantry Regiment constituting the main effort. The terrain and vegetation along the Villa Verde Trail were a sharp departure from what the division had become accustomed to in previous campaigns. Instead of steaming jungles or seas of mud, the soldiers fought at altitude on slopes covered by cogon grass and scrub pine. Tanks were critical to forward progress, but getting the vehicles up sixty-degree slopes required feats of ingenuity and endurance.[54]

Progress was slow in the mountainous, forested terrain, but the 127th Infantry was able to break through the Japanese outpost line within two days, decimating the Japanese *10th Reconnaissance Regiment* along the way. The 127th Infantry crossed the Cabalisian River, compelling the Japanese commander, Maj. Gen. Haruo Konuma, to commit the *2nd Tank Division*, itself badly battered from its earlier battles and now essentially functioning as infantry, to the fight.[55] The Japanese reinforcements arrived at Salacsac Pass on March 4, just in time to prevent the Americans from seizing it. Konuma ordered the division to hold the area at all costs.[56]

Beginning on March 7, the 127th Infantry attempted to penetrate the Japanese positions at Salacsac Pass, but the tortuous terrain and excellent Japanese defensive positions stymied the attackers. The Japanese main line of resistance consisted of a honeycomb of cave positions interconnected by tunnels. The Japanese positioned artillery pieces in caves; they would fire and then roll back into the interior for protection from counterbattery fire. "He [the Japanese soldier] defended his main line of resistance with fanatical zeal," recorded the 32nd Infantry Division after-action report. "Each enemy strongpoint fought to the last. The Jap remained in his cave or emplacement until he was destroyed or buried alive by demolition charges."[57] Napalm was particularly effective when it struck Japanese positions. Col. Shigia Kawai of the *2nd Tank Division* recalled, "Not only were the trees and vegetation burned in the fierce conflagration which resulted but the trenches and foxholes, as well, became holocausts as the napalm flowed through them."[58]

The terrain was particularly challenging. "Hills with nearly perpendicular slopes and deep, precipitous ravines made all movements exceedingly difficult," Krueger recalled, a situation made even worse by Japanese use of caves to cover and conceal their forces.[59] The terrain was terra incognito to the Red Arrow Division, which lacked maps of the area. When the battle for the Villa Verde Trail began, the only map available was on the scale of 1:250,000, completely useless for tactical maneuvering and fire support. The aerial photo interpretation team attached to the division produced

1:10,000 and 1:25,000 scale maps, but inadequate reproduction capabilities limited distribution. During the fighting for Salacsac Pass, even this large-scale map provided insufficient detail, requiring the photo interpretation team to produce a photo mosaic map with hill numbers overprinted on it.[60]

The terrain also made resupply especially difficult. Division engineers performed near miracles in constructing a military-grade road along the nineteen miles of the Villa Verde Trail in "rugged mountainous country where the conception of a truck road seemed ridiculous and impossible."[61] Radio reporter William Dunn christened the route the "baby Burma road."[62] Supplies had to be hand-carried from dumps below the Caraballo spur, a round-trip journey of nearly a week. Filipino laborers, who hauled ammunition and supplies to the troops on the front lines, made a tangible contribution to the fight. PCAU 18 supplied the 32nd Infantry Division with 12,321 civilian laborers in March, 23,502 in April, and 16,914 in May.[63]

By March 23, the 127th Infantry had lost a third of its strength, including nearly every company and battalion commander. Relief by the 128th Infantry was completed on March 25, but that regiment had no more success than its predecessor. On the night of March 31–April 1, a force of 250 Japanese launched a counterattack against the 3rd Battalion, 128th Infantry, which had just succeeded in seizing Hill 504, key terrain along the trail. Advancing behind a heavy artillery barrage, the attackers overwhelmed Company L. The 3rd Battalion counterattacked at 02:00 and restored the original line by dawn. The American infantry had used 1,800 grenades in the night melée, which killed more than 60 Japanese soldiers at the cost of 84 American casualties.[64]

By April 4, the 128th Infantry was 1,000 men understrength. I Corps narrowed the division zone to enable it to concentrate two regiments on the fight at Salacsac Pass, and, on April 7, the 126th and 128th Infantry Regiments continued the assault. The regiments clawed at the Japanese positions for ten days, gaining some key terrain, but making no major breakthroughs. By then both regiments had been badly depleted and were on the verge of combat-ineffectiveness. The Japanese *2nd Tank Division* had also suffered heavily in the assaults, but it had the advantage of holding prepared positions on the high ground.[65]

The 32nd Infantry Division made one final valiant effort to penetrate Salacsac Pass and seize Santa Fe, beginning on April 17, when the 127th Infantry went into the line once more in relief of the 128th Infantry. The grueling attack made slow progress, with Japanese counterattacks hampering progress. It was now the turn of the 126th Infantry to border on combat-ineffectiveness, and Maj. Gen. Gill had no choice other than to return the

128th Infantry to the fight on May 3 and employ a battalion of guerrillas, the 1st Battalion of the Buena Vista Regiment, in limited operations. The attack continued on May 8, with Japanese forces fighting to the death. The Red Arrow Division's fight ended twenty days later with the seizure of Salacsac Pass and the occupation of the small town of Imugan by the Filipino guerrillas. The next day the guerrillas linked up with the 126th Infantry, which had been attached to the 25th Infantry Division and trucked up Route 5 to advance toward Imugan from the east. The 32nd Infantry Division never did reach Santa Fe, which was left to the 25th Infantry Division.

The battles along the Villa Verde Trail had cost the 32nd Infantry Division 825 killed, 2,160 wounded, and 6,000 non-battle casualties – more than 80 percent of the 11,000 soldiers that had arrived with the division on Luzon.[66] Among the Americans killed were a regimental commander, two battalion commanders, and scores of company commanders and platoon leaders.[67] The fact that the division had destroyed the Japanese *2nd Tank Division* as a combat-effective unit and killed nearly 9,000 Japanese soldiers was of little solace.[68]

The other element of the I Corps main effort, the 25th Infantry Division's attack northwards along Route 5, was more successful. Attacks from February 21 to March 5 succeeded in clearing Route 5 between Puncan and Digdig, aided by the advance of the 35th Infantry Regiment along the sparsely defended Route 100 to the east. Lt. Gen. Swift, taking advantage of the unanticipated success, ordered the division to continue its attack north up Route 5 toward Putlan. The attack, commencing on March 7, was successful. The 35th Infantry again played a key role by enveloping Japanese forces to the east along a serviceable trail along the Bonga and Putlan Rivers, reaching Putlan on the evening of May 8. The 27th Infantry Regiment arrived along Route 5 the next day and spent a week clearing the area of Japanese forces. To this point, the advance had been spectacular by the standards of the northern Luzon campaign, but that progress was about to come to a screeching halt in front of the next objective: the high ground south of Santa Fe at Balete Pass.[69]

Steep, wooded terrain and Japanese resistance would combine to make the battle for Balete Pass a nightmare. Some ravines in the area were impassable, even to infantry. Observation and fields of fire were obstructed by thick tropical vegetation, limiting the effectiveness of artillery and airpower. With the difficult terrain came "engineering problems, which, at times, seemed almost impossible to surmount."[70] The *10th Division* was well dug in and positioned to prevent either an attack directly north along Route

9.3: Pfc. Thomas D. Flynn, Jr. (with TNT charge), Pfc. Lawrence Galvan, and Pfc. Javier Mazquez of the 2nd Battalion, 127th Infantry, 32nd Infantry Division clear a Japanese-occupied cave on the Villa Verde Trail, May 12, 1945. Japanese troops dug themselves into the mountains of Luzon in an attempt to inflict as many casualties as possible on US forces. Clearing these cave fortifications was a slow, time-consuming process. (Credit: US Army Signal Corps Photo)

5 or an enveloping maneuver on either flank. Its commander ordered the division to defend to the death: "Positions will not be yielded to the enemy even though you die. Our only path is victory or death; therefore, defend to the last man. Those who retreat without orders will be decapitated."[71] An attempt in the middle of March by the 35th Infantry Regiment to envelop Japanese positions along the Old Spanish Trail east of Route 5 was halted because of the impracticality of constructing a suitable supply road, given the clay soil, "which turned into impassable mud after two or three vehicles passed over a given spot."[72] The operation did compel the area commander, Maj. Gen. Haruo Konuma, to reinforce the defense with a regiment of paratroopers. Concurrent attacks by the 16th and 27th Infantry Regiments up Route 5 also met with limited success.[73]

9.4: Troops of the 25th Infantry Division near Balete Pass, Luzon, March 23, 1945. The fighting in northern Luzon was strategically unnecessary and killed thousands of US, Philippine, and Japanese troops before the Japanese surrender brought an end to the bloodletting. (Credit: US Army Signal Corps Photo)

At this point Maj. Gen. Mullins reoriented his forces to conduct a two-regiment attack to the east of Route 5, with another reinforced regiment attacking north up Route 5 to hold Japanese forces in position. The attack, which began on March 16, proceeded slowly against determined Japanese opposition. The 161st Infantry, attacking west of Route 5, took the better part of two weeks to gain possession of the two miles of Norton Ridge. Four 90mm antiaircraft guns winched up onto the ridge proved invaluable in destroying Japanese pillboxes and caves.[74] The 27th Infantry attacked up Myoko Ridge, hitting the Japanese main defensive positions on March 28. The 35th Infantry, attacking further to the east through trackless terrain, reached Mt. Kanami roughly two-and-a-half miles east of Balete Pass. Japanese reinforcements checked the advance and threatened the regiment's supply line, compelling Mullins once again to withdraw the 35th

Infantry from its attempted envelopment of Japanese positions, placing it along Route 5 between the 161st and 27th Infantry Regiments. The division was now more concentrated, a necessity given the strong Japanese forces defending Balete Pass.[75]

It took a month of slow, grinding fighting for the 161st and 35th Infantry Regiments to advance less than a mile to the destroyed barrio of Kapintalan in the face of stiff Japanese resistance. "The Japanese appreciation and organization of this terrain was of a very high order," recorded the division after-action report. "All commanding features were organized in detail and consisted of an elaborate integrated system of interconnected caves, pillboxes, and emplacements. A complete realization of our artillery and aerial supremacy was evidenced by the Japanese emplacement of their artillery in caves which afforded protection against bombing and counter-battery fire."[76] The 27th Infantry found the going no easier on Myoko Ridge. "As the push through the mountains drew nearer to Balete Pass, the actions of the separate regiments – though coordinated by Division and working toward the same ultimate goal – were often a world apart," recorded the division history. "In their respective zones the men fought a war of their own."[77] Foreseeing a long, grinding fight, Mullins had the foresight to open a rest camp near Puncan on April 6. One battalion from each regiment would receive a two-week rest while the other two continued fighting.[78]

Mullins had nearly despaired of reaching Balete Pass when the 27th Infantry discovered a gap in the Japanese defenses to the west of Mt. Myoko. On April 22, the regimental commander, Col. Philip F. Lindeman, ordered the 2nd Battalion to exploit the opportunity, while another battalion continued the assault on Mt. Myoko. The 2nd Battalion occupied Lone Tree Hill on April 25, and, two days later, troops were less than a mile from Balete Pass. Japanese resistance and supply shortages caused by difficult terrain, which forced carrying parties hauling supplies to slog for twelve hours to reach the battalion, forced a halt until a new supply route could be established. The 35th Infantry attacked along Kapintalan Ridge in an attempt to reach the 27th Infantry, while the 161st Infantry attempted to envelop Balete Pass from the west along Kenbu and Haruna Ridges. By May 4 the attacks had made enough progress that the final seizure of Balete Pass was conceivable with one more concerted attack, made feasible by the arrival of the 148th Infantry Regiment to clear Mt. Myoko and release other units to augment the main effort.[79]

The final advance commenced on May 4. The 2nd Battalion, 27th Infantry hit the main Japanese strongpoint on Kapintalan Ridge on May 5,

600 yards south of Lone Tree Hill, while the 1st Battalion, 35th Infantry attacked from the south. The battalions hammered away at the strongpoint for six days, finally overcoming Japanese resistance with the support of artillery, mortars, flamethrowers, and self-propelled artillery. Soldiers sealed more than 200 caves "so organized as to permit the Japanese to shift troops to meet an attack and then to shift the troops farther along the ridge line without coming into the open and exposing themselves."[80] The 27th and 35th Infantry effected a link-up on May 11. Nearly 1,000 Japanese dead littered the area, and an unknown number sealed inside caves.[81] On the division's eastern flank, the 148th Infantry seized and cleared Mt. Myoko by May 12. The presence of tanks in the attack on the ridge leading to Mt. Myoko surprised the Japanese and proved invaluable in the success of the assault.[82] The 3rd Battalion, 161st Infantry advanced along Haruna Ridge on May 4, while the 27th Infantry maneuvered along Wolfhound Ridge toward Route 5. On May 10, the 27th Infantry reached Balete Pass and linked up with elements of the 161st Infantry on Haruna Ridge, while the 35th Infantry cleared Route 5 north to Balete Pass, a task finished three days later.

It took from then until the end of May for the 25th Infantry Division to grind its way through the remaining Japanese resistance, descend into Santa Fe, and link up with the 32nd Infantry Division near Imugan along the Villa Verde Trail. The way into the Cagayan Valley was now open. The victory had been one of engineering and logistics as well as combat prowess. Division engineers constructed roads "over terrain, which upon first examination looked to be impassable." Some roads were so steep that vehicles had to be winched up them. Each regiment also used 300 to 1,800 Filipino carriers to haul supplies up the ridges in the absence of roads. Each battalion in the attack required a minimum of 300 carriers to supply its essential needs in combat. Small drop areas required more precision than was possible with C-47 cargo planes, so L-5 liaison planes were used to deliver supplies to isolated units. The small aircraft flew 746 sorties and dropped 143,162 pounds of supplies in this manner.[83]

Filipino guerrillas also had a role in the victory. Around 5,500 guerrillas served with the 25th Infantry Division during the Luzon campaign. Guerrilla units secured the division's flank along the Old Spanish Trail, patrolled supply routes, and guarded the division command post. Two organized units of Chinese guerrillas served with the 161st Infantry Regiment and performed well in combat. The guerrillas performed tasks that freed up combat formations to focus on more intensive missions against

Japanese forces. Although they were poorly equipped and lacking in training and discipline, the guerrillas "served as well as they knew."[84]

The Tropic Lightning Division paid a steep price for its accomplishment, incurring 685 killed (including the assistant division commander,
Brig. Gen. James L. Dalton II, one of only 11 US Army ground force general
officers killed by hostile fire in World War II) and 2,090 wounded in action
since the beginning of the operation on February 21. On the other hand,
the Japanese *10th Division* guarding Balete Pass was destroyed as an effective
unit, with nearly 8,000 soldiers killed in the fighting.[85]

The other prong of the I Corps attack in northern Luzon – toward Baguio –
was more successful. Beginning in the last week of February and continuing
to the middle of March, the 33rd Infantry Division (Maj. Gen. Percy
W. Clarkson) conducted aggressive patrolling along several avenues of
advance. Japanese forces strongly defended Route 11, which ran northwards
to Baguio, but patrols discovered much less opposition on the Tuba Trail
and the road from Caba to Galiano, both of which ran from the coast
eastward toward Baguio. Further north, Route 9, which ran from Bauang
on the coast east and then southeast to Baguio, appeared undefended. Had
Clarkson been allowed to focus his combat power on the latter route, he
might have succeeded in turning the Japanese flank and seizing Baguio. But
Swift was concerned about the lack of forces should something go wrong
and opted for a more conservative approach. He ordered Clarkson to
commit a regiment along Route 11 and conduct a reconnaissance in force
with a single battalion along Route 9.[86]

The 136th Infantry made predictably little progress along Route 11, but
the battalion committed to Route 9 advanced as far as Burgos on March 27,
meeting no opposition. There the advance halted, however, as the USAFIP-
NL regiment guarding the division's flank at San Fernando was repositioned north to open a new front in northern Luzon. Swift directed the
33rd Infantry Division to assume responsibility for San Fernando and
extended the division's boundary to the east to assist the hard-pressed
32nd Infantry Division, facing stiff opposition along the Villa Verde Trail.[87]

There matters stood until the arrival in late March of the 129th Infantry
Regiment, which had been garrisoning Manila with its parent unit, the 37th
Infantry Division. Clarkson directed the regiment to reconnoiter along
Route 9 toward Baguio. By April 1, the lead elements had reached Salat,
one mile short of the main Japanese defensive line, and by April 9 the
regiment had closed on the main Japanese defenses at Sablan. The success
was enough to convince SWPA to release the rest of the 37th Infantry

Division, minus one regiment, to Sixth Army for a two-division attack on Baguio.[88]

The attack commenced on April 12, with regiments attacking along the four lines of advance toward Baguio. The 136th Infantry, reinforced by the division reconnaissance troop and a battalion of Volckmann's guerrillas, advanced along Route 11; the 123rd Infantry advanced along the Tuba Trail; the 130th Infantry advanced along the Galiano road; and the 129th Infantry, the vanguard of the 37th Infantry Division, made the main effort down Route 9 into Baguio. The advances from the south made little headway, but the attacks down Route 9 and along the Tuba Trail proved decisive. Aided by artillery and tank fire, the 129th Infantry penetrated the Japanese defenses at Sablan on April 14. The 148th Infantry then passed into the lead along Route 9. The Japanese made a last desperate stand at the Irisan Gorge, where, from April 17 to 21, they held against fierce attacks. But skillful maneuvering and intensive fire support enabled the 148th Infantry to seize the key crossing. Along the Galiano road, the 130th Infantry was able to use the gains made by the Buckeyes to its north to envelop Japanese troops at Asin, thereby opening up that avenue of approach into Baguio.[89]

The Japanese could see the end nearing and evacuated President José P. Laurel and a few members of his collaborationist government to Japan. Others were left to fend for themselves, among them Manuel Roxas, Laurel's chief advisor, who, along with several other members of the collaborationist government, made his way to American lines. MacArthur, much to the chagrin of Roxas's political rival Sergio Osmeña, pardoned Roxas and promoted him to brigadier general; the rest were jailed pending trial for collaboration. MacArthur argued that Roxas had proved his loyalty by failing to reveal the presence of Dr. Emigdio Cruz, an envoy who had covertly traveled to Manila in 1943 to confer with Roxas and other Filipino leaders at the request of President Quezon. He had also requested evacuation from the Philippines when the Japanese broke the intelligence ring of which he was a part, although the operation to rescue him failed.[90] MacArthur clearly favored Roxas over Osmeña, and, although MacArthur did not openly support him, Roxas would end up winning the election for president in April 1946, defeating Osmeña in the process.[91]

I Corps, concerned about a possible Japanese troop concentration to the north near La Trinidad, ordered a temporary halt to shore up flank security, which proved unnecessary. The 33rd and 37th Infantry Divisions had by this time plowed through the strongest portions of the Japanese defenses.

Bowing to the inevitable, the Japanese commander, Maj. Gen. Naokata Utsunomiya, ordered a withdrawal to the north and northeast, which enabled 10,000 of his troops to escape the impending encirclement. On April 24, a patrol from the 129th Infantry entered Baguio, and the remainder of the regiment occupied the city two days later. The 33rd Infantry Division linked up with the Buckeyes in Baguio on April 29, ending the fight for the city.[92]

By that time, Baguio had been bombed and beaten into ruins. Felixberto C. Sta. Maria wrote, "When the airplanes and cannons got through with their job, Baguio was a local edition of the famous flattened cities of Germany . . .. Wave after wave of ferocious bombers came and went unloading their cargoes unopposed. Ugly craters gaped where trim, picturesque landscape [once] stood . . .. The toll in lives and property was enormous."[93] Although the Japanese were able to withdraw many of their troops from the Baguio front, nearly their entire complement of artillery had been destroyed in the fighting. Furthermore, the seizure of Japanese supply dumps placed their forces in severe supply difficulties, and malnutrition and sickness reduced the ranks of effective soldiers.

After a week of mopping up and securing La Trinidad, the 37th Infantry Division redeployed to Santa Fe, en route to its future battlefields in the Cagayan Valley. The 33rd Infantry Division reverted to a holding force, awaiting events elsewhere before continuing offensive operations.

Unlike most Filipino guerrilla organizations, Volckmann's USAFIP-NL would receive its own zone of operations, with the mission of clearing Luzon north of Vigan, harassing Japanese forces in the Cagayan Valley, and attacking from the west coast of Luzon along Route 4 toward the *Shobu Group* base at Bontoc. The seizure of Bontoc would isolate the bulk of Yamashita's forces, leaving them to eke out a subsistence-level existence in the Cordillera Central Mountains. The terrain along Route 4, while undeniably beautiful, was every bit as difficult to maneuver through as that along the Villa Verde Trail. Compounding the issue was the pending arrival of the monsoon season at the end of May, which would make Route 4 nigh on impassable to military traffic.[94]

The 15th Infantry Regiment, USAFIP-NL, was responsible for clearing northwestern Luzon and opening Route 3 along the coast south to Vigan. Under pressure from the guerrilla regiment, by early April the ill-trained and poorly supplied *Araki Force* in the area had withdrawn into the interior southeast of Vigan, and the coastal route was open all the way south to Lingayen Gulf. On April 10, the 15th Infantry attacked, forcing the *Araki*

Force to retreat roughly thirty miles to Gayaman, where its path south was blocked by the 121st Infantry Regiment, USAFIP-NL. The *Araki Force* then moved southeast into the trackless Cordillera Central, where starvation and disease decimated the force before it arrived in the tiny mountain village of Besao in the middle of May. Of the 8,000 troops who began the campaign in northwestern Luzon, only 1,500 arrived in Bontoc at the end of May. The rest had been killed or had scattered into the hinterland, to die by starvation or to be tracked down and killed by guerrillas before the war's end.[95]

Operations along Route 4 were not nearly as easy. Although a guerrilla company had occupied the town of Cervantes twenty miles inland from Libtong on February 24, the arrival of the *19th Division* in the area quickly reversed this gain. The guerrillas recovered the town on March 13, but needed reinforcement if they were to remain. Volckmann assembled a provisional battalion to hold Cervantes, but, on April 3, Japanese pressure once again forced the unit to vacate the town. In the meantime, Krueger had ordered Volckmann to attack along Route 4 toward Bontoc, a task that would consume USAFIP-NL for the next three months.[96]

Volckmann ordered the 121st Infantry, augmented by the provisional battalion already in place near Cervantes, to attack east along Route 4 toward Bontoc. Like all USAFIP-NL forces, the 121st Infantry lacked robust fire support, which forced it to depend on sporadic air support from the Fifth Air Force flying out of airstrips near Lingayen Gulf. Beginning on March 29, the regiment attacked toward Bessang Pass, about seven miles inland from Libtong. Here the ground rose nearly a mile, providing excellent defensive terrain for a regiment of the Japanese *19th Division* to dig itself in. By the middle of May, attacks by the 121st Infantry had made scant progress. On May 17, the Japanese counterattacked, driving the guerrillas back and dispersing one of the two battalions arrayed along the high ground astride Route 4. Only the arrival of the 15th Infantry, fresh from its success against the *Araki Force*, salvaged the situation. The 15th Infantry attacked to recover the lost ground, which it did by the end of the month.[97]

The seesaw fighting for Bessang Pass turned to the favor of the Americans after I Corps seized Santa Fe. At this point, Sixth Army gave operational control of Volckmann's forces to I Corps and directed Swift to provide the guerrillas with the wherewithal to seize Cervantes. I Corps returned the 66th Infantry Regiment, USAFIP-NL, to Volckmann's control and reinforced the drive along Route 4 with the 1st Battalion, 123rd Infantry and a battalion of 105mm howitzers, which augmented the guerrilla's own battalion of 75mm pack howitzers. The additional combat power enabled Volckmann to launch an attack on June 1 with three guerrilla regiments, with the regular US infantry battalion in reserve. The guerrillas made headway against the severely depleted and disease-ridden Japanese forces, finally occupying Bessang Pass on June 14. The next day the 15th Infantry secured Cervantes, putting the final touches on the battle that had begun in late March.[98]

With the *Shobu Group* increasingly hemmed into its mountain redoubt in the Cordillera Central, the final act in the Luzon campaign began to play out. After having destroyed the *2nd Tank* and *10th Divisions* in the fighting along the Villa Verde Trail and at Balete Pass, I Corps was advancing rapidly toward the southern entrance into the Cagayan Valley. Yamashita's goal was for the remnants of the forces fighting near Santa Fe to hold long enough to enable the *103rd* and *4th Air Divisions*, which had been garrisoned in the valley to gather the harvest upon which the *Shobu Group* relied for sustenance, time to withdraw westward and link up with the rest of the group's forces in the Cordillera Central.[99]

Sixth Army planned to use the 25th and 33rd Infantry Divisions in the invasion of Japan, so Krueger ordered the 37th Infantry Division, followed by the 6th Infantry Division, to continue the attack north into the Cagayan Valley, while the 32nd Infantry Division went into the line near Baguio. A small task force commanded by Maj. Robert V. Connolly would move up Route 3 to the northern tip of Luzon and seize the port of Aparri.[100]

The Buckeye Division began its attack on May 31 and made rapid progress against spirited but ineffective opposition. As the division smashed into the broad Cagayan Valley on June 14, the spearhead consisted of an armored column of tanks, tank destroyers, M7 self-propelled artillery, M16s (a half-tracked vehicle with quad .50-caliber machine guns mounted in the back), and M8 armored cars. The major challenges were the same as those during the advance down the central plain to Manila: the reconstruction of blown bridges across rivers and securing the line of communication to the rear.[101] Beightler rotated the lead regiment to keep fresh troops at the head of the division. The 37th Infantry Division was the main effort undertaken by the Sixth Army, which gave it all the air support "which it was possible to control on a narrow front." Six to eight flights, each consisting of twelve fighter-bombers, performed armed reconnaissance, and remained on call for close support of ground forces from dusk to dawn. During the Cagayan Valley fighting, the division was supported by 2,483 fighter-bomber sorties, which dropped 1,776 tons of bombs and 33,250 gallons of napalm.[102]

By June 16, the lead American forces were at Cauayan, an advance of seventy miles in just seventeen days. The 11th and 14th Regiments, USAFIP-NL, had by then cleared the valley west of the Cagayan River all the way north to Aparri, which Maj. Connolly's task force had besieged in conjunction with Volckmann's guerrillas. The 63rd Infantry Regiment, 6th Infantry Division went into action on June 13 by advancing northwest up Route 4 toward the heart of the *Shobu Group*'s redoubt in the Cordillera Central. The attacks shattered Yamashita's planned defensive lines, forcing him to plan a last-ditch stand in the nearly trackless Asin River Valley.[103]

The Buckeyes took only ten more days to secure the entire length of the Cagayan Valley. The lightning advance shattered the *Yuguchi Force*, the last remaining Japanese combat element in the area. On June 26, a motorized column led by tanks made contact with a battalion task force of the 11th Airborne Division, which had dropped near Aparri on June 23 and made its way south. The junction of these two forces ended the fighting in the Cagayan Valley. The 37th Infantry Division and its attachments would from that point onward patrol the Sierra Madre Mountains to the east, where upwards of 10,000 Japanese soldiers, most of them on the point of starvation, held out.[104]

US and Filipino forces continued to compress the remnants of the *Shobu Group* in their Cordillera Central redoubt, which came to be known as the Kiangan Pocket, but the campaign for northern Luzon was effectively finished. Japanese forces had long outlasted their supplies. By April, Japanese soldiers were receiving only 100–400 grams of rice (130–520 calories) each day; by June the ration was cut to just 50 grams of rice (65 calories) per day.[105]

MacArthur relieved Sixth Army of its duties in Luzon on June 30, declaring the campaign over. The next day Krueger "sent MacArthur a map of Luzon showing American and Japanese casualties to June 30, 'which,' Krueger added, 'may be of interest to you.' By that time Sixth Army counted 173,563 Japanese dead, or 20,000 more than Willoughby ever admitted were on the island."[106] Another 75,000 Japanese still lurked in various mountain hideaways, awaiting their fate.

Eighth Army assumed responsibility throughout the Philippines, with XIV Corps the operational headquarters on Luzon. There was plenty of mopping up duty left, but only the *Shobu Group* remained as a viable combat force, and it could not impact activities on Luzon beyond its redoubt in the Asin River Valley. Food was scarce, and troops subsisted on starvation rations of rice, sweet potatoes, and wild grasses.[107] The 6th and 32nd Infantry

Divisions and the USAFIP-NL regiments, now 21,000 strong and backed by 2 battalions of artillery, continued their attacks to reduce the pocket, albeit hampered by torrential summer rains.[108] "The object of our offensive campaign was to drive the enemy from the food-producing areas into the Sierra Madre Mountains, where their strength would diminish because of starvation and disease," Eichelberger later wrote. "In retrospect it seems to me that this campaign accomplished little and could have readily been foregone."[109] He was not wrong.

Psychological operators did their best to attempt to persuade the Japanese to save themselves by showering tons of paper on Japanese troops in an attempt to coerce their surrender. Between October 20, 1944, and the end of the war, the various commands in the Philippine Islands dropped 61,100,000 leaflets on Japanese positions.[110] As malnutrition and disease gripped the remaining Japanese in their mountain redouts, more of them became willing to consider surrender as an option.

MacArthur had by then moved on from supervising operations in the Philippines. His wife Jean, his son Arthur, Arthur's nanny Au Cheu, and aide Lt. Col. Sidney Huff had arrived from Australia on March 6, and "Sir boss" and his wife settled into a routine that rarely took the general away from Manila except for a visit to the Marakina Valley twenty miles northeast of Manila and one trip in June to visit Eighth Army forces in the south and to witness the Australian invasion of Borneo. MacArthur was one of the few – perhaps the only – US Army soldier deployed in an active theater of war who enjoyed the company of his family. Their presence kept him in rhythm, but also no doubt engendered a bit of jealousy from those who soldiered on until the end of the war alone.

On April 3, 1945, the US Joint Chiefs of Staff created US Army Forces, Pacific (AFPAC), with MacArthur as its commander. This headquarters, populated by officers from GHQ SWPA, assumed command over all Army and Army Air Forces units in the Pacific, with the exception of those in the North and Southeast Pacific and the Twentieth Air Force conducting the strategic bombing against Japan. AFPAC was stood up in Manila on April 6, and at that point SWPA faded from history. MacArthur became intimately involved in the planning for the invasion of Japan, essentially delegating operations in the Philippines to Krueger and Eichelberger.

After the end of the war, Yamashita descended from the Kiangan Pocket to surrender his forces to Maj. Gen. Beightler of the 37th Infantry Division. With communications tenuous, it took several days to convince Yamashita that Japan had surrendered. His headquarters received a telegram from the

Southern Expeditionary Army Group, flyers were dropped to inform Japanese troops of the surrender, and American attacks ceased. Yamashita was able to make contact with American commanders in his area, and he set out for Kiangan on August 31, arriving on September 2. He was driven to Bagabag and flew from there to Baguio. Instead of the 23,000 or so Japanese estimated by American intelligence officers, more than 40,000 Japanese soldiers in the Kiangan pocket marched into captivity.[111] Yamashita had succeeded in getting the most out of his troops and delaying the liberation of Luzon, but whether his achievement would have made any difference to the planned invasion of Japan is rendered moot by the dropping of the atomic bombs on Hiroshima and Nagasaki and the resulting Japanese surrender. During the six months of the Luzon campaign, the Japanese lost 248,000 combatants killed, captured, or dead from disease and starvation.[112]

One final act of redemption remained, but MacArthur was not present for it. Present in the room in Baguio where Yamashita signed the act of surrender of his troops in the Philippines were Lt. Gen. Arthur E. Percival, who, in February 1942, had surrendered Singapore to Yamashita in the largest surrender in British military history, and Lt. Gen. Jonathan Wainwright, who, in May 1942, had surrendered US and Filipino forces to Yamashita's predecessor as commander of the *14th Area Army,* Lt. Gen. Masaharu Homma, in the largest surrender in US military history. After a brief but dignified ceremony, Yamashita was led away to Bilibid Prison, where he would await trial as a war criminal.[113]

10

THE CENTRAL AND SOUTHERN PHILIPPINES

My many flights over Mindanao had convinced me that our job was to drive the Japanese into those barbarous wastes and that, once they were prisoners of the terrain, we should let them stay there and starve.[1]

Lt. Gen. Robert Eichelberger

Clearing the Central and Southern Philippines would liberate millions of Filipinos from Japanese occupation and eliminate the last bastions of Japanese resistance in the islands. MacArthur was willing to undertake these operations for the sake of the larger political, military, and humanitarian objectives at stake – the complete liberation of the Filipino people from Japanese control being the paramount goal. Air bases on Palawan and the Zamboanga Peninsula on Mindanao would also support further operations into the Dutch East Indies and complete the isolation of Japanese forces in the Visayas and on Mindanao.[2] MacArthur assigned these missions – the Victor series of operations in the Musketeer Operations Plan – to Lt. Gen. Robert Eichelberger's Eighth Army, which was already engaged in clearing the remaining Japanese forces from Leyte. For Eichelberger, as for MacArthur, "the Philippines made magic for me. I had served there as a young officer, and the lovely place names rang the bell of memory; they were pure music."[3]

MacArthur was determined to extend the Philippines campaign beyond Luzon, despite lack of specific authorization from the JCS, which had counted on Filipino guerrillas to liberate the remainder of the Philippines south of Leyte, Samar, Mindoro, and Luzon. In early February 1945, MacArthur informed the JCS that he would use US forces in his theater for "mopping up operations" in the Philippines. The Joint Chiefs were in Yalta for the Argonaut Conference, leaving them precious little time to discuss the matter. True to form when it came to supporting MacArthur's initiatives, Admiral King viewed such operations as an "undesirable waste of effort."[4] The Joint Chiefs (via Marshall) sent a query to MacArthur asking "to what extent in time and numbers do you consider it essential for

American divisions and air forces to be employed in clearing up the islands?"[5] MacArthur responded to Marshall on February 10, stating, "It is estimated that all the ground and air forces available to me will be required to clear the Philippines and that it will take at least six months. It is deemed essential that the strength of the SWPA remain unimpaired."[6]

On February 26, MacArthur sent a more detailed message specifying the operations SWPA would conduct to liberate the Central and Southern Philippines, as well as Australian operations to liberate portions of the Netherlands East Indies. The message listed the units involved in each operation and dates of execution. For the Philippines, these read:

A. Luzon – Sixth Army with 6th, 25th, 32nd, 33rd, 37th, 38th, 43rd, 1st Cavalry, and the 11th Airborne Divisions;

B. Visayas and Mindanao – Eighth Army:

    (1) Palawan 28 February with one RCT [regimental combat team] of 41st Division

    (2) Zamboanga 10 March with 41st Division less one RCT

    (3) Panay and Negros Occidental 25 March with 40th Division less one RCT

    (4) Cebu and Negros Oriental 25 March with the Americal Division less one RCT

    (5) Mindanao 12 April with 24th and 31st Divisions, with the 93rd Division being used to garrison liberated islands.[7]

Of course, by this date the invasion of Palawan was only two days away, leaving little time for the JCS to consider whether the campaign to liberate the Central and Southern Philippines was advisable.

Presumably, Marshall passed this message on to the Joint Chiefs and their planning staffs. On March 30, Marshall sent a message to MacArthur, noting that he "expected" the Joint Chiefs to task MacArthur with completing the occupation of Luzon, as well as conducting "such additional operations toward completing the liberation of the Philippines as can be mounted without prejudice to the accomplishment of the over-all objective," which was to force the unconditional surrender of Japan.[8] By that date, of course, operations in the Central and Southern Philippines were already well under way. The Joint Chiefs agreed on April 3 to allow MacArthur to "complete the occupation of Luzon and conduct such additional operations in the Philippines as required for the accomplishment of the over-all objective in the war against Japan."[9] The directive was squishy enough to allow MacArthur to complete the liberation of the Philippines as he saw fit. There matters stood, as the Joint Chiefs did not again deliberate regarding MacArthur's operations in the Philippines, most likely because MacArthur was using forces already allocated to his theater to pursue his goals, and they were not needed for the invasion of Okinawa. True to form, MacArthur took lack of objection from the JCS as consent for his planned operations.[10]

Operations would commence well before the typhoon season bore down on the Philippines. MacArthur provided Eichelberger with the forces required to undertake significant operations by stripping several combat divisions and other formations from Krueger's Sixth Army (much to Krueger's chagrin) and thereby delaying the destruction of Japanese forces in the mountainous interior of Luzon – an objective that was in any case much more questionable than liberating millions of Filipinos in the Visayas and on Mindanao. In all, Eighth Army would control X Corps and the Americal, 24th, 31st, 40th, and 41st Infantry Divisions and the 503rd Parachute Infantry Regiment, along with the normal reinforcing tank, artillery, engineer, and combat service support forces, and augmented by land-based airpower and minimal but sufficient naval forces. Large numbers of Filipino guerrillas would support Eighth Army, earning their rightful place among the forces of liberation.

The actual date of operations differed little from MacArthur's message to Marshall. Eichelberger's Eighth Army would seize Palawan (Victor III, February 28) and the Zamboanga–Sulu Archipelago (Victor IV, March 10), thereby isolating Japanese forces on Mindanao. Forces would then seize Panay (Victor I, March 18), Cebu (Victor II, March 26), and Negros (Victor I and II, March 29). The final operation would be the invasion of Mindanao (Victor V, April 17), on which the majority of Japanese forces in the Southern Philippines were stationed. In all of these operations, Eichelberger emphasized speed of execution to preclude Japanese forces from creating the type of defenses that had given the 32nd Infantry Division so much grief at Buna. His aggressiveness paid off in a rapid series of operations that liberated thirty islands in a matter of weeks.[11]

"Eighth Army had a young staff which was endowed with enterprise and daring," Eichelberger wrote in his memoir. "It worked out, intelligently and with mathematical accuracy, the hazards and supply realities of our landings. Never once were its calculations seriously in error."[12] The staff work had to be superb, for Eighth Army became the premier amphibious assault organization in the Southwest Pacific Theater. Between the middle of February and early April 1945, Eighth Army would conduct fourteen major and twenty-four minor amphibious assaults across hundreds of miles of the Philippines archipelago in what was a tour de force in

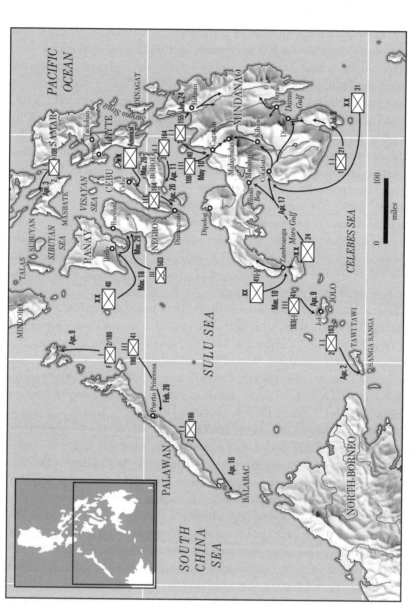

Map 10: Central and Southern Philippines, February–August 1945.

amphibious warfare. The techniques had not changed substantially since the first amphibious operations in SWPA in New Guinea, but now US forces had overwhelming air and naval superiority, making life easier for the invasion forces. Nevertheless, according to Vice Adm. Barbey, "each landing, regardless of size, was as meticulously planned and executed as if it were another Lingayen Gulf."[13] Multi-tasking was the order of the day in the Seventh Amphibious Force and in Eighth Army.

The *35th Army* in the Central and Southern Philippines had no "hope for anything more than to die while conducting a static defense."[14] Much of the army, including its commander, Gen. Sōsaku Suzuki, was trapped on Leyte. The other major concentration, the *100th Division* and about half of the *30th Division* that did not deploy to Leyte, was positioned on southeast Mindanao, where the Japanese had expected the American landings in the Philippines to begin. The *54th Independent Mixed Brigade* was on the Zamboanga Peninsula, the *55th Independent Mixed Brigade* was in the Sulu Archipelago, and about half of the *102nd Division* was distributed among Panay, Negros, Cebu, and Bohol. Gen. Suzuki was able to evacuate from Leyte to Cebu in March, but lost his life attempting to reach his forces in eastern Mindanao. The army chief of staff, Maj. Gen. Yoshiharu Tomochika, took command and finally reached Mindanao in late April. Most of his troops were poorly trained, ill-equipped, and psychologically unprepared for the intense combat that awaited them.[15]

The divisions of the Eighth US Army, on the other hand, while understrength, were for the most part combat-experienced killing machines by this point in the campaign. They had fought the Japanese on islands in the Southwest Pacific and on Leyte and Luzon in the Philippines. Commanders understood how to combine arms (infantry, tanks, artillery, engineers) and services (close air support and naval gunfire) to maximize combat effectiveness. Soldiers also knew how to survive in the difficult jungle environment. Troops were aware of the sanitation and prophylactic measures required to ward off malaria, scrub typhus, fungus, amoebic dysentery, and schistosomiasis (parasitic worms). "The rigors of tropical combat would not be a new experience to them," recorded the Eighth Army after-action report.[16]

Eighth Army operations would commence with the 41st Infantry Division (Maj. Gen. Jens A. Doe) assaulting Palawan, the Zamboanga Peninsula, and the Sulu Archipelago. Control of Palawan would ensure control of the Sulu Sea and shipping lanes running through the southern and western approaches of the South China Sea.[17] The 186th Infantry Regiment (Col. Oliver P. Newman) staged in Mindoro for the Palawan operation on February 9, 1945. The regiment departed on February 26 and arrived in Puerto Princesa Bay on Palawan two days later. The assault waves landed without opposition at 08:45. The 1st Battalion rapidly overran the airfield east of Puerto Princesa, while the 2nd Battalion occupied the town without resistance by early afternoon. The troops found only one in ten homes still standing, the remainder having been destroyed by the pre-assault bombardment. The battalions then fanned out in search of Japanese forces, finding little in the way of organized resistance other than one strong position on Hill 1445 north of Iratag, which was assaulted and overrun on March 7–8. GIs recovered the charred remains of the American prisoners murdered on December 14 by the Japanese and buried them with honors.[18] By the end of the month, Eighth Army considered the island liberated. The 2nd Battalion remained on Palawan to secure it in conjunction with Filipino guerrillas, while small amphibious operations liberated several small islands nearby. The airfield on Palawan was operational by March 20, but poor soil complicated its renovation and limited its effectiveness.[19]

The next objective was the Zamboanga Peninsula, control of which secured the Basilan Strait and the approaches leading to Borneo, as well as providing a base from which to support future operations in the Sulu Archipelago and eastern and central Mindanao.[20] Because the airfield on Palawan would not be completed in time to support the invasion of Zamboanga, planners decided to use a guerrilla-held airstrip at Dipolog in northern Zamboanga to stage a Marine fighter squadron, which could cover the landing beaches from there. Control of the airstrip behind Japanese lines proved critical to the forthcoming invasion. On March 8, two reinforced infantry companies from the 21st Infantry Regiment, 24th Infantry Division deployed via C-47 to the guerrilla-held strip and established a defensive perimeter in conjunction with local guerrilla forces.[21]

The 162nd Infantry waded ashore at San Mateo on the Zamboanga Peninsula at 09:15 on March 10 against light opposition, followed closely by the 163rd Infantry. The pre-invasion bombardment had forced the Japanese to vacate their prepared positions, if indeed they ever had the intention of defending the shoreline. At 17:00 the next day, the 3rd Battalion, 163rd Infantry occupied Zamboanga City, capital of Mindanao and the third-largest city in the Philippines, and cleared out Japanese snipers. The city, like so many others in the Philippines, had sustained substantial damage from the pre-invasion bombardment. Eichelberger observed that "the once beautiful town was a ruin. Between Japanese

dynamiting and devastation, and our aerial bombardment, the main buildings had become eyeless stone skeletons."[22] Nevertheless, the power plant
and water system were usable, and the docks were intact. Aviation engineers
had the San Roque airstrip operational within a few days. The regiments
then pursued the Japanese north into the "almost impenetrable rain
forests."[23]

Clearing the remainder of the peninsula was a difficult chore. The
Japanese had prepared an elaborate defense system on high ground consisting of trenches, bunkers, barbed wire, and log pillboxes. Bulldozers cut
roads behind the assault battalions, enabling supply and evacuation as they
forged deeper into the wilderness. Filipino guerrillas under the command
of Capt. Donald J. LeCouvre assisted by blocking a Japanese escape route up
the eastern shore of the peninsula. After slogging their way through the
fortified Japanese defensive zone, troops of the 41st Infantry Division finally
confronted the main Japanese position on Mount Capisan. The 163rd
Infantry, supported by a battalion of the 162nd Infantry, attacked the
position on March 25 and killed 3,000 Japanese soldiers. The division
then proceeded to inch its way up the Zamboanga Peninsula during the
rest of the month and through April, clearing the remnants of Japanese
forces wherever encountered. The 93rd Infantry Division ("Blue Helmets,"
commanded by Maj. Gen. Harry H. Johnson) arrived in July to secure the
peninsula.[24] By the end of the war, only 2,485 of the 8,900 Japanese troops
originally on the peninsula remained to enter into captivity.[25]

Landings in the Sulu Archipelago (Basilan, Tawi Tawi, Jolo, and Busanga)
followed the invasion of Zamboanga. The liberation of Basilan, which was
accomplished without opposition on March 16, was especially important,
providing access to an enormous rubber plantation that had survived the
war unscathed. The 2nd Battalion, 163rd Infantry landed on Tawi Tawi on
April 2 and had cleared the minimal Japanese forces from the island group
within five days. The remainder of the 163rd Infantry landed on Jolo on
April 9 and, together with Filipino guerrillas, destroyed the Japanese forces,
the largest concentrations of which were positioned on Mt. Daho in the
center of the island and on Mt. Tumatangus to the southwest, in a little more
than three weeks of fighting. The remnants were cleared by guerrilla patrols
and, beginning in the middle of June, by the 368th Infantry Regiment, 93rd
Infantry Division, which arrived to replace the 163rd Infantry.

The Sultan of Sulu, Muhammed Janail Abirir II, welcomed Col. William
J. Moroney as his troops liberated Jolo City. The sultan had surrendered to
the future commander of the American Expeditionary Forces in France

during World War I, Captain John J. Pershing, during the Philippine Insurrection but had remained loyal to the United States during the current war. The Japanese had stripped him of his most prized possessions, a saber presented to him by General Pershing and a rifle given to him by General Leonard Wood, but Colonel Moroney restored some of the sultan's prestige by presenting him with his own .45-caliber pistol. Civil affairs personnel alleviated malnutrition by distributing captured Japanese stockpiles of food, most of which had been stolen from the Filipinos, while guerrillas helped to organize local government. Engineers constructed an all-weather airfield on Sanga Sanga Island in the Tawi Tawi group, which was ready for operations on May 2.[26]

While the 41st Infantry Division was engaged on Palawan, the Zamboanga Peninsula, and the Sulu Archipelago, the 40th Infantry Division (Maj. Gen. Rapp Brush) was withdrawn from fighting on Luzon (minus the 108th Infantry, still fighting on Leyte) and assigned to the Eighth Army for the invasions of Panay and Negros (Victor I).[27] Guerrilla reports provided Eighth Army with extensive information on the composition and disposition of Japanese forces in the Visayas. By the time US forces returned to Panay, guerrilla leader Col. Macario Peralta had 22,600 men under his control, 8,000 of them armed. They controlled much of the interior of the island, having taken advantage of the departure of half of the Japanese garrison to fight a losing battle on Leyte.[28] The bulk of the garrison of 2,750 Japanese on Panay was located near Iloilo City, hemmed in by guerrilla formations in the surrounding hills. The division plan envisioned a landing south of Iloilo at Tigbauan, movement east to Iloilo, and then destruction of Japanese forces in the city. Afterwards, guerrillas would clear the remainder of the island.[29]

Guerrillas had constructed airfields in northern Panay, and the 40th Infantry Division took advantage of these to position artillery spotting aircraft two days in advance of the invasion on a beach near Tigbauan on March 18. The landing by the 185th Infantry was unopposed (indeed, the troops were greeted on the beach by Peralta's guerrillas in starched khaki uniforms), and the regimental combat team was firmly established ashore by evening.[30] While the 2nd Battalion, 160th Infantry moved north into the mountains to pursue the Japanese, the 185th Infantry attacked east to seize Iloilo. The next evening approximately 1,000 Japanese soldiers and 200 Japanese and Filipino civilians evacuated the city after setting fire to a number of buildings, breaking through guerrilla lines to the north.

American troops entered Iloilo the next morning and found the port facilities intact. In their customary display of gratitude, the Filipino residents welcomed their liberators with eggs, fruit, and candy. Eichelberger was there to savor the moment, "surrounded by a laughing, cheering, flower-throwing city population which seemed to have gone crazy with joy."[31] American soldiers also discovered grisly remains of Japanese atrocities. As the Japanese garrison of Iloilo withdrew, they drugged fifty bedridden Japanese military patients in the La Paz hospital before setting fire to the facility. Only a few patients escaped the inferno.[32]

The 40th Reconnaissance Troop and elements of the 185th Infantry pursued the Japanese, who disintegrated as an effective fighting force in their attempt to gain refuge in the mountains. Slowed down by the civilians in their midst, the retreating Japanese soldiers bayoneted sixty-two women

10.1: Maj. Gen. Rapp Brush, CG, 40th Infantry Division; Col. George W. Latimer, Chief of Staff, 40th Infantry Division; and Capt. Robert W. Munyon, aide de camp, land on Panay, March 18, 1945. True to form, MacArthur committed the Eighth Army to the liberation of the Central and Southern Philippines without explicit permission from the JCS. (Credit: US Army Signal Corps Photo)

and children south of Jimanban. Japanese soldiers also killed entire Filipino families before stealing their food. Airstrikes by Marine Corsairs and Army A-20 attack aircraft along with guerrilla ambushes added to the toll of Japanese killed. Small elements of the 2nd Battalion, 160th Infantry and the 185th Infantry landed on Guimaras Island and Inampulugan Island on March 22–23, finding only a tiny Japanese outpost on the latter island.[33]

As the 185th Infantry moved onward to invade Negros, the 2nd Battalion, 160th Infantry and Peralta's guerrillas took over the mission of eliminating the last remnants of Japanese resistance on Panay. By the end of March, the only Japanese unit capable of organized resistance was located at San Jose. On April 9–10, the Philippine 65th Infantry Regiment attacked and destroyed this concentration. A final airstrike northwest of Cabatuan on May 13 dispersed the last organized Japanese force on the island, leaving the remaining Japanese to eke out a miserable existence in the mountains.[34] At the end of the war, the Japanese commander on Panay, Lt. Col. Ryoichi Totsuka, led 1,558 men into captivity.[35]

The next target for the Sunburst Division was Negros, the fourth-largest island in the Philippines, occupied by 13,500 Japanese troops. By March 1945, Lt. Col. Salvador Abcede commanded 14,000 guerrillas on the island, half of them armed, and they controlled much of the interior. The 185th Infantry would land on the west coast south of the Bago River, and then drive north to seize Bacolod, Talisay, and Silay. Seizing the bridge over the Bago River intact was a key to the success of the landing, and a reinforced platoon was given the mission of landing three hours in advance of the amphibious assault force and taking the bridge. At 05:00 on March 29, the platoon landed and moved inland to the bridge, where, after a sharp firefight, it eliminated a small Japanese detachment and cut the control wires to the demolition charges. The 185th Infantry landed at 08:00 unopposed, crossed the intact bridge, and moved rapidly north along the coast. By the evening of Y-Day, the lead elements of the 185th Infantry were closing in on the southern outskirts of Bacolod.[36]

The Japanese decided not to defend Bacolod and evacuated the city on the night of March 29 after setting fire to the business district. American troops cleared the city of stay-behind snipers by noon the next day and continued up the coast to Talisay, assaulting and seizing the town against stiff Japanese resistance on April 2. Silay fell the next day. The main Japanese force withdrew east into the island's interior, pursued by the 40th Reconnaissance Troop and a battalion of the 160th Infantry.[37]

The 503rd Parachute Infantry, originally scheduled to drop by para-chute on Negros, instead landed by water on April 8 and moved into line on the northern flank of the 185th Infantry in preparation for the advance inland to destroy the main Japanese force in the interior of the island. The paratroopers' advance followed a road along a narrow, steep ridge, requir-ing significant engineer work to repair destroyed sections and widen it for military traffic, particularly tanks, upon which the advance depended. Japanese fortifications along the crest and in adjacent ravines had to be destroyed in a time-consuming process.

The 185th Infantry meanwhile seized Guimbalaon and continued east, meeting increased resistance as it entered the mountainous interior. On April 14, the regiment seized the high ground near San Juan and ran into major Japanese defensive positions along the Lantawan corridor. A two-week battle against the fortified Japanese brought the regiment to the western edge of Patag. By early May, the two regiments were prepared for a coordinated attack on Patag, which began on May 6. The 503rd Parachute Infantry was initially held up by Japanese forces in well-prepared positions along Banana Ridge, but the advance of the 185th Infantry to its south threatened to envelop the position, which the Japanese uncharacteristically abandoned instead of fighting to the death.[38]

The 160th Infantry Regiment, which landed on Y plus 1, occupied Concepcion and continued to the east on the southern flank of the 185th Infantry. The regiment faced Japanese resistance that became more ten-acious the closer the Americans got to the mountains. As troops fought upwards into heavy rain forest and steep mountains, the temperatures plummeted, necessitating the issuance of field jackets – a rarity in the Pacific War. The anchor of the Japanese defense was Dolan Hill, a position fortified with caves, tunnels, and mutually supporting pillboxes. After two days of artillery and air preparation, the 1st Battalion, 160th Infantry jumped off in what would become a fierce, multi-day battle for the key terrain. After several days of futile attacks, the infantry reached a small knoll near the crest on April 21 and dug in. Neither side would budge. Hundreds of Filipinos were employed to haul supplies up the hill along the "trail of a thousand steps," while engineers began construction of a winding road to the top.[39]

Faced with stalemate, American commanders decided to do what American forces in World War II did best – use massive amounts of fire-power against the Japanese positions. The Americans on the hill withdrew, and aircraft and artillery subjected the Japanese positions to four days of bombardment. On May 15, the infantry assaulted the hill under the cover of heavy artillery concentrations. At the top, they discovered the area cleared of vegetation, bare tree stumps, 41 destroyed pillboxes, and 200 Japanese bodies. Patrols continued down the sides of the hill, but found only a few dazed survivors, who put up no resistance.[40]

By the middle of May, only 500 Japanese remained capable of organized resistance in the Dolan Hill area. Nevertheless, the Japanese soldiers, in fortified positions along Terukuni and Kasagi Ridges, fought tenaciously. American patrols located strongpoints and brought them under artillery and mortar fire and aerial bombardment. The Japanese needed to move to areas where they could forage for food, but left forces behind on Hill 3355 to guard the retreat. The 503rd Parachute Infantry met stiff resistance, but took the hill on May 27. On the night of May 31, the remaining Japanese vacated their positions, withdrawing to the south and east. Japanese forces, now numbering fewer than 2,000 effectives suffering from malnutrition and disease, were nearing exhaustion. Japanese resistance was at an end. The scattered remnants of Japanese forces who did not surrender either eked out a meager existence in the jungle or were hunted down by Filipino guerrillas.[41] At the end of the war, 6,169 Japanese soldiers came out of the mountains to surrender.[42]

The Americal Division (Maj. Gen. William H. Arnold), minus the 164th Infantry Regiment in Eighth Army reserve, was notified to prepare for the invasion of Cebu on March 3, 1945.[43] The division was formed on the island of New Caledonia on May 27, 1942, by combining three infantry regiments from the Massachusetts, Illinois, and North Dakota National Guard "orphaned" by the transition of their parent divisions from a square (four-regiment) to a triangular (three-regiment) organization. Its name came from amalgamating "America" and "New Caledonia," and it was the only US division formed outside of the United States during World War II. The division participated in the Guadalcanal and Bougainville campaigns and was engaged in clearing operations on Leyte when notified for movement to Cebu.

Guerrilla forces numbering around 8,500 men under Lt. Col. James Cushing on Cebu, about a quarter of them armed, were attached to the division for the operation. According to the Eighth Army's operational report, Cushing "hated the Japanese and fought them fearlessly along with his men, who both liked and respected him."[44] The guerrillas helped a great deal in controlling key terrain and providing intelligence on Japanese forces. Cushing also visited the Americal Division headquarters before the invasion and passed on intelligence information that greatly assisted with planning.[45]

On March 26, following a one-hour-long pre-invasion bombardment, the 132nd and 182nd Infantry Regiments landed at 08:30 on a beach near Talisay, southwest of Cebu City. Although the beach was heavily mined, which resulted in the disabling of ten of the fifteen tracked landing vehicles (LVTs) in the first wave, it was sparsely defended. The assistant division commander, Brig. Gen. Eugene W. Ridings, reorganized the surviving LVTs and directed the opening and marking of lanes through the minefields, unjamming the troops and equipment that were piling up on the beach. By late morning the situation was under control and the regiments established a firm beachhead. The next day the 132nd Infantry advanced northeast and seized Cebu City, the second-largest city in the Philippines, with a pre-war population of 146,000, which the Japanese evacuated without a fight. Large portions of Cebu City had been destroyed, and the Filipinos there were on the verge of starvation, making civil relief and control of black markets imperative. Here as elsewhere in the islands, PCAUs performed yeoman service in conducting civil affairs operations.[46]

The 182nd Infantry advanced northeast to Pardo and established contact with Cushing's guerrillas, which had seized a critical water reservoir and distribution tank, but had yet to clear Japanese forces from the area. The Japanese main body had positioned itself northwest of Cebu City in heavily fortified positions along Babag Ridge. The 182nd Infantry began its attack against the Japanese positions on March 28 and "met fanatical resistance from the enemy who occupied formidable, prepared defensive positions." Company A, 182nd Infantry was annihilated when the Japanese detonated an ammunition cache under its position on Go Chan Hill.[47] Maj. Gen. Arnold committed his reserve, the 2nd Battalion, 132nd Infantry, in an attack on Japanese positions northwest of Basak. The remainder of the 132nd Infantry continued its advance north in an attempt to envelop Japanese positions. On March 30, the 182nd Infantry launched a coordinated attack that overran the first line of Japanese fortifications, but the positions extended in such depth that no quick breakthrough was possible.[48]

With concrete, coral, and log ceilings as thick as eight feet, Japanese fortifications on Babag Ridge rivaled those in the Hindenburg Line on the Western Front during World War I. "One hill . . . was found to be a labyrinth of tunnels. Three concrete lined ramps led into the hill. After some twisting and turning they met in the center . . . . Passageways averaged six feet high and were roofed with heavy boards and in some cases with concrete . . . . Innumerable other hills, constructed in the same manner, were found later virtually undamaged by air and artillery bombardment."[49] Infantry had to

10.2: Soldiers of the 3rd Battalion, 132nd Infantry wade ashore on Cebu, March 26, 1945. Eighth Army's amphibious blitzkrieg, with Lt. Gen. Robert Eichelberger's forces conducting thirty-eight amphibious landings in forty-four days, earned for it the nickname "Amphibious Eighth." (Credit: US Army Signal Corps Photo)

clear these complexes one position at a time using flamethrowers, grenades, and demolition charges, supported by tanks, self-propelled artillery, antiaircraft guns used in direct-lay mode, and close air support. Subjected to incessant firepower, "the Japs hung on. They were living underground, and were usually safe from anything except a direct hit."[50] For the next week and a half, progress was measured in hundreds of yards as the Americal troopers ground into the heavily fortified Japanese positions. Infantrymen repulsed a Japanese counterattack on April 5 only after every available man was put on the front line to hold it.

The arrival of the 164th Infantry from Eighth Army reserve on April 9 made possible a new plan of maneuver that would force the Japanese out of their positions. The regiment would envelop the Japanese right (southern) flank. On April 8–9, the 132nd Infantry shifted forces north and attacked the Japanese left flank to divert attention from the pending arrival of the

164th Infantry. The maneuver worked; on April 9 the Japanese, oblivious of troop movements to their south, attacked the 132nd Infantry in the pre-dawn hours and were repulsed "in bitter fighting."[51]

The 164th Infantry, minus the 3rd Battalion which would invade Bohol, assembled in the high ground to the southwest of Japanese lines, shielded by Filipino guerrillas who occupied the ground between it and the 182nd Infantry. The decisive battle for Babag Ridge commenced on April 12 with an attack by all three battalions of the 182nd Infantry supported by tanks, 90mm antiaircraft guns, artillery, airstrikes, and naval gunfire, with the 2nd Battalion, 132nd Infantry attacking on its right (northern) flank. The attack continued the next day against ferocious resistance, with the key terrain of Hill 21 seized only after a bayonet charge broke Japanese lines. The 164th Infantry had meanwhile infiltrated behind the Japanese positions on the ridge, and its appearance in their rear on the morning of April 13, while not decisive, helped to turn the course of the battle. Although the Japanese continued to resist for three more days, their position was becoming increasingly hopeless. The Japanese commander, Maj. Gen. Takeo Manjome, could either fight it out to the end or order a retreat. He chose the latter option, and on April 16 Japanese forces began the evacuation of Babag Ridge and moved north into the mountains, effectively ending the organized defense of the island. When the 164th and 132nd Infantry Regiments linked up on April 18, they overran the final Japanese positions on Babag Ridge.[52] Lt. Gen. Eichelberger labeled the fighting on Babag Ridge as "the toughest positions to reduce, considering the size of the forces involved, that I have ever seen," which was saying a lot, given that he had witnessed the bitter fighting at Buna.[53]

The Americal Division exploited the Japanese withdrawal by seizing key points along the coast, while Filipino guerrillas harassed the small groups of Japanese soldiers that had retreated into the mountainous interior of the island. The 3rd Battalion, 132nd Infantry conducted a shore-to-shore movement to seize Danao without opposition on April 20. The pursuit up the coastal highways was rapid and largely unopposed, with the exception of occasional roadblocks and minefields. From that point to the end of May, patrols probed into the mountainous interior "to locate and destroy the small hostile groups as they wandered about the hills seeking food, water and means of avoiding conflict with American and Guerrilla troops." In the first two weeks of June, a more organized operation to destroy the remnants of Japanese forces succeeded in breaking up any remaining organized units. On June 20, the Americal Division turned over the island to Cushing's guerrillas for garrison and patrolling, while SWPA developed the port facilities at Cebu City to enable the embarkation of a three-division corps for the planned invasion of Japan. In three months of fighting, the Americal Division and Filipino guerrillas had killed more than 5,000 Japanese soldiers.[54]

In comparison with Cebu, the other operations by the Americal Division were cake walks. Only 300 or so Japanese occupied Bohol, and thus Filipino guerrillas controlled most of the island. The 3rd Battalion, 164th Infantry landed at 07:00 on April 11 at Tagbilaran without opposition, as Filipino guerrillas under the command of Maj. Ismael P. Ingeniero had already secured the beaches. Extensive patrolling failed to locate the Japanese until April 15, when an organized defensive position was located north of Ginopolan. The 3rd Battalion concentrated to successfully attack the Japanese positions the next day. The battalion occupied the ridge and repulsed three counterattacks that night. On April 20, the attack continued onto a nearby hill, with similar success. Only small groups of Japanese remained to be eliminated by patrols or to slowly waste away in desolate condition in the hills. On May 7, the American forces completed movement back to Cebu, leaving the island in the hands of Filipino guerrillas.[55]

Given the rugged, mountainous terrain in the middle of Negros, operations to liberate the southern part of the island were conducted independently from operations in the northern part. The 164th Infantry, Americal Division, cleared southern Negros (Negros Oriental) while the 40th Infantry Division and the 503rd Parachute Infantry tackled the bulk of Japanese forces in the northern portion of the island. At 08:00 on April 26, the 164th Infantry assaulted the southeast coast of Negros near Dumaguete and landed without opposition. The 1st Battalion moved rapidly to occupy the town, securing it by 16:30. The regiment then advanced to the west, meeting firm Japanese opposition on high ground to the west of Dumaguete on April 29. Over the next month, the 1st Battalion conducted a slow, sustained advance up the ridges into the rain forest 4,000 feet above sea level. Only concentrated artillery barrages were able to blow the Japanese out of their prepared cave and pillbox positions. By the end of May, the Japanese had withdrawn into the deep interior of the island, protected in part by the onset of the monsoon season. On June 1, two US infantry companies moved by water to the southern end of Negros in order to move north in conjunction with guerrillas, but they encountered no Japanese forces and withdrew six days later. A final battle with Japanese forces west of Dumaguete from June 7 to 12 ended organized resistance, and on June 20 the 164th Infantry redeployed to Cebu.[56]

PCAUs were instrumental in providing relief to the hard-pressed Filipino people on the Visayan islands. Within a day of American landings, PCAUs were operating on Panay (PCAU 13) and Negros (PCAU 26), while PCAUs 15 and 24 supported operations on Cebu, Bohol, and Negros Oriental. They provided emergency relief and medical care and hired local Filipinos to serve as much-needed laborers to assist with logistics and transportation – just as Gen. MacArthur had envisioned in his meeting with President Roosevelt the previous summer. These units reestablished civil government, protected key installations, reopened schools, instituted measures to protect public health and sanitation, established hospitals, and promoted economic revitalization. They distributed clothing and other supplies to the civil population. PCAUs also exchanged currency for new Victory Series of Philippine Treasury Certificates, accredited by the US and Filipino governments.[57] According to the Eighth Army after-action report, "The work done by these units in preventing starvation, epidemics, and public disorder, and in restoring civil government to the Filipinos cannot be underestimated."[58] Civil affairs units had other unforeseen effects as well. According to the Americal Division, "When liberation came only the presence of the Americans prevented a period of liquidation and terror [against collaborators]."[59] The post-war political situation in the Philippines would indeed have looked much different had MacArthur's forces failed to liberate the island archipelago prior to V-J Day.

At the end of the war, around 17,500 Japanese soldiers in the Visayas came down from the mountains to surrender, slightly more than half of the 32,350 who defended the islands against the Eighth Army assaults. American casualties in the Visayas numbered 835 killed and 2,300 wounded.[60] Filipino casualties are unknown, but their sacrifices were vital to the liberation of their country. Guerrillas "did what they could. 'We remained,' they told their liberators, and were grateful that relief had come."[61]

MacArthur and his staff were delighted with Eighth Army's performance, especially the rapid pace of operations and its willingness to conduct operations without overwhelming material superiority. Eichelberger confided to his diary, "Steve [Chamberlin] said that the history of the Visayan campaign would some day be considered a classic."[62] Although the campaign did not receive a lot of attention either then or since, he was not wrong.

Mindanao, the second-largest and southernmost major island in the Philippines, would be invaded last.[63] It did not have to be taken; the war had long since passed the Japanese garrison by. But American prestige was on the line and the welfare of hungry Filipinos was at stake, and MacArthur therefore demanded Mindanao's liberation. "The dogfaces who fought and won this battle of 'prestige' fought it without enthusiasm," the historian of the 24th Infantry Division wrote, "but with a sullen and melancholy hatred."[64]

Mindanao was wild. Fertig's guerrillas might have known their way around the island, but, for US forces entering from the sea, "Maps depicted large expanses of the country in white patches and the legend 'unexplored.'"[65] The road network was primitive. The twisting and poorly maintained Highway 1 ran from Parang on Illana Bay east to Digos on Davao Gulf, a road distance of roughly 120 miles. The Sayre Highway ran from Macajalar Bay in northern Mindanao south to Kabacan, a road distance of roughly 150 miles, where it intersected Highway 1 in the center of the island. "Mindanao, if one excepted urban communities on the northern and southern seacoasts, was pretty much the same primitive land over which Pershing, Harbord, and Frank R. McCoy had campaigned thirty-odd years before," wrote Eichelberger, recalling the history of the Philippine Insurrection at the turn of the century.[66]

On Mindanao, Col. Wendell Fertig's guerrillas had by the spring of 1945 developed into one of the two strongest guerrilla forces in the Philippines, rivaling Col. Russell Volckmann's US Army Forces in the Philippines, Northern Luzon, for that honor. Eichelberger described Fertig as "a slim man with a pleasing manner, but he was fearless and there was iron in his soul."[67] Fertig had divided his 10th Military District into five divisions, totaling 1,680 officers and 23,817 enlisted soldiers, of whom 16,392 were armed. Fertig's headquarters, which had a full general and special staff laid out along American military lines, moved several times to evade detection and destruction by Japanese forces. One of Fertig's most trying tasks was finding the right leaders for each of the many organizations under his command. Many officers (Fertig included) attempted to assume ranks one or two grades higher than they had earned or deserved, while many Filipino guerrillas were utterly unsuited to military leadership. Fertig's great accomplishment, through "tact and sound leadership," was to bring "them all into the fold," including the difficult-to-handle Moros.[68]

By 1945, SWPA had transported roughly 500 tons of weapons, equipment, and supplies to Mindanao, which became a supply base for guerrillas elsewhere in the Philippines. Fertig's radio network had seventy stations. His guerrillas controlled three airfields at Dipolog, Lala, and Barobo, along with much of the interior of the island.[69] The strength of the guerrillas on

Mindanao was partly due to geography; the Japanese had confined their occupation to the coastal towns and cities and the roads connecting them, allowing Filipino guerrillas to control more than 85 percent of the island. Mindanao was also closer to SWPA's base in Australia than the remainder of the Philippines, easing the arming and resupply of Fertig's guerrillas. But their strength was also a strategic calculation, as SWPA had until September 1944 planned to invade Mindanao first before moving on to the other islands in the archipelago, as it was within range of land-based air cover from Morotai. Halsey's raids that month changed that calculation. Instead of being the first island to be liberated, Mindanao would become the last.

Air reconnaissance and guerrilla reports provided a clear picture of Japanese dispositions. Fertig's intelligence summaries kept SWPA intimately informed of Japanese strengths and dispositions on Mindanao. One such summary, dated October 31, 1944, was twenty-nine pages long and contained maps and diagrams of enemy dispositions, airfields, guerrilla and Japanese-held areas, guerrilla organization, and hiding places for Japanese ships, as well as exhibits on troop movements, patrols, ship sightings, guerrilla strength returns, and targeting information.[70]

Lt. Gen. Sōsaku Suzuki commanded the *35th Army* on Mindanao, composed of the *30th* and *100th Divisions*, the latter located in the vicinity of Davao City and the former guarding the northern coast of Mindanao and the Sayre Highway leading south into the island's interior. Both units were short of ammunition and critical supplies, as US submarines had severed the sea lines of communication to the island beginning the previous summer.[71] The *30th Division* had lost four of its nine infantry battalions to the fighting on Leyte. The *100th Division* was composed of unevenly trained personnel, and a third of the soldiers were poorly motivated Koreans. Its fire support amounted to ten artillery pieces and thirty naval guns, all of them short of ammunition.[72] The Eighth Army G-2 estimated that there were 34,000 Japanese troops on Mindanao, the largest garrison outside of Luzon. Fertig's intelligence officer estimated that there were 42,600 Japanese soldiers on Mindanao, which turned out to be nearly correct. The major concentration was from the *100th Division* near Davao Gulf, where the Japanese expected the invasion to commence. The poor transportation network and US air superiority would make any concentration of Japanese forces difficult.[73]

R-Day was set for April 17. Staging out of Leyte, X Corps (Maj. Gen. Franklin C. Sibert, whom Eichelberger had known since their assignment together as lieutenants in Panama) directed the operation. Eichelberger preferred a direct assault on Davao Gulf, but lack of naval support due to the ongoing campaign in Okinawa precluded that scheme. It was just as well, for Japanese troop concentrations and defenses were oriented on defending Davao from a seaward attack. Instead of assaulting Davao Gulf, X Corps would invade the west coast of Mindanao, where Japanese defenses were thin, but doing so would also "necessitate a backbreaking overland march" to reach the main Japanese defenses in the Davao region.[74]

The 24th Infantry Division (Maj. Gen. Roscoe B. Woodruff, the first captain of the West Point Class of 1915 – the "class the stars fell on"), staging out of Mindoro, and the 31st Infantry Division ("Dixie Division," commanded by Maj. Gen. Clarence A. Martin, who had served with Eichelberger at Buna), staging out of Morotai and Sansapor, would carry out landings in the Cotabato–Malabang area, develop a base area and airfields, and attack overland to Davao City. The Dixie Division hailed from the Deep South, including National Guard units from Alabama, Florida, Louisiana, and Mississippi. It had trained for three years in Camp Blanding, Florida; in the Louisiana and Carolina maneuvers; at Camp Bowie, Texas; at Camp Shelby, Mississippi; and finally at Camp Pickett, Virginia, prior to deploying overseas. The division fought in New Guinea and Morotai prior to its assignment to the Mindanao expedition. Despite the US Army's efforts, the 31st Infantry Division maintained its regional culture, including a vicious brand of Jim Crow racism that affected the way it treated friends and enemy alike.[75]

The Philippine 108th Division, commanded by guerrilla leader Lt. Col. Charles Hedges, supported by Marine aircraft, attacked the Japanese garrison at Malabang on March 17 and cleared the airfield and the area around the town by the middle of April. As a result, Eichelberger, aboard the command ship USS *Wasatch*, changed the invasion scheme while en route to Mindanao with the invasion force. X Corps sent only one reinforced battalion to land unopposed at Malabang, while the main force would land seventeen miles south at Parang. Even though Fertig assessed that any landings in the vicinity of Illana Bay would be unopposed, the pre-invasion bombardment commenced as scheduled.[76]

Nearly six months after the invasion of Leyte, the last major amphibious invasion in the Philippines began at 09:00 on April 17 with an assault on the Mindanao coast near Parang by the 19th Infantry Regiment, 24th Infantry Division. The Japanese were caught off balance, expecting instead a landing at Davao. Instead, American forces had landed on the other side of the island and were now headed to Davao from the opposite direction than expected. The only figure on the beach was a Filipina armed with an old American rifle, who greeted the soldiers with a hearty "Victoree – you are welcome."[77] By the end of the day, the Victory Division held thirty-five miles of coastline and was headed east to Davao, aided by the movement of forces via landing craft up the Mindanao River. Reconnaissance parties heading up the river into the heart of darkness reported "many crocodiles but no Japs."[78] Eichelberger compared the operation to the use of gunboats along the Mississippi River during the American Civil War.[79]

A boat battalion of the 3rd Engineer Special Brigade had traveled 1,000 miles from Lingayen Gulf to the mouth of the Mindanao River, arriving, "with amazing precision, in Moro Gulf just as the assault forces of the 24th Division arrived by naval escort," Eichelberger recalled. "It was the kind of timing that no commander in his right mind has any reason to expect."[80] The 19th and 21st Regimental Combat Teams of the 24th Infantry Division attacked east along the poorly maintained Highway 1 as well as sailing up the Mindanao River, and by R plus 5 had taken Kabacan, the southern terminus of the Sayre Highway, which led north to the Del Monte airstrips. The Japanese intelligence and communications system was so bad that it was four days before the *100th Division* commander knew the exact location of the American landings, and he only learned that the Americans had moved up the Mindanao River to Kabacan, with the 31st Infantry Division moving north from there along the Sayre Highway and the 24th continuing east toward Davao, from a commercial radio broadcast emanating from San Francisco.[81]

The 34th Infantry assumed the lead along Highway 1, reaching the Davao Gulf at Digos on April 27, 10 days and 110 miles from its start point on the beach at Parang.[82] There they found abandoned Japanese fortifications, facing the wrong direction. Eichelberger's emphasis on speed paid off handsomely. The pace of the advance had succeeded beyond MacArthur's wildest estimation; he had believed that it would take X Corps three to four months to cross the island and was massively appreciative of the lightning-quick drive.[83] "You run an army in combat just like I would like to have done it," MacArthur told his new favorite army commander.[84]

Geography and weather proved more formidable than the Japanese; at some points, the infantry found the ill-maintained Highway 1 to be "just a tunnel through green vegetation," while men became heat casualties by the score in the "moist, dank, and insufferably hot" climate.[85] According to battalion surgeon Captain George E. Morrissey, the "road looked as if a tornado had swept down [the] column of marching troops, scattering exhausted soldiers on each side. This is the type of weather that Filipinos will not go out in. It is entirely possible that the sun can kill a man."[86] Highway 1 was essentially abandoned in favor of the water route as the division's principal line of communication.

As it reached the east coast of the island, the 24th Infantry Division pivoted north. The 34th and 19th Infantry Regiments leap-frogged one another in the drive to Davao City. Japanese defenses, oriented east to defend against an amphibious invasion from Davao Gulf, proved useless against an advance from the south. By May 1, the lead elements of the 19th Infantry reached the city's outskirts, which it cleared within two days. Nearby, Japanese infantry had turned Hill 550 into a fortress, which was taken only after seventeen days of bombardment and infantry assault. Davao, subject to constant American bombing, was wrecked from end to end, and nearly bereft of inhabitants. "Well, there seems to be almost nobody around to be liberated," remarked Maj. William T. Cameron, head of PCAU 29.[87] But soon

> thousands of Filipinos straggled into Davao, a sick, famished, terrified horde. Madame Baldomera Sexon, the director of Davao's Mission Hospital, testified that some 25,000 Filipinos had died through starvation, disease and murder during Japanese rule. During later stages of the campaign, the Jap military embarked on an orgy of rape and murder which virtually exterminated the inhabitants of five outlying communities.[88]

If ever justification was needed for MacArthur's campaign to liberate the entire Philippine Archipelago, scenes such as those the GIs discovered at Davao were it.

While the Victory Division battled to reach Davao City, the Dixie Division, having landed in the wake of the 24th Infantry Division, began its attack north along the Sayre Highway, which was "at best a third rate road, and the seasonal rains and lack of maintenance had not improved it any."[89] Crossing the Pulangi River on April 27, the 2nd Battalion, 124th Infantry drove northward and at dusk encountered the lead elements of a Japanese battalion moving south. In the ensuing meeting engagement, the superior firepower of the Americans prevailed, forcing the Japanese to withdraw and enabling the Dixie Division to establish a solid presence north of the river.[90]

Terrain and weather combined to slow the advance, with nightly precipitation turning the main supply route into an impassable river of mud. Engineers were as critical as infantry in this advance; of the 159 bridges encountered in the 25-day advance, all but 2 had been destroyed either by the Japanese or by guerrillas. The 124th Infantry Regiment ran into difficulties when it encountered a series of steep gorges north of Kabacan. Infantry negotiated the steep slopes to clear the far sides, while engineers rigged cables to span the gorges and bulldozed tons of dirt into them. C-47 aircraft dropped supplies to the forward troops, which kept the advance going, and Marine SBD dive bombers provided close air support until artillery could move forward. Engineers ultimately built hundreds of bypasses, "and sixteen Bailey bridges and sixty-five wooded bridges were installed on the Sayre Highway."[91]

On May 3, the 124th Infantry Regiment reached the northwest terminus of the Kibawe–Talomo trail, which Maj. Gen. Sibert believed led to Davao Gulf. After conducting an aerial reconnaissance of the terrain southeast from Kibawe that confirmed Fertig's judgment that the trail was mostly "a figment of the imagination," Eichelberger limited the advance down the trail to a reinforced battalion.[92] "My many flights over Mindanao had convinced me that our job was to drive the Japanese into those barbarous wastes," Eichelberger confided in his memoirs, "and that, once they were prisoners of the terrain, we should let them stay there and starve."[93] Heavy rains now descended on Mindanao as the monsoon season arrived, making even the slightest ground movement difficult.

The main effort continued north, encountering heavy opposition in what the troops christened the Colgan Woods, named after a brave Catholic chaplain who risked (and ultimately gave) his life to minister to the needs of the wounded.[94] Here the Japanese had created a spider web of well-camouflaged foxholes, presenting the attacking forces with a difficult tactical problem, made worse by the delay in bringing up artillery because of the conditions along the Sayre Highway. The artillery finally arrived after a heroic effort by engineers to repair the road, and, after an intensive artillery barrage, the 124th Infantry cracked the Japanese line on May 12. Pvt. First Class William E. Hammer recalled the grisly scene in the aftermath of battle:

> Our company went in to bring the dead out. The area was devastated. Dead lay all about – ours and Japs. A Jap was pinned to a tree with a bayonet. And then there was a chaplain and several others huddled together. All were dead . . .. The hot tropical sun had already begun to bloat the bodies which created the most indescribable and unforgettable odor.[95]

The monsoon season turned the roads of Mindanao into streams of mud. Given the precarious state of the Sayre Highway, Eichelberger now decided to open a logistics node on the northern coast of Mindanao. On May 10, the 108th Infantry (detached from the 40th Infantry Division) landed unopposed at Macajalar Bay, the northern terminus of the Sayre Highway, with assistance from Filipino guerrillas, who cleared the beaches ahead of the landing.[96] The regiment then advanced south to link up with the 155th Regimental Combat Team of the 31st Infantry Division, which had leapfrogged past the 124th Infantry. The two forces converged at the village of Impalutao on May 23.[97] The Japanese in central Mindanao were now caught in a vise, "with only three alternatives left to them; death, surrender, or a retreat into the trackless jungle to the east of the Sayre Highway."[98]

Accompanied by Eichelberger, MacArthur sailed in the USS *Boise* from Manila past Mindoro to Mindanao, retracing his perilous journey from Corregidor in 1942, to celebrate the opening of the Sayre Highway with a parade by the 3rd Battalion, 108th Infantry on June 5.[99] The 120-mile "pounding and spine-cracking ride" round trip by jeep from Macajalar Bay to the 31st Infantry Division headquarters at Malaybalay, which MacArthur insisted upon undertaking rather than flying, took eight grueling hours. "General MacArthur and I are both lucky," Eichelberger wrote to his wife, "that we are not this moment looking up at the Sayre Highway – with the rain in our faces – from the ground floor of a canyon. What a road!"[100] MacArthur then stopped at Cebu, Negros, and Panay, before sailing onward to witness the Australian invasion of northwest Borneo on June 10. MacArthur finished his tour of the Eighth Army area by visiting Jolo, Davao, and Zamboanga City.

The 124th and 155th Infantry Regiments pursued the Japanese east into the mountains, held up by the tortuous terrain and atrocious weather as much as by Japanese defenses. The attack along the ridges to Silae broke the back of what was left of the *30th Division*, which retreated east toward the supposed sanctuary of the Agusan Valley. A battalion of the 155th Infantry moved up the Agusan River aboard landing craft, and, together with Fertig's guerrillas, they kept the Japanese remnants on the move. Surviving Japanese who were not killed by guerrillas or air raids succumbed to starvation and disease or eked out a meager existence in the mountains of eastern Mindanao.[101]

While the 31st Infantry Division attacked up the Sayre Highway to destroy the *30th Division*, the 24th Infantry Division attacked to destroy the *100th Division*, which was entrenched in the hills to the west of Davao City. The going was tough, with advances slow against determined Japanese resistance. The 21st and 34th Infantry Regiments

10.3: Gen. Douglas MacArthur; Maj. Gen. William H. Arnold, commanding general, Americal Division; and Lt. Gen. Robert L. Eichelberger, commanding general, Eighth Army, near Cebu City, June 6, 1945. This was MacArthur's last trip outside Manila until his journey to Tokyo to accept the Japanese surrender. (Credit: US Army Signal Corps Photo)

took most of May to pound their way through the strongest defenses in the center of the Japanese line, reaching the village of Tugbok by May 28. Exploiting Japanese weakness, Woodruff ordered the attack to continue in order to shatter the center of the Japanese line, while the 19th Infantry Regiment advanced to the north of the Davao River to link up with Filipino guerrillas and attack the easternmost Japanese positions in the vicinity of Mandog. By June 10, the *100th Division* was in full retreat. Elements of the division defended the road junction at Calinan and from there withdrew northwest to the barrio of Kibangay, but by the middle of July the Japanese troops in the area were running low on food. They withdrew into the mountains, there to endure a miserable existence until the end of the war, hunted by Filipino guerrillas.[102]

A battalion of the 167th Infantry meanwhile attacked southeast along the Talomo trail, ostensibly to fall on the rear of the *100th Division*. "The few ink scratches referred to on tactical maps as the Talomo Trail were at best a gross exaggeration of terminology," the division recorded in its operations report:

> From the origin of the trail at Kibawe to the Pulangi River there had once been a diminutive roadway which subsequent to the first few days of the operation had been reduced to a sea of viscous mud varying in depth from ankle to waist. East of the Pulangi River the so-called trail was an inferior foot path, through mountainous terrain, over which even the formerly dependable carabao could not be employed. Supply to the front was somewhat alleviated by the seizure of the drop area on the high plateau, but medical installations (excepting aid stations) could not be transported east of the river. Problems of evacuation were paramount. Casualties were carried over the rugged terrain by litter, taxing the soldier bearers to the utmost of their endurance.[103]

Despite these handicaps, the infantry attacked down the Kibawe–Talomo trail, "fighting through torrential rains in knee deep mud over what has truly been described as some of the world's worst terrain."[104] By the end of the war, the battalion was still thirty miles short of linking up with Filipino guerrillas in the vicinity of Kibangay.[105]

The last operation on Mindanao was an attack on Japanese units in the Sarangani Bay area, conducted by the 1st Battalion, 21st Infantry; Filipino guerrillas; and a provisional battalion comprised of antiaircraft units. The operation began on July 8 and ended with the conclusion of hostilities. Ironically, this was the site of the initial invasion of the Philippines as envisioned by SWPA in the summer of 1944; it turned out to be the final operation of the campaign.[106]

True to his nature of underestimating Japanese troop strength, MacArthur had told Eichelberger in May 1945 that "he did not believe there were four thousand Japanese left alive on Mindanao."[107] At the end of the war, Eighth Army calculated Japanese losses on Mindanao as 12,863 killed, 598 taken prisoner, and 22,441 surrendered after end of hostilities – 35,902 total, although this number does not include civilians who turned themselves in or those 8,000 or so Japanese who were killed or died of disease or starvation in the mountains and whose bodies were never located.[108] Of this number, guerrillas on Mindanao accounted for 8,316 Japanese fatalities – a full division of Japanese troops.[109] More importantly, their operations had kept the spirit of resistance alive and allowed Filipinos agency in the liberation of their homeland.

Eichelberger had a distinguished career in the Pacific War, rescuing operations gone amiss at Buna and Biak and outmaneuvering Japanese forces at Hollandia and on Mindanao. But his crowning achievement was the broader Visayan–Mindanao campaign, which liberated much of the Philippines and alleviated the suffering of the Filipino people under Japanese occupation at a modest cost in blood and treasure. This was an amphibious blitzkrieg, with Eighth Army conducting thirty-eight amphibious landings in forty-four days – nearly one a day – from February 19 to April 3, 1945, earning for it the nickname "Amphibious Eighth."[110]

MacArthur was generous in his praise of Eighth Army's accomplishments. "My heartiest commendations for the brilliant execution of the Visayan campaign," he wrote to Eichelberger. "This is a model of what a light but aggressive command can accomplish in rapid exploitation."[111] Eichelberger had accepted his assignments and pursued their accomplishment with the minimal forces SWPA had allocated to him. Eighth Army accomplished a great deal with the shipping and airpower available, in part by operating with less margin for error logistically than prescribed by doctrine. But it was a risk Eichelberger was willing to accept, given overwhelming US air and sea supremacy in the Central and Southern Philippines.[112]

His West Point classmate Lt. Gen. George S. Patton, Jr. gave Eichelberger perhaps the greatest compliment. Anticipating a transfer to the Pacific to fight the Japanese, Patton reflected on the challenges ahead. "In my limited experience with amphibious attacks, I found them the most dangerous form of sport yet devised," he wrote to Eichelberger. "If I should be so fortunate, I am going to sit at your feet and learn how to do it."[113]

11

REBIRTH

History will do its own winnowing.[1]

Yay Panlilio, *The Crucible*

The Japanese government sued for peace on August 10, and six days later the Japanese *Imperial General HQ* informed MacArthur it would probably take another twelve days to notify all units in the Philippines.[2] But convincing troops on the ground to surrender after the cessation of hostilities was often easier said than done. On Cebu, the Americal Division dropped leaflets on Japanese positions informing them of the surrender, but the Japanese rejected them as propaganda. Only after the Japanese were able to repair a wireless set and contact Tokyo to get direct word of the surrender did they agree to give up. American forces directed the Japanese to collection points, where they were disarmed, their wounded sent to hospitals, and the remainder placed in detention camps.[3] Stragglers, unaware of Japan's capitulation, continued to surrender for a year after the official ceremony in Tokyo Bay. Twenty Japanese soldiers who had been hiding in a jungle-filled ravine in a remote area of Corregidor did not surrender until January 1, 1946.[4] One officer, 2nd Lieut. Hiroo Onoda, held out on Lubang Island off the southeastern coast of Batangas until formally relieved of his duty on March 10, 1974, by his former commanding officer, Major Yoshimi Taniguchi, who was flown from Japan for the ceremony. Onoda received a hero's welcome in Japan.[5]

The survivors who surrendered were among the lucky few. Japanese casualties from October 20, 1944, to June 29, 1945, in the Philippines totaled 304,092 killed and 14,746 taken prisoner.[6] Sixth and Eighth Armies together destroyed twenty-three Japanese divisions: *1st, 8th, 10th, 16th, 19th, 23rd, 26th, 30th, 100th, 102nd, 103rd, 105th,* and *2nd Tank;* the *2nd Airborne Brigade* (reinforced to divisional strength); the *54th, 55th, 58th, 61st,* and *68th Independent Mixed Brigades* (reinforced to divisional strength); three divisional units organized from twenty-eight independent battalions known as the *Kobayashi, Suzuki,* and *Shimbu* commands; and three naval divisions.[7]

US forces in the Philippines campaign sustained 60,717 battle casualties, 16,233 of them killed in action or died of wounds.[8] Infantrymen sustained 90 percent of the battle casualties, and most of the non-battle casualties as well. Sixth Army alone suffered more than 93,000 non-battle casualties on Luzon, and although most of these soldiers returned to their units after a stay in the hospital, many others suffered life-long physical and mental debilitation from wounds and post-traumatic stress disorder. In the 38th Infantry Division, which is representative of other combat divisions, combat stress casualties represented nearly 10 percent of total casualties, clustered primarily in the infantry regiments.[9] Non-battle casualties in the Southwest Pacific Theater eclipsed battle casualties by a wide margin and exceeded those in other theaters of war, primarily due to the variety of diseases afflicting soldiers in SWPA as opposed to those found in other combat theaters. Malaria, which had ravaged American ranks in New Guinea, was controlled by Atabrine, reducing the incidence of the disease from 361 cases per 1,000 men in New Guinea to just 25–30 cases per 1,000 men in the Philippines.[10] Shortages of combat divisions meant that units fought for months on end without rest, exacerbating combat stress casualties; this was a problem in the European Theater of Operations as well.[11]

The Filipino people suffered more – by far – than either the Japanese or American forces and incurred the most civilian dead as a percentage of the pre-war population of any Asian nation, including China. Depending on the source consulted, the Philippines suffered between 3.5 and 5.6 percent dead (630,000 to 1 million people) out of a pre-war population of 18.1 million, ranking just behind Poland, the Soviet Union, Germany and Austria, Greece, Yugoslavia, and Hungary – all of them subject to Hitler's "Final Solution."[12]

There is no doubt that the treatment of the Filipino people by the *14th Area Army* and other Japanese forces was horrendous. Japanese soldiers killed noncombatants, tortured suspected guerrillas and their sympathizers, raped women, and looted Filipino food and possessions, often with abandon. Their rapacious conduct during the fighting for Manila contributed to the excessive death toll of civilians in that battle. The Filipino people wanted justice, and MacArthur, in his role as Supreme Commander for the Allied Powers, demanded accountability. He aimed the hand of justice at the commander of the *14th Area Army*, Gen. Tomoyuki Yamashita, and the commander of Japanese forces in the Philippines during the Bataan Death March, Lt. Gen. Masaharu Homma. MacArthur convened a military commission composed of five general officers – none of them with legal training – to try Yamashita on the charge of failing "to control the operations of the members of his command, permitting them to commit brutal atrocities and other high crimes against the people of the United States and its allies and dependencies, particularly the Philippines; and he, General Tomoyuki Yamashita, thereby violated the laws of war."[13] This would be the first time in history that a commander would be tried for the actions of his troops not because he ordered them to commit war crimes, or knew about their actions but did nothing to stop them, but because he failed to control their murderous conduct. "The charge against Yamashita," writes military lawyer and historian Allan Ryan, "thrust the principle of [command] responsibility into the realm of criminal accountability."[14]

Yamashita was arraigned on October 8, 1945, in the ballroom of the American High Commissioner's residence in Manila. The trial began on October 29, with prosecution witnesses detailing the grotesque actions of Japanese soldiers since the American invasion. Yamashita sat calmly, listening to the testimony. None of it directly linked him with the atrocities committed; the prosecution could not present a smoking gun to tie the general with orders to commit war crimes. Yamashita did not want to fight in Manila, and he had ordered the garrison to withdraw. Rear Adm. Iwabuchi had other ideas and disobeyed his orders, believing he had to first accomplish the missions given to him by his naval boss. Isolated in his headquarters in Baguio, Yamashita had no idea what was happening in Manila and most certainly did not order Japanese troops there – most of them naval forces – to run amok. The commission was not interested in his testimony.[15]

There was plenty of available evidence linking Japanese units to the wholesale slaughter of noncombatants in the guise of suppressing guerrillas, with some written evidence supposedly linking these actions to army orders, but the prosecution did not make the case. Evidence exists of Japanese officers writing in their diaries that they were eliminating entire villages on the orders of the *14th Area Army*.[16] The problem for the prosecution was that a written order never surfaced, other than one issued on October 11, 1944, for the suppression of armed guerrillas, which certainly did not include unarmed women and children.[17] Perhaps subordinate officers were merely using "army orders" as an excuse to justify their horrific actions. On the witness stand, Yamashita's chief of staff, Gen. Akira Mutō, denied that his commander had ever issued orders for the killing of noncombatant civilians.[18] More likely, subordinate unit commanders took Yamashita's order and twisted it to their own purposes. "Ultimately, the word 'guerrilla' evolved into the convenient euphemism to justify for the Japanese their act of dealing death, first to all males, and eventually to all Filipinos, including women and children," writes one Filipino historian. "The guerrilla was the enemy. All Filipinos were guerrillas. All Filipinos must be liquidated."[19] But the prosecution could not connect Yamashita to any of it.

It did not matter. The charge was not that Yamashita had ordered the atrocities, or that he had willingly allowed them to proceed. The charge was instead that the general had failed to prevent the atrocities, regardless of his ability to actually do so.[20] "How can I be convicted of crimes I didn't even know about?" Yamashita had rhetorically asked a reporter from the International News Service, Pat Robinson, before his trial had begun.[21] How indeed. On Friday, December 7, 1945 – four years after the Japanese attack on Pearl Harbor initiated the Pacific War – the military tribunal found Yamashita guilty as charged and sentenced him to death by hanging. The defense appealed the case to the US Supreme Court, which upheld the verdict on the basis of the Hague Convention of 1907, which the US Senate had ratified, despite the fact that criminal liability for command responsibility is not embedded in the law of war.[22] MacArthur approved the death sentence, which was carried out on February 23, 1946, at the prison camp of Los Baños, which had once housed US prisoners of war. Yamashita's ghost – the principle of command accountability for the actions of one's subordinates – is still with us today, regardless of how haphazardly it has been applied over the years.[23]

Homma followed Yamashita to the grave. A military tribunal held in the High Commissioner's residence in Manila from January 3 to February 11, 1946, convicted him on the basis of the actions of his troops during the Bataan Death March. He was executed by firing squad in Los Baños on April 3, 1946.

The twin drives in the Pacific under two commanders, Nimitz and MacArthur, worked better than the JCS had reason to believe. Operations in two separate theaters kept the Japanese on the horns of a dilemma and forced them to separate their forces to parry blows hundreds if not thousands of miles apart. The strategy worked because the United States could produce enough war matériel and field enough armies, air forces, and navies to sustain both arms of its Pacific advance, even as its armed forces focused their main effort on the defeat of Nazi Germany in Europe. Even then, SWPA's share of the American war effort never exceeded 15 percent of the total.[24]

In just nine months, the Philippines campaign isolated the Japanese homeland from its conquered empire to the south, made possible an air and sea blockade to prevent the resources of the Netherlands East Indies from reaching Japan, gained a base equivalent to the British Isles in size, liberated the Philippines and its people from Japanese occupation, freed Allied prisoners of war and civilian detainees held in camps in the Philippines, destroyed the majority of the remaining Japanese fleet, and destroyed several thousand aircraft.[25] The campaign gained ports and airfields that were needed to support an invasion of Japan, as the facilities in the Marianas and on Okinawa were insufficient to host the number of troops needed for that endeavor. The JCS at the time believed that the liberation of the Philippines was a necessary precondition to the invasion of Japan, and modern arguments to the contrary are reliant on a healthy dose of hindsight.[26]

Despite MacArthur's reliance on a staff created from a single service, joint operations in the Southwest Pacific were exceptional and are worthy of study in professional military educational institutions. SWPA undertook more amphibious landings – eighty-seven in all – than occurred in any other theater, the Central Pacific included. After Buna, MacArthur became a convert to island hopping, even to the extent of taking credit for perfecting the concept, which was more than a stretch of the truth and not one of his brightest moments. SWPA logisticians performed legendary feats of improvisation on a shoestring budget and made possible MacArthur's return to the Philippines.

Air support was crucial to the effectiveness of MacArthur's operations in the Philippines, as he lacked the number of troops otherwise required to destroy the Japanese forces in the islands. In a month and a half of fighting on Luzon between January 28 and March 10, 1945, the Fifth Air Force flew more than 24,000 sorties in support of ground forces, dropping nearly 12,000 tons of bombs and firing roughly 8 million rounds of .50-caliber ammunition in close support – and this amount despite the fact that MacArthur forbade use of air support in the Battle of Manila, which occurred during the period.[27] During the entire Luzon campaign, Fifth Air Force flew 57,663 close air support sorties, with Marine dive bombers accounting for 8,556 of them.[28] By the end of the campaign, commanders invariably preferred Marine close air support, which Marine airmen had honed to a fine art in the interwar period and in the early years of the Pacific War.[29]

Japanese forces fought well under difficult conditions. Yamashita was proud of the performance of his infantry. In an interview with several members of the Pacific War Board on September 8, 1945, at New Bilibid Prison, Yamashita stated, "If we had had your artillery and your air support, we would have won."[30] His plan to cede the central plain and fight in the mountains extended the Luzon campaign until the end of the war. MacArthur did not need to fight for the high ground, other than to secure the water sources for the city of Manila. He could have left Japanese forces in northern Luzon to wither on the vine, as US and Australian forces had done with the remaining Japanese on Bougainville in the South Pacific. But MacArthur was determined to liberate every last square inch of Philippine territory, and largely achieved that goal, albeit at a cost.

Filipinos fought for their own liberation as members of the resistance, examined below, and assisted US forces as guides or as day laborers in transportation, warehousing, construction, and other fields. They also governed liberated areas, reducing the workload on already overburdened PCAUs. Their support validated MacArthur's argument that SWPA could liberate the Philippines with a lean combat service support structure because of the presence of a loyal and cooperative population.

MacArthur was central to the Philippines campaign. Despite his self-centered posturing, his talents at the politico-strategic level were undeniable. Without his strategic acumen, the New Guinea campaign would have lasted much longer than it did or might not have been pursued at all, possibly resulting in JCS approval for what would have been a problematic and possibly disastrous invasion of Formosa. His arguments for the liberation of the Filipino people, who lived after all on American territory, melded political, humanitarian, and strategic concerns. If his political arguments overstepped the authority of a theater commander, they also resonated with the president, who agreed with him on the matter. MacArthur's strategic flexibility and willingness to accept calculated risks led to astonishing successes in the Admiralty Islands, at Hollandia, and in Leyte, which accelerated the campaign in the Southwest Pacific in ways that a more unimaginative commander might not have envisioned. He was the right commander for the Southwest Pacific Theater and expertly played his role. Redemption was his reward.

MacArthur, of course, had his faults. He was a Victorian man of destiny who wanted and needed to be seen as a great man on the stage of history, and thus was extremely proud, self-serving, sensitive to criticism, and unwilling to share the spotlight with others. His belief in his own infallibility and reluctance to consider contrary opinions led to errors of judgment that put his forces at risk on more than one occasion. MacArthur instilled confidence and engendered loyalty to those who served under him, and quickly replaced those he believed failed to support him. His detractors, many of whom originated from outside the organizations MacArthur commanded, viewed him as egotistical, haughty, willful, and aloof.[31]

MacArthur was intelligent and possessed a first-class mind, which did not always extend to his judgment of people. His choice of subordinates was sometimes questionable. He found excellent subordinate commanders in Kenney, Krueger, Kinkaid, Eichelberger, Whitehead, and Barbey. His staff was hard-working and loyal and some, such as deputy chief of staff Richard Marshall and the SWPA operations officer, Stephen Chamberlin, were excellent. But MacArthur held on to the Bataan Gang long after some of them, such as Sutherland and Willoughby, needed to be replaced, and he embraced others, such as Courtney Whitney, who should never have been brought onto the staff in the first place.

Even those who deeply admired MacArthur, such as Kenney, were not exceptionally close to him. "MacArthur was never able to develop a feeling of warmth and comradeship with those about him," writes Daniel Barbey, his exceptional amphibious force commander. "He had their respect but not their sympathetic understanding or their affection. He could not inspire [with] the electrifying leadership Halsey had. He was too aloof and too correct in manner, speech, and dress. He had no small talk, but when discussing military matters he was superb."[32] MacArthur was comfortable in small-group settings and used his aides as sounding boards.

MacArthur was loyal to those who were loyal to him, but the one thing he denied even his closest subordinates was publicity. MacArthur wanted to be known not just as a great strategic leader, but as a great battlefield commander as well. This meant denying publicity to the officers at those echelons. They would receive promotions and awards, but not public recognition, for their exploits.[33] Some officers, such as Krueger, were just fine with this limitation. Others, such as Eichelberger, were (understandably) resentful. The troops, of course, could not understand why the American people knew far more about units in the European Theater than they did about units in the Southwest Pacific. Patton's Third Army became the stuff of legend; Krueger's Sixth and Eichelberger's Eighth Armies were hidden under the cover of "MacArthur's forces" and buried deep in the history books.

Despite his belief in himself, MacArthur was not an exceptional operational and tactical leader. He often overlooked (or failed to appreciate) Japanese capabilities in his plans and orders, such as at Buna and Biak, and seriously underestimated Japanese strength on Luzon. Although he was personally courageous and visited the front lines on several occasions (going too far forward a few times), at other times he was ignorant of

11.1: General of the Army Douglas MacArthur, Supreme Allied Commander, in Manila, August 1945. By the end of the war, his redemption was complete, albeit at a cost. (Credit: US Army Signal Corps Photo)

conditions at the front, such as in Bataan, at Buna and Biak, in Leyte, and in Manila and northern Luzon. His visits to the frontlines, when they occurred, seemed to be more about satisfying his need to demonstrate personal courage than to inspire the soldiers under his command. As a result, MacArthur's soldiers never embraced him in the way that, say, Field Marshal William Slim's soldiers did.[34]

To many, MacArthur was and is an enigma.[35] He was a consummate actor who played the role a given situation called for, and thus different people viewed him differently depending on the performance.[36] "Once, when asked his opinion of MacArthur, Australian Field Marshal Thomas Blamey replied that 'the best and the worst things you hear about him are both true.'"[37] MacArthur would go on to become Supreme Commander for the Allied Powers in post-war Japan and play an enormously constructive role in the rehabilitation of that country. He would proceed to lead US and UN forces in Korea, resulting in another operational triumph at Inchon every bit as dramatic as the leap to Hollandia. True to form, MacArthur would then ignore intelligence regarding the buildup of Chinese forces and their intervention in the conflict. Determined to expand the war into China, MacArthur's statements delving into the realm of foreign policy led to his relief by President Harry S. Truman, who was not as forgiving of insubordination by the supreme commander as was his predecessor in office.

The Philippines were free, but they had been devastated by occupation and liberation. Manila, the scene of intense fighting in February 1945, was piled with rubble. Radio reporter William Dunn recorded, "Manila is a mess of crumbled rubble. On damp days you can still catch the stench of rotting human flesh beneath the piles of steel and masonry."[38] Most of it was Japanese, which Filipinos allowed to rot until American sanitation teams cleared the area. Aerial spraying aimed to reduce the population of flies and mosquitoes.[39] With so much untreated sewage, Sixth Army's sanitation experts were amazed that Manila escaped a cholera epidemic.

The rehabilitation of Manila was a major undertaking that consumed an enormous amount of attention from the SWPA civil affairs section. The fighting in Manila had left at least 100,000 Filipinos homeless. Fighting had destroyed a third of the city and left another third badly damaged. Public utilities such as electricity and water treatment were not operational. Filipinos were reliant on SWPA resources for food and medical care. The bulk of relief supplies, including food, came from the United States.[40]

By the end of the war, thirty PCAUs operated on every major island and in nearly every province in the Philippines. Col. George D. Sears was in charge of civil affairs for Sixth Army. The PCAUs under his control conducted civil relief operations and cared for refugees. They distributed captured Japanese food and medicines until supplies for civil relief arrived via ship. The Manila PCAU soup kitchens fed as many as 45,000 Filipinos each day.[41] PCAUs established food rationing systems in their areas to control the distribution of food as best as they could. Wages and prices were restored to pre-war levels, a measure intended to control inflation.[42]

But, with goods scare, the emergence of a thriving black market was inevitable. "Black-market operations assumed serious proportions as the campaign progressed," Gen. Krueger recalled. "Military property, principally food and clothing, but also medicines, was illicitly acquired by Filipinos by gift, barter or theft."[43] Staple commodities went for up to ten times the price set by the Commonwealth government. With just ten officers and thirty-nine enlisted men, PCAUs were unable to police the multitude of transactions in their areas.[44] The black market would abate only when the supply of much needed goods balanced demand.

President Osmeña did what he could to alleviate the suffering of his people, but he had little real power, which lay in MacArthur's and Washington's hands. MacArthur had the authority to appoint temporary officials to replace those of the collaborationist regime, and he gave preference to leaders of guerrilla units that he had recognized.[45] PCAUs removed Huks from office wherever they found them, which proved difficult in Pampanga because of the popularity of the group in that province.[46]

In May 1945, Osmeña accompanied Sen. Millard Tydings (Democrat, Maryland) and a nine-man Filipino Rehabilitation Commission to survey the Commonwealth's reconstruction and rehabilitation needs. "The commission has a heavy task in front of it," reported William Dunn. "Manila lay in ruins, along with a number of other cities and towns in the islands, goods are scarce, inflation rampant, and the black market booming. The situation cries out for 'the moral rebirth of a shaken nation.'"[47] As a start, the restored Commonwealth government lifted restrictions on churches and reopened schools, which had been forced to conduct lessons in Japanese during the occupation, if they were allowed to operate at all.[48]

Despite the challenges they faced, SWPA civil affairs officers met the needs of the majority of the Filipino people. "It should be pointed out that the effort to relieve the embattled City of Manila was in the discharge of an emergency responsibility of the United States which finds little precedent in our country's history," the civil affairs section recorded in its after-action report:

> However debatable may be some of the methods employed to meet this emergency, the fact remains that the responsibility was fully discharged – without incidence of starvation, without food riots or other disorders, and without serious threat of epidemic – from the time our forces entered the City to fight street by street for its occupation until normalcy had been restored and the responsibility transferred to the civil authorities.[49]

While civil affairs teams focused on the relief of the needs of the Filipino people, engineers went to work rebuilding the Commonwealth's infrastructure. The job began even as combat troops marched south toward Manila. The dry weather and expansive land mass of Luzon made the siting of logistical facilities and air bases much easier than on Leyte. Engineers and logisticians built Base M at Lingayen Gulf and Base R in Batangas to meet the immediate needs of the Sixth Army. Once the Battle of Manila was over, they developed Base X in the Manila area. This base included hospitals in a variety of civilian buildings and a purpose-built hospital complex at Mandaluyong on the southeastern edge of Manila. By September 30, Base X boasted 14,450 beds, which would have been filled to capacity had Operation Olympic, the invasion of Japan, occurred.[50] Thankfully, the end of the war made most of the hospital capacity superfluous, and it was quickly downsized.

Existing infrastructure required extensive rehabilitation. The lines of communication running south from Lingayen Gulf to Manila, primarily National Highways 3 and 5, required much needed repairs after years of neglect by Japanese occupation forces. The grading, rolling, and surfacing of these roads was a fairly straightforward task. More difficult was replacing the numerous destroyed bridges along the routes. The bridge across the Agno River twenty miles from the beaches of Lingayen Gulf along Highway 3 was a case in point. Four of the 13 160-foot spans had been demolished, requiring Sixth Army engineers to emplace float bridging to get the combat forces across. Engineers began repair of the bridge on January 21 by dropping the damaged trusses into the river and replacing them with triple-double Bailey bridging, which resembled a huge erector set. By February 4, the bridge was opened to thirty-five-ton traffic, allowing the pontoon bridge to be pulled up and moved further south, where additional crossings required its use.[51]

Manila was especially hard hit. The Japanese had destroyed all of the bridges across the Pasig River bisecting Manila, as well as the city's utilities, port facilities, power and water systems, and business establishments. What the Japanese didn't destroy, American artillery had devastated in the parts of the city that had become a battlefield. In the near term, the demolition of the water system that serviced Manila was of particular concern, as the use of untreated water could lead to an outbreak of cholera. The damage to the city's water system was extensive; upwards of 10,000 breakages in water mains caused the loss of 65 percent of the city's water through leakage. Quick action by the 1st Cavalry Division saved much of the Novaliches Reservoir from destruction, but enemy demolition parties damaged a portion of the aqueduct connecting the Novaliches Dam with the Balara Filters along with the outlet to the San Juan Reservoir. Engineer parties rerouted the water flow to bypass the damaged installations, restoring partial water service to Manila by February 21. The making of more permanent repairs to water lines "was a very slow and tedious process." Until then, engineers manned 30 water distribution points scattered throughout north-ern Manila, which provided 800,000 gallons per day, supported by 12 mobile purification units. By late May, water pressure had been restored to pre-war levels, and, by the end of July, "over 30 miles of storm drains, 105 miles of sanitary sewers, and 15 miles of open drainage ditches were cleaned, repaired, and restored to service." By the end of the war, engineers had repaired 60 percent of the damaged water lines, and, by the end of 1945, "the entire water system had been restored to operating condition."[52]

The electrical distribution system in Manila was in even worse shape. Japanese troops had systematically demolished the city's utilities as the Battle of Manila raged, including 80 percent of the electrical generating and distribution system. Until engineers could repair the system, which required shipment of new diesel generators and other parts from the United States, power to critical installations and utilities came from portable generators. There was never enough power to go around. Until more generators and a large floating power plant could arrive, the US Navy came to the rescue by sailing the destroyer escort USS *Wiseman* (DE 667) from Leyte to Manila. "Equipped with special transformers and control equipment which permitted its generators to run in parallel and transmit power at commercial voltages," the *Wiseman* supplemented the local power grid in Manila. The 3,500 kilowatts of electricity provided by the ship, however, was a drop in the requirement bucket. The floating power barge *Impedance*, which could generate 30,000 kilowatts of electrical power, was not due to arrive until September 1. In the meantime, the Navy sent another destroyer escort, the USS *Whitehurst* (DE 634), to augment the power grid. By November 1945, repairs to the electrical generating stations and power grid increased available power to Manila to 41,000 kilowatts, and the des-troyer escorts were released for other duties.[53]

Immediately after the fall of Manila, Army engineers and Navy Seabees, aided by hundreds of Chinese and Filipino laborers, went to work rehabilitat-ing the port of Manila and Subic Bay Naval Base. The extensive work involved removing most of the 600 sunken vessels within Manila harbor, restoring or building 24 Liberty ship berths, and dredging the harbors. By May 1945, Manila Harbor could handle 90,000 deadweight tons of cargo per week. Subic Bay was transformed into a major naval base, including an amphibious training center, a submarine base, a supply depot, and a degaussing station.[54] At the end of the war, four Seabee battalions were still working on the base, which would become the primary US naval facility in the Western Pacific during the Cold War. By the end of the year, Manila had room for thirty Liberty ships at a time, making it one of the largest port facilities in the world.[55]

The city of Manila would take years to recover, as artillery fire had destroyed 613 city blocks containing 11,000 buildings. The destruction rivaled that in the Allied cities of Nanjing, Warsaw, and Brest. The destruction encompassed many of the city's libraries and cultural artifacts. Tons of unexploded ordnance littered the city and had to be collected and disposed of before it claimed the lives of Manila's residents. Bulldozers cleared nearly 4,000 city blocks, while workers hauled away nearly 31,000 truckloads of debris. Aerial spraying aimed to reduce the population of flies and mosquitoes.[56]

The US Consulate General in Manila opined that rehabilitation of the city would require ten to fifteen years, which if anything was optimistic.[57] Congress passed the Philippine Rehabilitation Act in April 1946, which allocated $620 million for reconstruction activities, nearly $10 billion in 2024 dollars.[58] Even with extensive US assistance, Manila never regained its pre-war status as the "Pearl of the Orient."

Politics quickly came to the fore as liberation dawned. Of concern was when to convene the Commonwealth legislature, which had been elected in the fall of 1941 but had never met. Osmeña had wanted to weed out collaborators among the elected senators and representatives first, but, pressured by MacArthur and Manuel Roxas, who had been elected to the pre-war senate, he soon relented. In June 1945, the Philippine Congress convened in Manila, and, with a majority of senators having served in the collaborationist regime, they elected Roxas as president of the Senate. The legislators also made MacArthur an honorary citizen of the Philippines and provided other honors as well, perhaps none so moving to a soldier as to "be carried in perpetuity on the company rolls of the units of the Philippine Army and, at parade roll calls, when his name is called, the senior noncommissioned officer shall answer 'Present in Spirit.'"[59]

No issue was as incendiary as the treatment of collaborators. Osmeña attempted to empower guerrilla leaders and others who had refused to collaborate with the Japanese, to no avail.[60] Before his death, President Quezon argued that government officials remained at their posts by his order "to keep law and order [and] to protect the interests of the Filipino people."[61] He wrote passionately,

> These men did what they had been asked to do, while they were free, under the protection of their government. Today they are virtually prisoners of the enemy. I am sure they are only doing what they think is their duty. They are not traitors. They are the victims of the adverse fortunes of war and I am

sure they had no choice. Besides, it is most probable that they accepted their positions in order to safeguard the welfare of the civilian population in the occupied areas. I think, under the circumstances, America should look upon their situation sympathetically and understandingly.[62]

Of course, politics were also at play. Many collaborators were members of Quezon's political party, and Roxas was Quezon's protégé. They had cooperated with American officials and had been rewarded with legislation granting Philippine independence in 1946. Subjecting them to retribution for cooperating with the Japanese would remove the very force that had been most cooperative with American officials in the past, and, by implication, those best positioned to work with the United States in the future. Leaving the decision on what to do with these men to the Filipinos was not just goodwill, it was good politics.[63]

On the whole, Filipinos treated collaborators much more sympathetically than other nations did, for many viewed their service under the Japanese as a necessary evil to mitigate the worst of the occupation. Many of those who collaborated, being part of the Filipino elite, were elected to the government after the liberation. In contrast to the treatment meted out to collaborators in France, the Filipinos acted with compassion. "No people on earth had suffered more than the Filipinos," Carlos Romulo wrote. "But no mob vengeance was allowed to hold sway in the Philippines."[64] President Osmeña made it clear that collaborators would have their day in court, but he realized that their motives for collaboration differed. Some Filipinos needed to run the local governments under Japanese control "to protect the populations from the oppressors to the extent possible by human ingenuity and to comfort the people in their misery." The alternative was direct Japanese control or the empowerment of "unscrupulous Filipino followers capable of any treason to their people." Courts, not mob justice, would sort those who stayed in their positions out of fear of reprisals or to serve the people from those motivated by a genuine desire to see the Japanese succeed.[65]

MacArthur's intervention tilted the scales in favor of the Philippine establishment. He had already overlooked Roxas's collaboration with José Laurel's puppet government and had set him on a course to assume postwar power. On August 23, MacArthur went further, releasing upwards of 5,000 Filipinos suspected of collaboration, pending judicial hearings down the road.[66] This represented a victory for the Filipino elite, many of whom had cooperated with the Japanese occupiers during the war. Instead of facing trial, they instead "developed a well-organized propaganda campaign to persuade the world that all those who collaborated with the Japanese had done so only from" patriotic motives.[67] Only a handful of collaborators were ever tried, and even fewer convicted. The election of Roxas to the presidency in April 1946 ended further trials, and with them any chance that the pre-war elite would be held accountable for their collaboration with the Japanese. By giving Roxas his full support, MacArthur had tipped the scales of Philippine national politics in favor of the oligarchy that had held power before the war.[68]

Washington politics were also at play. Interior Secretary Harold Ickes was at odds with MacArthur and had different ideas about what should happen with the post-war Philippines. Ickes took a hard line on collaboration, but with ulterior motives. "Concern about collaboration of Roxas and others was centered more in Washington than in the Philippines," Paul Rogers believes. "The charge 'collaboration' was raised by those in the Interior Department who wanted to delay Philippine independence and, incidentally, to keep this small departmental empire intact for as long as possible."[69] Truman resisted Secretary Ickes's entreaty to appoint a High Commissioner to the Philippines and deferred to MacArthur on the administration of the Philippines, at least while the war lasted.[70] Instead, in late May the new US president sent a commission to study what should be done. After a few weeks in country, the commission reported that a general election should be held as soon as possible, and independence granted to a newly elected Filipino government. Wasting no time to throw his hat into the ring, Roxas declared himself a candidate for the presidency.[71]

Favored by MacArthur and the American military establishment and with control over the largest newspaper in the Philippines, the Manila *Daily News*, Roxas defeated Osmeña in the presidential election held on April 23, 1946. Roxas served as the last president of the Commonwealth of the Philippines and the first president of the Philippine Republic, which was ushered into existence on July 4, 1946. On hand to witness his inauguration was General of the Army Douglas MacArthur.

If any group of Filipinos deserved credit for the liberation of their homeland, it was the resistance. US Army officers at the time and official historians since understood the invaluable contribution made by the guerrillas as forces of liberation. They provided intelligence, assistance as guides, reconnaissance patrolling, combat power that augmented US forces in battle, and security for rear areas and lines of communication. "Their use for these purposes materially increased the number of American fighting men available for the mop-up of areas in which the Japanese survivors still retained some organization and fighting effectiveness," the Eighth Army reported.[72] Russell Volckmann agreed, writing, "Were it not for the fact that the Americans were operating in a territory where the natives are on their side, the liberation of the Philippines would have been more difficult, more costly in manpower and would have lasted longer."[73] Perhaps the greatest tribute was that of the official US Army historian of the liberation of the Philippines, Robert Ross Smith, who opined, "It is, indeed, difficult to imagine how the Southwest Pacific Area could have undertaken the reconquest of the Philippines without the predominately [sic] loyal and willing Filipino population."[74]

So what in the end did the resistance accomplish? For starters, the resistance kept lit the lamp of hope. More than a quarter million Filipinos participated in the resistance, and they believed in MacArthur's promise to return.[75] "His [MacArthur's] name was like an invocation to them [the Philippine people], a holy word that had special power and meaning. None of them doubted his promise to return, but they were anxious to learn when the invasion would come. We told them honestly that we did not know," opined guerrilla leader Edwin Ramsey.[76] Iliff David Richardson, who served with Col. Ruperto Kangleon on Leyte, stated, "We didn't expect to be able to win until MacArthur returned, but we did count on killing Japs and on keeping alive in the people the hope of eventual liberation."[77] Once SWPA made contact with the guerrillas, the provision of arms, ammunition, and supplies rekindled the people's faith in MacArthur's promise. "The Aid" long promised by the United States would arrive in due course and with it, liberation. The resistance also controlled a great deal of the islands. In truth, the Japanese controlled only the urban areas, major towns, and the routes in between. Filipinos and Americans established civil administration in areas controlled by guerrillas, which was much of the rural landmass of the islands. Even cities were contested in the sense that the resistance could limit local collaboration with Japanese forces.

Guerrillas and coast-watcher units provided a great deal of intelligence to SWPA, a flow that increased exponentially once SWPA was able to send radios to the islands. Intelligence summaries kept SWPA informed of Japanese strengths and dispositions in the Philippines, information that was often more accurate than that gained from radio intercepts and codebreaking.[78] Volckmann's intelligence on Japanese troop and naval movements, sent to G-2 SWPA in numerous reports, helped complete the picture of Japanese dispositions and intentions on Luzon prior to the landings at Lingayen Gulf in January 1945.[79] In that month alone, guerrillas sent 3,700 radio messages to SWPA, a testament to the robust intelligence and communications network they and AIB had established in the Philippines.[80]

The US National Archives II contains seventy boxes of carefully catalogued messages from various guerrilla leaders in the Philippines to MacArthur's HQ in Australia and later to Sixth and Eighth Army headquarters in the Philippines. There are roughly 300 messages per box, or approximately 21,000 messages in all. These reports detail Japanese troop identification and dispositions, activities of the collaborationist government, assessment of Allied air attacks, guerrilla personnel and supply status, weather and terrain reports, information on downed airmen, atrocities committed against civilians, and more. They show the importance of the guerrilla movement in developing the intelligence picture of the Philippines prior to MacArthur's return and in assisting Krueger and Eichelberger in their operations to liberate the islands.[81] As noted previously, order-of-battle intelligence based on these reports was often more accurate than assessments derived from Ultra, which had its own limitations. At the tactical level, "Guerrillas were a never ceasing fount of information but due to their tendency to estimate many times the actual strengths, most careful evaluation and verification was necessary."[82]

Direct action killed tens of thousands of Japanese soldiers, harassed Japanese units, and interdicted their lines of communication as the day of liberation approached. On Mindanao alone, in 1944 and 1945 guerrillas accounted for 8,316 Japanese fatalities – a full division of troops.[83] Volckmann's division in northern Luzon by the end of the war reported that it had killed 52,033 Japanese, while sustaining 1,395 killed and 3,385 wounded.[84] Even if these reports need to be taken with a measure of skepticism, the accomplishments of the guerrillas were nothing short of impressive, given the handicaps they needed to overcome to become combat-effective. Just as importantly, their operations had kept the spirit of resistance alive, while degrading Japanese defensive measures. Tens of thousands of Japanese troops were diverted to suppress the guerrillas, interfering with Japanese preparations to defend against an invasion.

After US combat forces returned to the Philippines, guerrilla units became adjuncts of American combat divisions and served honorably with them in the liberation of their country, presenting to the Japanese forces a complex and deadly hybrid threat.[85] Both Sixth and Eighth Armies made much more extensive use of guerrilla forces than originally anticipated. Volckmann's forces in northern Luzon added the equivalent of at least one infantry division to Krueger's force structure, partly compensating for the loss of five divisions to Eighth Army. Guerrillas often served as guides for liberating US troops, who were unfamiliar with the local physical and human terrain in the Philippines. Guerrillas guarded key logistical nodes and lines of communication. They also recruited and organized Filipino laborers and porters to support US forces logistically – an important contribution, given the poor condition of many roads in the Philippines, which made transportation difficult. For good reasons, after the war Filipinos would wear the mark of the guerrilla as a badge of distinction and honor, for it gave them agency in their own liberation.

The cost of liberation was steep. Out of a pre-war population of eighteen million, the Philippines lost one million souls during the war. Of Ramsey's 40,000 guerrillas, by the end of the war 5,000 had perished – one in eight.[86] But their sacrifice ensured the place of the Filipino guerrillas among the great resistance movements in the history of warfare. MacArthur acknowledged this fact in a message shortly after his return to Leyte:

> As Commander-in-Chief of the forces of liberation I publicly acknowledge and pay tribute to the great spiritual power that has made possible these notable and glorious achievements – achievements which find few counterparts in military history. Those great patriots, Filipino and American, both living and dead, upon whose valiant shoulders has rested the leadership and responsibility for the indomitable movement in the past critical period, shall, when their identities can be known, find a lasting place on the scroll of heroes of both nations – heroes who have selflessly and defiantly subordinated all to the cause of human liberty. Their names and their deeds shall ever be enshrined in the hearts of our two peoples in whose darkest hours they have waged relentless war against the forces of evil that sought, through ruthless brutality, the enslavement of the Filipino people.[87]

Russell Volckmann, who commanded some of the most effective guerrilla forces in the islands, praised the accomplishments of his men in his memoir, *We Remained*. Looking back on their accomplishments, Volckmann wrote:

> During three long years these men lived in extremes of sunstroke or cold, had put in tortuous hours on the trails or in demoralizing cramped hideouts, had felt ravenous hunger and the tension of being hunted like animals. They had known devout admiration and profound hatred; understanding, gentleness, and fanatic cruelty; the confusion of battle, the serenity of hypnotic tropical nights – always either married to the devil or close to God. Cut off from the outside world by the mountains, the sea, and a fanatic enemy, these men emerged among a strange people as determined, self-reliant, and resourceful leaders. In their violent

struggle, where the normal was strange and the abnormal common, they found a deep satisfaction in molding a machine capable of releasing tremendous violence against a despotic enemy. To a large degree, they were answerable only to themselves. They stood alone, with their failures mortgaged with human lives and their successes rewarded in new hope for a stricken people.[88]

In her memoir, *The Crucible*, guerrilla Yay Panlilio was more circumspect. Regarding the deeds of various guerrilla groups she wrote, "History will do its own winnowing."[89]

Indeed, history has done so. After the war, Chick Parsons became a citizen of the Philippine Republic and lived out his days in Manila. Wendell Fertig served on active duty until the mid 1950s and retired never having been awarded a general's star. He headed a Colorado mining company until his death in 1975. Along with Russell Volckmann and Colonel Aaron Bank, a former OSS operative who served with a Jedburgh team in France, he is credited with founding the US Army Special Forces, the vaunted Green Berets. Volckmann retired from the US Army as a brigadier general and spent the rest of his days as a furniture manufacturing executive. Three guerrillas would go on to become presidents of the Philippines: Ramon Magsaysay, Carlos Garcia, and Ferdinand Marcos. Magsaysay, Peralta, and Kangleon would become secretaries of national defense. Terry Adevoso served, at age thirty-one, as secretary of labor under Philippine President Ramon Magsaysay. Others rose to the top in the military or served in government as cabinet officials, senators, congressmen, and ambassadors. They sacrificed to help liberate their country, and in doing so became the heart and soul of the future Philippine Republic.

Carlos Romulo signed the United Nations Charter as the chief Philippine delegate. He would go on to serve eight Philippine presidents as resident commissioner of the Philippines to the United States Congress, secretary of foreign affairs, UN delegate, and secretary of education. As the ultimate honor, he served as president of the General Assembly of the United Nations in 1949–1950.

For her part, Yay Panlilio underplayed her service to the Philippines. "I'm no hero," she protested. "But I've walked with heroes."[90] President Harry S. Truman disagreed, awarding Panlilio the Medal of Freedom in 1950 for her contribution to the liberation of her homeland.

Acknowledgments

A book of this magnitude is always a corporate effort to some extent. Senior editor Michael Watson and his team at Cambridge University Press have been helpful at every stage of the publication process. Joe LeMonnier did his usual superb job with creating the maps.

I am particularly grateful to the archivists in multiple institutions who helped me collect the research for this study, among them Tim Nenninger and his staff at the Textual Records Branch of the National Archives at College Park, Maryland; Jim Zobel at the MacArthur Memorial Archives in Norfolk, Virginia; and the staffs at the Hoover Institution Library and Archives in Palo Alto, California, the US Army Heritage and Education Center in Carlisle, Pennsylvania, and the United States Military Academy Library at West Point, New York. The staff at the Still Picture Branch of the National Archives at College Park, Maryland, were superb in assisting me in locating most of the photos used in the book.

Richard Frank, the dean of Pacific War research, provided inspiration at the beginning of this project in 2015, when he and I discussed the concept at the annual meeting of the Society for Military History in Montgomery, Alabama. Rich, who is writing a trilogy on the history of the Asia–Pacific War, took the time to read the manuscript and provide extensive feedback and discussion of key points. I am sincerely indebted to him for his careful attention to detail, and for sharing the fruits of his research and experience with me.

Col. Mike Morris and Gordon Rudd of the Marine Corps School of Advanced Warfighting graciously allowed me to participate in one of their staff rides to the Pacific, during which Gordon and I were able to explore the battlefields of Leyte. Kojiro Yamada from NHK Japan TV also invited me to visit the battlefields of Manila, Lingayen Gulf, and Baguio with his crew in the filming of a documentary on the fighting in Luzon.

Dear friends Wick Murray and Lee Smith and Jeff and Nancy Kueffer allowed me to stay at their mountain homes in Tannersville, New York, and Burnsville, North Carolina, respectively, while writing this book. Wick has since moved on to the great history library in the sky, and I and his other friends and mentees will miss him dearly.

Finally, I owe a debt of gratitude to my wife Jana, not just for her lifelong companionship, but for proofreading every word of the manuscript, providing much needed criticism, and creating a first-class index.

Figures

Maps

Abbreviations

ABDA – American–British–Dutch–Australian Command
ACTS – Air Corps Tactical School
AFPAC – US Army Forces, Pacific
AGC – amphibious command ship
AIB – Allied Intelligence Bureau
AKA – amphibious cargo ship
APD – high-speed transport, converted destroyers or destroyer escorts
AT – Japanese convoy designation
ATIS – Allied Translator and Interpreter Section
BAR – Browning Automatic Rifle
BB – battleship
CA – heavy cruiser
CAF – Cagayan–Apayao Force
CAP – combat air patrol
CB – US Navy construction battalion, or "Seabees"
CCS – Combined Chiefs of Staff, composed of the British Imperial General
Staff and the American Joint Chiefs of Staff
CINC – Commander-in-Chief
CL – light cruiser
CTF – Commander, Task Force
CVE – escort carrier
DD – destroyer
DE – destroyer escort
FEAF – Far East Air Force
FS – chemical smoke screen
G-1 – personnel section or officer
G-2 – intelligence section or officer
G-3 – operations and plans section or officer
G-4 – logistics section or officer
GHQ – general headquarters
HQ – headquarters

IJN – Imperial Japanese Navy
JCS – Joint Chiefs of Staff (US)
LCI – landing craft, infantry
LCI(R) – landing craft, infantry (rocket)
LCM – landing craft, mechanized
LGAF – Luzon Guerrilla Armed Forces
LSM – landing ship, medium
LST – landing ship, tank
LVT – landing vehicle, tracked, or "Alligator"
MAG – Marine Aircraft Group
Magic – Cryptanalysis derived from the Japanese "Purple" diplomatic cipher
NARA II – National Archives II at College Park, Maryland
OSS – Office of Strategic Services
PA – Philippine Army
PBY – Consolidated PBY Catalina flying boat
PC – Philippine Constabulary
PCAU – Philippine Civil Affairs Unit
POA – Pacific Ocean Areas
PRS – Philippine Regional Section (Allied Intelligence Bureau)
PS – Philippine Scouts
PT – motor torpedo boat
RCT – regimental combat team
ROTC – Reserve Officers' Training Corps
SOP – standard operating procedure
SSO – Special Security Officer, charged with handling top-secret Ultra material
SWPA – Southwest Pacific Area
TA – Japanese convoy designation
Ultra – Cryptanalysis derived from Japanese and German military ciphers
USAFFE – US Army Forces in the Far East
USAFIP – US Army Forces in the Philippines (-NL, Northern Luzon)
USAHEC – US Army Heritage and Education Center, Carlisle, Pennsylvania
USFIP – US Forces in the Philippines
USMA – United States Military Academy at West Point, New York
VMF – Marine fighter squadron [(N) – night-capable]
WAC – Women's Army Corps

US Division Nicknames

11th Airborne Division – Angels
1st Cavalry Division – First Team
Americal Division – Americal
6th Infantry Division – Red Star
7th Infantry Division – Hourglass
24th Infantry Division – Victory
25th Infantry Division – Tropic Lightning
31st Infantry Division – Dixie
32nd Infantry Division – Red Arrow
33rd Infantry Division – Prairie
37th Infantry Division – Buckeye
38th Infantry Division – Cyclone
40th Infantry Division – Sunburst
41st Infantry Division – Jungleers
43rd Infantry Division – Winged Victory
77th Infantry Division – Statue of Liberty
81st Infantry Division – Wildcats
93rd Infantry Division – Blue Helmets
96th Infantry Division – Deadeyes

Note on Sources

Research on MacArthur's campaign in the Philippines begins at National Archives II in College Park, Maryland. Record Group 496, Records of General Headquarters, Southwest Pacific Area and United States Army Forces, Pacific, houses nearly 3.8 million pages of SWPA records, including a number of boxes of key papers collected during the war by SWPA Chief of Staff Richard K. Sutherland. RG 218, Records of the US Joint Chiefs of Staff, houses 17.7 million pages of records, but of particular use are the summaries of their meetings during the war. Record Group 407, Records of the Adjutant General's Office, houses more than 88 million pages of records including the orders, staff studies, intelligence summaries, logistical data, after action reports, and other paperwork of US divisions, corps, armies, and other military organizations. RG 165, Records of the War Department General and Special Staffs, houses nearly 36.8 million pages of records, including those records collected by the Operations Division History Unit during World War II, which were especially useful in tracking the discussions and decisions concerning the Philippines. RG 313, Records of Naval Operating Forces, houses more than seventy million pages of records of US naval forces, which were useful in constructing the history of the Battle of Leyte Gulf and other naval actions in the SWPA theater. Record Group 554, Records of General Headquarters, Far East Command, Supreme Commander Allied Powers, and United Nations Command, houses 13.6 million pages of records, which include a large amount of captured Japanese material and interrogations of Japanese officers, thankfully all translated into English. Finally, Record Group 457, Records of the National Security Agency/Central Security Service, houses nearly 4.5 million pages of records that include a great deal of declassified special intelligence (Ultra and Magic) from World War II.

The MacArthur Memorial Archives and Library in Norfolk, Virginia, houses documents on MacArthur's tenure as Philippine Military Advisor, his command of USAFFE, and his command of SWPA. Among the collection are key messages to/from MacArthur during the war, which duplicate those found in the National Archives but are easier to locate. The collection also includes MacArthur's private correspondence, which, concerning his private thoughts, regrettably is not extensive. Papers of Bonner Fellers, George Kenney, Richard J. Marshall, Weldon "Dusty" Rhoades, Richard K. Sutherland, Courtney Whitney, and Charles Willoughby are also in the collection. Papers of lesser-known figures such as Bonner Fellers, Richard J. Marshall, and Weldon "Dusty" Rhoades contain valuable insights. William Dunn was a radio reporter who accompanied MacArthur's return to Leyte and Luzon, and the archive houses transcripts of his broadcasts.

The US Army Heritage and Education Center in Carlisle, Pennsylvania, houses an extensive collection of papers and oral histories of US Army personnel in its archives. Among the collections and oral histories consulted for this book were those of Maj. Gen. Clovis Byers, Clyde D. Eddleman, Robert Eichelberger, Wendell Fertig, Maj. Gen. Edwin F. Harding, Aubrey Newman, Joseph Swing, and Russell Volckmann. The archive also houses Far East Command, Pacific Theater Historical Section interrogations of Japanese officials concerning their World War II experiences. Other sources located at USAHEC include articles written by returning junior officers at various professional military schools in the United States.

The Hoover Institution Archive houses various collections of papers, including those of William Hammer, Herbert "Gene" Hungerford, Edward Huxtable, Elizabeth James, John Sidney "Slew" McCain Sr., Henry Muller, Claude Owens, Raymond Tarbuck, Lee Telesco, and Laurence Wilson.

The Special Collections room of the United States Military Academy Library at West Point, New York, houses papers of graduates of the institution and their family members, including Amelia Mary Bradley, Oscar Griswold, Walter Krueger, Archie L. McMaster, and Emily Van Sickle.

Memoirs fill in gaps and add color that archival sources lack. Just before his death, MacArthur published *Reminiscences* (New York: McGraw-Hill, 1964), which is a self-serving account of the general's life and career but still useful. Memoirs of his subordinate commanders in SWPA include Daniel E. Barbey, *MacArthur's Amphibious Navy: Seventh Amphibious Force Operations, 1943–1945* (Annapolis, MD: United States Naval Institute, 1969); Lewis H. Brereton, *The Brereton Diaries* (New York: William Morrow, 1946), which must be treated with caution as the entries for the first days of the war in the Philippines were recreated from memory and are suspect; Robert L. Eichelberger, *Our Jungle Road to Tokyo* (New York City: Viking Press, 1950), along with his letters to his wife catalogued in Jay Luvaas, ed., *DEAR MISS EM: General Eichelberger's War in the Pacific, 1942–1945* (Westport, CT: Greenwood, 1972); George C. Kenney, *General Kenney Reports: A Personal*

History of the Pacific War (New York: Duell, Sloan and Pearce, 1949); Walter Krueger, *From Down Under to Nippon: The Story of Sixth Army in World War II* (Washington, DC: Combat Forces Press, 1953); and Jonathan M. Wainwright, *General Wainwright's Story: The Account of Four Years of Humiliating Defeat, Surrender, and Captivity* (Garden City, NY: Doubleday, 1946). MacArthur's chief of staff, Richard K. Sutherland, did not publish memoirs, but his stenographer did, and they are excellent: Paul P. Rogers, *The Good Years: MacArthur and Sutherland* (New York: Praeger, 1990), and *The Bitter Years: MacArthur and Sutherland* (New York: Praeger, 1991). Rogers was the only enlisted person who escaped to Australia with MacArthur's party. His is a unique view of the relationship between these two pivotal figures, one that is mostly sympathetic to both of them.

Memoirs of other senior leaders who played a role in the Pacific War include William F. Halsey and J. Bryan III, *Admiral Halsey's Story* (New York: Whittlesey-McGraw-Hill, 1947); Ernest J. King, *Fleet Admiral King: A Naval Record* (New York: W. W. Norton, 1952); and William D. Leahy, *I Was There: The Personal Story of the Chief of Staff to Presidents Roosevelt and Truman Based on His Notes and Diaries Made at the Time* (New York: Whittlesey House, 1950).

Other memoirs of note include William C. Chase, *Front Line General* (Houston: Pacesetter Press, 1975); William E. Dyess, *The Dyess Story: The Eye-Witness Account of the Death March from Bataan and the Narrative of Experiences in Japanese Prison Camps and of Eventual Escape* (New York: G. P. Putnam's Sons, 1944); Roger O. Egeberg, *The General: MacArthur and the Man He Called "Doc"* (New York: Hippocrene Books, 1983); Stephen M. Mellnik, *Philippine War Diary, 1939–1945* (New York: Van Nostrand Reinhold, 1969); Hiro Onoda, *No Surrender: My Thirty Year War*, trans. Charles S. Terry (New York and Tokyo: Kodansha International, 1974); William Rhoades, *Flying MacArthur to Victory* (College Station, TX: Texas A&M University Press, 1981); Manuel Luis Quezon, *The Good Fight* (New York: D. Appleton-Century, 1946); Carlos P. Romulo, *I Saw the Fall of the Philippines* (Garden City, NY: Doubleday, Doran, & Co., 1943) and *I See the Philippines Rise* (Garden City, NY: Doubleday, 1946); and Emily Van Sickle, *The Iron Gates of Santo Tomas: The Firsthand Account of an American Couple Interned by the Japanese in Manila, 1942–45* (Chicago: Academy of Chicago, 1992).

Biographers have also weighed into the history of the war in the Philippines with some excellent works. The best and most complete biography of MacArthur is D. Clayton James, *The Years of MacArthur*, 3 vols. (New York: Houghton Mifflin, 1970–1985). Other accounts include Clay Blair, *MacArthur* (Garden City, NY: Doubleday, 1972); Arthur Herman, *Douglas MacArthur: American Warrior* (New York: Random House, 2016); William Manchester,

American Caesar: Douglas MacArthur, 1880–1964 (Boston: Little, Brown, 1978); Geoffrey Perret, *Old Soldiers Never Die: The Life and Legend of Douglas MacArthur* (New York: Random House, 1996); Carol Morris Petillo, *Douglas MacArthur: The Philippine Years* (Bloomington, IN: Indiana University Press, 1981); Michael Schaller, *Douglas MacArthur: The Far Eastern General* (New York: Oxford University Press, 1989); and Charles A. Willoughby and John Chamberlain, *MacArthur: 1941–1951* (New York: McGraw-Hill, 1954). For a recent critical treatment, see James Ellman, *MacArthur Reconsidered: General Douglas MacArthur as Wartime Commander* (Essex, CT: Stackpole, 2023). Carol M. Petillo, "Douglas MacArthur and Manuel Quezon: A Note on an Imperial Bond," *Pacific Historical Review* 48, no. 1 (February 1979): 107–117, unlocked the mystery of Philippine President Manuel Quezon's payments to MacArthur and several of his staff officers.

Biographies of other key figures include Thomas B. Buell, *Master of Sea Power: A Biography of Fleet Admiral Ernest J. King* (Boston: Little, Brown, 1980); Thomas E. Griffith, Jr., *MacArthur's Airman: General George C. Kenney and the War in the Southwest Pacific* (Lawrence, KS: University Press of Kansas, 1998); Wilson Allen Heefner, *Twentieth Century Warrior: The Life and Service of Major General Edwin D. Patrick* (Shippensburg, PA: White Mane, 1995); Kevin C. Holzimmer, *General Walter Krueger: Unsung Hero of the Pacific War* (Lawrence, KS: University Press of Kansas, 2007); William M. Leary, ed., *We Shall Return! MacArthur's Commanders and the Defeat of Japan, 1942–1945* (Lexington: University Press of Kentucky, 1988), which includes eight chapter-length discussions of MacArthur and his subordinate commanders; John Kennedy Ohl, *Minuteman: The Military Career of General Robert S. Beightler* (Boulder, CO: Lynne Rienner, 2001); E. B. Potter, *Bull Halsey* (Annapolis, MD: Naval Institute Press, 1985) and *Nimitz* (Annapolis, MD: Naval Institute Press, 1976); John F. Shortal, *Forged by Fire: General Robert L. Eichelberger and the Pacific War* (Columbia, SC: University of South Carolina Press, 1987); Duane Schultz, *Hero of Bataan: The Story of General Jonathan M. Wainwright* (New York: St. Martin's Press, 1981); Gerald E. Wheeler, *Kinkaid of the Seventh Fleet: A Biography of Admiral Thomas C. Kinkaid, U.S. Navy* (Washington, DC: Naval Historical Center, 1995); and John F. Wukovits, *Devotion to Duty: A Biography of Admiral Clifton A. F. Sprague* (Annapolis, MD: Naval Institute Press, 1995).

The best historical accounts of the campaigns in the Philippines and Southwest Pacific remain the US Army official histories: Louis Morton, *Strategy and Command: The First Two Years* (Washington, DC: Office of the Chief of Military History, 1962); Maurice Matloff, *Strategic Planning for Coalition Warfare, 1943–1944* (Washington, DC: Office of the Chief of Military History, 1959); Louis Morton, *The Fall of the Philippines*

(Washington, DC: Office of the Chief of Military History, 1953); Samuel Milner, *Victory in Papua* (Washington, DC: Office of the Chief of Military History, 1957); John Miller, Jr., *Cartwheel: The Reduction of Rabaul* (Washington, DC: Office of the Chief of Military History, 1959); Robert Ross Smith, *The Approach to the Philippines* (Washington, DC: Office of the Chief of Military History, 1953); M. Hamlin Cannon, *Leyte: The Return to the Philippines* (Washington, DC: Office of the Chief of Military History, 1954); Robert Ross Smith, *Triumph in the Philippines* (Washington, DC: Office of the Chief of Military History, 1963); and Robert Ross Smith, "Luzon Versus Formosa," in Kent Roberts Greenfield, ed., *Command Decisions* (Washington, DC: Office of the Chief of Military History, 1960).

Reports of General MacArthur: The Campaigns of MacArthur in the Pacific, vol. I (Washington, DC: Center of Military History, 1966) was compiled and edited by Maj. Gen. Charles Willoughby with the assistance of Gordon Prange, himself a major historian of the Pacific War. Volume II (two parts) examines Japanese operations from captured documents and interviews. Willoughby and his G-2 Section also wrote a *History of Intelligence Activities under General MacArthur, 1942–1950* (Wilmington, DE: Scholarly Resources, 1983).

Official histories from air, naval, and marine historians are also excellent: Wesley Frank Craven and James Lea Cate, *The Army Air Forces in World War II*, vol. I: *Plans and Early Operations, January 1939 to August 1942* (Chicago: University of Chicago Press, 1948), and vol. V: *The Pacific: Matterhorn to Nagasaki, June 1944 to August 1945* (Chicago: University of Chicago Press, 1953); Frank O. Hough, *History of the U.S. Marine Corps Operations in World War II*, vol. I: *Pearl Harbor to Guadalcanal* (Washington, DC: Historical Branch, G-3 Division, US Marine Corps, 1959); George W. Garand, *History of the U.S. Marine Corps Operations in World War II*, vol. IV: *Western Pacific Operations* (Washington, DC: Historical Division, US Marine Corps, 1971); and Samuel Eliot Morison, *History of United States Naval Operations in World War II*, vol. III: *The Rising Sun in the Pacific, 1931–April 1942* (Boston: Little, Brown, 1948); vol. XII: *Leyte, June 1944–January 1945* (Boston: Little, Brown, 1953); and vol. XIII: *The Liberation of the Philippines: Luzon, Mindanao, the Visayas, 1944–1945* (Boston: Little, Brown, 1955). Office of the Chief Engineer, GHQ Army Forces Pacific, *Engineers of the Southwest Pacific, 1941–1945*, vol. VI: *Airfield and Base Development* (Washington, DC: GPO, 1951), details construction of the many airfields and bases in the Southwest Pacific.

Histories of the fall of the Philippines include William H. Bartsch, *December 8, 1941: MacArthur's Pearl Harbor* (College Station, TX: Texas A&M University Press, 2003), which is the most complete history of the destruction of the majority of the Far East Air Force after the Japanese strike on Pearl Harbor and supersedes Walter D. Edmonds, *They Fought with What They Had: The Story of the Army Air Forces in the Southwest Pacific, 1941–1942* (New York: Little, Brown, 1951); John Jacob Beck, *MacArthur and Wainwright: Sacrifice of the Philippines* (Albuquerque: University of New Mexico Press, 1974); James H. Belote and William H. Belote, *Corregidor: The Saga of a Fortress* (New York: Harper & Row, 1967); Richard Connaughton, *MacArthur and Defeat in the Philippines* (New York: Abrams Press, 2001); Christopher L. Kolakowski, *Last Stand on Bataan: The Defense of the Philippines, December 1941–May 1942* (Jefferson, NC: McFarland, 2016); Bill Sloan, *Undefeated: America's Heroic Fight for Bataan and Corregidor* (New York: Simon & Schuster, 2012); John C. Whitman, *Bataan: Our Last Ditch: The Bataan Campaign, 1942* (New York: Hippocrene Books, 1990); and Donald J. Young, *The Fall of the Philippines: The Desperate Struggle against the Japanese Invasion, 1941–1942* (Jefferson, NC: McFarland, 2015). Edward S. Miller, *War Plan Orange: The U.S. Strategy to Defeat Japan, 1897–1945* (Annapolis, MD: Naval Institute Press, 1991), details the four-decade history of the US joint plan to fight a war in the Pacific.

The Bataan Death March and prisoner experiences are detailed in Stanley L. Falk, *Bataan: The March of Death* (New York: W. W. Norton, 1962); Donald Knox, *Death March: The Survivors of Bataan* (New York: Harcourt Brace Jovanovich, 1981); and A. V. H. Hartendorp, *The Santo Tomas Story* (New York: McGraw-Hill, 1964).

The guerrilla war in the Philippines resulted in an enormous number of histories and memoirs, but no overarching history of the resistance. The best study to date is James Villanueva, *Awaiting MacArthur's Return: World War II Guerrilla Resistance against the Japanese in the Philippines* (Lawrence, KS: University Press of Kansas, 2022). Other works include Dirk Jan Barreveld, *Cushing's Coup: The True Story of How Lt. Col. James Cushing and His Filipino Guerrillas Captured Japan's Plan Z* (Philadelphia: Casemate, 2015); Lawrence M. Greenberg, *The Hukbalahap Insurrection* (Washington, DC: US Army Center of Military History, 1987); Philip Harkins, *Blackburn's Headhunters* (New York: W. W. Norton, 1955); Kent Holmes, *Wendell Fertig and His Guerrilla Forces in the Philippines* (Jefferson, NC: McFarland, 2015); Allison Ind, *Allied Intelligence Bureau: Our Secret Weapon in the War against Japan* (New York: David McKay, 1958); Benedict J. Kerkvliet, *The Huk Rebellion: A Study of Peasant Revolt in the Philippines* (Berkeley, CA: University of California Press, 1977); Robert Lapham and Bernard Norling, *Lapham's Raiders: Guerrillas in the Philippines, 1942–1945* (Lexington: University Press of Kentucky, 1996); Elmer N. Lear, "The Western Leyte Guerrilla Warfare

Forces: A Case Study in the Non-legitimation of a Guerrilla Organization," *Journal of Southeast Asian History* 9, no. 1 (March 1968): 69–94; Gamaliel L. Manikan, *Guerilla Warfare on Panay Island in the Philippines* (Manila: Sixth Military District Veterans Foundation, 1977); Scott A. Mills, *Stranded in the Philippines: Professor Bell's Private War against the Japanese* (Annapolis, MD: Naval Institute Press, 2009); Proculo L. Mojica, *Terry's Hunters (The True Story of the Hunters ROTC Guerrillas)* (Manila: Benipayo Press, 1965); Bernard Norling, *The Intrepid Guerrillas of North Luzon* (Lexington: University of Kentucky Press, 1999); Yay Panlilio, *The Crucible* (New York: Macmillan, 1950); Edwin Price Ramsey and Stephen J. Rivele, *Lieutenant Ramsey's War: From Horse Soldier to Guerrilla Commander* (New York: Knightsbridge, 1990); Jesus Villamor, *They Never Surrendered: A True Story of Resistance in World War II* (Quezon City: Vera-Reyes, 1982); Russell W. Volckmann, *We Remained: Three Years behind the Enemy Lines in the Philippines* (New York: W. W. Norton, 1954); and Yung Li Yuk-wai, *The Huaqiao Warriors: Chinese Resistance Movement in the Philippines, 1942–1945* (Manila: Ateneo de Manila University Press, 1996). Willoughby collected material gathered by his staff and published *The Guerrilla Resistance Movement in the Philippines* (New York: Vantage Press, 1972). William Wise details Chick Parsons's adventures in *Secret Mission to the Philippines: The Story of "Spyron" and the American–Filipino Guerrillas of World War II* (New York: E. P. Dutton, 1968). Finally, two novels are of significant historical interest. John Keats published a narrative of Wendell Fertig's war on Mindanao in *They Fought Alone* (New York: J. B. Lippincott, 1963), which must be checked against other sources for accuracy – for a critical review, see Clyde Childress, "Wendell Fertig's Fictional 'Autobiography': A Critical Review of *They Fought Alone*," *Bulletin of the American Historical Collection* 31, no. 1 (January 2003). Ira Wolfert wrote a novel about Iliff David Richardson, *American Guerrilla in the Philippines* (New York: Simon and Schuster, 1945), which in 1950 was adapted into a major motion picture.

Selected works analyzing facets of the war in the Southwest Pacific include Larry Alexander, *Shadows in the Jungle: The Alamo Scouts behind Japanese Lines in World War II* (New York: Caliber, 2009); Eric M. Bergerud, *Touched with Fire: The Land War in the South Pacific* (New York: Viking, 1996); Charles F. Brower, *Defeating Japan: The Joint Chiefs of Staff and Strategy in the Pacific War, 1943–1945* (New York: Palgrave Macmillan, 2012); Peter J. Dean, *MacArthur's Coalition: US and Australian Military Operations in the Southwest Pacific Area, 1942–1945* (Lawrence, KS: University Press of Kansas, 2018); Edward J. Drea, *MacArthur's Ultra: Codebreaking and the War against Japan, 1942–1945* (Lawrence, KS: University Press of Kansas, 1992), which is by far the best source on Ultra intelligence in the Southwest Pacific; and

Stephen R. Taaffe, *MacArthur's Jungle War: The 1944 New Guinea Campaign* (Lawrence, KS: University Press of Kansas, 1998).

There are only a few histories of the overall campaign to liberate the Philippines. William B. Breuer, *Retaking the Philippines: America's Return to Corregidor and Bataan, October 1944–March 1945* (New York: St. Martin's Press, 1986), is a thinly footnoted, popular account that covers MacArthur's return to the Philippines from the landing at Leyte in October 1944 through the retaking of Corregidor Island in March 1945. It blends a general overview of operations with detailed accounts of combat action, focusing on the retaking of Corregidor Island in February 1945. James P. Duffy, *Return to Victory: MacArthur's Epic Liberation of the Philippines* (New York: Hachette Books, 2021), is a lightly footnoted account of the liberation of the Philippines written for lay readers. The author provides a cursory overview of the guerrilla movement, incorrectly notes that Roosevelt significantly influenced the debate on whether to invade Luzon, ignores the impact of Ultra intelligence, devotes only a few pages to the campaign on Luzon after the battle for Manila, and completely omits discussion of several operations, such as the invasions of Negros and Mindanao. Stanley L. Falk, *Liberation of the Philippines* (New York: Ballantine Books, 1971), is a short, illustrated history of the campaign to liberate the Philippines also written for lay readers. Gerald A. Astor, *Crisis in the Pacific: The Battles for the Philippine Islands by the Men Who Fought Them – An Oral History* (New York: Donald J. Fine, 1996), combines a concise history of the campaign for the Philippines with oral histories of those who served.

Works on specific aspects of the campaign for the Philippines are more plentiful. The Battle of Leyte Gulf is especially well documented. Works include Thomas J. Cutler, *The Battle of Leyte Gulf: 23–26 October 1944* (New York: HarperCollins, 1994), and his edited volume, *The Battle of Leyte Gulf at 75* (Annapolis, MD: Naval Institute Press, 2019); James A. Field Jr., *The Japanese at Leyte Gulf: The Shō Operation* (Princeton: Princeton University Press, 1947); Kenneth Friedman, *Afternoon of the Rising Sun: The Battle of Leyte Gulf* (Novato, CA: Presidio, 2001); Edwin P. Hoyt, *The Battle of Leyte Gulf: The Death Knell of the Japanese Fleet* (New York: Weybright and Tailey, 1972); Samuel Eliot Morison, "The Battle of Surigao Strait," *US Naval Institute Proceedings* 84, no. 12 (1958): 31–53; John Prados, *Storm over Leyte: The Philippine Invasion and the Destruction of the Japanese Navy* (New York: Caliber, 2016); Carl Solberg, *Decision and Dissent: With Halsey at Leyte Gulf* (Annapolis, MD: Naval Institute Press, 1995); Mark E. Stille, *Leyte Gulf: A New History of the World's Largest Sea Battle* (Oxford: Osprey, 2023); H. P. Willmott, *The Battle of Leyte Gulf: The Last Fleet Action*

(Bloomington: Indiana University Press, 2005); and C. Vann Woodward, *The Battle for Leyte Gulf* (New York: Macmillan, 1947).

Histories of the Leyte campaign include Stanley L. Falk, *Decision at Leyte* (New York: W. W. Norton, 1966); Milan Vego, *The Battle for Leyte, 1944: Allied and Japanese Plans, Preparations, and Execution* (Annapolis, MD: Naval Institute Press, 2006); and articles that deal with specific aspects, including Leigh C. Fairbank, Jr., "Division Engineers, Part II: Leyte," *The Military Engineer* 39, no. 256 (February 1947): 56–63; and Frank E. Gillette, "Supply Problems on Leyte," *Military Review* 25, no. 1 (April 1945): 61–68.

The Luzon campaign has also generated substantial literature. The Battle of Manila is the focus of Alfonso J. Aluit, *By Sword and Fire: The Destruction of Manila in World War II, 3 February–3 March 1945* (Manila: National Commission for Culture and the Arts, 1994), which brings together first-person accounts of Filipinos caught up in the maelstrom of conflict in Manila in February 1945; Richard Connaughton, John Pimlott, and Duncan Anderson, *The Battle for Manila: The Most Devastating Untold Story of World War II* (Novato, CA: Presidio, 1995); James M. Scott, *Rampage: MacArthur, Yamashita, and the Battle of Manila* (New York: W. W. Norton, 2018); and most recently Nicholas Evan Sarantakes, *The Battle of Manila: Poisoned Victory in the Pacific War* (New York: Oxford University Press, 2025). Bataan and Corregidor's iconic status has led to several books, including Gerald M. Devlin, *Back to Corregidor: America Retakes the Rock* (New York: St. Martin's Press, 1992); Edward M. Flanagan, *Corregidor: The Rock Force Assault, 1945* (Novato, CA: Presidio, 1988); B. David Mann, *Avenging Bataan: The Battle of Zigzag Pass* (Raleigh, NC: Ivy House, 2002); and Kevin Maurer, *Rock Force: The American Paratroopers Who Took Back Corregidor and Exacted MacArthur's Revenge on Japan* (New York: Dutton Caliber, 2020). The raids on Cabanatuan and Los Baños prisoner of war camps have been extensively chronicled in Anthony Arthur, *Deliverance at Los Banos: The Dramatic True Story of Survival and Triumph in a Japanese Internment Camp* (New York: St. Martin's Press, 1985); William B. Breuer, *The Great Raid on Cabanatuan: Rescuing the Doomed Ghosts of Bataan and Corregidor* (Hoboken, NJ: John Wiley & Sons, 1994); Bruce Henderson, *Rescue at Los Baños: The Most Daring Prison Camp Raid of World War II* (New York: William Morrow, 2015); and Hampton Sides, *Ghost Soldiers: The Epic Account of World War II's Greatest Rescue Mission* (New York: Anchor, 2001). The fighting in northern Luzon is covered in Generoso P. Salazar, Fernando R. Reyes, and Leonardo Q. Nuval, *World War II in North Luzon, Philippines, 1941–1945* (Quezon City: University of the Philippines, 1992), which examines the conventional operations of USAFIP-NL units; and Robert M. Young, *Pacific Hurtgen: The*

American Army in Northern Luzon, 1945 (Washington, DC: Westphalia Press, 2017), which views the campaign in Luzon and in the Central and Southern Philippines after the seizure of Manila as unnecessary and wasteful of American lives for negligible strategic gains.

Air–ground operations in the Philippines are discussed in E. L. Jenkins, "Combined Air–Ground Operations on Luzon," *Military Review* 25, no. 11 (February 1946): 30–34; and Charles W. Boggs, *Marine Aviation in the Philippines* (Washington, DC: Historical Division, USMC, 1951).

Various issues are examined in Ronald K. Edgerton, "General Douglas MacArthur and the American Military Impact in the Philippines," *Philippine Studies* 25, no. 4 (1977): 420–440; and David Joel Steinberg, *Philippine Collaboration in World War II* (Ann Arbor, MI: The University of Michigan Press, 1967). Yamashita's trial is related from the viewpoint of his defense counsel in Frank A. Reel, *The Case of General Yamashita* (New York: Octagon, 1971), which is highly critical of MacArthur's administration of victor's justice. Allan A. Ryan, *Yamashita's Ghost: War Crimes, MacArthur's Justice, and Command Accountability* (Lawrence, KS: University Press of Kansas, 2012), is critical of the principle of command accountability that the trial established, and which has been used haphazardly since.

Unit histories, which vary in quality, include Francis D. Cronin, *Under the Southern Cross: The Saga of the Americal Division* (Washington, DC: Combat Forces Press, 1951); Bertram C. Wright, *The 1st Cavalry Division in World War II* (Tokyo: Toppan, 1947); Edward M. Flanagan, *The Angels: A History of the 11th Airborne Division* (Novato, CA: Presidio, 1989); 6th Infantry Division Public Relations Section, *The 6th Infantry Division in World War II, 1939–1945* (Washington, DC: Infantry Journal Press, 1947); Jan Valtin (Richard Krebs), *Children of Yesterday: The Twenty-Fourth Infantry Division in World War II* (New York: Readers' Press, 1946); Robert F. Karolevitz, *The 25th Infantry Division and World War II* (Baton Rouge, LA: Army and Navy Publishing, 1946); 31st Infantry Division Staff, *History of the 31st Infantry Division in Training and Combat, 1940–1945* (Baton Rouge, LA: Army and Navy Publishing, 1946); Christopher M. Rein, *Mobilizing the South: The Thirty-First Infantry Division, Race, and World War II* (Tuscaloosa: The University of Alabama Press, 2022); Public Relations Office, 32nd Infantry Division, *13,000 Hours: Combat History of the 32nd Infantry Division – World War II* (self-published,1945); John M. Carlisle, *Red Arrow Men: Stories about the 32nd Division on the Villa Verde Trail* (Nashville, TN: Battery Press, 1990); Historical Committee, 33rd Infantry Division, *The Golden Cross: A History of the 33rd Infantry Division in World War II* (Mt. Vernon, IN: Windmill, 1994);

Stanley A. Frankel, *The 37th Infantry Division in World War II* (Washington, DC: Infantry Journal Press, 1948); Peyton Hoge, *38th Infantry Division: Avengers of Bataan* (Atlanta: Albert Love, 1983); *40th Infantry Division: The Years of World War II, 7 December 1941–7 April 1946* (Baton Rouge, LA: Army & Navy Publishing, 1947); William F. McCartney, *The Jungleers: A History of the 41st Infantry Division* (Washington, DC: Infantry Journal Press, 1948); Hargis Westerfield, *41st Infantry Division: The Fighting Jungleers* (Paducah, KY: Turner, 1992); Joseph E. Zimmer, *The History of the 43rd Infantry Division, 1941–1945* (Baton Rouge: Army and Navy Publishing, 1947); 77th Infantry Division Historical Committee, *Ours to Hold High: The 77th Division in World War II* (Washington, DC: Infantry Journal Press, 1947); and Orlando R. Davidson, J. Carl Willems, and Joseph A. Kahl, *The Deadeyes: The Story of the 96th Infantry Division* (Washington, DC: Infantry Journal Press, 1947). The Fifth Air Force's history is related in Steve Birdsall, *Flying Buccaneers: The Illustrated History of Kenney's Fifth Air Force* (New York: Doubleday, 1977).

General histories of the Pacific War are useful to place the Philippines campaign in context. They include Peter Calvocoressi, Guy Wint, and John Pritchard, *Total War: The Causes and Courses of the Second World War*, vol. II: *The Greater East Asia and Pacific Conflict*, 2nd rev. ed. (New York: Pantheon, 1989); John Costello, *The Pacific War, 1941–1945* (New York: Quill, 1982); Grace Person Hayes, *The History of the Joint Chiefs of Staff in World War II: The War against Japan* (Annapolis, MD: Naval Institute Press, 1982); the trilogy by John C. McManus, *Fire and Fortitude: The US Army in the Pacific War, 1941–1943* (New York: Caliber, 2019), *Island Infernos: The US Army's Pacific War Odyssey, 1944* (New York: Caliber, 2021), and *To the End of the Earth: The US Army and the Downfall of Japan, 1945* (New York: Caliber, 2023); Williamson Murray and Allan R. Millett, *A War to Be Won: Fighting the Second World War* (Cambridge, MA: Belknap, 2000); Ronald H. Spector, *Eagle against the Sun: The American War with Japan* (New York: Free Press, 1985); John Toland, *But Not in Shame: The Six Months after Pearl Harbor* (New York: Random House, 1961) and *The Rising Sun: The Decline and Fall of the Japanese Empire: 1936–1945* (New York: Random House, 1970); and the trilogy by Ian W. Toll, *Pacific Crucible: War at Sea in the Pacific, 1941–1942* (New York: W. W. Norton, 2011), *The Conquering Tide: War in the Pacific Islands, 1942–1944* (New York: W. W. Norton, 2015), and *Twilight of the Gods: War in the Western Pacific, 1944–1945* (New York: W. W. Norton, 2020).

Notes

CHAPTER 1: CATASTROPHE

1. Frank Hewlett, Manila bureau chief for United Press International, 1942. Hewlett was the last reporter to leave Corregidor before it fell to the Japanese.
2. The costs of fighting on Okinawa eclipsed those incurred on any single island in the Philippines, but, taken as a whole, the casualties of the Philippine campaign were greater.
3. The best accounts remain the US Army official histories: Louis Morton, *The Fall of the Philippines* (Washington, DC: Office of the Chief of Military History, 1953); M. Hamlin Cannon, *Leyte: The Return to the Philippines* (Washington, DC: Office of the Chief of Military History, 1954); and Robert Ross Smith, *Triumph in the Philippines* (Washington, DC: Office of the Chief of Military History, 1963). Histories of the fall of the Philippines include John Jacob Beck, *MacArthur and Wainwright: Sacrifice of the Philippines* (Albuquerque: University of New Mexico Press, 1974); Richard Connaughton, *MacArthur and Defeat in the Philippines* (New York: Abrams Press, 2001); Christopher L. Kolakowski, *Last Stand on Bataan: The Defense of the Philippines, December 1941–May 1942* (Jefferson, NC: McFarland, 2016); the first volume of the US Army in the Pacific War trilogy by John C. McManus, *Fire and Fortitude: The US Army in the Pacific War, 1941–1943* (New York: Caliber, 2019); Bill Sloan, *Undefeated: America's Heroic Fight for Bataan and Corregidor* (New York: Simon & Schuster, 2012); Donald J. Young, *The Fall of the Philippines: The Desperate Struggle against the Japanese Invasion, 1941–1942* (Jefferson, NC: McFarland, 2015); and John C. Whitman, *Bataan: Our Last Ditch: The Bataan Campaign, 1942* (New York: Hippocrene Books, 1990). Histories of the liberation of the Philippines include Stanley L. Falk, *Liberation of the Philippines* (New York: Ballantine Books, 1971); William B. Breuer, *Retaking the Philippines: America's Return to Corregidor and Bataan, October 1944–March 1945* (New York: St. Martin's Press, 1986); James P. Duffy, *Return to Victory: MacArthur's Epic Liberation of the Philippines* (New York: Hachette, 2021); and the second and third volumes of the trilogy by John C. McManus: *Island Infernos: The US Army's Pacific War Odyssey, 1944* (New York: Caliber, 2021), and *To the End of the Earth: The US Army and the Downfall of Japan, 1945* (New York: Caliber, 2023). A more complete listing can be found in the Note on Sources.

4. The US Army divisions deployed to the Pacific were the Americal, 6th, 7th, 24th, 25th, 27th, 31st, 32nd, 33rd, 37th, 38th, 40th, 41st, 43rd, 77th, 81st, 93rd, 96th, 98th, 1st Cavalry, and 11th Airborne. In addition, the Philippine Division was stationed on Luzon, where it was destroyed in fighting in 1941–1942. Only the 27th and 98th Infantry Divisions did not serve in the Philippines.

5. The best and most complete biography of MacArthur is D. Clayton James, *The Years of MacArthur*, 3 vols. (New York: Houghton Mifflin, 1970–1985). Other significant accounts include William Manchester, *American Caesar: Douglas MacArthur, 1880–1964* (Boston: Little, Brown, 1978); Geoffrey Perret, *Old Soldiers Never Die: The Life and Legend of Douglas MacArthur* (New York: Random House, 1996); and Arthur Herman, *Douglas MacArthur: American Warrior* (New York: Random House, 2016). For a recent critical treatment, see James Ellman, *MacArthur Reconsidered: General Douglas MacArthur as Wartime Commander* (Essex, CT: Stackpole, 2023). A more complete listing can be found in the Note on Sources.

6. MacArthur would spend two decades as a captain, a typical career path in the post-Civil War US Army.

7. MacArthur spent a year in the Philippines before his tour was cut short by a bout of malaria.

8. Herman, *Douglas MacArthur*, 129.

9. Ibid., 108, 151.

10. After his divorce from his first wife and during his third tour in the Philippines, MacArthur also met a sixteen-year-old Filipina actress, Isabel Rosario Cooper, with whom he established an erotic relationship. He paid for her travel to the United States and put her up in an apartment in Georgetown as what people in that era would term a kept woman. MacArthur ended the relationship in 1933 when it threatened to become public. Vernadette Vicuña Gonzalez, *Empire's Mistress, Starring Isabel Rosario Cooper* (Durham, NC: Duke University Press, 2021).

11. Herman, *MacArthur*, 214–225.

12. Ibid., 248.

13. MacArthur chose President Quezon to be the child's godfather.

14. Arthur MacArthur III, an Annapolis graduate with a promising career in the US Navy, had died unexpectedly of appendicitis on December 2, 1923. Mary Pinkney Hardy MacArthur was MacArthur's closest confidant (with one exception – Douglas's relationship with Filipina actress Isabel Rosario Cooper, which he kept secret from his mother) and fiercest advocate throughout his life until her death in Manila on December 3, 1935, just after arriving in the Philippines with her son. Her passing left a huge emotional hole in MacArthur's life, one that his new wife Jean Faircloth would fill.

15. Paul P. Rogers, *The Good Years: MacArthur and Sutherland* (New York: Praeger, 1990), 39–40. Eisenhower's relationship with MacArthur never recovered; the two remained estranged until the end of their lives. Kerry Irish, "Dwight

Eisenhower and Douglas MacArthur in the Philippines: There Must Be a Day of Reckoning," *Journal of Military History* 74, no. 2 (April 2010): 439–473, 465.

16. To differentiate MacArthur's deputy chief of staff, Richard J. Marshall, from the US Army Chief of Staff, George C. Marshall, I will use their ranks and first names along with their last names unless the context in which they appear is clear.

17. Douglas MacArthur, *Reminiscences* (New York: McGraw-Hill, 1964), 103–104.

18. Morton, *The Fall of the Philippines*, 10–11.

19. The latter worry was certainly true of the communist-inspired Huk movement, which fought against the Japanese during World War II but later turned on the Philippine government. Herman, *MacArthur*, 267; Irish, "Dwight Eisenhower and Douglas MacArthur in the Philippines," 449.

20. Irish, "Dwight Eisenhower and Douglas MacArthur in the Philippines," 455–463.

21. Herman, *MacArthur*, 280–281; MacArthur, *Reminiscences*, 106.

22. Joint Board, "Symbols to represent foreign countries," October 29, 2004, https://web.archive.org/web/20161119113902/http://strategytheory.org/military/us/joint_board/Symbols%20to%20Represent%20Foreign%20Countries%20(1904).pdf.

23. For the evolution of War Plan Orange, see Edward S. Miller, *War Plan Orange: The U.S. Strategy to Defeat Japan, 1897–1945* (Annapolis: Naval Institute Press, 1991).

24. Ibid., Chapter 17.

25. Ronald H. Spector, *Eagle against the Sun: The American War with Japan* (New York: Free Press, 1985), 57.

26. Herman, *MacArthur*, 264.

27. Miller, *War Plan Orange*, 271.

28. Morton, *The Fall of the Philippines*, 62.

29. Miller, *War Plan Orange*, 55–56.

30. Sutherland's father, Howard Sutherland, had been a successful business executive and a former US representative and senator from West Virginia.

31. Carlos P. Romulo, *I Saw the Fall of the Philippines* (Garden City, NY: Doubleday, Doran, & Co., 1943), 131.

32. Rogers, *The Good Years*, 26.

33. Williamson Murray and Allan R. Millett, *A War to Be Won: Fighting the Second World War* (Cambridge, MA: Harvard University Press, 2000), 185.

34. Morton, *The Fall of the Philippines*, 24–27.

35. Ibid., 35. On October 1, 1941, the entire Philippine Army possessed only forty-eight 75mm guns.

36. Ibid., 27–28.

37. The Philippine Scouts were long-serving Filipino regulars assigned to the US Army and commanded for the most part by US Army officers.

38. Frank O. Hough, Verle E. Ludwig, and Henry I. Shaw, Jr., *Pearl Harbor to Guadalcanal: History of U.S. Marine Corps Operations in World War II*, vol. I

(Washington, DC: Historical Branch, US Marine Corps, 1993), Part IV. The 4th Marines were known as the "China Marines" due to their service on the Asian mainland since 1927.

39. United States Asiatic Fleet Locations, December 7, 1941, www.navsource.org/ Naval/usfb.htm.
40. Morton, *The Fall of the Philippines*, 33.
41. Ibid., 37.
42. Herman, *MacArthur*, 301–302; Manchester, *American Caesar*, 215.
43. Manchester, *American Caesar*, 216.
44. Charles O. Cook, Jr., "The Strange Case of Rainbow 5," *US Naval Institute Proceedings* 104, no. 8 (1978): 67–73.
45. Ibid., 42. The FEAF also controlled eighteen B-18, nine A-27, and twelve B-10 bombers; sixteen P-26 and fifty-two P-35 fighters; and fifty-eight other aircraft. None of these were modern combat aircraft.
46. Ibid., 43–45.
47. Lewis H. Brereton, *The Brereton Diaries* (New York: William Morrow, 1946), 32–33; William H. Bartsch, *December 8, 1941: MacArthur's Pearl Harbor* (College Station, TX: Texas A&M University Press, 2003), 219–224.
48. Brereton, *The Brereton Diaries*, 35–36.
49. Ibid, 35; MacArthur, *Reminiscences*, 113.
50. Brereton, *The Brereton Diaries*, 34–35; MacArthur, *Reminiscences*, 113.
51. Sun Tzu, *Art of War*, 3.18: Attack by Stratagem, https://suntzusaid.com/book/ 3/18.
52. Manchester, *American Caesar*, 187–188.
53. John T. Correll, "Disaster in the Philippines," November 1, 2019, www.airand spaceforces.com/article/disaster-in-the-philippines.
54. Brereton, *The Brereton Diaries*, 38–39.
55. Bartsch, *December 8, 1941*, 296.
56. Correll, "Disaster in the Philippines."
57. Bartsch, *December 8, 1941*, 300–302.
58. Ibid., 320–321.
59. Morton, *The Fall of the Philippines*, 88; Brereton, *The Brereton Diaries*, 44.
60. Walter D. Edmonds, "What Happened at Clark Field," *The Atlantic*, July 1951, www.theatlantic.com/magazine/archive/1951/07/what-happened-at-clark-fiel d/639484.
61. Bartsch, *December 8, 1941*, is the most complete history of the destruction of the majority of the FEAF hours after the Japanese strike on Pearl Harbor. It supersedes Walter D. Edmonds, *They Fought with What They Had: The Story of the Army Air Forces in the Southwest Pacific, 1941–1942* (New York: Little, Brown, 1951), and the official history, *The Army Air Forces in World War II*, vol. I: *Plans and Early Operations, January 1939 to August 1942* (Chicago: University of Chicago Press, 1948), 201–213.
62. MacArthur, *Reminiscences*, 117–118.

63. Brereton, *The Brereton Diaries*, 64–67.
64. "M'Arthur Denies Brereton Report," *New York Times*, September 28, 1946, 6.
65. Bartsch, *December 8, 1941*, 420–421.
66. Ibid., 421–424; Ellman, *MacArthur Reconsidered*, 42.
67. Edmonds, "What Happened at Clark Field."
68. Morton, *The Fall of the Philippines*, 94–95.
69. Ibid., 98.
70. Ibid., 107.
71. At the time, and even after the war, MacArthur contended that he fought outnumbered. The contemporary assertion could be chalked up to poor intelligence, but the post-war contention was pure fabrication. MacArthur, *Reminiscences*, 123–124.
72. Morton, *The Fall of the Philippines*, 125–132.
73. Jonathan M. Wainwright, *General Wainwright's Story: The Account of Four Years of Humiliating Defeat, Surrender, and Captivity* (Garden City, NY: Doubleday, 1946), 48.
74. Morton, *The Fall of the Philippines*, 136–138.
75. Ibid., 142–144.
76. Manchester, *American Caesar*, 242.
77. Morton, *The Fall of the Philippines*, 145.
78. For an analysis of these realities, see Louis Morton, *Strategy and Command: The First Two Years* (Washington, DC: Office of the Chief of Military History, 1962), 186–193.
79. Morton, *The Fall of the Philippines*, 148.
80. Dwight D. Eisenhower, *Crusade in Europe* (Garden City, NY: Doubleday, 1948), 21–22.
81. Morton, *The Fall of the Philippines*, 152.
82. Ibid., 155.
83. John W. Whitman, "Decision That Starved an Army," *Army Logistician* 95, no. 2 (1995): 36–39.
84. Morton, *The Fall of the Philippines*, 234.
85. Rogers, *The Good Years*, 135.
86. Morton, *The Fall of the Philippines*, 164–165.
87. Ibid., 166.
88. Ibid., 174.
89. Ibid., 177.
90. Ibid., 180n60.
91. Volckmann would survive the battle and the campaign, becoming one of the foremost leaders of Filipino guerrillas in northern Luzon from 1942 to 1945.
92. Morton, *The Fall of the Philippines*, 189.
93. Ibid., 197.
94. Ibid., 200–201.
95. Ibid., 207–208.

96. Ibid., 210.
97. Ibid., 220.
98. Ibid., 225.
99. Wainwright, *General Wainwright's Story*, 46.
100. Morton, *The Fall of the Philippines*, 238–241.
101. The 26th Cavalry (PS) was converted to a motorized squadron equipped with trucks and a mechanized unit equipped with M3 scout cars.
102. Morton, *The Fall of the Philippines*, 245–248.
103. USAFFE 311.23, MacArthur to Unit Commanders, January 5, 1942, Entry 540, Box 31, RG 496, NARA II.
104. Morton, *The Fall of the Philippines*, 259.
105. Ibid., 265–278; Herman, *MacArthur*, 380–381. MacArthur biographer William Manchester posits that, having promised reinforcements to the troops in Bataan, he couldn't face them knowing there would be no aid forthcoming. Manchester, *American Caesar*, 267.
106. Morton, *The Fall of the Philippines*, 285–290.
107. Ibid., 278–285.
108. Ibid., 290.
109. Ibid., 295.
110. Ibid., 296–306.
111. William E. Dyess, *The Dyess Story: The Eye-Witness Account of the Death March from Bataan and the Narrative of Experiences in Japanese Prison Camps and of Eventual Escape* (New York: G. P. Putnam's Sons, 1944), 43.
112. Ibid., 44–45.
113. Morton, *The Fall of the Philippines*, 306–311; Wainwright, *General Wainwright's Story*, 56–57.
114. Morton, *The Fall of the Philippines*, 314–317.
115. Ibid., 318–319.
116. Ibid., 319–324.
117. Ibid., 328–329.
118. Ibid., 329.
119. Ibid., 330–336.
120. On February 3, Lt. Willibald C. Bianchi of New Ulm, Minnesota, earned the Medal of Honor by personally assaulting two machine gun positions, knocking out one with a grenade before being overcome by several bullet wounds. He was evacuated and survived the campaign, only to be killed on January 9, 1945, when the unmarked Japanese ship in which he was being transported was hit by a 1,000-lb. bomb. The author was also born in New Ulm and is a member of American Legion Post 132, named after Bianchi and Cpl. Benjamin J. Seifert, New Ulm's first World War I casualty.
121. Morton, *The Fall of the Philippines*, 336–341.
122. Ibid., 342–345.
123. Ibid., 347, 350.

124. Morton, *Strategy and Command*, 190.

125. John Jacob Beck, *MacArthur and Wainwright: Sacrifice of the Philippines* (Albuquerque: University of New Mexico Press, 1974), 100.

126. For Quezon's views, see Manuel Luis Quezon, *The Good Fight* (New York: D. Appleton-Century, 1946), 268–276.

127. MacArthur, *Reminiscences*, 139.

128. Romulo, *I Saw the Fall of the Philippines*, 322.

129. MacArthur, *Reminiscences*, 140. Quezon suffered from tuberculosis and required evacuation both to form a government in exile and to get out of the fetid air of Malinta Tunnel. The US High Commissioner to the Philippines, Francis B. Sayre, and his wife left Corregidor three days later.

130. Sutherland was awarded $75,000; Marshall $45,000; and Huff $20,000. Rogers, *The Good Years*, 165. Huff was a naval lieutenant when he joined MacArthur as his naval adviser in 1935. In 1941, MacArthur transferred Huff to the US Army and commissioned him as a lieutenant colonel. Huff would spend most of the war as aide to MacArthur's wife Jean Faircloth.

131. Carol M. Petillo, "Douglas MacArthur and Manuel Quezon: A Note on an Imperial Bond," *Pacific Historical Review* 48, no. 1 (February 1979): 107–117.

132. USAFFE 311.23, MacArthur to Unit Commanders, January 15, 1942, Entry 540, Box 30, RG 496, NARA II.

133. Rogers, *The Good Years*, 143–144; Herman, *MacArthur*, 354; Manchester, *American Caesar*, 273–274.

134. Morton, *The Fall of the Philippines*, Chapter 22; D. Clayton James, *The Years of MacArthur*, vol. II: *1941–1945* (Boston: Houghton Mifflin, 1975), 84.

135. Morton, *The Fall of the Philippines*, 378.

136. James, *The Years of MacArthur*, vol. II, 89.

137. Morton, *The Fall of the Philippines*, 355–357; Morton, *Strategy and Command*, 194; MacArthur, *Reminiscences*, 140–141.

138. Wainwright, *General Wainwright's Story*, 5. Wainwright survived the war as a prisoner in Manchuria and met MacArthur again not in Bataan, but in Yokohama.

139. MacArthur refused to evacuate via submarine as doing so "would be too time-consuming." Rogers, *The Good Years*, 184. This seems unlikely to have been the real reason. More likely was MacArthur's claustrophobia, which would flare up in a submarine.

140. MacArthur, *Reminiscences*, 142.

141. The members of the party were Gen. MacArthur, his wife Jean, their four-year-old son Arthur, and the family's Chinese amah Loh Chiu (referred to by the MacArthurs as Au Cheu); his doctor, Maj. Charles H. Morhouse; Maj. Gen. Sutherland and Brig. Gen. Marshall; MacArthur's aide Lt. Col. Sidney Huff; Sutherland's aide Lt. Col. Francis H. Wilson; Rear Adm. Francis W. Rockwell and his chief of staff, US Navy Capt. Harold G. Ray; Col. Charles P. Stivers, G-1; Col. Charles A. Willoughby, G-2, and Capt. Joseph McMicking, Asst. G-2; Brig.

Gen. Spencer B. Akin, Signal Officer, and Lt. Col. Joe R. Sherr, Asst. Signal Officer; Brig. Gen. Hugh J. Casey, Engineer Officer; Brig. Gen. William F. Marquat, Anti-Aircraft Officer; Brig. Gen. Harold H. George, Air Officer; Maj. LeGrande A. Diller, Public Relations Officer; and MacArthur and Sutherland's stenographer, MSgt. Paul P. Rogers, who just a day earlier had been promoted from private.

142. Morton, *The Fall of the Philippines*, 357–360. MacArthur awarded all crew members of the four PT boats and the two B-17 bombers which carried his party to safety the Silver Star. From Batchelor Field near Darwin, MacArthur and his party flew by DC-3 to Alice Springs. Jean MacArthur decided that she had had enough of airplanes, and a special train was arranged to carry MacArthur and his family the rest of the way across the continent. The bulk of the party flew on to Melbourne to arrange his welcome.

143. Romulo, *I Saw the Fall of the Philippines*, 220.

144. USAFFE 311.23, Commanding General USAFFE to War Department, March 19, 1942, RG 496, Entry 540, Box 30, NARA II; Morton, *The Fall of the Philippines*, 363–366.

145. USAFFE 311.23, Commanding General, USFIP to Commanding General, USAFFE, March 27, 1942, Entry 540, Box 30, RG 496, NARA II.

146. Wainwright, *General Wainwright's Story*, 72.

147. Ibid., 63; Morton, *The Fall of the Philippines*, 369–371, 376–378.

148. Wainwright, *General Wainwright's Story*, 60.

149. USAFFE 311.23, Commanding General, USFIP to General Marshall, War Department, March 28, 1942, Entry 540, Box 30, RG 496, NARA II.

150. Morton, *The Fall of the Philippines*, Chapter 23.

151. Ibid., 421–422.

152. Ibid., 422–427.

153. Ibid., 427–431.

154. Ibid., 434–437.

155. Ibid., 438–440.

156. Ibid., 442–448.

157. Ibid., 448–453; MacArthur, *Reminiscences*, 146. MacArthur writes that Washington failed to approve his planned last-ditch offensive, and that, had Luzon Force executed his plans, the Bataan Death March "would never have taken place." Neither assertion is correct.

158. Morton, *The Fall of the Philippines*, 454–455; Wainwright, *General Wainwright's Story*, 83–84.

159. The last plane to depart Bataan, a patched-up J2F Duck amphibious biplane, carried MacArthur aide Carlos Romulo and five aviators to safety. Romulo, *I Saw the Fall of the Philippines*, 290–295.

160. Morton, *The Fall of the Philippines*, 458–466.

161. USAFFE 461, Wainwright to MacArthur, April 9, 1942, Entry 540, Box 45, RG 496, NARA II.

162. Stanley L. Falk, *Bataan: The March of Death* (New York: W. W. Norton, 1962), 57–62.
163. Ibid., 107–109.
164. Ibid., 143–158.
165. Ibid., 184–193.
166. Ibid., 194–200.
167. Dyess's description of his experiences during the death march are in Dyess, *The Dyess Story*, 68–97.
168. Falk, *Bataan*, Chapter 20.
169. For a discussion of the impact of organizational culture on military forces, see Peter R. Mansoor and Williamson Murray, *The Culture of Military Organizations* (New York: Cambridge University Press, 2019).
170. Morton, *The Fall of the Philippines*, 498–503.
171. Ibid., 503–506.
172. Ibid., 506–507.
173. Ibid., 510–513.
174. Ibid., 513–515.
175. Ibid., 516–519.
176. Ibid., 474.
177. James Black, Jr., "The Manila Harbor Forts: 1942," *Philippine Studies* 36, no. 2 (1988): 208–218.
178. Wainwright, *General Wainwright's Story*, 74.
179. Morton, *The Fall of the Philippines*, 493–497.
180. Ibid., 524.
181. Ibid., 536–541.
182. Romulo, *I Saw the Fall of the Philippines*, 132.
183. Morton, *The Fall of the Philippines*, 542–546; Wainwright, *General Wainwright's Story*, 98–109.
184. Morton, *The Fall of the Philippines*, 546–551.
185. For a detailed history of the 4th Marines at Corregidor, see Frank O. Hough, *History of the U.S. Marine Corps Operations in World War II*, vol. I: *Pearl Harbor to Guadalcanal* (Washington, DC: Historical Branch, G-3 Division, US Marine Corps, 1959).
186. Morton, *The Fall of the Philippines*, 554–564.
187. Wainwright, *General Wainwright's Story*, 122–123. Stimson and Marshall favored awarding Wainwright the Medal of Honor, but MacArthur, angry that Wainwright had ordered the surrender of all US forces in the Philippines and not just those on Bataan and Corregidor, vehemently argued against it. Wainwright, who was much more deserving of the honor than MacArthur, eventually received the medal after the war ended. James, *The Years of MacArthur*, vol. II, 150–151.
188. Wainwright, *General Wainwright's Story*, 128–143; Morton, *The Fall of the Philippines*, 565–573.
189. Ibid., 574–582.

CHAPTER 2: THE LONG ROAD BACK

1. *Reports of General MacArthur: The Campaigns of MacArthur in the Pacific*, vol. I (Washington, DC: Center of Military History, 1966), 161.
2. D. Clayton James, *The Years of MacArthur*, vol. II: *1941–1945* (Boston, MA: Houghton Mifflin, 1975), 133–141.
3. "I Came Through; I Shall Return," *The Advertiser* (Adelaide, South Australia), March 21, 1942, 1, https://trove.nla.gov.au/newspaper/article/48749454.
4. William Manchester, *American Caesar: Douglas MacArthur, 1880–1964* (Boston, MA: Little, Brown, 1978; New York: Dell, 1978), 311–312.
5. James, *The Years of MacArthur*, vol. II, 109.
6. Maurice Matloff and Edwin M. Snell, *Strategic Planning for Coalition Warfare, 1941–1942* (Washington, DC: Center of Military History, 1953), 169–172. The final division of responsibilities came into effect on April 18, 1942, after the British, Australian, New Zealand, and Dutch (in exile) governments agreed to it.
7. The Joint Chiefs of Staff reassigned Guadalcanal and Tulagi in the Solomon Islands to the South Pacific Theater of Operations on July 2, 1942.
8. For the organization of SWPA, see *Reports of General MacArthur*, Chapter 2. The following paragraphs are based on this source.
9. D. M. Horner, "Blamey and MacArthur: The Problem of Coalition Warfare," in William M. Leary, ed., *We Shall Return! MacArthur's Commanders and the Defeat of Japan, 1942–1945* (Lexington: University Press of Kentucky, 1988), 23–59, 24–27.
10. That directive, issued on March 30, stated in part, "As Supreme Commander you are not eligible to command directly any national force." James, *The Years of MacArthur*, vol. II, 120. The Australians accepted the arrangement, which minimized Blamey's role, with grace.
11. The 41st Infantry Division was known as the "Sunsetters," but would receive the nickname "Jungleers" during the New Guinea campaign.
12. Horner, "Blamey and MacArthur," 29.
13. Eichelberger relieved Maj. Gen. Edwin F. Harding at Buna and Maj. Gen. Horace Fuller on Biak. Jay Luvaas, ed., *DEAR MISS EM: General Eichelberger's War in the Pacific, 1942–1945* (Westport, CT: Greenwood, 1972), 4.
14. Samuel Milner, *Victory in Papua* (Washington, DC: Office of the Chief of Military History, 1957), 25–26.
15. Manchester, *American Caesar*, 407. Manchester cites a volume by historian Forrest Pogue as the source for this statement, but Pogue rebuffs this claim. See Forrest Pogue, "The Military in a Democracy: A Review: *American Caesar*," *International Security* 3, no. 4 (Spring, 1979): 58–80, 65.
16. Roger O. Egeberg, *The General: MacArthur and the Man He Called "Doc"* (New York: Hippocrene Books, 1983), 127–128.
17. Ranks are as of the summer of 1942; most of the staff received further promotion later in the war.

18. John C. McManus, *Fire and Fortitude: The US Army in the Pacific War, 1941–1943* (New York: Caliber, 2019), 67.

19. Anton Myrer, *Once an Eagle* (New York: Holt, Rinehart, and Winston, 1968).

20. D. Clayton James, "Historical Critique of [the movie] 'MacArthur'," December 17, 1976, Folder 27, Box 4, Papers of D. Clayton James, Special Collections Library Department, Mississippi State University, Starkville, Mississippi.

21. James, *The Years of MacArthur*, 77–78.

22. Paul P. Rogers, *The Good Years: MacArthur and Sutherland* (New York: Praeger, 1990), 139.

23. Ibid., 138, 231.

24. Ibid., 245.

25. Edward J. Drea, *MacArthur's Ultra: Codebreaking and the War against Japan, 1942–1945* (Lawrence, KS: University Press of Kansas, 1992), 17.

26. Charles A. Willoughby, *Maneuver in War* (Harrisburg, PA: Military Service Publishing, 1939).

27. James, *The Years of MacArthur*, 78–80.

28. Jack Torry, *Last One Out: Yates McDaniel: World War II's Most Daring Reporter* (Atglen, PA: Schiffer Military, 2021), 133.

29. Rogers, *The Good Years*, 275.

30. Ibid., 288.

31. Ian W. Toll, *Twilight of the Gods: War in the Western Pacific, 1944–1945* (New York: W. W. Norton, 2020), 35.

32. For an examination of the development of Eisenhower's headquarters and its approach to combined operations, see Carson Teuscher, "Allied Force: Coalition Warfare in the Mediterranean and the Allied Template for Victory, 1942–1943" (Ph.D. dissertation, Ohio State University, 2024).

33. For an examination of the organization of GHQ SWPA, see Peter J. Dean, *MacArthur's Coalition: US and Australian Military Operations in the Southwest Pacific Area, 1942–1945* (Lawrence, KS: University Press of Kansas, 2018), Chapter 3. The only Australian officer on the SWPA staff was a liaison officer.

34. Gerald E. Wheeler, "Thomas C. Kinkaid: MacArthur's Master of Naval Warfare," in William M. Leary, ed., *We Shall Return! MacArthur's Commanders and the Defeat of Japan, 1942–1945* (Lexington: University Press of Kentucky, 1988), 115–154, 118.

35. Rogers, *The Good Years*, 226.

36. Horner, "Blamey and MacArthur," 58.

37. Egeberg was MacArthur's personal physician, who became an aide to save him from the wrath of Lt. Gen. Sutherland and his Australian mistress, Elaine Bessemer Clark. Clark's husband, Capt. Reginald Bessemer Clark, had been captured in Malaya and spent the war in a Japanese prison camp. Sutherland was married with an adult daughter; Clark had a young son. The two did little to hide their affair, and MacArthur feigned indifference until Sutherland crossed the

line and brought his paramour forward to New Guinea and Leyte, resulting in the end of their close relationship. John C. McManus, *Island Infernos: The US Army's Pacific War Odyssey, 1944* (New York: Caliber, 2021), 174–177.

38. Rogers, *The Good Years*, 71.

39. Egeberg, *The General*, 42.

40. Ibid., 46.

41. Milner, *Victory in Papua*, 25.

42. Horner, "Blamey and MacArthur," 35. Horner calls this "one of the most controversial episodes in Australian military history."

43. Ibid., 37.

44. Louis Morton, *Strategy and Command: The First Two Years* (Washington, DC: Office of the Chief of Military History, 1962), 341–342.

45. For an examination of the offensive to seize Buna and Gona, see *Papuan Campaign: The Buna–Sanananda Operation (16 November 1942–23 January 1943)* (Washington, DC: War Department Historical Division, 1945) and Milner, *Victory in Papua*.

46. For an extended examination of Operation Cartwheel, see John Miller, Jr., *Cartwheel: The Reduction of Rabaul* (Washington, DC: Office of the Chief of Military History, 1959).

47. Eric M. Bergerud, *Touched with Fire: The Land War in the South Pacific* (New York: Viking, 1996), 129.

48. Ibid., 132–133.

49. John F. Shortal, *Forged by Fire: General Robert L. Eichelberger and the Pacific War* (Columbia, SC: University of South Carolina Press, 1987), 37.

50. Bergerud, *Touched with Fire*, 211.

51. Ibid., 213.

52. For a comprehensive assessment of the combat effectiveness of the 32nd Infantry Division entering the Buna campaign, see Milner, *Victory in Papua*, 132–137.

53. *Papuan Campaign*, 9–14.

54. Milner, *Victory in Papua*, 197.

55. Ibid., 169–170, 200.

56. Horner, "Blamey and MacArthur," 38.

57. Rogers, *The Good Years*, 326.

58. Robert L. Eichelberger, *Our Jungle Road to Tokyo* (New York City: Viking Press, 1950), 21. Eichelberger's chief of staff, Brig. Gen. Clovis Byers, hailed from Columbus, Ohio. He attended Ohio State University and was in the same fraternity (Phi Gamma Delta – albeit in different years) as Eichelberger, and, like his boss, he had left Columbus to attend West Point, where he graduated in 1920. He was Eichelberger's chief of staff when the latter officer commanded the 77th Infantry Division, and followed his boss to Australia when he took command of I Corps.

59. Interview with Maj. Gen. Byers and Lt. Gen. Eichelberger, June 1, 1950, OCMH WWII Pacific Interviews – Papua, USAHEC.

60. Shortal, *Forged by Fire*, 49–51.

61. Milner, *Victory in Papua*, 246.

62. Interview with Maj. Gen. Harding, December 10, 1947, OCMH WWII Pacific Interviews – Papua, USAHEC.

63. Eichelberger, *Our Jungle Road to Tokyo*, 24–32.

64. Urbana Force on the western part of the battlefield at Buna was named after Eichelberger's hometown, while Warren Force in the east was named after Harding's hometown. Both generals hailed from Ohio.

65. MacArthur awarded Staff Sgt. Bottcher a Distinguished Service Cross and a battlefield commission to the rank of captain. Milner, *Victory in Papua*, 244n25.

66. Milner, *Victory in Papua*, 238–259; Shortal, *Forged by Fire*, 54.

67. *Papuan Campaign*, 20; Herman S. Wolk, "George C. Kenney: MacArthur's Premier Airman," in William M. Leary, ed., *We Shall Return! MacArthur's Commanders and the Defeat of Japan, 1942–1945* (Lexington: University Press of Kentucky, 1988), 88–114, 100.

68. Milner, *Victory in Papua*, 264–265.

69. *Papuan Campaign*, 36–59.

70. Ibid., 70–80; James, *The Years of MacArthur*, vol. II, 274.

71. Miller, *Cartwheel*, 38.

72. *Papuan Campaign*, 81; James, *The Years of MacArthur*, vol. II, 280; Milner, *Victory in Papua*, 371. US Army and Marine dead numbered roughly 1,600 men on Guadalcanal. John Miller, Jr., *Guadalcanal: The First Offensive* (Washington, DC: Office of the Chief of Military History, 1949), 350.

73. Milner, *Victory in Papua*, 372.

74. MacArthur did award Eichelberger a Distinguished Service Cross, but the announcement of the award was lumped in with others awarded to members of his staff who had never crossed the Owen Stanley Mountains to visit Buna.

75. Shortal, *Forged by Fire*, 64–65.

76. Douglas MacArthur, *Reminiscences* (New York: McGraw-Hill, 1964), 169.

77. *Reports of General MacArthur: The Campaigns of MacArthur in the Pacific*, vol. I (Washington, DC: Center of Military History, 1966), 100.

78. *Reports of General MacArthur*, 42.

79. *Yank* 2, no. 4 (July 16, 1943): 17.

80. *Reports of General MacArthur*, 43.

81. Bergerud, *Touched with Fire*, 92–93; Robert J. T. Joy, "Malaria in American Troops in the South and Southwest Pacific in World War II," *Medical History* 43 (1999), 192–207; *Papuan Campaign*, 92–94.

82. Milner, *Victory in Papua*, 372.

83. Ibid.

84. Bergerud, *Touched with Fire*, 61.

85. MacArthur, *Reminiscences*, 157.

86. Rogers, *The Good Years*, 246.
87. Charles Willoughby and G-2 Section, SWPA, *History of Intelligence Activities under General MacArthur, 1942–1950* (microform), 11.
88. Ibid., 17–18.
89. Ibid., 29–33; History and Business of G-2 P.I. Section, January 18, 1946, Entry 123, Box 619, RG 496, NARA II.
90. *History of Intelligence Activities under General MacArthur*, 63–65.
91. Ibid., 59–62.
92. Ibid., 66–69. The best source on the creation and operations of the Central Bureau is Drea, *MacArthur's Ultra*.
93. The breaking of the naval code before the Battle of Midway was not the end of the story. Japanese naval codes changed periodically from late May 1942 until the end of 1944, resulting in a constant struggle to decrypt messages that used new codes, ciphers, and rules of usage. Beginning in January 1945, the breaking of the *Ransuuban* system resulted in US codebreakers reading the vast majority of Japanese communications that used the new code until the end of the war. Richard B. Frank, "Code Breaking in the Asia Pacific War: Struggle and Triumph, May 1942 to December 1944," draft manuscript submitted for publication in a collection in honor of David Horner.
94. Drea, *MacArthur's Ultra*, xi, 62; "History of the Operations of Special Security Officers Attached to Field Commands," Entry A1 9002, Box 14, RG 457, NARA II. Soldiers of the Australian 9th Division found a trunk with the entire cryptographic library of the Japanese 20th Division which had been discarded in a muddy pit in New Guinea during the Japanese retreat from Saidor. As soon as the material was cleaned and dried, the Central Bureau was translating 2,000 pages of coded messages a day. Lori S. Stewart, "Japanese Code Library Found in New Guinea," US Army Intelligence Center of Excellence, January 13, 2023, www.dvidshub.net/news/436784/japanese-code-library-found-new-guinea.
95. Drea, *MacArthur's Ultra*, 21–22.
96. Report of Special Security Representative, HQ Armed Forces Pacific, 1 January–1 December 1945, Entry A1 9002, Box 14, RG 457, NARA II.
97. *History of Intelligence Activities under General MacArthur*, 36.
98. Drea, *MacArthur's Ultra*, 24–25.
99. Ibid., 28.
100. Ibid., 30.
101. *History of Intelligence Activities under General MacArthur*, 40–44. The result of these leaflet drops was the surrender of just 950 Japanese soldiers, one for every 52,632 leaflets. Ibid., p. 49.
102. Ibid., 32–38. In all, AIB coordinated for the delivery of 325,000 pounds of supplies to agents and guerrilla forces. Ibid., 49.
103. Ibid., 45–46.
104. James, *The Years of MacArthur*, vol. II, 334–335; Manchester, *American Caesar*, 390–391.

105. *Reports of General MacArthur*, 100–101.

106. MacArthur, *Reminiscences*, 174.

107. In one amusing incident, Barbey tested a new craft called an "Alligator," a tracked landing craft that could crawl over coral reefs, by driving through the streets of Washington and crossing the Potomac River into a nearby lake. Upon emerging from the water after the successful test, the crew – including Barbey – was arrested for violating a wildlife sanctuary. Daniel E. Barbey, *MacArthur's Amphibious Navy: Seventh Amphibious Force Operations, 1943–1945* (Annapolis, MD: United States Naval Institute, 1969), 20.

108. Ibid., 21.

109. Ibid., 24.

110. Ibid.

111. *Reports of General MacArthur*, 107; Arthur Herman, *Douglas MacArthur: American Warrior* (New York: Random House, 2016), 462–465.

112. Kevin C. Holzimmer, *General Walter Krueger: Unsung Hero of the Pacific War* (Lawrence, KS: University Press of Kansas, 2007), 97.

113. Luvaas, *DEAR MISS EM*, 65.

114. Paul P. Rogers, *The Bitter Years: MacArthur and Sutherland* (New York: Praeger, 1991), 18

115. Holzimmer, *General Walter Krueger*, 102–103.

116. Biography of Lieutenant General Walter Krueger, Papers of Walter Krueger Jr., Box 12, USMA Library Special Collections; William M. Leary, "Walter Krueger: MacArthur's Fighting General," in William M. Leary, ed., *We Shall Return! MacArthur's Commanders and the Defeat of Japan, 1942–1945* (Lexington: University Press of Kentucky, 1988), 60–87, 60–64.

117. Rogers, *The Bitter Years*, 34–35.

118. Ibid., 93.

119. Ibid., 35.

120. Leary, "Walter Krueger," 65.

121. Luvaas, *DEAR MISS EM*, 214.

122. Ibid., 64. In his correspondence with his wife, Eichelberger referred to MacArthur as "Sarah" to escape the censor's pen. Sarah stood for Sarah Bernhardt, a self-absorbed French stage actress – a clear allusion to MacArthur's theatrics and vanity. When he thought better of MacArthur, which he did in 1945 when leading the Eighth Army in the liberation of the Central and Southern Philippines, Eichelberger referred to him in letters home as the "Big Chief."

123. Rogers, *The Bitter Years*, 56.

124. Barbey, *MacArthur's Amphibious Navy*, 170.

125. Shortal, *Forged by Fire*, 66–68. Eichelberger was a West Point classmate of Third Army commander Lt. Gen. George S. Patton, Jr., and Ninth Army commander Lt. Gen. William Simpson, and would have fought alongside them had one of these promotions been granted, perhaps even supplanting Omar Bradley as future commander of the 12th Army Group.

126. Luvaas, *DEAR MISS EM*, 65.

127. Rogers, *The Good Years*, 329.

128. George C. Kenney, *General Kenney Reports: A Personal History of the Pacific War* (New York: Duell, Sloan and Pearce, 1949), 114.

129. MacArthur, *Reminiscences*, 157.

130. Alexus Gregory Grynkewich, "'Advisable in the National Interest?' The Relief of General George C. Kenney," MA Thesis, University of Georgia, 1994, 25–26; Wolk, "George C. Kenney," 91.

131. Kenney, *General Kenney Reports*, ix–x.

132. Ibid., 44–45.

133. Ibid., 52–53.

134. Ibid., 53–59. One of the bomber pilots, Harl Pease Jr., was posthumously awarded the Medal of Honor for his heroic actions during the strike.

135. Ibid., 62–63.

136. James, *The Years of MacArthur*, vol. II, 199.

137. Manchester, *American Caesar*, 350.

138. Donald M. Goldstein, "Ennis C. Whitehead: Aerial Tactician," in William M. Leary, ed., *We Shall Return! MacArthur's Commanders and the Defeat of Japan, 1942–1945* (Lexington: University Press of Kentucky, 1988), 178–207, 192.

139. Kenney, *General Kenney Reports*, 73.

140. Ibid., 203–206; *Reports of General MacArthur*, 110–111; Miller, *Cartwheel*, 39–41. Kenney's memoir overstates Japanese losses, which nevertheless were considerable. A US Army Air Forces study corrected the inflated figures for Japanese losses initially reported by SWPA. James, *The Years of MacArthur*, vol. II, 298. For a concise account, see Sam McGowan, "Battle of the Bismarck Sea: A 15-Minute War in the South Pacific," Warfare History Network, March 2004, https://wa rfarehistorynetwork.com/article/battle-of-the-bismarck-sea-a-15-minute-war-i n-the-south-pacific.

141. *Reports of General MacArthur*, 111.

142. Kenney, *General Kenney Reports*, Chapter 9.

143. Horner, "Blamey and MacArthur," 42–43.

144. Miller, *Cartwheel*, 49–59.

145. Ibid., 50; Barbey, *MacArthur's Amphibious Navy*, 58–68.

146. *Reports of General MacArthur*, 120–121.

147. Kenney, *General Kenney Reports*, 276–279, 285. Kenney's headquarters overestimated the number of aircraft destroyed, a figure revised after the war when historians gained access to Japanese records. Miller, *Cartwheel*, 199n10.

148. The division's amphibious landing was the first by Australian forces since the ill-fated Gallipoli campaign in 1915.

149. *Reports of General MacArthur*, 122–124; Miller, *Cartwheel*, 200–221; Barbey, *MacArthur's Amphibious Navy*, 74. After the Lae operation, Seaman First Class Johnnie D. Hutchins was awarded the Medal of Honor posthumously for

guiding LST-473 clear of oncoming torpedoes after Japanese bombs wrecked the pilot house of the ship and mortally wounded him. Barbey, *MacArthur's Amphibious Navy*, 83.

150. Kenney, *General Kenney Reports*, 313; Bernhardt L. Mortensen, "Rabaul and Cape Gloucester," in Wesley Frank Craven and James Lea Cate, eds., *The Army Air Forces in World War II*, vol. V: *The Pacific: Matterhorn to Nagasaki, June 1944 to August 1945* (Chicago: University Press of Chicago, 1953), 311–358, 321. Japanese shipping losses were exaggerated by the aircrews and later revised downward, albeit still considerable.

151. Leading one B-25 squadron in the attack, Maj. Raymond H. Wilkins and his crew accounted for hits on a destroyer and a transport before antiaircraft fire downed their plane. Wilkins was posthumously awarded the Medal of Honor. Kenney, *General Kenney Reports*, 319–321; Mortensen, "Rabaul and Cape Gloucester," 325–326. The American losses in the raid on November 2 are certain, while Japanese losses were no doubt lower than those reported at the time.

152. Kenney, *General Kenney Reports*, 321.

153. Miller, *Cartwheel*, 312.

154. MacArthur, *Reminiscences*, 183–184.

155. In his memoir, Barbey relates an amusing story of an attempt by three Red Cross workers to establish a morale service facility at Cape Gloucester sometime after the landing by the 1st Marine Division. The commander of LST-457, former Congressman James Van Zandt of Pennsylvania, attempted to warn the three women away, describing the awful conditions ashore. But, armed with orders from GHQ SWPA, they demanded passage regardless. Upon arriving at the beachhead, Van Zandt reported "his arrival with 400 troops, 100 vehicles, 300 tons of bulk cargo, and 3 Red Cross girls and requesting instructions. The instructions came quickly: 'Land troops, vehicles, and cargo on Yellow Beach. Keep girls locked up and return to Buna.'" Barbey, *MacArthur's Amphibious Navy*, 125.

156. For an examination of the culture of the Imperial Japanese Army before and during World War II, see David Hunter-Chester, "Imperial Japanese Army Culture, 1918–1945: Duty Heavier Than a Mountain, Death Lighter Than a Feather," in Peter R. Mansoor and Williamson Murray, *The Culture of Military Organizations* (New York: Cambridge University Press, 2019), 208–225.

157. John Dower, *War without Mercy: Race and Power in the Pacific War* (New York: W. W. Norton, 1986).

158. Bergerud, *Touched with Fire*, 415.

159. The Allied fleet also included vessels from Australia, New Zealand, and the Netherlands.

160. Gerald E. Wheeler, *Kinkaid of the Seventh Fleet: A Biography of Admiral Thomas C. Kinkaid, U.S. Navy* (Washington, DC: Naval Historical Center, 1995), 343.

161. The Great White Fleet was the popular name for a US task force of sixteen battleships and their escorts that circumnavigated the earth from

December 16, 1907, to February 22, 1909, to showcase the global reach of the US Navy. The ships were painted white to highlight the peaceful nature of the voyage.

162. Wheeler, *Kinkaid of the Seventh Fleet*, 361.
163. Ibid., 375.
164. Ibid., 348–350; *Reports of General MacArthur*, 134.
165. Wheeler, *Kinkaid of the Seventh Fleet*, 353.
166. Ibid., 376–377.
167. Stephen R. Taaffe, *MacArthur's Jungle War: The 1944 New Guinea Campaign* (Lawrence, KS: University Press of Kansas, 1998), 228–229.
168. The 1st Cavalry Division had left its horses behind in the United States and operated as infantry, albeit with an organizational structure unique to a horse cavalry division.
169. Miller, *Cartwheel*, 316.
170. Kenney, *General Kenney Reports*, 359; Thomas E. Griffith, Jr., *MacArthur's Airman: General George C. Kenney and the War in the Southwest Pacific* (Lawrence, KS: University Press of Kansas, 1998), 151. Instead of firing on the circling aircraft, the Japanese defenders hid and held their fire, which confused the aerial observers.
171. Miller, *Cartwheel*, 321.
172. Larry Alexander, *Shadows in the Jungle: The Alamo Scouts behind Japanese Lines in World War II* (New York: Caliber, 2009), 80.
173. 1 CD G-2, Admiralties G-2 Periodic Reports, 25 February 1944, 901-2.1, RG 407, NARA II.
174. Barbey, *MacArthur's Amphibious Navy*, 151.
175. "Sketch History of the 1st Cavalry Brigade, 9 June 1944," 901-CC(1)-0.1, NARA II. Chase had big shoes to fill, as the pre-war commander of the 1st Cavalry Brigade was Brig. Gen. Jonathan Wainwright, who had been taken prisoner by Japanese forces after defending the Philippines in 1941–1942.
176. Lobit would earn a Distinguished Service Cross for his gallant leadership during the invasion of Los Negros.
177. Because MacArthur decided to accompany the invasion task force, Vice Adm. Kinkaid added two cruisers and four destroyers to the destroyer division initially tasked with supporting the invasion to provide the theater commander with adequate communications and protection. Miller, *Cartwheel*, 321–322.
178. Ibid., 326.
179. For its actions on February 29, 1944, the 2nd Squadron, 5th Cavalry was awarded a Distinguished Unit Citation.
180. Harold D. Steward, "The First Was First" (Manila, 1945), 901-0, RG 407, NARA II. Henshaw later drowned while trying to save a soldier's life when a boat in which he was riding sank off the coast of Los Negros.
181. Barbey, *MacArthur's Amphibious Navy*, 154.

182. 1 Cav Bde, 1 CD, Historical Report, 28 February–18 May 1944, 901-CC(1)-0.3, RG 407, NARA II.

183. Sergeant Troy A. McGill held his revetment single-handedly after most of his squad mates had died around him. When his rifle ammunition ran out, he leaped forward to club the attacking Japanese troops until they killed him. At dawn, his fellow soldiers counted more than 105 Japanese dead in front of the position; McGill was credited with 60 of them. Sergeant McGill was awarded a posthumous Medal of Honor for his heroic actions.

184. Major Bertram C. Wright, *The 1st Cavalry Division in World War II* (Tokyo: Toppan, 1947), 20.

185. 1 Cav Bde, 1 CD, Translation of Captured Situation and Operation Telegrams of Admiralty Garrison Unit, 29 February–18 March 1944, Telegram #137, 901-CC(1)-0.3, RG 407, NARA II.

186. 1 Cav Bde, 1 CD, Historical Report, 28 February–18 May 1944.

187. 8th Cavalry, Historical Report, Admiralties Campaign, 6 March–20 May 1944, Section 2, Lessons Learned, 901-CRG(8)-0.3, RG 407, NARA II.

188. HQ, 1 CD, "Historical Report of the Brewer Task Force (1st Cavalry Division) in the Admiralty Islands Campaign, 24 January–18 May 1944," 27 June 1944, 41–46, 901-0.3, RG 407, NARA II.

189. 1 CD, "Diary of the Admiralty Islands Campaign, 29 February 44–2 April 44," 901-0.3.0.50, RG 407, NARA II, 1.

190. Ibid., 49.

191. 1 CD Artillery, "Historical Record, Admiralty Islands Campaign, 26 February to 18 May 1944," 901-ART-0.3, RG 407, NARA II.

192. 1 CD, "G-3 Historical Report – Admiralty Islands Campaign," June 7, 1944, 901-3, RG 407, NARA II.

193. General Clyde D. Eddleman Oral History, USAHEC, 29.

194. 2 Cav Bde, 1 CD, "Historical Report, Leyte-Samar Is. Campaign, 20 Oct–25 Dec 1944," 9 Jan 1945, 1, 901-CC(2)-0.3, RG 407, NARA II.

195. 1 CD, Training Memorandum No. 2, 27 May 1944, 901–3.13, RG 407, NARA II.

196. It is noteworthy that "even Admiral King, MacArthur's bitterest critic among the Joint Chiefs, conceded that [the invasion of the Admiralties] had been 'a brilliant maneuver.'" Manchester, *American Caesar*, 397.

197. Miller, *Cartwheel*, 350.

198. 1 CD, "Diary of the Admiralty Islands Campaign, 29 February 44–2 April 44," 50.

199. Edward J. Drea, "Ultra Intelligence and General Douglas MacArthur's Leap to Hollandia, January–April 1944," *Intelligence and National Security* 5, no. 2 (1990): 323–349.

200. Rogers, *The Bitter Years*, 73.

201. Drea, *MacArthur's Ultra*, 104–105.

202. Robert Ross Smith, *The Approach to the Philippines* (Washington, DC: Office of the Chief of Military History, 1953), 11–12. Of course, because Ultra

intelligence indicated the absence of significant Japanese combat forces at Hollandia, the scheme was anything but reckless.

203. Rogers, *The Bitter Years*, 75.
204. Barbey, *MacArthur's Amphibious Navy*, 179.
205. Kenney, *General Kenney Reports*, 372–374. During the summer of 1944, the civilian air pioneer Charles Lindbergh visited the Southwest Pacific Theater. Kenney put him to work teaching his pilots how to extend the range of their P-38 fighters. Lindbergh flew on several dozen combat missions and even shot down a Japanese aircraft. His guidance helped to increase the combat radius of the P-38s from 400 to more than 700 miles, a significant development in a theater where long flights were common. Ibid., 412–415.
206. Barbey, *MacArthur's Amphibious Navy*, 162.
207. Smith, *The Approach to the Philippines*, 20–32; Wheeler, "Thomas C. Kinkaid," 124–125.
208. *Reports of General MacArthur*, 145.
209. By the end of the Hollandia operation, the Japanese had lost 452 airplanes to bombing and air-to-air combat. Kenney, *General Kenney Reports*, 393; Smith, *The Approach to the Philippines*, 50.
210. *General Kenney Reports*, 381.
211. Ibid., 387.
212. Ibid., 388. That dubious honor would fall to Adm. Halsey's Third Fleet, which encountered Typhoon Cobra in December 1944. It sank 3 ships, destroyed 100 aircraft, and drowned 790 sailors.
213. Eichelberger, *Our Jungle Road to Tokyo*, 107.
214. Taaffe, *MacArthur's Jungle War*, 88.
215. Eichelberger, *Our Jungle Road to Tokyo*, 110; Taaffe, *MacArthur's Jungle War*, 91–92; Smith, *The Approach to the Philippines*, 78–79.
216. Shortal, *Forged by Fire*, 83.
217. *Reports of General MacArthur*, 146–148.
218. MacArthur, *Reminiscences*, 184.
219. Toll, *Twilight of the Gods*, 39–42; Manchester, *American Caesar*, 417–419.
220. Drea, *MacArthur's Ultra*, 129–130.
221. Smith, *The Approach to the Philippines*, 152–205; *Reports of General MacArthur*, 156–160.
222. Drea, *MacArthur's Ultra*, 126.
223. *General Kenney Reports*, 395.
224. Smith, *The Approach to the Philippines*, 219–231; *Reports of General MacArthur*, 151–152.
225. Smith, *The Approach to the Philippines*, Chapter 10.
226. Ibid., Chapter 11.
227. Barbey, *MacArthur's Amphibious Navy*, 195.
228. *General Kenney Reports*, 394–395.
229. Barbey, *MacArthur's Amphibious Navy*, 202.

230. Smith, *The Approach to the Philippines*, 355–356; Drea, *MacArthur's Ultra*, 139–140; Wheeler, *Kinkaid of the Seventh Fleet*, 371.

231. Barbey, *MacArthur's Amphibious Navy*, 203.

232. Eichelberger, *Our Jungle Road to Tokyo*, 156; Holzimmer, *General Walter Krueger*, 165.

233. Luvaas, *DEAR MISS EM*, 128.

234. Shortal, *Forged by Fire*, 90–91.

235. Eichelberger, *Our Jungle Road to Tokyo*, 135–154; *Reports of General MacArthur*, 152–153.

236. *General Kenney Reports*, 400.

237. Ibid.

238. *Reports of General MacArthur*, 149.

239. Because of the excessive jump casualties in the first two drops, the third battalion arrived by landing craft.

240. *Reports of General MacArthur*, 153–156; Smith, *The Approach to the Philippines*, 406–424.

241. Smith, *The Approach to the Philippines*, 440–448.

242. *Reports of General MacArthur*, 160–161.

243. Drea, *MacArthur's Ultra*, 108–109.

244. *Reports of General MacArthur*, 164. According to the SWPA staff, US aircraft and ships sank more than 5,000 Japanese vessels, most of them small barges and coastal craft, during the New Guinea campaign.

CHAPTER 3: THE RESISTANCE

1. "We Knew a Few Things from the Japanese," *The Paltik* (official journal of the FACGF), February 26, 1945, in Fil-American Cavite Guerrilla Forces (FACGF), Narrative History, Entry 112, Box 600, RG 496, NARA II.

2. Other great resistance movements rivaling the Filipino guerrillas were the Yugoslavian partisans in the Balkans, the Chinese Communist guerrillas on the Asian mainland, and the Soviet guerrillas on the Eastern Front. All of them played an important and sometimes crucial role in liberating their homelands from foreign occupation. The best overall history of the guerrilla movement in the Philippines during World War II is James Villanueva, *Awaiting MacArthur's Return: World War II Guerrilla Resistance against the Japanese in the Philippines* (Lawrence, KS: University Press of Kansas, 2022).

3. Robert Lapham and Bernard Norling, *Lapham's Raiders: Guerrillas in the Philippines, 1942–1945* (Lexington: University Press of Kentucky, 1996), 13–14, 17–18. MacArthur promoted Thorp to lieutenant colonel in March 1942.

4. Ibid., 19.

5. Ibid., 22.

6. Herminia S Dizon, "The Complete Data Covering the Guerrilla Activities of the Late Col. Claude A. Thorp," Philippine Archives Collection (Guerrillas), Col. Claude A. Thorp file, Box 258, RG 407, NARA II.

7. Lapham and Norling, *Lapham's Raiders*, p. 129; Yung Li Yuk-wai, *The Huaqiao Warriors: Chinese Resistance Movement in the Philippines, 1942–1945* (Manila: Ateneo de Manila University Press, 1996), 90.

8. Lapham and Norling, *Lapham's Raiders*, 133–134.

9. Edwin Price Ramsey and Stephen J. Rivele, *Lieutenant Ramsey's War: From Horse Soldier to Guerrilla Commander* (New York: Knightsbridge, 1990), 115.

10. Lawrence M. Greenberg, *The Hukbalahap Insurrection* (Washington: US Army Center of Military History, 1987), 17.

11. Max Boot, *The Road Not Taken: Edward Lansdale and the American Tragedy in Vietnam* (New York: Liveright, 2018).

12. Lapham and Norling, *Lapham's Raiders*, 36.

13. The US National Archives Philippine Archives Collection lists 1,318 entries for guerrilla groups in the Philippines during World War II, albeit many of them subunits of larger commands. The list is available online at www.archives.gov/research/military/ww2/philippine/guerrilla-list-1.html.

14. Lapham and Norling, *Lapham's Raiders*, 77.

15. Ibid., 54–55.

16. Ramsey and Rivele, *Lieutenant Ramsey's War*, Chapter 1. Ramsey left Bataan as a lieutenant and was promoted to major after communications with SWPA were restored in July 1944.

17. Ibid., 60–68. Ramsey was wounded in the attack and received the Silver Star for his valor in action. Bob Seals, "Lieutenant Colonel Edwin P. Ramsey, USA-Ret," *On Point* (Summer 2011): 17–20, 19.

18. In 1943, Ramsey moved his area of operations south to Manila.

19. Ramsey and Rivele, *Lieutenant Ramsey's War*, 111.

20. Ibid., 112.

21. Ibid., 113.

22. Ibid., 142.

23. Ibid., 163.

24. Ibid., 262.

25. Anderson 8, June 18, 1944, AIB PRS, "Who's Who," Entry 110, Box 586, RG 496, NARA II.

26. HQ Philippines Command, U.S. Army Recognition Program of Philippine Guerrillas, c. 1949, RG 554, NARA II, https://catalog.archives.gov/id/692176 7, 23–24; Lapham and Norling, *Lapham's Raiders*, 111–112. USAFFE Luzon Guerrilla Army Forces was renamed USAFFE Luzon Guerrilla Forces on January 1, 1944, and Anderson's Command on January 1, 1945.

27. Ramsey and Rivele, *Lieutenant Ramsey's War*, 253; HQ Philippines Command, U.S. Army Recognition Program of Philippine Guerrillas, c. 1949, RG 554, NARA II, https://catalog.archives.gov/id/6921767, 21–22. Promoted to

colonel, Santos eventually commanded upwards of 8,500 soldiers in Bulacan organized in 10 regiments.

28. A conclusion arrived at by Robert Lapham and others as well. Lapham and Norling, *Lapham's Raiders*, 113–114.

29. Russell W. Volckmann, *We Remained: Three Years behind the Enemy Lines in the Philippines* (New York: W. W. Norton, 1954), 40.

30. Ibid., 88.

31. Ibid., 108.

32. Ibid., 120; Bernard Norling, *The Intrepid Guerrillas of North Luzon* (Lexington: University of Kentucky Press, 1999), 175–178. Moses and Noble were captured on June 2, 1943.

33. Volckmann, *We Remained*, 122–125.

34. Norling, *The Intrepid Guerrillas of North Luzon*, 26–28.

35. Ibid., 55.

36. Volckmann to Lapham, Msg. No. 117, June 14, 1944, Entry 112, Box 605, RG 496, NARA II.

37. Lapham and Norling, *Lapham's Raiders*, 115. Ramsey, however, states that Lapham agreed to serve as his deputy in the East Central Luzon Area Force since the former was the senior officer by virtue of date of rank. See Ramsey and Rivele, *Lieutenant Ramsey's War*, 160–161.

38. Jesus Villamor, *They Never Surrendered: A True Story of Resistance in World War II* (Quezon City: Vera-Reyes, 1982), 183.

39. AIB PRS, "Who's Who" card on Col. Hugh Straughn, Entry 110, Box 596, RG 496, NARA II. The Japanese executed Straughn along with Col. Thorp, Lt. Col. Noble, Captain Barker, Col. Nakar of the Philippine Army, and twenty-one enlisted men in October 1943 at Old Bilibid prison. G-2 Rear to G-2 ADVON, "Fate of Lt Col Martin Moses," November 14, 1945, G-2 SWPA, General Correspondence, Box 161, RG 496, NARA II.

40. Proculo L. Mojica, *Terry's Hunters (The True Story of the Hunters ROTC Guerrillas)* (Manila: Benipayo Press, 1965), 29.

41. Ibid., 61–65.

42. Yay Panlilio, *The Crucible* (New York: Macmillan, 1950), 22.

43. Ibid., 58.

44. Ibid., 59.

45. Mojica, *Terry's Hunters*, 274–275.

46. For a history of the Chinese resistance in the Philippines, see Li, *The Huaqiao Warriors*.

47. Anderson to CinC, SWPA, Subject: Chinese Guerrillas, August 6, 1944, Entry 112, Box 605, RG 496, NARA II.

48. Jose Fernandez, Jr., "Death Creates Converts," undated, Entry 112, Box 604, RG 496, NARA II.

49. The butterfly swing consisted of a prisoner, suspended by a rope tied to his lashed wrists behind his back, swinging under a tree branch by means of another rope tied to his testicles and yanked back and forth by a torturer.

50. Panlilio, *The Crucible*, 140; see also Ramsey and Rivele, *Lieutenant Ramsey's War*, 151–152.

51. Mojica, *Terry's Hunters*, 71.

52. Wendell W. Fertig, "Guerrillero," unpublished manuscript, Wendell W. Fertig Papers, USAHEC, VI:8.

53. Personal diary of a member of the 86th Airfield Bn, unspecified date in February 1945, Translations of Captured Enemy Documents, May 24, 1945, 901-2.9, RG 407, NARA II.

54. Lina C. Espino, "My Personal Experience during the Japanese Occupation," Laurence L. Wilson Papers, Hoover Institution Archives.

55. Vincente Co, "My Personal Experience during the Japanese Occupation," Laurence L. Wilson Papers, Hoover Institution Archives.

56. Esteban Cruz, "My Impression of the Japanese," Laurence L. Wilson Papers, Hoover Institution Archives.

57. Dionisia Cauam, "Reminiscences during the Japanese Occupation," Laurence L. Wilson Papers, Hoover Institution Archives.

58. Personal diary belonging to a member of the Fujita Unit (3rd Co.), 116th "Fishing" Battalion, Translations of Captured Enemy Documents, April 22, 1945, 901-2.9, RG 407, NARA II.

59. Diary presumably belonging to a member of Akatsuki 16709 Force, HQ XIV Corps, Captured Documents Batch #719, Item #13, March 2, 1945, 901-2.9, RG 407, NARA II.

60. HQ XIV Corps, Captured Documents Batch #1070, Item #13, April 1, 1945, 901-2.9, RG 407, NARA II.

61. HQ XIV Corps, Captured Documents Batch #1037, Item #25, March 29, 1945, 901-2.9, RG 407, NARA II.

62. In a controversial proceeding, a war crimes tribunal convened by Gen. Douglas MacArthur in Manila in October 1945 found Yamashita guilty of war crimes and sentenced him to death, a verdict that was carried out by hanging the following February. But Yamashita was not charged with ordering atrocities; rather, he was charged with not being able to control his troops. See Allan A. Ryan, *Yamashita's Ghost: War Crimes, MacArthur's Justice, and Command Accountability* (Lawrence, KS: University Press of Kansas, 2012).

63. Historical Record, Mindanao Guerrilla Resistance Movement, Tenth Military District from 16 September 1942 to 30 June 1945, Chapter XI, Japanese Atrocities, Wendell W. Fertig Papers, USAHEC.

64. Ibid.

65. Panlilio, *The Crucible*, 180–184.

66. Fertig, "Guerrillero," V:76–77.

67. For some of the more prominent literature on counterinsurgency, see David Galula, *Counterinsurgency Warfare: Theory and Practice* (Westport, CT: Praeger, 1964), Daniel Marston and Carter Malkasian, *Counterinsurgency in Modern Warfare* (Oxford: Osprey, 2010), US Army Field Manual 3-24, *Counterinsurgency* (2006), David J. Kilcullen, *Counterinsurgency* (Oxford: Oxford University Press, 2010), and Max Boot, *Invisible Armies: An Epic History of Guerrilla Warfare from Ancient Times to the Present* (New York: Liveright, 2013).

68. Benjamin F. Isidro, "My Impressions of the Japanese," Laurence L. Wilson Papers, Hoover Institution Archives.

69. Wendell Fertig Diary, April 11, 1943, Wendell Fertig Papers, USAHEC.

70. AIB, SWPA, "Statement of Mr. Edward M. Kuder to Dr. J. R. Hayden Regarding Events and Conditions in Lanao Immediately Preceding the War and from 8 December 1941 to 29 September 1943," Richard K. Sutherland Papers, Entry 19810, Box 48, RG 496, NARA II, 34–35.

71. Leoncio Mariano, Memo for the Precinct Commander re: Poster Found on Calle Azcarraga, April 4, 1944, PRS Records, Entry 112, Box 604, RG 496, NARA II.

72. HQ, Propaganda and Sabotage, Guerrilla Forces of the Commonwealth of the Philippines, Memo to CO 10th MD, Subject: Propaganda – Sabotage, February 15, 1944, PRS Records, Entry 112, Box 604, RG 496, NARA II.

73. For Cushing's exploits, see Norling, *The Intrepid Guerrillas of North Luzon*, 5–13.

74. Ibid., 137.

75. Volckmann, *We Remained*, 120–121.

76. D. Clayton James, *The Years of MacArthur*, vol. II: *1941–1945* (Boston: Houghton Mifflin, 1975), 105. Sharp was fifty-five years old and in ill-health; guerrilla life would most likely have killed him.

77. Mindanao Guerrilla Resistance Movement, 5; Louis Morton, *The Fall of the Philippines* (Washington, DC: Center of Military History, 1953), 576–577.

78. Eighth Army, Operational Monograph on the Panay Negros Occidental Operation (Victor I), 108-0, Box 2233, RG 407, NARA II, 12.

79. President Sergio Osmeña, head of the Philippine government in exile, ordered Confesor out of Panay early in 1945 to remove any chance of bloodshed. The guerrilla movement on Panay, as well as the conflict between Peralta and Confesor, is detailed in Gamaliel L. Manikan, *Guerrilla Warfare on Panay Island in the Philippines* (Manila: The Sixth Military District Veterans Foundation, Inc., 1977).

80. William Wise, *Secret Mission to the Philippines: The Story of "Spyron" and the American–Filipino Guerrillas of World War II* (New York: E. P. Dutton, 1968), 67.

81. Upon being informed by Fertig of his reasoning, Casey replied in a letter, "That's the stuff!" Letter, Casey to Fertig, August 22, 1943, Wendell Fertig Papers, USAHEC.

82. Fertig, "Guerrillero," V:32–33.

83. Morgan wanted to use Fertig as the face of the guerrilla movement, but coveted the power of command for himself. The two of them would vie for control until September 1943, when Fertig unceremoniously (and against orders) shipped Morgan back to Australia on a submarine, ostensibly to serve as the guerrilla liaison officer to SWPA headquarters. John Keats, *They Fought Alone* (New York: J. B. Lippincott, 1963), 82–89, 288–295. Although purportedly the story of Fertig and the guerrilla movement on Mindanao, this book must be read carefully and checked against other sources for accuracy as some parts of it contain invented conversations, much as Thucydides composed fictitious but plausible speeches to illustrate key moments in his history of the Peloponnesian War. For a critical review, see Clyde Childress, "Wendell Fertig's Fictional 'Autobiography': A Critical Review of *They Fought Alone*," *Bulletin of the American Historical Collection* 31, no. 1 (123) (January 2003), https://fireinthejungle.files.wordpress.com/2011/05/123_wendell_fertig_s .pdf. For a more balanced history of Fertig as a guerrilla commander, see Kent Holmes, *Wendell Fertig and His Guerrilla Forces in the Philippines* (Jefferson, NC: McFarland, 2015).
84. Keats, *They Fought Alone*, 101–106.
85. The Moro people of Mindanao, Palawan, and the Sulu Archipelago are a Muslim-majority ethnic group comprising roughly 5 percent of the Philippine population.
86. A close reading of Fertig's diary reveals this recurring medical ailment.
87. Mindanao Guerrilla Resistance Movement, 8–10.
88. AIB, SWPA, "Statement of Mr. Edward M. Kuder to Dr. J. R. Hayden Regarding Events and Conditions in Lanao Immediately Preceding the War and from 8 December 1941 to 29 September 1943," Papers of General Richard K. Sutherland relating to GHQ, SWPA, 1942–45, Entry 19810, Box 48, RG 496, NARA II, 22.
89. Keats, *They Fought Alone*, 86–89.
90. Ibid., 100.
91. Ibid., 122–125.
92. Ibid., 169.
93. Letter, Fertig to Casey, September 29, 1943, Wendell Fertig Papers, USAHEC.
94. "Statement of Mr. Edward M. Kuder," 30–32.
95. Fertig, "Guerrillero," VI:19.
96. Keats, *They Fought Alone*, 172.
97. Ibid., 175–176. The call-sign MSF stood for Mindanao Smith Fertig.
98. Fertig, "Guerrillero," VI:43.
99. Ibid., VI:44.
100. Fertig to MacArthur, February 20, 1943, Mindanao Guerrilla Resistance Movement, Chapter VI, 38.
101. Despite the geographical limitation of his command, Peralta was instrumental in developing the small guerrilla groups on Masbate, Marinduque, Mindoro,

and Palawan. According to the report of MacArthur's staff, "Colonel Peralta soon developed one of the most extensive and efficient intelligence systems in the Philippines." *Reports of General MacArthur: The Campaigns of MacArthur in the Pacific*, vol. I (Washington, DC: US Army Center of Military History, 1966), 316.

102. MacArthur to Fertig, February 21, 1943, Mindanao Guerrilla Resistance Movement, Chapter VI, 38–39; Keats, *They Fought Alone*, 187–188.

103. Keats, *They Fought Alone*, 243, 287.

104. Note from Willoughby to G-2 Philippines subsection, March 29, 1943, Entry 123, Box 621, RG 496, NARA II.

105. Ira Wolfert, *American Guerrilla in the Philippines* (New York: Simon & Schuster, 1945), 185.

106. Mindanao Guerrilla Resistance Movement, Chapter VI, 38–39.

107. Ibid., VI: 3–6.

108. Allison Ind, *Allied Intelligence Bureau: Our Secret Weapon in the War against Japan* (New York: David McKay, 1958), 10–12.

109. Charles A. Willoughby, *The Guerrilla Resistance Movement in the Philippines* (New York: Vantage Press, 1972), 40.

110. Norling, *The Intrepid Guerrillas of North Luzon*, 77–79. Although how the CAF was compromised is disputed, the radio itself might have given away the guerrillas' position through Japanese use of electronic direction finding. Remaining CAF personnel joined Volckmann's USAFIP-NL forces.

111. Ind, *Allied Intelligence Bureau*, 115.

112. On December 20, 1942, Lt. Frank H. Young and Mr. Albert Klestadt arrived in Brisbane. Young had departed central Luzon in July 1942 and journeyed via the Bicols, Samar, Leyte, Cebu, and Negros to Panay. There he joined Klestadt (a German civilian) and finished the trek to Australia via Zamboanga to Darwin, arriving after a five-month odyssey. "A Brief History of the G-2 Section, GHQ, SWPA, and Affiliated Units," in Charles Willoughby and G-2 Section, SWPA, *History of Intelligence Activities under General MacArthur, 1942–1950* (Wilmington, DE: Scholarly Resources, 1983), 7–8.

113. Thorp to MacArthur, "Guerrilla Warfare in Luzon," AIB PRS, Entry 112, Box 605, RG 496, NARA II.

114. Ind, *Allied Intelligence Bureau*, 115–116, 122.

115. Ibid., 118–119.

116. Letter from Quezon to MacArthur, March 4, 1943, Box 9, Folder 26 (Manuel Quezon), RG 10 (Personal Correspondence), MacArthur Memorial Archives.

117. SWPA G-2, "Calendar of Submarine Shipments to Philippine Guerrillas and Agents, December 1942–December 1944," Entry 123, Box 621, RG 496, NARA II.

118. Fertig Diary, March 6, 1943.

119. Ind, *Allied Intelligence Bureau*, 138.

120. Villamor, *They Never Surrendered*, 93.

121. Ibid., 96.

122. Ibid., 146.

123. Note from Willoughby to Philippines subsection, March 29, 1943, PRS Records, Entry 123, Box 621, RG 496, NARA II.
124. Villamor, *They Never Surrendered*, 86. Montelibano performed another function as well; in a civil ceremony, he married Villamor to a Filipina named Maria whom the major had met on Negros.
125. Ibid., 135.
126. Ind, *Allied Intelligence Bureau*, 134; Scott A. Mills, *Stranded in the Philippines: Professor Bell's Private War against the Japanese* (Annapolis, MD: Naval Institute Press, 2009).
127. Ind, *Allied Intelligence Bureau*, 137–138, 144–145.
128. Villamor, *They Never Surrendered*, 184–188.
129. Manuel Luis Quezon, *The Good Fight* (New York: D. Appleton-Century, 1946), 208.
130. Villamor, *They Never Surrendered*, 191; Ramsey and Rivele, *Lieutenant Ramsey's War*, 175–176; Douglas MacArthur, *Reminiscences* (New York: McGraw-Hill, 1964), 237.
131. Miguel Pendon, "Official Report of Personal Accomplishments as Guerrilla Chief," Lee Telesco Papers, Box 1, Hoover Institution Archives, 5–6.
132. David Joel Steinberg, *Philippine Collaboration in World War II* (Ann Arbor, MI: The University of Michigan Press, 1967).
133. Ramsey and Rivele, *Lieutenant Ramsey's War*, 181–182.
134. This was a half-truth; Parsons had indeed served as the Panamanian consul before the war, but was on active duty with the US Navy by the time the Japanese occupied Manila. Keats, *They Fought Alone*, 191–192.
135. Parsons was taken to Santiago Prison, where the Japanese tortured him. Without extracting any information, they eventually released him. Wise, *Secret Mission to the Philippines*, 48–51.
136. Ind, *Allied Intelligence Bureau*, 110.
137. Wise, *Secret Mission to the Philippines*, 74.
138. The shipment included radio transmitters and receivers, charging units, batteries, Philippine pesos, tools, wire, pistols, grenades, ammunition, drugs, surgical kits, vaccines, newspapers, magazines, soap, sewing kits, cigarettes, chocolate bars, clothing, buckwheat flour to make communion wafers for the fervently Catholic Filipino faithful, communion wine, and a set of lieutenant colonel insignia for Fertig. Money was crucial, as most areas under guerrilla control lacked a means of printing currency, without which the local economies could not function.
139. Fertig Diary, September 29, 1943.
140. Ind, *Allied Intelligence Bureau*, 164–167.
141. Ibid., 171.
142. GHQ SWPA, "The Guerrilla Resistance Movement on Panay and Neighboring Islands, 27 November 1944," Entry 1094, Box 258, RG 407, NARA II.

143. The intermediary between Kangleon and Fertig was Iliff David Richardson, who had served with Lt. John D. Bulkeley and Motor Torpedo Boat Squadron 3 (which evacuated MacArthur and his party from Corregidor) before the fall of the Philippines. In summer 1943, Richardson journeyed from Leyte to Mindanao to contact Fertig on Kangleon's behalf and was fortunate that Cdr. Chick Parsons was at Fertig's headquarters at the time. Richardson returned to Leyte with promises of aid and became Kangleon's chief of staff. His story is told in Wolfert, *American Guerrilla in the Philippines*, which was loosely adapted as a motion picture starring Tyrone Power in 1950.

144. For an examination of the competition for legitimacy between Miranda and Kangleon, see Elmer N. Lear, "The Western Leyte Guerrilla Warfare Forces: A Case Study in the Non-legitimation of a Guerrilla Organization," *Journal of Southeast Asian History* 9, no. 1 (March 1968): 69–94.

145. M. Hamlin Cannon, *Leyte: The Return to the Philippines* (Washington, DC: Center of Military History, 1954), 16–18.

146. Wise, *Secret Mission to the Philippines*, 111–114.

147. Dyess, Mellnik, and McCoy were part of a group of ten Americans who had escaped from Davao Penal Colony on Mindanao and made their way to Fertig's headquarters with the assistance of Filipino guerrillas. Most of the escapees stayed on to serve with the guerrillas until they were evacuated by submarine to Australia later in the war; one, Air Corps First Lieutenant Leo Boelens, would never make it back to the United States, as he died on Mindanao on a guerrilla operation. Holmes, *Wendell Fertig and His Guerrilla Forces in the Philippines*, 166–170.

148. Dyess recounted his story in William E. Dyess, *The Dyess Story: The Eye-Witness Account of the Death March from Bataan and the Narrative of Experiences in Japanese Prison Camps and of Eventual Escape* (New York: G. P. Putnam's Sons, 1944). The most recent and comprehensive account of the prisoners' escape from Davao Penal Colony and subsequent revelations about Japanese atrocities is John D. Lukacs, *Escape from Davao: The Forgotten Story of the Most Daring Prison Break of the Pacific War* (New York: Simon & Schuster, 2010).

149. John C. Shively, *Profiles in Survival: The Experiences of American POWs in the Philippines during World War II* (Bloomington: Indiana Historical Society Press, 2012), Chapter 7.

150. Mellnik would stay on in Australia to coordinate guerrilla activities in SWPA G-2. He later published a memoir of his wartime service: Stephen M. Mellnik, *Philippine War Diary, 1939–1945* (New York: Van Nostrand Reinhold, 1969). McCoy would return to duty as executive officer of the light cruiser USS *Cleveland*, which participated in the shelling of the island of Corregidor upon the return of US forces to the Philippines. Dyess would die in a training accident on December 22, 1943, when the P-38 Lightning aircraft he was piloting developed engine trouble and he flew it into the ground rather than bailing out to prevent the plane from crashing in an urban area and killing civilians there. Dyess Air Force Base near Abilene, TX, is named after him.

151. *Reports of General MacArthur*, vol. I, 313. Upon his return to Cebu, Cushing placed Estrella on trial for exceeding his authority; Estrella was later executed for his misdeeds. Villamor, *They Never Surrendered*, 262–263.
152. Ind, *Allied Intelligence Bureau*, 142–143.
153. Villamor, *They Never Surrendered*, 196–206.
154. "Cushing; background, mission and accomplishments," September 20, 1945, GHQ Messages in the Guerrilla Resistance Movement in the Philippines, 1943–1945, Box 514, RG 496, NARA II.
155. Koga had succeeded Admiral Isoroku Yamamoto, who had designed the attack on Pearl Harbor, on April 21, 1943, three days after US aircraft shot down Yamamoto's plane in an operation that may have been personally sanctioned by President Franklin Roosevelt.
156. Greg Bradsher, "The Z Plan Story," *Prologue* 37, no. 3 (Fall 2005), www.archives .gov/publications/prologue/2005/fall/z-plan; Dirk Jan Barreveld, *Cushing's Coup: The True Story of How Lt. Col. James Cushing and His Filipino Guerrillas Captured Japan's Plan Z* (Philadelphia: Casemate, 2015). The translated plan warned Spruance that the Japanese gambit was to lure the US battle fleet away from Saipan to allow land-based aircraft free rein to attack the invasion transports. Spruance was later criticized for his lack of aggressiveness in pursuing the Japanese fleet on the first day of the Battle of the Philippine Sea, but doing so would have opened the way for air attacks against the troop transports.
157. Quezon awarded Villamor the Philippine Medal for Valor, the highest military honor bestowed by the Philippine Commonwealth, for his actions in organizing the resistance in the Philippines.
158. Villamor, *They Never Surrendered*, 215–219, 244–251. Villamor became an American citizen in 1950.
159. Wolfert, *American Guerrilla in the Philippines*, 131.
160. From 1943 until September 1944, strategic plans (RENO III) called for the initial US invasion of the Philippines on Mindanao.
161. "A Brief History of the G-2 Section, GHQ, SWPA, and Affiliated Units," 46n12; *Reports of General MacArthur*, vol. I, 309.
162. All dates in this paragraph and the next are from SWPA G-2, "Calendar of Submarine Shipments to Philippine Guerrillas and Agents, December 1942–December 1944."
163. *Reports of General MacArthur*, vol. I, 301; Maj. Emigdio C. Cruz, "Personal Narrative of Major Emigdio C. Cruz, Jan 43–Feb 44," in GHQ, US Army Forces Pacific, *Intelligence Activities in the Philippines during the Japanese Occupation*, vol. II, documentary appendices, Appendix XX. Quezon awarded Cruz the Philippine Medal for Valor for his courageous expedition.
164. SWPA G-2, "Calendar of Submarine Shipments to Philippine Guerrillas and Agents, December 1942–December 1944."

165. MacArthur to President Franklin D. Roosevelt, July 20, 1943, Lee Telesco Papers, Box 1, Hoover Institution Archives.

166. The *Nautilus* had played a crucial part in the Battle of Midway. Early on the morning of June 4, the submarine attempted to torpedo the Japanese battleship *Kirishima* without effect, and in return was unsuccessfully hunted by the Japanese destroyer *Arashi*. While returning to the fleet, the *Arashi* was spotted by USS *Enterprise* air group Commander Wade McClusky, who followed it to the Japanese carrier group. In the ensuing attack, the *Enterprise*'s dive bombers destroyed the carriers *Kaga* and *Akagi*, while the USS *Yorktown*'s air group destroyed the *Soryu*, thereby significantly altering the balance of naval forces in the Pacific. Gordon W. Prange, *Miracle at Midway* (New York: Penguin, 1982), 260.

167. Naval History and Heritage Command, "Narwhal II (SC-1)," www.history.navy .mil/research/histories/ship-histories/danfs/n/narwhal-ii.html.

168. Fertig Diary, November 15, 1943.

169. Keats, *They Fought Alone*, 337–338.

170. The *Seawolf* was lost near Morotai while headed to Samar with personnel and supplies, most likely due to friendly fire from the USS *Rowell* (DE-403), on October 3, 1944. Naval History and Heritage Command, "Seawolf I (SS-197)," www.history.navy.mil/research/histories/ship-histories/danfs/s/sea wolf-i.html.

171. Seventh Fleet Intelligence Center, "Submarine Activities Connected with Guerrilla Organizations," www.history.navy.mil/research/library/online-read ing-room/title-list-alphabetically/s/submarine-activities-connected-with-guer rilla-organizations.html.

172. Lapham and Norling, *Lapham's Raiders*, 161.

173. Neil Shafer, *Philippine Emergency and Guerrilla Currency of World War II* (Racine, WI: Western Publishing Co., 1974).

174. "Currency in the Philippines, June 1943," Papers of General Richard K. Sutherland relating to GHQ, SWPA, 1942–45, Entry 19810, Box 48, RG 496, NARA II.

175. AIB (including its PRS) reported directly to Lt. Gen. Sutherland, with loose coordination through G-2, through May 1944. Maj. Gen. Willoughby developed his own Philippines section in late 1942 and augmented it in June 1944 when GHQ SWPA disbanded AIB PRS and distributed its functions among the various general staff sections.

176. Ind, *Allied Intelligence Bureau*, 174.

177. Memorandum for Record, "Clarification of AIB responsibility," May 29, 1943, Entry 123, Box 622, RG 496, NARA II.

178. Memo, Philippine Regional Section – Conference with C-in-C, May 30, 1943, Entry 123, Box 621, RG 496, NARA II.

179. See PRS to Chief of Staff, "Philippine Operations," May 27, 1942, and following exchange of memos with G-2 on May 28, 29, and 30 in G-2 Philippine Section, Entry 123, Box 622, RG 496, NARA II.

180. PRS, "Philippine Intelligence Coverage," June 24, 1943, Entry 19810, Papers of General Richard K. Sutherland relating to GHQ, SWPA, 1942–45, Entry 19810, Box 55, RG 496, NARA II.

181. C. A. McVittie, G-2 Rear Echelon, Memo, "Plans for Philippine Intelligence Net," August 22, 1943, Entry 123, Box 621, RG 496, NARA II.

182. A point made by the G-2 (citing advice from the recently returned Parsons, Mellnik, Dyess, and Smith) in a memo to the G1 on August 19, 1943, regarding the PRS plan. Entry 123, Box 622, RG 496, NARA II.

183. PRS to Chief of Staff, "Philippine Intelligence Plan," August 25, 1943, Papers of General Richard K. Sutherland relating to GHQ, SWPA, 1942–45, Entry 19810, Box 55, RG 496, NARA II.

184. Endorsement to G-2 memo, "Plans for Philippine Intelligence Net," August 31, 1943.

185. G-2 to PRS, August 28, 1943, Papers of General Richard K. Sutherland relating to GHQ, SWPA, 1942–45, Entry 19810, Box 55, RG 496, NARA II.

186. PRS to Chief of Staff, "Philippine Intelligence Plan," August 25, 1943.

187. Carlos P. Romulo, *I See the Philippines Rise* (Garden City, NY: Doubleday, 1946), 120–121.

188. The relay stations in the Philippines used inventive call letters such as ISRM, for "I Shall Return, MacArthur," and MACA, the signature MacArthur used on inter-office communications.

189. Ind, *Allied Intelligence Bureau*, 224–228; Bob Stahl, *You're No Good to Me Dead: Behind Japanese Lines in the Philippines* (Annapolis, MD: Naval Institute Press, 1995), 75.

190. Ind, *Allied Intelligence Bureau*, 183.

191. Ibid., 184–186; Report of Colonel J. K. Evans concerning the activities of Commander Charles Parsons, 28 October 1944, Box 57, Papers of General Richard K. Sutherland relating to GHQ, SWPA, 1942–45, Entry 19810, Box 55, RG 496, NARA II.

192. Villamor, *They Never Surrendered*, 215.

193. G-2 to CoS, August 15, 1943, Entry 123, Box 622, RG 496, NARA II.

194. G-2 to CoS, February 22, 1944, Entry 123, Box 622, RG 496, NARA II.

195. PRS to CoS, March 12, 1944, Box 622, Entry 123, RG 496, NARA II.

196. G-2 to CoS, March 17, 1944, Entry 123, Box 622, RG 496, NARA II.

197. G-2 to CoS, April 10, 1944, Entry 123, Box 622, RG 496, NARA II.

198. Memo, "Philippine Island Activities," April 13, 1944, Entry 123, Box 622, RG 496, NARA II.

199. PRS to G-2, April 13, 1944, and PRS to G-2, April 14, 1944, Entry 123, Box 622, RG 496, NARA II.

200. PRS to CoS, June 5, 1944, Entry 123, Box 622, RG 496, NARA II. Whitney continued to serve MacArthur as head of the Philippine affairs section (i.e.,

civil affairs officer) and was promoted to brigadier general in January 1945. He would continue to serve at MacArthur's side until the general's relief from command of US forces in Korea and retirement from active duty in 1951.

201. Willoughby to Mellnik, May 25, 1944, Entry 123, Box 622, RG 496, NARA II.
202. Ramsey to Commander 10th Military District, January 5, 1944, AIB PRS, Entry 112, Box 604, RG 496, NARA II.
203. Ramsey and Rivele, *Lieutenant Ramsey's War*, 205–206.
204. PRS Report 282, August 20, 1944, Entry 112, Box 600, RG 496, NARA II.
205. PRS, "Who's Who" card catalogue, Entry 110, Boxes 586–598, RG 496, NARA II.
206. Memo, "Ball; Background, Mission and Accomplishments," September 20, 1945, GHQ Messages in the Guerrilla Resistance Movement in the Philippines, 1943–1945, Entry 112, Box 508, RG 496, NARA II.
207. USAFIP-NL, After-Battle Report: United States Army Forces in the Philippines, North Luzon Operations, 9 January to 15 August 1945, 10 November 1945, 16–17, Russell W. Volckmann Papers, USAHEC, 15.
208. Ind, *Allied Intelligence Bureau*, 225.
209. Ramsey and Rivele, *Lieutenant Ramsey's War*, 248.
210. Ibid., 242–252.
211. *Reports of General MacArthur*, vol. I, 302.
212. Mojica, *Terry's Hunters*, 271.
213. Lapham and Norling, *Lapham's Raiders*, 121.
214. Ibid., 336; Panlilio, *The Crucible*, 165–169.
215. Mojica, *Terry's Hunters*, 411.
216. Ibid., 415–416.
217. USAFIP-NL, After-Battle Report, 15–17, 210. Once Sixth Army was established ashore on Luzon, the spigot of arms, ammunition, and supplies was turned on full blast and Volckmann's troops transformed into the equivalent of a US infantry division, albeit one that was not fully trained or equipped to the standards of other American forces.
218. Mojica, *Terry's Hunters*, 358.
219. Ramsey and Rivele, *Lieutenant Ramsey's War*, 258–260.
220. Ibid., 289.
221. Volckmann, *We Remained*, 175–176.
222. Keats, *They Fought Alone*, 366–367.
223. Mindanao Guerrilla Resistance Movement, Chapter VII, 3.
224. Ibid., VII:50.
225. Keats, *They Fought Alone*, 390–393.
226. Ibid., 404–406.
227. Fertig Diary, September 9, 1944.
228. Mindanao Guerrilla Resistance Movement, Chapter VII, 2.
229. Ibid., VI:10.
230. Fertig Diary, October 19, 1944.

231. Pertinent Data Re: Personnel of 10th Military District, August 15, 1944, Entry 123, Box 619, RG 496, NARA II. On August 15, 1944, Fertig commanded 72 US personnel, 2,366 officers, and 32,632 enlisted men. As of December 1943, 16,000 were armed, with another 9,300 weapons delivered after that date.
232. HQ, Sixth Army, "Recognition of Guerrilla Units," February 25, 1945, copy located in Operations Reports of the 25th Infantry Division, 325-0.3-0, Box 6933, RG 407, NARA II.
233. Ramsey and Rivele, *Lieutenant Ramsey's War*, 302.
234. Upon returning to the United States in the summer of 1945, Ramsey, now a lieutenant colonel, was diagnosed with malaria, amoebic dysentery, anemia, acute malnutrition, and general nervous collapse. Ibid., 333.
235. Lapham and Norling, *Lapham's Raiders*, 111.
236. Volckmann, *We Remained*, 180.

CHAPTER 4: THE DECISION

1. Douglas MacArthur, *Reminiscences* (New York: McGraw-Hill, 1964), 145.
2. The Japanese took 20,000 American and 70,000 Filipino military personnel into captivity in the Philippines, as well as interning 8,000 Allied civilians. Most of the Filipinos were paroled in the months following the surrender. Most of the American military prisoners were eventually shipped off to serve as forced laborers in Korea, Manchuria, and Japan. Only half of them ever saw home again. MacArthur Memorial staff, "The Price of Unpreparedness: POWs in the Philippines during World War II," MacArthur Memorial and Museum, Norfolk, VA, 2024.
3. Diary of Colonel Weldon "Dusty" Rhoades, October 14, 1944, Papers of Colonel Weldon "Dusty" Rhoades, Box 1, RG 28, MacArthur Memorial Archives.
4. Grace Person Hayes, *The History of the Joint Chiefs of Staff in World War II: The War against Japan* (Annapolis: Naval Institute Press, 1982), 367–372, 402.
5. Maurice Matloff, *Strategic Planning for Coalition Warfare, 1943–1944* (Washington, DC: Office of the Chief of Military History, 1959), 205–210; Robert Ross Smith, "Luzon versus Formosa," in Kent Roberts Greenfield, ed., *Command Decisions* (Washington, DC: Office of the Chief of Military History, 1960), 461–478, 462–463.
6. Hayes, *The History of the Joint Chiefs of Staff in World War II*, 504–507; Charles F. Brower, *Defeating Japan: The Joint Chiefs of Staff and Strategy in the Pacific War, 1943–1945* (New York: Palgrave Macmillan, 2012), 87.
7. *Reports of General MacArthur: The Campaigns of MacArthur in the Pacific*, vol. I (Washington, DC: Center of Military History, 1966), 168–169.
8. D. M. Horner, "Blamey and MacArthur: The Problem of Coalition Warfare," in William M. Leary, ed., *We Shall Return! MacArthur's Commanders and the Defeat of Japan, 1942–1945* (Lexington: University Press of Kentucky, 1988), 23–59, 50–52.
9. Hayes, *The History of the Joint Chiefs of Staff in World War II*, 604.

10. JCS to CINC SWPA (4785) and COMGENCENTPAC (729), March 2, 1944, Entry 422, Operations Division History Unit (Miscellaneous), Box 6, RG 165, NARA II.

11. The standard treatment of this debate is Smith, "Luzon versus Formosa."

12. Memo, SWPA to Chief of Staff, US Army, Subject: Strategy in the Pacific, March 8, 1944, Folder 5, Box 16, Message 79, RG 4, MacArthur Memorial Archives.

13. JCS to MacArthur and Nimitz, March 12, 1944, Message 85, Folder 5, Box 16, RG 4, MacArthur Memorial Archives; Robert Ross Smith, *The Approach to the Philippines* (Washington, DC: Office of the Chief of Military History, 1953), 9–12.

14. Smith, "Luzon versus Formosa," 463.

15. Ernest J. King, *Fleet Admiral King: A Naval Record* (New York: W. W. Norton, 1952), 541.

16. WARX50007, June 12, 1944, Entry 422, Operations Division History Unit (Miscellaneous), Box 6, RG 165, NARA II. Marshall, King, and Arnold were in England at the time for an inspection tour of the Normandy beachhead. They discussed the possible acceleration of operations in the Pacific with their British colleagues on June 14 at a conference in the War Cabinet Office in London. King, *Fleet Admiral King*, 552–553.

17. CX13891, June 18, 1944, Entry 422, Operations Division History Unit (Miscellaneous), Box 6, RG 165, NARA II.

18. Ibid.

19. WAR55718, Marshall to MacArthur "Eyes Only," June 24, 1944, Entry 422, Operations Division History Unit (Miscellaneous), Box 6, RG 165, NARA II.

20. Ibid.

21. Ibid.

22. Ibid.

23. MacArthur to Marshall, July 8, 1944, Folder 1, Box17, RG 4, MacArthur Memorial Archives.

24. Lisle Rose, "Planning the Penultimate Stages of the Pacific War," in Thomas J. Cutler, ed., *The Battle of Leyte Gulf at 75* (Annapolis, MD: Naval Institute Press, 2019), 38.

25. The President traveled aboard the heavy cruiser *Baltimore*, the only time he visited the Pacific theater during World War II.

26. MacArthur, *Reminiscences*, 196–197.

27. WDGS OPD, Memorandum for Record (OPD Executive File number 882), July 3, 1944, Entry 422, Operations Division History Unit (Miscellaneous), Box 47, RG 165, NARA II.

28. MacArthur to Marshall, July 18, 1944, Folder 1, Box 17, Message 80, USAPAC Records, RG 4, MacArthur Memorial Archives.

29. Marshall to MacArthur, July 18, 1944, Folder 1, Box 17, Message 81, USAPAC Records, RG 4, MacArthur Memorial Archives.

30. D. Clayton James, *The Years of MacArthur*, vol. II: *1941–1945* (Boston: Houghton Mifflin, 1975), 527–528; Thomas B. Buell, *Master of Sea Power: A Biography of Fleet Admiral Ernest J. King* (Boston: Little, Brown, 1980), 467.

31. William F. Halsey and J. Bryan III, *Admiral Halsey's Story* (New York: Whittlesey-McGraw-Hill, 1947), 195.

32. Weldon E. (Dusty) Rhoades, *Flying MacArthur to Victory* (College Station: Texas A&M University Press, 1987), 257.

33. Smith, "Luzon versus Formosa," 463.

34. Ian W. Toll, *Twilight of the Gods: War in the Western Pacific, 1944–1945* (New York: W. W. Norton, 2020), 90–91.

35. Samuel Eliot Morison, *History of United States Naval Operations in World War II*, vol. XII: *Leyte, June 1944–January 1945* (Boston: Little, Brown, 1953), 397.

36. MacArthur to Stimson, WD 567, Sig. Corps Q2786, October 10, 1943, Papers of General Richard K. Sutherland relating to GHQ, SWPA, 1942–45, Entry 19810, RG 496, NARA II.

37. MacArthur, *Reminiscences*, 197–198. As he went to bed that night, Roosevelt asked his personal physician for an aspirin, and to give him another when he woke up the following morning. "In all my life nobody has ever talked to me the way MacArthur did," he explained. William Manchester, *American Caesar: Douglas MacArthur, 1880–1964* (Boston: Little, Brown, 1978; New York: Dell, 1978), 427.

38. William D. Leahy, *I Was There: The Personal Story of the Chief of Staff to Presidents Roosevelt and Truman Based on His Notes and Diaries Made at the Time* (New York: Whittlesey House, 1950), 250.

39. For an examination of US Army–Marine relations in the Central Pacific campaign, see Sharon Tosi Lacey, *Pacific Blitzkrieg: World War II in the Central Pacific* (Denton, TX: University of North Texas Press, 2013).

40. James, *The Years of MacArthur*, 533; E. B. Potter, *Nimitz* (Annapolis, MD: Naval Institute Press, 1976), 318–319. See also a record of MacArthur's arguments in "Conference between General Giles and M/Gen. Handy," August 7, 1944, Entry 422, Operations Division History Unit (Miscellaneous), Box 6, RG 165, NARA II.

41. "Notes for Discussion with General Marshall" (OPD Executive File number 1120), undated, Entry 422, Operations Division History Unit (Miscellaneous), Box 47, RG 165, NARA II.

42. Ibid., 3.

43. Although they did not know it at the time, the Japanese largely agreed with MacArthur's assessment. Maj. Gen. Yoshiharu Tomochika, who served in Tokyo in the summer of 1944, stated after the war, "I am certain that the Japanese high command had no expectation whatever that the Americans would land on the Asiatic continent, because the Japanese could cut off lines of communication very easily if the Americans did not first take the Philippines." 10th Information and Historical Service, Eighth Army, "Staff Study of Operations of the Japanese 35th Army on Leyte," Part I, III:6.

44. "Notes for Discussion with General Marshall", 4–5.
45. Ibid., 6.
46. Ibid., 10–11.
47. Ibid., 3–4.
48. Ibid., 10.
49. Notes, Opening Meeting, "WIDEAWAKE" Conference, GHQ SWPA, Brisbane, July 20, 1944, Raymond D. Tarbuck Papers, Box 1, Hoover Institution Archives, 12.
50. Ibid., 15.
51. WARX 71483, 27 July 1944, Entry 422, Operations Division History Unit (Miscellaneous), Box 6, RG 165, NARA II.
52. Message C15689, Rear Echelon SWPA to War Department (MacArthur to Marshall "Eyes Only"), August 3, 1944, Entry 422, Operations Division History Unit (Miscellaneous), Box 6, RG 165, NARA II.
53. WAR-75632, August 4, 1944, Entry 422, Operations Division History Unit (Miscellaneous), Box 6, RG 165, NARA II.
54. M. Hamlin Cannon, *Leyte: The Return to the Philippines* (Washington, DC: Office of the Chief of Military History, 1954), 6–8.
55. Frank Futrell, "Prelude to Invasion," in Wesley Frank Craven and James Lea Cate, eds., *The Army Air Forces in World War II*, vol. V: *The Pacific: Matterhorn to Nagasaki, June 1944 to August 1945* (Chicago: University of Chicago Press, 1953), 275–322, 284.
56. Ibid.
57. CINCPOA to COMINCH, August 18, 1944, Entry 422, Operations Division History Unit (Miscellaneous), Box 6, RG 165, NARA II.
58. Copy of directive in OPD Executive File 1125, Entry 422, Operations Division History Unit (Miscellaneous), Box 47, RG 165, NARA II.
59. Memo, Conference between Rear Adm. Cooke and Rear Adm. Sherman, August 22, 1944, Entry 422, Operations Division History Unit (Miscellaneous), Box 6, RG 165, NARA II.
60. Hayes, *The History of the Joint Chiefs of Staff in World War II*, 615.
61. Smith, "Luzon versus Formosa," 471.
62. "Points to Be Taken Up with Admiral King Concerning His Memorandum," September 25, 1944, in Deputy Chief of Staff, SWPA, Memorandum for the Commander in Chief, October 7, 1944, Tab O, Entry 19810, Papers of General Richard K. Sutherland, General Correspondence, 1941–1945, RG 496, NARA II.
63. JCS 171st Meeting Minutes, September 3, 1944, CCS 334, Box 198, RG 218, NARA II.
64. Marshall's notes for the meeting state, "It is assumed that the Joint Chiefs of Staff will issue a directive for LEYTE operation in the near future. It is to be assumed that the SWPA will carry out that operation then directed to follow up with air neutralization of Luzon by air operations alone. The question is asked, 'What service and supporting troops can SWPA make available for the FORMOSA

operation?' The only answer that can be given is none." The notes went on to detail the shortage of service forces in SWPA, including the diversion of combat troops to act as laborers at supply bases. Notes on Release of Service and Supporting Troops from SWPA used in Presentation to JPS, September 4, 1944, Entry 19810, Box 40, Papers of General Richard K. Sutherland relating to GHQ, SWPA, 1942–45, RG 496, NARA II.

65. WD 825, Marshall to MacArthur, September 9, 1944, Entry 19810, Box 40, Papers of General Richard K. Sutherland relating to GHQ, SWPA, 1942–45, RG 496, NARA II. GHQ SWPA ultimately prepared three versions of the Philippines operations plan – Musketeer I, II, and III – which Admiral King inevitably called the Three Musketeers. Manchester, *American Caesar*, 430.

66. "Comparison of Luzon with Formosa as Logistic Bases for Operations against Japan," in Deputy Chief of Staff, SWPA, Memorandum for the Commander in Chief, October 7, 1944, Tab H.

67. Memorandum for Chief, Strategy and Policy Group, Subject: Pacific Strategy (OPD Executive File 1176), September 5, 1944, Entry 422, Operations Division History Unit (Miscellaneous), Box 47, RG 165, NARA II.

68. Ibid.

69. Deputy Chief of Staff, SWPA, Memorandum for the Commander in Chief, October 7, 1944.

70. JCS 172nd Meeting Minutes, September 5, 1944, CCS 334, RG 218, NARA II; Brower, *Defeating Japan*, 107–108. Although Leahy was supportive of MacArthur's arguments for invading Luzon, his support was not, as Brower contends, the decisive factor in the decision to bypass Formosa. In the end, logistical arguments were decisive in shaping the final outcome of the debate.

71. Operations Division memo to [US Army] Chief of Staff, September 5, 1944, Entry 422, Operations Division History Unit (Miscellaneous), Box 6, RG 165, NARA II.

72. Hayes, *The History of the Joint Chiefs of Staff in World War II*, 620.

73. *Reports of General MacArthur: The Campaigns of MacArthur in the Pacific*, vol. I (Washington, DC: Center of Military History, 1966), 174.

74. Admiral Ernest J. King, "Second Report to the Secretary of the Navy: Covering Combat Operations from 1 March 1944 to 1 March 1945," March 1945, Entry 422, Operations Division History Unit (Miscellaneous), Box 6, RG 165, NARA II, 103–133; Clark G. Reynolds, *The Fast Carriers: The Forging of an Air Navy* (Annapolis, MD: Naval Institute Press, 1968), 251.

75. Message 130300, Cdr 3rd Fleet to CINCPOA, September 13, 1944, Entry 422, Operations Division History Unit (Miscellaneous), Box 6, RG 165, NARA II.

76. Message 130813, CINCPOA to CINCSWPA, September 13, 1944, Entry 422, Operations Division History Unit (Miscellaneous), Box 6, RG 165, NARA II.

77. OCTAGON 24, JCS to Rear Echelon SWPA, September 13, 1944, Entry 422, Operations Division History Unit (Miscellaneous), Box 31, RG 165, NARA II.

78. Message CX17697, Rear Echelon SWPA to War Department, September 14, 1944, Entry 422, Operations Division History Unit (Miscellaneous), Box 6, RG 165, NARA II. Upon his return to Hollandia, MacArthur retroactively approved Sutherland's messages, but told him never to make key operational decisions on his behalf again. Paul P. Rogers, *The Bitter Years: MacArthur and Sutherland* (New York: Praeger, 1991), 163.

79. Edward J. Drea, *MacArthur's ULTRA: Codebreaking and the War against Japan, 1942–1945* (Lawrence: University Press of Kansas, 1992), 157–158.

80. Cannon, *Leyte*, 20.

81. OCTAGON 31A, JCS to MacArthur and Nimitz for action, September 15, 1944, Entry 422, Operations Division History Unit (Miscellaneous), Box 31, RG 165, NARA II; Maurice Matloff, *Strategic Planning for Coalition Warfare, 1943–1944* (Washington, DC: Office of the Chief of Military History 1959), 512–513.

82. For an intimate description of the fighting on Peleliu, see Eugene B. Sledge, *With the Old Breed: At Peleliu and Okinawa* (Novato, CA: Presidio, 1981); for the fighting by the 81st Infantry Division, see Bobby C. Blair and John Peter DeCioccio, *Victory at Peleliu: The 81st Infantry Division's Pacific Campaign* (Norman, OK: University of Oklahoma Press, 2011).

83. Futrell, "Prelude to Invasion," 313–314.

84. Daniel E. Barbey, *MacArthur's Amphibious Navy: Seventh Amphibious Force Operations, 1943–1945* (Annapolis, MD: United States Naval Institute, 1969), 227.

85. *Reports of General MacArthur*, 174–176.

86. "Seabees" was the US Navy's nickname for its construction battalions, or CBs.

87. Robert L. Eichelberger, *Our Jungle Road to Tokyo* (New York City: Viking Press, 1950), 163.

88. Office of the Chief Engineer, GHQ Army Forces Pacific, *Engineers of the Southwest Pacific, 1941–1945*, vol. VI: *Airfield and Base Development* (Washington, DC: GPO, 1951), 283.

89. Ibid., 284.

90. Ibid.

91. Ibid., 286.

92. Message C18103, GHQ SWPA to War Department, September 21, 1944, Entry 422, Operations Division History Unit (Miscellaneous), Box 6, RG 165, NARA II.

93. Diary of Richard J. Marshall, September 21, 1944, Papers of R. J. Marshall (Deputy COS to CG, SWPA), RG 29c, MacArthur Memorial Archives.

94. The worst argument among the JCS was undoubtedly the decision to invade Northwest Africa in November 1942. WD 849, R. J. Marshall to MacArthur, September 28, 1944, Entry 19810, Box 40, Papers of General Richard K. Sutherland relating to GHQ, SWPA, 1942–45, RG 496, NARA II.

95. Sig. Corps 287-28, CG, SWPA, to US Army Chief of Staff, Washington, DC, September 28, 1944, Entry 19810, Box 35, Papers of General Richard K. Sutherland relating to GHQ, SWPA, 1942–45, RG 496, NARA II.

96. Charles F. Romanus and Riley Sutherland, *Stillwell's Command Problems* (Washington, DC: Office of the Chief of Military History, 1956), 433–434.

97. Ibid., 435.

98. Brower, *Defeating Japan*, 99–102.

99. Smith, "Luzon versus Formosa," 473–474.

100. MG Richard Marshall to MacArthur, September 17, 1944, Message 53, Folder 2, Box 17, RG 4, MacArthur Memorial Archives.

101. Smith, "Luzon versus Formosa," 475.

102. Morison, *Leyte*, 17.

103. Memorandum for Chief of Staff, Subject: Future Operations in the Pacific (OPD Executive File number 1255), October 2, 1944, Entry 422, Operations Division History Unit (Miscellaneous), Box 48, RG 165, NARA II.

104. JCS 180th Meeting Minutes, October 3, 1944, CCS 334, RG 218, NARA II; JCS WARX 40782, October 3, 1944, Entry 422, Operations Division History Unit (Miscellaneous), Box 6, RG 165, NARA II; Matloff, *Strategic Planning for Coalition Warfare, 1943–1944*, 531.

105. Deputy Chief of Staff, SWPA, Memorandum for the Commander in Chief, October 7, 1944.

CHAPTER 5: LEYTE GULF

1. Commander, Task Unit 77.4.3, Subject: Action against the Japanese Main Body off Samar Island, 25 October 1944, October 29 1944, UD351, Box 261, RG 313, NARA II, 1–2.

2. W-43866 Washington to GHQ SWPA, 10 October 1944, Papers of Walter Krueger Jr., Box 9, USMA Library Special Collections.

3. M. Hamlin Cannon, *Leyte: The Return to the Philippines* (Washington, DC: Office of the Chief of Military History, 1954), 41–42; D. Clayton James, *The Years of MacArthur*, vol. II: *1941–1945* (Boston: Houghton Mifflin, 1975), 547–548. *Essex*-class fleet carriers were built as carriers from the keel up and carried 100 aircraft; *Independence*-class light carriers were built on cruiser hulls and carried 35 aircraft; *Casablanca*-class escort carriers were built on merchant ship hulls and carried 27 aircraft.

4. US Third Fleet, Action Report – Period 23–26 October 1944, Enclosure D, Composition of Forces, Record Group 313, UD351, Box 40, NARA II. Cited numbers are as of the morning of October 23. The fleet carrier *Bunker Hill* and two destroyers left on this day for repairs, rearmament, and provisioning at Manus Island.

5. Captain Raymond Tarbuck, USN, "PHILIPPINE INVASION, 'King-Two' Operation, General Headquarters Observer's Log," A-Day, October 20, 1944, Raymond D. Tarbuck Papers, Box 1, Hoover Institution Archives, 10.

6. Edwin P. Hoyt, *The Battle of Leyte Gulf: The Death Knell of the Japanese Fleet* (New York: Weybright and Talley, 1972), 10.

7. Samuel Eliot Morison, *History of United States Naval Operations in World War II,* Vol. XII: *Leyte, June 1944–January 1945* (Boston: Little, Brown, 1953), 91–95.

8. William F. Halsey and J. Bryan III, *Admiral Halsey's Story* (New York: Whittlesey-McGraw-Hill, 1947), 207–208.

9. Special Intelligence Bulletin No. 526, October 15/16, 1944, Entry A1 9002, Box 65, RG 457, NARA II.

10. Morison, *Leyte,* 106–107, 126. Aircraft from the escort carriers supporting the Seventh Fleet also struck Leyte, but the Japanese had already abandoned the airfields located on that island.

11. Ibid., 165n11.

12. Frank Futrell, "Leyte," in Wesley Frank Craven and James Lea Cate, eds., *The Army Air Forces in World War II,* vol. V: *The Pacific: Matterhorn to Nagasaki, June 1944 to August 1945* (Chicago: University of Chicago Press, 1953), 341–389, 347.

13. Milan Vego, *The Battle for Leyte, 1944: Allied and Japanese Plans, Preparations, and Execution* (Annapolis, MD: Naval Institute Press, 2006), 49.

14. Ibid., 53–54.

15. Ibid., 65–67.

16. Rear Admiral Tomiji Koyanagi, "With Kurita in the Battle of Leyte Gulf," in Thomas J. Cutler, ed., *The Battle of Leyte Gulf at 75* (Annapolis, MD: Naval Institute Press, 2019), 259–277, 260.

17. Far East Command, Pacific Theater Historical Section, Interrogations of Japanese Officials on World War II, interrogation of Vice Adm. Tasuku Nakazawa, Chief of the Operations Section, Imperial General HQ, USAHEC.

18. Edward J. Drea, *MacArthur's ULTRA: Codebreaking and the War against Japan, 1942–1945* (Lawrence: University Press of Kansas, 1992), 152–155.

19. Monograph #4, Record of Philippines Operations, Phase 3, Vol. I, Operational Preparations of the 14th Area Army in the P.I., E147(A1), Box 38, RG 554, NARA II, 2; Vego, *The Battle for Leyte,* 74.

20. One indication of the lack of defensive material is the near absence of mention by US troops of encountering barbed wire as they attacked Japanese defensive positions in the Philippines.

21. Cannon, *Leyte,* 22, 49.

22. Operational Preparations of the 14th Area Army in the P.I., 1–2.

23. 10th Information and Historical Service, Eighth Army, "Staff Study of Operations of the Japanese 35th Army on Leyte," Part I, II:2.

24. Monograph #6, Record of Philippines Operations, Phase 3, Supplement to Vol. 2, 35th Army Operations in the Leyte Area, E147(A1), Box 38, RG 554, NARA II, 10.

25. "Report of statements made by General YAMASHITA, Tokoyuki, Commander-in-Chief of Japanese Army Forces in the Philippines, Lt. General MUTO, Akira,

his Chief of Staff, in conversations with ATIS officers at New Bilibid Prison, MANILA," September 4–6, 1945, USAHEC, OCMH Files, Pacific Interviews, 7.

26. James M. Scott, *Rampage: MacArthur, Yamashita, and the Battle of Manila* (New York: W. W. Norton, 2018), 43–44.

27. Cannon, *Leyte*, 51.

28. Maj. Gen. Yoshiharu Tomochika, "The True Facts of the Leyte Operation," trans. 166th Language Det., November 5, 1946, USAHEC, 7. Maj. Gen. Yoshiharu Tomochika was the Deputy Chief of Staff of the Japanese 35th Army, responsible for the Leyte campaign.

29. Cannon, *Leyte*, 21.

30. 35th Army Operations in the Leyte Area, 10–11.

31. Tomochika, "The True Facts of the Leyte Operation," 13.

32. Ibid., 15.

33. Far East Command, Pacific Theater Historical Section, Interrogations of Japanese Officials on World War II, interrogation of Lt. Gen. Seizo Arisue, Chief of the Second Department, General Staff HQ, USAHEC.

34. Seventh Fleet, Report of Operation for the Capture of Leyte Island Including Action Report of Engagements in Surigao Strait and off Samar Island on 25th of October 1944, UD351, Box 45, RG 313, NARA II, 4–5.

35. Cannon, *Leyte*, 22–23.

36. William B. Breuer, *Retaking the Philippines: America's Return to Corregidor and Bataan October 1944–March 1945* (New York: St. Martin's Press, 1986), 35–36.

37. CINCSWPA to CINCPAC, Ultra message, October 15, 1944, Papers of Richard K. Sutherland, Folder 12, Box 5, RG 30, MacArthur Memorial Archives. US commanders lacked details of specific Japanese plans for the upcoming naval battle because of the introduction of a new Japanese naval code, Nan-62, on July 25, 1944, which remained unbreakable until the introduction of the *Ransuuban* system in December. Richard B. Frank, "Code Breaking in the Asia Pacific War: Struggle and Triumph, May 1942 to December 1944," draft manuscript submitted for publication in a collection in honor of David Horner.

38. James D. Hornfischer, *The Last Stand of the Tin Can Sailors* (New York: Bantam Dell, 2004), 98.

39. Report of Major John H. Gunn, October 23, 1945, in Report of Special Security Representative, HQ Armed Forces Pacific, 1 January–1 December 1945, Entry A1 9002, Box 14, RG 457, NARA II.

40. Seventh Fleet, Report of Operation for the Capture of Leyte Island, 8–10.

41. Orlando R. Davidson, J. Carl Willems, and Joseph A. Kahl, *The Deadeyes: The Story of the 96th Infantry Division* (Washington, DC: Infantry Journal Press, 1947), 21.

42. "Leyte Historical Report of the 24th Infantry Division Landing Team, 20 October 1944–25 December 1944," January 25, 1945, 324–0.3, Box 6612, RG 407, NARA II, 14.

43. Carlos P. Romulo, *I See the Philippines Rise* (Garden City, NY: Doubleday, 1946), 2. Romulo served as resident commissioner of the Philippines, a non-voting

delegate to the US House of Representatives, from 1944 to 1946. After the war, he served as the president of the UN General Assembly from 1949 to 1950 and president of the UN Security Council in 1957, 1980, and 1981.

44. Tarbuck, King-Two GHQ Observer's Log, A-Day, October 20, 1944, 10; Cannon, *Leyte*, 60–62.

45. Douglas MacArthur, *Reminiscences* (New York: McGraw-Hill, 1964), 215.

46. Tarbuck, King-Two GHQ Observer's Log, A-Day, October 20, 1944, 9.

47. MacArthur, *Reminiscences*, 215.

48. HQ, 1st Cavalry Division, "Historical Report of 1st Cavalry Division K-2 [King II] Operation, 20 October to 25 December 1944," March 4, 1945, 901-0.3, RG 407, NARA II, 17–18.

49. "Historical Report of 1st Cavalry Division K-2 [King II] Operation," 19.

50. Davidson, Willems, and Kahl, *The Deadeyes*, 21.

51. A square division was comprised of two infantry brigades, each with two infantry regiments, plus artillery and other combat and combat support units. From late 1939 to 1942, the US Army transitioned its infantry divisions to a triangular structure, which eliminated the brigade headquarters along with one of the infantry regiments.

52. Aubrey "Red" Newman, *Follow Me: The Human Element in Leadership* (Novato, CA: Presidio, 1981), 251–252.

53. "Leyte Historical Report of the 24th Infantry Division Landing Team," 22–23. During the attack, Private Harold H. Moon, who had been released from a stint in the guardhouse to participate in the invasion, earned the Medal of Honor for his courageous actions in defending his position when the others in his squad had been killed. Newman, *Follow Me*, 303–304.

54. Office of the Chief Engineer, GHQ Army Forces Pacific, *Engineers of the Southwest Pacific, 1941–1945: Airfield and Base Development* (Washington, DC: GPO, 1951), 290.

55. Cannon, *Leyte*, 84.

56. History of the Special Security Officer, Headquarters Sixth Army, 6 October 1944–8 August 1945, in Report of Special Security Representative, HQ Armed Forces Pacific, 1 January–1 December 1945, Entry A1 9002, Box 14 RG 457, NARA II.

57. James, *The Years of MacArthur*, vol. II, 554–555. The photo is so iconic that the Filipinos created a larger-than-life monument depicting the scene at the site of Red Beach on Leyte, which celebrates "Leyte Landing Day" as a provincial holiday each year on October 20.

58. MacArthur, *Reminiscences*, 216–217.

59. William Manchester, *American Caesar: Douglas MacArthur, 1880–1964* (Boston: Little, Brown, 1978; New York: Dell, 1978), 257.

60. James, *The Years of MacArthur*, vol. II, 559.

61. Romulo, *I See the Philippines Rise*, 105.

62. Letter from Sergio Osmeña to Gen. Douglas MacArthur, October 20, 1944, Folder 65, Box 8, RG 10 (Personal Correspondence), MacArthur Memorial Archives.
63. James, *The Years of MacArthur*, vol. II, 560.
64. Message, President Franklin D. Roosevelt to MacArthur, October 21, 1944, Papers of General Richard K. Sutherland relating to GHQ, SWPA, 1942–45, Entry 19810, RG 496, NARA II.
65. General George C. Kenney Diary, October 20, 1944, Box 2, RG 54 (Papers of General George C. Kenney), MacArthur Memorial Archives.
66. George C. Kenney, *General Kenney Reports: A Personal History of the Pacific War* (New York: Duell, Sloan and Pearce, 1949), 449.
67. Ibid., 451.
68. 221148OCT1944 MacArthur to COM3RDFLT, Action Reports, October 29, 1944, John S. McCain Papers, Box 1, Hoover Institution Archives.
69. MacArthur, *Reminiscences*, 218.
70. *Reports of General MacArthur: The Campaigns of MacArthur in the Pacific*, vol. I (Washington, DC: Center of Military History, 1966), 318.
71. Monograph #84 (Navy), Philippine Area Naval Operations, Part III: Leyte, E147 (A1), Box 51, RG 554, NARA II, 45.
72. Far East Command, Pacific Theater Historical Section, Interrogations of Japanese Officials on World War II, interrogation of Lt. Col. Yorio Ishikawa, 14th Area Army staff, USAHEC.
73. Vego, *The Battle for Leyte*, 210.
74. Ibid, 210–211.
75. James A. Field Jr., *The Japanese at Leyte Gulf: The Shō Operation* (Princeton: Princeton University Press, 1947), 12.
76. Clark G. Reynolds, *The Fast Carriers: The Forging of an Air Navy* (Annapolis, MD: Naval Institute Press, 1968), 159.
77. Field, *The Japanese at Leyte Gulf*, 25.
78. Ibid., 16.
79. Ibid., 17; MIS SWPA, Summary of Enemy Dispositions, October 1944, Box 18, RG 3, MacArthur Memorial Archives.
80. For the establishment of the first kamikaze formations, see Rikihei Inoguchi and Tadashi Nakajima, *The Divine Wind: Japan's Kamikaze Force in World War II* (Annapolis, MD: Naval Institute Press, 1958).
81. The term "kamikaze" refers to the Divine Wind (typhoon) that destroyed a Mongol invasion fleet in 1281. The Japanese high command had planned for the use of suicide weapons long before the formation of a kamikaze squadron in the Philippines. Ian W. Toll, *Twilight of the Gods: War in the Western Pacific, 1944–1945* (New York: W. W. Norton, 2020), 195.
82. Dwight C. Shepler, USNR, Report of Duty during period 1 December 1944 to 20 March 1945, Raymond D. Tarbuck Papers, Box 2, Hoover Institution Archives, 1. "Flash Red" meant that enemy planes were approaching.

83. Hoyt, *The Battle of Leyte Gulf*, 43–44.

84. For a good discussion of the naming convention for the Japanese order of battle, see Toll, *Twilight of the Gods*, 213n. Also see H. P. Willmott, *The Battle of Leyte Gulf: The Last Fleet Action* (Bloomington: Indiana University Press, 2005), 73–74; and Field, *The Japanese at Leyte Gulf*, 12–15.

85. Morison, *Leyte*, 160–164; Willmott, *The Battle of Leyte Gulf*, 74.

86. Field, *The Japanese at Leyte Gulf*, 30–31.

87. Ibid., 55; Anthony P. Tully, *Battle of Surigao Strait* (Bloomington: Indiana University Press, 2009), 52.

88. Field, *The Japanese at Leyte Gulf*, 31–32, 35–36.

89. C. Vann Woodward, *The Battle for Leyte Gulf* (New York: Macmillan, 1947; repr. Nashville: Battery Press, 1989), 34.

90. For an examination of the US submarine campaign in the Pacific, see Clay Blair, Jr., *Silent Victory: The U.S. Submarine War against Japan* (Philadelphia: Lippincott Williams & Wilkins, 1975).

91. MIS, G2, SWPA, Special Intelligence Bulletin No. 530, October 19–20, 1944, appendix "Enemy Capabilities of Naval Reaction to Allied Landings in the Philippines, 20 October 1944," A1 9002, Box 65, RG 457, NARA II.

92. Reynolds, *The Fast Carriers*, 258.

93. Breuer, *Retaking the Philippines*, 75.

94. Woodward, *The Battle for Leyte Gulf*, 30.

95. Reynolds, *The Fast Carriers*, 256.

96. Field, *The Japanese at Leyte Gulf*, 50. Vice Adm. Kurita and his staff, which had been aboard the *Atago*, transferred to a destroyer and later to the battleship *Yamato*.

97. 231240 Oct. 1944, John S. McCain Papers, Box 1, Hoover Institution Archives.

98. Thomas J. Cutler, *The Battle of Leyte Gulf: 23–26 October 1944* (New York: HarperCollins, 1994), 106–107.

99. Woodward, *The Battle for Leyte Gulf*, 35–39.

100. Field, *The Japanese at Leyte Gulf*, 50.

101. McCain's son, John S. McCain, Jr., commanded a submarine during World War II and would rise to the rank of admiral and command of US Pacific Command during the Vietnam War. McCain's grandson, John S. McCain III, was a naval aviator who spent six years in a North Vietnamese prisoner of war camp. He retired as a captain to run for political office in Arizona, serving two terms in the House of Representatives and six terms in the US Senate and running for president in the 2008 election as the nominee of the Republican Party. John S. McCain Sr. would not live to see any of this, for he died of a heart attack at his home in Coronado, California, four days after the surrender ceremony in Tokyo Bay.

102. US Third Fleet, Action Report – 23–26 October 1944, 2; US Third Fleet, War Diary, 1 October to 31 October 1944, P88, Box 238, RG 313, NARA II, 26.

103. US Third Fleet, Action Report – 23–26 October 1944, Enclosure A (Messages), 8–9.

104. Tully, *Battle of Surigao Strait*, 62–64.

105. Ibid., 82–83; US Third Fleet, Action Report – 23–26 October 1944, Enclosure A (Messages), 10; Woodward, *The Battle for Leyte Gulf*, 52–53. Illustrating the effectiveness of the Filipino guerrillas, the pilot who was shot down in the attack on Nishimura's task group, Cdr. Fred E. Bakutis, rafted ashore on Negros and was eventually returned to American control.

106. US Third Fleet, Action Report – 23–26 October 1944, 3; Woodward, *The Battle for Leyte Gulf*, 53–54.

107. Woodward, *The Battle for Leyte Gulf*, 70.

108. A. Denis Clift, "Leyte Gulf Reminiscences," in Thomas J. Cutler, ed., *The Battle of Leyte Gulf at 75* (Annapolis, MD: Naval Institute Press, 2019), 17–29, 20–21. McCampbell was awarded the Medal of Honor for his actions at Leyte Gulf and in the Battle of the Philippine Sea. He ended the war with thirty-four aerial combat victories, the top naval ace in US history.

109. Woodward, *The Battle for Leyte Gulf*, 56–57.

110. Ibid., 66–69.

111. War Diary, USS *Birmingham* (CL-62), October 1944, P88, Box 124, RG 313, NARA II, 21.

112. Ibid., 24.

113. Ibid., 23–24.

114. According to James Field, "the state of pilot training and the quality of Japanese communications were too poor to offer hope of success in the always difficult problem of coordinating land-based air operations with a surface fleet." Field, *The Japanese at Leyte Gulf*, 60.

115. Woodward, *The Battle for Leyte Gulf*, 60–63; Field, *The Japanese at Leyte Gulf*, 66–67.

116. Mark E. Stille, *Leyte Gulf: A New History of the World's Largest Sea Battle* (Oxford: Osprey, 2023), 136; Hoyt, *The Battle of Leyte Gulf*, 126, 132.

117. Koyanagi, "With Kurita in the Battle of Leyte Gulf," 265.

118. Karl Zingheim, "Sibuyan Sea: The Price of Daring," in Thomas J. Cutler, ed., *The Battle of Leyte Gulf at 75* (Annapolis, MD: Naval Institute Press, 2019), 117–135, 126–127.

119. Woodward, *The Battle for Leyte Gulf*, 76–78; Field, *The Japanese at Leyte Gulf*, 67–70.

120. Field, *The Japanese at Leyte Gulf*, 72.

121. US naval aviators downed upwards of 600 of the 1,000 aircraft the Japanese committed to the air battle over Formosa. Cutler, *The Battle of Leyte Gulf*, 71.

122. Field, *The Japanese at Leyte Gulf*, 65–66.

123. Ibid., 63.

124. Ibid., 73.

125. Woodward, *The Battle for Leyte Gulf*, 132.

126. US Third Fleet, Action Report – 23–26 October 1944, Enclosure A (Messages), 19.

127. Woodward, *The Battle for Leyte Gulf*, 72.
128. US Third Fleet, Action Report – 23–26 October 1944, 3–4.
129. Ibid., 4.
130. Ibid., 4–5.
131. Ibid., Enclosure D.
132. For more on Halsey's thinking, see Fleet Admiral William F. Halsey, Jr., "The Battle for Leyte Gulf," in Thomas J. Cutler, ed., *The Battle of Leyte Gulf at 75* (Annapolis, MD: Naval Institute Press, 2019), 225–236, 229.
133. Zingheim, "Sibuyan Sea: The Price of Daring," 127.
134. Halsey's intelligence staff believed that the Japanese were luring Halsey's fleet to the north to open the way for Kurita's fleet to transit San Bernardino Strait, but Halsey's chief of staff, Rear Admiral Robert Carney, rejected their assessment. Carl Solberg, *Decision and Dissent: With Halsey at Leyte Gulf* (Annapolis, MD: Naval Institute Press, 1995), 120–126.
135. Cutler, *The Battle of Leyte Gulf*, 210–213.
136. Reynolds, *The Fast Carriers*, 269–270.
137. US Third Fleet, Action Report – 23–26 October 1944, 5.
138. Seventh Fleet, Report of Operation for the Capture of Leyte Island, 14–15.
139. Ibid., 15–16.
140. Tully, *Battle of Surigao Strait*, 44–48.
141. Ibid., 30–33.
142. Ibid., 81.
143. Ibid., 99–101. The senior surviving officer of Nishimura's force wrote that Nishimura sped up to arrive at Surigao Strait well in advance of the Second Striking Force, deliberately desynchronizing the plan, because he did not want to come under Vice Adm. Shima's command. See James A. Field Jr., "Leyte Gulf: The First Uncensored Japanese Account," in Thomas J. Cutler, ed., *The Battle of Leyte Gulf at 75* (Annapolis, MD: Naval Institute Press, 2019), 243–258, 253.
144. Cutler, *The Battle of Leyte Gulf*, 185.
145. Field, *The Japanese at Leyte Gulf*, 83–86.
146. Seventh Fleet, Report of Operation for the Capture of Leyte Island, 18; David Sears, "Wooden Boats at War: Surigao Strait," www.historynet.com/wooden-boats-at-war-surigao-strait.
147. Seventh Fleet, Report of Operation for the Capture of Leyte Island, 18.
148. A. Denis Clift, "Leyte Gulf Reminiscences," 22.
149. Tully, *Battle of Surigao Strait*, 152–154.
150. One of the torpedoes that hit the *Yamashiro* was part of a second salvo of 5 torpedoes launched by the USS *Bennion* at 3,000 yards – pointblank range. Adm. James L. Holloway III, "Second Salvo at Surigao Strait," in Thomas J. Cutler, ed., *The Battle of Leyte Gulf at 75* (Annapolis, MD: Naval Institute Press, 2019), 319–328, 328.
151. Tully, *Battle of Surigao Strait*, 171.

152. Ibid., 190. The Seventh Fleet operations report claims that the order for the battleships to open fire came at 03:33, but apparently Oldendorf delayed the command of execution.

153. "Crossing the T" on an enemy fleet meant that a force's guns could be trained broadside on an approaching line of ships in column formation, subjecting them to concentrated fire. Samuel Eliot Morison, "The Battle of Surigao Strait," *US Naval Institute Proceedings* 84, no. 12 (1958): 31–53.

154. Stille, *Leyte Gulf*, 153.

155. Vice Adm. Jesse B. Oldendorf, "Admiral Oldendorf Comments on the Battle of Surigao Strait," in Thomas J. Cutler, ed., *The Battle of Leyte Gulf at 75* (Annapolis, MD: Naval Institute Press, 2019), 237–242, 240.

156. Woodward, *The Battle for Leyte Gulf*, 119–120; Field, *The Japanese at Leyte Gulf*, 89; Seventh Fleet, Report of Operation for the Capture of Leyte Island, 18–20.

157. Tully, *Battle of Surigao Strait*, 216.

158. Woodward, *The Battle for Leyte Gulf*, 122–123; Field, *The Japanese at Leyte Gulf*, 92; Morison, *Leyte*, 232–233.

159. Shima's flagship, the heavy cruiser *Nachi*, would be sunk in Manila Bay on November 5 by aircraft from the USS *Lexington* and the USS *Ticonderoga*.

160. Woodward, *The Battle for Leyte Gulf*, 127.

161. Gerald E. Wheeler, *Kinkaid of the Seventh Fleet: A Biography of Admiral Thomas C. Kinkaid U.S. Navy* (Washington, DC: Naval Historical Center, 1995), 396.

162. Cutler, *The Battle of Leyte Gulf*, 177–178.

163. Roger O. Egeberg, *The General: MacArthur and the Man He Called "Doc"* (New York: Hippocrene Books, 1983), 73; James, *The Years of MacArthur*, vol. II, 562.

164. Woodward, *The Battle for Leyte Gulf*, 134–135.

165. Ibid., 139–140; US Third Fleet, Action Report – 23–26 October 1944, 6; Halsey and Bryan, *Admiral Halsey's Story*, 222.

166. Field, *The Japanese at Leyte Gulf*, 94–96, 119–122.

167. Although many of the transports, having disgorged their troops and cargo, had already departed, the critical supply vessels that held Sixth Army's logistical wherewithal in their holds remained in Leyte Gulf.

168. MacArthur, *Reminiscences*, 229.

169. Field, *The Japanese at Leyte Gulf*, 100.

170. Reynolds, *The Fast Carriers*, 268–269.

171. Nimitz also believed that Task Force 34 was guarding San Bernardino Strait.

172. Cutler, *The Battle of Leyte Gulf*, 170–171.

173. Wheeler, *Kinkaid of the Seventh Fleet*, 400.

174. Cutler, *The Battle of Leyte Gulf*, 159.

175. Ibid., 216.

176. Seventh Fleet, Report of Operation for the Capture of Leyte Island, 25.

177. 260001 Oct. 1944, CTU 77.4.3 to CTF 77, John S. McCain Papers, Box 1, Hoover Institution Archives; Hornfischer, *The Last Stand of the Tin Can Sailors*, 132–137.

178. Seventh Fleet, Report of Operation for the Capture of Leyte Island, 27.

179. Halsey and Bryan, *Admiral Halsey's Story*, 219.

180. Morison, *Leyte*, 336; Paul Stillwell, "'Where Is Task Force 34?' The Frustration of Admiral Lee," in Thomas J. Cutler, ed., *The Battle of Leyte Gulf at 75* (Annapolis, MD: Naval Institute Press, 2019), 101–116, 113–114.

181. Hornfischer, *The Last Stand of the Tin Can Sailors*, 177.

182. Upon the ship's commissioning, Evans told the crew who were present, "I intend to go in harm's way and anyone who doesn't want to go along had better get off right now." At Leyte Gulf, Evans kept that promise. Lt. Robert C. Hagen, USNR, as told to Sidney Shalett, "We Asked for the Jap Fleet – and Got It," *Saturday Evening Post*, May 26, 1945.

183. Hornfischer, *The Last Stand of the Tin Can Sailors*, 179.

184. Ibid., 185; Hoyt, *The Battle of Leyte Gulf*, 210–211.

185. Hagen, "We Asked for the Jap Fleet."

186. Hoyt, *The Battle of Leyte Gulf*, 215.

187. Capt. Walter Karig, Lt. Cdr. Russell L. Harris, and Lt. Cdr. Frank A. Manson, "Jeeps versus Giants," in Thomas J. Cutler, ed., *The Battle of Leyte Gulf at 75* (Annapolis, MD: Naval Institute Press, 2019), 289–303, 298.

188. Edward J. Huxtable, Commanding Officer, Composite Squadron Ten, 1943–1945, "Some Recollections," Edward J. Huxtable Papers, Hoover Institution Archives, 19.

189. Woodward, *The Battle for Leyte Gulf*, 182. The best account of Taffy 3's action is Hornfischer, *The Last Stand of the Tin Can Sailors*. The survivors of the *Hoel* and *Johnston* remained in the water for two days and two nights before rescue came. Of the 186 men on the *Johnston* who were able to abandon ship, 141 lived through the ordeal. Cdr. Evans, regrettably, was not one of them. Only 82 sailors from the *Hoel* survived; 252 were listed as missing or dead. For his bravery in fighting his ship to the bitter end even while seriously wounded, Evans was posthumously awarded the Medal of Honor.

190. Woodward, *The Battle for Leyte Gulf*, 188–189; Hornfischer, *The Last Stand of the Tin Can Sailors*, 310–312. For his actions, Lt. Cdr. Fowler was awarded the Navy Cross. The *Chokai* was deliberately sunk by torpedoes from a Japanese destroyer later that night while trying to make its way north to San Bernardino Strait. For more information on the fates of the *Chikuma* and *Chokai*, see Anthony P. Tully, "Solving Some Mysteries of Leyte Gulf: The Fate of the *Chikuma* and *Chokai*," *Warship International*, no. 3 (2000): 248–256.

191. A flight of three Avenger torpedo bombers from the *Ommaney Bay* finished off the cruiser around 14:00. Tully, "Solving Some Mysteries of Leyte Gulf," 250–251.

192. Seventh Fleet, Report of Operation for the Capture of Leyte Island, 32; Field, *The Japanese at Leyte Gulf*, 123.

193. Hornfischer, *The Last Stand of the Tin Can Sailors*, 243–246; Woodward, *The Battle for Leyte Gulf*, 197.

194. Seventh Fleet, Report of Operation for the Capture of Leyte Island, 32.

195. Woodward, *The Battle for Leyte Gulf*, 214.

196. The survivors of the *Gambier Bay* lashed life rafts and floating debris together to stay afloat. They remained in the water for forty hours before being rescued; two were killed by sharks. Brief of Action Report of U.S.S. *Gambier Bay* (Capt. W. V. R. Vieweg), Action Culminating in Its Loss 25 October, 20 December 1944, CINCPAC Records, P88, Box 124, RG 313, NARA II.

197. Morison, *Leyte*, 156.

198. Seventh Fleet, Report of Operation for the Capture of Leyte Island, 29–30; Memorandum for General MacArthur from Admiral Kinkaid, October 20, 1944, Papers of General Richard K. Sutherland relating to GHQ, SWPA, 1942–45, Entry 19810, Box 59, RG 496, NARA II.

199. Tarbuck, King-Two GHQ Observer's Log, A+5, October 25, 1944, 24–25.

200. US Third Fleet, Action Report – 23–26 October 1944, Enclosure A (Messages), 32.

201. Halsey and Bryan, *Admiral Halsey's Story*, 219–220.

202. US Third Fleet, Action Report – 23–26 October 1944, Enclosure A (Messages), 33.

203. Ibid., 34.

204. "The rules for padding specified that it may not consist of familiar words or quotations, it must be separated from the text by double consonants, and it must not be susceptible to being read as part of the message." E. B. Potter, *Nimitz* (Annapolis, MD: Naval Institute Press, 1976), 339. In this case, the padding failed on two counts; it could be read as part of the message, and it was a familiar quotation from Lord Alfred Tennyson's poem "The Charge of the Light Brigade," which read in part, "When can their glory fade? O the wild charge they made! All the world wonder'd." October 25, the day of the battle off Samar, was also the anniversary of the Battle of Balaklava, during which the famous charge occurred. The encoder at Nimitz's headquarters had clearly erred. According to Halsey, Nimitz "blew up when I told him about it; he tracked down the little squirt and chewed him to bits, but it was too late then; the damage had been done." Halsey and Bryan, *Admiral Halsey's Story*, 221. In fact, this admonishment did not happen, but the offending ensign was transferred out of the CINCPAC communications section. Potter, *Nimitz*, 351. October 25 also happened to be St. Crispin's Day and the anniversary of the Battle of Agincourt.

205. Halsey and Bryan, *Admiral Halsey's Story*, 220.

206. Ibid., 221.

207. Field, *The Japanese at Leyte Gulf*, 109; Seventh Fleet, Report of Operation for the Capture of Leyte Island, 30. Kurita was unaware that his cruisers had closed the range to the American carriers.

208. Commander, Task Unit 77.4.3, Subject: Action against the Japanese Main Body off Samar Island, 25 October 1944, October 29, 1944, UD351, Box 261, RG 313, NARA II, 2.

209. Samuel Eliot Morison, *The Two-Ocean War: A Short History of the United States Navy in the Second World War* (Boston: Little, Brown, 1963), 461.

210. There is a good analysis of the possible reasons for Kurita's decision to withdraw in Kenneth I. Friedman, *Afternoon of the Rising Sun: The Battle of Leyte Gulf* (Novato, CA: Presidio, 2001), 339–345.

211. Message 281445, CTF 77 to COMINCH (King), CINCPAC (Nimitz), COM 3rd Fleet (Halsey), COM 7th Fleet, CINCSWPA (MacArthur), COMAIRPAC (Kenney), Papers of General Richard K. Sutherland relating to GHQ, SWPA, 1942–45, Entry 19810, Box 59, RG 496, NARA II.

212. "Action against the Japanese Main Body off Samar Island," 1–2.

213. Potter, *Nimitz*, 344.

214. For a good summary of the various reasons given for Kurita's actions, see Toll, *Twilight of the Gods*, 294–300.

215. Field, *The Japanese at Leyte Gulf*, 109.

216. Friedman, *Afternoon of the Rising Sun*, 345.

217. Field, *The Japanese at Leyte Gulf*, 142–143; Koyanagi, "With Kurita in the Battle of Leyte Gulf," 268–269.

218. Koyanagi, "With Kurita in the Battle of Leyte Gulf," 275–276.

219. The *Suwanee* was hit again by a kamikaze the next day, damaging the ship further.

220. Seventh Fleet, Report of Operation for the Capture of Leyte Island, 29, 31.

221. Tarbuck, King-Two GHQ Observer's Log, A+5, October 25, 1944, 27.

222. Halsey and Bryan, *Admiral Halsey's Story*, 229.

223. Ibid., 232.

224. Ibid; Potter, *Nimitz*, 346–347.

225. Toll, *Twilight of the Gods*, 172.

226. US Pacific Fleet, Second Carrier Task Force, Narrative Report of Task Group 38.1 Operations, October 2–29, 1944, John S. McCain Papers, Box 3, Hoover Institution Archives.

227. Woodward, *The Battle for Leyte Gulf*, 214. Because of the extended range to the target, McCain ordered his planes equipped with fuel drop tanks, which prevented them from carrying more effective, but heavier, torpedoes.

228. US Third Fleet, Action Report – 23–26 October 1944, 7–8.

229. Ibid., 7.

230. Field, *The Japanese at Leyte Gulf*, 122.

231. The Essex-class fleet carrier *Wasp* (CV-18) in this battle should not be confused with the carrier *Wasp* (CV-7), which was sunk by a Japanese submarine on September 15, 1942.

232. Ibid., 132–134, Woodward, *The Battle for Leyte Gulf*, 222–225.

233. Daniel E. Barbey, *MacArthur's Amphibious Navy: Seventh Amphibious Force Operations, 1943–1945* (Annapolis, MD: United States Naval Institute, 1969), 271–275.

234. Koyanagi, "With Kurita in the Battle of Leyte Gulf," 272.

235. Woodward, *The Battle for Leyte Gulf,* 229.

236. Message 291312Z, MacArthur to COM Third Fleet, Papers of General Richard K. Sutherland relating to GHQ, SWPA, 1942–45, Entry 19810, Box 59, RG 496, NARA II. Paul Rogers contends, "Sutherland himself had been humiliated and had been hurt by MacArthur, and he left the message for the future. He recorded what he obviously felt was a serious indictment of MacArthur's character." Paul P. Rogers, *The Bitter Years: MacArthur and Sutherland* (New York: Praeger, 1991), 201–202.

237. Kenney, *General Kenney Reports,* 170.

238. Reynolds, *The Fast Carriers,* 281.

239. Trent Hone, "Halsey's Decision," in Thomas J. Cutler, ed., *The Battle of Leyte Gulf at 75* (Annapolis, MD: Naval Institute Press, 2019), 81–100, 96.

240. The last major sortie of the Japanese fleet, by the battleship *Yamato,* the light cruiser *Yahagi,* and eight destroyers on April 7, 1945, resulted in the sinking of all of the vessels with the exception of three destroyers in the naval equivalent of a banzai charge that never contacted the US fleet off of Okinawa. Toll, *Twilight of the Gods,* 582–589.

CHAPTER 6: THE BATTLE FOR LEYTE

1. Roger O. Egeberg, *The General: MacArthur and the Man He Called "Doc"* (New York: Hippocrene Books, 1983), 75.

2. M. Hamlin Cannon, *Leyte: The Return to the Philippines* (Washington, DC: Office of the Chief of Military History, 1954), 85; Douglas MacArthur, *Reminiscences* (New York: McGraw-Hill, 1964), 221.

3. Edward J. Drea, *MacArthur's ULTRA: Codebreaking and the War against Japan, 1942–1945* (Lawrence: University Press of Kansas, 1992), 168.

4. Far East Command, Pacific Theater Historical Section, Interrogations of Japanese Officials on World War II, interrogation of Col. Shujiro Kobayashi, Tactical Staff (Operations) Officer of the Fourteenth Area Army, USAHEC.

5. Monograph #4, Record of Philippines Operations, Phase 3, Vol. I, Operational Preparations of the 14th Area Army in the P.I., E147(A1), Box 38, RG 554, NARA II, 30; Monograph #6, Record of Philippines Operations, Phase 3, Supplement to Vol. 2, 35th Army Operations in the Leyte Area, E147(A1), Box 38, RG 554, NARA II, 34. The Japanese *Imperial General HQ* was likewise convinced that the decisive battle should be fought on Leyte. Milan Vego, *The Battle for Leyte, 1944: Allied and Japanese Plans, Preparations, and Execution* (Annapolis, MD: Naval Institute Press, 2006), 199. According to Maj. Gen. Yoshiharu Tomochika, chief

of staff of the Japanese *35th Army*, the Imperial Japanese Navy hid its true losses at Leyte Gulf because it "could not stand the humiliation of revealing its actual, heavy losses to the Army." 10th Information and Historical Service, Eighth Army, "Staff Study of Operations of the Japanese 35th Army on Leyte," Part I, III:13.

6. Monograph #5, Record of Philippines Operations, Phase 3, Vol. 2, 14th Area Army Command in the Leyte Opns, E147(A1), Box 38, RG 554, NARA II, 5; interrogation of Col. Shujiro Kobayashi.

7. "Report of statements made by General YAMASHITA, Tomoyuki, Commander-in-Chief of Japanese Army Forces in the Philippines, Lt. General MUTO, Akira, his chief of staff, in conversations with ATIS officers at New Bilibid Prison, MANILA," September 4–6, 1945, USAHEC, OCMH Files, Pacific Interviews, 7–8.

8. 35th Army Operations in the Leyte Area, 33–34.

9. Maj. Gen. Yoshiharu Tomochika, "The True Facts of the Leyte Operation," trans. 166th Language Det., November 5, 1946, USAHEC, 15.

10. 1st Cavalry Division, G-1 Weekly Reports (Leyte), 20–25 October 1944, Annex 7, Civilian Population, 901-1.1, RG 407, NARA II, 1.

11. Radio broadcast, October 22, 1944, William Dunn Radio Transcripts, Folder 42, Box 3, RG 52, MacArthur Memorial Archives.

12. Carlos P. Romulo, *I See the Philippines Rise* (Garden City, NY: Doubleday, 1946), 122.

13. William C. Chase, *Front Line General* (Houston: Pacesetter Press, 1975), 67–68.

14. Captain Raymond Tarbuck, USN, "PHILIPPINE INVASION, 'King-Two' Operation, General Headquarters Observer's Log," A+3, October 20, 1944, Raymond D. Tarbuck Papers, Box 1, Hoover Institution Archives, 17.

15. Radio broadcast, October 30, 1944, William Dunn Radio Transcripts, Folder 42, Box 3, RG 52, MacArthur Memorial Archives.

16. Romulo, *I See the Philippines Rise*, 132.

17. D. Clayton James, *The Years of MacArthur 1941–1945* (Boston: Houghton Mifflin, 1975), 561. The house was built by Walter Scott Price, a US Army engineer who stayed in the Philippines after the Spanish–American War, married a local Filipina, and raised a family in Tacloban.

18. HQ, 1st Cavalry Division, "Historical Report of 1st Cavalry Division K-2 [King II] Operation, 20 October to 25 December 1944," March 4, 1945, 901-0.3, RG 407, NARA II, 24–28.

19. "Leyte Historical Report of the 24th Infantry Division Landing Team, 20 October 1944–25 December 1944," January 25, 1945, 324-0.3, Box 6612, RG 407, NARA II, 26.

20. Ibid., 28.

21. Ibid., 103–104.

22. Ibid., 36–37.

23. Capt. Paul Austin, Co. F, "A Captain's Collection," unpublished manuscript, Aubrey S. Newman Papers, Box 3, USAHEC.

24. "Leyte Historical Report of the 24th Infantry Division Landing Team," 40–41.
25. Aubrey S. Newman, "After Action Battle Report," unpublished draft manuscript, Aubrey S. Newman Papers, Box 2, USAHEC, 14–18.
26. "Leyte Historical Report of the 24th Infantry Division Landing Team," 44.
27. Ibid., 47.
28. Ibid., 48.
29. Orlando R. Davidson, J. Carl Willems, and Joseph A. Kahl, *The Deadeyes: The Story of the 96th Infantry Division* (Washington, DC: Infantry Journal Press, 1947), 21.
30. Ibid., 32–33.
31. Ibid., 47–48.
32. Sgt. George N. Meyers, "Mountain Warfare on ATTU," *Yank* 2, no. 2 (July 2, 1943), 3–4.
33. 7th Infantry Division, Operation Report, King II, Annex 5: Detailed Division Narrative, 307-3, Box 6134, RG 407, NARA II, 11–14.
34. Monograph #6, 51.
35. 7th Infantry Division, Operation Report, King II, Annex 5, 14–18.
36. Cannon, *Leyte*, 244.
37. Egeberg, *The General*, 75.
38. Ibid., 79.
39. Ibid., 79.
40. Ibid. 83.
41. Ibid., 82.
42. Letter, Bonner Fellers to his wife Dorothy, November 5, 1944, Bonner F. Fellers Papers, RG 44a Series I: Correspondence, Folder 24, Box 1, MacArthur Memorial Archives.
43. Romulo, *I See the Philippines Rise*, 161.
44. George C. Kenney, *General Kenney Reports: A Personal History of the Pacific War* (New York: Duell, Sloan and Pearce, 1949), 463.
45. Romulo, *I See the Philippines Rise*, 159.
46. "Leyte Historical Report of the 24th Infantry Division Landing Team," 51–52.
47. Ibid., 53.
48. Ibid., 124.
49. Bertram C. Wright, *The 1st Cavalry Division in World War II* (Tokyo: Toppan, 1947), 75.
50. Chase, *Front Line General*, 69.
51. Headquarters, 1st Cavalry Division, "Souvenir Battle Diary," 1945, 901-0, RG 407, NARA II, 6.
52. "Historical Report of 1st Cavalry Division K-2 [King II] Operation," 29–30.
53. "Souvenir Battle Diary," 7.
54. 96th Infantry Division, Operation Report, King Two, March 17, 1945, 396-0.3, RG 407, NARA II, 64.

55. Brig. Gen. Henry J. Muller, Jr., "Listen as You Have Never Listened Before," unpublished manuscript, Henry J. Muller Papers, Hoover Institution Archives, 13.

56. Davidson, Willems, and Kahl, *The Deadeyes*, 55.

57. Ibid., 57.

58. Ibid., 59.

59. Muller, "Listen as You Have Never Listened Before," 18–19. Homma was relieved of command after the Bataan campaign and forced into retirement in 1943. He never set foot on Leyte, which is why he was apprehended in Japan after the surrender.

60. Fifty-nine of the 164 graduates of the class of 1915 pinned on general's stars, more than for any other class in the history of West Point. Other members of the class of 1915 included future five-star generals Dwight Eisenhower and Omar Bradley and future four-star generals James Van Fleet and Joseph T. McNarney.

61. Muller, "Listen as You Have Never Listened Before," 14–15. Muller's comment about the rest of Leyte being mapped in great detail was, of course, not true.

62. Ibid., 16.

63. "Address by Brigadier General Henry Muller to the Manila Liberation Commemoration 1945–1999," February 5, 1999, Henry J. Muller Papers, Hoover Institution Archives, 4.

64. Colonel Haugen, Orin D. "Hard Rock," http://511pir.com/officers-biograph ies/165-colonel-orin-d-hard-rock-haugen.

65. Freda Brinson, "Soldiers Battled Enemies, Filthy Conditions, Foreign Disease, and Wounds That Linger in the Aftermath," December 7, 2013, www.aapc.com/ blog/26557-wwii-military-health-in-the-pacific.

66. Public Relations Office, 32nd Infantry Division, *13,000 Hours: Combat History of the 32nd Inf Division – World War II* (1945), 22.

67. "The Commander's Appreciation of Logistics," lecture delivered to the Army War College, January 3, 1955, Box 12, Papers of Walter Krueger Jr., USMA Library Special Collections, 9.

68. Captain George E. Morrissey, Medical Corps, "The Philippine Campaign of 1st Bn. 34th Infantry," entry for October 30, 1944, Aubrey S. Newman Papers, Box 3, USAHEC.

69. Letter, Bonner Fellers to his wife Dorothy, November 8, 1944, Bonner F. Fellers Papers, Folder 24, Box 1, RG 44a (Series I: Correspondence), MacArthur Memorial Archives.

70. Elizabeth L. James, unpublished diary, November 9, 1944, Elizabeth L. James Papers, Hoover Institution Archives.

71. Radio broadcast, November 9, 1944, William Dunn Radio Transcripts, Folder 43, Box 3, RG 52, MacArthur Memorial Archives.

72. Muller, "Listen as You Have Never Listened Before," 12–13.

73. "Leyte Historical Report of the 24th Infantry Division Landing Team," 5.

74. Ibid., 11, 133–134.

75. Public Relations Office, 32nd Infantry Division, *13,000 Hours*, 21–22.
76. "Leyte Historical Report of the 24th Infantry Division Landing Team," 52–53.
77. Ibid., 119.
78. 1 CD, "Historical Report of 1st Cavalry Division K-2 [King II] Operation, 20 October to 25 December 1944," March 4, 1945, 901-0.3, RG 407, NARA II, 43–44.
79. 1 Cavalry Brigade, "Historical Report, 12 Oct–25 Dec 1944," January 10, 1945, 901-CC(1)-0.3, RG 407, NARA II, 5.
80. 2 Cavalry Brigade, 1 CD, "Historical Report, Leyte-Samar Is. Campaign, 20 Oct–25 Dec 1944," January 9, 1945, 1, 901-CC(2)-0.3, RG 407, NARA II, 17.
81. 1 Cavalry Brigade, "Historical Report, 12 Oct–25 Dec 1944," S-4 summary, January 10, 1945, 901-CC(1)-0.3, RG 407, NARA II, 5.
82. 1 CD, G-1 Weekly Report, 15–22 November 1944, Annex 5 (Civilian Population), 901-1.21, RG 407, NARA II.
83. 1 CD, G-1 Weekly Report, 20–25 October 1944, Annex 7 (Civilian Population), 901-1.21, RG 407, NARA II.
84. 1 CD, G-1 Weekly Report, 8–15 November 1944, Annex 6 (Civilian Population), 901-1.21, RG 407, NARA II.
85. "Leyte Historical Report of the 24th Infantry Division Landing Team," 115.
86. The basic policy was outlined in SWPA Staff Memorandum 35, "Civil Administration and Relief in the Philippines," August 30, 1944. Civil Affairs Section, US Army Forces Pacific, "Report on Philippine Civil Affairs," August 25, 1945, Papers of General Richard K. Sutherland relating to GHQ, SWPA, 1942–45, Entry 19810, RG 496, NARA II, 6.
87. 1 CD, "Historical Report of 1st Cavalry Division K-2 [King II] Operation," 22–23.
88. Ibid., 21–23.
89. "Leyte Historical Report of the 24th Infantry Division Landing Team," 30.
90. "Report on Philippine Civil Affairs," 11, 31–32; David Smollar, "'Hard, Bitter, Unpleasantly Necessary Duty': A Little-Known World War II Story of the Philippines," *Prologue* (Summer 2015), 6–15, www.archives.gov/publications/prologue/2015/summer.
91. Smollar, "Hard, Bitter, Unpleasantly Necessary Duty," 8. Rauh graduated first in his Harvard Law School class and clerked on the Supreme Court before being commissioned in the Army of the United States. He would go on after the war to become a noted civil rights advocate and attorney. President Bill Clinton awarded Rauh the Presidential Medal of Freedom in 1993.
92. MacArthur, *Reminiscences*, 235.
93. MacArthur to Maj. Gen. John Hilldring, Director of the Civil Affairs Division, War Department, September 2, 1944, Entry 19810, Box 40, Papers of General Richard K. Sutherland relating to GHQ, SWPA, 1942–45, RG 496, NARA II.
94. MacArthur, *Reminiscences*, 236–237.
95. "Report on Philippine Civil Affairs," 14.
96. James, *The Years of MacArthur*, vol. II, 582–583.

97. Egeberg, *The General*, 81.

98. Frank E. Gillette, "Supply Problems on Leyte," *Military Review* 25, no. 1 (April 1945): 61–68, 61.

99. William M. Leary, "Walter Krueger: MacArthur's Fighting General," in William M. Leary, ed., *We Shall Return! MacArthur's Commanders and the Defeat of Japan, 1942–1945* (Lexington: University Press of Kentucky, 1988), 60–87, 71–72.

100. "The Commander's Appreciation of Logistics," lecture delivered to the Army War College, January 3, 1955, Box 12, Papers of Walter Krueger Jr., USMA Library Special Collections, 8.

101. Daniel E. Barbey, *MacArthur's Amphibious Navy: Seventh Amphibious Force Operations, 1943–1945* (Annapolis, MD: United States Naval Institute, 1969), 216.

102. Office of the Chief Engineer, GHQ Army Forces Pacific, *Engineers of the Southwest Pacific 1941–1945*, vol. VI: *Airfield and Base Development* (Washington, DC: GPO, 1951), 287–288.

103. GHQ SWPA, Staff Study, King-Two, 4 ed., September 20, 1944, Entry 166, Box 796 (SWP ACS G-4 Staff Studies), RG 496, NARA II.

104. Office of the Chief Engineer, GHQ Army Forces Pacific, *Engineers of the Southwest Pacific*, vol. VI, 290–291.

105. Ibid., vol. VI, 306–308.

106. Ibid., vol. VI, 291–292.

107. Samuel Eliot Morison, *History of United States Naval Operations in World War II*, vol. VI: *Leyte, June 1944–January 1945* (Boston: Little, Brown, 1958), 166n12.

108. *Reports of General MacArthur: The Campaigns of MacArthur in the Pacific*, vol. I (Washington, DC: Center of Military History, 1966), 224.

109. Walter Krueger, *From Down Under to Nippon: The Story of Sixth Army in World War II* (Washington, DC: Combat Forces Press, 1953), 165.

110. Daniel E. Barbey, *MacArthur's Amphibious Navy: Seventh Amphibious Force Operations, 1943–1945* (Annapolis, MD: United States Naval Institute, 1969), 262.

111. Frank Futrell, "Leyte," in Wesley Frank Craven and James Lea Cate, *The Army Air Forces in World War II*, vol. V: *The Pacific: Matterhorn to Nagasaki, June 1944 to August 1945* (Chicago: University of Chicago Press, 1953), 341–389, 368–369.

112. General George C. Kenney Diary, October 25, 1944, RG 54 (Papers of General George C. Kenney), MacArthur Memorial Archives.

113. Kenney Diary, October 26, 1944.

114. Radio broadcast, October 28, 1944, William Dunn Radio Transcripts, Folder 42, Box 3, RG 52, MacArthur Memorial Archives.

115. Futrell, "Leyte," 369.

116. Kenney to Arnold, October 28, 1944, Kenney Diary.

117. Arnold to Kenney, November 3, 1944, Kenney Diary.

118. Kenney to Arnold, December 18, 1944, Kenney Diary.

119. Bong died in a crash on August 6, 1945, while testing the new P-80A "Shooting Star" jet fighter. The second top-scoring ace of the Pacific War, Maj. Thomas McGuire, reached thirty-eight kills before dying in a crash on the island of Negros on January 7, 1945.

120. Office of the Chief Engineer, GHQ Army Forces Pacific, *Engineers of the Southwest Pacific*, vol. VI, 298–299.

121. Futrell, "Leyte," 374, 383–384; Charles W. Boggs, *Marine Aviation in the Philippines* (Washington, DC: Historical Division, USMC, 1951), 30–31.

122. Office of the Chief Engineer, GHQ Army Forces Pacific, *Engineers of the Southwest Pacific 1941–1945*, vol. VI, 299.

123. Ibid., 300.

124. Futrell, "Leyte," 373.

125. Office of the Chief Engineer, GHQ Army Forces Pacific, *Engineers of the Southwest Pacific 1941–1945*, vol. VI, 303.

126. Message 010703, CTF 77 (Kinkaid) to CINCSWPA; Papers of General Richard K. Sutherland relating to GHQ, SWPA, 1942–45, Entry 19810, RG 496, NARA II.

127. Message 010831, CTF 77 (Kinkaid) to COMFEAF (Kenney), CINCSWPA, CINCPAC, COM 7th Fleet, COMGEN 5th Air Force; Papers of General Richard K. Sutherland relating to GHQ, SWPA, 1942–45, Entry 19810, RG 496, NARA II.

128. Message 011335, COM 3rd Fleet (Halsey) to CINCSWPA (MacArthur); Message 011651, CTG 78.2 to CTG 77.1 (Adm Weyler); Papers of General Richard K. Sutherland relating to GHQ, SWPA, 1942–45, Entry 19810, RG 496, NARA II.

129. Futrell, "Leyte," 372.

130. Gerald E. Wheeler, *Kinkaid of the Seventh Fleet: A Biography of Admiral Thomas C. Kinkaid U.S. Navy* (Washington, DC: Naval Historical Center, 1995), 408, 410.

131. Samuel Eliot Morison, *History of United States Naval Operations in World War II*, vol. XIII: *The Liberation of the Philippines: Luzon, Mindanao, the Visayas, 1944–1945* (Boston: Little, Brown, 1959), 53; William B. Breuer, *Retaking the Philippines: America's Return to Corregidor and Bataan: October 1944–March 1945* (New York: St. Martin's Press, 1986), 99.

132. Cannon, *Leyte*, 221. After realizing the battle for Leyte was likely lost, Terauchi moved the *Southern Expeditionary Army Group* headquarters from Manila to Saigon in the middle of November.

133. Special Intelligence Bulletin No. 543, November 1/2, 1944, Entry A1 9002, Box 65, RG 457, NARA II.

134. Special Intelligence Bulletin No. 551, November 9/10, and Special Intelligence Bulletin No. 552, November 10/11, 1944, Entry A1 9002, Box 65, RG 457, NARA II.

135. Cannon, *Leyte*, 99–102; Monograph #84 (Navy), Philippine Area Naval Operations, Part III: Leyte, E147(A1), Box 51, RG 554, NARA II, 97–110; Monograph #6, 62.

136. Monograph #84, 97–110, Cannon, *Leyte*, 99–101; Drea, *MacArthur's ULTRA*, 178.

137. Vincent P. O'Hara, "After the Battle: Sea Power and the Ormoc Campaign," in Thomas J. Cutler, ed., *The Battle of Leyte Gulf at 75* (Annapolis, MD: Naval Institute Press, 2019), 156–171, 158.

138. Monograph #6, 37, 46.

139. Krueger, *From Down Under to Nippon*, 166.

140. O'Hara, "After the Battle," 160–161.

141. Drea, *MacArthur's ULTRA*, 184.

142. Ibid., 161–162.

143. Boggs, *Marine Aviation in the Philippines*, 33–37.

144. Drea, *MacArthur's ULTRA*, 175–178.

145. Ibid., 170–171; Krueger, *From Down Under to Nippon*, 169.

146. SWPA G-2 Advon, Memo #2 to CinC & C/S, November 6, 1944, Entry 45, Box 324, RG 496, NARA II.

147. SWPA G-2 Advon, Memo #3 to CinC & C/S, November 8, 1944, Entry 45, Box 324, RG 496, NARA II.

148. Leyte Historical Report of the 24th Infantry Division Landing Team, 20 October 1944–25 December 1944, 54.

149. Ibid., 105.

150. Ibid., 63–64.

151. Ibid., 161.

152. Ibid., 111–112.

153. Ibid., 72. The battalion's casualties totaled 31 dead and 55 wounded, while 241 non-battle casualties suffered from skin disorders, trench foot, and battle fatigue.

154. Ibid., 74.

155. Morrissey, "The Philippine Campaign of 1st Bn. 34th Infantry," entry for November 21, 1944.

156. Leyte Historical Report of the 24th Infantry Division Landing Team, 80. The 1944 game, played at Yankee Stadium, is still the worst defeat in Notre Dame football history. Lt. Col. Clifford was awarded the Distinguished Service Cross for his actions on Kilay Ridge, and his battalion was awarded a Distinguished Unit Citation.

157. Ibid., 76.

158. Morrissey, "The Philippine Campaign of 1st Bn. 34th Infantry," entry for November 14, 1944.

159. Leyte Historical Report of the 24th Infantry Division Landing Team, 64.

160. By the end of the campaign, Sixth Army was short nearly 24,000 officers and enlisted soldiers from its authorized strength. Cannon, *Leyte*, 222.

161. Ibid., 174–175. Letter, Irving to Sutherland, January 20, 1945, Papers of General Richard K. Sutherland relating to GHQ, SWPA, 1942–45, SLD, Entry 19810, Box 60, RG 496, NARA II. MacArthur, realizing the injustice of the relief, gave Irving command of the 38th Infantry Division shortly before the war ended.

162. 32nd Infantry Division, Report after Action, Leyte Engagement or K-2 Operation, 16 November–25 December 1944, 332-0.3, Box 7793, RG 407, NARA II, 6.

163. 32nd Infantry Division History, 332-0, Box 7793, RG 407, NARA II, 5.

164. 10th Information and Historical Service, Eighth Army, "Staff Study of Operations of the Japanese 35th Army on Leyte," Part I, IV:33.

165. 32nd Infantry Division, Report after Action, Leyte Engagement, 7–8.

166. Ibid., 11.

167. Ibid.

168. Ibid., 25.

169. 1 CD, "Historical Report of 1st Cavalry Division K-2 [King II] Operation," 38–43.

170. Ibid., 45–46.

171. Ibid., 49.

172. 7th Cavalry, "Historical Report, Leyte Campaign, 20 Oct–25 Dec 1944," 901-CRG(7)-0.3, RG 407, NARA II, 11–12.

173. Davidson, Willems, and Kahl, *The Deadeyes*, 59.

174. Ibid., 61.

175. Ibid., 63.

176. Ibid., 69.

177. Cannon, *Leyte*, 296.

178. Joseph B. Seay, "The 11th Airborne Division in the Leyte Mountain Operation," *Military Review* 29, no. 6 (September 1949): 17–24, 18.

179. Ibid., 22.

180. 11 Airborne Division, "Historical Summary, 25 February 1943 to 10 February 1945," March 12, 1945, 311-0.1, RG 407, NARA II, 4.

181. 11 Airborne Division, "History," May 13, 1945, 311-0.1, RG 407, NARA II, 11.

182. Gillette, "Supply Problems on Leyte," 66.

183. Drea, *MacArthur's ULTRA*, 175; Cannon, *Leyte*, 100–101.

184. Monograph #5, Record of Philippines Operations, Phase 3, Vol. 2, 14th Area Army Command in the Leyte Opns, E147(A1), Box 38, RG 554, NARA II, 6; Cannon, *Leyte*, 254.

185. Cannon, *Leyte*, 257–265.

186. Monograph #5, 9–11; Monograph #6, 81.

187. Monograph #6, 85.

188. Muller, "Listen as You Have Never Listened Before," 7.

189. Ibid., 22.

190. Monograph #6, 84; Cannon, *Leyte*, 299–300.

191. Bad weather on Luzon forced the cancelation of the second and third lifts.

192. Staff Sergeant W. E. Lindau, 11th Airborne Division History, Feb. 1943–May 1945, 311-0.1, RG 407, NARA II, 14; Monograph #6, 24–33. Japanese transports headed for Tacloban and Dulag airfields were either shot down or crash-landed, killing all the paratroopers aboard. Cannon, *Leyte*, 305.

193. Sixth US Army, "Report of the Leyte Operation, 20 October 1944–25 December 1944," CARL, 72.

194. Cannon, *Leyte*, 302–305; 11 Airborne Division, "History," 9–10. During the fighting PFC Ova A. Kelley charged into a Japanese formation and disorganized it with rifle fire and grenades. His actions inspired the other men in his company, who proceeded to eliminate the Japanese position near the San Pablo airfield. Kelley was killed during the fighting and was awarded a posthumous Medal of Honor for his actions. Davidson, Willems, and Kahl, *The Deadeyes*, 68–69.

195. Tomochika, "The True Facts of the Leyte Operation," 28.

196. 11 Airborne Division, "Report after Action with the Enemy, Operation King II, Leyte Campaign," May 28, 1945, 311-0.3, RG 407, NARA II, 5.

197. "Dear General: World War II Letters, 1944–1945," letter dated December 24, 1944, Joseph Swing Letters to Peyton C. March, Joseph Swing Papers, USAHEC.

198. Monograph #6, 86.

199. Krueger, *From Down Under to Nippon*, 175.

200. The 77th Infantry Division, nicknamed the "Statue of Liberty Division" because of the division's origins in New York state during World War I, was activated on March 25, 1942, and trained in the United States for two years prior to its deployment to Hawai'i. It had landed on Guam in conjunction with the 3rd Marine Division on July 21, 1944, and fought for eighteen days before the island was secured. Leyte would be the division's second combat action.

201. Cannon, *Leyte*, 276–277.

202. Krueger, *From Down Under to Nippon*, 177.

203. Ibid., 178–179.

204. HQ, 77th Infantry Division, G-3 Operation Summary, 23 November–25 December 1944, 377-0.3, Box 9790, RG 407, NARA II, 10.

205. Kenney, *General Kenney Reports*, 487–488; Cannon, *Leyte*, 281–282; Futrell, "Leyte," 381–382.

206. Comments on Chapters XV, XVII, XVIII, XIX and XX of *The United States Army in World War II*, in M. Hamlin Cannon, *Leyte: Return to the Philippines*, Andrew D. Bruce Papers, Box 6, AHEC, 3.

207. 77th Infantry Division, G-3 Operation Summary, 23 November–25 December 1944, 11.

208. "Staff Study of Operations of the Japanese 35th Army on Leyte," Part I, II:10.

209. Monograph #6, 97, 101.

210. Futrell, "Leyte," 381.

211. Dwight C. Shepler, USNR, Report of Duty during period 1 December 1944 to 20 March 1945, Raymond D. Tarbuck Papers, Box 2, Hoover Institution Archives, 3.

212. Cannon, *Leyte*, 283.

213. 77th Infantry Division, G-3 Operation Summary, 23 November–25 December 1944, 12–14.

214. Ibid., 15.

215. Ibid., 17.

216. Ibid., 18–19.

217. Monograph #5, Record of Philippines Operations, Phase 3, Vol. 2, 14th Area Army Command in the Leyte Opns, E147(A1), RG 554, Box 38, 13.

218. 77th Infantry Division, G-3 Operation Summary, 23 November–25 December 1944, 21.

219. Leigh C. Fairbank, Jr., "Division Engineers, Part II: Leyte," *The Military Engineer* 39, no. 256 (February 1947): 56–63.

220. 77th Infantry Division, G-3 Operation Summary, 23 November–25 December 1944, 39.

221. Ibid., 27–28.

222. Organizational History, Leyte Operation, 16 November 1944–2 January 45, 332-0.3, Box 7794, RG 407, NARA II, 32.

223. 32nd Infantry Division, Supplemental Historical Report after Action, 26 December 1944–21 January 1945, 332-0.3, Box 7794, RG 407, NARA II, 3.

224. 1st Cavalry Division, Battle Diary, 901-0, RG 407, NARA II.

225. HQ, 77th Infantry Division, G-3 Operation Summary, 23 November–25 December 1944, 32–39.

226. Special Intelligence Bulletin No. 594, December 22/23, 1944, Entry A1 9002, Box 65, RG 457, NARA II.

227. Radio broadcast, December 26, 1944, William Dunn Radio Transcripts, Folder 45, Box 3, RG 52, MacArthur Memorial Archives; James, *The Years of MacArthur*, vol. II, 591.

228. Lt. Gen. Kenney's and Maj. Gen. Marshall's Australian secretaries, Beryl Stevenson and Louise Mowat, also received commissions as WACs at the same time, albeit as 1st Lieutenants. Paul P. Rogers, *The Bitter Years: MacArthur and Sutherland* (New York: Praeger, 1991), 67–68.

229. Ibid., 164. Kenney and Richard Marshall also brought their Australian secretaries to Hollandia, but, unlike Clark, they could actually type. Manchester, *American Caesar*, 404.

230. Rogers, *The Bitter Years*, 80–83, 163; Egeberg, *The General*, 59, 61.

231. Manchester, *American Caesar*, 404.

232. Egeberg, *The General*, 92–93.

233. Ibid., 93.

234. James, *The Years of MacArthur*, vol. II, 598.

235. A comprehensive narration of this incident and its implications for the relationship between MacArthur and Sutherland can be found in Rogers, *The Bitter Years*, 211–217.

236. James, *The Years of MacArthur*, vol. II, 596, 598.

237. Eighth Army, Leyte Mop-up Operation, 108-0, Box 2233, RG 407, NARA II, 30.

238. Jay Luvaas, ed., *DEAR MISS EM: General Eichelberger's War in the Pacific, 1942–1945* (Westport, CT: Greenwood, 1972), 172.

239. Ibid., 196.

240. Eighth Army, Leyte Mop-up Operation, 88.

241. Robert L. Eichelberger, *Our Jungle Road to Tokyo* (New York: Viking, 1950), 181; Cannon, *Leyte*, 368.

242. 10th Information and Historical Service, Eighth Army, "Staff Study of Operations of the Japanese 35th Army on Leyte," Part I, II:11–12.

243. Cannon, *Leyte*, 367–368.

244. *Reports of General MacArthur*, 240n98.

245. "Japanese Airplane Losses," Philippines–Formosa–Ryukyus, Kenney Diary, February 10, 1945.

246. Futrell, "Leyte," 375.

247. MacArthur, *Reminiscences*, 234.

CHAPTER 7: THE INVASION OF LUZON

1. Russell Volckmann, *We Remained* (New York: W. W. Norton, 1954), 188.

2. "World Battlefronts: Old Soldier," *Time*, January 29, 1945.

3. Lt. Gen. George Kenney to Gen. H. H. Arnold, Subject: Operations in the Pacific, November 22, 1944, Entry 422, Box 48, Operations Division History Unit (Miscellaneous), RG 165, NARA II.

4. Robert Ross Smith, *Triumph in the Philippines* (Washington, DC: Office of the Chief of Military History, 1963), 21–22.

5. General George C. Kenney Diary, November 26, 1944, RG 54 (Papers of General George C. Kenney), MacArthur Memorial Archives.

6. Ibid.

7. Kenney Diary, November 30, 1944.

8. Gerald E. Wheeler, *Kinkaid of the Seventh Fleet: A Biography of Admiral Thomas C. Kinkaid, U.S. Navy* (Washington, DC: Naval Historical Center, 1995), 413.

9. Message 86, MacArthur to Marshall, November 30, 1944, War Department Messages #801–900, 9 August 1944–28 December 1944, Folder 2, Box 17, USAPAC Records, RG 4, MacArthur Memorial Archives.

10. Smith, *Triumph in the Philippines*, 45–46.

11. The attack on the *Nashville* killed 133 men, including Brig. Gen. Dunckel's chief of staff and several other senior officers, and wounded 190 others. MacArthur had considered sailing on the *Nashville* to observe the Mindoro landing, but his staff had

thankfully talked him out of it because of the threat of kamikaze attacks, which materialized. Samuel Eliot Morison, *History of United States Naval Operations in World War II*, vol. XIII: *The Liberation of the Philippines: Luzon, Mindanao, the Visayas, 1944–1945* (Boston: Little, Brown, 1955), 23–24; D. Clayton James, *The Years of MacArthur*, vol. II: *1941–1945* (Boston: Houghton Mifflin, 1975), 608.

12. Frank Futrell, "Mindoro," in Wesley Frank Craven and James Lea Cate, eds., *The Army Air Forces in World War II*, vol. V: *The Pacific: Matterhorn to Nagasaki, June 1944 to August 1945* (Chicago: University of Chicago Press, 1953), 390–412, 397.

13. Wheeler, *Kinkaid of the Seventh Fleet*, 414. To compensate for the kamikaze threat, the complement of aircraft aboard the large Essex-class carriers was changed from thirty-eight fighters, thirty-six dive bombers, and eighteen torpedo bombers to seventy-three fighters, fifteen dive bombers, and fifteen torpedo bombers. The fast carrier task groups also developed new tactics, techniques, and procedures to ensure that kamikazes could not approach without detection. Morison, *The Liberation of the Philippines*, 54–55.

14. John Curatola, "Typhoon Cobra: Halsey Versus Mother Nature," The National World War II Museum, October 1, 2024, www.nationalww2museum.org/war/a rticles/typhoon-cobra-halsey-versus-mother-nature.

15. Bob Drury and Tom Clavin, *Halsey's Typhoon: The True Story of a Fighting Admiral, an Epic Storm and an Untold Rescue* (New York: Atlantic Monthly Press, 2006).

16. Office of the Chief Engineer, GHQ Army Forces Pacific, *Engineers of the Southwest Pacific, 1941–1945*, vol. VI: *Airfield and Base Development* (Washington, DC: GPO, 1951), 316.

17. Futrell, "Luzon," 398–399.

18. Smith, *Triumph in the Philippines*, 49–51.

19. Futrell, "Luzon," 401.

20. Smith, *Triumph in the Philippines*, 52.

21. George C. Kenney, *General Kenney Reports: A Personal History of the Pacific War* (New York: Duell, Sloan and Pearce, 1949), 497.

22. Futrell, "Luzon," 411.

23. Robert D. Eichelberger, *Our Jungle Road to Tokyo* (New York: Viking, 1950), 204.

24. Smith, *Triumph in the Philippines*, 27.

25. Edward J. Drea, *MacArthur's Ultra: Codebreaking and the War against Japan, 1942–1945* (Lawrence, KS: University Press of Kansas, 1992), 180.

26. Smith, *Triumph in the Philippines*, 27–28.

27. Drea, *MacArthur's Ultra*, 181.

28. General Clyde D. Eddleman Oral History, Clyde D. Eddleman Papers, USAHEC, 11–12.

29. Ibid., 12–13.

30. Volckmann, *We Remained*, 177–179.

31. Ibid., 181.

32. For an extended discussion of Willoughby's assessment of Japanese strength on Luzon, see Drea, *MacArthur's Ultra*, Chapter 7.

33. Ibid., 182.
34. Ibid., 186.
35. Report of statements made by General Yamashita, Tokoyuki, Commander-in-Chief of Japanese Army Forces in the Philippines, Lt. General Muto, Akira, his Chief of Staff, in conversations with ATIS officers at New Bilibid Prison, MANILA, September 4–6, 1945, OCMH Files, Pacific Interviews, USAHEC, 6.
36. Smith, *Triumph in the Philippines*, 93.
37. Report of statements made by General Yamashita and Lt. General Muto, 2.
38. GHQ, US Army Forces Pacific, "Enemy on Luzon: An Intelligence Summary," 26–38.
39. Smith, *Triumph in the Philippines*, 89.
40. Monograph #7, Record of Philippines Operations, Phase 3, Vol. 3, Luzon Operations, E147(A1), Box 39, RG 554, NARA II, 9–11.
41. Monograph #8, Record of Philippines Operations, Phase 3, Supplement to Vol. 3, Shimbu Group Operations, E147(A1), Box 39, RG 554, NARA II, 3.
42. Historical Division, Eighth Army, "Staff Study of Japanese Operations on Luzon, P.I.," March 22, 1949, Part I, 8.
43. Smith, *Triumph in the Philippines*, 94–96.
44. Headquarters, 14th Area Army, January 1, 1945, "Instructions to Organic and Attached Units Awaiting the Decisive Battle of Luzon," OCMH Files, Pacific Interviews, USAHEC.
45. James, *The Years of MacArthur*, vol. II, 613.
46. Staff Study, M-1 Operation, 7 October 1944, Box 27, Folder 4, RG 30 (Papers of Richard K. Sutherland), MacArthur Memorial Archives; Sixth US Army, Report of the Luzon Campaign, 9 January 1945–30 June 1945, Vol. I, Combined Arms Research Library, Ft. Leavenworth, KS, 7–9. Mike-I, or M-I, was a component of Operations Plan Musketeer III for the liberation of the Philippines, published on September 26, 1944.
47. The 25th Infantry Division had a unique history, being formed during the war from two regiments of the Old Hawaiian Division (27th and 35th Infantry), and a National Guard regiment (161st Infantry) from the Pacific Northwest. The division was seasoned in Guadalcanal, New Georgia, and Vella Lavella under the command of Maj. Gen. J. Lawton Collins prior to the Luzon campaign. It enjoyed more than a year of rest and training in New Zealand and New Caledonia prior to its commitment on Luzon.
48. "XIV Corps Operations on Luzon," Papers of Oscar W. Griswold, Box 1A, USMA Library Special Collections, 11–13.
49. Smith, *Triumph in the Philippines*, 54–55.
50. Ibid., 57.
51. Lieut. Dwight C. Shepler, Report of Duty during period 1 December 1944 to 20 March 1945, Raymond D. Tarbuck Papers, Box 2, Hoover Institution Archives, 6.
52. Douglas MacArthur, *Reminiscences* (New York: McGraw-Hill, 1964), 240.
53. Sixth US Army, Report of the Luzon Campaign, 15.

54. Roger O. Egeberg, *The General: MacArthur and the Man He Called "Doc"* (New York: Hippocrene Books, 1983), 104.
55. Bonner Fellers to his wife, January 2, 1945, Folder 1, Box 2, RG 44a (Series I: Correspondence), MacArthur Memorial Archives. MacArthur, of course, would have asked the Lord for further benevolence if forces under his command had invaded Japan, and he no doubt beseeched the Lord for generosity when he gambled on the invasion of Inchon during the Korean War.
56. MacArthur, *Reminiscences*, 240.
57. Futrell, "Luzon," 406. McGuire would tragically die on January 7, 1945, in a crash on Negros while pursuing a Japanese Zero.
58. Diary of Lieutenant General O. W. Griswold, Oscar W. Griswold Papers, USAHEC.
59. Besides the *Long*, kamikazes also hit the battleships *New Mexico* and *California*, the cruisers *Minneapolis*, *Australia*, *Louisville*, and *Columbia* (twice), five destroyers, another minesweeper, an aviation tender, and a fast transport destroyer (APD). Daniel E. Barbey, *MacArthur's Amphibious Navy: Seventh Amphibious Force Operations, 1943–1945* (Annapolis, MD: United States Naval Institute, 1969), 297.
60. Gerald E. Wheeler, "Thomas C. Kinkaid: MacArthur's Master of Naval Warfare," in William M. Leary, ed., *We Shall Return! MacArthur's Commanders and the Defeat of Japan, 1942–1945* (Lexington: University Press of Kentucky, 1988), 115–154, 149.
61. Trent Hone, "Countering the Kamikaze," *Naval History Magazine* 34, no. 5 (October 2020), www.usni.org/magazines/naval-history-magazine/2020/octo ber/countering-kamikaze; Morison, *The Liberation of the Philippines*, 55–58.
62. Sixth US Army, Report of the Luzon Campaign, 15.
63. XIV Corps, After Action Report, M-1 Operation, July 29, 1945, https://cgsc.co ntentdm.oclc.org/digital/collection/p4013coll8/id/4680, 29.
64. Griswold Diary, January 8, 1945. Emphasis in the original.
65. By the end of January, the Japanese had only ten serviceable planes left on Luzon. Monograph #7, 51.
66. Smith, *Triumph in the Philippines*, 65–66.
67. Letter from Douglas MacArthur to Jean MacArthur, January 8, 1945, Folder 21, Box 7, RG 10 (Personal Correspondence), MacArthur Memorial Archives.
68. Smith, *Triumph in the Philippines*, 67–69; "XIV Corps Operations on Luzon," 42.
69. "XIV Corps Operations on Luzon," 49–50.
70. Griswold Diary, January 8, 1945.
71. Volckmann, *We Remained*, 182.
72. Shepler, Report of Duty, 7–8.
73. Ibid., 8.
74. James, *The Years of MacArthur*, vol. II, 621.
75. Stanley A. Frankel, *The 37th Infantry Division in World War II* (Washington, DC: Infantry Journal Press, 1948), 225.

76. Monograph #4, Record of Philippines Operations, Phase 3, Vol. I, Operational Preparations of the 14th Area Army in the P.I., E147(A1), Box 38, RG 554, NARA II, 9.

77. Ibid., 21.

78. USAFIP, After-Battle Report: United States Army Forces in the Philippines, North Luzon Operations, 9 January to 15 August 1945, November 10, 1945, Russell W. Volckmann Papers, USAHEC, 42.

79. "Staff Study of Japanese Operations on Luzon, P.I.," Part I, 13.

80. USAFIP-NL, G-3 Periodic Report No. 5, 27 January to 3 February 1945, Russell W. Volckmann Papers, USAHEC.

81. "XIV Corps Operations on Luzon," 73.

82. Letter, Bonner Fellers to his wife Dorothy, January 9, 1945, Bonner F. Fellers Papers, Folder 24, Box 1, RG 44a (Series I: Correspondence), MacArthur Memorial Archives.

83. Volckmann, *We Remained,* 188–189.

84. See Williamson Murray and Peter R. Mansoor, eds., *Hybrid Warfare: Fighting Complex Opponents from the Ancient World to the Present* (New York: Cambridge University Press, 2012).

85. Volckmann, *We Remained,* 195–196.

86. The 43rd Infantry Division was composed of units from Maine, Vermont, Rhode Island, and Connecticut. Inducted into Federal service on February 24, 1941, it had trained at Camp Blanding, FL, Camp Shelby, MS, and Fort Ord, CA, including participation in maneuvers in Louisiana and the Carolinas, prior to deployment to New Caledonia. The division had combat experience in the Russell Islands, New Georgia, and Aitape in New Guinea in 1943 and 1944 before its assignment to the Luzon campaign. Joseph E. Zimmer, *The History of the 43rd Infantry Division, 1941–1945* (Baton Rouge: Army and Navy Publishing, 1947), 9–10, 19–34.

87. Smith, *Triumph in the Philippines,* 77–87.

88. Sixth US Army, Report of the Luzon Campaign, 19–20.

89. Report After Action: Operations of the 37th Infantry Division, Luzon P.I., 1 November 1944 to 30 June 1945, 337-0, Box 8601, RG 407, NARA II, 196.

90. Sixth US Army, Report of the Luzon Campaign, 21–22.

91. Monograph #4, 41.

92. Walter Krueger, *From Down Under to Nippon: The Story of Sixth Army in World War II* (Washington, DC: Combat Forces Press, 1953), 227; Smith, *Triumph in the Philippines,* 131–132.

93. Smith, *Triumph in the Philippines,* 133.

94. Egeberg, *The General,* 106.

95. The SWPA staff study for the Luzon operation stated, "Development in the Lingayen Gulf area will be very limited in character. It will consist of minimum installations necessary to land and forward required equipment and supplies to support the forces. Installations will be of a temporary nature and of a type

which can be readily abandoned or displaced forward upon the capture of Manila. The principle will be observed that, following the capture of Manila, all logistic services and installations will be established in that area and the Lingayen Gulf area will be abandoned as a principal port of entry." GHQ, SWPA, Staff Study, Operation Mike-One, October 7, 1944, Entry 146, Box 729, RG 496, NARA II, 16.

96. Drea, *MacArthur's Ultra*, 193.
97. Krueger, *From Down Under to Nippon*, 227–228.
98. Eddleman Oral History, 32.
99. Griswold Diary, January 14, 1945.
100. Letter, Bonner Fellers to his wife Dorothy, January 16, 1945, Bonner F. Fellers Papers, Folder 24, Box 1, RG 44a (Series I: Correspondence), MacArthur Memorial Archives.
101. Paul P. Rogers, *The Bitter Years: MacArthur and Sutherland* (New York: Praeger, 1991), 236.
102. Ibid., 243–245, 252. Sutherland did get his teeth fixed in Brisbane; of course, he also spent time each day with his Australian WAC girlfriend.
103. Drea, *MacArthur's Ultra*, 191.
104. "Cabanbang Party; Background, Mission and Accomplishments," September 20, 1945, GHQ Messages in the Guerrilla Resistance Movement in the Philippines, 1943–1945, Box 508, RG 496, NARA II. SWPA received 1,108 messages from this station alone.
105. Cabanbang to GHQ, January 13, 1945, Msg. 793, GHQ Messages in the Guerrilla Resistance Movement in the Philippines, 1943–1945, Box 514, RG 496, NARA II.
106. Egeberg, *The General*, 114–115.
107. Ibid., 116.
108. Gen. Tomoyuki Yamashita, Statement on the Philippine Operations in 1944–1945, September 1945, in GHQ Far East Command, *Statements of Japanese Officials on World War II*, 497.
109. Krueger, *From Down Under to Nippon*, 228–229; Sixth US Army, Report of the Luzon Campaign, 22–23; Smith, *Triumph in the Philippines*, 142–143.
110. I Corps, History of the Luzon Campaign, January 8, 1946, https://cgsc.con tentdm.oclc.org/digital/api/collection/p4013coll8/id/3367/download, 36.
111. Sixth US Army, Report of the Luzon Campaign, 25–27.
112. Smith, *Triumph in the Philippines*, 165.
113. "Enemy on Luzon: An Intelligence Summary," 73.
114. Sixth US Army, Report of the Luzon Campaign, 24.
115. Smith, *Triumph in the Philippines*, 177–178; Sixth US Army, Report of the Luzon Campaign, 29.
116. XIV Corps, After Action Report, M-1 Operation, 68–72.
117. Griswold Diary, January 28, 1945.
118. Frankel, *The 37th Infantry Division in World War II*, 237.

119. Sixth US Army, Report of the Luzon Campaign, 26.

120. Smith, *Triumph in the Philippines*, 212.

121. Strength figures based on 1 CD G-1 Daily Report, 2 February 1945, 901-1.1, RG 407, NARA II.

122. 1 Cav Bde, "Historical Report, 12 Oct–25 Dec 1944," 10 January 1945, 901-CC (1)-0.3, RG 407, NARA II, 5. Appendix IV.

123. 2 Cav Bde, "Official Historical Report of the 2nd Brigade Combat Team, 27 Jan 1945–30 June 1945," 9 July 1945, 901-CC(2)-0.3, RG 407, NARA II, 3.

124. HQ, 1 CD, "Historical Report of the 1st Cavalry Division in the Luzon Campaign, 27 Jan 45–30 June 45," July 12, 1945, 901-0.3, RG 407, NARA II, 1.

125. Egeberg, *The General*, 113.

126. Ibid., 116.

127. Ibid., 123.

128. Ibid., 120–123.

129. Ibid., 159.

130. Eichelberger, *Our Jungle Road to Tokyo*, 181–182.

131. Griswold Diary, January 26, 1945.

132. Radio broadcast, January 15, 1945, William Dunn Radio Transcripts, Folder 46, Box 3, RG 52, MacArthur Memorial Archives.

133. MacArthur, *Reminiscences*, 241–242.

134. Dunn radio broadcast, January 15, 1944.

135. Radio broadcast, January 22, 1945, William Dunn Radio Transcripts, Folder 46, Box 3, RG 52, MacArthur Memorial Archives.

136. Sixth US Army, Report of the Luzon Campaign, 30; *Reports of General MacArthur: The Campaigns of MacArthur in the Pacific*, vol. I (Washington, DC: US Army Center of Military History, 1966), 321.

137. Krueger, *From Down Under to Nippon*, 237–239.

138. Sixth US Army, Report of the Luzon Campaign, 31. Full-length treatments of the Cabanatuan Raid include William B. Breuer, *The Great Raid on Cabanatuan: Rescuing the Doomed Ghosts of Bataan and Corregidor* (Hoboken, NJ: John Wiley & Sons, 1994) and Hampton Sides, *Ghost Soldiers: The Epic Account of World War II's Greatest Rescue Mission* (New York: Anchor, 2001).

139. Smith, *Triumph in the Philippines*, 310.

140. The 38th Infantry Division was a National Guard division from Indiana, Kentucky, and West Virginia. Activated on January 17, 1941, the division trained at Camp Shelby, MS, Camp Gordon Johnston, FL, and Camp Livingston, LA, including participation in maneuvers in Louisiana in 1941 and 1942. The division deployed to Hawai'i in 1943 and then to Oro Bay, New Guinea, prior to its entry into combat in the latter stages of the Leyte campaign in December 1944. Luzon would be the division's first significant combat action.

141. Smith, *Triumph in the Philippines*, 310–313. Magsaysay was appointed secretary of national defense in 1950 and would be elected president of the Philippines in 1953.

142. Ibid., 315–322. For an in-depth look at the battle for Zig Zag Pass, see B. David Mann, *Avenging Bataan: The Battle of Zigzag Pass* (Raleigh, NC: Ivy House, 2002).

143. Smith, *Triumph in the Philippines*, 323–330.

144. Ibid., 331–334.

145. History of the 40th Infantry Division: The Luzon Operation, 340-0.2, Box 8871, NARA II, 16–17.

146. Smith, *Triumph in the Philippines*, 202–208; Sixth US Army, Report of the Luzon Campaign, 42.

147. Sixth US Army, Report of the Luzon Campaign, 32.

148. Smith, *Triumph in the Philippines*, 190.

149. 6th Infantry Division Public Relations Section, *The 6th Infantry Division in World War II, 1939–1945* (Washington, DC: Infantry Journal Press, 1947), 98–99.

150. Ibid., 99–100.

151. Capt. Robert F. Karolevitz, ed., *The 25th Division: World War 2*, March 26, 1947 (published by unit), copy located at 325-0, Box 6929, NARA II, 109.

152. Smith, *Triumph in the Philippines*, 197–199. The 25th Infantry Division counted more than 2,650 Japanese dead and 142 destroyed tanks in the battle for Lupao. Karolevitz, *The 25th Division*, 112.

153. Sixth Army viewed the situation differently, believing that the use of the *2nd Tank Division* in a massed counterattack against Sixth Army's eastern flank would have seriously delayed the army's advance and caused higher casualties. In any case, US airpower would have destroyed the division once it came into the open. Sixth US Army, Report of the Luzon Campaign, 44.

154. Ibid., 35–36, 43–44.

155. Radio broadcast, January 16, 1945, William Dunn Radio Transcripts, Folder 46, Box 3, RG 52, MacArthur Memorial Archives; MacArthur, *Reminiscences*, 246. For the history of the Santo Tomas internment camp, see A. V. H. Hartendorp, *The Santo Tomas Story* (New York: McGraw-Hill, 1964).

156. Stephen L. Moore, "The Heroes of Palawan – How Survivors of a Japanese Massacre Lived to Tell the Tale of Atrocities in the Philippines," December 2, 2016, https://militaryhistorynow.com/2016/12/02/the-heroes-of-palawan-how-survivors-of-a-japanese-massacre-lived-to-tell-the-tale-of-atrocities-in-the-philippines.

157. Ibid.

158. Cabais to General MacArthur, Message 4, January 1, 1945, Folder 9, Box 21, RG 16, MacArthur Memorial Archives. The sender was Master Sgt. Eutiquio Cabais, a member of the Filipino 5218 Reconnaissance Battalion, who had been sent into Palawan in August 1944 to set up a Coastwatching station.

159. Seven other prisoners also escaped and eventually made their way to guerrilla camps and from there to Morotai via seaplane. CINCPAC/CINCPOA, E&E

Report No. 23, February 15, 1945, Claude M. Owens Papers, Box 2, Hoover Institution Archives.

160. Krueger, *From Down Under to Nippon*, 227.
161. Comments by General Walter Krueger, US Army, Retired, on "Triumph in the Philippines," draft manuscript, Papers of Walter Krueger Jr., USMA Library Special Collections, Box 12, 2.
162. Sixth US Army, Report of the Luzon Campaign, 31.
163. Griswold Diary, January 30, 1945.
164. 1 CD, "Historical Background, The Luzon Campaign, First Cavalry Division," January 28, 1947, 901-0, RG 407, NARA II, 4.
165. Krueger, *From Down Under to Nippon*, 241. Brig. Gen. Eddleman recalled, "It was the old man's [64th] birthday . . . . We went to the building where his company had been billeted and to where his noncom associates had given him a farewell party. And to this beautiful house where the company commander and the first lieutenant lived. And we went in there and there was a sleezy looking Filipino down on the first floor, and a well dressed woman. When we got upstairs, there was some good looking gals that came out of the room. When we got in the jeep, an MP called the aide aside and said, 'What was General Krueger doing in that whore house?' He did not know it until I told him about it after the war." Eddleman Oral History, 38–39.
166. Eddleman Oral History, 31.
167. Sixth US Army, Report of the Luzon Campaign, 32.
168. Frankel, *The 37th Infantry Division in World War II*, 238.
169. Operations of the 37th Infantry Division, Luzon P.I., 37.
170. Sixth US Army, Report of the Luzon Campaign, 32.
171. Frankel, *The 37th Infantry Division in World War II*, 240.
172. Ibid.
173. William C. Chase, *Front Line General* (Houston: Pacesetter Press, 1975), 83.
174. Fifth Cavalry Historical Report, Luzon, July 12, 1945, 901-CRG(5)-0.3, Box 13299, RG 407, NARA II, 3.
175. Charles W. Boggs, *Marine Aviation in the Philippines* (Washington, DC: Historical Division, USMC, 1951), 68.
176. Ibid., 75–78.
177. 1 CD, "Historical Background, The Luzon Campaign," 9.
178. Chase, *Front Line General*, 84.
179. Radio broadcast, February 2, 1945, William Dunn Radio Transcripts, Folder 46, Box 3, RG 52, MacArthur Memorial Archives.
180. 1 CD, "Historical Background, The Luzon Campaign, First Cavalry Division," 9.
181. Krueger, *From Down Under to Nippon*, 243.
182. Sutton was awarded the Distinguished Service Cross for his actions.
183. Captain Thomas A. Barrow, "Breakthrough to Manila," The Armored School, Fort Knox, KY, April 22, 1948, USAHEC.
184. Fifth Cavalry, Historical Report, Luzon Campaign, 6.

185. For a first-person account of the stand-off in the Education Building, see Rupert Wilkinson, "Standoff at Santo Tomas," April 2014, www.historynet.co m/standoff-santo-tomas/?f.

186. "XIV Corps Operations on Luzon," 131.

187. 1 CD, "Historical Background, the Luzon Campaign, First Cavalry Division," 15. Sgt. John J. Gallagher of G Troop, 8th Cavalry rushed an enemy bunker to destroy a Japanese machine gun crew with his tommy gun. When all the troop's officers and first sergeant were killed or wounded, Gallagher took charge and led the troop until the end of the battle, repelling three Japanese counter-attacks. He was awarded the Distinguished Service Cross.

188. Ibid., 14. Brig. Gen. Chase was awarded the Distinguished Service Cross for his leadership of the flying column into Manila.

189. Frankel, *The 37th Infantry Division in World War II*, 254.

190. Ibid., 252. Maj. Gen. Beightler was unhappy about losing the race to Manila, and after the war accused Gen. Krueger of prejudice in stacking the deck against the National Guard, which he believed was denied the rightful honor of liberating the city. John Kennedy Ohl, *Minuteman: The Military Career of General Robert S. Beightler* (Boulder, CO: Lynne Rienner, 2001), 172.

191. Ibid., 242; James M. Scott, *Rampage: MacArthur, Yamashita, and the Battle of Manila* (New York: W. W. Norton, 2018), 222–224.

192. Emily Van Sickle, unpublished manuscript, "How Far the Dawn," Emily Van Sickle Papers, USMA Library Special Collections, 4. See also her memoir, Emily Van Sickle, *The Iron Gates of Santo Tomás: The Firsthand Account of an American Couple Interned by the Japanese in Manila, 1942–45* (Chicago: Academy of Chicago, 1992).

193. Ibid., 359.

194. Herbert E. "Gene" Hungerford, unpublished manuscript, "The Wall to Freedom," vol. 1, Herbert E. Hungerford Papers, Hoover Institution Archives, Chapter 1, Section 5.

195. Radio broadcast, February 4, 1945, William Dunn Radio Transcripts, Folder 46, Box 3, RG 52, MacArthur Memorial Archives.

196. HQ, Fifth Cavalry, Historical Report, Luzon Campaign, 12 July 1945, 901-CRG (5)-0.3, RG 407, NARA II, 8; Wilkinson, "Standoff at Santo Tomas."

197. Hungerford, "The Wall to Freedom," Chapter 3, Section 1.

198. Dunn radio broadcast, February 4, 1945.

199. Fifth Cavalry, Historical Report, Luzon Campaign, 7–8.

200. Ibid., 8–9.

201. Hungerford, "The Wall to Freedom," Chapter 2, Section 4.

202. Frankel, *The 37th Infantry Division in World War II*, 255.

203. MacArthur, *Reminiscences*, 246.

204. Ibid., 248–249.

205. Griswold Diary, February 4, 1945.

206. Fifth Cavalry Historical Report, Luzon, 7–8.

207. Wilkinson, "Standoff at Santo Tomas."
208. "XIV Corps Operations on Luzon," 132.
209. Amelia Mary Bradley, unpublished memoirs, Amelia Mary Bradley Papers, USMA Library Special Collections.
210. Frankel, *The 37th Infantry Division in World War II*, 255.
211. "Lo Joe," unpublished memoirs of Archie L. McMaster, Papers of Archie L. McMaster, USMA Library Special Collections.
212. MacArthur, *Reminiscences*, 248; Egeberg, *The General*, 135–136.
213. Chase, *Front Line General*, 96.
214. MacArthur, *Reminiscences*, 247; Egeberg, *The General*, 139.
215. Chase, *Front Line General*, 98.
216. Egeberg, *The General*, 135–143.
217. Smith, *Triumph in the Philippines*, 221–222.
218. Eichelberger, *Our Jungle Road to Tokyo*, 188–189.
219. Smith, *Triumph in the Philippines*, 224.
220. Jay Luvaas, ed., *DEAR MISS EM: General Eichelberger's War in the Pacific, 1942–1945* (Westport, CT: Greenwood, 1972), 208.
221. Smith, *Triumph in the Philippines*, 225; Eichelberger, *Our Jungle Road to Tokyo*, 190. The gorge at this point was 250 feet wide and 85 feet deep, making a bypass difficult at best. The 11th Airborne Division also lacked the bridging material necessary to span the gap if the Japanese succeeded in destroying the bridge, which they had wired for demolition.
222. 11th Airborne Division, Report after Action with the Enemy, Operation Mike VI, Luzon Campaign, 31 January–30 June 1945, January 24, 1946, 311-0.3, RG 407, NARA II, 16.
223. Smith, *Triumph in the Philippines*, 226.
224. 11th Airborne Division, Report after Action with the Enemy, Operation Mike VI, 4.
225. Ibid., 226–227.
226. 11th Airborne Division, Historical Narrative: Operation Mike Six, 31 January–5 February 1945, 311-0.3, RG 407, NARA II, 3; Eichelberger, *Our Jungle Road to Tokyo*, 194. Soule was awarded the Distinguished Service Cross for his actions on Tagaytay Ridge that day.
227. Futrell, "Luzon," 427.
228. 11th Airborne Division, "Luzon," August 3, 1945, 311-0, RG 407, NARA II, 2.
229. John F. Shortal, *Forged by Fire: General Robert L. Eichelberger and the Pacific War* (Columbia: University of South Carolina Press, 1987), 109–111.
230. Staff Sergeant W. E. Lindau, "11th Airborne Division History, Feb. 1943–May 1945," undated, 311-0.1, RG 407, NARA II.
231. Edwin B. Jeffress, Operations of the 2nd Battalion, 511th Parachute Infantry (11th Airborne Division) in the Battle for Southern Manila, 3–10 February, Advanced Infantry Officers Course 1948–1949, Ft. Benning, GA, https://mco

ecbamcoepwprd01.blob.core.usgovcloudapi.net/library/DonovanPapers/ww ii/STUP2/G-L/JeffressEdwinB%20%20CPT.pdf, 19.

232. Ibid., 19–23; Eichelberger, *Our Jungle Road to Tokyo*, 196. Tech. Sgt. Steele was later killed in the fighting in Manila. He was posthumously awarded the Distinguished Service Cross for his actions at Imus.

233. Lindau, "11th Airborne Division History," 18.

234. Smith, *Triumph in the Philippines*, 231. During the night, the 11th Airborne Division chief of staff, Col. Irvin R. Schimmelpfennig, was killed while reconnoitering a bypass. 11th Airborne Division, Historical Narrative: Operation Mike Six, 4.

235. Lindau, "11th Airborne Division History," 18.

236. Smith, *Triumph in the Philippines*, 234.

237. 11th Airborne Division, Report after Action with the Enemy, Operation Mike VI, 4.

238. Shortal, *Forged by Fire*, 113.

239. Luvaas, *DEAR MISS EM*, 198–199.

240. Sixth US Army, Report of the Luzon Campaign, 36.

CHAPTER 8: THE BATTLE OF MANILA

1. Stanley A. Frankel, *The 37th Infantry Division in World War II* (Washington, DC: Infantry Journal Press, 1948), 296.

2. Robert Ross Smith, *Triumph in the Philippines* (Washington, DC: Office of the Chief of Military History, 1963), 237–240.

3. *United States v. Tomoyuki Yamashita*, December 5, 1945, 3912–3913, https://maint .loc.gov/rr/frd/Military_Law/pdf/Yamashita-trial_Vol_21-34.pdf .

4. Richard B. Frank, *Guadalcanal: The Definitive Account of the Landmark Battle* (New York: Penguin, 1992), Chapter 18.

5. XIV Corps, "Japanese Defense of Cities as Exemplified by the Battle for Manila," July 1, 1945, https://cgsc.contentdm.oclc.org/digital/api/collection/p4013col l8/id/2947/download; Smith, *Triumph in the Philippines*, 240–242. These missions included holding Nichols Field and the Cavite naval base area, directing suicide boat operations, and destroying all naval installations and supplies in the area.

6. Report of statements made by General Yamashita, Tokoyuki, Commander-in-Chief of Japanese Army Forces in the Philippines, Lt. General Muto, Akira, his Chief of Staff, in conversations with ATIS officers at New Bilibid Prison, MANILA, September 4–6, 1945, OCMH Files, Pacific Interviews, USAHEC, 6.

7. Smith, *Triumph in the Philippines*, 242–243.

8. Ibid., 246–248; XIV Corps, "Japanese Defense of Cities as Exemplified by the Battle for Manila," 3–13.

9. Smith, *Triumph in the Philippines*, 246.

10. Ibid.
11. Shimbu Group Headquarters, January 16, 1945, "Outline of Instructions Regarding the Shimbu Group's Combat in the Manila Area," OCMH Files, Pacific Interviews, USAHEC.
12. Smith, *Triumph in the Philippines*, 249.
13. Jack Torry, *Last One Out: Yates McDaniel: World War II's Most Daring Reporter* (Atglen, PA: Schiffer Military, 2021), 182.
14. CG SWPA to CG Eighth Army, February 5, 1945, Papers of General Richard K. Sutherland relating to GHQ, SWPA, 1942–45, Entry 19810, RG 496, NARA II. At the urging of Griswold, MacArthur lifted the restriction on the use of unobserved artillery fire on February 10.
15. Sixth US Army, Report of the Luzon Campaign, 9 January 1945–30 June 1945, Vol. I, Combined Arms Research Library, Ft. Leavenworth, KS, 36.
16. Frankel, *The 37th Infantry Division in World War II*, 266. Lt. Col. George T. Coleman, the commander of the 2nd Battalion, 145th Infantry Regiment, was killed leading the final attack on the Japanese positions in the Tondo District.
17. Sixth US Army, Report of the Luzon Campaign, 37.
18. Smith, *Triumph in the Philippines*, 256–257.
19. Ibid., 260n.
20. D. Clayton James, *The Years of MacArthur*, vol. II: *1941–1945* (Boston: Houghton Mifflin, 1975), 640.
21. Diary of Lieutenant General O. W. Griswold, USA, February 7, 1945, Oscar W. Griswold Papers, USAHEC.
22. Frankel, *The 37th Infantry Division in World War II*, 269–271.
23. Ibid., 273.
24. Both Reese and Rodriguez were awarded the Medal of Honor, the former posthumously.
25. Both Harrell and Muenster were awarded the Distinguished Service Cross.
26. Cicchetti was awarded a posthumous Medal of Honor.
27. Frankel, *The 37th Infantry Division in World War II*, 273–274.
28. Ibid., 275.
29. Smith, *Triumph in the Philippines*, 260–264. Restrictions on the use of airpower remained in effect, however.
30. Griswold Diary, February 10, 1945.
31. Report After Action: Operations of the 37th Infantry Division, Luzon P.I., 1 November 1944 to 30 June 1945, 337-0, Box 8601, RG 407, NARA II, 51.
32. John Kennedy Ohl, *Minuteman: The Military Career of General Robert S. Beightler* (Boulder, CO: Lynne Reinner, 2001), 184.
33. Letter, Bonner Fellers to his wife Dorothy, February 10, 1945, Bonner F. Fellers Papers, Folder 1, Box 2, RG 44a (Series I: Correspondence), MacArthur Memorial Archives.

34. Smith, *Triumph in the Philippines*, 265–266; 11th Airborne Division, Report after Action with the Enemy, Operation Mike VI, Luzon Campaign, 31 January–30 June 1945, January 24, 1946, 311-0.3, RG 407, NARA II, 4–5.

35. 11th Airborne Division, Report after Action, Operation Mike VI, 5; 11th Airborne Division, "Luzon," August 3, 1945, 311-0, RG 407, NARA II, 2.

36. Edwin B. Jeffress, Operations of the 2nd Battalion, 511th Parachute Infantry (11th Airborne Division) in the Battle for Southern Manila, 3–10 February, Advanced Infantry Officers Course 1948–1949, Ft. Benning, GA, https://mcoec bamcoepwprd01.blob.core.usgovcloudapi.net/library/DonovanPapers/wwii/STUP2/G-L/JeffressEdwinB%20%20CPT.pdf, 27.

37. Ibid., 33.

38. Smith, *Triumph in the Philippines*, 268. Haugen died of wounds on February 22 while being medically transported to Biak. Colonel Haugen, Orin D. "Hard Rock," http://511pir.com/officers-biographies/165-colonel-orin-d-hard-rock-haugen.

39. Robert D. Eichelberger, *Our Jungle Road to Tokyo* (New York: Viking, 1950), 197.

40. Smith, *Triumph in the Philippines*, 266–267.

41. Sixth US Army, Report of the Luzon Campaign, 38.

42. 11th Airborne Division, Report after Action, Operation Mike VI, 6.

43. Fifth Cavalry, Historical Report, Luzon Campaign, July 12, 1945, 901-CRG(5)-0.3, RG 407, NARA II, 13.

44. 1st Cavalry Division, Historical Report, 24 January–30 June 1945, July 10, 1945, 901-CC(1)-0.3, RG 407, NARA II; Smith, *Triumph in the Philippines*, 269–270.

45. Smith, *Triumph in the Philippines*, 271–272.

46. Ibid., 272–273.

47. Ibid., 273–274; XIV Corps, After Action Report, M-1 Operation, July 29, 1945, https://cgsc.contentdm.oclc.org/digital/collection/p4013coll8/id/4680, 95–96; 11th Airborne Division, Report After Action, Operation Mike VI, Luzon Campaign, January 24, 1946, 6.

48. American assault techniques are detailed in XIV Corps, "Japanese Defense of Cities as Exemplified by the Battle for Manila," 21–26.

49. Frankel, *The 37th Infantry Division in World War II*, 278.

50. XIV Corps, "Japanese Defense of Cities as Exemplified by the Battle for Manila," 22.

51. XIV Corps, After Action Report, M-1 Operation, 99–100; Frankel, *The 37th Infantry Division in World War II*, 277.

52. Radio broadcast, February 12, 1945, William Dunn Radio Transcripts, Folder 46, Box 3, RG 52, MacArthur Memorial Archives.

53. XIV Corps, After Action Report, M-1 Operation, 100; Frankel, *The 37th Infantry Division in World War II*, 276; Smith, *Triumph in the Philippines*, 282.

54. GHQ, US Army Forces Pacific, "Enemy on Luzon: An Intelligence Summary," 76–77.

55. Radio broadcast, February 16, 1945, William Dunn Radio Transcripts, Folder 46, Box 3, RG 52, MacArthur Memorial Archives.
56. Letter, Bonner Fellers to his wife Dorothy, February 14, 1945, Bonner F. Fellers Papers, Folder 1, Box 2, RG 44a (Series I: Correspondence), MacArthur Memorial Archives.
57. History of the 12th Cavalry Regiment during the Luzon Campaign, July 11, 1945, 901-CRG(12)-0.3, Box 13315, RG 407, NARA II, 10.
58. Ibid., 10–11; Fifth Cavalry, Historical Report, Luzon Campaign, 15–16; Smith, *Triumph in the Philippines*, 277–279.
59. XIV Corps, After Action Report, M-1 Operation, 104; Smith, *Triumph in the Philippines*, 279.
60. Griswold Diary, February 17, 1945, Oscar W. Griswold Papers, USAHEC.
61. Letter, Bonner Fellers to his wife Dorothy, February 16, 1945, Bonner F. Fellers Papers, Folder 1, Box 2, RG 44a (Series I: Correspondence), MacArthur Memorial Archives.
62. XIV Corps, After Action Report, M-1 Operation, 108; Smith, *Triumph in the Philippines*, 282; Frankel, *The 37th Infantry Division in World War II*, 278–279.
63. Frankel, *The 37th Infantry Division in World War II*, 284.
64. Wielding his 2.36-inch rocket launcher, Pfc. Paul B. Hoffner moved forward to a position from which he launched nine rounds at Japanese positions in a convent adjoining St. Theresa Church, destroying three emplacements. He was awarded the Distinguished Service Cross for his actions. Frankel, *The 37th Infantry Division in World War II*, 285.
65. Ibid., 284–285; Smith, *Triumph in the Philippines*, 283.
66. Frankel, *The 37th Infantry Division in World War II*, 285–286.
67. XIV Corps Operations on Luzon, undated, Papers of Oscar W. Griswold, USMA Library Special Collections, 187–188.
68. Frankel, *The 37th Infantry Division in World War II*, 286–287.
69. Smith, *Triumph in the Philippines*, 285.
70. Frankel, *The 37th Infantry Division in World War II*, 287.
71. Ibid., 288.
72. Operations of the 37th Infantry Division, Luzon P.I., 69.
73. Japan was not a signatory to the convention, so technically its use of the hospital as a military fortification did not violate a treaty obligation but was merely an uncivilized act of war.
74. Frankel, *The 37th Infantry Division in World War II*, 281; Smith, *Triumph in the Philippines*, 287.
75. Frankel, *The 37th Infantry Division in World War II*, 281–283.
76. Whether or not the 148th Infantry Regiment seized the Medical School is a point of contention – Smith, *Triumph in the Philippines*, 288n. I find it doubtful that the regiment would have abandoned the structure prior to its relief, as the official history alleges. More likely is that the Buckeyes never took the building, leaving it to the 5th Cavalry Regiment to assault.

77. Fifth Cavalry, Historical Report, Luzon Campaign, 17.
78. Ibid., 17–18.
79. Ibid., 18–19.
80. Ibid., 19.
81. Ibid., 19–20.
82. Ibid., 21–22.
83. Ibid., 22–23.
84. Ibid., 20–21. GIs recaptured University Hall the next morning.
85. History of the 12th Cavalry Regiment during the Luzon Campaign, 12.
86. Ibid., 13.
87. Interrogation Report, XIVCAEI 0063, March 18, 1945, Entry 441, Box 2708, RG 496, NARA II, 17.
88. Douglas MacArthur, *Reminiscences* (New York: McGraw-Hill, 1964), 247.
89. Griswold Diary, February 18–22, 1945.
90. Frankel, *The 37th Infantry Division in World War II*, 283.
91. Griswold Diary, February 17, 1945.
92. XIV Corps, After Action Report, M-1 Operation, 114.
93. Radio broadcast, February 21, 1945, William Dunn Radio Transcripts, Folder 46, Box 3, RG 52, MacArthur Memorial Archives.
94. CG SWPA to CG Sixth Army, February 17, 1945, Papers of General Richard K. Sutherland relating to GHQ, SWPA, 1942–45, Entry 19810, RG 496, NARA II.
95. Griswold Diary, February 17, 1945.
96. XIV Corps, After Action Report, M-1 Operation, 114.
97. Ibid., 116.
98. Captain Glenn A. Steckel, "The Role of Field Artillery in the Siege on Intramuros, Manila, P. I.," The Armored School, Fort Knox, KY, May 7, 1948, USAHEC; XIV Corps, After Action Report, M-1 Operation, 120; Smith, *Triumph in the Philippines*, 295–296.
99. Steckel, "The Role of Field Artillery in the Siege on Intramuros," 10–12.
100. XIV Corps, After Action Report, M-1 Operation, 121.
101. Radio broadcast, February 24, 1945, William Dunn Radio Transcripts, Folder 46, Box 3, RG 52, MacArthur Memorial Archives.
102. Richard Connaughton, John Pimlott, and Duncan Anderson, *The Battle for Manila: The Most Devastating Untold Story of World War II* (London: Bloomsbury, 1995), 167; XIV Corps, After Action Report, M-1 Operation, 123–124.
103. Herbert E. "Gene" Hungerford, unpublished manuscript, "The Wall to Freedom," Vol. I, Herbert E. Hungerford Papers, Hoover Institution Archives, Chapter 3, Section 2.
104. Frankel, *The 37th Infantry Division in World War II*, 289.

105. Steckel, "The Role of Field Artillery in the Siege on Intramuros," 14; XIV Corps, After Action Report, M-1 Operation, 123; Smith, *Triumph in the Philippines*, 298.

106. Connaughton, Pimlott, and Anderson, *The Battle for Manila*, 110.

107. 129th Infantry Regiment, Report of Atrocities at Fort Santiago, Luzon, March 2, 1945, Claude M. Owens Papers, Box 2, Hoover Institution Archives.

108. XIV Corps Operations on Luzon, 204.

109. Smith, *Triumph in the Philippines*, 300–301.

110. Ohl, *Minuteman*, 193.

111. History of the 12th Cavalry Regiment during the Luzon Campaign, 14. During the fight for the Customs Building, the newly installed commander of E Troop, 2nd Squadron, 5th Cavalry Regiment, Lt. John J. Gregory, was seriously wounded in the hip. Pfc. William J. Grabiarz tried to recover his stricken commander, but was wounded in turn. Grabiarz shielded Lt. Gregory with his own body and was killed in the process, but saved his commander's life. For his actions Grabiarz received a posthumous Medal of Honor. Fifth Cavalry, Historical Report, Luzon Campaign, 24.

112. Frankel, *The 37th Infantry Division in World War II*, 293.

113. Smith, *Triumph in the Philippines*, 302.

114. Ibid., 303.

115. Fifth Cavalry, Historical Report, Luzon Campaign, 26.

116. Ibid., 27.

117. Smith, *Triumph in the Philippines*, 303–304.

118. Fifth Cavalry, Historical Report, Luzon Campaign, 27.

119. Ibid., 28.

120. Frankel, *The 37th Infantry Division in World War II*, 294.

121. Fifth Cavalry, Historical Report, Luzon Campaign, 28.

122. Ibid., 29.

123. Frankel, *The 37th Infantry Division in World War II*, 293. Iwabuchi might have committed ritual suicide before the end of the battle, although the sources are unclear.

124. Fifth Cavalry, Historical Report, Luzon Campaign, 29.

125. Frankel, *The 37th Infantry Division in World War II*, 295.

126. Sixth US Army, Report of the Luzon Campaign, 40. The official US Army history lists Japanese dead in Manila at 12,500, with another 3,500 men killed on the outskirts. The rest of the garrison presumably made their way across the Marikina River into the mountains to the east to join the *Shimbu Group*. Smith, *Triumph in the Philippines*, 307.

127. XIV Corps, "Japanese Defense of Cities as Exemplified by the Battle for Manila," 26.

128. Griswold Diary, March 3, 1945.

129. Ibid., 50; John C. McManus, *To the End of the Earth: The US Army and the Downfall of Japan, 1945* (New York: Caliber, 2023), 97.

130. The Japanese had invaded the north side of the tail of Corregidor on the night of May 5–6, 1942 and lost half their assault force in the first wave. Louis Morton, *The Fall of the Philippines* (Washington, DC: Office of the Chief of Military History, 1953), 555–557.

131. Sixth US Army, Report of the Luzon Campaign, 49–50.

132. General George C. Kenney Diary, February 7, 1945, Box 2, RG 54 (Papers of General George C. Kenney), MacArthur Memorial Archives. Kenney made good on his promise; between 26 January and 16 February, the 5th and 13th Air Forces dropped 2,331 tons of bombs on Corregidor. Ibid., February 14, 1945.

133. Sixth US Army, Report of the Luzon Campaign, 51–52.

134. Ibid.

135. Letter, Bonner Fellers to his wife Dorothy, February 16, 1945.

136. Roger O. Egeberg, *The General: MacArthur and the Man He Called "Doc"* (New York: Hippocrene Books, 1983), 146–147.

137. The town, not the brewery.

138. William C. Chase, *Front Line General* (Houston: Pacesetter Press, 1975), 107.

139. Egeberg, *The General*, 149.

140. Ibid., 151.

141. Walter Krueger, *From Down Under to Nippon: The Story of Sixth Army in World War II* (Washington, DC: Combat Forces Press, 1953), 267.

142. Sixth US Army, Report of the Luzon Campaign, 53; E. L. Jenkins, "Combined Air–Ground Operations on Luzon," *Military Review* 25, no. 11 (February 1946): 30–34.

143. Sixth US Army, Report of the Luzon Campaign, 53–54; Smith, *Triumph in the Philippines*, 341–344.

144. Sixth US Army, Report of the Luzon Campaign, 53.

145. Ibid., 54.

146. Chase, *Front Line General*, 110.

147. MacArthur, *Reminiscences*, 250.

148. Krueger, *From Down Under to Nippon*, 269.

149. MacArthur awarded Jones a Distinguished Service Cross for his command of Rock Force on Corregidor, while Rock Force was awarded a Distinguished Unit Citation.

150. General Clyde D. Eddleman Oral History, Clyde D. Eddleman Papers, USAHEC, 36; Smith, *Triumph in the Philippines*, 348–349. Histories of the recapture of Corregidor include E. M. Flanagan, *Corregidor: The Rock Force Assault, 1945* (Novato, CA: Presidio, 1988); Gerard M. Devlin, *Back to Corregidor: America Retakes the Rock* (New York: St. Martin's Press, 1992); and Kevin Maurer, *Rock Force: The American Paratroopers Who Took Back Corregidor and Exacted MacArthur's Revenge on Japan* (New York: Dutton Caliber, 2020).

151. 38th Infantry Division, "The Avengers of Bataan: Report on the M-7 Operation, 19 January to 30 June 1945," 338-0, Box 8795, RG 407, NARA II, 50–54.

152. Ibid., 55–60; C. R. Bathurst, "Report on Engineer Operations in the Recapture of Fort Drum," *Military Review* 25, no. 9 (December 1945): 17–20.

153. Smith, *Triumph in the Philippines*, 357.

154. 11th Airborne Division, History, May 13, 1945, 311-0.1, RG 407, NARA II, 21.

155. Yung Li Yuk-wai, *The Huaqiao Warriors: Chinese Resistance Movement in the Philippines, 1942–1945* (Manila: Ateneo de Manila University Press, 1996), 87.

156. 11th Airborne Division, History, 21–22; 11th Airborne Division, Luzon, August 3, 1945, 311-0, RG 407, NARA II, 3; Proculo L. Mojica, *Terry's Hunters (The True Story of the Hunters ROTC Guerrillas)* (Manila: Benipayo Press, 1965), 602; Yung Li Yuk-wai, *The Huaqiao Warriors*, 87. Brig. Gen. Courtney Whitney of MacArthur's staff witnessed the operation aboard an amphibious vehicle.

157. "Address by Brigadier General Henry Muller to the Manila Liberation Commemoration 1945–1999," February 5, 1999, Henry J. Muller Papers, Hoover Institution Archives, 8.

158. Griswold Diary, February 24, 1945. For a complete history of the raid, see Anthony Arthur, *Deliverance at Los Banos: The Dramatic True Story of Survival and Triumph in a Japanese Internment Camp* (New York: St. Martin's Press, 1985) and Bruce Henderson, *Rescue at Los Baños: The Most Daring Prison Camp Raid of World War II* (New York: William Morrow, 2015).

159. The official US Army historian puts the number of civilian dead in the Battle of Manila at 100,000, but this publication did not appear until 1963, and the figure appears without attribution. The number of civilians killed in the fighting was likely far fewer. Smith, *Triumph in the Philippines*, 307. For an extended discussion of the number of Filipinos who died in Manila, see Richard B. Meixsel, "Did 100,000 Civilians Die in the Battle of Manila in 1945? – Robert Ross Smith's *Triumph in the Philippines* and the Story of a Number," https://corregidor.org/refdoc/Reference_Reading/Meixsel/DID-100,000-CIVILIANS-DIE-IN-THE-BATTLE-OF-MANILA-IN-1945-/index.html. A number of the Filipinos' stories are related in Alfonso J. Aluit, *By Sword and Fire: The Destruction of Manila in World War II, 3 February–3 March 1945* (Manila: National Commission for Culture and the Arts, 1994).

160. Prosecution Exhibit 393, Yamashita War Crimes Tribunal, *United States of America vs. Tomoyuki Yamashita*, Claude M. Owens Papers, Box 2.

161. XIV Corps Operations on Luzon, 144.

162. By far the best account of the atrocities in Manila is James M. Scott, *Rampage: MacArthur, Yamashita, and the Battle of Manila* (New York: W. W. Norton, 2018).

163. XIV Corps Operations on Luzon, 166.

164. Copy of the order in XIV Corps Operations on Luzon, 166.

165. Ibid., 144–145.

166. Ibid., 171; Aluit, *By Sword and Fire*, 229–232.

167. *United States of America vs. Tomoyuki Yamashita*, Exhibit 108, Testimony of Zenaida G. R. Lyons, US Army Forces in the Western Pacific, Military Commission Papers, Box 2, Hoover Institution Archives.

168. XIV Corps Operations on Luzon, 200.

169. Ibid., 201–202.

170. Scott, *Rampage*, 279–282.

171. United States Senate, "Sack of Manila," June 16, USAHEC, 1945, 4–8.

172. HQ, XIV Corps, Report of Investigation of Alleged Atrocities by Members of the Japanese Imperial Forces in Manila and other parts of Luzon, Philippine Islands, April 9, 1945, Papers of Oscar W. Griswold, Box 4, USMA Library Special Collections, 40.

173. Aluit, *By Sword and Fire*, 405.

174. Smith, *Triumph in the Philippines*, 307.

175. Hungerford, "The Wall to Freedom," Chapter 3, Section 6.

176. Ibid.

177. Amelia Mary Bradley, unpublished memoirs, Amelia Mary Bradley Papers, USMA Library Special Collections, 2.

178. Ibid., 4.

179. Letter from Pvt. Thomas M. Woebke to Mr. and Mrs. John H. Woebke, April 15, 1945, transcript in author's possession. Thomas Woebke is the author's maternal uncle.

180. MacArthur, *Reminiscences*, 251.

181. James, *The Years of MacArthur*, vol. II, 645.

182. MacArthur, *Reminiscences*, 251.

183. Ibid., 251–252; James, *The Years of MacArthur*, vol. II, 647–648.

CHAPTER 9: CLEARING LUZON

1. Capt. Robert F. Karolevitz, ed., *The 25th Division: World War 2*, March 26, 1947 (published by unit), copy located at 325-0, Box 6929, NARA II, 116.

2. US forces had cleared the Japanese from the islands of Attu and Kiska in the Aleutians for similar reasons.

3. Robert Ross Smith, *Triumph in the Philippines* (Washington, DC: Office of the Chief of Military History, 1963), 364. Krueger received his fourth star on March 5, 1945.

4. Edward J. Drea, *MacArthur's Ultra: Codebreaking and the War against Japan, 1942–1945* (Lawrence, KS: University Press of Kansas, 1992), 200.

5. GHQ, US Army Forces Pacific, "Enemy on Luzon: An Intelligence Summary," 89–90.

6. Walter Krueger, *From Down Under to Nippon: The Story of Sixth Army in World War II* (Washington, DC: Combat Forces Press, 1953), 322–323.

7. For a narrative of Alamo Scout activities during the liberation of the Philippines, see Larry Alexander, *Shadows in the Jungle: The Alamo Scouts behind Japanese Lines in World War II* (New York: NAL Caliber, 2009).

8. WD 936, February 22, 1945, Papers of General Richard K. Sutherland relating to GHQ, SWPA, 1942–45, Entry 19810, RG 496, NARA II.

9. HQ, Sixth Army, Prisoner of War Preliminary Interrogation Reports, 21 December 1944–27 June 1945, as well as reports from associated corps and divisions in Entry 441, Box 2707, RG 496, NARA II.

10. Smith, *Triumph in the Philippines*, 366–369; Sixth US Army, Report of the Luzon Campaign, 9 January 1945–30 June 1945, Vol. I, Combined Arms Research Library, Ft. Leavenworth, KS, 57.

11. XIV Corps, After Action Report, M-1 Operation, July 29, 1945, https://cgsc.co ntentdm.oclc.org/digital/collection/p4013coll8/id/4680, 137–142.

12. The 2nd Squadron, 7th Cavalry was awarded a Distinguished Unit Citation for its role in the fighting around Antipolo.

13. Sixth US Army, Report of the Luzon Campaign, 61–62; Smith, *Triumph in the Philippines*, 375–377.

14. Smith, *Triumph in the Philippines*, 379–381; XIV Corps, After Action Report, 152.

15. Joseph E. Zimmer, *The History of the 43rd Infantry Division, 1941–1945* (Baton Rouge, LA: Army and Navy Publishing, 1947), 67.

16. Smith, *Triumph in the Philippines*, 382–383. Brig. Gen. Charles E. Hurdis assumed command of the 6th Infantry Division. For an account of Patrick's death, see Wilson Allen Heefner, *Twentieth Century Warrior: The Life and Service of Major General Edwin D. Patrick* (Shippensburg, PA: White Mane, 1995), 140–143.

17. Sixth US Army, Report of the Luzon Campaign, 72.

18. Smith, *Triumph in the Philippines*, 385–389.

19. Ibid., 392–396.

20. Smith, *Triumph in the Philippines*, 396–397.

21. 6th Infantry Division, Operations Report – Luzon Campaign, 9 January–30 June 1945, 17 July 1945, 306-0.3, Box 6037, RG 407, NARA II, 74.

22. Ibid., 398–403; 38th Infantry Division, "The Avengers of Bataan: Report on the M-7 Operation, 19 January to 30 June 1945," 338-0, Box 8795, RG 407, NARA II, 105.

23. 6th Infantry Division, Operations Report – Luzon Campaign, 404.

24. Sixth US Army, Report of the Luzon Campaign, 74–75; Frank Futrell, "Luzon," in Wesley Frank Craven and James Lea Cate, *The Army Air Forces in World War II*, vol. V: *The Pacific: Matterhorn to Nagasaki, June 1944 to August 1945* (Chicago: University of Chicago Press, 1953), 413–447, 436.

25. Futrell, "Luzon," 436.

26. Sixth US Army, Report of the Luzon Campaign, 75–76.

27. 7th Cavalry, Historical Report, Luzon Campaign, 27 January–30 June 1945, 901-CRG(7)-0.3, RG 407, NARA II, 24.

28. Ibid., 29.

29. Ibid., S-2 Annex, 49.

30. Krueger, *From Down Under to Nippon*, 324.

31. Smith, *Triumph in the Philippines*, 415–422.

32. Ibid., 426.
33. 11th Airborne Division, Report after Action with the Enemy, Operation Mike VI, Luzon Campaign, 31 January–30 June 1945, January 24, 1946, 311-0.3, RG 407, NARA II, 57.
34. Smith, *Triumph in the Philippines*, 428–430.
35. Swing to March, March 4, 1945, "Dear General: World War II Letters, 1944–1945," Joseph Swing Papers, USAHEC.
36. 11th Airborne Division, Report after Action with the Enemy, Operation Mike VI, 9–10.
37. Smith, *Triumph in the Philippines*, 431–432.
38. Ibid., 433.
39. Ibid., 433–434.
40. Ibid., 434–435.
41. The International Military Tribunal for the Far East Digital Collection, University of Virginia School of Law, http://imtfe.law.virginia.edu/collec tions/page-1-7144.
42. Smith, *Triumph in the Philippines*, 436–437.
43. Ibid., 438–439.
44. Ibid., 439–444.
45. Ibid., 444–445.
46. Ibid., 449–453; Krueger, *From Down Under to Nippon*, 321–322.
47. Smith, *Triumph in the Philippines*, 461.
48. Ibid., 463.
49. 32nd Infantry Division, After-action Report, Luzon, January 27–June 30, 1945, 332-0.3, Box 7794, NARA II, 24.
50. The 33rd Infantry Division was a National Guard unit from Illinois. It arrived in July 1943 in Hawai'i, where it guarded the island and conducted jungle warfare training. After further training in New Guinea and deployments to Wakde and Morotai, the division deployed in January 1945 to Luzon, where it relieved the 43rd Infantry Division in preparation for operations to seize Baguio.
51. USAFIP, After-Battle Report: United States Army Forces in the Philippines, North Luzon Operations, 9 January to 15 August 1945, November 10, 1945, Russell W. Volckmann Papers, USAHEC, 12–13.
52. Smith, *Triumph in the Philippines*, 465–467; Russell W. Volckmann, *We Remained: Three Years behind the Enemy Lines in the Philippines* (New York: W. W. Norton, 1954), 216.
53. Krueger, *From Down Under to Nippon*, 328.
54. Public Relations Office, 32nd Infantry Division, *13,000 Hours: Combat History of the 32nd INF Division – World War II*, 332-0, Box 7793, NARA II, 25.
55. By the middle of February, the *2nd Tank Division* had lost 2,000 men along with 90 percent of its tanks and 70 percent of its artillery in earlier fighting. Historical Division, Eighth Army, "Staff Study of Japanese Operations on Luzon, P.I.,"

March 22, 1949, Interrogation of Col. Shigia Kawai, 2nd Tank Division, Operational Summary, 5.

56. Smith, *Triumph in the Philippines*, 492–495.
57. 32nd Infantry Division, After-action Report, Luzon, "Japanese Defensive Tactics along the Villa Verde Trail," G-2 Annex, 7.
58. "Staff Study of Japanese Operations on Luzon," Interrogation of Col. Shigia Kawai, 2nd Tank Division, Operational Summary, 20.
59. Krueger, *From Down Under to Nippon*, 260.
60. 32nd Infantry Division, After-action Report, Luzon, G-2 Annex, 2.
61. Ibid., Engineer Annex, 1.
62. Radio broadcast, May 29, 1945, William Dunn Radio Transcripts, Folder 50, Box 3, RG 52, MacArthur Memorial Archives.
63. 32nd Infantry Division, After-action Report, Luzon, Civil Affairs Annex, 2.
64. Ibid., 30.
65. Smith, *Triumph in the Philippines*, 498–505.
66. Ibid., 505–511.
67. 32nd Infantry Division, After-action Report, Luzon, 54.
68. Ibid., G-2 Annex, 4.
69. Smith, *Triumph in the Philippines*, 512–516.
70. Operations of the 25th Infantry Division, Luzon, P.I., 17 January–30 June 1945, 325-0.3, Box 6932, NARA II, 35.
71. Karolevitz, ed., *The 25th Division*, 116.
72. Operations of the 25th Infantry Division, Luzon, P.I., 48.
73. Smith, *Triumph in the Philippines*, 516–522.
74. Karolevitz, ed., *The 25th Division*, 134, 139.
75. Operations of the 25th Infantry Division, Luzon, P.I., 54; Smith, *Triumph in the Philippines*, 522–525.
76. Operations of the 25th Infantry Division, Luzon, P.I., 55.
77. Karolevitz, ed., *The 25th Division*, 133.
78. Ibid., 134.
79. Smith, *Triumph in the Philippines*, 526–531; Operations of the 25th Infantry Division, Luzon, P.I., 61–62.
80. Operations of the 25th Infantry Division, Luzon, P.I., 67.
81. Karolevitz, ed., *The 25th Division*, 140–141; Operations of the 25th Infantry Division, Luzon, P.I., 67.
82. Karolevitz, ed., *The 25th Division*, 137.
83. Operations of the 25th Infantry Division, Luzon, P.I., 69–71.
84. Ibid., 180–181.
85. Smith, *Triumph in the Philippines*, 534–537. To honor Dalton's memory, on September 12, 1945, Commonwealth Act No. 679 changed the name of Balete Pass to Dalton Pass, which it remains today.
86. Smith, *Triumph in the Philippines*, 472–475.
87. Ibid., 475–476.

88. Ibid., 479.
89. Ibid., 480–485.
90. Ronald K. Edgerton, "General Douglas MacArthur and the American Military Impact in the Philippines," *Philippine Studies* 25, no. 4 (1977): 420–440, 430n33.
91. D. Clayton James, *The Years of MacArthur*, vol. II: *1941–1945* (Boston: Houghton Mifflin, 1975), 691–693; Douglas MacArthur, *Reminiscences* (New York: McGraw-Hill, 1964), 236–237; Roger O. Egeberg, *The General: MacArthur and the Man He Called "Doc"* (New York: Hippocrene Books, 1983), 172.
92. Smith, *Triumph in the Philippines*, 485–486.
93. Felixberto C. Sta. Maria, "The Story of Baguio," in Laurence L. Wilson, "Baguio: The Main City of the Mountain Province, P.I. during the Japanese Occupation," Laurence L. Wilson Papers, Hoover Institution Archives.
94. Smith, *Triumph in the Philippines*, 541–544.
95. Ibid., 546–547.
96. Ibid., 548–549.
97. Ibid., 550–552.
98. Ibid., 553–556.
99. Ibid., 560–561.
100. In a reverse of the usual command arrangements, Connolly's task force fell under the command of Volckmann's guerrilla headquarters. Krueger, *From Down Under to Nippon*, 310.
101. Report After Action: Operations of the 37th Infantry Division, Luzon P.I., 1 November 1944 to 30 June 1945, 337-0, Box 8601, RG 407, NARA II, 139.
102. Ibid., 151–152.
103. Smith, *Triumph in the Philippines*, 562–568.
104. Operations of the 37th Infantry Division, Luzon P.I., 121–149; 11th Airborne Division, Report after Action with the Enemy, Operation Mike VI, 9; Smith, *Triumph in the Philippines*, 569–571. Task Force Connolly had taken Aparri on June 23 and elements were on the ground to meet the paratroopers when they landed.
105. Monograph #8, Record of Philippines Operations, Phase 3, Supplement to Vol. 3, Shimbu Group Operations, E147(A1), Box 39, RG 554, NARA II, 19.
106. Drea, *MacArthur's Ultra*, 200.
107. Far East Command, Pacific Theater Historical Section, Interrogations of Japanese Officials on World War II, interrogation of Col. Naotake Utsunomiya, Asst. Chief of Staff, 14th Area Army, USAHEC.
108. Smith, *Triumph in the Philippines*, 572–577.
109. Robert L. Eichelberger, *Our Jungle Road to Tokyo* (New York: Viking, 1950), 254.
110. SWPA, "Psychological Warfare … Its Role in the Philippines," Entry 441, Box 2717, RG 496, NARA II.
111. Gen. Yamashita stated that he had 40,000 troops with him at the end of the war, half of whom were effective. Gen. Tomoyuki Yamashita, Statement on the Philippine Operations in 1944–1945, September 1945, in GHQ Far East

Command, *Statements of Japanese Officials on World War II*, 497. Smith, *Triumph in the Philippines*, 579, puts the figure at 50,000.

112. Krueger, *From Down Under to Nippon*, 318.

113. Jonathan M. Wainwright, *General Wainwright's Story: The Account of Four Years of Humiliating Defeat, Surrender, and Captivity* (Garden City, NY: Doubleday, 1946), 282–286.

CHAPTER 10: THE CENTRAL AND SOUTHERN PHILIPPINES

1. Robert L. Eichelberger, *Our Jungle Road to Tokyo* (New York: Viking, 1950), 239.

2. Robert Ross Smith, *Triumph in the Philippines* (Washington, DC: Office of the Chief of Military History, 1963), 583–584.

3. Ibid., 201.

4. Historian Ronald Spector agrees, labeling the campaign in the Central and Southern Philippines "militarily pointless" and downplaying its humanitarian goals. Ronald Spector, *Eagle against the Sun: The American War with Japan* (New York: Free Press, 1985), 526–527. The antipathy between King and MacArthur was, of course, mutual.

5. JCS 189th Meeting Minutes, February 7, 1945, CCS 334, RG 218, NARA II.

6. MacArthur to Marshall, February 10, 1945, Entry 184, Box 852, RG 496, NARA II.

7. MacArthur to Marshall, February 26, 1945, WD937, RG 4, MacArthur Memorial Archives.

8. MacArthur to Marshall, March 30, 1945, WD953, RG 4, MacArthur Memorial Archives.

9. Grace Person Hayes, *The History of the Joint Chiefs of Staff in World War II: The War against Japan* (Annapolis, MD: Naval Institute Press, 1982), 692–693.

10. Samuel Eliot Morison, *History of United States Naval Operations in World War II*, vol. XIII: *The Liberation of the Philippines: Luzon, Mindanao, the Visayas, 1944–1945* (Chicago: University of Illinois Press, 1958), 214.

11. John F. Shortal, *Forged by Fire: General Robert L. Eichelberger and the Pacific War* (Columbia: University of South Carolina Press, 1987), 115–116.

12. Eichelberger, *Our Jungle Road to Tokyo*, 202.

13. Daniel E. Barbey, *MacArthur's Amphibious Navy: Seventh Amphibious Force Operations, 1943–1945* (Annapolis, MD: United States Naval Institute, 1969), 310.

14. Smith, *Triumph in the Philippines*, 587.

15. Ibid., 587–588.

16. Eighth Army, Operational Monograph on the Panay Negros Occidental Operation (Victor I), 108-0, Box 2233, RG 407, NARA II, 30.

17. GHQ, SWPA, Operations Instructions 89, February 6, 1945, 98 GHQ1-3.17, Box 791, RG 407, NARA II.

18. Barbey, *MacArthur's Amphibious Navy*, 314.
19. William F. McCartney, *The Jungleers: A History of the 41st Infantry Division* (Washington, DC: Infantry Journal Press, 1948), 140–141; Eighth Army, Operational Monograph on the Palawan Operation (Victor III), 108-0, Box 2234, RG 407, NARA II, 62.
20. GHQ, SWPA, Operations Instructions 91, February 14, 1945, 98 GHQ1-3.17, Box 792, RG 407, NARA II.
21. Eighth Army, Operational Monograph on the Palawan Operation (Victor IV), 108-0, Box 2234, RG 407, NARA II, 9, 31.
22. Eichelberger, *Our Jungle Road to Tokyo*, 207.
23. McCartney, *The Jungleers*, 145–147.
24. The 93rd Infantry Division was comprised of Black soldiers led by mostly white officers. SWPA used it primarily for labor and security duties, because of endemic racism that left senior officers suspicious of its combat capabilities.
25. Ibid., 148; Smith, *Triumph in the Philippines*, 597.
26. Ibid., 597–599; McCartney, *The Jungleers*, 149–153.
27. GHQ, SWPA, Operations Instructions 93, February 22, 1945, 98 GHQ1-3.17, Box 792, RG 407, NARA II.
28. Operational Monograph on the Panay Negros Occidental Operation, 12. Smith, *Triumph in the Philippines*, 601–602. Lt. Gen. Robert Eichelberger decorated Peralta with a Distinguished Service Cross for his role in organizing and leading the guerrillas on Panay.
29. Operational Monograph on the Panay Negros Occidental Operation, 21–23.
30. Ibid., 37.
31. Eichelberger, *Our Jungle Road to Tokyo*, 209.
32. Operational Monograph on the Panay Negros Occidental Operation, 44–45; *40th Infantry Division: The Years of World War II, 7 December 1941–7 April 1946* (Baton Rouge, LA: Army & Navy Publishing, 1947), 120–124.
33. *40th Infantry Division*, 123–124.
34. Ibid., 124.
35. The Panay Negros Occidental Operation, 130.
36. *40th Infantry Division*, 127.
37. Ibid., 127–129.
38. Ibid., 129–131.
39. Ibid., 131–133.
40. Ibid., 133–134.
41. Ibid., 134–135.
42. The Panay Negros Occidental Operation, 130.
43. GHQ, SWPA, Operations Instructions 94, March 2, 1945, 98 GHQ1-3.17, Box 792, RG 407, NARA II.
44. Eighth Army, Operational Monograph on the Cebu–Bohol Negros Oriental Operation (Victor II), 108-0, Box 2233, RG 407, NARA II, 13.
45. Ibid., 28.

46. After Action Report, Americal Infantry Division, V-2 Operation, 300-0.3, Box 4803, RG 407, NARA II, 2–4; Smith, *Triumph in the Philippines*, 612.

47. Smith, *Triumph in the Philippines*, 614.

48. After Action Report, Americal Infantry Division, V-2 Operation, 4–6.

49. "Story of the Americal Division," 300-0.1, Box 4801, RG 407, NARA II, 4.

50. Ibid.

51. After Action Report, Americal Infantry Division, V-2 Operation, 8–9.

52. Ibid., 10–11.

53. "Story of the Americal Division," 3.

54. After Action Report, Americal Infantry Division, V-2 Operation, 11–15; Smith, *Triumph in the Philippines*, 617.

55. After Action Report, Americal Infantry Division, V-2 Operation, 17–18.

56. Ibid., 21–26.

57. Eighth Army, Operational Monograph on the Cebu–Bohol Negros Oriental Operation, 25–26.

58. The Panay Negros Occidental Operation, 129.

59. After Action Report, Americal Infantry Division, V-2 Operation, 20.

60. Smith, *Triumph in the Philippines*, 618–619.

61. Eighth Army, Operational Monograph on the Cebu–Bohol Negros Oriental Operation, 15.

62. Jay Luvaas, ed., *DEAR MISS EM: General Eichelberger's War in the Pacific, 1942–1945* (Westport, CT: Greenwood, 1972), 247–248.

63. GHQ, SWPA, Operations Instruction 97, March 11, 1945, 98 GHQ1-3.17, Box 792, RG 407, NARA II.

64. Jan Valtin (Richard Krebs), *Children of Yesterday: The Twenty-Fourth Infantry Division in World War II* (New York: Readers' Press, 1946), 387.

65. Ibid., 356.

66. Eichelberger, *Our Jungle Road to Tokyo*, 217.

67. Ibid.

68. Historical Record, Mindanao Guerrilla Resistance Movement, Tenth Military District from 16 September 1942 to 30 June 1945, Chapter 11, Japanese Atrocities, Wendell W. Fertig Papers, USAHEC, 50.

69. Eighth Army, Operational Monograph on the Mindanao Operation (Victor V), 108-0, Box 2234, RG 407, NARA II, 16–17. Fertig reported that he had nearly 35,000 guerrillas under his control, although only two-thirds of them were armed, which probably explains the difference in numbers between his report and the number given in the Eighth Army monograph.

70. Copy in Mindanao Guerrilla Resistance Movement.

71. 10th Information and Historical Service, Eighth Army, "Staff Study of Japanese Operations on Mindanao Island," Narrative of Operations of the 100th Japanese Infantry Division, 7.

72. Ibid., 22.

73. Eighth Army, Operational Monograph on the Mindanao Operation, 18–21; Smith, *Triumph in the Philippines*, 621–623.
74. Eichelberger, *Our Jungle Road to Tokyo*, 218.
75. The best study of the 31st Infantry Division in World War II is Christopher M. Rein, *Mobilizing the South: The Thirty-First Infantry Division, Race, and World War II* (Tuscaloosa: The University of Alabama Press, 2022).
76. Eighth Army, Operational Monograph on the Mindanao Operation, 52–53; Mindanao Guerrilla Resistance Movement, Chapter 7, 7.
77. Valtin, *Children of Yesterday*, 356–357.
78. Ibid., 357.
79. Eichelberger, *Our Jungle Road to Tokyo*, 221; Morison, *The Liberation of the Philippines*, 244–245.
80. Eichelberger, *Our Jungle Road to Tokyo*, 220.
81. "Staff Study of Japanese Operations on Mindanao Island," 13.
82. Maj. Gen. R. B. Woodruff, "Their Last Stronghold: A Narrative Account of the 24th Infantry Division on Mindanao," 1945, 324-0.3, Box 6613, RG 407, NARA II, 3–6.
83. Eichelberger, *Our Jungle Road to Tokyo*, 223.
84. Shortal, *Forged by Fire*, 124.
85. Eichelberger, *Our Jungle Road to Tokyo*, 220.
86. Captain George E. Morrissey, Medical Corps, "The Philippine Campaign of 1st Bn. 34th Infantry," entry for April 23, 1945, Aubrey S. Newman Papers, Box 3, USAHEC.
87. Valtin, *Children of Yesterday*, 84.
88. Woodruff, "Their Last Stronghold," 7–11.
89. Eighth Army, Operational Monograph on the Mindanao Operation, 312.
90. Rein, *Mobilizing the South*, 202–204. For this battle and ensuing operations in the Colgan Woods, the 2nd Battalion, 124th Infantry was awarded a Distinguished Unit Citation.
91. Eichelberger, *Our Jungle Road to Tokyo*, 228.
92. Smith, *Triumph in the Philippines*, 639–640.
93. Eichelberger, *Our Jungle Road to Tokyo*, 239.
94. Capt. (Father) Aquinas T. Colgan received the Distinguished Service Cross for his heroism.
95. William E. Hammer, "Recollections," William E. Hammer Papers, Hoover Institution Archives, 37.
96. *Reports of General MacArthur: The Campaigns of MacArthur in the Pacific*, vol. I (Washington, DC: US Army Center of Military History, 1966), 312.
97. *40th Infantry Division*, 140.
98. Eighth Army, Operational Monograph on the Mindanao Operation, 308; 31st Infantry Division, Operations Report – Mindanao, 22 April–30 June 1945, 331-0.3, Box 7733, RG 407, NARA II, 25.
99. *40th Infantry Division*, 141.

100. Eichelberger, *Our Jungle Road to Tokyo*, 241.

101. Smith, *Triumph in the Philippines*, 642–644.

102. "Staff Study of Japanese Operations on Mindanao Island," 18–22.

103. 31st Infantry Division, Operations Report – Mindanao, 34.

104. *History of the 31st Infantry Division in the Pacific* (NP, 1947), 331-0, Box 7733, NARA II, 23–24.

105. Smith, *Triumph in the Philippines*, 645.

106. Eighth Army, Operational Monograph on the Mindanao Operation, 309.

107. Eichelberger, *Our Jungle Road to Tokyo*, 244.

108. Ibid., 311; Smith, *Triumph in the Philippines*, 647.

109. Historical Record, Mindanao Guerrilla Resistance Movement, Chapter 8, 2.

110. Historical Section, Eighth Army, *Amphibious Eighth* (1948).

111. Eichelberger, *Our Jungle Road to Tokyo*, 202.

112. Ibid., 233.

113. Luvaas, *DEAR MISS EM*, 24.

CHAPTER 11: REBIRTH

1. Yay Panlilio, *The Crucible* (New York: Macmillan, 1950), 58.

2. Eighth Army, Operational Monograph on the Panay Negros Occidental Operation (Victor I), 108-0, Box 2233, RG 407, NARA II, 131–132.

3. Eighth Army, Operational Monograph on the Cebu–Bohol Negros Oriental Operation (Victor II), 108-0, Box 2233, RG 407, NARA II, 131–133.

4. *Reports of General MacArthur: The Campaigns of MacArthur in the Pacific*, vol. I (Washington, DC: US Army Center of Military History, 1966), 465.

5. Hiroo Onoda, *No Surrender: My Thirty-Year War*, trans. Charles S. Terry (New York and Tokyo: Kodansha International, 1974).

6. GHQ SWPA, Psychological Operations Section, Japanese Statistical Trends, Entry 441, Box 2701, RG 496, NARA II.

7. *Reports of General MacArthur*, vol. I, 357.

8. The official US Army dates of the Philippines campaign are October 17, 1944, to July 4, 1945. Statistical and Accounting Branch, Office of the Adjutant General, US Army, "Army Battle Casualties and Nonbattle Deaths in World War II, 7 December 1941–31 December 1946," Department of the Army, June 1, 1953, 94.

9. 38th Infantry Division, "The Avengers of Bataan: Report on the M-7 Operation, 19 January to 30 June 1945," 338-0, Box 8795, RG 407, NARA II, 182.

10. William F. McCartney, *The Jungleers: A History of the 41st Infantry Division* (Washington, DC: Infantry Journal Press, 1948), 154.

11. Robert Ross Smith, *Triumph in the Philippines* (Washington, DC: Office of the Chief of Military History, 1963), 652–653. For a discussion of the impact of the shortage of combat divisions on the combat effectiveness of the Army of the

United States, see Peter R. Mansoor, *The GI Offensive in Europe: The Triumph of American Infantry Divisions, 1941–1945* (Lawrence, KS: University Press of Kansas, 1999).

12. The higher figure is from Ronald E. Dolan, ed., *Philippines: A Country Study* (Washington, DC: US Library of Congress, 1991), 41; the lower figure and comparison data are from "Total Second World War Fatalities as a Share of Pre-war Populations per Country or Region between 1939 and 1945," Statista, www .statista.com/statistics/1351638/second-world-war-share-total-population-loss.

13. Allan A. Ryan, *Yamashita's Ghost: War Crimes, MacArthur's Justice, and Command Accountability* (Lawrence, KS: University Press of Kansas, 2012), 61.

14. Ibid., 62.

15. Ibid., 164–167.

16. See Chapter 3.

17. Ryan, *Yamashita's Ghost*, 210.

18. Ibid., 179. Mutō would be tried and convicted by the International Military Tribunal for the Far East for his role in the Nanjing massacre and executed on December 23, 1948, alongside Gen. Hideki Tojo, the Japanese prime minister who oversaw Japan's decision to go to war with the United States and other nations in the Asia–Pacific region.

19. Alfonso J. Aluit, *By Sword and Fire: The Destruction of Manila in World War II, 3 February–3 March 1945* (Manila: National Commission for Culture and the Arts, 1994), 382–383.

20. Ryan, *Yamashita's Ghost*, 251.

21. James M. Scott, *Rampage: MacArthur, Yamashita, and the Battle of Manila* (New York: W. W. Norton, 2018), 466.

22. Ryan, *Yamashita's Ghost*, 294–295.

23. No one was held accountable for the My Lai massacre in the Vietnam War, for instance, leading one to conclude that command accountability is applied only in victor's justice. Lawyer and historian Allan Ryan writes, "But Yamashita's ghost lingers in the law. Born in an unprecedented and ambiguous charge by a vindictive American general, nurtured by a misbegotten trial by his subordinates, deferentially upheld by America's highest court, shaped by two panels of American judges at Nuremberg, and incorporated into official American policy and international tribunals, it has loomed over the international law of war far too long." Ibid., 341.

24. William Manchester, *American Caesar: Douglas MacArthur, 1880–1964* (Boston: Little, Brown, 1978; New York: Dell, 1978), 328.

25. *Reports of General MacArthur*, vol. I, 357.

26. For the alternative argument that the Philippines campaign was unnecessary and wasteful, see Robert M. Young, *Pacific Hurtgen: The American Army in Northern Luzon, 1945* (Washington, DC: Westphalia Press, 2017).

27. Frank Futrell, "Luzon," in Wesley Frank Craven and James Lea Cate, eds., *The Army Air Forces in World War II*, vol. V: *The Pacific: Matterhorn to Nagasaki, June 1944 to August 1945* (Chicago: University Press of Chicago, 1953), 413–447, 441.

28. Charles W. Boggs, *Marine Aviation in the Philippines* (Washington, DC: Historical Division, USMC, 1951), 106.

29. Smith, *Triumph in the Philippines*, 655; Robert L. Eichelberger, *Our Jungle Road to Tokyo* (New York: Viking, 1950), 250.

30. Pacific Warfare Board Report no. 69, "Japanese High Command Estimate of the Effectiveness of American Artillery and Air Support in the Philippine Operations," September 21, 1945, Entry 535, Box 3019, RG 496, NARA II.

31. D. Clayton James, *The Years of MacArthur*, vol. II: *1941–1945* (Boston: Houghton Mifflin, 1975), 665.

32. Daniel E. Barbey, *MacArthur's Amphibious Navy: Seventh Amphibious Force Operations, 1943–1945* (Annapolis, MD: United States Naval Institute, 1969), 232.

33. Jay Luvaas, ed., *DEAR MISS EM: General Eichelberger's War in the Pacific, 1942–1945* (Westport, CT: Greenwood, 1972), 283–284, 293.

34. Slim had a natural rapport with his soldiers. "He thought, he *knew*, at our level; it was that, and the sheer certainty that was built into every line of him, that gave Fourteenth Army its overwhelming confidence; what he promised, that he would surely do. And afterwards, when it was over and he spoke of what his army had done, it was always 'you', not even 'we', and never 'I.'" For that, his troops respected and embraced him. George MacDonald Fraser, *Quartered Safe Out Here: A Recollection of the War in Burma* (London: Harvill, 1993), 37.

35. For an assessment of differing views of MacArthur, see Cole Kingseed, "Will the Real MacArthur Please Wade Ashore," *Army* (July 2020), 40–43.

36. James, *The Years of MacArthur*, vol. II, 666.

37. D. M. Horner, "Blamey and MacArthur: The Problem of Coalition Warfare," in William M. Leary, ed., *We Shall Return! MacArthur's Commanders and the Defeat of Japan, 1942–1945* (Lexington: University Press of Kentucky, 1988), 58.

38. Radio broadcast, May 8, 1945, William Dunn Radio Transcripts, Folder 50, Box 3, RG 52, MacArthur Memorial Archives.

39. James M. Scott, *Rampage: MacArthur, Yamashita, and the Battle of Manila* (New York: W. W. Norton, 2018), 433.

40. Civil Affairs Section, US Army Forces Pacific, Report on Philippine Civil Affairs, August 25, 1945, Papers of General Richard K. Sutherland relating to GHQ, SWPA, 1942–45, Entry 19810, RG 496, NARA II, 67–74.

41. Walter Krueger, *From Down Under to Nippon: The Story of Sixth Army in World War II* (Washington, DC: Combat Forces Press, 1953), 322.

42. Report on Philippine Civil Affairs, 73.

43. Krueger, *From Down Under to Nippon*, 325.

44. Report on Philippine Civil Affairs, 71.

45. Ronald K. Edgerton, "General Douglas MacArthur and the American Military Impact in the Philippines," *Philippine Studies* 25, no. 4 (1977): 420–440, 428.
46. Ibid., 437.
47. Radio broadcast, May 24, 1945, William Dunn Radio Transcripts, Folder 50, Box 3, RG 52, MacArthur Memorial Archives.
48. Carlos P. Romulo, *I See the Philippines Rise* (Garden City, NY: Doubleday, 1946), 143–147.
49. Report on Philippine Civil Affairs, 85.
50. Office of the Chief Engineer, GHQ Army Forces Pacific, *Engineers of the Southwest Pacific, 1941–1945*, vol. VI: *Airfield and Base Development* (Washington, DC: GPO, 1951), 366.
51. Ibid., 337.
52. Ibid., 362–363, 365.
53. Ibid., 364–365.
54. Degaussing neutralized the magnetic field generated by a ship's hull, making it less susceptible to magnetic mines.
55. Office of the Chief Engineer, GHQ Army Forces Pacific, *Engineers of the Southwest Pacific, 1941–1945*, vol. VI, 357–358, 367.
56. Scott, *Rampage*, 426–427, 433.
57. Ibid., 362.
58. James, *The Years of MacArthur*, vol. II, 514.
59. Ibid., 698; Douglas MacArthur, *Reminiscences* (New York: McGraw-Hill, 1964), 265–266.
60. Manchester, *American Caesar*, 491.
61. Paul P. Rogers, *The Bitter Years: MacArthur and Sutherland* (New York: Praeger, 1991), 130.
62. Ibid., 130.
63. Ibid.
64. Romulo, *I See the Philippines Rise*, 131.
65. Ibid., 153–154.
66. James, *The Years of MacArthur*, vol. II, 699.
67. Ibid., 699.
68. Ibid., 700–701.
69. Rogers, *The Bitter Years*, 292.
70. Paul McNutt arrived as High Commissioner in September 1945, after MacArthur had already left Manila for Japan. Edgerton, "General Douglas MacArthur and the American Military Impact in the Philippines," 425.
71. Rogers, *The Bitter Years*, 293.
72. Eighth Army, Leyte Mop-up Operation, 108-0, Box 2233, RG 407, NARA II, 89.
73. USAFIP, After-Battle Report: United States Army Forces in the Philippines, North Luzon Operations, 9 January to 15 August 1945, November 10, 1945, Russell W. Volckmann Papers, USAHEC, 139.
74. Smith, *Triumph in the Philippines*, 658.

75. Ronald E. Dolan, ed., *Philippines: A Country Study* (Washington, DC: US Library of Congress, 1991), 40.

76. Edwin Price Ramsey and Stephen J. Rivele, *Lieutenant Ramsey's War: From Horse Soldier to Guerrilla Commander* (New York: Knightsbridge, 1990), 161.

77. Ira Wolfert, *American Guerrilla in the Philippines* (New York: Simon and Schuster, 1945), 111.

78. One such summary sent by Wendell Fertig from Mindanao, dated October 31, 1944, was twenty-nine pages long and contained maps and diagrams on Japanese dispositions, airfields, guerrilla- and Japanese-held areas, guerrilla organization, and hiding places for Japanese ships, as well as exhibits on troop movements, patrols, ship sightings, guerrilla strength returns, and targeting information. Copy in Historical Record, Mindanao Guerrilla Resistance Movement, Tenth Military District from 16 September 1942 to 30 June 1945, Wendell W. Fertig Papers, USAHEC.

79. Message Nr. 58 from Volckmann to MacArthur on December 31, 1944, correctly stated, "Reports to date indicate that in the event of an Allied landing at Aparri or Lingayen Gulf, the enemy plans to conduct main defence [sic] not at the beach but back beyond the range of naval bombardment." Russell W. Volckmann Papers, USAHEC.

80. "A Brief History of the G-2 Section, GHQ, SWPA, and Affiliated Units," in Charles Willoughby and G-2 Section, SWPA, *History of Intelligence Activities under General MacArthur, 1942–1950* (Wilmington, DE: Scholarly Resources, 1983), 31.

81. GHQ Messages in the Guerrilla Resistance Movement in the Philippines, 1943–1945, Boxes 506–575, RG 496, NARA II.

82. 38th Infantry Division, "The Avengers of Bataan: Report on the M-7 Operation, 19 January to 30 June 1945," 338-0, Box 8795, RG 407, NARA II, 142.

83. Historical Record, Mindanao Guerrilla Resistance Movement, VIII: 2.

84. USAFIP, "After-Battle Report: United States Army Forces in the Philippines, North Luzon Operations, 9 January to 15 August 1945," November 10, 1945, Russell Volckmann Papers, USAHEC, 139.

85. For more on the concept of hybrid threats, see Williamson Murray and Peter R. Mansoor, eds., *Hybrid Warfare: Fighting Complex Opponents from the Ancient World to the Present* (New York: Cambridge University Press, 2012).

86. Ramsey and Rivele, *Lieutenant Ramsey's War*, 332.

87. *Reports of General MacArthur*, vol. I, 325.

88. Russsell W. Volckmann, *We Remained: Three Years behind the Enemy Lines in the Philippines* (New York: W. W. Norton, 1954), 183.

89. Panlilio, *The Crucible*, 58.

90. Romulo, *I See the Philippines Rise*, 177.

Index